CASES AND MATERIALS ON CONSTITUTIONAL AND ADMINISTRATIVE LAW

SECOND EDITION

BY

GEOFFREY WILSON
M.A., LL.B.

Professor of Law, Warwick University and Barrister at Law of Gray's Inn

CAMBRIDGE UNIVERSITY PRESS

CAMBRIDGE

LONDON · NEW YORK · MELBOURNE

Published by the Syndics of the Cambridge University Press
The Pitt Building, Trumpington Street, Cambridge CB2 1RP
Bentley House, 200 Euston Road, London NW1 2DB
32 East 57th Street, New York, NY 10022, USA
296 Beaconsfield Parade, Middle Park, Melbourne 3206, Australia

First published 1966
Second edition 1976
Reprinted 1977 1979

First printed in Great Britain by
The Eastern Press Limited
London and Reading

Reprinted in Great Britain
at the University Press, Cambridge

Library of Congress Cataloguing in Publication Data
Wilson, Geoffrey Philip.
Cases and materials on constitutional and administrative law.
(Cambridge legal case book series)
Includes index.
1. Great Britain – Constitutional law – Cases.
2. Administrative law – Great Britain – Cases. I. Title. II. Series.
KD3930.A7W5 1976   342′.41   75–6005

ISBN 0 521 20816 5 hard covers
ISBN 0 521 09959 5 paperback

For the 1977 reprint of the paperback version it has been possible to replace the account of the Prevention of Terrorism Act 1974 with an account of the Prevention of Terrorism Act 1976.

CAMBRIDGE LEGAL CASE BOOK SERIES

CASES AND MATERIALS
ON CONSTITUTIONAL
AND ADMINISTRATIVE LAW

PREFACE TO THE SECOND EDITION

The present edition of this book follows the pattern of the first in abandoning an exclusively court-oriented approach to the study of constitutional and administrative law and in taking a broader view of the constitutional arrangements of the United Kingdom than had been customary in the past. This is not simply a question of including materials other than the reports of decided cases, though this is in itself an important aspect of a broader approach. It is also a question of giving more attention than had been customary to those parts of the constitution which have commonly been grouped together under the general heading of the Conventions of the Constitution. In the absence of a written constitution which can be regarded as the supreme law of the land, and more particularly in the absence of a Constitutional or Supreme Court, it makes little sense to confine oneself to the decisions of the ordinary courts, which at best can give only a partial and fragmented picture of the overall structure, of which the courts themselves are merely one element. To do so, moreover, is to ignore the very institutions, procedures and principles which constitute the hard core of the British Constitution, in particular those which centre on the Government and Parliament and their relations with one another.

It has been a particular weakness of public law in the United Kingdom in the past that this is exactly what has happened. With very few exceptions public lawyers have abandoned to students of politics and politicians the study of those parts of the constitution which form the country's claim to be a parliamentary democracy. Both students of law and law teachers have found other branches of public law more accessible and more appealing. Dull and difficult though much of administrative law, for example, may often be, it is at least capable of being reduced to the familiar routine of the study of reports of decided cases and the application of rules culled from them to hypothetical sets of facts, which is the traditional mode of legal study in the United Kingdom. It can be taught, too, in a way which can find a ready response among students, at the general level of concern about the problems of supervising and controlling the activities of public authorities and officials, holding a balance between the need for discretion and the need to secure that decisions are fairly and openly made within the limits of the law, and at the more particular level of concern about the problems of housing, the environment, town and country planning, social security or government aid to industry, which can crop up in administrative law cases.

And the same is true of the field of civil liberties. This too is an area where decided cases can be made to play a central part and where the subject matter finds an immediate response. Younger law teachers in particular have been attracted to the problems of race relations, police powers, the right to protest and demonstrate, freedom of speech and the role of the state as guardian of morals, all areas where the intellect can be stimulated and nourished by strong feelings.

There are also substantive reasons why these fields should have been more cultivated than the more general parts of constitutional law. The grants of powers to public authorities and officials have in the past constantly outpaced the development of a legal framework of principles and procedures for their exercise and the provision of remedies for their abuse. For a long time it was left largely to the courts and lawyers to develop this framework, unassisted by the legislature, and in this period in particular it was the urgent task of academic lawyers to try to introduce some kind of order into the field and create a body of administrative law which would both explain the reactions of the courts and provide guides and pointers to future developments. This continues to be necessary, even though the legislature, assisted by such bodies as the Council on Tribunals, makes a more substantial contribution than it did in the past to the development of this field of public law. So too, in the absence of any documents setting out and guaranteeing basic rights in the United Kingdom, even though it is a signatory of the European Convention of Human Rights, it has always been the particular responsibility of lawyers and the courts to act as guardians of basic liberties, to be alert to the growth of new problem areas, and to develop old and devise new remedies to deal with changing situations and to give expression to changes in values. The concern shown by public lawyers in this area has always been and will continue to be an integral and central part of the tradition of public law in the United Kingdom.

The parliamentary system has by contrast rarely been a popular subject of study among lawyers. The relevant materials differ in style and content from reported cases and are not susceptible to the same case study treatment. Unlike the closely reasoned judgments of Her Majesty's judges, which it is at least plausible to attempt to arrange in some kind of coherent scheme, a task which is made easier by the fact that the judges themselves have an obligation to show how their particular decisions fit into the overall picture of the relevant legal rules, the materials relevant to the study of the parliamentary system are more diffuse, much fuzzier at the edges – and often at the centre as well – much less conclusive in style, generally less accessible and often brought into existence by people who have no obligation to go beyond their immediate task and attempt to show how what they are doing fits into the general scheme of things. It may be, too, that the difficulty of separating out the merely political from the more properly constitutional and even a certain disenchantment with the parliamentary system itself have prevented many lawyers from taking its study seriously. The fact that the normal methods used to test a student's knowledge of legal cases cannot be used in this area only tends to reinforce the law teacher's scepticism about its relevance and the law student's apprehension.

The neglect of the parliamentary system is understandable but there are a number of reasons why it is time for a change. Two in particular stand out. The first is the intrinsic importance of the subject matter. Whatever one may think either of the effectiveness of the parliamentary system or the validity of the current descriptions of it which prevail in the textbooks, it is nonetheless the basis of the constitutional arrangements that we have. Indeed it is possible to put it more strongly even than that. It lies at the very heart of our notion of ' constitutionalism ' itself, the notion, that is, that it is proper to conduct the debates about fundamental issues and the struggles between different groups and interests in the community within the framework of a ' Constitution '. Both constitutionalism and the parliamentary system that we have today are the products of the same ideas and the same strivings and it is not at all easy in the United Kingdom context to separate the two. Historical accident has long protected us from any sharp revolutionary breaks in our constitutional development. The present arrangements have every appearance of having grown organically and being in some way deep-rooted in the character and consciousness of the British people. One result of this is that the British have never had to think through from top to bottom what is the point of having a constitution, to what principles and values it should give expression, and which institutions and procedures are best suited to meet the needs of the time and the expectations of the British people. And yet this is the stance that a student of the constitution must adopt. He must be in a position to look at the British Constitution as he might look at the constitution of any other country, and be in a position to ask why it is as it is and whether it could be different. And this is particularly important at the present time since it is clear that the present arrangements, and certainly the rather simple model of them that has been inherited from the past, are under strain. The product for the most part of struggles and developments of the nineteenth and early twentieth centuries, they now have to cope with conditions and meet expectations that were then not really thought of. One very clear example is the impact of Britain's participation in the European Community. Even more important is the vastly increased responsibility that Governments now undertake in relation to the general working of the economy, and the necessity of their securing the support of major interests in the community if this responsibility is to be carried out. And quite apart from the challenges to the existing structure which result from changed conditions and the changed role of Government there are also challenges like those resulting from the demands for more openness in Government and for more opportunities to participate in and exercise an influence on the formation and application of legislative and administrative policy, both at central and local level. These developments not only present challenges to the existing structures but also to the student of constitutional law. The relative neglect of this aspect of public law has already made it possible for out-of-date models of the constitution to prevail when developments have left them far behind. The first task is therefore to bring these oversimplified models up to date. The second task is more difficult. It involves considering the institutions and procedures which at present prevail and asking to what extent they are adequate to perform existing tasks and achieve existing goals, and to what extent they need to be modified to perform new tasks and achieve new goals and/or to give expression to new standards and values which did not exist when they were first established. The position in this area of public law is rather like the position in the early days of administrative law. Those actively engaged in Government are far more concerned to deal with current problems in a politically decisive way than to consider the long-term constitutional implications of what they are doing. It is one of the differences between the role of the constitutional lawyer in the United Kingdom and his colleagues in other countries that whereas the latter are working for the most part within the framework of an existing constitution which sets out the basic procedures, standards and principles which are to be observed in the government of the country, the former has the responsibility of constantly re-creating and redrafting the constitution in the light of the developments which take place before him. In this he is rather like the private lawyer in relation to decided cases and to private law in general. He too has the task of attempting to explain the latest developments and to show how they fit in with the principles, rules and values which had hitherto been regarded as prevailing. Both start too with general notions of the principles and values which underlie the whole system, in the case of the private lawyer the notion of the legal way of doing things, and for the public lawyer the constitutional way of doing things. In each case it is the task of the student to try to get some idea of what this involves and in particular what this involves in the United Kingdom context. From this point of view the present is a particularly favourable time. It is just at the time that institutions, procedures and principles are being challenged that they are likely to be discussed, and this is what has happened. The materials which follow give some examples of these discussions.

The second reason for giving due consideration to the parliamentary system goes back to what was said earlier about the partial and fragmented nature of an exclusively court-oriented approach to the study of constitutional and administrative law, and has to do with the unity of the subject and of the subject matter of a public lawyer's concerns. To treat the various parts or aspects of public law as if they existed in self-contained compartments, to ignore the relationship between them and in particular to ignore the part played by the parliamentary system in the overall pattern, is to obscure this unity and the unity of values and principles which bind the various parts together. One can see this, for example, if one considers the demand for more open government. The contexts in which this demand is relevant range all the way from the doctrine of Cabinet secrecy, through the Government's relations with pressure groups and the boards of the nationalised industries, Green Papers, Parliamentary Questions, the Parliamentary Commissioner, the powers and privileges of Select Committees, access to public records, the Official Secrets Acts, the publicity of judicial proceedings and local authority meetings, to the doctrine of Crown privilege, the principles of natural justice and procedure at public inquiries. And much the same is true of the demand for greater participation, where the contexts range all the way from Parliament to the private firm. Nor is it simply a question of the parliamentary system forming part of the context in which subjects like administrative law or civil liberties need to be considered. They are all part and parcel of the same context, namely the constitutional arrangements of the United Kingdom, which provide the formal framework within which, in the last resort, basic questions of political, economic and social concern are expected to be resolved.

There is another reason too for emphasising the underlying unity of the system and the importance of the parliamentary system within it. As was suggested earlier one of the reasons for the comparative neglect of the parliamentary system by lawyers and law students has been that its relevance to matters of immediate concern is often more difficult to grasp than that of a particular case, especially a particular case in the courts. Yet the very elements of a particular case which convey this sense of its relevance are often merely examples of more general principles and issues which are not only to be found expressed elsewhere in the system but which often lie at the heart of the parliamentary system, where they can be more clearly identified and more comprehensively discussed than in the context of any individual case. It makes little sense, for example, to concentrate on an individual case in which a Minister's decision has been challenged because he failed to give an objector sufficient information or a sufficient opportunity to state his case beforehand and ignore the more general questions of openness and participation, or to get excited over a case in which a hotel proprietor is claiming compensation for the compulsory acquisition of his property or a worker is claiming that he is entitled to the payment of benefit during a strike and ignore the more general question of parliamentary supervision of the Government's handling of the economy on which the value of the property, the compensation or benefit or the continuance of the worker's job depends; or to be concerned about the right to demonstrate and ignore the more general question of the institutional and procedural opportunities available to influence and participate in central and local government decision-making; or to ignore the link between the use of demonstrations, public inquiries, and even trials in courts as opportunities for exercising pressure, securing publicity and debate, and the asumptions on which the parliamentary system and the system of local government themselves rest. To concentrate always on the individual case, on the end product, on the pathological situation is like chasing the tail of the dog. It is tinkering. And if the public lawyer is to do anything more than patch up parts of the machinery that are malfunctioning, he must take a broader view than the individual case that is likely to end up on his doorstep or than any one area of public law that may for convenience have been hived off for the sake of doing some more concentrated work upon it.

The questions of openness and participation which are the hallmark of a democracy provide important perspectives for a study of the British Constitution and assist in giving a unity to the various parts. They are both issues of current concern. There is a third issue which is also fundamental and related more to the liberal aspect of the liberal democratic values of which the United Kingdom constitutional arrangements are intended to be an expression, and that is the question of the measures such a state can take in its own self-defence, the maintenance of order and the integrity of its institutions and the protection of its citizens. Hitherto this question has arisen mostly in time of war. In peacetime it has centred on measures for dealing with problems of security against spies and on the exercise of police powers. Events in Northern Ireland have brought home to the United Kingdom issues which have been glossed over in the past because the problems which they raised had hitherto been confined to the colonies. The rise of the urban guerrilla in the United Kingdom now raises more directly than ever before the question of the extent to which the problems he creates justify a departure from the normal processes and principles that prevail in peacetime and also questions about the use of the armed forces in the maintenance of order at home. As a result the present edition contains more materials on these questions than even existed at the time the first was published.

Although relative importance has generally been the reason for including topics in the materials which follow, unimportance has not always been the criterion for excluding them. Putting together a book of reasonable size and cost is like putting together a course that must last so long and no longer. The final decision as to what should go in and what not is bound in the end to seem somewhat arbitrary. As a result there are important topics which are not represented in the materials which follow. The chapter which I have omitted with the greatest reluctance is on citizenship, immigration and race relations. There is no mention either of devolution – though here the report of the Royal Commission on the Constitution provides an up-to-date discussion of the main issues – or the European Convention of Human Rights, trade unions, the media, education or the role of the state as guardian of public morals; and the materials have their customary English bias. On the other hand more space has been given to other topics than they received in the first edition.

Many of the changes in the present edition are the result of events that have occurred since the first edition was published in 1967. One event that can find no place in the text and yet is as important for the study of constitutional and administrative law as any there mentioned is the death of Professor Stanley de Smith. The world of legal scholarship is far too small and too thinly populated to suffer the loss of one of its leaders without acknowledgment. If this book is big enough to include a circular from the Department of the Environment on publicity in relation to planning applications, it is certainly big enough to lament the loss of a colleague. The general standing of law teachers in the United Kingdom is lower than in some other countries where their writings play a larger part in the development of the law. But in the field of public law the courts in the United Kingdom play a much less conspicuous part than they do in the field of private law. There is a sense in which both constitutional and administrative law are the creation of writers like Professor de Smith, and the whole field of public law will miss his quality of quiet rationality, of which it always stands so much in need.

I wish to express my gratitude to the following for permission to quote extracts in this edition: the Controller of Her Majesty's Stationery Office for permission to include extracts from official publications including Hansard; The Times Newspapers Limited for extracts from 'The Times Law Reports'; Butterworth & Company Limited for extracts from the *All England Law Reports*; P.L.D. Publishers for extracts from the *All-Pakistan Legal Decisions*; Associated Book Publishers Limited for an extract from *The British Cabinet* by J. P. Mackintosh; Professor D. N. MacCormick and Associated Book Publishers Limited; Jonathan Cape Limited for extracts from *The Cabinet* by Patrick Gordon-Walker; C.M.L.R. Limited for extracts from *Common Market Law Reports*; Barrie & Jenkins Limited for extracts from Viscount Samuel's *Memoirs*; Incorporated Council of Law Reporting for England & Wales; Charles Knight & Company Limited for extracts from *Local Government Reports*; The Law Book Company Limited for an extract from Commonwealth Law Reports; Lloyds of London Press Limited for an extract from *Lloyds List Reports*; Oxford University Press for an extract from 'The Monarch and the Selection of a Prime Minister' by Graeme C. Moodie in *Political Studies,* © Oxford University Press, 1957; The Hansard Society for extracts from *Parliamentary Affairs*; P. J. Madgwick for an extract from his article 'Resignations' published in *Parliamentary Affairs*; W. Green & Son Limited for an extract from the *Scots Law Times*; The Scottish Council of Law Reporting for extracts from *Session Cases*; D. G. Williams of Emmanuel College, Cambridge, for an extract from 'Protest and Public Order' in the *Cambridge Law Journal*; and Leonard Tivey for an extract from his article 'The Political Consequences of Economic Planning.'

It pleases me also to be able to thank once again Mrs Elizabeth Anker in the Government Publications Department in the University of Warwick library for helping me to track down references and quotations which had gone astray, and of course my wife and family for their infinite patience.

Warwick   Geoffrey Wilson
September 1975

CONTENTS

STATUTES AND STATUTORY INSTRUMENTS

Numbers in heavy type refer to the pages at which contents of the statutes are set out

xvii

CASES

Numbers in heavy type refer to the pages at which contents of the cases are set out

COMMAND PAPERS AND PARLIAMENTARY PAPERS

Numbers in heavy type refer to the pages at which the contents are set out

Command papers and government publications

CHAPTER I

THE MONARCHY

Instead of adapting to changing political circumstances and expectations by abandoning the monarchy and establishing a republic with a new written Constitution – though there have been republican stirrings, especially in the 1870s – the United Kingdom adapted its monarchical institutions by retaining the form of monarchy but subjecting the monarch himself to an increasing number of restrictions. Some of them were formal and statutory, such as the provision in the Bill of Rights denying the monarch the power to tax without the consent of Parliament. But the most important were the result of political practices which developed into constitutional conventions. Indeed so much importance came to be attached to these conventions that many have ceased to be a description of political practice based on precedent and have come to be regarded as part of the formal constitutional structure of the country, and as such would be embodied in a written Constitution were the United Kingdom to adopt one. The most important and general of these conventions affecting the Queen is that in all ordinary affairs of Government she acts on the advice of her Ministers for the time being, the Ministers themselves being represented in this context by the Prime Minister. The Queen's most important independent constitutional functions have to do with the fact that she is the formal source of the Government's authority – she appoints the Prime Minister – and that she is the ultimate custodian of the constitution – in the last resort she may dismiss a Government or refuse her consent to legislation. Her powers under the first head are regulated by well established conventions. Those under the second are emergency powers and their scope is uncertain. In a situation in which it would be plausible to consider the exercise of those powers it would be difficult to disentangle constitutional propriety from political wisdom. The lessons of 1912 seem to be that it is difficult for the monarch to behave with constitutional propriety unless all the other actors in the scene do so as well and that it is hard to envisage a situation in which the exercise of the emergency powers would be effective, or more important, where they could be exercised without bringing the monarch into the political arena and putting the monarchy itself at risk.

I. THE REVOLUTION SETTLEMENT

The formal starting point of the present constitutional arrangements is 1689. It was then that a revolutionary [1] break with the past was made and

---

[1] i.e. in a legal sense. The Convention Parliament Act 1688, the Bill of Rights 1689, and the Crown and Parliament Recognition Act 1690 all pur-

a new line of succession established. It was then, too, that the Bill of
Rights was passed, which is the nearest the United Kingdom has to a
basic constitutional document. Its inadequacies in this respect are typical.
Formally it is not basic. Being a statute it can be repealed like any other
statute without any special procedure being adopted. Its provisions are
limited for the most part to dealing with the contemporary crisis. It
makes no attempt to provide a comprehensive constitutional framework
for the future. It is principally concerned with legitimating the new line
of succession to the throne and redressing the grievances alleged against
James II. In spite of its limitations, however, it has come to be regarded
as an important constitutional expression of the political settlement of a
large number of controversies that had troubled the seventeenth century
and as the legal foundation of the most important constitutional developments that occurred in the eighteenth and nineteenth centuries, which, in
their turn have determined the basic structure of the United Kingdom's
present constitutional arrangements. It expressly settled the question
whether it was lawful for the Government to tax without the consent of
Parliament and, although it refers expressly only to the suspending and
dispensing power in relation to legislation it confirmed the principle expressed by Coke L.C.J. in the *Case of Proclamations* (below, p. 7) that
the King could not change the law by proclamations issued by virtue of
the royal prerogative. Further it echoed his view that the prerogative
itself was part of the ordinary law of the land and that it was for the
courts to determine its content and scope. It confirmed too by implication
the abolition of special prerogative courts such as the court of Star
Chamber. There is in it no mention of Prime Minister, Cabinet, the
doctrine of Ministerial responsibility, appropriation, the Consolidated Fund
or audits and accounts. But it is on the twin pillars of the necessity of
parliamentary consent for taxation and legislation, asserted expressly and
by implication by the Bill of Rights, that the whole classical theory of
the Constitution, of which these form essential elements, was subsequently
based.

BILL OF RIGHTS (1689)   [1 Will. & Mary Sess. 2. ch. 2]

Whereas the lords spirtuall and temporall and com̄ons assembled at
Westminster lawfully fully and freely representing all the estates
of the people of this realme did upon the thirteenth day of February
in the yeare of our Lord one thousand six hundred eighty eight
present unto their Majesties then called and known by the names
and stile of William and Mary Prince and Princesse of Orange being
present in their proper persons a certaine declaration in writing
made by the said lords and com̄ons in the words following viz.

Whereas the late King James the Second by the assistance of

---

ported to give validity to the events of 1689. But the new regime's validity
is in fact based on its general acceptance and the political weakness of its
Stuart rivals.

diverse evill councillors judges and ministers imployed by him did endeavour to subvert and extirpate the Protestant religion and the lawes and liberties of this kingdom . . .

And whereas the said late King James the Second haveing abdicated the government and the throne being thereby vacant his Highnesse the Prince of Orange (whom it hath pleased Almighty God to make the glorious instrument of delivering this kingdome from popery and arbitrary power) did (by the advice of the lords spirituall and temporall and diverse principall persons of the commons) cause letters to be written to the lords spirituall and temporall being protestants and other letters to the several countyes cityes universities boroughs and cinque ports for the choosing of such persons to represent them as were of right to be sent to Parlyament to meete and sitt at Westminster upon the two and twentyeth day of January in this yeare one thousand six hundred eighty and eight in order to such an establishment as that their religion lawes and liberties might not againe be in danger of being subverted, upon which letters elections haveing beene accordingly made.

And thereupon the said lords spirituall and temporall and commons pursuant to their respective letters and elections being now assembled in a full and free representative of this nation takeing into their most serious consideration the best meanes for attaining the ends aforesaid doe in the first place (as their auncestors in like case have usually done) for the vindicating and asserting their auntient rights and liberties, declare

That the pretended power of suspending of laws or the execution of laws by regall authority without consent of Parlyament is illegall.

That the pretended power of dispensing with laws or the execution of laws by regall authoritie as it hath been assumed and exercised of late is illegall.

That the commision for erecting the late court of commissioners for ecclesiastical causes and all other commissions and courts of like nature are illegal and pernicious.

That levying money for or to the use of the Crowne by ptence of prerogative without grant of Parlyament for longer time or in other manner then the same is or shall be granted is illegal.

That it is the right of the subjects to petition the King and all commitments and prosecutions for such petitioning are illegal.

That the raising or keeping a standing army within the kingdome in time of peace unlesse it be with consent of Parlyament is against law.

That the subjects which are protestants may have arms for their defence suitable to their conditions and as allowed by law.

That election of members of Parlyament ought to be free.

That the freedome of speech and debates or proceedings in Parlyament ought not to be impeached or questioned in any court or place out of Parlyament.

That excessive baile ought not to be required nor excessive fines imposed nor cruell and unusuall punishments inflicted.

That jurors ought to be duly impannelled and returned . . .

That all grants and promises of fines and forfeitures of particular persons before conviction are illegal and void.

And that for redresse of all grievances and for the amending strengthening and preserveing of the lawes of Parlyaments ought to be held frequently.

And they doe claime demand and insist upon all and singular the premises as their undoubted rights and liberties. . . To which demand of their rights they are particularly encouraged by the declaration of his Highnesse the Prince of Orange as being the onely meanes for obtaining a full redresse and remedy therein. Haveing therefore an intire confidence that his said Highnesse the Prince of Orange will perfect the deliverance soe farr advanced by him and will still preserve them from the violation of their rights which they have here asserted and from all other attempts upon their religion rights and liberties. The said lords spirituall and temporall and commons assembled at Westminster doe resolve that William and Mary Prince and Princesse of Orange be and be declared King and Queene of England France and Ireland and the dominions thereunto belonging to hold the crowne and royall dignity of the said kingdomes and dominions to them the said prince and princesse dureing their lives and the life of the survivour of them. . .

Upon which their said Majestyes did accept the crowne and royall dignitie of the kingdoms of England France and Ireland and the dominions thereunto belonging. . . And thereupon their Majestyes were pleased that the said lords spirituall and temporall and commons being the two Houses of Parlyament should continue to sitt and with their Majesty's royall concurrence make effectuall provision for the settlement of the religion lawes and liberties of this kingdome soe that the same for the future might not be in danger againe of being subverted, to which the said lords spirituall and temporall and commons did agree and proceede to act accordingly. Now in pursuance of the premisses the said lords spirituall and temporall and commons in Parlyament assembled for the ratifying confirming and establishing the said declaration and the articles clauses matters and things therein contained by the force of a law made in due forme by authority of Parlyament doe pray that it may be declared and enacted that all and singular the rights and liberties asserted and claimed in the said declaration are the true auntient and indubitable rights and liberties of the people of this kingdome and soe shall be esteemed allowed adjudged deemed and taken to be and that all and every the particulars aforesaid shall be firmly and strictly holden and observed as they are expressed in the said declaration. And all officers and ministers whatsoever shall serve their Majestyes and their successors according to the same in all times to come.

And the said lords spirituall and temporall and commons ... doe hereby recognize acknowledge and declare that King James the Second haveing abdicated the government and their Majestyes having accepted the crowne and royall dignity as aforesaid their said Majestyes did become were are and of right ought to be by the lawes of this realme our soveraigne liege lord and lady King and Queene of England France and Ireland and the dominions thereunto belonging... And... the said lords spirituall and temporall and commons doe beseech their Majestyes that it may be enacted established and declared that the crowne and regall government of the said kingdoms and dominions with all and singular the premisses thereunto belonging and appertaining shall bee and continue to their said Majestyes and the survivour of them dureing their lives and the life of the survivour of them and that the entire perfect and full exercise of the regall power and government be onely in and executed by his Majestie in the names of both their Majestyes dureing their joynt lives and after their deceases the said crowne and premisses shall be and remaine to the heires of the body of her Majestie and for default of such issue to her royall Highnesse the Princess Anne of Denmarke and the heires of her body and for default of such issue to the heires of the body of his said Majestie...

And whereas it hath beene found by experience that it is inconsistent with the safety and welfaire of this protestant kingdome to be governed by a popish prince or by any King or Queene marrying a papist the said lords spirituall and temporall and commons doe further pray that it may be enacted that all and every person and persons that is are or shall be reconciled to or shall hold communion with the see or church of Rome or shall professe the popish religion or shall marry a papist shall be excluded and be for ever uncapeable to inherit possesse or enjoy the crowne and government of this realme and Ireland and the dominions thereunto belonging or any part of the same or to have use or exercise any regall power authoritie or jurisdiction within the same And in all and every such case or cases the people of these realmes shall be and are hereby absolved of their allegiance and the said crowne and government shall from time to time descend to and be enjoyed by such person or persons being protestants as should have inherited and enjoyed the same in case the said person or persons soe reconciled holding communion or professing or marrying as aforesaid were naturally dead And that every King and Queene of this realme who at any time hereafter shall come to and succeede in the imperiall crowne of this kingdome shall on the first day of the meeting of the first Parlyament next after his or her comeing to the crowne sitting in his or her throne in the House of Peeres in the presence of the lords and commons therein assembled or at his or her coronation before such person or persons who shall administer the coronation oath to him or her at the time of his or her takeing the said oath (which shall first happen) make subscribe and audibly repeate the declaration mentioned in the Statute made in the thirtyeth yeare of the raigne of King Charles the Second entituled An Act for the more effectuall preserveing the Kings person and government by disableing papists from sitting in either House of Parlyament . . .[2]

2. And . . . from and after this present session of Parlyament noe dispensation by non obstante of or to any statute or any part thereof shall be allowed but . . . the same shall be held void and of noe effect except a dispensation be allowed of in such statute and except in such cases as shall be specially provided for by one or more bill or bills to be passed dureing this present session of Parliament . . .[3]

---

[2] [The declaration was as follows: ' I *A.B.* doe solemnly and sincerely in the presence of God professe testifie and declare that I do believe that in the sacrament of the Lords Supper there is not any transubstantiation of the elements of bread and wine into the body and blood of Christ at or after the consecration thereof by any person whatsoever; and that the invocation or adoration of the Virgin Mary or any other saint, and the sacrifice of the masses as they are now used in the Church of Rome are superstitious and idolatrous, and I doe solemnly in the presence of God professe and testifie and declare that I doe make this declaration and every part thereof in the plaine and ordinary sense of the words read unto me as they are commonly understood by English protestants without any evasion, equivocation or mentall reservation whatsoever and without any dispensation already granted me for this purpose by the Pope or any other authority or person whatsoever or without any hope of any such dispensation from any person or authority whatsoever or without thinking that I am or can be acquitted before God or man or absolved of this declaration or any part thereof although the Pope or any other person or persons or power whatsoever should dispense with or annull the same, or declare that it was null and void from the beginning.'

See now the Accession Declaration Act, 1910, which substitutes for this declaration: ' I [*here insert the name of the Sovereign*] do solemnly and sincerely in the presence of God profess, testify and declare that I am a faithful Protestant, and that I will, according to the true intent of the enactments which secure the Protestant succession to the Throne of my Realm, uphold and maintain the said enactments to the best of my powers according to law.']

[3] On the general question of the legitimacy of governments cp. the cases of *Madzimbamuto* v. *Lardner-Burke* and *Carl Zeiss Stiftung* v. *Rayner & Keeler Ltd.* (*No. 2*) below p. 255 and p. 519.

THE CASE OF PROCLAMATIONS
(1611) 12 Co.Rep. 74; 77 E.R. 1352

Lord Justice Coke records that he was sent for by the king and asked whether he could prohibit new buildings in and about London, and the making of starch from wheat, by royal proclamation. Coke asked for time to consult his fellow judges.

In the same term it was resolved by the two Chief Justices, Chief Baron, and Baron Altham, upon conference betwixt the Lords of the Privy Council and them, that the King by his proclamation cannot create any offence which was not an offence before; for then he may alter the law of the land by his proclamation in a high point: for if he may create an offence where none is, upon that ensues fine and imprisonment; also that the law of England is divided into three parts, common law, statute law, and custom; but the King's proclamation is none of them; also malum aut est malum in se, aut prohibitum, that which is against common law is malum in se, malum prohibitum is such an offence as is prohibited by Act of Parliament, and not by proclamation.

Also, it was resolved, that the King hath no prerogative but that which the law of the land allows him. But the King for the prevention of offences may by proclamation admonish his subjects that they keep the laws, and do not offend them; upon punishment to be inflicted by the law. Lastly, if the offence be not punishable in the Star Chamber, the prohibition of it by proclamation cannot make it punishable there; and after this resolution, no proclamation imposing fine and imprisonment was afterwards made.

II. THE APPOINTMENT OF A PRIME MINISTER

The main rule governing the appointment of a Prime Minister is that the leader of the party which commands a majority, usually as a result of a general election, is entitled to be invited to form a Government. When no party has secured an overall majority the practice has differed slightly according to circumstances. In 1923 the Conservative Government under Baldwin failed to secure an overall majority but remained the largest party. It met the House of Commons, was defeated and Baldwin then resigned. The King sent for the leader of the second largest party, MacDonald. The Conservative Government under Baldwin again failed to secure an overall majority in 1929, but this time the Labour Party had the largest number of seats and Baldwin resigned straight away without meeting Parliament. The King sent for MacDonald as leader of the party with the largest number of seats who again formed a Government, with the discriminating support of the Liberals. In 1974 Mr Heath's

Conservative Government failed to secure either an overall majority or the largest number of seats and resigned after he had failed to secure the support of the Liberals or of any of the other minority parties. The Queen then sent for Mr Wilson, the leader of the party with the largest number of seats.

In the past uncertainty has been caused on the resignation of a Conservative Prime Minister because of the absence of any regular procedure within the party for choosing a successor. The recent establishment of an election procedure by that party should have removed that problem. Up to that time there was a danger that the monarch might in effect be called upon to choose a leader for the party. This is what happened in 1923, when the King chose Baldwin in preference to Lord Curzon, it being clear that the Conservative party had a majority in the House of Commons but not clear who would command the greatest confidence among its supporters. A similar problem arose in 1940 when Chamberlain decided to resign as head of a Conservative Government in order that a Coalition Government might be formed, though in this case it is clear that in the end it was not the King, who seems to have preferred Lord Halifax, but the party leaders themselves who settled that Churchill was the most appropriate choice. These last two incidents are chiefly of importance today as occasions on which it could be argued that a possible candidate for the office of Prime Minister was rejected because he was a peer. It is worth noting, however, that there were other reasons for the choice that was made, in particular in the Curzon–Baldwin case, and that precedent is less important than principle in establishing the case against having a peer as Prime Minister.

Normally, therefore, the monarch's role in the appointment of a Prime Minister is minimal. George V did, however, play some part in the process of selection on two occasions, in circumstances which could recur. In 1916 when Asquith resigned as Prime Minister of a Coalition government the King sent for Bonar Law as the leader of the second largest party in the House of Commons. This was, however, a time when party lines were blurred. On the Unionist side Sir Edward Carson had already resigned from the Government and become the centre for some Unionist opposition to it. And on the Liberal side Lloyd George had himself precipitated the crisis by his criticism of the way in which Asquith was conducting the war effort and by his proposals for change. In this he had the support of both Liberals and Unionists. The situation was moreover exceptional in that it was widely felt that there should not be an election because of the disruption it would cause in time of war. When Bonar Law, without any prospect of a dissolution, failed to form a Government the King played a small part by acting as host to the party leaders in an effort to encourage them to come to some agreement. Eventually he invited Lloyd George to form a Government. More controversial was the part he played, or appeared to play, in 1931. This now remains the most important of the episodes in which doubt has arisen as to who should be invited to form a Government.

Baldwin–Curzon, 1923

In May 1923 Bonar Law, the Conservative Prime Minister, resigned on grounds of ill-health. There were two possible successors, Lord Curzon, the Foreign Secretary, who had been Deputy Prime Minister in Bonar Law's absence, and Stanley Baldwin, the Chancellor of the Exchequer. King George V, having consulted leaders of the Conservative party through his private secretary, decided to invite Baldwin to form a Government.

... I endeavoured gradually to break to Lord Curzon that, while estimating at its highest value the predominant position occupied by Lord Curzon in the Government, and indeed in the political life of the country, His Majesty, after due consideration, felt compelled, though with great regret, to ignore the personal elements, and to base his choice upon what he conceived to be the requirements of the present times: viz. the continuance of the Prime Minister in the House of Commons. That His Majesty recognised that this matter was one of the few in which the Sovereign and no one else is personally responsible, and that he believed he would not be fulfilling his trust were he now to make his selection of Prime Minister from the House of Lords ...

[Memorandum of the King's private secretary, Lord Stamfordham, 22 May 1923 [4]]

On 28 May 1923 the Conservative members of both Houses met to elect Baldwin the new Leader of the Party. A resolution to this effect was moved by Lord Curzon, who said in the course of his speech:

In a sense it may be said that the choice of Mr Stanley Baldwin as Leader of the whole Conservative Party has been determined by the action of the King. But we all felt, and I am sure you will agree, that it was right that the choice of the Sovereign should be ratified and confirmed by the vote of the entire Party so that Mr Baldwin in taking up his task may feel that he is the leader who is acclaimed by every section of the party.

[*Gleanings and Memoranda* (June 1923), p. 633 [5]]

On this occasion George V wrote in his diary 'There are really no precedents for the present situation. I must use my judgment as each case arises.'

Churchill–Halifax, 1940

In May 1940 after a critical debate on the conduct of the war, in which some eighty members of the Conservative party had failed to support the

---

[4] Royal Archives. Quoted Harold Nicolson, *George V* (1952), p. 377.
[5] Cited R. T. McKenzie, *British Political Parties* (1955), p. 41.

Government in the division lobbies, the Prime Minister, Neville Chamberlain, approached the leaders of the Labour party with a view to forming a Coalition Government. The Labour party refused to join a Government with Chamberlain at its head. The choice of his successor lay between Churchill and Lord Halifax.

... At 11 o'clock I was again summoned to Downing Street by the Prime Minister. There once more I found Lord Halifax. We took our seats at the table opposite Mr Chamberlain. He told us that he was satisfied that it was beyond his power to form a National Government. The response he had received from the Labour leaders left him in no doubt of this. The question therefore was whom he should advise the King to send for after his own resignation had been accepted. His demeanour was cool, unruffled, and seemingly quite detached from the personal aspect of the affair. He looked at us both across the table.

I have had many important interviews in my public life, and this was certainly the most important. Usually I talk a great deal, but on this occasion I was silent. Mr Chamberlain evidently had in his mind the stormy scene in the House of Commons two nights before, when I had seemed to be in such heated controversy with the Labour Party. Although this had been in his support and defence, he nevertheless felt that it might be an obstacle to my obtaining their adherence at this juncture. His biographer, Mr Feiling, states definitely that he preferred Lord Halifax. As I remained silent, a very long pause ensued. It certainly seemed longer than the two minutes which one observes in the commemorations of Armistice Day. Then at length Halifax spoke. He said that he felt that his position as a Peer, out of the House of Commons, would make it very difficult for him to discharge the duties of Prime Minister in a war like this. He would be held responsible for everything, but would not have the power to guide the Assembly upon whose confidence the life of every government depended. He spoke for some minutes in this sense, and by the time he had finished it was clear that the duty would fall upon me – had in fact fallen upon me. Then, for the first time, I spoke. I said I would have no communication with either of the Opposition Parties until I had the King's Commission to form a Government. On this the momentous conversation came to an end, and we reverted to our ordinary easy and familiar manners of men who had worked for years together and whose lives in and out of office had been spent in all the friendliness of British politics. I then went back to the Admiralty, where, as may well be imagined, much awaited me.

[W. S. Churchill, *The Second World War* (1948), vol. 1, *The Gathering Storm*, p. 523]

The Prime Minister recapitulated the position, saying he had made up his mind that he must go, and that either Churchill or I must take his place. He would serve under either. It would therefore be necessary to see the Labour people before they went to Bournemouth, where they were about to hold a party conference, and ask them whether they would in principle be prepared to join the Government (*a*) under the present Prime Minister or (*b*) under some other Prime Minister. David Margesson said that unity was essential and that he did not think this could be secured under Chamberlain. He did not at that moment pronounce definitely between Churchill and myself, I then said that I thought for the reasons given the Prime Minister must probably go, but that I had no doubt at all in my mind that for me to succeed him would create a quite impossible situation. Apart altogether from Churchill's qualities as compared with my own at this particular juncture, what in fact would be my position? Churchill would be running Defence, and in this connection one could not but remember how rapidly the relationship between Asquith and Lloyd George had broken down in the first war, and I should have no access to the House of Commons. The inevitable result would be that, outside both these points of vital contact, I should speedily become a more or less honorary Prime Minister, living in a kind of twilight just outside the things that really mattered. I might if necessary have prayed in aid the experience of Lord Rosebery as Prime Minister with Sir William Harcourt leading the House of Commons but Churchill, with suitable expressions of regard and humility, having said he could not but feel the force of my words, the Prime Minister reluctantly and Churchill evidently with much less reluctance finished by accepting my view.

[The Earl of Halifax, *Fulness of Days* (1957), p. 219]

I saw the Prime Minister after tea. He told me that Attlee had been to see him & had told him that the Labour Party would serve in the new administration of a new Prime Minister but not one with himself as P.M. He then told me he wished to resign so as to make it possible for a new Prime Minister to form a Government. I accepted his resignation, & told him how grossly unfairly I thought he had been treated, & that I was terribly sorry that all this controversy had happened. We then had an informal talk over his successor. I, of course, suggested Halifax, but he told me that H. was not enthusiastic, as being in the Lords he could only act as a shadow or a ghost in the Commons, where all the real work took place. I was disappointed over this statement, as I thought H. was the obvious man, & that his peerage could be placed in abeyance for the time being. Then I knew that there was only one person whom I could send for to form a Government who had the confidence of the country, & that was Winston. I asked Chamberlain his advice, & he told me Winston was the man to send for. I said goodbye to Chamberlain & thanked him for all his help to me, & repeated that I would greatly regret my loss at not having him as my P.M. I sent for Winston & asked him to form a Government. This he accepted & told me he had not thought this was the reason for my having sent for him. He had thought it possible of course, & gave me some of the names of people he would ask to join his government. He was full of fire & determination to carry out the duties of Prime Minister.

[Diary of King George VI, Friday 10 May 1940 [6]]

The formation of the National Government, 1931

The Labour party had taken office as a minority government in 1929. They soon ran into a major economic crisis.

On August 11th the Prime Minister ... held a meeting of a special Committee of the Cabinet. They decided to take into formal consultation the leaders of the Conservative and Liberal parties. On August 13th MacDonald and Snowden had a conversation with Baldwin, who had come back from Aix-les-Bains, and Neville Chamberlain; and afterwards with myself. We were told in outline the facts as they then stood. ... The Ministers communicated to us the measures they proposed to present to their colleagues.

In the next week the currency position was no better, while the political situation was worsened by a grave division in the Cabinet. The Prime Minister and the Chancellor of the Exchequer had presented a bold and comprehensive plan, which would cover the deficits completely, but only a minority of their colleagues supported them ... On August 19th the Cabinet sat for nine hours, but could not reach agreement. The representatives of the other parties were summoned to a joint conference at Downing Street on the following morning.

On this occasion the Conservatives were Mr Neville Chamberlain and Sir Samuel Hoare ... I had asked to be accompanied by Sir Donald Maclean ... MacDonald and Snowden were again the spokesmen for the Government. We were all of one mind as to the policy to be pursued. ... On the question of maintaining the value of the £ there was no division of opinion, inside the Cabinet or out. The question was only as to ways and means ... [W]e went through the Chancellor of the Exchequer's proposals point by point. The

[6] Royal Archives. Quoted Sir J. W. Wheeler Bennett, *King George VI* (1958), p. 443.

Conservative and Liberal leaders agreed to recommend our parties to support them. The disagreement in the Cabinet continued. We met again on August 21st, and twice on the 22nd. At the final meeting, at nine o'clock that night, the Prime Minister told us that the Cabinet deadlock could not be overcome and that he had decided to resign.

[Viscount Samuel, *Memoirs* (1945), pp. 202–3]

His Majesty reached Euston shortly after eight on the morning of Sunday, August 23: two hours later he received the Prime Minister at Buckingham Palace.

Mr MacDonald explained that the Government were urgently seeking to obtain further loans or credits in New York and Paris to a total of one hundred million pounds. . .

Mr MacDonald at the same time warned the King that it was possible that certain of his most influential colleagues in the Cabinet, and notably Mr Arthur Henderson and Mr William Graham, would not consent to these economies now tentatively put to New York. If they were to resign from the Government it would not be possible for him to carry on the administration without their assistance. The resignation of the Labour Government as a whole would then become inevitable.

The King, on receiving this intimation, decided that the correct constitutional course was immediately to consult the leaders of the Conservative and Liberal Oppositions. Mr Baldwin . . . could not be located: it was thus . . . that Sir Herbert Samuel was the first of the two leaders to furnish His Majesty with advice. Sir Herbert, who reached the Palace shortly after noon, told the King that, in view of the fact that the necessary economies would prove most unpalatable to the working class, it would be to the general interest if they could be imposed by a Labour Government. The best solution would be if Mr Ramsay MacDonald, either with his present, or with a reconstituted Labour Cabinet, could propose the economies required. If he failed to secure the support of a sufficient number of his colleagues, then the best alternative would be a National Government composed of members of the three parties. It would be preferable that Mr MacDonald should remain Prime Minister in such a National Government. Sir Herbert made it clear at the same time that such a non-party Government should only be constituted ' for the single purpose of overcoming the financial crisis '.

At 3.0 that afternoon, Mr Baldwin in his turn came to Buckingham Palace. The King asked him whether he would be prepared to serve in a National Government under Mr Ramsay MacDonald. Mr Baldwin answered that he would be ready to do anything to assist the country in the present crisis. Even if Mr MacDonald insisted on resigning, he, Mr Baldwin, would be ready to carry on the Government if he could be assured of the support of the Liberal Party in effecting the necessary economies. In that event, once the crisis had been surmounted, he would ask His Majesty for a dissolution and go to the country. To this the King agreed. . .

That evening the Cabinet received a telegram from Messrs. J. P. Morgan and Co. intimating that no help could be possible without economies which had the support of the Bank of England and the City.

Having read to the Cabinet a telegram from J. P. Morgan and Co., the Prime Minister made a strong personal appeal to his colleagues to accept the revised schedule of economies even though they comprised a 10% cut in the dole . . . [I]f . . . any senior Minister felt it necessary to resign rather than to consent to such a measure, then the Government must resign as a whole.

It was immediately evident that many important Ministers, with Mr Arthur Henderson at their head, were determined never to consent to any reduction in the benefit. The Prime Minister then stated that he proposed immediately to inform the King of what had passed in Cabinet and to advise His Majesty to summon a conference between Mr Baldwin, Sir Herbert Samuel and himself for the following morning. The Cabinet authorised the Prime Minister to inform His Majesty that they had placed their resignations in his hands. . .

Mr MacDonald reached the Palace at 10.20:

'The Prime Minister', wrote Sir Clive Wigram [the King's private secretary], 'looked scared and unbalanced. He told the King that all was up and that at the Cabinet 11 had voted for accepting the terms of the Bankers and 8 against. The opposition included Henderson, Graham, Adamson, Greenwood, Clynes, Alexander, Addison and Lansbury. In these circumstances the Prime Minister had no alternative than to tender the resignation of the Cabinet.

The King impressed on the Prime Minister that he was the only man to lead the country through this crisis and hoped he would reconsider the situation. His Majesty told him that the Conservatives and Liberals would support him in restoring the confidence of foreigners in the financial stability of the country.

The Prime Minister asked whether the King would confer with Baldwin, Samuel and himself in the morning. His Majesty willingly acceded to this request. . .'

The King's diary for Monday, August 24, is written with his habitual avoidance of exaggeration. . .

Sir Clive Wigram's memorandum of what happened during the Conference is more detailed and informative:

' At 10 a.m. the King held a Conference at Buckingham Palace at which the Prime Minister, Baldwin and Samuel were present. At the beginning, His Majesty impressed upon them that before they left the Palace some communiqué must be issued, which would no longer keep the country and the world in suspense. The Prime Minister said that he had the resignation of his Cabinet in his pocket, but the King replied that he trusted there was no question of the Prime Minister's resignation: the leaders of the three Parties must get together and come to some arrangement. His Majesty hoped that the Prime Minister, with the colleagues who remained faithful to him, would help in the formation of a National Government, which the King was sure would be supported by the Conservatives and the Liberals. The King assured the Prime Minister that, remaining at his post, his position and reputation would be much more enhanced than if he surrendered the government of the country at such a crisis. Baldwin and Samuel said that they were willing to serve under the Prime Minister, and render all help possible to carry on the Government as a National Emergency Government until an emergency bill or bills had been passed by Parliament, which would restore once more British credit and the confidence of foreigners. After that they would expect His Majesty to grant a dissolution. To this course the King agreed. During the Election the National Government would remain in being, though of course each Party would fight the Election on its own lines.

At 10.35 a.m. the King left the three Party leaders to settle the details of the communiqué to be issued, and the latter said they would let His Majesty know when they were ready.

About 11.45 the King was requested to return to the Conference, and was glad to hear that they had been able to some extent to come to some arrangement. A Memorandum had been drawn up which Baldwin and Samuel could place before their respective colleagues, but the Prime Minister said that he would not read this out in Cabinet as he should keep it only for those who remained faithful to him. . . It is quite understood that, up to now, the Cabinet had not resigned. His Majesty congratulated them on the solution of this difficult problem, and pointed out that while France and other countries existed for weeks without a Government, in this country our constitution is so generous that leaders of Parties, after fighting one another for months in the House of Commons, were ready to meet together under the roof of the Sovereign and sink their own differences for a common good and arrange as they had done this morning for a

National Government to meet one of the gravest crises that the British Empire had yet been asked to face.

At the end of the Conference the following communiqué was issued to the Press:

> "His Majesty the King invited the Prime Minister, Mr Stanley Baldwin and Sir Herbert Samuel to Buckingham Palace this morning, and the formation of a National Government is under consideration. A fuller announcement will be made later." '

The Prime Minister then informed the Cabinet that it had been decided to form a ' Cabinet of Individuals ' to deal with the emergency. All except J. H. Thomas, Philip Snowden and Lord Sankey refused to join him.

At 4.0 p.m. Mr Ramsay MacDonald again drove to Buckingham Palace:

> ' The Prime Minister ', wrote Sir Clive Wigram, ' arrived looking worn and weary and was received by the King. The Prime Minister tendered his resignation as Prime Minister of the Labour Government which the King accepted. The King then invited him to form a National Administration. Mr Ramsay MacDonald accepted the offer, and kissed hands on his appointment as the new Prime Minister.'

[Harold Nicolson, *King George V* (1952), pp. 460ff]

Mr MacDonald at the Palace meeting on the Monday morning agreed to the formation of a National Government, with himself as Prime Minister, without a word of previous consultation with any of his Labour colleagues. He knew he would have the great majority of the Labour Cabinet against him, and practically the whole of the Parliamentary Labour Party. He had, in fact, at that time, no assurance that he could take any of his late colleagues with him. Mr Baldwin and Sir Herbert Samuel were in a different position. They could count confidently on carrying their Parties with them. Mr MacDonald at the best could not hope to have the support of more than a mere handful of Labour members.

It was a very strange thing that Mr MacDonald should have taken this grave step without informing some at least of his Labour colleagues of his intention. He did tell his Cabinet, as I have mentioned, that he intended to advise the King to call the Opposition leaders into consultation, but this was not understood either by them or the Labour Cabinet as the prelude to a National Government.

[Viscount Snowden, *An Autobiography* (1934), p. 952]

In an analysis of the constitutional aspects of the crisis which appeared in the autumn of 1931, Leonard Woolf wrote: [7] ' the action of the King and Prime Minister may have been technically constitutional, but if the Crown and the head of a Party Government act as they did, a fair and honest working of a democratic system on the model of the British Constitution is impossible '. His argument was that the Constitution, ' in so far as it is democratic ', rests upon the party system, that the Prime Minister is appointed because he commands the support of his party and not, normally, because of his individual qualifications; and that, despite the fact that MacDonald did not command the support of his party, he was yet appointed in his capacity as party leader. Woolf continued: ' It is said that the King personally induced Mr MacDonald to do this. If so, he was doing something which may prove highly dangerous to the Crown. For, in effect, he was making an individual Prime Minister though he had no support for his Government in the House of Commons, except by a process of camouflage and jugglery ', a precedent which could easily be used to establish something like a dictatorship.

Laski was also an exponent of this type of criticism. . . [8] Basically, he argued along lines similar to Woolf's. Thus, he attacked MacDonald for not advising the King to send for Baldwin or for Arthur Henderson. ' Either of these courses [he argued] would have been strictly constitutional since it would have taken account of the fact that Mr MacDonald was not the Prime Minister as Mr MacDonald but as the leader of a party within whose discretion it was to unmake him as leader if it so desired. . . [O]nce Mr MacDonald dissented from the policy of his party, his significance in our politics became purely personal in character; it can only have become more than that by the significance which the King chose to attach to him at a period of crisis.' [9]

[Graeme C. Moodie, *The Monarch and the Selection of a Prime Minister : A Reexamination of the Crisis of 1931*. V. Political Studies (1957), p. 5]

III. THE DISSOLUTION OF PARLIAMENT

Lord Haldane's memorandum, 1916

When Asquith resigned in 1916 the question arose whether Bonar Law could make his acceptance of the task of forming a Government conditional on the King dissolving Parliament to give him an opportunity to

---

[7] ' A constitutional revolution ', *Political Quarterly*, 2 (1931), 475–7.

[8] His most detailed and effective criticism is to be found in ' The crisis and the Constitution ', a pamphlet published in 1932. But see also his *Parliamentary Government in England* (1938), pp. 402–8.

[9] ' The crisis and the Constitution ', p. 33.

strengthen his position in the House of Commons. Lord Stamfordham, the King's private secretary, wrote to Lord Haldane, a former Lord Chancellor: 'Will you be very kind and tell me, if the King were asked to dissolve Parliament as a condition of anyone undertaking to form a Government, could his Majesty constitutionally refuse to do so?' The following is Lord Haldane's reply.

1. The Sovereign ought at no time to act without the advice of a responsible Minister, excepting when contemplating the exercise of his prerogative right to dismiss Ministers. The only Minister who can properly give advice as to a Dissolution of Parliament is the Prime Minister.

2. The Sovereign, before acting on advice to dissolve, ought to weigh that advice. His Majesty may, instead of accepting it, dismiss the Minister who gives it, or receive his resignation. This is the only alternative to taking his advice.

3. It follows that the Sovereign cannot entertain any bargain for a Dissolution merely with a possible Prime Minister before the latter is fully installed. The Sovereign cannot, before that event, properly weigh the general situation and the Parliamentary position of the Ministry as formed.

[Memorandum of Lord Haldane, 5 December 1916 [10]]

Labour Government, 1950

In February 1950 the Labour party was returned to power with an overall majority of eight. There was some discussion as to the circumstances in which the King could refuse the grant of a further dissolution of Parliament if it were advised by Prime Minister Attlee in the hope of increasing his majority. The following letters discussing the issue were written to the Editor of *The Times*.

Sir, There seems to be an impression in some quarters that if the Government were to be defeated in the Commons on an important vote in present circumstances the Prime Minister would have the right to demand a dissolution of Parliament. This is unsound constitutional doctrine: Mr Attlee would have no such 'right'. The classic passage on the subject is contained in a speech made by Mr Asquith – no mean authority on such a matter – on December 18, 1923, just after the first MacDonald Government was formed. He said: 'The dissolution of Parliament is in this country one of the prerogatives of the Crown. It is not a mere feudal survival, but it is a part, and I think a useful part, of our constitutional system . . . It does not mean that the Crown should act arbitrarily and without the advice of responsible Ministers, but it does mean that the Crown

[10] Royal Archives. Quoted Nicolson *op. cit.* p. 289.

is not bound to take the advice of a particular Minister to put its subjects to the tumult and turmoil of a series of General Elections so long as it can find other Ministers who are prepared to give contrary advice. The notion that a Minister who cannot command a majority in the House of Commons . . . is invested with *the right* to demand a dissolution is as subversive of constitutional usage as it would, in my opinion, be pernicious to the paramount interests of the nation at large.'

The situation envisaged is one of the rare surviving cases in which the Sovereign exercises his own discretion in deciding upon his public action... If, therefore, the Government were overthrown by an adverse vote, it would be an error to suppose that the King had no option. The King's Government would have to be carried on, and the question for the Sovereign to resolve would be whether someone else should be invited to form a Government. It may be, with party representation so nearly equal on either side, that the alternative Government could not be formed or would not last, in which case another General Election becomes unavoidable. But, be that as it may, it seems important to recognise how that would come about, and not to suppose that the Sovereign is constitutionally bound to act on the advice of a Minister who is unable to carry on.

House of Lords, April 22   Yours faithfully,
                                                            SIMON

[*The Times*, 24 April 1950]

Sir, In spite of the authority due to his eminence both in law and in politics, I think that Lord Simon is on unsound and dangerous ground when he suggests . . . that the King might properly refuse to accept the advice of the Prime Minister to dissolve Parliament. It is in the highest degree desirable that the King should remain *au dessus le combat* in respect of political manœuvres not only in actuality but in appearance. By refusing to accept a Prime Minister's advice the King would put the Opposition into office, thereby in effect giving them the opportunity of choosing the occasion for a General Election, which would expose him to criticism. Although such conduct may have been still possible in Victorian times, when it was much debated, I submit that the march of political development has made it no longer justifiable. Moreover, it is very important that in such circumstances the King should be bound by a clear and simple rule which there can be no mistaking, and this is exactly what the convention that he must accept the advice of his Prime Minister provides . . .

                                                            Yours faithfully,
House of Lords, April 24   CHORLEY

[*The Times*, 26 April 1950]

Sir, Lord Simon's letter shows that in Mr Asquith's view – expressed immediately before the formation of the first MacDonald Government and not 'just after', as Lord Simon says – it was the right of the Crown to refuse a dissolution to a Prime Minister defeated in the House of Commons. But it is surely of at least equal importance to remember that this is a prerogative which has been exercised on no occasion since the Reform Bill of 1832; that when Queen Victoria considered exercising it in 1858 she was strongly advised by Lord Aberdeen, whom she consulted informally as a former Prime Minister who was not a supporter of the Government, against taking 'an unusual and, he believed he might say, an unprecedented course'; and that when she again considered exercising it in 1886, at a time when she was very strongly prejudiced against the Government of the day, even the Leader of the Opposition warned her of the 'undesirable' consequence that if 'tempestuous times should follow, the responsibility would be thrown on her'; and that in 1924, following upon Mr Asquith's statement, King George V appears to have had no hesitation in granting a dissolution to Mr MacDonald, in spite of the fact that this involved the country in its third General Election within two years . . .[11]

House of Commons, April 24

Yours faithfully,
Roy Jenkins

[*The Times*, 26 April 1950]

Sir, . . . This 'difficult and intricate question' (as Anson called it) cannot be dogmatically answered without considering the circumstances in which it arises. In our constitution, unlike that of the United States, the legislature has not a fixed period of life, but may be brought to an end at any time before five years are up by an exercise of the prerogative. Is it really suggested that, however recent the last General Election may be and whatever its result, the Prime Minister has the absolute right to require the Crown to put its subjects to the 'tumult and turmoil' of another General Election within a few weeks of the last? And if the result of the second election does not suit him, can he claim a third? On the contrary I conceive that the Sovereign has the duty, in the case of a freshly elected Parliament at any rate, of considering whether government could be carried on under another head, and that if he thinks it can, he is acting constitutionally and in the best interests of the country in preferring this alternative. I am not presuming to suggest what might happen at the present time, but I am maintaining an abstract

[11] [In fact the King granted the dissolution with great reluctance, as he had when Baldwin requested a dissolution in 1923. See Harold Nicolson, *King George V*, pp. 380 and 400.]

proposition, which I think can be established by taking instances which have actually occurred.

Supposing that, as the result of a General Election, a Prime Minister finds himself left with the support of only a minority in the new House of Commons. He is under no obligation to resign immediately, and his Government may decide to meet the House when it assembles. An amendment to the Address is then carried against them, as happened in 1892. When this happens, can the defeated Prime Minister go to the Sovereign and demand another General Election, and is the Sovereign bound to grant his request? Of course not. But why not? Because there is an alternative Government available, without sending the electorate again to the polls. Or again, supposing that a Government which is normally supported by a majority is defeated by a snap vote, the result of which can be rectified or overlooked. Can the Prime Minister have the right to claim a dissolution, perhaps in the hope of turning his small majority into a larger one? Surely the whole thing depends on the actual circumstances, and the Sovereign, in the discharge of his heavy responsibility, may consider the circumstances; and one relevant circumstance may be that Parliament is only a few weeks old.

Everybody will agree that the King should manifestly remain *au dessus du combat*, but this result is not necessarily secured in all circumstances by ' taking the advice of a particular Minister to put his subjects to the tumult and turmoil of a series of General Elections so long as he can find other Ministers who are prepared to give contrary advice '. That is what Mr Asquith said, and it seems to me, with all respect to those who assert the contrary, that the British constitution is not quite so wooden as they suppose. The danger of laying down a universal negative is that it can be upset by instances to the contrary such as the above. It is one of the advantages of having a constitution which is mainly unwritten that its proper working can always be adjusted to the public interest and to common sense. How things might work out in present circumstances is not for your correspondents to decide, or even to speculate. But I venture to maintain that the proposition of Mr Asquith, formulated in words based on almost unrivalled practical contact with constitutional issues, is correct.

Yours faithfully,
House of Lords, April 26

SIMON

[*The Times*, 27 April 1950]

Sir, On the outbreak of war in 1939 General Hertzog, then Prime Minister of the Union of South Africa, proposed to his Parliament a resolution that South Africa should declare neutrality. This was opposed by General Smuts, and after debate General Hertzog was defeated in the House of Assembly by a majority of 13. General Hertzog thereupon advised the Governor-General, the late Sir Patrick Duncan, to dissolve Parliament. Sir Patrick Duncan refused the advice and sent for General Smuts, who formed a Government which carried on successfully, albeit with a small majority, until that Parliament expired by effluxion of time in accordance with statute in 1943.

Was Sir Patrick Duncan wrong, as apparently Lord Chorley and Mr Roy Jenkins, M.P., would have it? . . .

April 26
                                        Yours faithfully,
                                        DOUGAL O. MALCOLM
[*The Times*, 27 April 1950]

Sir, It is surely indisputable (and common sense) that a Prime Minister may ask – not demand – that his Sovereign will grant him a dissolution of Parliament; and that the Sovereign, if he so chooses, may refuse to grant this request. The problem of such a choice is entirely personal to the Sovereign, though he is, of course, free to seek informal advice from anybody whom he thinks fit to consult.

In so far as this matter can be publicly discussed, it can be properly assumed that no wise Sovereign – that is, one who has at heart the true interest of the country, the constitution, and the Monarchy – would deny a dissolution to his Prime Minister unless he were satisfied that: (1) the existing Parliament was still vital, viable, and capable of doing its job; (2) a General Election would be detrimental to the national economy; (3) he could rely on finding another Prime Minister who could carry on his Government, for a reasonable period, with a working majority in the House of Commons. When Sir Patrick Duncan refused a dissolution to his Prime Minister in South Africa in 1939, all these conditions were satisfied: when Lord Byng did the same in Canada in 1926,[12] they appeared to

[12] [In September 1925 the Liberal Government under Mr Mackenzie King had failed to secure a majority of seats at the General Election but had managed to remain in power with the support of the Progressive and Labour parties. In June 1926 the Governor-General, Lord Byng, refused the Prime Minister's request for a dissolution after he had ascertained that Mr Meighen, the leader of the Opposition Conservative party, was prepared to form a Government with the support of the Agricultural party. Mr Mackenzie King therefore resigned and Mr Meighen was invited to form a Government. Within three days, the new Conservative Government was defeated in the House by one vote, after the Agricultural party had failed to support it. When the Conservative Prime Minister in his turn asked Lord Byng to dissolve Parliament, he granted his request. At the election, the Liberals were returned with a large majority and their success was regarded as a vote of censure on Lord Byng who was strongly criticized for granting to the Conservatives what he had refused the Liberals.]

be, but in the event the third proved illusory.

I am, &c., SENEX [13]

April 29

[*The Times*, 2 May 1950]

IV. THE DISMISSAL OF MINISTERS

The Home Rule crisis, 1912–14

In 1906 the Liberal party was returned to power with a large majority.[14] In 1909 the House of Lords, which had already rejected and mutilated other Bills sent up from the House of Commons, rejected the Finance Bill embodying the Budget proposals of the Chancellor of the Exchequer, Lloyd George. This was a serious interference with the Commons' traditional right to determine money matters. It was defended on the grounds that the measure was more than a mere financial measure and amounted to a social reform for which the Government had no mandate. The Prime Minister, Asquith, advised King Edward VII to dissolve Parliament, and a General Election was held in January 1910. The Liberal party's majority was greatly reduced but it was able to stay in power with the support of the Labour party and the Irish Nationalists.[15] The Government was now determined that the power of the House of Lords to force a Government to choose between abandoning legislation which it considered vital and advising a dissolution of Parliament should be removed. As it was unlikely that the House of Lords would readily acquiesce in any weakening of its own powers, the Prime Minister advised King George V, who had succeeded his father in May 1910, that it might be necessary to create five hundred peers to make sure that the Government was able to command a majority in the House of Lords in favour of the necessary legislation.[16] King George V not unnaturally insisted that before he could consent to such drastic action he must be satisfied that the Government had the support of the electorate for the measure. Having extracted from the King a secret pledge that he would create peers if the Government could win electoral support for a Parliament Bill to reduce the powers of the Lords, Prime Minister Asquith advised a dissolution. At the General Election in December 1910, the Liberal party's majority disappeared but it was still able to stay in power with the sup-

[13] [J. Wheeler-Bennett, in his biography of George VI, notes that ' Senex ' was Sir Alan Lascelles, the King's private secretary.]

[14] Liberals 400, Conservatives 157, Irish Nationalists 83, Labour 30.

[15] Liberals 275, Conservatives 273, Irish Nationalists 82, Labour 40.

[16] There were precedents for such a manœuvre though these had been on a much smaller scale. Queen Anne had created twelve peers in 1712 to secure a majority in the Lords in favour of the Treaty of Utrecht. William IV had very reluctantly agreed to create some sixty peers to carry through the Reform Bill of 1832, though in the event this did not prove necessary as a sufficient number of peers followed the lead of the Duke of Wellington and refrained from voting against the Bill.

port of the Labour and Irish members.[17] The King's readiness to create peers was made known, and the Parliament Act (below, p. 239) was passed by the House of Lords without their actual creation being necessary.

No sooner had this crisis passed than another, which had been in the background from the beginning of the controversy over the powers of the House of Lords, came to the fore. The main feature of the Parliament Act was that it took away the power of the House of Lords to reject legislation outright and gave it instead a power to delay it for two years. This meant that it was now possible for the first time to pass legislation without the consent of the Upper House. One of the issues which had for a long time troubled English politics was the question of Home Rule for Ireland. It was supported by the Liberal party and by the Irish Nationalists who derived most of their strength from southern Ireland. It was opposed by the Conservative and Unionist party and a great part of the people living in the northern Irish counties of Ulster. Until the passing of the Parliament Act, no Bill granting Home Rule to Ireland could have been passed without the consent of the House of Lords where the Conservative strength was overwhelming. In April 1912 the Liberal Government introduced a Home Rule Bill in the House of Commons with the intention that it should become law after two years under the Parliament Act, even if it were rejected by the House of Lords. It aroused violent opposition. There were threats that if the Bill became law, a provisional Government would be established in northern Ireland, and volunteer forces were raised in both southern and northern Ireland. Those who wanted the Union with England to be preserved, or at least special provision made for Ulster, were strongly supported by the leaders of the Conservative Opposition. The Opposition argued that the Government had no mandate for the Bill, as the last two elections had been fought over entirely different issues. They alleged that the Bill was part of a corrupt parliamentary bargain between the Government and the Irish Nationalists and was in fact the latter's reward for their support of the Government in cutting down the powers of the Lords. It became their avowed object to force the Government to hold an election. From a constitutional point of view, it was clear that now that the power of the House of Lords to force a dissolution, as they had done over the Budget of 1909, had been so drastically reduced, the King was the only person who conceivably still had the power to insist on an election being held before the Bill was passed, either by persuasion or, if this failed, by refusing his assent to the Home Rule Bill until an election had been held, or, in the last resort, by dismissing the Government and inviting someone to form a Government who would advise him to dissolve Parliament so that an election could be held. The Opposition leaders put their views to the King in two memoranda, one of which is printed below. That the King felt the force of these arguments and the dangers inherent in the situation can be seen from his letter to the Prime Minister, to which

[17] Liberals 272, Conservatives 272, Irish Nationalists 84, Labour 42.

Asquith replied with a statement of the orthodox view of the position of a constitutional monarch in the twentieth century.

In the event, the outbreak of war prevented matters coming to a head. The King, however, had prepared a memorandum with the help of Lord Loreburn, which probably reflected his final view, though it was never sent to the Prime Minister. The views expressed in it suggest that even if there may still be occasions on which the King would be justified in exercising the power to refuse his assent to legislation or to dismiss his Ministers, the very occasions on which the situation was serious enough to justify such action would be occasions when matters had gone too far for the action to have a tranquillizing effect.

MR LAW ON ULSTER'S RESISTANCE
JUSTIFICATION OF FORCE
GREAT DEMONSTRATION AT BLENHEIM
(From our special correspondent)

Mr Bonar Law, who was received with cheers, said: — . . . The Parliament Bill was not carried for nothing. It was carried in order that the Government might be able to force through Parliament Home Rule proposals which at the election were carefully hidden from the people of this country, and which they did not dare even to mention in their election addresses – proposals which they are trying to carry, not only without the consent, but, as we know and as they know, against the will of the people of this country.

The Chief Liberal Whip has told us also that the Home Rule Bill will be carried through the House of Commons before Christmas. Perhaps it will. (A Voice.—'Perhaps it won't.') I do not know. But I do know this – that we do not acknowledge their right to carry such a revolution by such means. We do not recognize that any such action is the constitutional government of a free people. We regard them as a revolutionary committee which has seized by fraud upon despotic power. (Cheers.) In our opposition to them we shall not be guided by the considerations, we shall not be restrained by the bonds, which would influence us in an ordinary political struggle. We shall use any means (loud cheers), whatever means seem to us likely to be most effective . . . to deprive them of the power which they have usurped and to compel them to face the people whom they have deceived. Even if the Home Rule Bill passes through the House of Commons, what then? I said in the House of Commons, and I repeat here, that there are things stronger than Parliamentary majorities.

. . . Nations, and great nations, have, indeed, taken up arms to prevent their subjects from seceding, but no nation will ever take up arms to compel loyal subjects to leave their community. (Cheers.) I do not believe for a moment that any Government would ever dare to make the attempt, but I am sure of this – that, if the attempt were made, the Government would not succeed in carrying Home Rule. They would succeed only in lighting fires of civil war. . . . While I had still in the party a position of less responsibility than that which I have now I said that in my opinion if an attempt were made without the clearly expressed will of the people of this country, and as part of a corrupt Parliamentary bargain, to deprive these men of their birthright, they would be justified in resisting by all means in their power, including force. (Cheers.) I said so then, and I say now, with a full sense of the responsibility which attaches to my position, that if the attempt be made under present conditions I can imagine no length of resistance to which Ulster will go in which I shall not be ready to support them and in which they will not be supported by the overwhelming majority of the British people. (The audience rose from their seats and cheered this declaration for some minutes.)

[*The Times*, 29 July 1912]

If the Home Rule Bill passes through all its stages under the Parliament Act and requires only the Royal Assent the position will be a very serious and almost an impossible one for the Crown. The Unionist Party will hold that, as the Constitution is admittedly in suspense (for the duty of carrying out the Preamble of the Parliament Act [18] is admitted by the Government) and as it is at the least doubtful, and in view of the by-elections more than doubtful whether the Government have the approval of the country, the position is precisely similar to what it would be if the Government supported by the House of Commons asked the Sovereign to use the Royal Prerogative to overcome the opposition of the House of Lords. In such circumstances Unionists would certainly believe that the King not only had the Constitutional right but that it was his duty before acting on the advice of his Ministers to ascertain whether it would not be possible to appoint other Ministers who would advise him differently and allow the question to be decided by the country at a General Election. The last precedent prior to the Parliament Act which B.L. can recall was the Reform Bill of 1832. On that occasion B.L. believes, without having the opportunity of refreshing his memory, that though an election had been fought specially on the issue of the Reform Bill the King did not consent to the creation of the new Peers till he had sent for the Leader of the Conservative Party and ascertained from him that he was not prepared to take the responsibility of forming a Government. Such would be the view of the Unionist Party.

[18] [See below, p. 239.]

The Radical Party, on the other hand, would almost certainly maintain that the veto of the Sovereign had fallen completely into desuetude, and that the duty of the King was to regard the passage of the Home Rule Bill under the Parliament Act as final and give his assent to it as a matter of course. In reality it does not matter which of these views is constitutionally sound. In any case, whatever course was taken by H.M., half of his people would think that he had failed in his duty, and in view of the very bitter feelings which by that time would have been aroused, the Crown would, B.L. fears, be openly attacked by the people of Ulster and their sympathisers if he gave his assent to the Bill, and by a large section of the Radical Party if he took any other course. Such a position is one in which the King ought not to be placed, and B.L. is of the opinion that if his Majesty put the case strongly to the Prime Minister he would feel that it was his duty to extricate the King from so terrible a dilemma. B.L. also ventures to suggest to H.M. that when any crisis arises it might be well to consult informally Mr Balfour or Lord Lansdowne or himself, and he assures H.M. that any advice given under such circumstances would not be influenced by Party considerations.

[Rough draft of a memorandum submitted by Bonar Law to King George V, September 1912 [19]]

Although I have not spoken to you before on the subject, I have been for some time very anxious about the Irish Home Rule Bill, and especially with regard to Ulster. The speeches not only of people like Sir Edward Carson, but of the Unionist Leaders, and of ex-Cabinet Ministers; the stated intention of setting up a provisional Government in Ulster directly the Home Rule Bill is passed; the reports of Military preparations, Army drilling etc.; of assistance from England, Scotland and the Colonies; of the intended resignation of their Commissions by Army Officers; all point toward rebellion if not Civil War; and, if so, to certain bloodshed. Meanwhile, there are rumours of probable agitation in the country; of monster petitions; Addresses from the House of Lords; from Privy Councillors; urging me to use my influence to avert the catastrophe which threatens Ireland. Such vigorous action taken, or likely to be taken, will place me in a very embarrassing position in the centre of the conflicting parties backed by their respective Press. Whatever I do I shall offend half the population. One alternative would certainly result in alienating the Ulster Protestants from me, and whatever happens the result must be detrimental to me personally and to the Crown in general. No Sovereign has ever been in such a

[19] Quoted Robert Blake, *The Unknown Prime Minister* (1955), p. 150.

position, and this pressure is sure to increase during the next few months.

In this period I shall have a right to expect the greatest confidence and support from my Ministers, and, above all, from my Prime Minister. I cannot help feeling that the Government is drifting and taking me with it. Before the gravity of the situation increases I should like to know how you view the present state of affairs, and what you imagine will be the outcome of it. On the 24th July I saw Mr Birrell, who admitted the seriousness of the outlook. He seemed to think that perhaps an arrangement could be made for Ulster to 'contract out' of the Home Rule scheme, say for 10 years, with the right to come under the Irish Parliament, if so desired, after a referendum by her people, at the end of that period. But it was for the Opposition to come forward with some practical proposal to this effect.

Is there any chance of a settlement by consent as suggested by Lord Loreburn, Lord Macdonnell, Lord Dunraven, Mr W. O'Brien, Mr Birrell, Lord Lansdowne, Mr Bonar Law and others? Would it be possible to have a Conference in which all parties should take part, to consider the whole policy of devolution, of which you, in introducing the Home Rule Bill in April 1912, said 'Irish Home Rule is only the first step'? Would it not be better to try to settle measures involving great changes in the Constitution, such as Home Rule all round, Reform of the House of Lords etc., not on Party lines, but by agreement?

[Memorandum handed by King George V to Asquith, 11 August 1913 [20]]

... In old days, before our present Constitution was completely evolved, the Crown was a real and effective, and often a dominating, factor in legislation. Its powers were developed to considerable lengths by such Kings as Henry VIII, and enforced with much suppleness and reserve by Queen Elizabeth; but the Tudor Sovereigns had a keen eye and a responsive pulse to the general opinion of the nation. The Stuarts, who followed, pushed matters to extremes, with the result that Charles I lost his head and James II his throne. The Revolution put the title to the Throne and its prerogatives on a Parliamentary basis, and, since a comparatively early date in the reign of Queen Anne, the Sovereign has never attempted to withhold his assent from a Bill which had received Parliamentary sanction.

We have had, since that date, Sovereigns of marked individuality, of great authority, and of strong ideas (often, from time to time,

[20] Royal Archives. Quoted Nicolson, *op. cit.* p. 223.

opposed to the policy of the Ministry of the day), but none of them – not even George III, Queen Victoria, or King Edward VII – have ever dreamt of reviving the ancient veto of the Crown. We have now a well-established tradition of 200 years, that, in the last resort, the occupant of the Throne accepts and acts upon the advice of his Ministers. The Sovereign may have lost something of his personal power and authority, but the Crown has been thereby removed from the storms and vicissitudes of party politics, and the monarchy rests upon a solid foundation which is buttressed, both by long tradition, and by the general conviction that its impersonal status is an invaluable safeguard for the continuity of our national life.

It follows that the rights and duties of a constitutional monarch in this country in regard to legislation are confined within determined and strictly circumscribed limits. He is entitled and bound to give his Ministers all relevant information which comes to him; to point out objections which seem to him valid against the course which they advise; to suggest (if he thinks fit) an alternative policy. Such intimations are always received by Ministers with the utmost respect, and considered with more care and deference than if they proceeded from any other quarter. But, in the end, the Sovereign always acts upon the advice which Ministers, after full deliberation and (if need be) reconsideration, feel it their duty to offer. They give that advice well knowing that they can, and probably will, be called to account for it by Parliament.

The Sovereign undoubtedly has the power of changing his advisers, but it is relevant to point out that there has been, during the last 130 years, one occasion only on which the King has dismissed a Ministry which still possessed the confidence of the House of Commons. This was in 1834, when William IV (one of the least wise of British monarchs) called upon Lord Melbourne to resign. He took advantage (as we now know) of a hint improvidently given by Lord Melbourne himself, but the proceeding was neither well advised nor fortunate. The dissolution which followed left Sir R. Peel in a minority, and Lord Melbourne and his friends in a few months returned to power, which they held for the next six years. The authority of the Crown was disparaged, and Queen Victoria, during her long reign, was careful never to repeat the mistake of her predecessor.

The Parliament Act was not intended in any way to affect, and it is submitted has not affected, the Constitutional position of the Sovereign. It deals only with differences between the two Houses. When the two Houses are in agreement (as is always the case when there is a Conservative majority in the House of Commons), the

Act is a dead letter. When they differ, it provides that, after a considerable interval, the thrice repeated decision of the Commons shall prevail, without the necessity for a dissolution of Parliament. The possibility of abuse is guarded against by the curtailment of the maximum life of any given House of Commons to five years.

Nothing can be more important, in the best interests of the Crown and of the country, than that a practice, so long established and so well justified by experience, should remain unimpaired. It frees the occupant of the Throne from all personal responsibility for the acts of the Executive and the Legislature. It gives force and meaning to the old maxim that ' the King can do no wrong '. So long as it prevails, however objectionable particular Acts may be to a large section of his subjects, they cannot hold him in any way accountable, and their loyalty is (or ought to be) wholly unaffected. If, on the other hand, the King were to intervene on one side, or in one case – which he could only do by dismissing Ministers in *de facto* possession of a Parliamentary majority – he would be expected to do the same on another occasion, and perhaps for the other side. Every Act of Parliament, of the first order of importance, and only passed after acute controversy, would be regarded as bearing the personal *imprimatur* of the Sovereign. He would, whether he wished it or not, be dragged into the arena of party politics; and at a dissolution following such a dismissal of Ministers as has been just referred to, it is no exaggeration to say that the Crown would become the football of contending factions.

This is a Constitutional catastrophe which it is the duty of every wise statesman to do the utmost in his power to avert.

[Memorandum presented to King George V by Prime Minister Asquith, September 1913 [21]]

The bill for the better Government of Ireland having now passed through the necessary stages, the King concludes that, by the terms of the Parliament Act, it will come on, automatically, for his Assent unless the House of Commons direct to the contrary.

Much has been said and written in favour of the proposition that the Assent of the Crown should be withheld from the measure. On the other hand, the King feels strongly that that extreme course should not be adopted in this case unless there is convincing evidence that it would avert a national disaster, or at least have a tranquillizing effect on the distracting conditions of the time. There is no such evidence.

[Letter drafted by King George V to Asquith on 31 July 1914 [22]]

[21] Royal Archives K. 2553 (2) 10.
[22] Royal Archives. Quoted Nicolson, *op. cit.* p. 234.

V. THE STATUS OF CONSTITUTIONAL CONVENTIONS AFFECTING THE CROWN

The following passage, written in the context of the role of the monarch in the appointment of a Prime Minister, in fact, applies more generally to the conventions regulating the conduct of the monarch, and indeed to the status of constitutional conventions generally.

The second assumption, which must now in part be discarded, is that problems about constitutional behaviour can be discussed as if they were almost entirely matters for intellectual debate and argument. In fact, of course, constitutional rules are the product of, for example, the distribution of power in society as well as of the relative rational appeal of conflicting arguments. This is particularly obvious if one reflects upon the nature of the conventions governing the behaviour of the Monarch. These conventions have arisen gradually out of changing political circumstances. Following upon changes in the distribution of power within this country, and the demand that government become accountable and responsive to new elements within the community, the Crown, if it was to survive as an object of general loyalty, had progressively to surrender the claim to exercise its full legal powers. Given that the Crown was to continue as Head of State and the symbol of national unity or, in other words, if it was to be free from serious political opposition, there was no politically feasible alternative to its becoming increasingly non-political and non-governmental. Being relatively irremovable, the Crown could only survive, in the face of demands for governmental accountability, by ceasing to be an active force in an ever-widening field of government. In the same way the House of Lords, in order to remain as the second chamber, has had to shed much of its powers, just as the United Kingdom has had to confer Dominion status upon the more restless and self-reliant of its colonies in order to maintain any form of close association with them. And, Dicey notwithstanding, the ultimate sanctions for obeying the conventions which have developed in this manner can only consist of the very forces which stimulated their evolution or adoption.

. . . It is primarily for this reason, incidentally, that constitutional precedents are not binding as such, but only in so far as they indicate the nature of the behaviour required by political circumstances. To put this yet another way, it may be said that in the case of the conventions surrounding the Monarch, more obviously even than with other constitutional rules, the constitutional and political limits to the use of power tend to coincide . . . [G]iven the nature and development of the conventions relating to the Monarchy, it is important that no Monarch act in such a way as to arouse the opposition of any powerful group in the community, lest this lead eventually to the undermining of the whole position and strength of the Monarchy itself (or, less drastically, of an individual Monarch); and from this it follows that criticism of a Monarch's action, in so far as it may reflect the beginning of such opposition, provides some ground for thinking it undesirable that such an action should be repeated. It is not criticism *per se* that is important, but criticism backed by power, actually or potentially. . .

[Graeme C. Moodie, *op. cit.* p. 18]

Compare the statement of Viscount Radcliffe in *Adegbenro* v. *Akintola* [1963] A.C. 614, 628. In talking of the principle that 'subject to questions as to the right of dissolution and appeal to the electorate, a Prime Minister might not remain in office as such once it has been established that he has ceased to command the support of the majority of the House ', he noted: ' But, when that is said, the practical application of these principles to a given situation, if it arose in the United Kingdom, would depend less upon any simple statement of principle than upon the actual facts of that situation and the good sense and political sensitivity of the main actors called up to take part.'

And see the speech of Baldwin, below p. 59.

CHAPTER II

THE GOVERNMENT

The role of Government

7. The role of government has greatly changed. Its traditional regulatory functions have multiplied in size and greatly broadened in scope. It has taken on vast new responsibilities. It is expected to achieve such general economic aims as full employment, a satisfactory rate of growth, stable prices and a healthy balance of payments. Through these and other policies (e.g. public purchasing, investment grants, financial regulators) it profoundly influences the output, costs and profitability of industry generally in both the home and overseas markets. Through nationalisation it more directly controls a number of basic industries. It has responsibilities for the location of industry and town and country planning. It engages in research and development both for civil and military purposes. It provides comprehensive social services and is now expected to promote the fullest possible development of individual human potential. All these changes have made for a massive growth of public expenditure. Public spending means public control. A century ago the tasks of government were mainly passive and regulatory. Now they amount to a much more active and positive engagement in our affairs.

8. Technological progress and the vast amount of new knowledge have made a major impact on these tasks and on the process of taking decisions; the change goes on. Siting a new airport, buying military supplies, striking the right balance between coal, gas, oil, and nuclear-powered electricity in a new energy policy – all these problems involve the use of new techniques of analysis, management and co-ordination.

9. There has also been a complex intermingling of the public and private sectors. This has led to a proliferation of para-state organisations: public corporations, nationalised industries, negotiating bodies with varying degrees of public and private participation, public participation in private enterprises, voluntary bodies financed from public funds. Between the operations of the public and the private sectors there is often no clear boundary. Central and local government stand in a similarly intricate relationship; central government is generally held responsible for services that it partly

33

or mainly finances but local authorities actually provide. As the tasks of government have grown and become more complex, so the need to consult and co-ordinate has grown as well.

10. The time it takes to reach a decision and carry it out has often lengthened. This is partly because of technological advance and the resulting complexity, e.g. of defence equipment. Another reason is that the public and Parliament demand greater foresight and order in, for example, the development of land, the transport system and other resources, than they did in the past.

11. Governments also work more and more in an international setting. The improvement in communications and the greater interdependence of nations enlarges the difficulties as well as the opportunities of government.

[Report of the Committee on the Civil Service 1966-8. Cmnd. 3638 (June 1968)]

I. GOVERNMENT DEPARTMENTS

THE PRIME MINISTER (MR HAROLD WILSON): . . . Changes in the central machinery of government, which go on all the time under every Government, reflect, or should reflect, the changing nature of the problems facing the country and the Government, though, inevitably, they also reflect the administrative ideas and working methods of the Prime Minister of the day, whoever he may be, and his colleagues. For example, even if they had been dealing with almost exactly the same problems at the same time, Lloyd George would have had very different ideas on government machinery and working than, say, Clem Attlee. Or, if they had been working and living at the same time, Baldwin would have had very different ideas from those of Gladstone or Peel. Thus, because they do reflect the views of Governments, quite apart from the problems with which they must deal, questions of the machinery of government and organisation, even the existence of particular Departments, inevitably become a matter of controversy, for example, between Government and Opposition, but also non-politically between hon. Members even within the same party and between experts in administration studying all these problems.

[773 H.C.Deb. 5s. c. 1556. 21 November 1968]

The Executive in the United Kingdom is organised on a functional basis. This distributes the responsibilities of the central Government between Departments in a number of groups, which are as homogeneous as possible and provide the Ministers concerned with a set of interrelated functions for which they can reasonably be expected, subject to the collective endorsement of the Cabinet, to be accountable to Parliament...

The application of this principle has led to an aggregation of functions which were previously exercised in separate Departments into a smaller number of large Departments... Thus, several Departments which were originally responsible for various different aspects of social security were first grouped together in a Ministry of Social Security; and that, in turn, has now been combined with the Department responsible for policy on the health services in a single Department of Health and Social Security under one Minister, the Secretary of State for Social Services. Similarly, in the environmental field the individual Departments which were responsible... for... housing, local government, transport and public buildings have been grouped together in a single Department of the Environment under one Minister, the Secretary of State for the Environment.

One advantage of this process... is that virtually all Departments now have at their head a Minister who has a strong claim to be a member of the Cabinet; and at the same time it has been possible to reduce the size of the Cabinet to the more compact and manageable figure of 19... A second advantage is the greater scope which this grouping of functions gives for the resolution within a single Department of the differences which used to arise between different Departments...

On the other hand the creation and development of these very large Departments have brought fresh problems. In part these lie in the internal management of organisations which are so large. This is not just a question of numbers but more particularly of complexity of issues, and this makes it more difficult for a single Minister to find time to deal with the range of issues with which he will be faced.[1] For example, the responsibilities of the Department of Trade and Industry encompass control of most of the public sector, nationalised industries, the relations with private sector industry, the promotion of exports and other issues such as civil aviation and marine services. The Secretary of State in charge of the Department is supported by other Ministers, to whom he devolves the supervision of particular sub-groups of functions. But the ultimate responsibility remains his; and the larger the Department and the wider the range of its functions, the heavier is the burden of that responsibility.

During the period of growth of the very large Departments, other forces have influenced the development of the machinery of Government... [W]hile the Cabinet Office retains its role of providing both an impartial service for the Cabinet itself and for its com-

---

[1] For the effect of this and the growth in complexity of government activity generally on the doctrine of Ministerial responsibility see below p. 165.

mittees, and a machinery for the resolution of inter-departmental disputes, its functions have been enlarged by the addition of a new body called the Central Policy Review Staff (CPRS). This body... is responsible for helping Ministers to distinguish the wood from the trees by keeping their main policy objectives firmly in view and reminding them, as appropriate, of the need to relate separate collective decisions to the totality of those objectives... As such, it is not the monopoly of any single Minister: it is at the service of all Ministers impartially and its programme of work is approved by the Cabinet as a matter of collective judgment.

[T. H. Caulcott, 'Developments in the organisation of Government Departments', *Management Services in Government*, vol. 28, no. 2 (1973), p. 68]

The Ministers of the Crown (Transfer of Functions) Act, 1946

THE LORD PRESIDENT OF THE COUNCIL (MR HERBERT MORRISON): ... The tasks of the government are so complex and develop so rapidly that Ministers can fairly ask Parliament to grant them some little latitude in adapting the executive machinery from time to time... [A] great many ministerial functions are not regulated by statute at all and these functions can be redistributed among Ministers as administrative needs may, from time to time, require... But those functions which have been assigned to particular Ministers by statute [2] cannot, under the present law, be transferred to another Minister without full-dress legislation...

In the Government's view, it is much more reasonable that the simple issue whether a particular function should be transferred from one Minister to another should be presented to Parliament for their yea or nay in the form of an Order in Council subject to a negative Resolution.[3]...

The view we have taken is that the distribution of particular functions between the various Departments is primarily a matter of domestic convenience in the administration of the Government of the day. Nevertheless, the view is also taken by us that these changes . . . are a matter of interest to Parliament and there ought to be a system of Parliamentary checks and supervision.

Clause 1 (2) provides that a Department may be dissolved and its functions transferred elsewhere by Order in Council. This is not a case of transfer of some of the functions of one Ministry to another; it is the greater issue of the dissolution of a Ministry... We thought

---

[2] For an example of the significance of this, see the case of *Lavender* v. *Minister of Housing and Local Government*, below p. 570. Contrast the freedom of Ministers to redistribute Parliamentary Questions among themselves.

[3] For the significance of these distinctions see below p. 239.

that . . . the complete disappearance of a State Department is a rather more serious matter than a mere transfer of function. Therefore, Clause 3 (1) provides that these Orders in Council shall be subject to affirmative Resolution procedure; that is, they cannot come into force without the specific approval of the two Houses of Parliament. Clause 2 enables the title of a Minister to be changed by Order instead of by full-dress legislation. This is a mere change of designation, of title and style. Such a change may be desirable in consequence of a transfer of functions, but there is no reason why it should not be made at any time . . .

[I]t is perhaps helpful to point out . . . what they do not authorise the Executive to do by Order in Council. First, an Order in Council under this Bill cannot set up a new Ministry, nor yet recreate a Ministry which has once been dissolved. Second, though it may reduce, it cannot increase the number of Ministers entitled to sit in the House of Commons. . .[4] Third . . . an Order in Council cannot make a temporary function permanent nor add in any way to its duration. Fourth, it cannot grant to any Minister any new function which would require statutory cover and is not already on the Statute Book. Nor, on the other hand, can it abolish or modify any statutory duty or restriction which Parliament has imposed on Ministers in the exercise of their statutory powers. Fifth, the Bill deals only with Ministers, and therefore could not be used to reallocate any of the functions of those statutory boards and commissions which have been deliberately set up by Parliament from time to time on a rather different footing from ordinary Government departments. If the Government wished to do any of these things . . . they would, as at present have to come to Parliament with specific legislation. . .

[Second Reading. 418 H.C.Deb. 5s. c. 454. 25 January 1946]

The Ministers of the Crown (Transfer of Function) Act, 1946, together with the Ministers of the Crown Act, 1964, have since been consolidated in the Ministers of the Crown Act, 1975.

THE MINISTERS OF THE CROWN ACT, 1975 [Ch. 26]

1. (1) Her Majesty may by Order in Council—
   (a) provide for the transfer to any Minister of the Crown of any functions previously exercisable by another Minister of the Crown;
   (b) provide for the dissolution of the government department in the charge of any Minister of the Crown and the transfer

---

[4] The number of Ministers who can sit in the House of Commons at any one time is regulated by the House of Commons (Disqualification) Act, 1957, as amended by the Ministers of the Crown Act, 1964.

to or distribution among such other Minister or Ministers of the Crown as may be specified in the Order of any functions previously exercisable by the Minister in charge of that department;

    (c) direct that functions of any Minister of the Crown shall be exercisable concurrently with another Minister of the Crown, or shall cease to be so exercisable.

(2) An Order in Council under this section may contain such incidental, consequential and supplemental provisions as may be necessary or expedient for the purpose of giving full effect to the Order, including provisions—

    (a) for the transfer of any property, rights and liabilities held, enjoyed or incurred by any Minister of the Crown in connection with any functions transferred or distributed;

    (b) for the carrying on and completion by or under the authority of the Minister to whom any functions are transferred of anything commenced by or under the authority of a Minister of the Crown before the date when the Order takes effect;

    (c) for such adaptations of the enactments relating to any functions transferred as may be necessary to enable them to be exercised by the Minister to whom they are transferred and his officers . . .

    (e) for the substitution of the Minister to whom functions are transferred for any other Minister of the Crown in any instrument, contract, or legal proceedings made or commenced before the date when the Order takes effect.

4. If Her Majesty is pleased by Order in Council to direct that any change shall be made in the style and title of a Minister of the Crown, the Order may contain provisions substituting the new style and title—

    (a) in the enactments . . . relating to the Minister;

    (b) in any instrument, contract, or legal proceedings made or commenced before the date when the Order takes effect.

5. (1) No order in Council which provides for the dissolution of a government department shall be made under this Act unless, after copies of the draft thereof have been laid before Parliament, each House presents an Address to Her Majesty praying that the Order be made.

(2) An Order in Council under this Act, not being an Order made in pursuance of such an Address as aforesaid, shall be laid before Parliament and shall be subject to annulment in pursuance of a resolution of either House of Parliament. . . .

(5) Nothing in this Act shall prejudice any power exercisable by virtue of the prerogative of the Crown in relation to the functions of Ministers of the Crown.

II. THE CABINET AND THE CO-ORDINATION
OF GOVERNMENT ACTIVITIES

5. But before dealing – either generally or in detail – with Departmental organisation, some reference must be made to the functions and procedure of the Cabinet, which is the mainspring of all the mechanism of Government. Its constitution and the methods of its procedure must depend to a large extent on the circumstances of the time, on the personality of the Prime Minister, and on the capacities of his principal colleagues. But we may be permitted to offer some general observations on the purposes which the Cabinet is, in our view, intended to serve, and the manner in which these purposes can most effectually be carried out.

6. The main functions of the Cabinet may, we think, be described as: —

   (*a*) the final determination of the policy to be submitted to Parliament;
   (*b*) the supreme control of the national executive in accordance with the policy prescribed by Parliament; and
   (*c*) the continuous co-ordination and delimitation of the activities of the several Departments of State.

7. For the due performance of these functions the following conditions seem to be essential, or, at least, desirable: —

   (i) The Cabinet should be small in number – preferably ten or, at most, twelve;
   (ii) it should meet frequently;
   (iii) it should be supplied in the most convenient form with all the information and material necessary to enable it to arrive at expeditious decisions;
   (iv) it should make a point of consulting personally all the Ministers whose work is likely to be affected by its decisions; and
   (v) it should have a systematic method of securing that its decisions are effectually carried out by the several Departments concerned.

8. It is scarcely necessary to consider whether these conditions were fulfilled by the Cabinets and the Cabinet procedure to which we had become accustomed in the generation which preceded the outbreak of the war. It is sufficient to point out that during the war an entirely new type of Cabinet has been evolved, with new methods of procedure.

The Report of the War Cabinet for 1917 (Cd. 9005) opens with the following statement: —

' The most important constitutional development in the United Kingdom during the last year has been the introduction of the War Cabinet system. This change was the direct outcome of the War itself. As the magnitude of the War increased, it became evident that the Cabinet system of peace days was inadequate to cope with the novel conditions. The enlarged scope of Government activity and the consequent creation of several new departments, made a Cabinet, consisting of all the Departmental Ministers meeting under the Chairmanship of the Prime Minister, far too unwieldy for the practical conduct of the War. It was extremely difficult for so large a body to give that resolute central direction which became more imperative the more the population and resources of the nation had to be organised for a single purpose – the defeat of German militarism.'

9. It seems probable that the constitution and procedure of the War Cabinet will not be found entirely suitable to the conditions which will prevail when peace has been restored. But we think that many of the considerations above mentioned will be found to apply with equal force; and that a rearrangement of the supreme direction of the executive organisation as it formerly existed has been rendered necessary, not merely by the war itself, but by the prospect after the war.

Such a rearrangement has been attempted, and the question whether it has yet assumed an adequate form, or works as efficiently as it might, is quite a different question from whether it is possible to return to the old order of things. We feel confident that the latter question must be answered in the negative.

10. Whether the new type of Cabinet should consist of Ministers in charge of the principal Departments of State, or of Ministers ' without portfolio ' able to concentrate their whole attention upon the problems submitted for their consideration, or of Ministers of both kinds, are questions which we do not propose to discuss here. But we think that there is one feature in the procedure of the War Cabinet which may well assume a permanent form, namely, the appointment of a Secretary to the Cabinet charged with the duty of collecting and putting into shape its agenda, of providing the information and material necessary for its deliberations, and of drawing up records of the results for communication to the Departments concerned.

[Report from the (Haldane) Committee on the Machinery of Government. Cd. 9230 (1918)]

THE PRIME MINISTER (MR CHURCHILL): . . . I want to begin by communicating to the House the main ideas which I have formed . . .

upon the machinery for conducting the war. I have reached the conclusion that in the present circumstances a War Cabinet composed of four or five men free from Departmental duties would not give the best results. . . Some may say that that system assisted to carry us to victory in the last war. I saw the system at close quarters, and I do not think that it was in practice altogether what it was represented to be in theory. The War Cabinet of those days was largely an instrument designed to give the great men who then conducted our affairs wide powers to deal with matters over the whole field, and in practice the meetings of that body . . . were attended by very much larger numbers than those who now grace our Council Board. Personally I have formed the view that it is better that there should be in the responsible directing centres of Government some, at any rate, of the key Ministers. There is the Minister for Foreign Affairs . . . the Chancellor of the Exchequer . . . the Minister of Labour . . . the Minister of Aircraft Production. . . Then there are the Defence Ministers, the three Service Ministers. But, as the Prime Minister under this arrangement, which the House has approved, is also the Minister of Defence, he represents those Departments in the War Cabinet. We make altogether eight, and yet we hold a great many of the key offices in our body. I think it is better to work in that way than to have five Ministers entirely divorced from their Departments, because that means that when a discussion has taken place in the Cabinet, the leaders of these Departments have to be summoned, and the whole business has to be gone over again in order to learn what it is they think they can do and to persuade them and convince them that it is necessary to do what has been decided upon.

The House must not underrate the power of these great Departments of State. I have served over twenty years in Cabinets, in peace and war, and I can assure the House that the power of these great Departments of State is in many cases irresistible because it is based on knowledge and on systematised and organised currents of opinion. You must have machinery which carries to the Cabinet with the least possible friction the consent and allegiance of these great Departments. It is not a question of loyalty. It is a question of honest differences of opinion which arise, and there are many matters to be settled and decided which would not arise in the ordinary Departmental mind. There are great difficulties in dealing with Departments of State unless the key Departments are brought into the discussion in the early stages and, as it were, take part in the original formation and initiation of our designs. . . We live in a country where His Majesty's Cabinet governs, subject to the continual superintendence, correction and authority of Parliament. In the last resort, only the Cabinet can exert the necessary authority over all these Departments... How then is this process to be achieved, with the minimum of action and the minimum of pressure? There is the problem for which I ventured, very respectfully, to offer a solution in the recent announcement of the formation of Government Committees... Every British Cabinet in the last 30 or 40 years has conducted a large part of its work by Cabinet Committees. Instead of the whole Cabinet sitting there hour after hour, they appoint four or five Ministers to go into this or that particular matter, to hammer it out among themselves, and then to come back and advise the parent body. Such Committees are often based upon the Ministers, the co-ordination of whose Departments is essential to the solution of the problem. They have the strongest incentive to agree because they are all colleagues... and if they do agree, they can make their Departments carry out their decisions, and carry them out with alacrity and good will. This was the system which I applied to the Ministry of Munitions in August 1917... and this is the system, which, *mutatis mutandis*, I have applied now to the two extraordinarily difficult and vital spheres of our life which are covered by the Import Executive and the Production Executive... I see... that some critics have asked, ' Are you not overburdening, these Ministers, each with his own Department, by making this one chairman, and these others members of this Imports and Production Executive? If they have to do all this work on these Executives how are they going to do their own work? ' But this is exactly their own work. This is the particular work they have to do. The management of these affairs and its interplay with other Departments constitutes the major problem before each of them...

[368 H.C.Deb. 5s. c. 258. 22 January 1941]

The Overlords, 1951–3

When Sir Winston Churchill formed his Conservative Government in October 1951, he appointed Lord Leathers Secretary of State for the Co-ordination of Transport, Fuel and Power, and Lord Woolton Lord President of the Council with special responsibility for the co-ordination of Food and Agriculture.

These appointments were criticized by the Opposition on two grounds. The first was that they weakened the responsibility of the Ministers appointed in the normal way to run the Departments whose activities were to be co-ordinated by the ' Overlords '. The second was the fact that both co-ordinating Ministers were in the House of Lords and so not personally responsible to the House of Commons.

In reply to a number of questions, the Government attempted a reasoned defence of the appointments on 6 May 1952.

THE PRIME MINISTER [MR CHURCHILL]: ... Every Departmental Minister is responsible to Parliament for the policy and administration of his Department. This is a fundamental principle in our system of Parliamentary democracy. But it is an equally respectable and necessary principle that Ministers as a body are collectively responsible for Government policy as a whole. This means that a Minister's personal responsibility for his Departmental policy must be exercised in harmony with the views of his Ministerial colleagues. The work of the so-called ' co-ordinating Ministers ' is an aspect of collective responsibility. In former days all reconciliation of Departmental policies was done in the Cabinet, of which all Departmental Ministers were members, or by the Prime Minister himself. But for many years past, Prime Ministers have from time to time entrusted to a senior colleague the duty of keeping a general oversight, on the Cabinet's behalf, over subjects of special importance not falling wholly within the jurisdiction of a single Department of State. These tasks have usually been assigned to holders of the old offices involving no heavy Departmental duties, notably the offices of Lord President and Lord Privy Seal. An early example of this was the arrangement by which in 1929 Mr Ramsay MacDonald assigned to Mr J. H. Thomas, as Lord Privy Seal, a special responsibility for co-ordinating measures for dealing with unemployment.

With the growing complexity of Government business, and the increasing extent to which policies have to be administered jointly by two or more Departments, Prime Ministers have found it increasingly convenient to ask senior Ministers to act in a co-ordinating role. And in recent times this arrangement has been more regularly adopted because, under modern conditions which have called into existence so many new Departments of State, the Cabinet no longer normally includes all Ministers in charge of Departments. This has led to the development of the system of standing Cabinet Committees, which assist the Cabinet in discharging its collective business and include Departmental Ministers who are not themselves members of the Cabinet. The chairmanship of these standing Committees has normally been assumed by senior Ministers without Departmental duties; and it is mainly in their capacity as Chairmen of these Committees that these Ministers have exercised their co-ordinating functions, subject to Cabinet review. This is a natural evolution in the processes of conducting the collective business of Government, and there is nothing new about it.

During the war the Lord President of the Council, in particular, discharged extensive co-ordinating responsibilities on this basis; and it is well-known that similar arrangements were in force during the period of office of the late Government. The responsibilities assigned under the present Government to Lord Woolton and Lord Leathers carry this development a stage further in one respect, and in one respect only, namely, that the specific area of co-ordination assigned to each of them was publicly announced on his appointment. Indeed, so far as concerns my noble Friend, Lord Leathers, it was made explicit in his title... Lord Leathers' co-ordinating functions do not differ, in the constitutional sense, from those of my noble Friend, Lord Woolton.

The co-ordinating Ministers have no statutory powers. They have, in particular, no power to give orders or directions to a Departmental Minister. A Departmental Minister who is invited by a co-ordinating Minister to adjust a Departmental policy to accord with the wider interests of the Government as a whole always has access to the Cabinet; and, if he then finds that he cannot win the support of his Ministerial colleagues, he should accept their decisions. No Departmental Minister can, of course, be expected to remain in a Government and carry out policies with which he disagrees. Thus, the existence and activities of these co-ordinating Ministers do not impair or diminish the responsibility to Parliament of the Departmental Ministers whose policies they co-ordinate. Those Ministers are fully accountable to Parliament for any act of policy or administration within their Departmental jurisdiction. It does not follow that the co-ordinating Ministers are ' non-responsible '. Having no statutory powers as co-ordinating Ministers, they perform in that capacity no formal acts. But they share in the collective responsibility of the Government as a whole, and, as Ministers of the Crown, they are accountable to Parliament...

Mr C. R. Attlee: Is it not clear that the difficulty has arisen in the naming of certain Ministers as co-ordinators? ... [H]itherto the practice of co-ordination, whether through chairmen of committees, or senior Ministers, has always been one which has been kept within the Government circle and not announced in public. The right hon. Gentleman has announced in public that certain Ministers have co-ordinating powers, and that has led to the difficulty of deciding where the responsibilities of one end and those of another begin. I do not think that the right hon. Gentleman has made it in the least clear who actually makes decisions on policy on such matters as these where they are co-ordinated by other Ministers...

The Prime Minister: On the general question, I gather that the Leader of the Opposition thinks that all these difficulties would have been smoothed away if, for instance, my noble Friend, Lord Leathers, had been appointed Minister without Portfolio?

Mr Attlee *indicated assent.*

THE PRIME MINISTER: That, I think, is a much less precise and clear-cut solution than that which I have ventured to place before the House. . .

MR ATTLEE: Is the right hon. Gentleman aware that this attempt at over-precision is a source of the difficulty? If we attempt to be precise in laying down the exact responsibility in a Government where there is collective responsibility, we run into difficulties. The right hon. Gentleman will remember that, excepting certain well-defined cases, such as defence, mention was never made as to what Minister presided over a Cabinet Committee, because Questions should be put to Departmental Ministers and not to senior Ministers, and we do not yet know what the noble Lord, Lord Leathers, does in respect of transport. No one can question him, and we cannot find out what he does; and so far as we can find out, decisions on transport are not taken by him nor by the Minister of Transport nor by the Cabinet, but by the right hon. Gentleman.

THE PRIME MINISTER: If the gravamen of the charge against me is that I have not succeeded in hushing it all up as well as the right hon. Gentleman did, I can bear that with composure. . .

MR HERBERT MORRISON: As the Prime Minister has indicated, the case of the late Mr J. H. Thomas was publicly announced, and he was held responsible to Parliament in respect of the broad policy regarding unemployment. As in the case of Lord Woolton and Lord Leathers their duties were publicly announced, including the implication that they were not only co-ordinating Ministers but, certainly in the case of Lord Leathers and, I think, of Lord Woolton, supervising Ministers, will the Prime Minister clearly tell the House that, as these have been announced as was done in the case of Mr Thomas, he rejects the statement made by the Lord President in another place to the effect that in this respect he, the noble Lord, was not accountable to Parliament? [5] Will the Prime Minister definitely uphold the doctrine that once it is announced that Ministers are responsible for certain things, it follows that they must accept responsibility to Parliament?

THE PRIME MINISTER: I am quite sure that Lord Woolton fully accepts accountability to Parliament. . .

[500 H.C.Deb. 5s. c. 188. 6 May 1952]

The experiment lasted until 1953. In November 1952 Lord Salisbury succeeded Lord Woolton as Lord President of the Council but without

---

[5] [During a debate in the House of Lords on 30 April 1952 Lord Woolton had said ' In my view, the work of the co-ordinators is not a responsibility to Parliament; it is a responsibility to the Cabinet ' (176 H.L.Deb. 5s. c. 475).]

taking over his co-ordinating functions. Although Lord Leathers did not resign until August 1953, the experiment seems to have been over before then. On 24 March 1953 Mr Morrison asked the Prime Minister whether the doctrine of supervising Ministers as distinct from co-ordinating Ministers, as announced in the Press at the time the Government was formed, had been abandoned. The Prime Minister replied: 'No. I think that would be going too far. But I think it may be admitted that the need which I found so very important in time of war has not presented itself in the same precise form now that we are at peace' [513 H.C.Deb. 5s. c. 615].

Cabinet Committees were early set up to discharge a function on behalf of the Cabinet... In 1903 Balfour set up the first standing committee – the Committee of Imperial Defence ... the first Cabinet body to have a secretariat... During the first world war very many committees were set up, in a haphazard way... In the second world war, as in the first, a full-fledged committee system was developed, but a more coherent one. This system became the basis for peace time Cabinets from the end of the war onwards... Attlee was the first Prime Minister to have in peacetime a permanent structure of Cabinet Committees... The pattern established by Attlee was continued by subsequent Conservative Prime Ministers and became the standard structure of the Cabinet system of the 1950s and 1960s. The original type of *ad hoc* committee continued to be used alongside the organised structure of standing committees...

The Prime Minister sets up and disbands committees, appoints the chairmen and members and sets the terms of reference. Normally, besides the Ministers departmentally concerned, some other Ministers are put on committees to ensure that policies are broadly considered. Ministers can be represented by their junior Ministers. Often a non-departmental Minister is in the chair: indeed a Cabinet today needs some such Ministers for this purpose – probably about four...

A major innovation made by Mr Harold Wilson was to raise the authority of Cabinet Committees... In 1967 Mr Harold Wilson informed the Cabinet of his view that a matter could be taken to the Cabinet from a committee only with the agreement of the chairman. In exercising his discretion the chairman would consider the degree of disagreement in the Committee or the intrinsic importance of the issue or its political overtones. In cases of dispute the question could be brought to the Prime Minister himself. Although this did not take away the constitutional right of a Cabinet Minister to bring any matter to the Cabinet including a question settled in a committee, in practice this right was greatly attenuated. This considerably reduced the pressure of business in the Cabinet. The value and appropriateness of the committee system from Attlee's time was demonstrated by the fate of the attempt made by Churchill, when he succeeded Attlee in 1951, to introduce Overlords charged with the duty of co-ordinating a number of related departments. The Opposition at once pointed out that responsibility of Ministers to Parliament was blurred.

Who was to answer for policy, the departmental Minister or the co-ordinating Overlord? In April 1952 Lord Woolton said that the Overlords were responsible to the Cabinet and not to Parliament. By August 1953 Sir Winston Churchill abandoned the idea. ' Now that we are in smoother waters ' he announced, ' we can rely on the normal methods of Cabinet procedure to secure co-ordination between the departments '.

By ' normal methods ' Churchill meant the committee system dating from 1945. It had by now become the natural and accepted way of running Cabinet government. As with many constitutional innovations, including originally the Cabinet itself, an attempt was made to cast a veil of secrecy over Cabinet Committees. They came, however, to form so essential a part in the working of the Cabinet that secrecy gradually broke down. It became widely felt that the public had a right to know at least the organisation of the Cabinet system, which was the seat and centre of political authority in the country...[6]

[Patrick Gordon-Walker, *The Cabinet* (1970), p. 40]

There has nevertheless been a traditional reluctance to reveal the system of committees operating at any particular time. Consider e.g. the exchange between Mr Paton and Mr Morrison:

MR PATON (*Norwich*): ... As I understand it there are Ministerial committees ... dealing with the mass of information that is flowing to them... Is it the Cabinet as a whole that makes the executive decisions at the highest level? ...

MR MORRISON: ... I cannot take my hon. Friend too far into the secrets of the Cabinet organisation... The Cabinet is responsible for the acts of the Government... How the Cabinet does its business, and to what extent it delegates certain things to Cabinet committees is ... the Cabinet's business... I can only assure my hon. Friend that decisions on policy, according to the nature of the decisions and of their importance, the significance and also the degree

[6] Gordon-Walker prints a list of Cabinet Committees down to 1964 at p. 176.

to which they may cause trouble and controversy in the House of Commons or the country are settled at the appropriate level. . . These things are settled by a Committee wherever possible.

[419 H.C.Deb. 5s. c. 2131. 28 February 1946]

Cp. also the following extract from the memorandum from the Cabinet Office to the Committee on s. 2 of the Official Secrets Act, 1911 (Cmnd. 5104 (1972)):

' 5. . . . It is generally known that in addition to the Cabinet itself there are a number of Ministerial and Official committees. The decisions of these committees, as indeed the decisions of individual Ministers, are as much decisions of the Government as are the decisions of the Cabinet itself. No Government, therefore, disclose the list of their committees their membership or scope, for to do so would be liable to impair collective responsibility as well as detract from the individual responsibility of Ministers. If, for example, it were known that a certain decision had been taken in a certain committee, the impression could be created that named Ministers were dissociated from it or on the contrary especially closely associated with it; and the decision could be attributed to the committee rather than to the Minister within whose responsibility it falls.'

THE PRIME MINISTER (MR HAROLD WILSON): . . . Perhaps I might refer to another proposal in the field of machinery of government made by the right hon. Gentleman the Leader of the Opposition, when he aired his ideas recently for a very much smaller Cabinet either than the present one or the Cabinet of our immediate predecessors . . . not, I hasten to add . . . the concept of a small Cabinet of non-Departmental Ministers on the lines of war Cabinets. . .

Indeed, during the last war Sir Winston Churchill soon found it necessary to bring back into the Cabinet Departmental heads such as the Chancellor of the Exchequer and others whom he had left outside. In any case, the problems of peace are very different from the organisation of war.

However, I should like to tell the House that a Cabinet of, say, 11 or 12, containing senior Ministers responsible for a wide range of Departments, is one I have examined very, very carefully on a number of occasions. In view of the interest taken in such an idea, perhaps I might give the House the reasons why, after very careful thought, I have on each occasion come to reject it.

First, I think that there is a very real problem of divided Ministerial responsibility. The system of overlords has been tried – for example, in the early 1950s – but it manifestly did not work. It is tempting, I think, to conceive of the idea of one Minister in overall charge of, shall we say, the economic and industrial Departments with subordinate Ministers of Cabinet rank outside the Cabinet in charge of, perhaps, finance, trade, labour, power, agriculture, transport, technology, but under the direct control of the super Minister; or to conceive of a super-Minister for the Social Services overlording not only my right hon. Friend's new Department, but housing and local government and education... I am quite clear in my own mind that the divided Ministerial responsibility involved would cause it to fail.

My second reason is that in the modern world it is inconceivable that the important sectors of our national life, and particularly those employed in and concerned with those particular sectors, should have only a secondary level Minister not in the Cabinet. There are right hon. Gentlemen on the other side who will remember the furore caused by the exclusion from the 1951 Cabinet of the Minister of Education and the justifiable anger it created among teachers, local education authorities, and officers and others concerned with education. Now, with the much greater responsibilities of the Secretary of State for Education and Science, one could imagine the feelings not only of those I have mentioned, but of the universities and the scientists as well. Again, the exclusion of, for example, agriculture or trade or transport, or the others I have mentioned, would create similar problems – problems measured, not merely by decibels of protest, but by the realities of administration.

The third reason, which I need only mention for hon. Members to work out the implications... is the fact that in any overlord grouping or regrouping – this would apply whether there were separate Ministers and Departments outside the Cabinet or whether there were great federations under a single Minister – there would inevitably be, whether in the economic or in the social grouping, certain Departments which had full Great Britain responsibility and others where the Scottish and Welsh responsibilities had been devolved to the Secretaries of State for Scotland and Wales...

I am sure that... the right hon. Gentleman... will probably reach the conclusion, as I have done, that what he is seeking to achieve can best be done by Cabinet Committees, the central ones presided over by the Prime Minister and others by other senior Ministers, not excluding committees under less senior Ministers, including some which have demonstrated the greatest vigour – committees, composed of junior Ministers presided over by one of their fellows...

[773 H.C.Deb. 5s. c. 1559. 21 November 1968]

One characteristic of the next period... is the emergence of the 'giant' departments... They are unitary departments, with one Cabinet Minister in charge, with the full statutory powers and responsibility to Parliament; and one Permanent Secretary responsible to him. This is a different concept from that of an 'overlord' Minister over two or more Ministers, introduced in the 1951 Conservative Government and abandoned because of the clash between the 'overlords'' responsibility for the Minister's work and their responsibility to Parliament... The 'giant' department is constitutionally just like any other department but much bigger. It is likely to have at least another Minister, in addition to its head, of status equivalent to that of a Minister not represented in the Cabinet... it will have one or more Second Permanent Secretaries... the advantages which are hoped for are set out in last October's White Paper 'The reorganisation of Central Government'... The biggest danger is that of excessive pressure on the Ministers; and linked with this is the danger of muddle and conflict between the Ministers... For Ministerial operation, the limiting factor on the size of the 'giant' is the amount of the department's business that must go to Cabinet and the Minister's ability to absorb and handle it. However effectively the Minister devolves the work on to his junior colleagues, the load of departmental Cabinet business is inescapable. If it stops the Cabinet Minister from doing the rest of his Cabinet and political work, his contact with Parliament, and his activities outside, the system becomes unmanageable.

There is no sure way round this difficulty. There have been many cases of having two Cabinet Ministers in one department... But this is inconsistent with the idea of a small Cabinet; and it is difficult to justify the concept of a 'giant' department with more work of national and political importance to the Cabinet than its Minister can comprehend and handle. The same argument refutes the idea of allowing the No 2 Minister to attend the Cabinet for particular business. If the Cabinet business cannot be handled effectively by the one Cabinet Minister, the department is too big.

On the other hand, the Minister's load can be greatly eased if the fields of responsibility of his No 2's are clearly enough defined to enable the No 2's to be accepted by Parliament as the spokesmen in all but the most critical occasions (which the Minister will be handling in Cabinet anyway); and it is important too that the outside interests involved in the department's work (industry, local government etc) shall be content to see the No 2 and not insist on seeing the Minister. There is enough experience so far to suggest that this can be achieved, provided that it is known that the Minister will always back up the No 2. The position of the 'second-tier' Minister is different from that of any Minister in the past; he has much less final responsibility than that which was formerly carried by a Minister in charge of a Department but not in the Cabinet (and often much more difficult and politically sensitive questions to handle); but he has much more final responsibility than Ministers of State have normally had...

[Sir Richard Clarke, *New Trends in Government*, Civil Service College Studies I (1971), p. 1]

III. THE PRIME MINISTER AND THE CABINET

The post-war epoch has seen the final transformation of Cabinet Government into Prime Ministerial government... Even in Bagehot's time it was probably a misnomer to describe the Premier as chairman, and *primus inter pares*... Since then his powers have been steadily increased, first by the centralisation of the party machine under his personal rule, and secondly by the growth of a centralised bureaucracy, so vast that it could no longer be managed by a Cabinet behaving like a board of directors or an old-fashioned company. Under Prime Ministerial government, secondary decisions are normally taken either by the department concerned or in Cabinet committee, and the Cabinet becomes the place where busy executives seek formal sanction for their actions from colleagues usually too busy – even if they do disagree – to do more than protest. Each of these executives, moreover, owes his allegiance not to the Cabinet collectively but to the Prime Minister who gave him his job, and who may well have dictated the policy he must adopt...
' Every Cabinet Minister is in a sense the Prime Minister's agent – his assistant. There's no question about that. It is the Prime Minister's Cabinet, and he is the one person who is directly responsible to the Queen for what the Cabinet does. If the Cabinet discusses anything it is the Prime Minister who decides what the collective view of the Cabinet is. A Minister's job is to save the Prime Minister all the work he can. But no Minister can make a really important move without consulting the Prime Minister, and if the Prime Minister wanted to take a certain step the Cabinet Minister concerned would either have to agree, argue it out in Cabinet, or resign.' [7]

But ... the old doctrine of collective Cabinet responsibility is scrupulously maintained and enforced, even though many of the decisions for which members must assume responsibility have been taken above their heads and without their knowledge. And this collective responsibility now extends downwards from the Cabinet through the Ministers outside the Cabinet, to the Parliamentary Under-Secretaries and even to the Private Parliamentary Secre-

---

[7] See Lord Home, *The Observer*, Sunday 16 September 1962.

taries. Under this doctrine, today, about a third of the Government's parliamentary strength is automatically required not merely to accept but actively to support policy decisions which, if they are of great importance, will nearly always have been taken by one man after consultation with a handful of advisers he has picked for the occasion...

Of course ... it (the Cabinet) retains very real reserve powers which can on occasion be suddenly and dramatically used for good or for ill. A Prime Minister, for instance, can be unseated by his colleagues; and it is this fact with which the constitutional purists seek to justify the distinction they still make between Presidential and Prime Ministerial government. A President, we are told, cannot be removed before the end of his term of office; a Prime Minister can be.

The distinction is valid provided we observe that a British party leader exerts such power and patronage within the machine that he can never be removed in real life by public, constitutional procedure. The method employed must always be that of undercover intrigue and sudden unpredicted *coup d'etat*. The intra-party struggle for power that is fought in the secret committees, and in the lobbies, may suddenly flare up round the Cabinet table. But if it does, the proceedings there will only be a ritual, and the real fight will have finished before they begin.

The decline of the Cabinet has been concealed from the public eye even more successfully than its rise to power in Bagehot's era. Here was a secret of our modern English Constitution which no-one directly concerned with Government – whether minister, shadow minister or civil servant – was anxious to reveal. Yet, despite the thick protective covering of prerogative and constitutional convention under which our government is still conducted, there must come occasions on which the drapery is whisked aside, and the reality of power revealed. One such occasion was when Sir Winston, shortly after he took office in 1951, announced that the first British A-bomb had been successfully tested. The Premier was careful to pay his tribute to his predecessor, for making the initial decision and sanctioning the huge expenditures that had never been revealed to Parliament. Very soon it was common knowledge that this decision had been taken by Mr Attlee without any prior discussion in the Cabinet, and that he had not revealed it to any but a handful of trusted friends. Another occasion which showed the new role of the Cabinet under Prime Ministerial government was the Suez crisis. Lord Avon took the decisions and prepared the plans for the Anglo-French attack on Port Said without Cabinet consultation, and with the assistance of only a handful of his colleagues and per-

manent advisers. After the secret was revealed, he was able until he
fell ill to enforce collective responsibility on a Cabinet only informed of his policy when it was already doomed to failure. He has
been blamed for the policy; but no one has suggested that he acted
unconstitutionally. Here then it was demonstrated that a British
Premier is now entitled on really momentous decisions to act first,
and then to face his Cabinet with the choice between collective
obedience or the political wilderness. . .

In theory – but also in practice – the British people retains the
power not merely to choose between two Prime Ministers, and
two parties, but to throw off its deferential attitude and reshape the
political system, making the parties instruments of popular control,
and even insisting that the House of Commons should once again
provide the popular check on the executive. . . Already there are
signs of popular protest against the growing ineffectiveness of Parliament and the oligarchic tendencies inherent in our modern two-
party machine politics. Perhaps the secret of Prime Ministerial
government discussed in these pages will be as rapidly overtaken by
events as Bagehot's English Constitution was when it appeared in
1867.

[R. H. Crossman, Introduction to Walter Bagehot, *The English Constitution* (1963), pp. 51ff]

While British government in the latter half of the nineteenth
century can be described simply as Cabinet government, such a
description would be misleading today. Now the country is governed
by the Prime Minister, who leads, co-ordinates and maintains a
series of Ministers all of whom are advised and backed by the Civil
Service. Some decisions are taken by the Prime Minister alone,
some in consultation between him and the senior ministers, while
others are left to heads of departments, to the full Cabinet, one of
the many Cabinet Committees, or to the permanent officials. Of
these bodies the Cabinet holds the central position because, though
it does not often initiate policy or govern in that sense, it is the
place where disputes are settled, where major policies are endorsed
and where the balance of forces emerges if there is disagreement.
In the end, most decisions have to be reported to the Cabinet and
Cabinet Ministers are the only ones who have the right to complain
if they have not been informed or consulted. The precise amount
of power held by each agency and the use made of the Cabinet
depends on the ideas of the Premier and the personnel and situation
with which he has to deal . . . There is no single catchphrase that
can describe this form of government, but it may be pictured as a
cone. The Prime Minister stands at the apex supported by and

giving point to a widening series of rings of senior ministers, the Cabinet, its committees, non-Cabinet ministers, and departments. Of these rings, the only one above the level of the Civil Service that has formal existence and acts as a sort of appeal for the lower tiers is the Cabinet...

[E]ven when a decision has been tracked down to the Cabinet, this does not necessarily mean that it was reached by the body of ministers sitting round the table in the Cabinet room. The Cabinet itself has become a highly organised business meeting and a vast amount of work is done, but at the expense of much prior consultation and the delegation of many decisions to Cabinet committees. The arrangements have now become sufficiently formal for the Cabinet Office to compile a book of Cabinet committees giving the membership of each committee on the left hand page and the terms of reference on the right, and a book of Cabinet precedents and procedure explaining how various types of business should be arranged and submitted. In such a highly organised body with a long agenda to be covered, there is little time for debate, and as a result there has been a natural tendency for the influential members to have informal meetings with the Prime Minister or to settle matters at personal interviews with him. Naturally these discussions are held to clear the ground and establish the actual points on which Cabinet decisions are required but, in the hands of some Prime Ministers the effect may be to weight the scales against possible criticism in the Cabinet and even, on some occasions, to withdraw matters from the purview of the Cabinet. Here again, the situation can only be covered by a description of the practice of recent Prime Ministers and their relations with their colleagues.

[J. P. Mackintosh, *The British Cabinet* (1968), pp. 529 and 10]

MR GEORGE BROWN: ... I do not propose today to go into the history of my various disagreements with Government decisions, and even more, with the way in which they have been increasingly made and the considerations on which they were so often based ... But in view of some of the wilder speculations and exaggerations over the weekend, I feel I owe it to the House and to my right hon. Friends on this side of the House, in particular, and, if I may say so, to myself, to say why I decided to resign at this time.

It was not despite the gravity of the situation; it was, in a sense, because of it. It is in just such a situation that it is essential for Cabinet Government to be maintained if democracy is to be assured, and equally it is in just such a situation that temptation to depart from it is at its greatest. Power can very easily pass not merely from

Cabinet to one or two Ministers, but effectively to sources quite outside the political control altogether. [HON. MEMBERS: ' Oh.']

It is open to anyone to challenge my judgment of the situation on Thursday night, when it was learned that the Prime Minister and two other Ministers were already at the Palace, or to feel that I exaggerated the dangers in it. But I am very conscious of past parallels in my own political lifetime, and felt strongly enough on the issue to gather some of my colleagues together and to protest then. When that protest was virtually brushed aside on the basis that what I had done was in itself irregular, I felt that the time had come to leave the Government.

[761 H.C.Deb. 5s. c. 55. 18 March 1968]

The term ' inner Cabinet ' is a misnomer. It is in no sense a Cabinet and must be distinguished from a Cabinet Committee. An inner Cabinet has no organic or set place in the Cabinet structure: it is no more than an informal, small group of friends or confidants of the Prime Minister drawn from members of his Cabinet... The question of Attlee's responsibility for the decision on the atom bomb and of Eden's for the decision on Suez involves consideration of the ' partial Cabinet '. A partial Cabinet is different from an inner Cabinet in that it is an organised part of the Cabinet system. Typically a partial Cabinet is a standing or *ad hoc* committee pre-sided over by the Prime Minister, which may – in matters of great moment and secrecy – prepare policies in detail and sometimes take decisions without prior consultation with the Cabinet as a whole. The Cabinet is in due course informed and consulted. The partial Cabinet depends upon a distinction among members of the Cabinet that is analogous to the arrangements for the distribution of Foreign Office telegrams. For a long time these have necessarily been sent to Ministers on a selective basis; some may be seen only by the Prime Minister and the Foreign Secretary... The cases of Attlee and Eden were not ... startling departures: they fit into a pattern that started earlier and continued later. I myself knew about the decision to make the atom bomb. The use of the Woomera range in Australia was involved and as Commonwealth Secretary I was a member of the Cabinet Committee dealing with the matter. We were making decisions that were continuous, highly technical and which related to military and scientific secrets of other countries besides our own. There was no question of the Prime Minister alone making decisions. A number of senior Ministers shared in every decision...

The day after Nasser seized the Suez Canal a Cabinet Committee of seven was set up on July 27, 1956. This committee supervised

detailed negotiations in the complex and rapidly changing developments of the next few months, which were also holiday months. The
Prime Minister and the Foreign Secretary handled the details of the
Anglo–French military preparations. The Cabinet met on September 11. On October 18, the Cabinet was informed of the plan for
the invasion of the Canal area. The Cabinet Committee drafted an
ultimatum to Israel and Egypt. In meetings on October 24 and 25
the Cabinet made the final decision and approved the terms of the
ultimatum. At this meeting one Minister is said to have complained
of the shortage of time for making decisions. But no Cabinet
Minister resigned... A partial Cabinet contains influential members of the Cabinet who can be said to represent it in the sense that
collectively they carry very great influence within it. These members must be unanimous or nearly so before a partial Cabinet can
function as such: otherwise there would be no certainty, and
indeed little hope, of carrying the Cabinet...

[Patrick Gordon-Walker, *op. cit*. pp. 39ff]

Although by the 1950s and 1960s the office of Prime Minister had
risen greatly in status, although the Prime Minister had acquired
an authority different in kind from that of his colleagues, he was
still not independent of the Cabinet. The Cabinet remained the sole
source of political authority. On occasion and for a while a partial
Cabinet could act in its name: but the power of a partial Cabinet
always depended upon the assurance that a sufficient number of
leading Ministers shared in its decisions to secure the full authority
of the Cabinet in the end. A strong Prime Minister can be very
strong.[8] He can sometimes commit the Cabinet by acts or words.
But he cannot *habitually* or often do so. A Prime Minister who
habitually ignored the Cabinet, who behaved as if Prime Ministerial
government were a reality – such a Prime Minister could rapidly
come to grief. He would be challenged by his colleagues in the
Cabinet and on occasion overridden. Theoretically a Prime Minister
could dismiss all his Ministers; but then he would present his critics
in the party with potent leadership: Mr Macmillan's mass dismissals

[8] MR AUSTEN CHAMBERLAIN (155 H.C.Deb. 5s. c. 220, 13 June 1922): ' I
  understand the right hon. Gentleman is anxious least the effect of the
  Cabinet Secretariat should be to exalt the Prime Minister... of the day,
  into a position of pre-eminence that he has never yet occupied... and
  give him a control of the Cabinet which is novel... I can assure him
  that that is not the effect of the Secretariat... I would say that the
  position of the Prime Minister has always had special weight in Cabinet
  deliberations. . . But what his actual position is and what his influence is,
  depends upon the man himself.'

in 1962 were generally held to have weakened him. Macmillan was less dominant in his new Cabinet than in his old. . .

The truth is that the Cabinet and the party inside and outside Parliament do indeed find the Prime Minister an indispensable asset and that gives him eminent power. But equally the Prime Minister cannot dispense with party, Parliament and Cabinet. Occasionally a great matter of policy may be dealt with by a partial Cabinet: but the normal, regular and natural procedure is for the Cabinet to discuss and decide all great issues and emergencies. . . On all such matters the Prime Minister's views will carry great weight with the members of the Cabinet; but he cannot . . . ignore their views. . . The Prime Minister can exercise his greatly enhanced powers only if he carries his Cabinet with him. . .

[Patrick Gordon-Walker, *op. cit.* p. 95]

IV. COLLECTIVE RESPONSIBILITY [9]

THE MARQUESS OF SALISBURY: . . . My Lords, my noble Friend [the Earl of Derby] pointed out several measures of the Government to which in the public eye he was an assenting party. He did not, he said, in reality assent to all; one was a compromise, while to another, he was persuaded by some observations which fell from the Chancellor of the Exchequer, which appeared to be founded on a mistake. Now, my Lords, am I not defending a great Constitutional principle, when I say that, for all that passes in Cabinet, each member of it who does not resign is absolutely and irretrievably responsible, and that he has no right afterwards to say that he agreed in one case to a compromise, while in another he was persuaded by one of his Colleagues. Consider the inconvenience which will arise if such a great Constitutional law is not respected. . . It is, I maintain, only on the principle that absolute responsibility is undertaken by every Member of a Cabinet who, after a decision is arrived at, remains a Member of it, that the joint responsibility of Ministers to Parliament can be upheld, and one of the most essential conditions of Parliamentary responsibility established.

[239 Parl.Deb. 3s. c. 833. 8 April 1878]

Cabinets have sometimes included people notoriously in disagreement with major lines of policy; for example, the Free Trader Churchill sat in Baldwin's Cabinet of 1925–9, a supposedly protectionist Cabinet, and got much of his own way. Some matters of high policy have been left as ' open questions '; Women's Suffrage was

[9] For the related principle of Cabinet secrecy see below p. 436.

such in the Asquith and Lloyd George Cabinet. This applies, of course, to matters on which action is not yet taken. But even when action has been completed, it has always been acceptable for a Minister to make private reservations, including recording his dissent in the Cabinet minutes.[10] It has sometimes even been acceptable for a dissentient Minister to make public reservations. Of this the most striking example is Lord Birkenhead. In commending the Equal Franchise Bill to the House of Lords in 1928 he cheerfully admitted he was opposed to the Bill:

'... I have been a member of the Cabinet with a very slight interruption for thirteen years, and I can hardly recall a single measure of first-class importance on which all members of the Cabinet had precisely the same views...

Through my own attitude there runs a golden vein of consistency. I was against the extension of the franchise to women. I am against the extension of the franchise to women...

I have spent nearly the whole of my political life in giving wise advice to my fellow-countrymen, which they have almost invariably disregarded, and if I had resigned everytime that my wise and advantageous advice was rejected I should seldom, indeed, during that critical period, have been in office.'[11]

In addition to these cases of non-operation of the convention, there is the ' agreement to differ ' of 1931–2, when three liberal and Free Trading Ministers stayed in MacDonald's Cabinet, but with liberty to oppose (i.e. speak against) protectionist measures. This open breach of the precedent was proposed on grounds of national crisis: ' an exception to a very sound constitutional principle which can only be justified by exceptional circumstances...' (Lord Hailsham). The Lord Chancellor (Sankey) went a little farther: with large cabinets dealing with a great range of subjects, ' the doctrine of collective responsibility remained as an ideal to be aimed at, but not always one to be realised...' He doubted whether ' it will ever be possible to get a large Cabinet to be unanimous on every subject '.[12]

[P. J. Madgwick, *Resignations : 20 Parliamentary Affairs* (winter 1966–7), pp. 260–1]

The agreement to differ, 1932

In January 1932, after the National Government under MacDonald had won an overwhelming victory at the General Election, a committee of

[10] For examples see Mackintosh, *The British Cabinet*, pp. 445–6.
[11] 71 H.L.Deb. 5s. c. 252–3 (22 May 1928).
[12] 83 H.L.Deb. 5s. c. 543–6 (10 February 1932).

the Cabinet recommended a general tariff of 10% as one of the measures to meet the financial and economic crisis. The Liberal members of the Government, Sir Herbert Samuel, Sir Donald Maclean and Sir Archibald Sinclair, and Lord Snowden, threatened to resign. They were only persuaded to remain in the Government on the understanding that the normal practice of members of the Government taking collective responsibility for its measures would be abandoned and that they would be free to speak and vote against any proposals involving the imposition of tariffs. The Government made the following announcement.

' The Cabinet has had before it the report of the Committee on the Balance of Trade, and after prolonged discussion it has been found impossible to reach a unanimous conclusion on the Committee's recommendations. The Cabinet, however, is deeply impressed with the paramount importance of maintaining national unity in presence of the grave problems that now confront this country and the whole world. It has accordingly determined that some modification of usual Ministerial practice is required and has decided that Ministers who find themselves unable to support the conclusions arrived at by the majority of their colleagues on the subject of import duties and cognate matters are to be at liberty to express their views by speech and vote. The Cabinet, being essentially united on all other matters of policy, believes that by this special provision it is best interpreting the will of the nation and the needs of the time ' (*The Times*, 23 January 1932).

On 8 February the Opposition moved a vote of censure on the Government.

MR LANSBURY: I beg to move, ' That this House can have no confidence in a Government which confesses its inability to decide upon a united policy and proposes to violate the long-established constitutional principle of Cabinet responsibility by embarking upon tariff measures of far-reaching effect which several of His Majesty's Ministers declare will be disastrous to the trade and industry of the country...'

THE LORD PRESIDENT OF THE COUNCIL (MR BALDWIN): ... The Motion says that the Government have no united policy. Let us look at the result of the Divisions to-night and to-morrow! The Motions in support of the Government will be carried by larger majorities than have ever been seen in the House before on matters of similar importance. But in studying this Motion we have to devote our minds to the meaning of the word ' Constitution ', and how far we are deviating in the course we are taking from what is constitutional... The first thing to get clear in our minds is that our Constitution, more than any Constitution in the world, is a living organism...

The historian can tell you probably perfectly clearly what the constitutional practice of this country was at any given period in

the past, but it would be very difficult for a living writer to tell you
at any given period in his lifetime what the Constitution of the
country is in all respects, and for this reason, that at almost any
given moment of our lifetime there may be one practice called
'Constitutional' which is falling into desuetude and there may be
another practice which is creeping into use but which is not yet
called 'Constitutional'. There may be changes on the horizon to be
seen only by some man of vision. I was interested to find last night,
when I had finished making the notes for my speech, that that very
point – I think it is an obvious one – was taken by no less an
authority than Walter Bagehot in the preface to the second edition
of his work on the Constitution, when he had cause to write of the
great changes in constitutional practice which had occurred in the
short seven years since the first edition was published. . .

The very Cabinet system itself . . . for quite a generation after the
first germs of the system appeared in Charles II's reign was
denounced as unconstitutional. . . To-day, a very favourite phrase
used by Members of Parliament is 'legislators'. We have all been
called 'legislators', but legislation is an extremely modern function.
As recently as the time of Chatham you will find that throughout
his Administration practically no important changes were made in
the law. You will find in the time of his son, William Pitt, that he
never thought of resigning office if legislation introduced by his
Government into Parliament failed to pass. Was his position at that
time constitutional? These are difficult questions to answer. I would
ask the House for one moment to contrast the position of William
Pitt with that of Sir Henry Campbell-Bannerman on the Cordite
Vote in the House of Commons, which is in the memory of many
of us.[13]

[13] ['The Liberal government had been desperately clinging for life to a small
majority of about a dozen, when there came on for debate a motion to
reduce the salary of the Secretary of State for War [Campbell-Bannerman],
made in order to draw attention to an alleged lack of cordite. The whips
sitting by the regular entrance of the House had in their tally the usual
majority for the government; but a score of Tories had gone from the
Palace Yard directly to the terrace, without passing through the ordinary
coat-room entrance. When the division-bell rang they came straight from
the terrace to the House, and to the surprise no less of the tellers than of
every one else the government was defeated by a few votes. This was
clearly a "snap" division, which would not ordinarily have been treated
as showing a lack of confidence in the ministry. But the time comes when
a tired man in the sea would rather drown than cling longer; and that was
the position of Lord Rosebery's government' (A. L. Lowell, *The Government of England* (1912), vol. 1, p. 466).

This was in 1895 and was the last occasion on which a Government
which had started life with a majority resigned following a defeat in
Parliament.]

Sir Henry Maine ... showed in very few words the position of the British Government and the British Cabinet for about a third of the eighteenth century. George I and George II cared a great deal about Hanover and being Kings of Hanover, and much less about England and being Kings of England. So there was a tacit understanding between the Whig aristocracy and these two Monarchs that the Whig aristocracy should concern itself with England, and the Kings should concern themselves with Hanover. But when George III came, he cared very little for Hanover and a great deal for England. He cared a great deal for being King of England, he hated the Cabinet system and he wanted to be, as King of England, the dictator of English policy. He refused to submit to the Cabinet. Was his position constitutional at that time or not? A very difficult question to answer. Up to that point you have innumerable instances of Ministers both voting and speaking against the Measures and policy of their own Government. The success of those votes and those speeches depended largely upon the character of the man who was at the top. It was an easier thing to speak against Newcastle than it had been to speak against Walpole. It was done, and done repeatedly, up to North's time.

As to the position of the Prime Minister, it is only within the time and the memories of those sitting here that the Prime Minister's place has appeared in the official precedence of this country. When did the Prime Minister's position become constitutional? That is not an easy question to answer. The real struggle began in the reign of George III. The whole struggle of the eighteenth century was the struggle between the King and the Ministers. Two points of view were held. One point of view was that each Minister, as a servant of the Crown, was responsible for his own Department, with little or no reference to his colleagues. The second view was that Ministers were a homogeneous body, with one Minister to direct and give unity. The King, of course, favoured the first view, because by that means, and that means alone, he could control the policy of this country. The struggle went on for nearly a generation, and the King lost. Probably the event that marked the end of that long constitutional struggle was the dismissal of Thurlow, the last Minister to claim that he had a right to the King's ear as Lord Chancellor and Keeper of the King's Conscience. It was not the mere fact of having conversation with the Monarch that mattered, but the fact that Ministers could discuss with him behind the back of their own leader, and if the King happened to be an extraordinarily able politician he could split any British Government into fragments at any time. So there was a great principle at the back of that struggle.

It was Pitt who ultimately made responsible Ministers the true source of power, and formed the system of government which has lasted practically until the present time... It is inconceivable to-day that the Monarch could play the party game that was played in those days... Going back to George III's time, the peril of the country through the great French War caused the struggle between the Crown and the Ministers to cease, and collective responsibility became the rule. It had grown... with the growth of parties. It was not necessary to the formation of party itself that it came in, but it came in to fight the party of the King's friends. That was how the battle went on, first as against the King's friends and then to maintain the position of the Government in Parliament. That has been the fact ever since. As party government grew and strengthened in this country, so that rule became essential for the maintenance of party government. Party discipline is necessary to party survival. It is not always put as crudely as that in this House, but it is put as crudely as that by Professor Lowell, of Harvard University...

To-day, whatever the right hon. Gentleman may say, we have a National Government. In other words, it is not the Government of one party. It is a Government consisting of representatives of the three parties. [HON. MEMBERS: ' No! ']... Therefore, the great principle for which the fight for a century and more went on is not at stake here. The fate of no party is at stake in making a fresh precedent for a National Government. Had the precedent been made for a party Government, it would have been quite new, and it would have been absolutely dangerous for that party.

Domestically the tariff issue is one of great importance. Internationally for the Government the world problems are infinitely more difficult, and... we believe that it would have been a grave matter for the world at large if, within a few months of the inauguration of this Government, there had been a secession of any section of its Members. It is very interesting that all the dissentient voices in this matter come from those who would like to see the Government split. You ask, is what we are doing constitutional? I remember very well – and it shows how at times questions are asked, and at other times silence is maintained – after the General Election of 1929 having a discussion with many of my friends as to whether we should resign at once or meet Parliament. Some of my friends... took the view that the constitutional position was to meet Parliament and accept our dismissal by Parliament. I took the view, that whatever had been the constitutional position, under universal suffrage the situation had altered; that the people of this country had shown plainly that whether they wanted hon. Members opposite or not, they certainly did not want me, and I was going to get out as soon as I could. My colleagues agreed with me, but I do not remember right hon. Gentlemen opposite asking me whether I behaved constitutionally. They were getting into our places before we had time to move. Is our action constitutional? Who can say what is constitutional in the conduct of a national Government? It is a precedent, an experiment, a new practice, to meet a new emergency, a new condition of things, and we have collective responsibility for the departure from collective action. Whatever some ardent politicians may think, it is approved by the broad common sense of the man-in-the-street. The success or failure of this experiment will depend on one thing only, and that is the spirit in which it is conducted. I have every hope . . . that this experiment may be so conducted that it may prove successful, and that the judgment of future generations will be that the House of Commons by the vote to-night took a step of wisdom and common sense.

[261 H.C.Deb. 5s. c. 515. 8 February 1932]

The Opposition motion was defeated by 438 votes to 38. In the event the experiment did not last long. In September 1932 Samuel, Sinclair and Snowden (Maclean had died in June) resigned over the Ottawa agreements which gave preference to goods coming from the Dominions over those coming from other countries.

CHAPTER III

THE CIVIL SERVICE

The role of the Civil Service

12. ... [T]he modern Civil Service must be able to handle the social, economic, scientific and technical problems of our time, in an international setting. Because the solutions to complex problems need long preparation, the Service must be far-sighted; from its accumulated knowledge and experience, it must show initiative in working out what are the needs of the future and how they might be met. A special responsibility now rests upon the Civil Service because one Parliament or even one Government often cannot see the process through.

13. At the same time, the Civil Service works under political direction and under the obligation of political accountability. This is the setting in which the daily work of many civil servants is carried out; thus they need to have a lively awareness of the political implications of what they are doing or advising. The Civil Service has also to be flexible enough to serve governments of any political complexion – whether they are committed to extend or in certain respects to reduce the role of the State. Throughout, it has to remember that it exists to serve the whole community, and that imaginative humanity sometimes matters more than tidy efficiency and administrative uniformity...

27. Civil servants work in support of Ministers in their public and parliamentary duties. Some of them prepare plans and advise on policy, assembling and interpreting all the data required, e.g. for a decision on a new social security policy, a change in defence policy, a new national transport policy or a new international joint project in the technical field . . . They prepare legislation and assist Ministers with its passage through Parliament. They draft regulations and answers to Parliamentary Questions. They produce briefs for debates and the mass of information which the constitutional principle of parliamentary and public accountability requires. Increasingly, senior civil servants now appear before Parliamentary Committees . . .

28. Operating policies embodied in existing legislation and implementing policy decisions take up most of the time of most civil servants. There are taxes to be collected, employment and social

security offices to be run. There is a mass of individual case-work both in local offices and in the central departments of state. New policy may require the creation of a new administrative framework. There are major programmes to be managed and controlled, such as the planning and engineering of motorways from their initial location and design to the finished construction; the design of Polaris installations and other military works; the management of international programmes like Concorde; the vast range of scientific research and development and of government procurement; the central responsibility for the nationalised industries and for the state of the economy.

29. Some of the work involves the Civil Service in complex relationships with other bodies which are partners in the execution of government policy or are directly affected by it. They include local authorities and nationalised industries in the first category and a multitude of organised interests in the second ...

[Report of the Committee on the Civil Service, 1966–8. Cmnd. 3638 (June 1968)]

The Northcote–Trevelyan Report, 1854

It cannot be necessary to enter into any lengthened argument for the purpose of showing the high importance of the Permanent Civil Service of the country in the present day. The great and increasing accumulation of public business, and the consequent pressure upon the Government, need only be alluded to; and the inconveniences which are inseparable from the frequent changes which take place in the responsible administration are matters of sufficient notoriety ...

It would be natural to expect that so important a profession would attract into its ranks the ablest and the most ambitious of the youth of the country; that the keenest emulation would prevail among those who had entered it; and that such as were endowed with superior qualifications would rapidly rise to distinction and public eminence. Such, however, is by no means the case. Admission into the Civil Service is indeed eagerly sought after, but it is for the unambitious, and the indolent or incapable, that it is chiefly desired. Those whose abilities do not warrant an expectation that they will succeed in the open professions, where they must encounter the competition of their contemporaries, and those whom indolence of temperament, or physical infirmities unfit for active exertions, are placed in the Civil Service, where they may obtain an honourable livelihood with little labour, and with no risk, where their success depends upon their simply avoiding any flagrant misconduct, and attending with moderate regularity to routine duties; and in which they are secured against the ordinary consequences of old age, or failing health, by an arrangement which provides them with the means of supporting themselves after they have become incapacitated . . . It is not our intention to suggest that all public servants entered the employment of the Government with such views as these; but we apprehend that as regards a large proportion of them, these motives more or less influenced those who acted for them in the choice of a profession; while, on the other hand, there are probably very few who have chosen this line of life with a view to raising themselves to public eminence . . .

There are, however, numerous honourable exceptions to these observations, and the trustworthiness of the entire body is unimpeached. They are much better than we have any right to expect from the system under which they are appointed and promoted.

Having thus touched upon some of the difficulties . . . what is the best method of providing . . . a supply of good men, and of making the most of them after they are admitted?

The general principle . . . which we advocate is, that the public service should be carried on by the admission into its lower ranks of a carefully selected body of young men, who . . . should be made constantly to feel that their promotion and future prospects depend entirely on the industry and ability with which they discharge their duties, that with average abilities and reasonable application they may look forward confidently to a certain provision for their lives, that with superior powers they may rationally hope to attain to the highest prizes in the Service, while if they prove decidedly incompetent, or incurably indolent, they must expect to be removed from it.

The first step towards carrying this principle into effect should be the establishment of a proper system of examination before appointment, which should be followed, as at present, by a short period of probation . . .

We accordingly recommend that a central Board be constituted for conducting the examination of all candidates for the public service whom it may be thought right to subject to such a test. Such board should be composed of men holding an independent position, and capable of commanding general confidence; should either include, or have the means of obtaining the assistance of persons experienced in the education of the youth of the upper and middle classes, and persons who are familiar with the conduct of official business. It should be made imperative upon candidates for admission to any appointment (except in certain cases which will presently be noticed), to pass a proper examination before the Board, and obtain from them a certificate of having done so . . .

In the examination which we have recommended, we consider that the right of competing should be open to all persons, of a given age, subject only, as before suggested, to the necessity of their giving satisfactory references from persons able to speak to their moral conduct and character, and of producing medical certificates to the effect that they have no bodily infirmity likely to incapacitate them for the public service . . .

The choice of the subjects to be comprehended in the examination, as well as the mode in which the examination should be conducted should, of course, be left to the Board of Examiners. We will therefore only indicate the advantage of making the subjects as numerous as may be found practicable, so as to secure the greatest and most varied amount of talent for the public service. Men whose services would be highly valuable to the country might easily be beaten by some who were their inferiors, if the examination were confined to a few subjects to which the latter had devoted their exclusive attention; but if an extensive range were given, the superiority of the best would become evident. Besides, an opportunity would be afforded for judging in what kind of situation each is likely to be most useful; and we need hardly allude to the important effect which would be produced upon the general education of the country, if proficiency in history, jurisprudence, political economy, modern languages, political and physical geography, and other matters, besides the staple of classics and mathematics, were made directly conducive to the success of young men desirous of entering into the public service. Such an inducement would probably do more to quicken the progress of our Universities, for instance, than any legislative measures that could be adopted.

It would probably be right to include in the examination some exercises directly bearing upon official business; to require a precis to be made of a set of papers, or a letter to be written under given circumstances; but the great advantage to be expected from the examinations would be, that they would elicit young men of general ability, which is a matter of more moment than their being possessed of any special requirements. Men capable of distinguishing themselves in any of the subjects we have named, and thereby affording a proof that their education has not been lost upon them, would probably make themselves useful wherever they might be placed . . .

[Report of Sir Stafford Northcote and Charles Trevelyan on the Organisation of the Permanent Civil Service 1854, P.P. XXVII 1]

98. . . . We think it will be generally accepted that the community must suffer if the present tradition is impaired whereby a non-

political Civil Service carries out impartially the tasks required of it by Governments of different political complexions. A corollary of this is that in the matter of recruitment and dismissal there must be no question of patronage or manipulation of appointments and that no improper influence should be exercised by tampering with the salaries of particular posts or individuals. The State as employer must therefore limit its freedom of action, in a way that a private employer need not, to secure, particularly in the higher Civil Service, immunity from political and personal pressures. This requires that recruitment procedures leading to admission to the established Civil Service should be more formal than those outside and should not be changed at short notice; that there should be a greater degree of security of tenure than is necessarily found outside; that the salaries of all posts in the Service should be public knowledge and should not be susceptible of arbitrary variation; from which it follows that there must be a high degree of standardisation in pay and conditions of service. Thus the State must enter into relationships with its employees which are more formal than those in the generality of other employments, and it can have no secrets, either from the Service generally or from the public, about the pay and conditions it offers to any of its staff . . .

[Report of the Royal Commission on the Civil Service, 1953–5. Cmd. 9613 (1955–6)]

19. . . . [T]here is not enough contact between the Service and the rest of the community . . . Partly this is a consequence of a career service. Since we expect most civil servants to spend their entire working lives in the Service, we can hardly wonder if they have little direct and systematic experience of the daily life and thought of other people. . .

123. . . . Nevertheless, we are convinced that, both in the public interest and also for the health of the service itself, effective steps must be taken to ensure a very much larger and freer flow of men and women between the Service and outside employments than there has been in the past. . .

125. . . . For example, the present system by which professional economists come into the Service from the universities for a few years and then return, perhaps to come back again for further spells later, has been of great value . . . In the various administrative groups similar short term appointments for those with relevant experience in industry, commerce or the universities could also bring advantages. . .

128. Determined efforts are needed to bring about the temporary interchange of staff with private industry and commerce, nationa-

lised industry and local government on a much larger scale than hitherto. War-time experience proves beyond doubt the value of such movement in promoting mutual knowledge and understanding. Coming at the right stage, experience in a changed environment can also be of decisive importance in the individual's development. . .

129. Several times in recent years Ministers have brought in professional experts and advisers of their own. These have been personal appointments in the sense that they have been individuals known to the Ministers concerned, who have judged that their individual qualities and experience could be of special help to them in their departments. We welcome this practice . . . We are satisfied that a Minister should be able to employ on a temporary basis such small numbers of experts as he personally considers he needs to help and advise him. . .

134. We have recommended a much greater flexibility of movement between the Civil Service and other employments. We think however that it should remain a career service in the sense that most civil servants should enter at young ages with the expectation, but not the guarantee, of a life-time's employment; and that the great majority of those who come to occupy top jobs will in practice be career civil servants. There are in our view substantial reasons why this should continue to be so: —

(a) Our avowed aim is to create a Civil Service that is truly professional. . . Long experience and accumulated knowledge are essential parts of this concept. While it involves a constant inflow of new men and ideas from outside, it must also involve for the majority a professional career in the Service.

(b) Civil servants must be able to give forthright advice to their superiors and to Ministers without fearing that a clash of views might lead to dismissal from the Service.

(c) Really able young men are more likely to come into the Service if they know that the top jobs are open to them; if too many of the senior posts were filled from outside the Service, this would produce frustration among those already in the Service and discourage recruitment.

(d) At a time when there is greater intermingling between the public and private sectors, and when the decisions of civil servants are of immediate concern to firms and other organisations, we want to see a substantial increase in the flow of staff, both long-term and short-term, between the Service and commerce and industry. But this should take place in a professional atmosphere fostered by the fact that the majority of civil servants expect to remain in the Service for a life-time's career. It is important that civil servants should not come to think of those who do business with their departments as their prospective employers, and that firms, which are increasingly required to reveal their technical and financial affairs to government, should be able to do so with confidence. . .

[Report of the Committee on the Civil Service, 1966–8. Cmnd. 3638]

109. . . . It has been alleged that the practice under which government servants are taken into the employment of armament firms, or given directorships, during their service or at or after retirement from the public service is objectionable. . . [T]he allegation is that it creates a relationship between firms and officials of the departments in which the complete independence of the latter in regard to the placing of contracts is likely to be endangered or prejudiced. . . Witnesses have been at pains to assert that it is no more than the suggestion of a possibility and that they make no specific charge. It has not been alleged by anyone that any public servant has at any time allowed his independence to be in any way impaired. We have no reason to believe, and do not believe, that the practice in question has been or is likely to be the occasion of any weakening of departmental independence; it is a practice which has obvious advantages in a system under which the government collaborates with private industry, and we do not propose that it should be discontinued. So far as concerns the proper conduct of civil servants and government officials generally, the matter is not confined to the particular case of employment by armament firms, and in general we are satisfied that the question of the conduct of public officials in regard to such matters may safely be left to the discretion of the service itself, in confident reliance upon the meticulous sense of public duty by which the service as a whole is inspired.

110. We cannot, however, regard as satisfactory the position under which armament firms are free to recruit ex-officials and ex-officers of the Army, Navy and Air Force at their own discretion, and we cannot ignore the suspicions which arise from the practice, however ill-founded they may be. We therefore recommend that officers, whether serving or retired, should not enter the service of armament firms in any capacity without the specific approval of the Minister in charge of their department. . .

[Report of the Royal Commission on the Private Manufacture of and Trading in Arms. Cmd. 5292 (October 1936) [1]]

[1] See also the report of the Board of Inquiry appointed by the Prime Minister to investigate certain discussions engaged in by Permanent Secretary to the Air Ministry, Cmd. 5254, August 1936.

As stated at the end of paragraph 15 of Cmd. 5451 ('Statement relating to Report of the Royal Commission on the Private Manufacture of and Trading in Arms, 1935–36'), the question of the acceptance of business appointments by officers of the Crown Services is one which 'calls for careful study, and is not being overlooked'. . . .

3. . . . His Majesty's Government recognise that there should be no possibility of a suggestion – however unjustified – in the public mind that members of those Services might be influenced in the course of their official relations with business concerns by hopes or offers of future employment in any of those concerns.

4. . . . His Majesty's Government in no sense imply that there is anything intrinsically improper or undesirable in Officers, on retirement at the end of their Service career, accepting business appointments. But they realise that there are types of case which might lend themselves to misunderstanding, and they have decided to require Government assent to the acceptance of appointments within these types.

5. These would include businessess and other bodies—
   (*a*) which are in contractual relationship with the Government;
   (*b*) which are in receipt of subsidies or their equivalent from the Government;
   (*c*) in which the Government is a shareholder;
   (*d*) which are in receipt from the Government of loans, guarantees or other forms of capital assistance;
   (*e*) with which Services or Departments or Branches of Government are, as a matter of course, in a special relationship;
and semi-public organisations brought into being by the Government and/or by Parliament.

6. In such cases all Officers of the rank of Assistant Under-Secretary of State (or Principal Assistant Secretary or, in Missions abroad, Ministers), Rear-Admiral, Major-General, Air Vice-Marshal – and above – will be required to obtain the assent of the Government before accepting an offer of employment.

In addition, in each of the four Services there are posts of a special or technical character not covered by the preceding sentence to which a similar requirement will apply. Lists of such posts will be prepared in the respective Departments in conjunction with the Treasury, to ensure parity of treatment.

7. The prior assent of the Government will take the form of approval by the Minister concerned after consultation with the

Treasury; but, after the lapse of two years from the date of retirement, such assent will no longer be required.

8. The like principles will apply in the case of Officers who, in exceptional circumstances, may wish to resign from the Services to take up outside occupations.

[Memorandum on the Subject of the Acceptance of Business Appointments by Officers of the Crown Services. Cmd. 5517 (July 1937)]

In a memorandum on the subject to the Committee on the Civil Service 1966–68 the Treasury noted:

' 4. In practice applications for permission to accept outside appointments have rarely been refused. But this does not necessarily mean that the policy has been ineffective. It is likely that the mere existence of the control has discouraged individuals from considering offers of employment about which they themselves felt doubtful. Moreover it ensures that Departments have prior knowledge of cases which might conceivably cause embarrassment, gives them a chance to consider the lines on which they could reply to criticism, and in some cases to attach conditions to their assent.

5. Whether by accident or design, the policy has been administered over the years in such a way that public complaint about particular appointments has been avoided, while industry and business have benefited by a small but steady intake of people with experience of public administration. We believe that it is in the public interest that this intake should continue. But if it is to continue it is most important to avoid public controversy over any particular case. Such controversy would do damage not only in the individual case but generally.'

Note that similar problems can arise in relation to the appointment of ex-Ministers.

1. POLITICAL NEUTRALITY

The Report of the Masterman Committee, 1948

In 1948 following representations from the staff side of the Civil Service National Whitley Council about the restrictions on the political activities of civil servants, the Government appointed a committee under the chairmanship of J. C. Masterman to examine the existing limitations and make recommendations as to any changes that might be desirable. It reported as follows:

38. ... The public interest demands, at least amongst those employees of the State who correspond with the common conception of the Civil Service, a manner of behaviour which is incompatible with the overt declaration of party political allegiance.

39. This incompatibility is obvious in the case of the Administrative Class who are the advisers of Ministers and assist in the making of policy. Their role in the formulation of policy decisions and their close relationship with Ministers clearly require an attitude of mind

with which the public advocacy of party political views would be inconsistent. . .

40. . . . In present conditions a Minister coming into a Department is able to rely on entirely loyal service to his ideas from all civil servants alike. He has no reason even to consider whether any particular civil servant, is, or is not, in sympathy with his political views. He is indeed able to assume that, whatever the civil servant's sympathies, they would not affect his advice on the facts in any given case. The disadvantages of departing from this position are obvious.

41. Only a very small proportion of the Service is, however, in close contact with Ministers. Those who are responsible for advising Ministers amongst a variety of other duties are to be found mainly among the higher Administrative ranks. The whole Administrative Class numbers only about 3,500 men and women, most of whom are stationed in Headquarters Departments in the Whitehall area. . .

42. Outside the Whitehall Ministries the Civil Service is a very large and widely spread body of men and women who are engaged not in advising Ministers but in the conduct of practical business. They are employed in various Headquarters branches, such as those of the Admiralty at Bath and the Ministry of National Insurance at Newcastle-on-Tyne, and in regional and local offices all over the country. In the latter, to a greater degree than in White-hall, the work brings all ranks down to quite junior officials into intimate relationship with every section of the community. The duties performed by them are broadly of three types, although each merges into the other: —

(*a*) duties involving the exercise of a large measure of discretion;
(*b*) duties which, while requiring powers of interpretation in given circumstances, are closely governed by Acts of Parliament, regulations or departmental instructions;
(*c*) duties of a partially or wholly routine character.

In these cases, the essential factor is the relation of civil servants with the public rather than their relations with the Minister. First the work of these civil servants must in fact be completely impartial. Secondly, the public as a whole and the Press must be satisfied in their own minds that no suggestion of political bias enters into their treatment of individuals. The importance of these considerations can hardly be exaggerated today when vital decisions on claims for social benefits, assessment to tax, liability to various forms of national service, entitlement to certain rationed commodities, and many other aspects of daily life are being taken by officials often of humble rank. Whether we consider the man-in-the-street seeking employment, the professional man applying for a supplementary allowance of petrol, or the member of the business community dealing with the various economic controls now operated by the Civil Service, the life of every citizen is being directly and acutely affected by all grades of the hierarchy. In these circumstances, public faith in the non-political and impartial attitude of the Civil Service as a whole would be quickly shaken if individual civil servants were known or even suspected, rightly or wrongly, to be not in fact detached from party allegiance.

43. There is finally to be considered the harmful effect upon the Service itself if the political allegiance of individual civil servants became generally known to their superior officers and colleagues. If a Minister began to consider whether A, on account of his party views, might be more capable of carrying out his policy than B, the usefulness of B would be limited and the opportunities of A would be unfairly improved. This would become known, and a tendency to trim the sails to the prevailing wind would be one consequence. Another would be a cynicism about the reasons for promotion, very damaging to morale. If it be thought that we have exaggerated this risk, we would point to the experience of those countries which are suffering from the consequences of taking a course different from our own. The danger is, we believe, a real one. It may result from only small beginnings, but, once begun, it produces a snowball effect, which is difficult, if not impossible, to check. Once a doubt is cast upon the loyalty of certain individuals or upon the equity of the promotion-machinery, an atmosphere of distrust may rapidly pervade an office and affect the arrangement of the work and damage the efficiency of the organisation. . .

45. It follows, in our opinion, that the principle hitherto observed in the Civil Service, that a civil servant maintains a certain reserve in political matters and does not put himself forward prominently on one side or the other, is plainly right for that part of the Service popularly associated with the phrase ' white collar workers '. The practice of reticence in public is necessary to the maintenance of this attitude. Nothing crystallizes views like the expression of them in controversy, and it would be harder ever afterwards for a civil servant to advise his Minister or his senior officers in a sense contrary to the party line if he had once publicly declared his adhesion to party doctrine. He must regard his powers as an advocate as being always at the service not of a party doctrine but of an administrative ideal. There is, of course, also the consideration that, even if he could keep his party views absolutely separate from his judgment of a particular question, as some contend he can, it would be almost impossible for him to convince other people that he had done so.

46. We have considered the argument advanced by the Staff Side that civil servants themselves can be trusted to exercise political rights in a way not detrimental to the public interest. This might seem an attractive suggestion, but in our view it relies too much on the traditional Civil Service attitude to public affairs which has been formed by decades of training and experience under the present convention. It does not follow that if the convention were modified civil servants would act and speak with the same reticence and wariness which they show at present. An announcement that civil servants were free to engage in political activity would fundamentally alter the point of view of the Service, at all events of its younger members. It would undoubtedly be a shock to public opinion, accustomed as it is to the tradition of a non-political Service. The Staff Side themselves appear to realise the risks inherent in such a change, as they do not exclude the possibility that individual civil servants, if allowed complete freedom, might create an intolerable situation for their Departments and become liable to disciplinary action. A few bad cases which attracted public attention would reduce public confidence in the Service as a whole. But in our view it would be inequitable to penalise an officer who erred in ignorance, and difficult for a Department to take disciplinary measures against him if he used his discretion unwisely. It seems to us that it is in the interests of the individual as well as the Department that there should be some protection against the creation of an intolerable situation, both by a general code of behaviour and, where the need arises, by explicit prohibitions. We see nothing derogatory in the existence of such rules. Moreover, if no rules existed, departmental case law would be bound to grow up out of decisions on individual cases; such decisions would often have to be sought by the staff themselves. We think that many civil servants would welcome some guidance in advance.

48. . . . The public service should, in our view, consistently be given the benefit of any doubt. Any weakening of the existing tradition of political impartiality would be the first step towards the creation of a 'political' Civil Service. . . Even the smallest move down that slope might eventually lead to the evils of the spoils system. Though it is impossible to measure accurately the possible effects of changes in the present system in this country, we are convinced that any such change would be fraught with dangerous possibilities, and that it would be a retrograde step, detrimental to both the public interest and the interest of the Civil Service itself. . .

[Report of the Committee on the Political Activities of Civil Servants. Cmd. 7718 (1948–9)]

285. We considered whether we should recommend that Ministers at the head of departments should be served by a personal *cabinet* on the French model, or alternatively that they should make a substantial number of largely personal and political appointments to positions at the top of their departments as in the United States. These are both devices that could be used to strengthen the Minister's control of the departmental policy-making process and to increase the sensitiveness with which the department responds to the needs of Parliament and the public. We have welcomed . . . the introduction of the practice whereby Ministers make a small number of temporary appointments. We think it important that Ministers should be free to arrange for the holders of such appointments to be closely associated with the work of the many ' official ' committees (i.e. committees of civil servants without ministerial membership) which make an essential contribution to policy-making; the work of these committees places a heavy responsibility on civil servants to ensure that the choices subsequently presented to Ministers are not unduly circumscribed [2] . . . [W]e also propose that the Minister should be assisted by a Senior Policy Adviser as well as by the Permanent Secretary and we suggested that the Minister's own methods of working would determine the pattern of relationships at the top and the precise division of responsibilities. These developments should increase the control of Ministers over the formulation of policy in their departments. In the light of them (taken in conjunction with our proposals in the next paragraph), we see no need for ministerial *cabinets* or for political appointments on a large scale.

286. A related issue is the extent to which a Minister should be free to change the staff immediately surrounding him. There is no problem about those who have been personally appointed on a temporary basis by his predecessor; when a new Minister comes in, they will go anyway. Thus the issue really arises only over the positions of the Permanent Secretary, the Senior Policy Adviser and the Private Secretary. Because of the nature of the Private Secretary's duties, he must be personally acceptable to his Minister; there should therefore, in our view, be no obstacle in the way of a Minister's selecting from within the department, or on occasion more widely within the Service, as his Private Secretary the individual best

---

[2] ' One of us (Dr Norman Hunt) considers that junior Ministers should also be members of the more important of these committees. At present junior Ministers are sometimes not in a position to make a full contribution to departmental work. Their inclusion in official committees could strengthen the political direction of departments.'

suited to his ways of working; no stigma should attach to a person who is moved out of this job. As far as Senior Policy Advisers are concerned (whether career civil servants or those appointed from outside the Service on a short-term basis), we would hope that, as they will be selected for this job as men of technical competence and vitality, Ministers will not normally wish to replace them. This must however be possible when a new Minister finds the current holder of this office too closely identified with, or wedded to, policies that he wishes to change; or when an adviser's capacity for producing and making use of new ideas declines. It should be more exceptional, however, for a Minister to change his Permanent Secretary. Ministers change often, whereas the running of a department requires continuity. Even so, Ministers should not be stuck with Permanent Secretaries who are too rigid or tired. Any changes of this kind affecting Senior Policy Advisers or Permanent Secretaries will require the most careful consideration by the Head of the Civil Service and the Prime Minister, whose joint task it is in this context to safeguard the political neutrality of the higher Civil Service.

[Report of the Committee on the Civil Service, 1966–8. Cmnd. 3638]

The case of Duck Island and the pigeon nuisance, 1972

As a result of complaints to Ministers from their own backbenchers that the Opposition was monopolising questions to the Minister for Housing and Reconstruction the latter asked his Department to prepare a bank of Questions which could be passed to Government backbenchers for use at Question time in the House of Commons. Officials in the Housing and Construction side of the Department were sent a minute from the Parliamentary Clerk in the Minister's office which stated:

'When the Department is next 1st for Questions on Wednesday 31 March, the majority of Questions that will be reached orally have been tabled by Labour Members, thus pushing out any (perhaps useful) Questions tabled to Ministers by Tory M.P.s. Mr. Amery, in discussion with Mr. Churchill, therefore, has decided that for the next 1st Order Question time . . . we will try and make sure that the first 50 odd Questions tabled are from Tory M.P.s, by "feeding" Questions to them. To do this, I should be grateful if all Directors/Under-Secretaries would furnish me with up to 10 Questions, if possible, so that I can ask Mr. Churchill to farm these out to friendly M.P.s for tabling (there is no need to forward me the answers until you have received the Parliamentary Question folders).'

The propriety of this action was considered by the Select Committee on Parliamentary Questions [H.C. 393 1971–72, 17 July 1972]. It said:

'36. In considering the implications of the evidence submitted to them, Your Committee have distinguished between the use by the Government of "inspired" oral and written Questions to enable them to give information to the House, and the preparation of a " bank " of Questions the answers to which are of secondary importance [3] to their use as a means of increasing the proportion of Questions on the Order Paper favourable to the Government. The use of " inspired " written Questions, and the alternative of volunteering Statements to the House, sometimes in written form, have been considered this Session by the Select Committee on Procedure (H.C. 217) and Your Committee do not deal with that matter. On the issues before them, they have come to the following conclusions:...

   (3) there is nothing wrong in Members accepting ideas for Questions, or draft Questions, from outside sources and taking upon themselves the responsibility of tabling them;

   (4) it is not the role of the Government machine to seek to redress the party balance of Questions in the Order Paper, and civil servants should not in future be asked to prepare Questions which have this object.'

The Committee also took evidence from Sir William Armstrong, the Head of the Home Civil Service, on the general question of the extent to which civil servants should assist Ministers in the performance of their party political rather than their governmental functions.

SIR WILLIAM ARMSTRONG, G.C.B., M.V.O., Head of the Home Civil Service and Permanent Secretary, Civil Service Department, called in and examined. 4 February 1972.

133. ....– The overwhelming presumption is that a Civil Servant carries out the instructions of a Minister and, unless there are reasons to the contrary, that is what he does. I suppose it arises mostly in relation to Ministerial powers. Ministers are frequently wanting to do things and it has to be pointed out to them that they do not have the powers to do them. Subject to that sort of thing, the overwhelming presumption is that Civil Servants will carry out the instructions of Ministers. There is one area that is an exception to this which I felt to be relevant... That is the rules regarding the position of Accounting Officers. With the Committee's permission I will read from a document called ' Government Accounting ' which is a public document on sale at the Stationery Office. Section ' C ' in this document describes the duties of the Accounting Officer and paragraphs 8 and 9 deal with disagreements between a Minister and the Accounting Officer. They say: ' 8. It may happen that an Accounting Officer disagrees with his Minister on a matter of importance affecting the efficient and economic administration of his

---

[3] E.g. ' to ask the Secretary of State for the Environment what steps he is taking to combat the pigeon nuisance in public buildings '; and ' to ask the Secretary of State for the Environment whether, in view of the success of flood-lighting of Duck Island in St. James Park, he has considered extending the lighting further.'

Department and thus the Accounting Officer's duty to Parliament. In such a case the Accounting Officer is expected to place on record his disagreement with any decision which he considers he would have difficulty in defending before the Public Accounts Committee as a matter of prudent administration. Having done so, he must, if the Minister adheres to the decision, accept it and, if necessary, support his defence of the action taken by reference to the policy ruling of the Minister. 9. Alternatively the matter of the Accounting Officer's disagreement and his protest may be one which involves his personal accountability on a question of the safeguarding of public funds or the formal regularity or propriety of expenditure. In that case he should state in writing his objection and the reason for it and carry out the Minister's decision only on a written instruction from the Minister overruling his objection. He should then inform the Treasury of the circumstances and communicate the papers to the Comptroller and Auditor General. Provided that this procedure has been followed, the Public Accounts Committee may be expected to acquit the Accounting Officer of any personal responsibility for the transaction.' I think that shows my point: that the overwhelming presumption is that even in these very extreme circumstances the Minister's instructions, if need be under protest in these particular areas, will be carried out. Then there is another area of understanding which I thought was relevant to this: the well-known rule that Ministers of a current Government are not entitled to ask to see the papers of a previous administration. That is a convention. There is no legal basis for it but it is one which, in my experience, each Government has accepted on coming into office. It is a self-denying ordinance which each Government has imposed on itself. It is occasionally necessary for Civil Servants to draw the attention of Ministers to this self-denying ordinance they have imposed on themselves. If a request, notwithstanding that, is made, the Civil Servant has the right to refuse; but I have never known of any difficulty arising in relation to that. Then there is another series of understandings which relate to the Civil Service in connection with party political activities. It is a rule that a Minister may not use his Department to do the duties of a constituency secretary – the duties which, if he were an ordinary Member of Parliament, he would have to do with his constituency secretary. The Department will, of course, deal with matters raised by his constituents as with any other Members of Parliament's letters, but there must be somebody who is not a Civil Servant and who acts as constituency secretary. On occasions it is perfectly obvious that there is not enough work for a full-time person and there may be the arrangement of part-time constituency work/part-time other work in the Minister's private office. Nevertheless, the principle is there, that the Minister himself should pay the salary of a constituency secretary or for that part of the time of a person which is engaged on that work. It is equally an understanding that if a Minister is going to a party meeting and making a party political speech he may not issue that speech through the departmental press office and use the Government distribution machinery to make that speech available to the Press. That must be done through the party's own Press machinery. There is no ban on the provision of information by Civil Servants for inclusion in such a speech. On the matter of party conferences, again the position is similar. There is no ban on the provision of information for inclusion in the speeches at a party conference but the departmental press office must not take part in any publicity to be given to the speeches and no Civil Servants should be present at a party conference. The only exception is that if a Minister with heavy departmental duties, such as the Prime Minister, the Foreign Secretary and the Chancellor of the Exchequer, finds it necessary to have a Private Secretary with him so that he may continue his departmental duties, while at the Party Conference, then he may do that. There were two points that at the time struck me as relevant about this: that in this understanding which has grown up and been confirmed by successive governments of the two sides it is quite clear that Civil Servants may – and indeed, it is taken for granted that they do – provide information for use on these party occasions; secondly, that all of these things relate to party political proceedings outside Parliament and there are no rules or regulations about what happens in Parliament itself. It is quite clear that in this House a Minister's political persona comes together with his ministerial persona. In a sense this is the most political occasion of all. Nevertheless, it is the occasion where he is behaving as a Minister. For that reason there are no rules, understandings, conventions limiting the help which Civil Servants may give to their Ministers in Parliament. I myself and other Civil Servants have taken part in what I might call various stratagems: arranging to talk out a motion or a Private Member's Bill, arranging the order of clauses in a Bill to fit with anticipated action in Parliament, reducing the number of clauses in a Bill so as to reduce the number of occasions when a debate on a clause stand part can take place and arranging to prolong debates on some subjects so as either to avoid altogether debates on other subjects or have them occur at a time of day or on a particular day of the week or month when it was thought that this would be more favourable to the Government. This kind of stratagem has been part of my parliamentary life and there are, as I say, no rules against it.

SIR ROBIN TURTON. 134. Sir William, apart from these under-standings you have talked about, surely the habit of 'inspired' questions has been a well-recognised thing in departments and has been practiced from administration to administration? – Yes, indeed. I was taking that for granted. There is absolutely no doubt about that at all.

135. Have there previously been banks of 'inspired' questions? – I have no idea.

MR LYON. 136. I gather that you take the view that what a Minister orders his Civil Servants to do is constitutionally correct unless hitherto there has been laid down some regulation forbidding this particular practice? – A regulation, understanding, convention, statute.

137. That is, some kind of instruction? – Yes.

138. But are there not things about the use of Civil Servants by party politicians which none the less might strike you as reprehen-sible, even if there are no instructions or understandings about it? – There might be, but I do not think that would constitute a reason for saying that they were improper or that the Civil Servant would be entitled to refuse.

139. Supposing, however, that the Minister were to say he wanted his Parliamentary Secretary to go with him to a party meeting in his constituency and to sit behind him in order that he should feed him with information on the platform in order to reply to difficult ques-tions that might be asked by the audience, would you regard that as being proper? – Your question is intended to relate to his Private Secretary. You said 'Parliamentary Secretary' and there is nothing more usual than that. But his Private Secretary, no. That is clearly ruled out by the existing understandings . . . so the civil servant has the right to refuse.

140. Does there seem to you to be any difficulty in him making available to members of his party who are not Ministers the resources of the Civil Service so that he can better do his job as an ordinary back-bench Member of Parliament? – Is there any diffi-culty in a Minister using Civil Servants to provide information to back benchers?

141. Yes? – No, there is no difficulty at all if a Minister wishes to do that. If some of the information . . . were officially secret and related to national defence or something like that, we would point this out to him . . . This goes on continuously. We provide at the request of Ministers information about our doings in the Civil Service Department to a group of interested Members of Parliament on both sides and we have done this with both administrations.

142. In the course of a series of minutes provided by the

Minister . . . there is one . . . from Mr Clifford the Parliamentary Clerk in the Ministry, which sets out quite explicitly that the aim of this practice we are investigating ' is to oust Opposition questions on first order days '. . . Did it not strike you . . . as being odd that Civil Servants were being used in that way? – Odd? It certainly was unusual, but that was not the question I was asked by Ministers. The question I was asked was, was it improper? . . .

144. You had never heard of it before? – No.

145. Did you tell the Minister that. . .? – This took place at a meeting at which a number of other people said they had heard of it before and referred to cases where it had happened.

146. But did you yourself say you had never heard of it before? – No. I did not rest my advice on precedent at all.

147. You rested your advice on the absence of any precedent? – The absence of any ban on it, yes.

148. The mere fact that there was in this area no law meant that it must be correct? – It meant that Ministers must be free to do what they set out to do.

149. But surely that would be to put an enormous power in the hands of Ministers in relation to the Civil Service if they were able to do as they willed, unless there had hitherto been some kind of instruction or understanding by Parliament about the use of civil servants in this area? – I believe that to be the fact: that Ministers do have that power, yes . . .

MR ORME. 153. Would you not agree that an Opposition has difficulties, in the sense that it is not backed by what is supposed to be an independent Civil Service, as is the Government . . .? – . . . I would agree.

MR CUNNINGHAM. 178. When on the Sunday you felt you ought to find out whether the Civil Servants writing these minutes had in fact received instructions from Ministers to do so, had they not received instructions you would have regarded these minutes as improper? – Yes, I should. I do not think it is any part of a Civil Servant's duty to take the initiative, as would be the case if he were doing this without instructions.

179. . . . – [I]f the proposition described in this minute had been one dreamed up by Civil Servants without reference to Ministers, that would have seemed to me to be quite an improper thing for Civil Servants to do . . .

182. If a Minister told a Civil Servant, ' I want to make a speech roundly condemning the previous government of a different party and I want you to dig up everything you can against them and write a speech of that party character ', do you think that that would be a desirable instruction for a Minister to give to a Civil Servant? –

I am not sure that it is within my province to say whether it is desirable. If the question is, should the Civil Servant refuse the answer is clear: no, he should not. The attitude of the Civil Servant who got such an instruction would be seen in the character of the draft he produced, just as I suggest you can see the attitude of the Civil Servants in the DoE from the character of the questions they put forward.

183. Do you think . . . that that impartiality would be better pre-served by this practice not taking place or by it taking place? – . . . I am very, very keen that what I believe to be the Civil Service's just reputation for impartiality – political impartiality, impartiality between the two parties – should be preserved. There are several sorts of impartiality, but what we are talking about here is impar-tiality between the two parties. What I feel to be important is that Ministers from the day they come into office after a general election should feel that they can trust their Civil Service advisers and that a situation of mutual confidence should be established between them. It is, of course, with the idea of maintaining that impartiality that we say the papers and secrets of a previous administration are not available to the next, so that the current administration can feel its secrets are not going to be available to the next. From that point of view, every Civil Servant likes to see his Minister playing, shall I say, a healthy part in Parliament. He is unhappy if he feels that he is getting on to the edge of things or if he is doing something which would not look too good if it were found out. On the other hand, as I have said, stratagems of a wide variety of kinds are a familiar feature of all this, and the fact that I do not happen to have met this one before does not mean I have not met others of a rather similar kind. That one accepts as expressions of the party battle, and what one hopes is that the party battle will go on vigorously and one's Minister will play a vigorous part in it.

MR ONSLOW. 184. From what you have said I imagine there have been stratagems of similar kinds under all the administrations you have been connected with in the Parliamentary context? – Yes, that is right, and of the kind I referred to: arranging to keep a debate going on one motion so that there will not be time for the following one, which seems to me to be very close to this; arranging, either in relation to a series of adjournment debates, or Private Members' motions or things of that kind, to keep a debate going on a particular amendment so that a difficult clause will not arise until some parti-cular time of the day or will start the next day with it – all this kind of thing.

185. And all this would or could, presumably, have been the result of discussions between Ministers and Civil Servants such as

yourself, of which no record would necessarily have been kept? –
Yes, that is right.

186. And this would be the normal practice? – I would expect so,
yes.

187. Although, of course, the effect is that the Government of the
day gains a tactical advantage on the Floor of the House over the
Opposition of the day? – That is right.

188. But this is the purpose and the conceded purpose, and one in
which the Civil Service is simply serving the party in power? – Yes.

189. And the true impartiality of the Civil Service is that it serves
either party when it is in power, irrespective of any political alignment of its own? – Yes.

190. But the Civil Service is not charged with being impartial as
between the Government and the Opposition? – That is correct.

191. Indeed, it would be wrong if it were to seek to be impartial
between the Government and the Opposition? – I would think that
the whole system would break down.

192. And in so far as there is any obligation upon anyone to see
that the Opposition get a fair crack of the whip, this rests upon the
Speaker or whoever else is occupying the chair? – Yes.

193. And it would be wholly wrong for the Civil Service to seek
to carry out a function which properly belongs to the Speaker or
whoever is in the chair? – Utterly wrong. . .

MR LYON. 198. . . . I can see how you might want to arrange to
have a debate go on for a certain time in order to preclude debate on
the next amendment: therefore you would have to have Back Bench
Members of Parliament ready to speak. But did the Civil Service
arrange that or the Minister? – No, the Parliamentary Private
Secretary – as he did in this case.

199. But all that that meant was that the Parliamentary Private
Secretary went around and got his mates to come into the debate.
The Civil Service did not take part? – They may have taken part to
the extent that information collected for the purposes of the debate
for the use of the Minister and available to the Parliamentary
Private Secretary could have been spread around.

200. You mean that the brief may have been duplicated and given
to other Members? – Not necessarily duplicated, but points out of it.

201. That would be simply a method of distributing what was
already in existence for the Minister? – Surely.

202. And not putting the Civil Service at the service of Back
Bench Members of Parliament? – You can put it that way, yes. I
think the distinction becomes a very fine one.

203. It may be fine but is it there? – If the minute that we have
all been reading had said, 'The Minister is anxious to see that in

every possible way publicity is given to the Government's record in housing and in the other fields for which he is responsible, and will everybody please suggest topics and provide material so that this can be done ', that would indeed have put the Civil Servants to as much or perhaps rather more work. Had he then taken those and plucked some questions out of them, the same result would have been secured. The same amount of work would have been done, but the minutes would not have been so attractive to the *Sunday Times*.

204. And there would have been a clear dividing line. You say it is a fine one but is it a dividing line? – I think it is a fig leaf myself, not a dividing line.

205. You said there was a meeting about having a statement made in the House about this matter at which the Lord President presided and that two people, one a Minister and one a Civil Servant, may have mentioned some previous occasion when this had been done? – Yes.

206. Could you tell us who was at the meeting? – To the best of my recollection, the Lord President, the Chief Whip, the Secretary of State for the Environment, the Minister for Housing and Construction, the Chief Whip's Private Secretary, one or two of the Prime Minister's Private Secretaries and I believe – and this is where I was hesitating – the Private Secretaries of the Lord President and the Secretary of State. By this time I was not quite too sure who was down at the other end of the room. . .

CHAIRMAN. 220. Would it not be another stratagem which has happened in all administrations that Private Members' Bills are prepared which are handed to Members not only of the Government party but sometimes also of the Opposition party and that these Private Bills are prepared in Government Departments? – Yes.

MR CUNNINGHAM. 221. What is the stratagem there? Is that a stratagem of the kind you were thinking of? – It could be. It could be to persuade a Member to introduce this Bill rather than another one that he might have had it in mind to introduce.

[Report from the Select Committee on Parliamentary Questions. H.C. 393 of 1971–2, 17 July 1972]

II. ANONYMITY [4]

3. The doctrine on the need for anonymity is vague, and practice varies not only from Department to Department but also from subject to subject and from situation to situation. . .

[4] For other aspects of anonymity, see below pp. 155ff.

4. Already – but to a limited extent – civil servants are identified publicly with their responsibilities. Thus:

(i) senior civil servants give oral evidence to the Public Accounts Committee, the Estimates Committee and the Select Committee on Nationalised Industries; they are excused from answering questions on matters of policy, but this does not, in practice, exclude very much;

(ii) some civil servants – and especially members of the professional grades – read papers, make speeches, or otherwise take part in public discussion, on such occasions as formal enquiries, local government committee meetings, or professional gatherings; their views appear in professional publications, and (in a limited way because the issues are seldom of sufficiently general interest) in the national press, on the radio or even on television; and

(iii) as a matter of everyday routine, civil servants consult particular sections of outside opinion about the evolution and application of policy. For this purpose, a number of Departments have consultative committees on particular subjects. These consultations are usually confidential. Informal contacts with interested individuals (including academics) are quite common. The machinery of the Economic Development Committees and the Regional Development Committees was set up to provide opportunities for exchanges of this kind.

5. In our view these contacts are insufficient and can give an impression outside the Service that civil servants are not fully in touch with public opinion. . .

7. Of course, a policy of greater openness has its risks:

(i) there is the risk of starting rumour: if civil servants take part in discussions on a particular proposal then it may be taken to indicate future Government intentions;

(ii) there is the risk that individual civil servants will be regarded as supporting or opposing particular policies, or measures, and their views may be thought to be at variance with those of their Minister (or a successor Minister);

(iii) the civil servant may imply that he dissents from settled policy, whereas in no public exchange would it be permissible for this to happen.

All these could be embarrassing to Ministers as well as to officials.

8. We think, however, that these risks are acceptable, both in general and as they affect the interests of our members. We do not envisage our members participating in the more artificial confrontations of television journalism, or in any exchange where objectivity is at a discount. Moreover, a civil servant who participates in open

exchanges would be foolish to commit himself to outright support of a proposed policy and the rejection of all its alternatives; it is usually possible to discuss policies and their implications intelligently and informedly without plumping for one course to the exclusion of all others. We think that, for the rest, the more generally that open participation in these exchanges is accepted and practised, then the less significance will be read into this participation in itself and the less importance will be attached to the occasional embarrassment. In some areas of policy there may even now be little room for development in these directions, and in a few there are special problems of security. But in most areas we think the emphasis should be on taking and creating opportunities for informed discussion, rather than on avoiding it, and that this change of attitude would make a valuable and substantial difference to the quality of the work of the Service.

9. We see open exchanges as being particularly valuable in the exploration of long-term policy options, in the explanation of settled policy, and in discussion of its application. The risks of embarrassment are greatest when policy is in the later stages of formation at or near Ministerial level. At this stage it would rarely be opportune for officials to take part in the more open type of discussion. But the more professional or academic the forum in which the discussion is held, the smaller the risk of subsequent embarrassment, and, in general, the greater the value of the discussion to all participants. As a rather obvious working rule it could be said that the less appropriate the occasion is for officials to speak then the more appropriate it may be for Ministers to do so.

[Memorandum by the Association of First Division Civil Servants to the Committee on the Civil Service, 1966–8. Cmnd. 3638 (June 1968)]

283. ... [T]he traditional anonymity of civil servants is already being eroded by Parliament and to a more limited extent by the pressures of the press, radio and television; the process will continue and we see no reason to seek to reverse it. Indeed we think that administration suffers from the convention, which is still alive in many fields, that only the Minister should explain issues in public and what his department is or is not doing about them. This convention has depended in the past on the assumption that the doctrine of ministerial responsibility means that a Minister has full detailed knowledge and control of all the activities of his department. This assumption is no longer tenable. The Minister and his junior Ministers cannot know all that is going on in his department, nor can they nowadays be present at every forum where legitimate questions are raised about its activities. The consequence is that

some questions go unanswered. In our view, therefore the convention of anonymity should be modified and civil servants, as professional administrators, should be able to go further than now in explaining what their departments are doing, at any rate so far as concerns managing existing policies and implementing legislation.

284. We do not under-estimate the risks involved in such a change. It is often difficult to explain without also appearing to argue; however impartially one presents the facts, there will always be those who think that the presentation is biased. It would be unrealistic to suppose that a civil servant will not sometimes drop a brick and embarrass his Minister. We believe that this will have to be faced and that Ministers and M.P.s should take a tolerant view of the civil servant who inadvertently steps out of line. On balance we think it best not to offer any specific precepts for the progressive relaxation of the convention of anonymity. It should be left to develop gradually and pragmatically. . .

[Report of the Committee on the Civil Service, 1966–8. Cmnd. 3638 (June 1968)]

29. It has . . . long been the practice for civil servants to explain the work of their departments, and also to describe Government policy, to House of Commons Select Committees, to bodies representative of particular sections of the community and to individual firms or members of the public. In many cases what they have had to say has been subsequently published. The information officers of Government departments are particularly concerned with explaining Government policy, and where necessary Government organisation, to the public as their full time work. In addition, senior civil servants concerned with implementing and advising on policy have increasingly taken part in interviews with the press and on radio and television, and have spoken at public conferences and other meetings. Particularly in those departments which have local offices, it is also common practice for officers to accept invitations to describe at meetings of local organisations particular policies and procedures and the main reasons for them. This trend is likely to continue. The names and appointments of particular officials working in different branches of Government departments, corresponding to the main divisions of policy, are readily ascertainable from published works of reference.

30. It will, of course, be necessary to ensure that further developments on these lines are encouraged in such a way as not to prejudice the confidential basis of the relationship between Ministers and their officials. The risk must be avoided of officials becoming personally identified with a particular line of advice on a particular

issue of policy or exposed to pressure to discuss in what respects their advice has not been accepted by Ministers. It is clearly right that officials should not be drawn into expressing personal views on policy matters which could be represented as in conflict with those of their Ministers, or as reflecting any political bias. The main responsibility for explaining policy to Parliament and the public must continue to rest with Ministers. For this reason the Government agree with the view of the Fulton Committee that the increased participation of civil servants in the task of explaining the work and organisation of the Government to the public should be allowed to develop 'gradually and pragmatically'. But they are in no doubt that this development should be encouraged.

[Information and the Public Interest. Cmnd. 4089 (June 1969)]

III. SECURITY [5]

The purge procedure

THE PRIME MINISTER [MR ATTLEE]: I desire to make a statement in regard to certain matters of employment in the Civil Service. . . Experience, both in this country and elsewhere, has shown that membership of, and other forms of continuing association with, the Communist Party may involve the acceptance by the individual of a loyalty, which in certain circumstances can be inimical to the State. . . It is not suggested that in matters affecting the security of the State all those who adhere to the Communist Party would allow themselves thus to forget their primary loyalty to the State. But there is no way of distinguishing such people from those who, if opportunity offered, would be prepared to endanger the security of the State in the interests of another Power. The Government have, therefore, reached the conclusion that the only prudent course to adopt is to ensure that no one who is known to be a member of the Communist Party, or to be associated with it in such a way as to raise legitimate doubts about his or her reliability, is employed in connection with work, the nature of which is vital to the security of the State. The same rule will govern the employment of those who are known to be actively associated with Fascist organs.

I should emphasise that this action is being taken solely on security grounds. The State is not concerned with the political views, as such, of its servants, and as far as possible alternative employment on the wide range of non-secret Government work will be found for those who are deemed for the reason indicated to be unsuitable for secret work. It may, however, happen that it is impossible to find

[5] See also below pp. 440ff.

suitable employment elsewhere in the Civil Service for individuals with specialist qualifications and in such cases there may be no alternative to refusal of employment or dismissal.

[448 H.C.Deb. 5s. c. 1703. 15 March 1948]

The conference of Privy Councillors on Security, 1956

The Conference was set up following the defection of Burgess and Maclean 'to examine the security procedures now applied in the public service'. A statement was subsequently made of the substance of those parts of the report which the Government was prepared to make public.

4. ... The Conference point out that, whereas once the main risk to be guarded against was espionage by foreign Powers carried out by professional agents, to-day the chief risks are presented by Communists and by other persons who for one reason or another are subject to Communist influence. The Communist faith overrides a man's normal loyalties to his country and induces the belief that it is justifiable to hand over secret information to the Communist Party or to the Communist foreign Power. This risk from Communists is not, however, confined to party members, either open or underground, but extends to sympathisers with Communism.

5. At one time the Fascist ideology also presented considerable security risks. Although to-day the chief risk is that presented by Communism, the security arrangements instituted in 1948 were directed, and will continue to be directed, against Communism and Fascism alike. In this paper for convenience and brevity the term 'Communism' is used to cover Communism and Fascism alike.

6. One of the chief problems of security to-day is thus to identify the members of the British Communist Party, to be informed of its activities and to identify that wider body of those who are both sympathetic to Communism, or susceptible to Communist pressure and present a danger to security. Thereafter steps must be taken to see that secret information is not handled by anyone who, for ideological or other motives, may betray it.

7. Her Majesty's Government agree with this broad analysis and will continue to base their policy on preventing persons of this nature from having access to secret information. . . .

10. Some of the recommendations of the Conference deal with what may be called the relation between security risks and defects of character and conduct. The Conference recognise that to-day great importance must be paid to character defects as factors tending to make a man unreliable or expose him to blackmail, or influence by foreign agents. There is a duty on Departments to inform themselves of serious failings such as drunkenness, addiction to drugs, homo-

sexuality or any loose living that may seriously affect a man's reliability.

12. While confining themselves to the security aspect of these defects of character and conduct, the Conference also record the view that in individual cases or in certain sections of the public service, a serious character defect may appropriately be the determining factor in a decision to dismiss a particular individual or to transfer him to other work.

13. The Conference also recommend that it should be recognised that the fact that a public servant is a Communist not only bars his employment on secret duties, but may also in some Departments have an unfavourable effect on his prospects of promotion.

14. The Conference also make a series of recommendations which turn on the risk presented by those in regard to whom there is no evidence that they are themselves members of the Communist Party, but evidence exists of Communist sympathies or of close association with members of the Communist Party.

15. The Conference is of the opinion that in deciding these difficult and often borderline cases, it is right to continue the practice of tilting the balance in favour of offering greater protection to the security of the State rather than in the direction of safeguarding the rights of the individual. They recommend that an individual who is living with a wife or husband who is a Communist or a Communist sympathiser may, for that reason alone, have to be moved from secret work, and that the same principle should be applied in other cases of a like nature.

16. The Conference recognise that some of the measures which the State is driven to take to protect its security are in some respects alien to our traditional practices. Thus, in order not to imperil sources of information, decisions have sometimes to be taken without revealing full details of the supporting evidence. Again, it is sometimes necessary to refuse to employ a man on secret duties, or in those cases where no alternative work can be found for him in the public service, to refuse to employ him at all, because after the fullest investigation doubts about his reliability remain, even although nothing may have been proved against him on standards which would be accepted in a Court of Law. . .

The Conference approve the Tribunal (commonly known as the Three Advisers) set up in 1948 to hear appeals from civil servants threatened on security grounds with transfer from secret duties or, when that is not practicable, with dismissal from the Service. This machinery should continue; and the person whose continued employment in Government Service is called in question on account of Communist association or sympathies will be able to have his case considered by it. The Conference also recommend that the terms of reference of the Three Advisors should be widened so as to enable them to present a fuller report to the responsible Minister. . .

19. The Conference point out that, while an individual can be arrested on suspicion that he is about to attempt to convey secret information to a foreign Power, he must be brought before the courts on a charge without delay. The time required to collect evidence upon which a charge can be based is often long, and the Conference dismiss any suggestion that power should be sought to detain persons for an unlimited period without preferring charges against them, on the grounds that this would run counter to this country's traditional principles of individual freedom, and would be most unlikely to be approved by Parliament in time of peace. They also come to the conclusion that legislation which would permit arrest and detention, without a charge being preferred, for a short specified period, say, fourteen days, would not be much help. The Conference also consider that the withdrawal of a passport could not be relied upon to prevent a United Kingdom citizen in connivance with a foreign Power from leaving the country.

20. For these reasons the Conference recommend that no additional powers should be sought to detain suspects or prevent them leaving the country. . .

[Statement of the Findings of the Conference of Privy Councillors on Security. Cmd. 9715 (1956)]

Any civil servant who is regarded as a security risk has a right of appeal. The detailed procedure in such cases was given to the House of Commons by Mr Enoch Powell, as Financial Secretary to the Treasury, in a written answer on 29 January 1957.

MR POWELL: . . . 1. The Minister [6] will have before him information on which to decide whether the reliability of the civil servant is *prima facie* to be regarded as in doubt on security grounds. A civil servant will be so regarded if:

(a) he is, or is to be, employed in connection with work the nature of which is vital to the security of the State; and simultaneously;

(b) he is or has recently been a member of the British Communist [7] Party, or in such a way to raise reasonable doubts about his reliability, is or has recently been sympathetic to

---

[6] That is, the Minister responsible for the Department to which the Civil Servant belongs.

[7] In this statement of Procedure, for convenience and brevity the term ' Communist ' is hereafter used to cover Communist and Fascist alike.

Communism, associated with Communists or Communist sympathisers or is susceptible to Communist pressure.

No statement of general application can be made as to what constitutes sympathy or association under (*b*) above. Each case will be assessed in the light of the particular facts.

2. If the Minister rules that there is a *prima facie* case, the civil servant is at once to be so informed and will normally be sent on special leave with pay, care being taken as far as possible not to disclose the reasons for his absence to his colleagues.

3. The civil servant will at the same time be given any particulars, such as the date of his alleged membership, or the nature of the alleged sympathies or associations, that might enable him to clear himself. There will however have to be limits to the information given for he cannot be given such particulars as might involve the disclosure of the sources of the evidence.

4. At the same time the civil servant will be asked to say whether he accepts or denies the allegation. If he accepts the allegation he will be dealt with as described in paragraphs 9 and 10 below. If he does not admit the allegation he shall have fourteen days in which to make written representations to the Minister if he so wishes.

5. The Minister will reconsider his *prima facie* ruling in the light of any representations the civil servant may make. If the Minister decides that there is no reason for varying it, the civil servant shall be so informed and shall then have seven days in which to decide whether to ask for a reference to the Three Advisers. If he does not ask for such a reference he will be dealt with as in paragraph 8 below. If he does ask for a reference to the Three Advisers the latter will be asked to consider the case as soon as possible.

6. The function of the Three Advisers is set out in their terms of reference.[8] Where there is no suggestion of Communist or Fascist associations or sympathies, cases of character defects will not be referred to the tribunal, and appeals will be dealt with under the normal disciplinary procedure of Departments.

7. In discharging their functions the Advisers will take into account the representations made by the civil servant. They will hear him in person, if he so wishes. He may also ask third parties to testify to them as to his record, reliability and character but he may not be accompanied and/or represented by a third party before them. In the special circumstances of these cases the proceedings must be governed by the requirement that neither sources of evidence nor evidence which might involve the disclosure of sources can be given to the person concerned. The Advisers will therefore

[8] [See below.]

count it as an important part of their functions to see that anyone appearing before them can make his points effectively and will adapt their procedure in such a way as to give him the best possible opportunity of bringing out the points which he wishes to bring to their notice.

8. On receiving the report of the Three Advisers, the Minister will reconsider his *prima facie* ruling and if he decides to uphold it, he will give the civil servant an opportunity of making representations to himself or his representative before action is finally taken. Similar opportunity will be given when the civil servant does not wish his case to go to the Advisers.

9. If the *prima facie* ruling is finally upheld, a civil servant will be posted to or retained in a non-secret branch within his own Department, or, if this is not practicable, will be posted to a non-secret branch in another Department. If he belongs to a category which it is impossible to employ in any other than a secret branch, or if his qualifications or experience are such that no alternative employment elsewhere in the Government service can be found, he will have to be dismissed unless he accepts the option, which should always be afforded in such cases, of resigning. . .

[563 H.C.Deb. 5s. c. 152 (Written Answers). 29 January 1957]

The terms of reference of the Three Advisers are as follows:

' 1. It is the policy of Her Majesty's Government that no one who is or has recently been a member of the British Communist Party or of a Fascist organisation or who, in such a way as to raise legitimate doubts about his reliability, is or has recently been sympathetic to Communism or Fascism or associated with Communists [9] or Communist sympathisers or is susceptible to Communist pressure, should be employed in connection with work the nature of which is vital to the security of the State.

2. You have been appointed to advise Ministers in any cases referred to you whether in your opinion their *prima facie* ruling that an individual comes under paragraph 1 has or has not been substantiated. In doing so you should answer the following questions:

(i) Are there or are there not reasonable grounds for supposing that the individual has or has recently had Communist sympathies or associations of the type described in paragraph 1 above?

(ii) If you are in doubt about the answer to (i) above, how do you assess the evidence whether presented to you or elicited at the hearing before you?

3. In answering these questions your aim should be to give the Minister the utmost help in deciding himself what course to take.

[9] In these terms of reference for convenience and brevity the term ' Communist ' is hereafter used to cover Communist and Fascist alike.

4. If you agree with the *prima facie* ruling you should specify your grounds. If you do not agree with the *prima facie* ruling or do not reach a firm opinion in any instance you should assess the evidence for the Minister reporting the weight which you have attached to particular factors.

5. You should in all cases take precautions to safeguard any very secret sources from which any of the information bearing on the conclusions has been obtained.

6. In the appreciation of a case defects of an individual's character should be taken into account when they bear upon his reliability in the general context of Communist associations or sympathies. (Where no question of such associations or sympathies arises, cases of character defects will not be referred to you, but appeals will be dealt with under the normal disciplinary procedure of Departments.)

7. A decision on what employment is to be regarded as involving " connection with work the nature of which is vital to the security of the State " is not one for you but for Ministers in charge of Departments. Your functions do not extend beyond advising Ministers as set out above ' [563 H.C.Deb. 5s. c. 155 (Written Answers). 29 January 1957].

Positive vetting

The ' purge procedure ' applies to all civil servants employed in connexion with work the nature of which is vital to the security of the State. In addition, those employed on exceptionally secret work are subject to a further procedure known as ' positive vetting '.

52. In January 1952 the Government announced that Civil Servants employed on exceptionally secret work would be subject to special enquiries. This procedure, known as Positive Vetting, is aimed at establishing the general integrity of the person concerned. The range of posts to which it applies consists of:

(a) Those which involve regular and constant access to the most highly classified defence information or material.

(b) Those giving access to the more highly classified categories of atomic energy information.

(c) In addition, Under-Secretaries and candidates under consideration for promotion to that rank are in all cases subject to Positive Vetting, regardless of the posts which they occupy, since any Civil Servant at this level must be regarded as likely to have access to highly secret information.

The Positive Vetting process consists of the following stages:

(i) a check with the Security Service, to ascertain whether intelligence records contain any adverse information about the individual in question (which in practice means traces of Communist association or sympathies or of other forms of subversive activity);

(ii) completion by the subject of a standard security questionnaire (in which he is asked, *inter alia*, whether he has or has ever had any connexion or sympathies with Communist or Fascist organisations);

(iii) letters to two referees named by the subject asking for information bearing on his reliability and character;

(iv) a field investigation into his character and circumstances.

[Security Procedures in the Public Service. Cmnd. 1681 (1961–2)]

The Radcliffe Committee on Security Procedures in the Public Service, 1961

(1) *The nature of the threat to security*

2. The evidence that we heard satisfies us that to-day much the most serious source of danger lies in the intelligence services of the Soviet *bloc* which, there is reason to suppose, are co-ordinated as between the various countries taking part. These services must be envisaged as steadily at work in this country collecting information for intelligence purposes and trying to break through our screen of protective security to get at the secrets we wish to preserve. In this work they are prepared to employ all the most up-to-date resources of espionage and they look for useful agents or instruments where-ever skill or occasion presents an opportunity.

3. The activities of the Communist Party of Great Britain are not of the same order as a threat to security. It is not the policy of the party, according to our information, to give its members, open or secret, any encouragement to undertake espionage, although this policy might, of course, be changed in changing conditions. Nor should the instruments of the Russian Intelligence Service be en-visaged as selected either necessarily or essentially on ideological grounds. Any form of sympathy or compulsion that can be laid hold of will serve its turn and among these compulsions fear, pressure, and mercenary motives are as strong as any other.

4. We have thought it necessary to say this in explanation of the background against which we have approached the recommenda-tions contained in our Report, because, as will be seen, our assess-ment is materially different in emphasis from that made by the Conference of Privy Councillors in 1956 – the last occasion upon which our subject was considered in any comprehensive form on behalf of the Government. . .

5. In our view this assessment would not by itself be a satisfactory guide for future action for the following reasons:

(*a*) It seems to suggest that the central problem of security is to exclude Communists from access to State secrets. For the reasons which we have given we believe that the central threat lies further back than the British Communist Party.

(*b*) The whole of our investigation has led us to conclude that nothing is more important to effective security than the basic measures of physical security, if well planned and consistently carried out. Safeguarding premises, documents, and cyphers and eliminating carelessness are of the first importance. No system of personnel security, however much elaborated, can be effective enough to modify their primary value.

(*c*) Counter-espionage against enemy agents is an indispensable part of the defensive system. None of the various defensive measures can safely be neglected in reliance on another; but one real success in counter-espionage can have positive results more far-reaching than all the rest.

(2) *Civil Service staff associations and trade unions*

33. We enquired into the penetration by Communists of the Civil Service staff associations and trade unions and were disturbed at the number of Communists and Communist sympathisers who are holding positions in those bodies either as permanent full-time paid officials or as unpaid officers or members of executive committees. We understand that there is no evidence that the Communists have made any exceptional effort to gain control of these unions, but they appear in fact to have achieved a higher degree of penetration here than in almost any other sector of the trade union movement. No evidence has been brought to our knowledge that Communist union officers, whether serving on a paid or unpaid basis, have been detected in any form of espionage. Nevertheless, we regard this presumably deliberate massing of Communist effort in the Civil Service unions as most dangerous to security, however one defines it.

34. We suggest, therefore, that it would be reasonable to establish the right of any Department in respect of establishments or staff employed on secret work to deny access to or to refuse to negotiate (either by correspondence or face to face) with a named trade union official whom it had reason to believe to be a Communist under the definition used in the purge procedure.[10] We envisage that the Department would be required to challenge the union official formally, as in the purge procedure, and that he would have a right of appeal to the Three Advisers.

(3) *Government contractors*

98. Many Government contracts, particularly in the defence field, are subject in whole or part to security classification and the protection of classified information and material in the hands of Government contractors is an important element in the security

---

[10] [The Government accepted this recommendation and put it into effect in June 1962.]

system. The security arrangements among Government contractors are broadly similar to those in Government Departments. The main features of the system are as follows. In addition to the general sanctions of the Official Secrets Acts the contractor is required to undertake certain measures set out in detail in a security clause which is included as a standard condition in all Government contracts which have a classified content. This provides for the exclusion from access to classified information of any person who does not need such access for the proper performance of the contract, or who (unless the Department specifically consents) is an alien or is not the servant of the contractor, or whom the Department has required to be excluded; it gives the Department a right to be supplied with full particulars of all persons handling classified information, to inspect the security arrangements of the firm, to control the placing of sub-contracts and so on. Failure to carry out these security obligations gives the Department the right to terminate the contract.

99. Either before or (more usually) after the contract has been signed the Department sends the contractor written instructions (in a letter usually called the 'secret aspects letter') defining the security classification which is to be applied to each part of the contract. In principle the application of the purge procedure and positive vetting to contractors' employees is on the same basis as in the public service. In practice these personnel security procedures, though sometimes calling for delicate handling, do not appear to present contractors with major difficulties or embarrassment.[11]

[Security Procedures in the Public Service. Cmnd. 1681 (1961–2)]

On 23 January 1964 the Government announced that in future investigations into security breaches would be conducted by a Standing Security Commission. Its terms of reference are: 'If so requested by the Prime Minister, to investigate and report upon the circumstances in which a breach of security is known to have occurred in the public service and upon any related failure of departmental security arrangements or neglect of duty; and, in the light of any such investigations, to advise whether any change in security arrangements is necessary or desirable.' The responsibility of individual civil servants is usually the subject of a separate inquiry to see whether any disciplinary action needs to be taken.

---

[11] [The application of the appeal procedure to the employees of Government contractors following a recommendation of the Conference of Privy Councillors was announced by the Lord Chancellor during a debate on the case of Mr Lang, an assistant solicitor at Imperial Chemical Industries. He had been dismissed after the Government had made it clear that he should not be allowed access to Government contracts placed with I.C.I. which were classified as secret (197 H.L.Deb. 5s. c. 1226ff. 21 June 1956).]

CHAPTER IV

THE COMPOSITION OF PARLIAMENT

I. THE QUALIFICATIONS OF ELECTORS

REPRESENTATION OF THE PEOPLE ACT, 1949
[12, 13 & 14 Geo. 6. ch. 68]

1. (1)... [T]he persons entitled to vote as electors at a parliamentary election in any constituency shall be those resident there on the qualifying date who, at that date and on the date of the poll, are of full age and not subject to any legal incapacity to vote and either British subjects or citizens of the Republic of Ireland:

Provided that a person shall not be entitled to vote as an elector in any constituency unless registered there in the register of Parliamentary electors to be used at the election, nor, at a general election, to vote as an elector in more than one constituency . . .

171. . . . '[L]egal incapacity' includes (in addition to any incapacity by virtue of any subsisting provision of the common law [1]) any disqualification imposed by this Act [2] or any other Act.[3]. . .

REPRESENTATION OF THE PEOPLE ACT, 1969
[Ch. 15]

1. (1) For purposes of the Representation of the People Acts a person shall be of voting age if he is of the age of eighteen years or over; and, if otherwise qualified, a person who is of voting age on the date of the poll at a parliamentary . . . election shall be entitled to

---

[1] [For example, peers. The House of Commons passes the following resolution at the beginning of each session: 'Resolved, that no Peer of the Realm, except Peers of Ireland, hath any right to give his vote in the Election of any Member to serve in Parliament.']

[2] [S. 140 of the Act provides that a person found personally guilty of corrupt practices shall for five years be incapable of being registered as an elector or voting at any parliamentary election. If found personally guilty of an illegal practice the incapacity only applies to the particular constituency.]

[3] [For example, the Peerage Act, 1963, which provides in s. 6: 'A woman who is the holder of a hereditary peerage . . . shall be subject to the same disqualifications in respect of membership of the House of Commons and elections to that House as a man holding that peerage '.]

vote as an elector, whether or not he is of voting age on the qualifying date.

(2) A person, if otherwise qualified, shall accordingly be entitled to be registered in a register of parliamentary electors . . . if he will attain voting age before the end of the twelve months following the day by which the register is required to be published; but, if he will not be of voting age on the first day of those twelve months—

(a) his entry in the register shall give the date on which he will attain that age; and

(b) until the date given in the entry he shall not by virtue of the entry be treated as an elector for any purposes other than purposes of an election at which the day fixed for the poll is that or a later date . . .

4. (1) A convicted person during the time that he is detained in a penal institution in pursuance of his sentence shall be legally incapable of voting at any parliamentary or local government election.

(2) For this purpose—

(a) 'convicted person' means any person found guilty of an offence (whether under the law of the United Kingdom or not), including a person found guilty by a court martial under the Army Act 1955, the Air Force Act 1955 or the Naval Discipline Act 1957 or on a summary trial under section 49 of the Naval Discipline Act 1957, but not including a person dealt with by committal or other summary process for contempt of court; and

(b) 'penal institution' means an institution to which the Prison Act 1952, the Prisons (Scotland) Act 1952 or the Prison Act (Northern Ireland) 1953 applies; and

(c) a person detained for default in complying with his sentence shall not be treated as detained in pursuance of the sentence, whether or not the sentence provided for detention in the event of default, but a person detained by virtue of a conditional pardon in respect of an offence shall be treated as detained in pursuance of his sentence for the offence.

(3) It is immaterial for purposes of this section whether a conviction or sentence was before or after the passing of this Act . . .

II. THE QUALIFICATIONS OF CANDIDATES

There are no residential or property qualifications. Any British subject who can find ten electors in the constituency to support his nomination and £150 deposit, which he will forfeit if he fails to poll one-eighth of the votes cast, can become a candidate, provided he is not a peer, a clergyman of the Church of England, a Minister of the Church of Scotland or a Roman Catholic priest, a bankrupt, someone disqualified after having been found guilty of a corrupt or illegal practice at an election, or the holder of an office which disqualifies him by virtue of the House of Commons Disqualification Act, 1957.

HOUSE OF COMMONS DISQUALIFICATION ACT, 1957 [5 & 6 Eliz. 2. ch. 20]

1. (1) Subject to the provisions of this Act, a person is disqualified for membership of the House of Commons who for the time being—

   (*a*) holds any of the judicial offices specified in Part I of the First Schedule to this Act;

   (*b*) is employed in the civil service of the Crown, whether in an established capacity or not, and whether for the whole or part of his time;

   (*c*) is a member of any of the regular armed forces of the Crown;

   (*d*) is a member of any police force maintained by a police authority;

   (*e*) is a member of the legislature of any country or territory outside the Commonwealth; or

   (*f*) holds any office described in Part II or Part III of the said First Schedule.

   (2) A person who for the time being holds any office described in Part IV of the said First Schedule is disqualified for membership of the House of Commons for any constituency specified in relation to that office in the second column of the said Part IV . . .

   (4) Except as provided by this Act, a person shall not be disqualified for membership of the House of Commons by reason of his holding an office or place of profit under the Crown or any other office or place; and a person shall not be disqualified for appointment to or for holding any office or place by reason of his being a member of that House . . .

5. (1) If at any time it is resolved by the House of Commons that the First Schedule to this Act be amended, Her Majesty may by Order in Council amend that Schedule accordingly . . .

6. (1) Subject to any order made by the House of Commons under the following provisions of this section,—

(*a*) if any person disqualified by this Act . . . is elected as a member of that House . . . his election shall be void; and

(*b*) if any person being a member of that House becomes disqualified by this Act . . . his seat shall be vacated.

(2) If in a case falling or alleged to fall within the foregoing subsection it appears to the House of Commons that the grounds of disqualification or alleged disqualification under this Act . . . have been removed, and that it is otherwise proper so to do, the House may by order direct that any such disqualification . . . shall be disregarded for the purposes of this section:

Provided that no such order shall affect the proceedings on any election petition or any determination of an election court, and this subsection shall have effect subject to the provisions of subsection (5) of section one hundred and twenty-four of the Representation of the People Act, 1949 (which relates to the making of an order by the House of Commons when informed of a certificate and any report of an election court) . . .

7. (1) Any person who claims that a person purporting to be a member of the House of Commons is disqualified by this Act, or has been so disqualified at any time since his election, may apply to Her Majesty in Council . . . for a declaration to that effect.

(2) Section three of the Judicial Committee Act, 1833 (which provides for the reference to the Judicial Committee of the Privy Council of appeals to Her Majesty in Council) shall apply to any application under this section as it applies to an appeal to Her Majesty in Council from a court.

(3) Upon any such application . . . the applicant shall give such security for the costs of the proceedings, not exceeding two hundred pounds, as the Judicial Committee may direct.

(4) For the purpose of determining any issue of fact arising on an application under this section the Judicial Committee may direct the issue to be tried—

(*a*) if the constituency for which the respondent purports to be a member is in England or Wales, in the High Court. . .

and the decision of that Court shall be final.

(5) Subject as hereinafter provided, a declaration may be made in respect of any person under this section whether the grounds of the alleged disqualification subsisted at the time of his election or arose subsequently:

Provided that no such declaration shall be made—

(*a*) in the case of disqualification incurred by any person on grounds which subsisted at the time of his election, if an election petition is pending or has been tried in which his disqualification on those grounds is or was in issue;

(*b*) ... if an order has been made by the House of Commons under subsection (2) of section six of this Act. ...

9. A person shall not be disqualified for membership of the House of Commons by reason of his having any pension from the Crown or by reason of any such contract, agreement or commission for or on account of the public service as is described in the House of Commons Disqualification (Declaration of Law) Act, 1931 ...[4]

The First Schedule which lists the disqualifying offices is divided into four parts. The First Part lists judicial offices which disqualify. It includes such offices as Judge of the High Court or Court of Appeal, Circuit Judge, Stipendiary Magistrate and the National Insurance Commissioners.

The Second Part lists those Commissions, Tribunals, and other bodies of which all members are disqualified. It includes the Boards of the Nationalised Industries, the Independent Broadcasting Authority, the Restrictive Practices Court, the Council on Tribunals, the Lands Tribunal, the National Insurance Advisory Committee and the University Grants Committee.

The Third Part lists other disqualifying offices. These include Ambassadors, Boundary Commissioners, the Comptroller and Auditor-General, Civil Service Commissioners, Governors of the British Broadcasting Corporation and the Governor and Deputy Governor of the Bank of England.

The Fourth Part lists offices which disqualify for particular constituencies. It includes Lords Lieutenant and Sheriffs as regards any constituency within the counties in which they hold office.

III. THE ORGANISATION OF CONSTITUENCIES AND THE SYSTEM OF VOTING

The United Kingdom is divided into single member constituencies. At an election the candidate in each constituency with the largest number of votes wins the seat. The delicate task of drawing constituency boundaries is entrusted in the first instance to independent Boundary Commissions for England, Wales, Scotland, and Northern Ireland operating according to rules laid down in the House of Commons (Redistribution of Seats) Acts, 1949 and 1958. The object has been to try and remove

---

[4] [The Select Committee on the Bill, in recommending this change in the law, noted: ' 7 ... Your Committee are anxious that neither here nor elsewhere where the practice and procedure of the British House of Commons are studied and appreciated should it be thought that the suggested repeal of the existing law indicates the least inclination by the House to tolerate any form of corruption connected with Government contracts. Nothing could be further from the intention of Your Committee: enquiry and evidence have satisfied them that the House has ample powers, quite apart from the legislation to be repealed, to deal with any improper or dishonourable conduct in connection with Government contracts by Government or by any member ' (H.C. 349 of 1955–6).]

the issue from party political interference. At the same time, however, neither Parliament nor Governments have felt willing to make the recommendations of the Commissions conclusive, any more than they regard the recommendations of a Speakers' Conference, the more informal device adopted to seek all party agreement on other questions of electoral reform, as conclusive. Individual Members of Parliament wish to modify recommendations from time to time, and Governments also have either asked Boundary Commissions to think again as in 1948, or even, as in 1969, advised Parliament to vote against all the proposals because it felt they were being made at an inopportune time. The statutory Boundary Commissions and the informal Speakers' Conferences provide the first examples so far mentioned of a problem that frequently recurs throughout the materials in this book, that is the tension between the desire to take some issues out of the field of party influence and yet retain some degree of Ministerial responsibility and Parliamentary control.

The system of voting

THE SECRETARY OF STATE FOR THE HOME DEPARTMENT (MR JAMES CALLAGHAN): . . . I thought that it would be as well to make at least a comment on one matter that your conference [5] considered and rejected, and which the Government agree with you in rejecting. I refer to the single transferable vote system. This . . . system was rejected by your conference by 19 votes to one.

As I understand, this system provides that constituencies return not one Member but several Members, and the elector is invited to arrange the candidates in the order of his choice by putting the figure 1, 2, 3, or whatever it may be, against their names. To ensure election, a candidate need not obtain majority of the votes polled: what he has to do is to get that proportion of votes which, for a certainty, secure the election of a candidate. Candidates in a three-Member constituency would need to get more than 25 per cent. of the votes. This number is called a quota. At the first count, first votes only are reckoned and the surplus votes of candidates who have received more than their quota are then transferred to the name marked ' 2 ', and the process continues until all the seats are filled.

There are a number of refinements of that system, but that is basically the start of it. As I understand, the proportional representation of parties that would ensue under this system could not be obtained in a constituency with less than three Members, and the view has been expressed that the best representation is obtained on the basis of an average constituency of from three to seven Members.

That, to me, is the beginning of the major objection. If I take the mean between those figures and refer to a constituency with five

[5] [i.e. the Speakers' Conference which reported in 1968 (Cmnd. 3550)].

Members it would mean in the first place that in the United Kingdom we would be reduced to about 100 constituencies. That would be the basis of election in this country and I believe very strongly that to have no more than 100 constituencies would mean that the link between the Member and his constituency would be lost. All of us who have experience of this link attach very great value to it. It is difficult enough now in all conscience to get to know 50,000 or 60,000 electors and it would be obviously impossible to get to know 300,000 electors, or even more if that quota were used.

But, of course, there is another major purpose of an election which the advocates of the single transferable vote will not recognise, although the British electorate recognises it. It is, as I mentioned earlier – and I put it in deliberately – one of the major purposes of an election not only to choose the Member, but to elect a Government. Under the system we now have, a member of the public chooses his Government best by choosing between those candidates whose parties will form a Government. I regret this on behalf of the Liberal Party, but it is the way in which the system works.

It is this system of Parliamentary government which should not be undermined, and we would weaken the rôle of the Government – we can argue about whether it is going too far or not far enough – and weaken the opportunity for effective central government if this system were to be adopted. As I read history, that is also the view of the electors. They have expressed it time after time during General Elections when third parties have not prospered when they have been on an optional basis.

I have tried to be as objective about it as I could because I understand that I am touching on a sore spot, but that is one of the inexorable facts of life that third parties come up against when a General Election arises. I do not know for what reason your conference rejected the concept of the single transferable vote, Mr Speaker, but it is for that reason that I do so, and the Government have decided that we should stick to the system we now have.

[770 H.C.Deb. 5s. c. 43. 14 October 1968]

Cp. the statement of Herbert Morrison:

'The noble Lady asked, as she had every right to ask, whether the Government were determined to resist proportional representation or the alternative vote. Believe me, I do not say this out of mere partisan considerations, neither does the Labour Party, but our honest view is that proportional representation is not conducive to the best form of Parliamentary government. We have come really to believe that after years of argument. There used to be a strong body of opinion in the Labour Party in favour of it, but after years of argument that is our conclusion.

' The alternative vote is somewhat better, but that, on the other hand, would lead to not too pleasant bargaining between political competitors, which is not to the good. It is much better that the parties should fight, and that the party which gets the most votes, let us hope, should come out on top. I admit that that does not necessarily follow. I admit all the mathematical criticisms against the existing system. I admit that a mathematical case and a theoretical case can be made against it. I admit that governments do not always represent the majority of the electorate. That happens to both sides. On the whole, the Left have had the worst of it up to now, although at the moment we are not doing badly. It happens both ways, but, broadly speaking, the system works. I would sooner have governments with strength and power behind them – even though I do not agree with them – so long as they observe the democratic forms, than a Parliament which can only live by the making and unmaking and re-making of Coalitions and bargains of all sorts.' [447 H.C.Debs. 5s. c. 1111. 17 February 1948]

The organisation of constituencies

HOUSE OF COMMONS (REDISTRIBUTION OF SEATS) ACT, 1949   [12, 13 & 14 Geo. 6. ch. 66]

1. (1) For the purpose of the continuous review of the distribution of seats at parliamentary elections, there shall be four permanent Boundary Commissions, namely a Boundary Commission for England . . . for Scotland . . . for Wales and . . . for Northern Ireland.

(2) The Boundary Commissions shall be constituted in accordance with the provisions of Part I of the First Schedule . . . and their procedure shall be regulated in accordance with Part III of that Schedule.

2. (1) Each Boundary Commission shall keep under review the representation in the House of Commons of the part of the United Kingdom with which they are concerned and shall . . . submit to the Secretary of State reports, with respect to the whole of that part of the United Kingdom, either—

   (a) showing the constituencies into which they recommend that it should be divided in order to give effect to the rules set out in the Second Schedule to this Act; or

   (b) stating that, in the opinion of the Commission, no alteration is required to be made in respect of that part of the United Kingdom in order to give effect to the said rules.

(3) Any Boundary Commission may also from time to time submit to the Secretary of State reports with respect to the area comprised in any particular constituency or constituencies in the part of the United Kingdom with which they are concerned, showing the

constituencies into which they recommend that that area should be divided in order to give effect to the rules set out in the said Second Schedule.

(4) Where a Commission intend to consider making a report under this Act, they shall, by notice in writing, inform the Secretary of State accordingly, and a copy of the said notice shall be published—

    (*a*) in a case where it was given by the Boundary Commission for England or the Boundary Commission for Wales, in the London Gazette...

(5) As soon as may be after a Boundary Commission have submitted a report to the Secretary of State under this Act, he shall lay the report before Parliament together, except in a case where the report states that no alteration is required to be made in respect of the part of the United Kingdom with which the Commission are concerned, with the draft of an Order in Council for giving effect, whether with or without modifications, to the recommendations contained in the report.

3. (1) A report of a Boundary Commission under this Act showing the constituencies into which they recommend that any area should be divided shall state, as respects each constituency, the name by which they recommend that it should be known, and whether they recommend that it should be a county constituency or a borough constituency.

(2) The draft of any Order in Council laid before Parliament by the Secretary of State under this Act for giving effect, whether with or without modifications, to the recommendations contained in the report of a Boundary Commission may make provision—

    (*a*) for any matters which appear to him to be incidental thereto or consequential thereon...

(3) Where any such draft gives effect to any such recommendations with modifications, the Secretary of State shall lay before Parliament together with the draft a statement of the reasons for the modifications.

(4) If any such draft is approved by resolution of each House of Parliament, the Secretary of State shall submit it to His Majesty in Council.

(5) If a motion for the approval of any such draft is rejected by either House of Parliament or withdrawn by leave of the House, the Secretary of State may amend the draft and lay the amended draft before Parliament, and if the draft as so amended is approved by resolution of each House of Parliament, the Secretary of State shall submit it to His Majesty in Council.

(6) Where the draft of an Order in Council is submitted to His Majesty in Council under this Act, His Majesty in Council may make an Order in terms of the draft which shall come into force on such date as may be specified therein and shall have effect notwithstanding anything in any enactment:

Provided that the coming into force of any such Order shall not affect any parliamentary election until a proclamation is issued by His Majesty summoning a new Parliament, or affect the constitution of the House of Commons until the dissolution of the Parliament then in being.

(7) The validity of any Order in Council purporting to be made under this Act and reciting that a draft thereof has been approved by resolution of each House of Parliament shall not be called in question in any legal proceedings whatsoever.

SCHEDULES [6]

FIRST SCHEDULE

Part I. *Constitution*

1. The Speaker of the House of Commons shall be the chairman of each of the four Commissions.

2. The Commission for England shall consist of the chairman [and a judge as deputy chairman] and two other members of whom one shall be appointed by the Secretary of State and the other by the Minister of Housing and Local Government.[7]

Part II. *Officers and expenses*

1. (1) The Secretary of State may, at the request of any Commission, appoint one or more assistant Commissioners to inquire into, and report to the Commission upon, such matters as the Commission think fit.

Part III. *Procedure*

3. Where a Commission have provisionally determined to make recommendations affecting any constituency, they shall publish in at least one newspaper circulating in the constituency a notice stating—

(a) the effect of the proposed recommendations and (except in a case where they propose to recommend that no alteration be made in respect of the constituency) that a copy of the recommendations is open to inspection at a specified place within the constituency; and

[6] [As amended by the Act of 1958. The words in square brackets were added in 1958.]

[7] [The Commissions for Wales and Scotland are constituted in the same way. In the case of Northern Ireland, both members are appointed by the Secretary of State.]

(*b*) that representations with respect to the proposed recommendations may be made to the Commission within one month
after the publication of the notice;

and the Commission shall take into consideration any representations duly made in accordance with any such notice.

4. A Commission may, if they think fit, cause a local inquiry to
be held in respect of any constituency or constituencies.

5. (1) Subsections (2) and (3) of section two hundred and ninety
of the Local Government Act, 1933 (which relate to the attendance
of witnesses at inquiries) shall apply in relation to any local inquiry
which the Commission for England or the Commission for Wales
may cause to be held in pursuance of this Act.

SECOND SCHEDULE

RULES FOR REDISTRIBUTION OF SEATS

1. The number of constituencies in the several parts of the United
Kingdom set out in the first column of the following table shall be
as stated respectively in the second column of that table—

Part of the United Kingdom.	*No. of Constituencies.*
Great Britain	Not substantially greater or less than 613.
Scotland	Not less than 71.
Wales	Not less than 35.
Northern Ireland ...	12.

2. Every constituency shall return a single member.

3. There shall continue to be a constituency which shall include
the whole of the City of London and the name of which shall refer
to the City of London.

4. (1) So far as is practicable having regard to the foregoing
rules—

(*a*) in England and Wales,—

  (i) no county or any part thereof shall be included in a constituency which includes the whole or part of any other
  county or the whole or part of a ... metropolitan
  borough [8] ...

  (iii) no metropolitan borough or any part thereof shall be included in a constituency which includes the whole or part
  of any other metropolitan borough ...

5. The electorate of any constituency shall be as near the

---

[8] [S. 4 (2) of the London Government Act, 1963, provides that the reference
to metropolitan boroughs is to be construed as a reference to a London
borough as established by that Act.]

electoral quota as is practicable having regard to the foregoing rules; and a Boundary Commission may depart from the strict application of the last foregoing rule if it appears to them that a departure is desirable to avoid an excessive disparity between the electorate of any constituency and the electoral quota, or between the electorate thereof and that of neighbouring constituencies in the part of the United Kingdom with which they are concerned.

6. A Boundary Commission may depart from the strict application of the last two foregoing rules if special geographical considerations, including in particular the size, shape and accessibility of a constituency, appear to them to render a departure desirable.

7. In the application of these rules to each of the several parts of the United Kingdom for which there is a Boundary Commission—

(a) the expression ' electoral quota ' means a number obtained by dividing the electorate for that part of the United Kingdom by the number of constituencies in it existing on the enumeration date;

(b) the expression ' electorate ' means—

(i) in relation to a constituency, the number of persons whose names appear on the register of parliamentary electors in force on the enumeration date under the Representation of the People Acts for the constituency;

(ii) in relation to the part of the United Kingdom, the aggregate electorate as hereinbefore defined of all the constituencies therein;

(c) the expression ' enumeration date ' means, in relation to any report of a Boundary Commission under this Act, the date on which the notice with respect to that report is published in accordance with section two of this Act.

THE HOUSE OF COMMONS (REDISTRIBUTION OF SEATS) BILL, 1958

THE SECRETARY OF STATE FOR THE HOME DEPARTMENT AND LORD PRIVY SEAL (MR R. A. BUTLER): ... This Bill makes certain amendments to the House of Commons (Redistribution of Seats) Act, 1949... There is probably general agreement on ... basic principles and this Bill does not affect them. But, as was indicated in the debates on the last general review of constituencies in December 1954, and January 1955, experience of the working of the present law has shown that some changes are needed... The Government, naturally, thought it right in a matter of this constitutional importance to discuss the proposals we had in mind with the leaders of the other parties... and... substantial agreement was reached on the proposals now contained in the Bill... The two changes made by Clause 1 are: first, the deputy-chairman of each Commission will, in future, be a judge. This follows the present practice in Scotland... The second change is that the Registrar-General, the Director of Ordnance Survey and the Commissioner of Valuation for Northern Ireland will become assessors and will cease to be members of the respective Commissions. These officials are at present members of the Commissions because of their expert knowledge. There was some feeling in the House on the occasion of the last general review... that while the Commissions should continue to have the benefit of expert knowledge of these officials, it would be better if the latter had no responsibility for the framing of the Commission's proposals. The result is that each Commission will consist of Mr Speaker as chairman, a High Court judge as deputy-chairman and two members appointed by the appropriate Ministers. In the case of the Commission for England and Wales that will be one member appointed by the Home Secretary and one member appointed by the Minister of Housing and Local Government... The Government intend... that the Ministerial appointments shall in each case be made in agreement with the other political parties, subject to the proviso that the Minister of Housing and Local Government will continue to appoint persons with a knowledge of local government...

Clause 2... extends the interval between general reviews of constituencies. The present intervals are three years minimum and seven years maximum. In the debates on the last general review... there appeared to be general agreement... that these intervals were too short, having regard to the upsets which redistribution is bound to cause in many cases, and that, as suggested by the Boundary Commission for England in... its First Report, the interval between reviews should be lengthened... The intervals proposed are ten years minimum and fifteen years maximum. Initially, these intervals will run from the date of the last reports of the Commissions. These were presented in November 1954... The Commissions need at least a year, more likely eighteen months... so that the next general review would probably start not earlier than some time in 1963... Ten years... should be long enough to ensure a reasonable period of stability and it will mean that at least one more General Election will take place before the next general review.

On the other hand, it should be short enough to ensure that gross differences or discrepancies between electorates of different constituencies are not allowed to continue uncorrected for too long... The Commissions already have power, under Section 2 (3) of the

1949 Act, to make recommendations affecting individual constituencies between general reviews. This is . . . a general power . . . but it is one . . . which hitherto has been used only to adjust constituency boundaries to local government boundaries, and we think rightly so. A major alteration can hardly be made to one constituency in isolation. It is almost bound to affect neighbouring constituencies over a gradually widening radius owing to the ripples which are created, and there would be a real risk of a series of alterations which might go far to stultify the whole purpose of extending the intervals between general reviews. . .

The third main proposal of the Bill – more flexibility in the application of the redistribution rules – is contained in Clause 2 (2). Section 2 (1) of the Act has the effect of requiring Commissions to aim at giving full effect to the redistribution rules in the Second Schedule to the Act on the occasion of each general review. This means, among other things, that they are obliged, in many cases, to recommend changes which would produce greater mathematical equality between constituencies even though the electorates of the existing constituencies concerned are not abnormal.

This gave rise, not unnaturally, to a good deal of upset and resentment in a number of constituencies on the occasion of the last review, and the Boundary Commission for England reported that some relaxation of the rules might well be considered. The Bill accordingly relieves the Commissions of the obligation to give full effect in all instances of the redistribution rules. It requires them to take account of the inconvenience and breaking of local ties which follow upon constituency changes. To sum it up, the effect of the Bill is to bring in a presumption against making changes unless there is a very strong case for them.

The Commissioners, however, will still be required to comply with Rule 4 of the redistribution rules. . . This provides that as far as practicable constituency boundaries should be kept in line with local government boundaries. . .

Before leaving the redistribution rules, perhaps I should refer to a matter which received a good deal of attention in the debates on the last general review, namely, the question of the relative electorates of county and borough constituencies. It was at that time a matter of some controversy. . .

On the occasion of the last review, the right hon. Member for South Shields (Mr Ede), pointed out that he had contested both rural and urban constituencies and knew the extra strain placed on a candidate in a county division. He said: 'I do not think there is any very serious difference of opinion as to the fact that there should be some weighting '. – (OFFICIAL REPORT, 16th December, 1954; Vol. 535, c. 2189.)

The Government share the view expressed by the right hon. Gentleman. He also said that the amount of that weighting was a matter of legitimate controversy, and he used these words:

> ' It may well be a good thing, before any alteration is made in the law, to give consideration to the point as to what is an appropriate differentiation between rural and urban seats to see if we can arrive at some generally agreed proportion.' (OFFICIAL REPORT, 26th January, 1955; Vol. 536, c. 356.)

The Government have considered this matter. Our present conclusion is that it is not the sort of matter that we can easily write into the redistribution rules. We feel that we must leave this to the good sense of the Boundary Commissions.

I now come to Clause 3, which provides for a separate electoral quota for each part of the United Kingdom.

The electoral quota means, at present, the average electorate of all constituencies in Great Britain, but the Great Britain average is not appropriate to the differing circumstances of England, Scotland and Wales, nor is it consistent with the fixed allocation of seats to Scotland and Wales – and consequently of that to England – contained in Rule 1 of the redistribution rules in the Second Schedule to the Act of 1949.

Clause 4 of the Bill refers to the publication of notices and the holding of local inquiries. Subsection (1) provides that where a Commission revises a proposed recommendation after publishing its notice of it, it must publish a notice of the revised recommendation. . . The Clause also obliges a Commission to hold a local inquiry if, on notice of a recommendation being published, and objection to that recommendation is made by a local authority, or at least 100 electors in the constituency affected. This applies both to an original recommendation and, in general, to a revised recommendation.

The proviso to Clause 4 (2) has the effect, however, that where a Commission has already held an inquiry into its original recommendation it need not hold a further inquiry into a revised recommendation if after considering all the circumstances, it is of the opinion that a further local inquiry would not be justified. These provisions . . . relate to local hearings in the constituencies affected.

We have also considered, in our discussions with the leaders of the other parties a suggestion made by the 1942 Committee on Electoral Machinery, whose recommendations paved the way for much of the present redistribution law – that, in addition to the local hearings, each Commission should sit, under its deputy-chairman, ' to hear any representations from the chief or national officers of the principal party organisations with respect to the provisional proposals '.

I have written to Mr Speaker, as chairman of the Commission, expressing on behalf of the Conservative Party the hope that the Commissions will be prepared to implement this suggestion. I understand from Mr Speaker . . . that the other two parties sitting here have also already written to Mr Speaker in the same sense. . .

[Second Reading. 582 H.C.Deb. 5s. c. 226. 11 February 1958]

HOUSE OF COMMONS (REDISTRIBUTION OF SEATS) ACT, 1958   [6 & 7 Eliz. 2. ch. 26]

1. (1) The deputy chairman of each Boundary Commission . . . shall be a judge who—
   (*a*) in the case of the Commission for England shall be a judge of the High Court appointed by the Lord Chancellor [9] . . .
(2) The officers of each Commission shall include two assessors who shall be (*a*) in the case of the Commission for England, the Registrar General for England and Wales and the Director General of Ordnance Survey [10]. . .

2. (1) After the coming into force of this Act a Boundary Commission's report under subsection (1) of section two of the principal Act shall be submitted not less than ten or more than fifteen years from the date of the submission of the Commission's last report under that subsection. . .

(2) It shall not be the duty of a Boundary Commission, in discharging their functions under the said section two, to aim at giving full effect in all circumstances to the rules set out in the Second Schedule to the principal Act, but they shall take account, so far as they reasonably can, of the inconveniences attendant on alterations of constituencies other than alterations made for the purposes of rule 4 of those rules, and of any local ties which would be broken by such alterations; and references in that section to giving effect to those rules shall be construed accordingly.

4. (1) Where a Boundary Commission revise any proposed recom-

[9] [The same provision is made for Wales. In Scotland the judge is a judge of the Court of Session appointed by the President of the Court. In Northern Ireland the judge is a judge of the High Court of Northern Ireland appointed by the Chief Justice.]

[10] [The same provision is made for Wales. In Scotland the Registrar-General for Scotland is appointed and in Northern Ireland the Registrar-General for Northern Ireland and the Commissioner of Valuation for Northern Ireland.]

mendations after publishing a notice of them under paragraph 3 of Part III of the First Schedule to the principal Act, the Commission shall comply again with that paragraph in relation to the revised recommendations, as if no earlier notice had been published.

(2) Where, on the publication of the notice under the said paragraph 3 of a recommendation of a Boundary Commission for the alteration of any constituencies, the Commission receive any representation objecting to the proposed recommendation from an interested authority or from a body of electors numbering one hundred or more, the Commission shall not make the recommendation unless, since the publication of the said notice, a local inquiry has been held in respect of the constituencies under paragraph 4 of the said Part III:

Provided that, where a local inquiry was held in respect of the constituencies before the publication of the said notice, this subsection shall not apply if the Commission, after considering the matters discussed at the local inquiry, the nature of the representations received on the publication of the said notice and any other relevant circumstances, are of opinion that a further local inquiry would not be justified.

(3) In the last foregoing subsection, ' interested authority ' and ' elector ' respectively mean, in relation to any recommendation, a local authority whose area is wholly or partly comprised in the constituencies affected by the recommendation and a parliamentary elector for any of these constituencies, and for this purpose ' local authority ' means the council of any county, or any borough (including a metropolitan borough) or of any urban or rural district.

Report of the Boundary Commission for England, 1969
Procedure of the Commission

12. The Rules required us to conduct our general review on the basis of the parliamentary electorates existing when we announced our intention. The General Register Office provided us with particulars of the electorates of each administrative area as at 15th February 1965, the Ordnance Survey prepared for us maps showing in detail all the administrative areas of England, and the Ministry of Housing and Local Government supplied us with information on housing and development. With this information before us we framed our provisional recommendations and published them locally.

13. We did not invite suggestions before making our provisional recommendations. We considered that it was better for us from our independent position to take the first step of preparing provisional

recommendations based on the information available to us without regard to any conflicting suggestions we might receive. There still remained the possibility of unsolicited suggestions reaching us but we considered that, were we to take account of them, it would be unfair to those holding contrary opinions who had not chosen to put suggestions to us and we decided not to consider any *ex parte* suggestions sent to us prior to the publication of our provisional recommendations. In the event, few such suggestions were received and the local inquiry procedure gave ample opportunity for the consideration of counter-proposals.

14. As required by the 1949 and 1958 Acts, we published our proposals in local newspapers circulating in the constituencies affected. We gave more publicity to our proposals than the statutes demanded and in all 651 notices of our provisional recommendations were inserted in newspapers. We also issued a series of press releases describing with the aid of outline maps the general effect of our recommendations.

15. Where our provisional recommendations involved changes in constituencies we arranged for a copy of the recommendations, with a map illustrating the boundaries, to be made available for public inspection at a local authority office or other suitable place within the constituency. The addresses of the offices at which inspection could be made were included in the local press notices. . .

16. After considering all the representations submitted against our provisional recommendations, we arranged for the holding of local inquiries where these were obligatory and, in the light of the reports on these, published revised recommendations where we thought necessary. The procedure was then repeated – representations against revised recommendations were considered, further local inquiries were held where we considered they were justified, and modified recommendations were published in some areas in the same manner as for provisional and revised recommendations. So we reached our final recommendations . . .

Local Inquiries

17. The notices advertising our proposals included a statement that any representations relating to the proposals should be addressed to the Commission in accordance with the statutory provisions within one month of the date of publication. Under section 4 (2) of the 1958 Act we were obliged to hold local inquiries where objections were lodged by a body of one hundred or more parliamentary electors in the affected constituency or by an interested local authority, and although this procedure added substantially to the time required to complete a general review, the local informa-

tion which it produced was invaluable to us in reaching our final recommendations.

18. At our request the Home Secretary appointed ... twenty-three assistant Commissioners ... to hold inquiries on our behalf. ...

19. Notices advertising the holding of local inquiries were published in local newspapers in exactly the same way as the notices advertising our provisional recommendations. Copies of the representations addressed to the Commission were placed on deposit for public inspection at addresses listed in the notices. Copies of representations were also distributed to local authorities and other bodies who had shown an interest. As a result of the experience of the first batch of local inquiries, explanatory statements of the reasons for our provisional recommendations were made available at all subsequent inquiries.

20. No statutory rules governed the conduct of the local inquiries. We took the view that, although only certain types of local representation could compel the holding of an inquiry, not only were we not precluded from considering other representations, but also it would be inconsistent with the objects of the inquiry procedure if we restricted the scope of an inquiry to the examination of representations made by local electors, particularly since the matters to be examined might affect the allocation of seats throughout England as a whole. We therefore did not impose any limitation as to the persons who could be heard at local inquiries.

21. Where we decided, after considering the report of a local inquiry, to revise our recommendations, it was necessary under the 1958 Act for the revised recommendations to be published in exactly the same way as the original provisional recommendations. Copies of the assistant Commissioner's report were deposited for public inspection with the revised recommendations and a map. Where we adhered to our provisional recommendations after holding a local inquiry, copies of the assistant Commissioner's report were made available near the end of our review when it was clear that we would not be making any further recommendations for the area.

22. In all, 70 local inquiries were held into our recommendations, including 7 second or re-opened inquiries. As a result of these, in 40 cases we decided to publish revised or modified recommendations.

Discussions with Political Parties

23. In 1942 the Committee on Electoral Machinery (Cmd. 6408) suggested that, apart from local inquiries held under the statutory arrangements, each Commission should also sit under its Deputy Chairman ' to hear any representations from the Chief or National Officers of the principal Party organisations with respect to the pro-

visional proposals '. It was made evident in the House of Commons during the Second Reading debate on the 1958 Redistribution Bill that the three principal parties were anxious to see the suggestion adopted. Indeed the leaders of the parties wrote to the Chairman of the four Boundary Commissions expressing the hope that the Commissions would be prepared to implement it. We adopted the suggestion and a meeting with the chief officers of the parties represented in the House of Commons was arranged shortly after the announcement of the general review. A further 7 meetings were held with the chief officers as the review proceeded. . .

Principles of the Review

28. We . . . began the review with the intention of avoiding, where possible, proposals that would change constituency boundaries for the sake of adjustments in the size of the electorates. We also considered it reasonable to assume that each existing constituency normally represents a community with its own distinct character, problems and traditions. Ties of many sorts may exist within this local community and we believe it to be proper for these ties, whatever they may be, to be taken fully into account before a constituency is disturbed. We were, however, not inclined to accept the argument put forward at some inquiries that ' local ties ' could refer only to the specific ties of political life that would be broken by redistribution. . .

Size of electorates

32. In 1954 when the electoral quota was 57,122 the Commission did not recommend the creation of constituencies with electorates of less than 40,000 or more than 80,000. . . The 1965 electoral quota for England calculated according to rule 7 (i.e. the total English electorate of 30,025,849 divided by 511, the existing total number of seats) was 58,759. We decided that the limits of 40,000 and 80,000 . . . could readily be applied in this review, but while in 1954 80% of the constituencies recommended by the Commission fell within the range of 45,000 to 65,000, it was our aim, taking account of the higher quota, to concentrate electorates between 50,000 and 70,000.

Urban and rural electorates

33. In their initial report of 1947 (Cmd. 7260) the Commission took the view that, in general, urban constituencies could more conveniently support large electorates than rural constituencies, and they recommended an upper limit for urban constituencies of 90,000 electors, or about 1½ times the then English electoral quota. This recommendation was modified by Parliament, additional constitu-

encies being created in a number of the large boroughs. Nevertheless in their 1954 report the Commission saw no reason to recede from the view expressed in the initial report. . .

36. We considered whether we should give some weighting in favour of rural constituencies and in particular whether there were rural counties with special problems of their own that deserved more than their strict entitlement of seats. The Rules do not provide for any distinction between the size of electorates in rural and urban constituencies nor do they allow for the allocation of additional seats to rural counties. As we understand them, the Rules require a common electoral quota to be applied to all constituencies whatever their character although Rule 6 does give us discretion to depart from the strict application of Rules 4 and 5 where special geographical considerations make it desirable.

37. It can be argued that extensive rural constituencies with possibly poor communications present problems for the Member of Parliament in representing his constituency, for the public in meeting their Member, and for local political party organisations. These problems, however, may not be so great today as in the past. On the contrary, it has been argued that a Member representing a borough constituency, more accessible as he is to the electorate, may be faced with more community problems than a Member for a county constituency. Our discussions with the chief officers of the political parties led us to the view that the arguments were evenly balanced and that there was no obvious case for deliberately seeking to create constituencies with smaller electorates in the rural areas. We did, however, take account of Rule 6 (special geographical considerations) in certain exceptional areas.

[Report of the Boundary Commission for England. Cmnd. 4084 (June 1969)]

HARPER v. *HOME SECRETARY* [1955] 1 Ch. 238

Court of Appeal

In this action the Mayor of Manchester and a member of the city council challenged the validity of the 1954 report of the English Boundary Commissioners in which they made recommendations for the Manchester area. Their report had already been presented to Parliament by the Home Secretary in accordance with s. 2 (5) of the Act of 1949, and had been approved by both Houses. It was therefore now the duty of the Home Secretary, under s. 3 (4) of the Act, to present the draft of the Order in Council giving effect to the recommendations to Her Majesty in Council to be embodied in an Order.

The plaintiffs claimed (i) a declaration that the report had not been made in accordance with the rules laid down in the Second Schedule of the Act and was therefore not a report within the meaning of s. 2 (5); (ii) a declaration that it was not therefore a report which the Home Secretary was required to lay before Parliament; (iii) a declaration that the Home Secretary was therefore not under an obligation to present the draft Order to Her Majesty in Council; and (iv) an injunction to restrain the Home Secretary from presenting it to her Majesty in Council.

Events moved very rapidly. The plaintiffs made an *ex parte* application to Roxburgh J. on Friday, 17 December 1954. He granted an interim injunction until the following Tuesday. On Monday, 20 December the Court of Appeal heard an appeal from his decision.

EVERSHED M.R. ... It is plain that the form of the action is an unusual one... [T]he plaintiffs seek an injunction to restrain the Secretary of State from presenting to Her Majesty in Council a draft order, which has already received the approval of both Houses of Parliament. It is therefore obvious that the court is concerned with matters which at any rate come somewhat near to touching on the relative spheres of Parliament and the courts. [He then set out relevant provisions of the Act and continued:] On this matter I have myself come to a clear conclusion that there is no ground for saying that the report, as I read it, was ... a substantial departure, or was indeed any departure, from the rules which the Commission had to have in mind...

My reading of these rules and of the whole Act is that it was quite clearly intended that, in so far as the matter was not within the discretion of the Commission, it was certainly to be a matter for Parliament to determine. I find it impossible to suppose that Parliament contemplated that, on any of these occasions when reports were presented, it would be competent for the court to determine and pronounce on whether a particular line which had commended itself to the Commission was one which the court thought the best line or the right line – whether one thing rather than another was to be regarded as practicable, and so on. If it were competent for the courts to pass judgments of that kind on the reports, I am at a loss to see where the process would end and what the function of Parliament would then turn out to be.

If that is the right view, then, as I think, everything else follows. Sir Andrew indeed conceded that, unless it could be said that the report was vitiated by the commissioners' misdirection of themselves so as to be, in effect, no report at all, his cause of action was destroyed in limine. I find it unnecessary to say what the court would say or should do if the commission on the face of a report made recommendations which were manifestly in complete disregard of the Act of 1949 and of the rules thereunder. I find it difficult to think that Parliament would pass them by unnoticed; but, if Parliament none the less adopted them, I find it unnecessary to say what view the court might take.

In *Hammersmith Corporation* v. *Boundary Commission for England*,[11] arising out of the same report, which came before Harman J., the remedy sought by representatives of certain other constituencies was against the Boundary Commission itself, and not the Home Secretary. The judge there said: ' This is not a matter in which I ought to be asked to interfere or in which any good purpose would be served by my seeking to do so. I do not think questions of jurisdiction really need be debated at this stage. I shall assume that I can, if necessary, express an opinion as to the proceedings of the Boundary Commission, without going beyond the functions of this court, but I am satisfied that I should certainly serve no useful object by doing so, and that the machinery set up under this Act does not leave any room which makes it appropriate for the court to intervene either at this or at any other stage.' I must say that I find myself in agreement with the view that obviously commended itself to Harman J.

Sir Andrew referred us to one or two cases, and on those I ought to say a few words. In *Rex* v. *Electricity Commissioners*,[12] the court granted a writ of prohibition against the Electricity Commissioners. But, in that case, what the Electricity Commissioners were told to do was to prepare certain schemes which would become orders on their confirmation, first by the Minister, and later by the resolution of the House. They would always be the orders of the commissioners, and the Act, which imposed on them the duty of making these schemes, plainly imposed on them quasi-judicial functions. . . If the Boundary Commission had been given similar functions, and if it had become manifest at some stage or on any occasion that they were exceeding them, it might well be that the court would think it right to make a prerogative order of prohibition or mandamus to compel them to perform their functions properly. I observe that Atkin L.J. forbore from expressing any view as to what the court would do if Parliament had, in fact, approved the order which the commissioners had been restrained from proceeding to make.

The other case to which Sir Andrew referred was *Attorney-General of New South Wales* v. *Trethowan*,[13] in order to show that the court will in appropriate cases grant injunctions and grant them ex parte to prevent someone in the position of a Minister from taking a bill or order, or whatever it might be, to the Sovereign or the Sovereign's representative for the purpose of its becoming law.

[11] *The Times*, 15 December 1954.
[12] [1924] 1 K.B. 171.   [13] [1932] A.C. 526.

But that was a case where the legislature concerned, namely, the legislature of New South Wales, had under the Australian Constitution strictly limited legislative functions; and it having been shown that the proposed Act of Parliament had disregarded the provision in the Constitution which required a particular sanction on the part of the electorate, the courts in Australia restrained members of the Legislative Council, other than the plaintiffs, who were suing, from proceeding to take the measure for the approval of the Governor-General; and the Privy Council here affirmed them. That seems to me to be quite a different case from the present. We are in no sense here concerned with a Parliament or legislature having limited legislative functions according to the constitution.

I do not, therefore, think that those two cases carry Sir Andrew any further on his road. The Attorney-General said that, apart from the question of the effect of the report and the proposed Order in Council, the courts had in any case no more power to grant the injunction against the Secretary of State than they would have to prevent a Minister, or the other appropriate persons concerned, from taking to the Sovereign a Bill that has duly passed its third reading in each of the two Houses for the royal assent; and a reference was made by him to *Reg.* v. *Lords Commissioners of the Treasury.*[14] I do not find it necessary to express my views on that broad proposition, save to say that, in my judgment, *Reg.* v. *Lords Commissioners of the Treasury* seems to me to be of a wholly different character from that with which we are now concerned.

But I return at the end of my judgment to the point which I mentioned earlier and on which I would say one final word, namely, the question of the defendant to this action. I have said that the defendant is ' the Secretary of State for the Home Department ' – sued, that is to say, by his official title as a Minister of the Crown. It is said by Sir Andrew that, since the report disregarded the rules in the Act of 1949, therefore it is not a report within the meaning of the Act, and that the Secretary of State has neither the duty to the House or to anyone else, nor the power or authority, to take this proposed Order in Council to Her Majesty. I am not myself satisfied that Sir Andrew is not in this respect upon the horns of a dilemma. If the whole thing is a nullity and all he seeks to do is to restrain a particular individual, who happens at the moment to be the Secretary of State for the Home Department, I am not satisfied that he ought not to sue him in his personal capacity as for an ordinary wrong – though, in that case, it would not be clear to me what breach of duty to the plaintiffs he was engaged in committing. On the other hand, if he does sue him, and rightly sues him, in his capacity as Secretary of State for the Home Department, then I am

14 (1872) L.R. 7 Q.B. 387.

not satisfied (though I express no final view on it, as we have not heard full argument) that the role is one which, having regard to the terms of the Crown Proceedings Act, 1947, will lie. And I am not satisfied, having regard to section 21 of that Act, that, on this alternative, the plaintiff could, in any event, obtain an injunction; but I find it unnecessary to do more than mention that caution on this point,[15] for, in my judgment, the answer to this case is that the plaintiffs have not established a prima facie case to my satisfaction that the report, which was presented and which has formed the basis of all that subsequently happened, was otherwise than in accordance with the powers vested in the Boundary Commission; and more particularly that the resolutions which the Houses of Parliament passed and under which the Secretary of State has acted and is purporting to act contained in them, so to speak, any infection of invalidity.

Therefore, I think that this ex parte injunction ought not to have been granted and I would allow the appeal against it.

JENKINS and HODSON L.JJ. concurred.   *Appeal allowed*

IV. THE ELECTION CAMPAIGN

The election campaign is regulated by Part II of the Representation of the People Act, 1949. It operates by providing that certain acts are to be corrupt or illegal offences or illegal practices. Those guilty of them are liable to criminal penalties and may also be disqualified for the future from voting or standing as a candidate. In an extreme case an Election Court provided for by the Act may declare an election invalid. One of the chief aims of the Act is to limit the amount spent by candidates. This it attempts to do by insisting that a candidate appoint an election agent (if he does not he is treated as if he was his own agent) and providing that all major expenses should only be incurred by him or on his authority. He is required after the election to return an account of expenses to show that he has kept within the permitted maximum. Many of the provisions are relics of the nineteenth-century successes in establishing purity in elections, such as the provisions against bribery, corruption and treating. Others seem designed to prevent candidates appearing to have wider support than in fact they have, e.g. by paying people to display posters, or using improper means to persuade, e.g. by paying canvassers. The prohibition against bands and banners was repealed in 1969.

REPRESENTATION OF THE PEOPLE ACT, 1949
[12, 13 & 14 Geo. 6. ch. 68] [16]

55. (1) Not later than the latest time for the delivery of notices of withdrawals for an election, a person shall be named by or on behalf of each candidate as the candidate's election agent. . .

---

[15] [See *Merricks* v. *Heathcote-Amory* (below, p. 267).]
[16] As amended by the Representation of the People Act, 1969.

(2) A candidate may name himself as election agent. . .

63. (1) No expenses shall, with a view to promoting or procuring the election of a candidate at an election, be incurred by any person other than the candidate, his election agent and persons authorised in writing by the election agent on account—

   (*a*) of holding public meetings or organising any public display; or

   (*b*) of issuing advertisements, circulars or publications; or

   (*c*) of otherwise presenting to the electors the candidate or his views or the extent or nature of his backing or disparaging another candidate:

Provided that paragraph (*c*) of this subsection shall not—

   (i) restrict the publication of any matter relating to the election in a newspaper or other periodical or in a broadcast made by the British Broadcasting Corporation or the Independent Television Authority; or

   (ii) apply to any expenses not exceeding in the aggregate the sum of ten shillings which may be incurred by an individual and are not incurred in pursuance of a plan suggested by or concerted with others, or to expenses incurred by any person in travelling or in living away from home or similar personal expenses.

(2) Where a person incurs any expenses required by this section to be authorised by the election agent, that person shall within fourteen days after the date of publication of the result of the election send to the appropriate officer a return of the amount of those expenses . . . accompanied by a declaration . . . giving particulars of the matters for which the expenses were incurred:

Provided that this subsection shall not apply to any person engaged or employed for payment or promise of payment by the candidate or his election agent. . .

(5) If any person incurs, or aids, abets, counsels or procures any other person to incur, any expenses in contravention of this section, or knowingly makes the declaration required by subsection (2) thereof falsely, he shall be guilty of a corrupt practice, and if a person fails to send any declaration or return or a copy thereof as required by this section he shall be guilty of an illegal practice:

Provided that—

   (*a*) the court before whom a person is convicted under this subsection may, if they think it just in the special circumstances of the case, mitigate or entirely remit any incapacity imposed by virtue of section one hundred and fifty-one of this Act; and (*b*) a candidate shall not be liable, nor shall his election be avoided, for a corrupt or illegal practice under this sub-section committed by an agent without his consent or connivance.

(6) Where any act or omission of an association or body of persons, corporate or unincorporated, is an offence declared to be a corrupt or illegal practice by this section, any person who at the time of the act or omission was a director, general manager, secretary or other similar officer of the association or body, or was purporting to act in any such capacity, shall be deemed to be guilty of that offence, unless he proves that the act or omission took place without his consent or connivance and that he exercised all such diligence to prevent the commission of the offence as he ought to have exercised having regard to the nature of his functions in that capacity and to all the circumstances. . .

80. (1) No person shall with intent to influence persons to give or refrain from giving their votes at a parliamentary or local government election, use, or aid, abet, counsel or procure the use of any television or other wireless transmitting station outside the United Kingdom for the transmission of any matter having reference to the election otherwise than in pursuance of arrangements made with the British Broadcasting Corporation for it to be received and re-transmitted by that Corporation, or of an arrangement made with the Independent Television Authority or a programme contractor . . . for it to be received by the Authority or contractor and re-transmitted by the Authority.

(2) An offence under this section shall be an illegal practice:

Provided that the court before whom a person is convicted of an offence under this section may, if they think it just in the special circumstances of the case, mitigate or entirely remit any incapacity imposed by virtue of section one hundred and fifty-one of this Act.

(3) Where any act or omission of an association or body of persons, corporate or unincorporated, is an illegal practice under this section, any person who at the time of the act or omission was a director, general manager, secretary or other similar officer of the association or body, or was purporting to act in any such capacity, shall be deemed to be guilty of the illegal practice, unless he proves that the act or omission took place without his consent or conni-vance and that he exercised all such diligence to prevent the com-mission of the illegal practice as he ought to have exercised having regard to the nature of his functions in that capacity and to all the circumstances. . .

94. (1) No payment or contract for payment shall for the pur-pose of promoting or procuring the election of a candidate at an

election be made to an elector or proxy for an elector on account of the exhibition of, or the use of any house, land, building or premises for the exhibition of, any address, bill or notice, unless it is the ordinary business of the elector or proxy as an advertising agent to exhibit for payment bills and advertisements and the payment or contract is made in the ordinary course of that business...

96. If a person is, either before, during or after an election, for the purpose of promoting or procuring the election of a candidate, engaged or employed for payment as a canvasser, the person so engaging or employing him and the person so engaged or employed shall be guilty of illegal employment...

99. (1) A person shall be guilty of a corrupt practice if he is guilty of bribery...

100. (1) A person shall be guilty of a corrupt practice if he is guilty of treating...

101. (1) A person shall be guilty of a corrupt practice if he is guilty of undue influence.

(2) A person shall be guilty of undue influence—

> (a) if he, directly or indirectly, by himself or by any other person on his behalf, makes use of or threatens to make use of any force, violence or restraint, or inflicts or threatens to inflict, by himself or by any other person, any temporal or spiritual injury, damage, harm or loss upon or against any person in order to induce or compel that person to vote or refrain from voting, or on account of that person having voted or refrained from voting...

103. ... ' election expenses '... means expenses incurred, whether before, during or after the election, on account of or in respect of the conduct or management of the election.

SECOND SCHEDULE
PARLIAMENTARY ELECTIONS RULES
Nomination

7. (1) Each candidate shall be nominated by a separate nomination paper...

(2) The nomination paper shall state the full names, place of residence and (if desired) description of the candidate...

(3) The description (if any) shall not exceed six words in length, and need not refer to his rank, profession and calling so long as, with the other particulars of the candidates, it is sufficient to identify him [17]...

---

[17] The prohibition of any reference to the candidate's political activities or affiliations was removed by s. 12 of the Representation of the People Act, 1969.

8. (1) The nomination paper shall be subscribed by two electors as proposer and seconder, and by eight other electors as assenting to the nomination. . .

9. (1) A person shall not be validly nominated unless his consent . . . in writing . . . is delivered at the place and within the time for the delivery of nomination papers. . .

(2) A candidate's consent . . . shall contain a statement that he is aware of the provisions of the House of Commons Disqualification Act, 1957, and that, to the best of his knowledge and belief, he is not disqualified for membership of the House of Commons.

10. (1) A person shall not be validly nominated unless the sum of one hundred and fifty pounds is deposited by him or on his behalf with the returning officer at the place and during the time for delivery of nomination papers. . .

Contested elections

18. The votes at the poll shall be given by ballot, the result shall be ascertained by counting the votes given to each candidate and the candidate to whom the majority of votes have been given shall be declared to have been elected. . .

50. Where, after the counting of votes (including a re-count) is completed an equality of votes is found to exist between any candidates and the addition of a vote would entitle any of those candidates to be declared elected, the returning officer shall forthwith decide between the candidates by lot, and proceed as if the candidate on whom the lot falls had received an additional vote.

REPRESENTATION OF THE PEOPLE ACT, 1969
[Ch. 15]

9. (1) Pending a parliamentary . . . election it shall not be lawful for any item about the constituency or electoral area to be broadcast from a television or other wireless transmitting station in the United Kingdom if any of the persons who are for the time being candidates at the election takes part in the item and the broadcast is not made with his consent; and where an item about a constituency or electoral area is so broadcast pending a parliamentary election there, then if the broadcast either is made before the latest time for delivery of nomination papers, or is made after that time but without the consent of any candidate remaining validly nominated, any person taking part in the item for the purpose of promoting or procuring his election shall be guilty of an illegal practice, unless the broadcast is so made without his consent.

(2) For purposes of subsection (1) above—

(*a*) a parliamentary election shall be deemed to be pending during the period ending with the close of the poll and beginning—

(i) at a general election, with the date of the dissolution of Parliament or any earlier time at which Her Majesty's intention to dissolve Parliament is announced; or

(ii) at a by-election, with the date of the issue of the writ for the election or any earlier date on which a certificate of the vacancy is notified in the Gazette in accordance with the Recess Elections Act 1784, the Election of Members during Recess Act 1858, the Bankruptcy (Ireland) Amendment Act 1872 or the Bankruptcy Act 1883...

R. v. *TRONOH MINES LTD.* [1952] 1 All E.R. 697

Central Criminal Court

On 19 October 1951, six days before the General Election, Tronoh Mines Ltd. published an advertisement in *The Times* headed 'Interim statement on dividend limitation'. In it the company criticized the financial policy of the Labour Party and in particular its proposal to limit company dividends. It went on to say that 'the nation, let alone your valuable companies in Malaya, cannot survive if the worm of socialism is permitted to continue to eat into the very core of its economic life... The coming general election will give us all an opportunity of saving the country from being reduced through the policies of the Socialist government to a bankrupt Welfare State. We need a new and strong government with Ministers who may be relied upon to encourage business enterprise and initiative, under the leadership of one who has, through the whole of his life, devoted himself to national and not sectional interests...'

The Company, its secretary, and The Times Publishing Company were subsequently charged under s. 63 (1) of the Representation of the People Act with unlawfully incurring expenses in issuing an advertisement with a view to promoting or procuring the election of a candidate other than the Labour Party's candidate at the parliamentary election held in the constituency of the cities of London and Westminster for which the writ had been issued on 6 October. They were also charged with incurring the expenses with a view to promoting or procuring the election of the Conservative candidate in the same constituency.

McNAIR J. On the view I take of the construction of s. 63 (1) of the Representation of the People Act, 1949, this is not a case which I can properly leave to the jury. For the purpose of the observations which I am about to make, I assume that the jury could properly find on the evidence that the object, or, possibly, the primary object, of incurring the expenditure in question was to advance the prospects of the anti-Socialist cause generally, that those who incurred those expenses had in mind the general election of 1951, and that they desired to achieve their object by securing the election of a majority of candidates who were against the Socialist government, though, if the matter had been left to the jury, the jury might well have taken the view that they were not the objects or the primary objects. The indictment contains two counts, charging the defendants with acting contrary to s. 63 (1) (*b*) and s. 63 (5) of the Act of 1949... Counsel for the defendants have submitted that, on the proper or reasonable construction of that section, the evidence tendered by the Crown does not establish any act which is prohibited by it. Section 63 (1) prohibits the incurring of expense on account of (*a*) holding public meetings, (*b*) issuing advertisements, or (*c*) ' otherwise presenting to the electors the candidate or his views or the extent or nature of his backing or disparaging another candidate '. It seems to me that (*c*) necessarily imports that the particular items specified in (*a*) and (*b*) must also, if they are to be caught by the prohibition, be items which have the effect of ' presenting to the electors the candidate or his views or the extent or nature of his backing or disparaging another candidate '. If this result had not been intended, it seems to me that para. (*c*) would have run: ' of presenting to the electors, whether by means specified in para. (*a*) or para. (*b*), or in any other way, the candidate or his views...' Furthermore, the Interpretation Act, 1889, s. 1 (1), provides that, unless the context otherwise requires, words importing the singular include the plural, and I think that the context here does not necessarily require that references to the election of a candidate at an election mean a candidate at a particular election and not candidates at elections generally. On the whole, therefore... I think that the construction contended for by the defence on this point is correct. It is not, however, necessary in a criminal case such as this to go to that length. It is sufficient to say that, in my judgment, it is a reasonable and possible construction. For, in the construction of a penal statute – to use the words of LORD SIMONDS in *Howell* v. *Falmouth Boat Construction, Ltd.*[18] – ' a man should not be put in peril on an ambiguity '.

I have reached the decision that on the evidence no reasonable jury could find that the advertisement in question was presenting to the electors of any constituency any particular candidate, still less presenting to the electors of the constituency of the cities of London and Westminster either the Conservative candidate or any candidate other than a Socialist candidate or his views.

Counsel for the defendants, Tronoh Mines, Ltd. and Mr Barrenger, also contended that this construction is supported by the consideration that s. 63 (1) does not prohibit the incurring of expendi-

---

[18] [1951] 2 All E.R. 281.

ture of the nature covered by the section absolutely, but only sub modo, and, therefore, the fact that the section itself provides no way in which the particular form of advertisement in question, namely, an advertisement in a national newspaper, which circulates generally throughout the country, supporting the views of a particular party and not those of a particular candidate, can be authorised, lent strong support to the view that the particular form of advertisement in question was not prohibited. If expenses incurred on account of the items specified in (a) (b) and (c), being supported in writing by the election agent, are permissible and authorised by the election agent, then, by virtue of subsection (2), the person who incurs them has to make a return to the returning officer of the amount of those expenses, stating the election at which and the candidate in whose support they were incurred. The prescribed form referred to in subsection (3) is set out in the Representation of the People Regulations, 1950 (S.I. 1950, No. 1254), which took effect after approval by resolution of both Houses of Parliament, and is Form W., and it is clear that that form is inappropriate for making a return of expenses of the kind with which we are here concerned. There is no way in which the expenditure, on the hypothesis I have stated, incurred in relation to all elections can be apportioned for the purpose of any particular return for a particular election. That consideration alone seems to me to lend strong support to the view that the section is not intended to prohibit expenditure incurred on advertisements designed to support, or having the effect of supporting, the interest of a particular party generally in all constituencies, at any rate at the time of a general election, and not supporting a particular candidate in a particular constituency.

Counsel for The Times Publishing Co., Ltd. has based an argument on the general structure of the group of section – ss. 60 to 78 – headed ' Election expenses '. Those words, ' Election expenses ', are, according to recognised canons of construction, to be regarded as forming part of the statute itself, and may, at any rate in the case of doubt but, probably in all cases, be used to provide the key to the general construction of each section which follows under that heading. Election expenses are defined in s. 103 as follows:

' " Election expenses " in relation to an election means expenses incurred, whether before, during or after the election, on account of or in respect of the conduct or management of the election.'

The result of s. 171 (1) is that ' election ' here means a parliamentary election, and that term ' parliamentary election ' is itself defined by s. 17 (1) of the Interpretation Act, 1889, in terms which make it plain that it means an election for a particular constituency and not a panoply of elections commonly known as a general election.

Accordingly, it seems to me that this group of sections is dealing with an election for a particular constituency, and it would be contrary to the ordinary canons of construction to impose the prohibition of s. 63 (1) in the circumstances of the present case. In other words, what is prohibited by this section is the incurring of expenditure of one of these particular categories which has the effect of supporting a particular candidate or candidates in a particular constituency, which, if authorised by the election agent, would form part of the election expenses for that constituency and thus be subject to the statutory maximum of expenditure for that constituency, I, therefore, accept the submission of counsel for The Times Publishing Co., Ltd. that s. 63 (1) does not prohibit expenditure, the real purpose or effect of which is general political propaganda, even although that general political propaganda does incidentally assist a particular candidate among others. There may be instances where there has been an incursion by a party or body into an election, but there is no evidence or suggestion of anything of that kind in the present case. Certain of the cases to which I have been referred (including *Lambeth, Kennington Division Case, Crossman* v. *Davis* [19] and *Shoreditch, Haggerston Division Case, Cremer* v. *Lowles* [20]), draw this distinction, and, although those were decisions on earlier legislation, it does not seem to me that in any relevant respect their validity has been altered by the Act of 1918, the Act of 1948, or the consolidated Act of 1949.

... Furthermore, the conclusion which I have reached on the general construction of the section renders it unnecessary for me to express any final view on the question whether the proof of intention, object, or view to promote or procure the election of candidates generally of one particular party or in opposition to one particular party in all elections held at one general election could be sufficient evidence, on which a jury could act, of specific intent such as is charged in the present case, viz., the intent of promoting or procuring the election of a particular candidate or candidates at a particular election. But I must say, having listened to the arguments on this point, I am strongly of the opinion that in a case such as this it would be necessary to prove affirmatively the specific intent relating to the particular election.

Verdict : ' Not Guilty ' on both counts

V. ELECTORAL REFORM

The Representation of the People Act assumes that the only important contest is on the constituency level and that the election is

[19] (1886) 54 L.T. 628; 4 O'M. & H. 93.   [20] (1896) 5 O'M. & H. 68.

decided in the last few weeks before the poll. Even on the constituency level the law invites disregard. The sanction against abuse – an election petition – has not been employed by any major party since 1929. This is not because malpractices are never suspected (although serious ones must have been very rare) but because the process of petitioning is expensive and uncertain. As one senior official said: ' If we lost a seat by one vote and·I could clearly prove illegal practices by the other side I wouldn't try. It would cost perhaps £5,000 and they might be able to show that our man had slipped up in some way. But worse than that, it might start tit-for-tat petitions and no party could afford a lot of them. On the whole, we're both law-abiding and it's as well to leave each other alone.' [21]

It is surely anomalous for the law to regulate in such detail what may be done or spent on behalf of individual candidates and to ignore what is done on the national level to return or defeat parties. It is now generally accepted that people vote for a party more than for a candidate and that countrywide trends are more important than any local efforts in determining the outcome. There is nothing in the law to prevent the parties – or private groups, such as business associations or trade unions – from intervening in the political argument on a national scale during the election campaign itself. In 1959 the opponents of nationalisation exercised a prudent restraint in suspending their efforts when the election was announced; almost certainly they would have been within their legal rights if they had gone on.

It would not be very difficult to draft laws to control the amounts spent nationally during the campaign period by interested organisations. Much greater ethical and practical problems are involved if restrictions against pre-campaign activities are considered. By bringing public-relations techniques into politics, the Conservative Central Office may have opened a Pandora's box, for what it did between 1957 and 1959 far from exhausted the possibilities of the PR approach. Great hesitation should be felt about placing any restraint on the freedom to advocate ideas. There would, moreover, be great

---

[21] [The Committee on Electoral Reform noted (Cmd. 7286 (1947–8), para. 54): ' It may be argued that it is not satisfactory that the vindication of electoral law should rest so largely on civil proceedings undertaken at considerable financial risk by the political parties or individual electors. The integrity of elections, it may be said, concerns the community as a whole and not merely the electors of a particular constituency.... Irregularities at elections should not be regarded as a private wrong which an individual must come forward to remedy, but as attempts to wreck the machinery of representative government and as an attack upon national institutions which the nation should concern itself to repel.' It suggested that the Treasury Solicitor might be the appropriate person to carry out this duty. The suggestion has not been taken up.]

technical difficulties in regulating the use of public-relations techniques, as there would be in restricting pre-campaign expenditure by the parties or by private groups. On the other hand, particularly with a close election in prospect, it would be possible to make nonsense of the present limitations, by increasingly intensive pre-campaign expenditure. The necessity for legislation has still to be proved. The case for an examination of the situation seems overwhelming.

[David Butler and Richard Rose, *The British General Election of 1959* (1960), Appendix v]

COMPANIES ACT, 1967 [Ch. 81]

19. (1) If a company (not being the wholly owned subsidiary of a company incorporated in Great Britain) has, in a financial year, given money for political purposes or charitable purposes or both, there shall (if it exceeded £50 in amount) be contained in the directors' report relating to that year, in the case of each of the purposes for which money has been given, a statement of the amount of money given therefor and, in the case of political purposes for which money has been given, the following particulars, so far as applicable, namely—

(*a*) the name of each person to whom money has been given for those purposes exceeding £50 in amount and the amount of money given;

(*b*) if money exceeding £50 in amount has been given by way of donation or subscription to a political party, the identity of the party and the amount of money given.

(2) The foregoing subsection shall not have effect in the case of a company which, at the end of a financial year, has subsidiaries which have, in that year given money as mentioned in the foregoing subsection, but is not itself the wholly owned subsidiary of a company incorporated in Great Britain; but in such a case there shall (if the amount of money so given in that year by the company and the subsidiaries between them exceed £50) be contained in the directors' report relating to that year, in the case of each of the purposes for which money has been given by the company and the subsidiaries between them, a statement of the amount of money given therefor and, in the case of political purposes for which money has been given, the like particulars, so far as applicable, as are required by the foregoing subsection.

(3) For the purposes of this section a company shall be treated as giving money for political purposes if, directly or indirectly,—

(a) it gives a donation or subscription to a political party of the United Kingdom or of any part thereof; or

(b) it gives a donation or subscription to a person who, to its knowledge, is carrying on, or proposing to carry on, any activities which can, at the time at which the donation or subscription was given, reasonably be regarded as likely to affect public support for such a political party as aforesaid.

(4) For the purposes of this section, money given for charitable purposes to a person who, when it was given, was ordinarily resident outside the United Kingdom shall be left out of account. . . .

The Speaker's Conference, 1969

A conference of representatives of the different parties sitting under the chairmanship of the Speaker has been one informal device adopted in the past in an effort to secure so far as possible agreement between the parties on matters of electoral reform. The most conspicuously successful of these was the first under Mr Speaker Lowther in 1917 which preceded the Representation of the People Act, 1918. That of 1929 under the same chairman, though he had by then ceased to be Speaker, was a failure. A third conference in 1944 also achieved a fair degree of agreement but led to charges of breach of faith by the Conservative Opposition when the Labour Government after it had come to power in 1945 refused to implement all its recommendations. The Speaker's Conference of 1969 was less controversial though by no means all of its recommendations were accepted. One of its recommendations related to public opinion polls.

'31. There should be no broadcast, or publication in a newspaper or other periodical, of the result of a public opinion poll or of betting odds on the likely result of a parliamentary election during the period of seventy-two hours before the close of the Poll. (The Conference decided by a majority to recommend this restriction; Ayes 9, Noes 5. The period of seventy-two hours was agreed to by a majority; Ayes 11, Noes 6). . .'

The Government did not accept this recommendation.

The Secretary of State for the Home Department (Mr James Callaghan): . . . Your recommendation, Sir, about public opinion polls and betting odds is, as far as I can make out, very controversial. . . . The argument for this restriction seems to be that the publication of the results of an opinion poll and of betting odds might cause an uncertain elector to vote for the party leading the poll, on the ground, I suppose, of jumping on the band-wagon, and that the results of an opinion poll published on the eve of the poll can be misleading since they might relate to a poll which had been conducted the previous week.

It is also suggested – and I share this view very strongly, although it is a personal one and I could not allow it to influence me – that the publication of betting odds does tend to bring an election into disrepute. . . .

I do not know whether there is any evidence that electors are influenced in the way I have described – indeed it would be possible to argue that the result of an opinion poll might be to rally the party which is not leading the poll, and to lead its supporters to say, ' We cannot bear the other chaps at any price. We had better go out and vote after all.' I do not know how one settles this question, and I do not think that there is any prospect of reaching a certain judgment on it. In any case, a restriction on the publication of these polls implies that people cannot be trusted with the vote, and many people outside Parliament would question the right of Parliament to determine what it is proper for electors to read in helping them to make up their minds as to how they should vote.

Merely restricting the publication of betting odds would not prohibit betting. The ban would not, as far as I can see, produce the ' quiet period ' that Mr Speaker's Conference wanted. Newspapers would be able to publish other political material, they could comment on the results of a public opinion poll published earlier if they wished. It would not be beyond the bounds of imagination for a newspaper to get round any restrictions, for example, by publishing the results of a poll on the popularity of the party leaders.

That would be something outside the subject we are discussing. Some people might feel that it would be advantageous to have such a poll and I do not think, at present, that I would want to restrict publications of that sort. The difficult practical questions that would arise would be how does one sever the publication of the results of a poll, which would be prohibited, from the publication of general statements or comments on the subject of public opinion? Would we prohibit reporting by United Kingdom newspapers and broadcasting agencies, or would we cast the net wider so as to prevent all possible forms of evasion? It would be a difficult and elaborate enterprise and I do not believe that it would succeed. It seems that when the arguments are not conclusive, and the practical difficulties are so daunting, the right course is to leave matters as they stand, and that is what I propose.

Mr J. J. MENDELSON (*Penistone*): My right hon. Friend said that he does not know what the reasoning was at Mr Speaker's Conference. Does not this point in the direction of changing our archaic system of not allowing arguments and speeches in committee to be published? The case for this conclusion is much more complex, and by necessity my right hon. Friend has been forced to leave out some of the reasoning behind it. Would he give his support to changing procedure?

MR CALLAGHAN: I do not think that arises from what I am saying this afternoon. We are debating this subject, and I have no doubt but that the views advanced in Mr Speaker's Conference will find an outlet on the Floor of the Chamber. I do not imagine that there will be any unrehearsed arguments at the end of the day. I prefer not to go further with the question raised.

[770 H.C.Deb. 5s. c. 43. 14 October 1968]

Matters which were considered by the Conference and on which they decided not to recommend any change in the law

4. Whether voting should be made compulsory. . .

8. The present relative majority system of election in single-member constituencies (The voting on the question that there should be no change in the law was; Ayes 19, No 1. A motion ' That parliamentary elections should be conducted in accordance with the single transferable vote system, more appropriately known as preferential voting with quota counting, in constituencies consisting of from 3 to 7 members, had been rejected, the voting being; Ayes 1, Noes 19). . .

20. Provisions relating to undue influence. . .

22. Cost of election petitions. . .

28. A proposal that bye-elections should be held within a certain time of a vacancy occurring. . .

29. Whether election law should require the source and amount of expenditure by political parties on general political propaganda between elections to be declared.

30. Whether expenditure on general political propaganda during the course of an election campaign should be subject to the provisions relating to election expenses in section 63 of the Act of 1949.

31. Whether the amount of the candidate's deposit, at present £150, should be altered; whether a lower proportion of the total votes cast, at present one-eighth, should be sufficient to secure return of the deposit; and whether any such alteration should be supplemented by a requirement that a nomination paper should be subscribed by a substantial number of electors.

32. Whether candidates' expenses should be met out of public funds.

[Final Report of the Speaker's Conference on Electoral Law. Cmnd. 3550]

CHAPTER V

THE RESPONSIBILITY OF
MINISTERS TO PARLIAMENT

There is no single doctrine of ministerial responsibility. It is a phrase which is used in a number of different senses. In the first place it describes the basic convention of constitutional monarchy – that it is the Queen's Ministers who are responsible for the government of the country. She acts on their advice. These Ministers are responsible to Parliament and owe their position to the fact that they command a majority in Parliament. That responsibility is both individual and collective. They are collectively responsible for the government of the country. They are expected to put proposals to Parliament as a body, support them as a body and resign as a body if they are defeated. This means that in the normal course of events they should be agreed on basic issues of policy, or at least that they should not carry their disagreement into the open. There have been exceptions but so far they have remained exceptions. In particular once a decision has been made Ministers are expected to stand by it and defend it, whatever their own private views. A Minister who finds himself unable to do this should resign and if he does not resign will usually be dismissed by the Prime Minister. The maintenance of collective responsibility is normally assisted in the first place by the fact that the members of the Government all belong to the same political party so that the constitutional doctrine is reinforced by party discipline and by the party's own instinct for self-preservation. Indeed the constitutional doctrine itself probably rests not only on the view that it is essential for the working of Parliamentary Government as we know it, but also that it helps to strengthen party cohesion and assists the maintenance of strong political parties. The present constitution seems to attach some importance to the principle of the strong political party – the most conspicuous expression of this being the system of voting which tends to exaggerate the majority of the winning party. It is often difficult in fact when one sees collective responsibility being enforced to know whether this is attributable to the constitutional doctrine, or to the application of party discipline, as the two merge into one another. Collective responsibility is assisted in the second place by the convention that discussions within the Government and in particular the Cabinet, are confidential and should not be made public. This aspect of collective responsibility is discussed below at p. 436.

The individual responsibility of Ministers is to the Government as a whole, and in particular the Prime Minister, who appointed and can dismiss them, and to Parliament. It is related to the organisation of the Government into departments with Ministers at their head. Ministers are primarily responsible for policy in the area of the Government's activities

137

which has been entrusted to them, for the exercise of their and their department's powers and the running of their departments. Numerous statutes emphasise the individual responsibility of Ministers by granting powers to them individually rather than to the Government as a whole, and the courts have taken the same view (see e.g. *Lavender* v. *Minister of Housing and Local Government*, below, p. 570; contrast the freedom which Ministers have to redistribute Questions among themselves). A Minister is not only expected to run his department and initiate and carry out policy in its sphere of activities but also to present, explain and defend the policy and the work of the department in Parliament. This involves piloting new legislation through Parliament, introducing and winding up debates and answering Questions. Normally he will be backed up in all this by the Government as a whole. If not he may be forced to resign, though it is not so much Parliament as his colleagues and the backbenchers in his own party, and in the last resort the Prime Minister, that will effectively determine whether he should go or stay, if he does not go voluntarily. It is rare for the Government to abandon a Minister in this way. The resignation of Sir Samuel Hoare is the most conspicuous example. Individual resignations are more frequently due to disagreements within the Government or acts of personal indiscretion, whether in Parliament, as in the case of Dalton and Profumo, or outside as with Lord Lambton and Earl Jellicoe.

In recent years it has not been Ministers' responsibility for policy that has attracted attention but their responsibility for the working of their departments. Here the principle of ministerial responsibility is joined by that of the anonymity of the civil service. This is another phrase which has more than one meaning. One aspect of anonymity has already been mentioned. It describes the wall that is commonly put round the activities of civil servants as advisers of Ministers and which is defended as being essential if they are to give frank advice to Ministers and if the convention is to be preserved that policies should be seen as the policies of Ministers and not of individual civil servants. It is a device to reduce their direct involvement in matters of political controversy. It involves not simply the anonymity of civil servants but the anonymity of the whole process and is part of that secrecy of British Government which is criticised when more openness is being advocated. But the principle of anonymity extends beyond the practice of not associating particular civil servants by name with particular policies to the practice of not naming individual civil servants associated with an example of faulty administration. Parliamentary criticism of the administration of a Department is expected to be expressed in terms of criticism of the Minister at its head. He takes the responsibility for the proper running of his Department and for taking such disciplinary measures as may be necessary. There is not only a wall around the policy making functions of the department but around its administrative functions as well.

In the past there has been one major exception to the maintenance of this wall and the anonymity of civil servants behind it. That has been when allegations of misconduct in which public interest has been aroused have led to the appointment of a committee or tribunal of inquiry with the express object of getting at the facts in order to restore public confidence. In these circumstances it has been common to publish the facts, name those responsible for any misconduct or faulty administration that has occurred, and also to announce what disciplinary action has been taken. This is not intended to affect the Ministers' responsibility in the matter. Indeed the most outstanding example of a resignation of a Minister following criticism of the civil servants in his department, in the Crichel Down case, followed such an inquiry. But apprehension has been expressed in other cases, notably that of the collapse of the Vehicle and General Insurance Company to the effect that the two principles of ministerial responsibility and anonymity of the civil service may become confused in such a case and that when a civil servant has been named the Minister may attempt to pass responsibility on to him as well. The tendency to play down the responsibility of Ministers in such circumstances has been reinforced by the growth of departments and the complexity of their activities. In any event the resignation of the Minister in the Crichel Down case was exceptional. In that respect the Ferranti case (below p. 164) was far more typical.

Discontent with the operation of the principle of ministerial responsibility in its relationship to faulty administration led in 1965 to the appointment of the Parliamentary Commissioner. Members of Parliament no longer have to be satisfied with answers to complaints made by Ministers on behalf of their civil servants but can take their complaints to the Commissioner, who has the power to conduct an investigation behind the wall and report his findings together with any recommendation he may have as regards redress. Although his powers extend to the investigation of complaints against specific individuals, safeguards are built into his procedures by the Parliamentary Commissioner Act, 1967, which he has supplemented in his own practice to protect their position. It is not his practice to name civil servants involved nor is his establishment intended to affect the principle that the Minister remains responsible. There is now therefore a method of going behind the back of the Minister in cases in which no exceptional public interest has been aroused and without breaching the principle of anonymity. Indeed when the Select Committee on the Parliamentary Commissioner tried to follow through the gap made by the Commissioner and identify particular civil servants involved in the Sachsenhausen case they were rebuffed by the Foreign Office and the Attorney-General on the grounds that this was the Minister's responsibility. It seems likely though that the provision of a regular method for the investigation of allegations of maladministration will make still more formal the Minister's acceptance of overall responsibility for the working of his department. This already seems to have happened in relation to the investigations of security cases, whether by special inquiry or now by the Security Commission. Here it seems to be the practice to identify individual civil servants who may have been careless by their office only. The whole area of security, however, including ministerial responsibility for breaches of security is clouded by the practice of keeping many of the facts relating to such breaches secret.

There are two further aspects which have attracted attention.

A Minister is responsible for policy in the field of his activities and for the performance of the functions that have been entrusted to him or his department. An important question which frequently recurs, and which may in itself raise important constitutional issues, is whether a particular function should be entrusted to him in the first place, and, if it is not, what the extent of his responsibility for the performance of that function should be. Should jurisdiction over restrictive practices be entrusted to a tribunal for which a Minister should be responsible or to the courts? Should a function be entrusted to a Minister or a local authority and if the latter what powers should the Minister retain in connection with its performance? Should the question whether a non-patrial should be refused entry to the country in the public interest be entrusted to an independent tribunal or be decided by the Home Secretary? Should responsibility for giving financial assistance to private firms be the responsibility of a department advised if need be by an independent committee or by an independent body subject only to general powers of ministerial control? The tendency to create semi-autonomous bodies to assist in the performance of governmental functions, whether they be bodies like the Boundary Commissions, or more importantly bodies in the economic field such as the National Board for Prices and Incomes, the National Economic Development Council, the Bank of England, and the nationalised industries, has often obscured the real responsibility for decisions and made Parliamentary supervision on the basis of the principle of ministerial responsibility alone difficult. And the obscurity has been increased by the growth of grey areas in which Ministers and the Government exercise influence or exhort in situations in which they have no statutory authority or in which they are unwilling to use such authority as they have, yet where the exhortation may be difficult to refuse.

Some of these problems have emerged most clearly in relation to the nationalised industries, but they are by no means confined to them. The response in Parliament to the nationalised industries was first to adapt the traditional methods of Parliamentary Questions and ministerial responsibility so far as possible to the new situation and then, after some hesitation, to establish a Select Committee with the specific task of conducting a direct examination of those responsible for the running of the nationalised industries as well as officials and Ministers in the sponsoring Departments. In 1969 this Committee's terms of reference were extended to include some at least of the activities of the Bank of England. The parliamentary response to other developments in the economic field has necessarily been more general and has culminated in the recent establishment of an Expenditure Committee which has been designed in part to investigate and report on the problems of the economy as a whole, concentrating in the first instance on the problems of public expenditure, but including as well such problems as those relating to the general relationships between government and industry. The importance of these developments can hardly be exaggerated. Those who by their practice established the present principles of the constitution did so when the Government's role in the economy was minimal. It has now become one of the key tests of the satisfactoriness of the United Kingdom's present constitutional arrangements.

It is not however the only one. For another major development which has raised problems about the traditional methods of securing accountability to Parliament of the activities of the Government has been Britain's entry into the European Economic Community. Some of the problems thus raised are touched on below at p. 300.

There is one last aspect of the principle of ministerial responsibility that should be mentioned. It is part of the 'strong government' syndrome. It involves the assertion that, given the principle of Ministerial responsibility to Parliament, Governments should be left free to take such action as they may think best, subject to their ability to carry Parliament, with the support of their majority in it, with them. This is seen at its most conspicuous in foreign affairs which has always been a no-man's land of constitutional law. In direct contradiction to this assertion however there has been an increasing demand for wider participation in the formulation of policy at all levels of government, local as well as central, and the provision of information which will make that participation possible. This question of the openness of and participation in the processes of government is discussed further below at p. 435.

I. DEFEAT IN THE HOUSE OF COMMONS

A Government holds office because it commands a majority in the House of Commons. If it loses its majority it should resign or the Prime Minister should request a dissolution. The best evidence that it has lost its majority is when it is defeated on a vote of confidence or on a matter which the Government regard as sufficiently important to treat as a vote of no confidence. Governments suffer defeats from time to time, e.g. on Committee stages of Bills, though usually they will take steps to reverse these decisions at a later stage in the Bill's progress. Such defeats do not put their tenure of office in jeopardy. Minority governments or governments with a very small majority, the kind whose strength in the House of Commons at any particular time can be affected by such things as illnesses and unavoidable absences, are a special case.

Labour Government, 1924

In the General Election in December 1923 the Conservative Government under Baldwin won the largest number of seats, but failed to win an overall majority and on an amendment to the Address in Reply to the King's Speech was defeated by a combination of Labour and Liberal votes. Baldwin resigned and MacDonald, as leader of the second largest party, formed the first Labour Government with the discriminating support of the Liberals.

THE PRIME MINISTER (MR J. RAMSAY MACDONALD): ... For the time
being no party in this House has a majority. The party opposite is the
largest of the three, but on account of the circumstances of the
Election, it is impossible for this House to ask them to remain in
power. As the second party, the Labour party has accepted the responsibility of office. I think that that will necessitate some alteration in
our House of Commons habits. I think that we will have less to say
about party . . . and that we shall lay more and more emphasis upon
the responsibility of individual Members of this House. . . It puts me
in this position, however: I have a lively recollection of all sorts of
ingenuities practiced by Oppositions in order to spring a snap division upon a Government, so that it might turn it out upon a defeat.
I have known bathrooms downstairs utilised, not for their legitimate
purpose, but for the illegitimate purpose of packing as many Members surreptitiously inside their doors as their physical limitations
would allow. I have known an adjoining building, where there happens to be a convenient Division bell, used for similar purposes. I
have seen the House, practically empty when the bells began to
ring, suddenly transformed into a very riotous sort of market-place
by the inrush of Members, doing their best for their nation, for the
House of Commons and for their party, to find a Government nap-
ping, and to turn it out upon a stupid issue.

I am going out on no such issue. . . The Labour Government will
go out if it be defeated upon substantial issues, issues of principle,
issues that really matter. It will go out if the responsible leaders of
either party or any party move a direct vote of no confidence, and
carry that vote. But I propose to introduce my business, knowing
that I am in a minority, accepting the responsibilities of a minority,
and claiming the privileges that attach to those responsibilities. If
the House on matters non-essential, matters of mere opinion, matters that do not strike at the root of the proposals that we make, and
do not destroy fundamentally the general intentions of the Government in introducing legislation – if the House wish to vary our proposition, the House must take the responsibility for that variation –
then a division on such amendments and questions as those will not
be regarded as a vote of no confidence.

[169 H.C.Deb. 5s. c. 749. 12 February 1924]

The Prime Minister eventually advised a dissolution after the Government
had been defeated over the Campbell Case (below, p. 515), a matter
which, at the end of the debate, Lieut.-Commander Kenworthy said was
'not a sufficiently grave matter for which to inflict 600 elections on the
country'. The debate, on 8 October 1924, was opened by Sir Robert
Horne for the Conservative party with the motion 'That the conduct of

His Majesty's Government in relation to the institution and subsequent withdrawal of criminal proceedings against the editor of the *Worker's Weekly* is deserving of the censure of this House.' Sir John Simon for the Liberals moved an amendment to this motion calling for the appointment of a Select Committee on which, because of the balance of parties in the House, the Government would have been in the minority. The Prime Minister announced that the Government would treat both motions as matters of confidence. The Conservatives decided to support the Liberal amendment which was carried against the Government by 364 votes to 198 (177 H.C.Deb. 5s. c. 581ff.).

Labour Government, 1974

At the General Election in February 1974 no party secured an overall majority. Mr Wilson formed a Government as leader of the largest party.

THE PRIME MINISTER (MR HAROLD WILSON): . . . The Government intend to treat with suitable respect, but not with exaggerated respect, the results of any snap vote or any snap Division. . .

In case of a Government defeat, either in such circumstances or in a more clear expression of opinion, the Government will consider their position and make a definitive statement after due consideration. But the Government will not be forced to go to the country except in a situation in which every hon. Member in the House was voting knowing the full consequences of his vote.

MR HEATH: I suspect that the statement which the Prime Minister has made is of considerable significance, particularly to him. But will he kindly explain how he proposes to ascertain that every hon. Member of the House who was voting was in full possession of his judgment?

THE PRIME MINISTER: . . . What I am trying to say is that a snap Division or even, perhaps in some cases, a more substantial one . . . would not necessarily mean, and would not, indeed, immediately mean, any fundamental decision about the future of the Government or about a dissolution. I am saying that if there were to be anything put to the House which could have those consequences, every hon. Member would have it explained to him in the House by the Government before he voted. . .

MR HEATH: I am sorry to interrupt the Prime Minister again, but this matter is obviously of great importance. Is he saying that no matter how major a question it is, if the Government themselves do not warn the House of Commons that they will resign afterwards, the Government will then refuse to resign?

THE PRIME MINISTER: The right hon. Gentleman knows the difference between a snap Division – he knows the difference between a Division which was not a snap Division but a considered one, as he found a number of times – and a vote of confidence. It is a vote of confidence about which I am speaking. . . In other words, we shall provide a recount.

[870 H.C.Deb. 5s. c. 70. 12 March 1974]

II. THE RESPONSIBILITY OF INDIVIDUAL MINISTERS

(i) Acts of policy

Sir Samuel Hoare, 1935

Sir Samuel Hoare became Foreign Secretary in June 1935. In October Italy, under Mussolini, invaded Abyssinia. The League of Nations declared Italy to be an aggressor and authorized the application of economic sanctions against her. At the same time it appointed a committee to seek a settlement of the problem. Its leading members were M. Laval, the French Foreign Minister, and Sir Samuel Hoare. In November there was a General Election. In its manifesto the Government declared its support for the League of Nations and collective resistance to aggression. It won a majority of 250 seats.

On 9 December it was announced in the French press that the Foreign Secretary, on his way to a holiday in Switzerland, had reached agreement with Laval as to the basis of a settlement which was to be recommended to Italy and Abyssinia. There was some debate in the House of Commons on 10 December, and a further debate was fixed for 19 December. By that time it had become clear that the proposals, which involved ceding some of Abyssinia to Italy and treating other areas of it as spheres of influence reserved to Italy, were extremely unpopular. On 18 December it was announced that the Government had reversed its previous decision accepting the proposals and that the Foreign Secretary had resigned.

The debate the next day began with a personal statement from Sir Samuel Hoare in which he maintained that the terms proposed were the only terms likely to be an acceptable basis for a settlement.

'SIR SAMUEL HOARE: . . . So far as the judgment of others is concerned, I am painfully aware that a great body of opinion is intensely critical of the course that I adopted. Knowing my own deficiencies, having no illusions about my own abilities, I should naturally have wished to accept the view of this great body of men and women from one end of the country to the other, but, looking at the situation as I see it, looking back at the position in which I was placed a fortnight ago, I say to the House that I cannot honestly recant. I sincerely believe that the course that I took was the only course that was possible in the circumstances. . . In any case, there is the hard ineluctable fact that for the time being I feel that I have not got the confidence of the great body of opinion in the country, and I feel that it is essential for the Foreign Secretary, more than any other Minister in the Government, to have behind him the general approval of his fellow-countrymen. I have not got that general approval behind me today. As soon as I realised this fact, without any prompting, without any suggestion from anyone, I asked the Prime Minister to accept my resignation ' [307 H.C.Deb. 5s. c. 2016].

Mr Attlee, for the Opposition, then moved (c. 2017): ' That the terms put forward by His Majesty's Government as a basis for an Italo-Abyssinian settlement reward the declared aggressor at the expense of the victim, destroy collective security, and conflict with the expressed will of the country and with the Covenant of the League of Nations, to the support of which the honour of Great Britain is pledged; this House, therefore, demands that these terms be immediately repudiated.'

' For our part ', he said in his speech, ' we cannot accept, unless we have very positive evidence, the right hon. Gentleman being made the scapegoat for acts for which, I believe, I shall show that the Government have taken collective responsibility. If it is right for the right hon. Gentleman to resign, then it is right for the Government to resign.'

THE PRIME MINISTER (MR BALDWIN): . . . We were not aware until it had been accomplished that an agreement had been come to. It was not until breakfast time on Monday morning [9 December] that I received a letter from my right hon. Friend urging that the Cabinet might endorse what he had done, as he believed it to be a necessary piece of work at the moment. Almost immediately afterwards, and before we had time to study the documents, the leakage took place. . . We were summoned to consider whether we would endorse the action of our colleague or whether we would repudiate it. There was no time, as it seemed to us then, for discussion owing to the leakage that had taken place. We had to decide quickly because we knew that a storm of questions would be upon us and that the matter would be raised in this House. We none of us liked the proposals; we thought they went too far. . . Here, although we were all responsible, the chief responsibility was mine, as it must be, and I decided at once that I must support the colleague who was not present to give his reasons, not present to be examined. . . I can quite see, looking back, that I ought at any cost to have fetched back my colleague from Switzerland. . . If I thought of it, I dismissed it in a moment because I knew how necessary rest was for him. His health had been causing me anxiety. . . You may say that it was an act of weakness on my part. It certainly was an error of judgment. It certainly was an error with which we were all concerned, but for which I am chiefly responsible. . . Since the War there has grown up, largely owing to the functioning of the League of Nations, a practice for Ministers in high positions to have discussions with one another on the Continent and sometimes to reach conclusions, but there is a real difficulty in maintaining that liaison which ought to be maintained with the Cabinet at home. . .

MR LEES SMITH: Before the Prime Minister passes from that

point, will he allow me to put a question, for I am sure he wishes to make this clear? He received this communication at breakfast time, and he has explained how he had to take a difficult personal decision. But there was a Cabinet meeting at 6 o'clock on the Monday night, and it is necessary to make it clear whether his decision was placed before the Cabinet and became, therefore, the collective responsibility of the Government.

THE PRIME MINISTER: . . . The responsibility was that of myself and my colleagues, and it is the responsibility of each and all of us. I think that everyone who has had Cabinet experience will admit that that is the position. . . I am coming shortly to what is the position of the Government but I would like to make clear that never throughout that week had I or any one of my colleagues any idea in our own minds that we were not being true to every pledge we had given in the Election. [HON. MEMBERS: ' Oh! '] . . . I was not expecting that deeper feeling which was manifested by many of my hon. Friends and friends in many parts of the country on what I may call the ground of conscience and of honour. The moment I am confronted with that I know that something has happened that has appealed to the deepest feelings of our countrymen, that some note has been struck that brings back from them a response from the depths. I examined again all that I had done, and I felt that with that feeling, which was perfectly obvious, there could not be the support in this country behind those proposals even as terms of negotiation. . . [T]he proposals are absolutely and completely dead. This Government is certainly going to make no attempt to resurrect them. . .

[307 H.C.Deb. 5s. c. 2032. 19 December 1935]

The debate ended with a division on an amendment moved by Earl Winterton (c. 2052): ' to leave out from " That " to the end of the Question, and to add instead thereof " This House, holding that any terms for settling the Italian-Abyssinian dispute should be such as the League can accept, assures His Majesty's Government of its full support, in pursuing the foreign policy outlined in the Government manifesto and endorsed by the country at the recent general election." ' This was carried by 397 votes to 165.

Sir Samuel Hoare returned to office as First Lord of the Admiralty in June 1936.

(ii) Parliamentary Questions

3. The rules for Questions, as set out in May's Parliamentary Practice (18th ed. pp. 232 et seq.), are derived in the main from decisions given over a long period by successive Speakers in relation to individual Questions.

4. The definition of an admissible Question is one which asks for information or action. . .

5. To be in order, a Question must relate to a matter within the Government's responsibility or one which could be made so by administrative or legislative action. . . [T]he point of Questions is to hold the Government responsible, and not merely to raise interesting general topics of the day, or the affairs of institutions for whom the Government is not answerable. . .

6. . . . [A] Question must not already be covered by a . . . refusal to answer given in the same Session. Furthermore, Questions on some subjects are out of order because refusals to answer, by successive administrations, have been so consistent that it has been ruled that such subjects cannot be raised by way of Questions. Examples of this class, are Questions that relate to details of arrangements for national security; to the use of Ministerial reserve powers relating to the content of the broadcasting authorities' programmes; and to matters of detail within the day-to-day responsibilities of nationalised boards.

7. The ability of the Government to block questioning by means of a refusal to answer is a consequence of its being under no obligation to answer any particular Question at all. This right is so powerful a protection against legitimate enquiry, however, that although no instances of abuse have been drawn to Your Committee's attention, they consider that the present absolute rule against Questions refused an answer should be modified. To abandon the rule altogether would be to invite Questions that were merely argumentative, and the valuable distinction between questioning and debate would be lost. (For example, Questions asking a Minister to withdraw a particular Bill could rapidly reach the proportions of a campaign.) Your Committee recommend, however, that where a Minister has refused to take the action or give the information asked for in a Question he should be able to be asked the same Question in three months' time. In relation to those matters which are currently considered to be closed altogether, Ministers should be able to be asked once every Session whether they will now answer such Questions. In this way, Governments will be required regularly to review their policy in regard to refusing to answer Questions, and their mere refusal will not close the issue. . .

APPENDIX 9

Matters about which successive Administrations have refused to answer Questions

Memorandum by the Principal Clerk of the Table Office

Agriculture

Day to day matters of agricultural marketing boards.
Day to day matters of British Sugar Corporation.
Day to day matters of Meat and Livestock Commission ...
Day to day matters of White Fish Authority ...

Attorney General

Details of investigations by Director of Public Prosecutions.
Day to day administration of the Legal Aid Scheme.
Particulars of inquiries made by the Queen's Proctor.

Defence

Details of arms sales.
Operational matters.
Contract prices.
Costs of individual aircraft etc.
Details of research and development ...

Education

Curricular matters.
Discipline in schools.
Detailed expenditure within universities.
The Arts Council (no intervention on policy, or statistics of individual grants).
Instructions to research councils.

Employment

Strike statistics for individual firms.
Numbers employed in individual firms.
Detailed matters of Industrial Training Boards ...
Day to day workings of the National Dock Labour Board.
Forecasts of future levels of unemployment.
Forecasts of future trends in incomes.

Environment

Forecasts of housing starts.
Council house waiting lists.
Rents for Government offices.
Sports Council.

Exchequer
Economic and budgetary forecasts.
Bank rate.
Exchange Equalisation Account.
Government borrowing.
Sterling Balances.
Tax affairs of individuals or companies.
Day to day matters of the Bank of England.
Commercial activities of British Petroleum . . .

Foreign and Commonwealth
Proceedings of Commonwealth Sanctions Committee.
Supply of arms . . .
Elections in Security Council.
Ministerial meetings of W.E.U.; N.A.T.O. Council.
Attendance records at Council of Europe.
O.E.C.D. meetings.

Home
Telephone tapping.
Names of prohibited immigrants.
Regional seats of government.
Security source operations.
Operational matters for the police . . .

Northern Ireland
Intelligence sources.

Posts and Telecommunications
Programme content.

Prime Minister
Telephone tapping.
Cabinet Committees.
Cost of the ' hot line '.
Security arrangements at Chequers.
Detailed arrangements for the conduct of Government business.
List of future engagements.

Social Services
Purchasing contracts in the N.H.S.
Reasons for appointing individual members of hospital boards . . .
Day to day running of General Practice Finance Corporation.
Personal information gained from social security schemes.

Trade and Industry
Commercial activities of the Overseas Marketing Corporation . . .
Relations between E.C.G.D. and individual exporters.

Reasons for refusal to refer mergers to Monopolies Commission.

Names of complainants about companies.

Individual transactions between National Film Finance Corporation and customers.

Day to day matters for English Tourist Board.

Details of defence research establishments.

Details of research contracts.

Forecast of price movements.

Advice from Economic Planning Councils.

Details of financial assistance to individual companies.

Individual applicants for I.D.C.'s . . .

Nationalised Industries

Day to day matters.

Statistics other than national.

Matters of commercial confidence.

[Report from the Select Committee on Parliamentary Questions. H.C. 393 of 1971–2, 17 July 1972]

On 18 December 1972 the Government accepted and the House of Commons agreed to the recommendations made by the Select Committee to the effect that there should be a regular revision of the classes of Questions which Ministers were not prepared to answer [848 H.C.Deb. 5s. c. 1070].

Commander Crabb (presumed death)

THE PRIME MINISTER (SIR ANTHONY EDEN): . . . It would not be in the public interest to disclose the circumstances in which Commander Crabb is presumed to have met his death.

While it is the practice for Ministers to accept responsibility I think it necessary, in the special circumstances of this case, to make it clear that what was done was done without the authority or the knowledge of Her Majesty's Ministers. Appropriate disciplinary steps are being taken.

MR DUGDALE: Is the Prime Minister aware that that is one of the most extraordinary statements made by a Prime Minister in the House of Commons, and that, whatever he may say to the contrary it is a complete evasion of Ministerial responsibility? May I ask him one or two questions? Whether he will answer them or not appears doubtful. First why was Commander Crabb diving in the close vicinity of the Soviet cruiser which was here on a friendly visit? Secondly why, and under whose authority, was a police officer sent to the hotel at which Commander Crabb was staying, and why did he order the leaves to be torn from the register showing the names both of Commander Crabb and of the man with whom he stayed? Further, what was the name of that older man and why did the police officer threaten the hotel keeper with action under the Official Secrets Act if he did not allow that to be done?

THE PRIME MINISTER: I thought it right to make the statement which I have made to the House, and I have nothing to add to it. . .

MR SHINWELL: The right hon. Gentleman has just told the House that he proposes to take disciplinary action. Will he be good enough to say against whom he is taking disciplinary action, and for what reason he is taking this disciplinary action?

THE PRIME MINISTER: No, Sir. What I have said in my statement was that disciplinary steps are being taken. That is so. . .

MR DUGDALE: In view of the Government's most unsatisfactory Answer, I beg to ask leave to move the Adjournment of the House under Standing Order No. 9 to call attention to a definite matter of urgent public importance, namely, the failure of Her Majesty's Government to give a satisfactory explanation to the country about the events connected with the disappearance of Commander Crabb.

MR SPEAKER: This application is covered by authority. When a Minister refuses to answer a Question on the grounds of public interest, it has been ruled in the past – and I adhere to it myself – that that is a matter which cannot be raised under the Standing Order. Therefore, I must decline to admit the right hon. Member's application.[1]

[552 H.C.Deb. 5s. c. 1220. 9 May 1956]

[1] On 30 May 1956, the Government published the text of Notes exchanged between it and the Soviet Government over the incident. The translation of the Soviet Government's Note read:

' The Embassy of the Union of Soviet Socialist Republics in Great Britain presents its compliments to the Foreign Office and has the honour to state as follows:

During the stay of the Soviet warships at Portsmouth, at 7.30 hours on 19th April, three sailors of the Soviet vessels discovered a diver swimming between the Soviet destroyers at their moorings at the South River jetty. The diver, dressed in a black light-diving suit with flippers on his feet, was on the surface of the water for the space of one or two minutes and then dived again under the destroyer " Smotryashchie ".

The Commander of the Soviet warships, Rear-Admiral V. F. Kotov, in conversation with the Chief of Staff of the Portsmouth naval base, Rear-Admiral Burnett, drew attention to the fact of the appearance of the diver near the anchorages of the Soviet vessels, immediately alongside the destroyers.

Rear-Admiral Burnett categorically denied the possibility of the appearance of a diver alongside the Soviet vessels and declared that at the time no diving operations of any kind were being carried out. In reality, how-

The matter was raised again on 14 May 1956.

MR HUGH GAITSKELL (*Leeds, South*) . . . [T]he Opposition . . . recognise the unfortunate necessity in present conditions, for secret services. . . Also we fully appreciate that details of the activities of these services cannot be disclosed as are the activities of other Government Departments. . . However . . . Parliament accepts that situation, and refrains from pressing these matters, and . . . Ministers exercising their undoubted rights, refuse to give information on what I think may be regarded as certain generally accepted assumptions.

These assumptions are: first, that the operations of these services are ultimately and effectively controlled by Ministers or by a Minister; secondly, that their operations are secret; thirdly, that what they do does not embarrass us in our international relations. And perhaps one might add, fourthly, that what they do appears, as far as we can make out, to be reasonably successful – [*Laughter.*] – in this sense, that if there were a widespread feeling that the secret services were extremely incompetent and inept, then it would be the duty of hon. Members to raise the matter.

It is an unfortunate fact that, in the episode which we are

---

ever, as appears from information reported in the British Press of 30th April last, there is confirmation of the fact that the British Naval Authorities were actually carrying out secret diving investigations in the vicinity of the anchored Soviet vessels at Portsmouth. Moreover, the carrying out of these investigations caused a fatality to a British diver. It is sufficient to quote that the " Daily Sketch " in reporting the loss of the diver Crabb, stated as follows: —

" He went into the water for the last time at Stokes Bay, Portsmouth, on secret investigatory work near to the anchorage of the Soviet cruiser ' Ordzhonikidze '."

Attaching as it does important significance to such an unusual occurrence as the carrying out of secret diving operations alongside Soviet warships visiting the British Naval Base at Portsmouth, the Embassy would be grateful to the British Foreign Office to receive an explanation on this question. *London, 4th May,* 1956.'

The Foreign Office replied:

' The Foreign Office presents its compliments to the Embassy of the Union of Soviet Socialist Republics and has the honour to make the following reply to the Embassy's note of 4th May.

As has already been publicly announced, Commander Crabb was engaged on diving tests and is presumed to have met his death whilst so engaged.

The diver, who as stated in the Soviet note was observed from the Soviet warships to be swimming between the Soviet destroyers, was presumably Commander Crabb. His approach to the destroyer was completely unauthorised and Her Majesty's Government desire to express their regret at the incident. FOREIGN OFFICE, S.W.1., *9th May,* 1956.'

discussing, none of these four conditions appears to have been fulfilled. . .

Now may I say a word about Ministerial responsibility in this matter. It is the custom for Ministers to cover up any decision by a civil servant; that is to say, normally the Minister not merely takes responsibility but appears to have taken that decision himself, whether, in fact, he did so or not. Even when this is not done and, of course, there are quite a number of occasions when it would be pedantic to insist that it should be done; when, in fact, a Minister comes to the House, and says, ' One of my officials made a mistake ', thereby implying that he, the Minister, was not directly responsible for that mistake, nevertheless it is a sound and vital constitutional principle that the Minister takes responsibility for what has happened.

That is a principle which I venture to say is fundamental to our democracy, because if we were to depart from it, it would imply that the Civil Service in some way or other was independent and not answerable to this House. Of course, the extent to which we condemn a Minister for an act of one of his officers, or a failure by one of his officers, obviously depends on the circumstances. There are minor occasions when a Minister admits that something has gone wrong and the House accepts it and the matter is left. . . [N]one of us would ask that the Prime Minister should disclose what ought not to be disclosed. . . Subject to this . . . it is the duty of any Opposition . . . to probe any weakness or what appears to be blunders or mistakes in Government administration.

Mr. Gaitskell then asked a number of questions about the events surrounding the incident e.g. the level at which the decision to undertake the enterprise was taken and who authorised the destruction of the pages in the hotel register which were said to have recorded that Commander Crabb had stayed there.

[W]hile we must be careful . . . democracy also must be made to work. We as the Parliament in a democracy, have the right to have our fears allayed, our anxieties extinguished; or at any rate we have the right to be satisfied that the Government are taking steps to put matters right.

THE PRIME MINISTER (SIR ANTHONY EDEN) . . . We are dealing tonight, I must say frankly to the House, with circumstances in which no Government here or in any other country, I believe, would say more than I am prepared to say to the House tonight; nor is there anything contrary to our practice, as the House knows, in taking this action. It is often done in defence. A classic example was the atomic bomb, where the whole expenditure – £100 million – was concealed in the Estimates for a number of years.

Similarly in international affairs. . . it is often contrary to the public interest to disclose the details of correspondence with a foreign Government or to reveal the course of negotiations with a foreign Government leading up to treaties or other agreements. . .

Again, to take our domestic affairs, there are many things which the Home Secretary, for instance, is not obliged to state publicly. He has not to disclose the grounds on which he has decided to deport an alien or those on which he grants or refuses a certificate of naturalisation. The right hon. Gentleman has spoken very freely about the secret services and speculated about their control, their organisation, and their efficiency. I am sorry to have to say that I am not prepared to discuss those matters in the House. It is easy – and I am not complaining – for the right hon. Gentleman to suggest or imply that all is not well. I could not answer him, because I could not answer him either generally or in detail without disclosing matters which, as he must recognise, must remain secret. That is why it is not the practice . . . to discuss these matters openly in the House, and I am not prepared to break that precedent.

I think it must be clear that it must be left to the discretion of Ministers to decide these matters. Only the Minister can judge; his discretion in this particular respect is absolute. It should be clear from this practice that the Minister cannot disclose the reasons for his decision. Obviously, if he were to disclose his reasons, it would be disclosing what he judged to be contrary itself to the public interest. . .

[T]herefore on this particular aspect of the matter I must tell the House now that I have not one word more to say than I announced on Wednesday. But I should like to comment on the second part of the statement which I made in the House last week. . .

I then took the exceptional course of making it plain that what was done was done without the authority of Her Majesty's Ministers. . .

We all know, in fact, that many actions are taken by servants of the Crown for which the authority of Ministers is not asked and, of course, that must always be so in any complex society such as ours today. The right hon. Gentleman is perfectly correct in saying that on these occasions it is nonetheless accepted that Ministers of the Government, collectively, are responsible to Parliament for the actions of officials.

I pondered long before I departed from that axiom in this case. . . In this instance there were special circumstances which, I judged, compelled me to state that what happened, or was thought to have happened, had been done without the authority of Ministers.

At that time my colleagues and I had been conducting important discussions with the Soviet leaders. We were completely unaware of any episode of this kind. Had I not made that clear publicly, doubt would inevitably have been thrown on the sincerity of our position during those discussions. That is a very serious and a very exceptional situation, but it explains to the House why, on that account, I thought it right to take the very unusual course I did of making that statement. . .

Having made it clear that what was done without the authority of Ministers I also found it necessary to let it be known that disciplinary steps were being taken. That in itself is, in part, an answer to what the right hon. Gentleman has just said. It shows that the Government are determined that the proper measures of control and authority should be exercised by Ministers in all matters of this kind.

[552 H.C.Deb. 5s. c. 1751. 14 May 1956]

(iii) Acts of civil servants

Crichel Down, 1954

Crichel Down was an area of land in Dorset compulsorily acquired by the Air Ministry in 1937 for use as a bombing range. When the Ministry no longer needed it after the war, it was transferred to the Ministry of Agriculture, where it was administered by an independent Agricultural Land Commission, set up under the Agriculture Act, 1947. The Commission decided that the best way to farm it was to equip it as a single unit and then let it (although it was made up of parcels of land taken from the estates of a number of previous owners). A number of local farmers applied to be considered as tenants and were told they would be sent details when the land became available. More important however was the interest shown by Commander Marten whose wife had succeeded to the ownership of one of the estates from which land had been taken in the first place. Even before the Commission had decided what to do with the land he had asked whether he could buy back the land that had been acquired from her estate. His first request was refused because it was mistakenly believed by the Commission that the Minister had no power to sell. This mistake had been discovered by the time he approached the Parliamentary Secretary to the Ministry of Agriculture through his Member of Parliament and repeated his request. The Parliamentary Secretary requested a report on the desirability of selling back the land. The report which he received advised against it. What he did not know, however, was that the report had been compiled by Mr Brown, a relatively junior subordinate, who for no clear reason had been told that his inquiries were to be confidential and that in particular he was not to approach the former owners, even though one of the crucial issues was whether the land could be better farmed from their land or as a single unit. As a result the report contained mis-statements of fact, including the statement that the land had been voluntarily acquired by the Air Ministry, in the first place, and that it had been in a bad condition. Reservations expressed about the financial viability of the Commission's proposals which had been inserted by one of his superiors disappeared on the way up the hierarchy. The land was in fact offered to the Crown Lands Commission, the body responsible for administering the hereditary estates of the Crown, who found a tenant, Mr Tozer, for it. The previous applications from local farmers were overlooked. When they were remembered Mr Eastwood, the Permanent Commissioner of Crown Lands, suggested to Mr Thompson, Crown Lands agent in Dorset, that something should be done to make it appear that their applications had been considered, and Mr Wilcox, an Under-Secretary at the Ministry, agreed. A request by Commander Marten to rent the whole area and farm it from his estate was rejected after some delay on the grounds that Crown Lands were already committed to Mr Tozer.

Eventually Commander Marten and a number of local landowners petitioned the Minister for an inquiry. The Minister, Sir Thomas Dugdale, appointed Sir Andrew Clark to conduct it. It was in his report that the facts finally emerged.

Sir Andrew Clark's conclusions [2]

(i) When the Minister came to his decision in December 1952, that as a matter of policy Crichel Down ought to be equipped and farmed as one unit, the true facts and considerations were not fully brought to his notice. The facts were assumed by the Ministry to have been correctly stated in Mr Brown's report, which they were not. The true financial position, in particular, had never been brought to the notice of the Ministry.

(ii) The Land Commission were a comparatively new body, very anxious to gain experience by trying their hand at a new and interesting venture such as equipping Crichel Down as a model farm, and in their eagerness to ensure that they were not deprived of the opportunity they adopted an irresponsible attitude towards the expenditure of public money and they were not always as frank with the Ministry as they might have been.

(iii) There was a lamentable exhibition of muddle and inefficiency over obtaining the report that was called for from the Lands Service in July 1952.

(iv) There was a most regrettable attitude of hostility to Lieut.-Commander Marten evinced by some of the officials involved. There was no excuse for this attitude. It was engendered solely by a feeling of irritation that any member of the public should have the temerity to oppose or even question the acts or decisions of officials of a Government or State Department.

(v) The attitude adopted by Mr Thomson and Mr Eastwood, that they were already too far committed to Mr Tozer when they heard of the previous applications, was wholly unjustified and was dictated solely by

[2] Report of the public inquiry into the disposal of land at Crichel Down (Cmd. 9176).

a determination not to allow anything to interfere with the plans they had in mind. The improper suggestion that the previous applicants should be misled needed no further comment.

(vi) There was no trace in this case of anything in the nature of bribery, corruption or personal dishonesty.

The Prime Minister appointed a small committee to consider whether any of the civil servants whose conduct was criticized by Sir Andrew Clark should be transferred. They made the following comment on Sir Andrew Clark's report:

' Apart altogether from the treatment of the claims of former owners or of other applicants for tenancies, Sir Andrew Clark's Report is critical of the administrative handling öf the disposal of Crichel Down in a number of respects – for example, the assessment of the financial implications, the preparation of reports, and the briefing of the Minister. His criticisms are in the main expressed in terms of the actions of individual officers. Having had the opportunity of considering not only the report but also the observations of the men concerned, and of questioning them on the sequence of events, we think it material to record our strong impression that some part of the deficiencies disclosed in the handling of this case may have been due as much to the organisational relationship between the headquarters of the Ministry of Agriculture and Fisheries, the Agricultural Land Commission and the Agricultural Land Service as to the faults of individuals' (Cmd. 9220 (1953–4)).

On 15 June 1954 Sir Thomas Dugdale made a statement in the House of Commons. This was followed by a debate on 20 July.

THE MINISTER OF AGRICULTURE (SIR T. DUGDALE): . . . Sir Andrew Clark states in Conclusion 25 of his Report that ' there was no trace in this case of anything in the nature of bribery, corruption or personal dishonesty.' The Inquiry has thus achieved my main purpose, which was to deal with any rumours and suggestions of this kind.

The Report contains criticisms of the actions and conduct of the Agricultural Land Commission and of a number of individuals. So far as those criticised are persons – and most of them are – for whose conduct I am answerable as a Minister of the Crown, the responsibility rests with me. That responsibility I wholly accept.

I have naturally given to those who are criticised an opportunity of making to me such observations as they wished on those parts of the Report which referred to them. Having considered the observations and explanations I have received, I must in fairness say that I have formed a less unfavourable view of many of the actions taken by those concerned than appears in the Report.

Mistakes and errors of judgment were made which those concerned regret as much as I do; and steps are being taken, so far as possible to see that these do not happen again. In view of the nature of the errors themselves and of the public way in which they have been exposed, I am satisfied that no further action by me in relation to them is necessary...

I will make a statement, on behalf of the Government, on the general policy relating to the disposal of land purchased compulsorily for public purposes as soon as a debate can be arranged...

[528 H.C.Deb. 5s. c. 1745. 15 June 1954]

THE MINISTER OF AGRICULTURE (SIR THOMAS DUGDALE): ...When in 1950 the Air Ministry no longer required the land, the Ministry of Agriculture took it over for agricultural use. My predecessor... in 1950 placed it under the management of the Agricultural Land Commission, the members of which are independent persons and not officials... [T]he Commission... came to the conclusion that... this area of 725 acres was likely to be more productive as one farm with a resident farmer than if farmed as the outlying land of neighbouring farms... [T]he Commission took the view that financially the scheme was justified...

When Commander Marten approached us in June, 1952, the matter had to be considered entirely afresh, this time from the angle of possible resale to the successors of the former owners...

The Commission reconsidered the matter and its advice was the same as its conclusion in August, 1950...

In deciding what advice to give me, it had to assess all the relevant factors, and for this purpose it is naturally supplied with information and advice by the officers serving it. The Commission has all this information and advice before it when discussing and formulating its own conclusions, but... having decided upon the opinion which, as a Commission, it wishes to give to me, it is no part of its duty to supply me also with the material which it has considered in reaching its conclusions.

After all, one of the advantages of seeking the views of an independent body like the Commission is that it can sift the evidence and reach a considered opinion in the light of that evidence, and, in accordance with its normal practice, the Commission did not attach to the considered opinion in this case which it sent me any of the material which had been placed before it, whether it was in favour of or contrary to the views which the Commission expressed. I am satisfied that there was no question of the Commission deliberately withholding information from me which it was part of its duty to pass on.

After receiving the Commission's advice. I thought it right, in the circumstances, to ask Lord Carrington, the Joint Parliamentary Secretary, to go down and make a personal inspection to see if he concurred in the views expressed. This he did, and again, looking at the matter purely from the point of view of agricultual management, he came to the conclusion that the proposal to equip the land as one farm was right.

This was the position towards the end of 1952. . .

. . . It is true that at that time both the Land Commission and I were under certain misapprehensions about both the condition of the land when the Air Ministry acquired it in 1937 and the form of acquisition of most of it. These questions, though clearly important, do not, I think, affect the core of the agricultural management problem which had to be decided in 1952.

I decided that I had no reason to reject the advice that I had received on the agricultural and financial merits. . .

I had now to decide whether, in spite of that, I should nevertheless sell the land back to the successors of the former owners because of the claim that Commander Marten was pressing for the return of his wife's property. The moral aspect of this claim was fully argued before I reached my decision. It is true, as I have said, that I was told incorrectly that the land from the Crichel and Langton Estates had been sold voluntarily, but I did not at the time regard the difference between voluntary and compulsory purchase as decisive. I recognised that the land owners concerned would have known that, failing agreement, compulsory powers could be exercised. . . I decided that the right course was to go ahead with the equipment of the land as one farm, and I gave instructions accordingly. I accept full responsibility for that decision, and I have endeavoured to explain to the House the reasons which led me to it. . .

Now I come to the next part of the story. I come to the sale to the Commissioners of Crown Lands. As the House will know, the Commissioners are in effect a body of trustees whose duty it is to administer the hereditary estates of the Crown. The capital remains the property of the Crown, but the income is surrendered to Parliament in exchange for the Civil List. Their Statutes provide for the reinvestment in land of any money which they receive from the sale of land. At that time I knew that they were looking out for land to purchase. I knew also that if they brought the Crichel Down land on condition that they equipped it, they could be relied on to observe that condition. They were approached, and their officials went into the whole question.

Although I am, *ex officio*, a Commissioner of Crown Lands as well as the Minister of Agriculture, the two offices are quite separate, and I need hardly say that I did not in any way intervene in these investigations to influence the recommendation that the officials would make . . . Their first step was to approach a possible tenant, who said that he would be ready to pay £3 an acre for the land equipped in an agreed way... They felt, therefore, that the proposition was a reasonable one... Crown Lands, therefore, decided to accept the proposal, and I approved of it in my double capacity as Minister of Agriculture and Commissioner of Crown Lands. The proposal went forward with Treasury consent.

I admit at once that it was most regrettable – and I make no attempt to excuse it – that the promises made on behalf of the Land Commission to previous applicants for the land that their applications would be considered in due course were not brought to the notice of those handling the matter until after Crown Lands felt that they were under a moral obligation to the prospective tenant. Had Crown Lands not taken this view, it would have been possible, even at that stage, to have advertised the tenancy, although such a procedure would have been unusual, because Crown Lands had not at that time decided to buy the land...

I should like to say a word about the conduct of the civil servants concerned. General issues of great constitutional importance arise in this regard... I am quite clear that it would be deplorable if there were to be any departure from the recognised constitutional position. I, as Minister, must accept full responsibility to Parliament for any mistakes and inefficiency of officials in my Department, just as, when my officials bring off any successes on my behalf, I take full credit for them. Any departure from this long-established rule is bound to bring the Civil Service right into the political arena, and that we should all, on both sides of the House, deprecate most vigorously... I would only add, at this stage, that it should not be thought that this means that I am bound to endorse the actions of officials, whatever they may be, or that I or any other Minister must shield those who make errors against proper consequences...

The accusation has been made publicly that officials wilfully misled me. Although there were certain inaccuracies and deficiencies in the information given me, when I took my decision, I had the main facts before me, and my advisers were certainly not guilty of wilfully misleading me. I underline the word ' wilfully.'

I now turn to the question of disciplinary action. The conduct of the civil servants concerned has been the subject of a public inquiry and of a report and, as a result, they have received public censure and reprimand. This in itself is a most severe punishment. I still hold the view which I expressed in the original statement I made in this House on 15th June, but there does remain the question as to what action may be necessary to maintain public confidence in the administration of Departments. The Government thought it right that the need for any such action should be further reviewed. My right hon. Friend the Prime Minister arranged for a small advisory

Committee of experienced persons to review this aspect of the matter...

The committee consisted of Sir John Woods, a former Permanent Secretary of the Board of Trade and now a director of the English Electric Co. and other companies, Sir Maurice Holmes, a former Permanent Secretary of the Ministry of Education, and Sir Harry Pilkington...

The Committee states that there are five civil servants whose actions are criticised with varying degrees of severity in Sir Andrew Clark's Report. Having studied the Report, read the observations submitted to me by these five officers and interviewed them, it reached a conclusion in the case of Mr Eastwood, the Permanent Commissioner of Crown Lands, that his usefulness as a public servant would be impaired if he were to remain in his present post. It recommends, therefore, that he should be transferred to other duties. Three of the four other officers involved are not now employed on the work on which they were engaged when dealing with the Crichel Down case, and the Committee recommends no action in regard to them... The Government fully accept this advice and are taking steps to give early effect to it...

I have already announced that there is to be an independent review of the organisation for administering Crown Lands. In addition, I am arranging for a thorough examination of the organisation and methods adopted within the Ministry and the Agricultural Land Commission for dealing with transactions in agricultural land. This examination will include the work of the Agricultural Land Service both at headquarters and in the provincial centres and counties.

I turn to the question of the disposal of agricultural land... After discussion with the Commission, I decided early last year that, after any necessary improvement, land should be sold wherever this can suitably be done...

This leads me to the general question of the policy which the Government have had under consideration for some time, namely, the disposal of agricultural land which was acquired compulsorily or under threat of compulsion and is no longer required for the purpose for which it was acquired. The extent of this problem should not be exaggerated. Departments do not normally buy land outright unless they expect to need it permanently. The question of releasing it, therefore, seldom arises, except when there has been extensive acquisition on threat of war or during war. Current cases are mostly concerned with acquisitions immediately before the war or during the war. The long-term problem should be a very small one indeed.

The Government have decided that where agricultural land which was acquired compulsorily or under threat of compulsion is no longer wanted by the original acquiring Department or immediately by any other Government Department possessing compulsory purchase powers for a purpose for which the use of those powers would be justified, then the land will be sold. This means that transfers of such land from one Government Department to another will not be made in future unless at the time of transfer the receiving Department could and would have bought the land compulsorily if it had been in private ownership. There is one exception which we must make to this rule, and that is where agricultural land has been so substantially altered in character while in possession of a Government Department that if it were sold it could not be used for agriculture in the same way as when it was originally acquired. . .

Where land is to be sold in accordance with the general policy I have just outlined, the Government have considered what attitude to adopt towards claims by former owners or their successors to buy it back. The Government recognise that the former owner or certain of his successors may fairly claim that they should be given a special opportunity to buy such land. . .

[T]he Government will in future consider each case on its merits with the desire that, where circumstances show that the land can properly be offered to a former owner or his successor who can establish his claim, this will be done at a price assessed by the district valuer as being the current market price.[3]

Having now had this opportunity of rendering account to Parliament of the actions which I thought fit to take, I have, as the Minister responsible during this period, tendered my resignation to the Prime Minister, who is submitting it to the Queen.

THE SECRETARY OF STATE FOR THE HOME DEPARTMENT (SIR DAVID MAXWELL-FYFE): . . . There has been criticism that the principle [of Ministerial responsibility] operates so as to oblige Ministers to extend total protection to their officials and to endorse their acts, and to cause the position that civil servants cannot be called to account and are effectively responsible to no one. That is a position which I believe is quite wrong. . . It is quite untrue that well-justified public criticism of the actions of civil servants cannot be made on a suitable occasion. The position of the civil servant is that he is wholly and directly responsible to his Minister. It is worth stating again that he holds his office ' at pleasure ' and can be dismissed at any time by the Minister; and that power is none the less real because it is seldom used. The only exception relates to a small number of senior posts, like permanent secretary, deputy secretary, and principal financial officer, where, since 1920, it has been necess-

---

[3] On this point see further below, p. 184.

ary for the Minister to consult the Prime Minister, as he does on appointment.

I would like to put the different categories where different considerations apply. . . [I]n the case where there is an explicit order by a Minister, the Minister must protect the civil servant who has carried out his order. Equally, where the civil servant acts properly in accordance with the policy laid down by the Minister, the Minister must protect and defend him.

I come to the third category, which is different. . . Where an official makes a mistake or causes some delay, but not on an important issue of policy and not where a claim to individual rights is seriously involved, the Minister acknowledges the mistake and he accepts the responsibility, although he is not personally involved. He states that he will take corrective action in the Department. I agree with the right hon. Gentleman that he would not, in those circumstances, expose the official to public criticism. . .

But when one comes to the fourth category, where action has been taken by a civil servant of which the Minister disapproves and has no prior knowledge, and the conduct of the official is reprehensible, then there is no obligation on the part of the Minister to endorse what he believes to be wrong, or to defend what are clearly shown to be errors of his officers. The Minister is not bound to defend action of which he did not know, or of which he disapproves. But, of course, he remains constitutionally responsible to Parliament for the fact that something has gone wrong, and he alone can tell Parliament what has occurred and render an account of his stewardship. The fact that a Minister has to do that does not affect his power to control and discipline his staff. One could sum it up by saying that it is part of a Minister's responsibility to Parliament to take necessary action to ensure efficiency and the proper discharge of the duties of his Department. On that, only the Minister can decide what it is right and just to do, and he alone can hear all sides, including the defence.

It has been suggested in this debate, and has been canvassed in the Press, that there is another aspect which adds to our difficulties, and that is that today the work and the tasks of Government permeate so many spheres of our national life that it is impossible for the Minister to keep track of all these matters. I believe that that is a matter which can be dealt with by the instructions which the Minister gives in his Department. He can lay down standing instructions to see that his policy is carried out. He can lay down rules by which it is ensured that matters of importance, of difficulty or of political danger are brought to his attention. Thirdly, there is the control of this House, and it is one of the duties of this House to see that that control is always put into effect.

... As I have said, it is a matter for the Minister to decide when civil servants are guilty of shortcomings in their official conduct. Normally, the Civil Service has no procedure equivalent to a court-martial, or anything of that kind. There have in the past been a few inquiries to establish the facts and the degree of culpability of individuals, but the decision as to the disciplinary action to be taken has been left to the Minister...

[530 H.C.Deb. 5s. c. 1285. 20 July 1954]

The Ferranti case, 1964

In his report for the year 1962–63 the Comptroller and Auditor-General drew attention to the fact that the amount allowed for direct labour and overheads in a guided missile contract between the Ministry of Aviation and Ferranti Ltd. exceeded the actual cost by 70% or £2·7 million, even though the figures relating to the actual costs were in the hands of the Ministry's accountants at the time the prices were fixed. On 24 January 1964 the Chancellor of the Exchequer and the Minister of Aviation appointed a committee under Sir John Lang ' to investigate the circumstances in which the prices agreed by the Ministry of Aviation for a contract for the supply of guided weapons may have allowed an excessive profit to the firm concerned; and to recommend whether any changes in organisation or procedure are necessary to ensure better assessment of prices for similar contracts in the future '.

In its First Report [Cmnd. 2428] the Committee concluded:

' 66. Three criticisms can be made of the Ministry. The first is that they placed reliance on their technical cost estimating organisation in an extremely advanced and complex technical field without the means of checking the accuracy of their estimates by reference to actual prime costs achieved. The second is that there was no effective collaboration between branches which should have been working together towards the common goal of fair and reasonable prices. This collaboration exists for aircraft and aero-engine contracts, but the Ministry failed to recognise its importance in other contracts. The third criticism is that the handling of the Mk. I Bloodhound production contracts revealed, in all the Directorates concerned, a lack of direction and a lack of drive in making the best use of the Ministry's resources.'

Ferranti, Ltd. agreed to pay back £4,250,000.

The report was debated on 30 July 1964.

THE MINISTER OF AVIATION (MR JULIAN AMERY) ... Sir John Lang found in his Report a central mistake on the Ministry's part from which the others have flowed. The Technical Costs branch miscalculated the direct labour content of the job by over 100%... That mistake was magnified by the addition of overheads calculated at the rate of 500%... This ... was the basic mistake but there were two chances ... to remedy it. The estimates ... were made at the end of 1959. The prices were not agreed until the end of 1960 and 1961. At that time the job had been largely completed and we could have insisted on looking at the work and calling for figures... This was not done... There was a second chance. This was to compare the figure for direct labour in the overhead calculations of the accounting services with the estimates of direct labour by technical costs. This was not done ... Sir John shows where our organisation went wrong. He does not show so clearly why it went wrong... I have started a stringent investigation into the question of personal responsibility in all this... The investigation is only beginning and we would not hesitate to take disciplinary action if it were proved to be necessary. I come now to the question of ministerial responsibilities. I think that it would be wholly unsuitable in a matter of this kind where the taxpayers' interest as has been proved, has been adequately defended, to make any charge against any Minister [An Hon. Member: ' This is absurd '] – in this affair. I have studied very carefully the records of resignations in matters of varying kinds over the last 50 years. Sir Austen Chamberlain is, I think, always regarded as the Minister who showed the most punctiliousness in a matter of resignation and his responsibility for the matter in question was very tenuous.

Mr DENIS HEALY (*Leeds, East*): The right hon. Gentleman is not a judge.

Mr AMERY ... I freely admit that mistakes have ... been made by my Department: but I am sure that the House will recognise that the task of the Contracts Division is an immensely difficult one. It is costing at the frontiers of knowledge and estimating the cost of the unknown... [W]ith it goes a great deal of routine, and even tedious work. It is not easy ... to get the right men in the right quantities to staff the Technical Costs branch. I believe that the Bloodhound I incident is the exception to the general course of contracts between the Government and industry. This is one occasion, the only one I have come across, where the Contracts branch of my Department has actually overestimated the cost of a project. The Department nearly always underestimated the cost and comes back for more... I freely agree that what has happened shows the need for an overhaul...

[699 H.C.Deb. 5s. c. 1815. 30 July 1964]

The collapse of the Vehicle and General Insurance Company, 1971
In 1971 A Tribunal of Inquiry was appointed under the Tribunals of Inquiry (Evidence) Act, 1921 (below p. 548) to inquire into the circum-

stances surrounding the collapse of the Vehicle and General Insurance
Co. One of the subjects into which it was directed to inquire was
'Whether there was negligence or misconduct by persons in the service
of the Crown directly or indirectly responsible for the discharge, in
relation to those companies [i.e. the Vehicle and General Insurance
Company and its subsidiaries] of functions under the Insurance Companies Acts 1958–67.' On this part of its terms of reference the Tribunal
commented: ' 3 . . . This necessarily involves investigation of the conduct
of individuals, including the investigation of possible ministerial responsibility for action or inaction, and of departmental policy and practice.'
In describing the general scope of their inquiry it said:

8. Pursuant to the statutes the Department has certain duties and
powers, many of the powers being discretionary. Whether or not a
discretionary power could and should have been used in relation to
the Company at various dates has been a crucial question in the
Inquiry. Whether or not to exercise a discretionary power involved
the obtaining of factual information and making a value judgment
on the facts. . .

9. This Inquiry has been mainly concerned with the conduct of
the Department and its officers in relation to the discharge of their
functions under the Acts in respect of the Company and its subsidiaries. What were their powers? Were the powers fully understood?
Did circumstances exist to the knowledge of the Department, and if
so when, in which the Department could have exercised power to
require information, to appoint inspectors to look into the affairs of
the Company, to place a restriction upon the business of the Company, or to petition the Court for an order that the Company should
be wound up? If such a power could have been exercised but was
not exercised, then why not; and was the omission to exercise the
power prudent or imprudent or negligent? Could and should any
action have been taken by the Department short of the exercise of
formal powers? These are some of the important questions to which
we have sought the answers. Another central issue is whether the
loss suffered by policyholders and shareholders was brought about
by any impropriety, negligence or misconduct.

The organisation and function of the Department
60. The Department responsible for discharging the functions of the
Government in relation to the Insurance Companies Acts 1958 to
1967 is the Board of Trade which on 20 October, 1970, merged with
the Ministry of Technology to become the Department of Trade and
Industry. The Department now employs some 26,000 non-industrial
staff and has about 70 Under-Secretaries: in 1961 the Board had
about 7,000 staff and 17 Under-Secretaries. Throughout the period

the Department has been headed by a President or Secretary of State who has been assisted by a number of junior Ministers. Responsibility for insurance has always rested with the President or Secretary of State himself, assisted by one junior Minister. In the period with which we are concerned the Presidents or Secretary of State have been Mr Edward Heath to September, 1964; Mr Douglas Jay to August, 1967; Mr Anthony Crosland to October, 1969; Mr Roy Mason to June, 1970; Mr Michael Noble; and since July, 1970 Mr John Davies.

61. The proportion of the work of the Department that is referred to Ministers is very small – well under 1%. The Ministers give political direction to the Department's operation and pilot legislation through Parliament. Once the legislation has been passed and any Ministerial guidance has been given, the civil servants are expected to take entire charge of the administration unless there are any problems about which they need guidance from higher up, or unless there are any matters of particular political sensitivity about which they think Ministers would wish to know.

62. The Permanent Secretary has the overall responsibility for the organisation and work of the Department. . . Because of the size of the Department and the range of policy issues involved the Permanent Secretary is now supported by two Second Permanent Secretaries. These have within the areas of work allocated to them full delegated responsibility both in relation to Departmental Ministers and, as Accounting Officers, to Parliament. The Permanent Secretary himself takes responsibility for a group of Divisions within the Department: this group includes the Insurance and Companies Division. Within this group there are six officers at Deputy Secretary level, to each of whom about five Under-Secretaries or specialists of equivalent grade are responsible. Each Under-Secretary is responsible for the area of work allocated to him. It is the normal practice in the Department, a practice found to be desirable in the light of experience, that almost all the work allocated to a Division is dealt with in full and finally at the level of Under-Secretary or below, and that only when there is a clear reason for making an exception is a matter referred higher by the Under-Secretary.

63. The work of the Insurance and Companies Division covers not only insurance but also companies legislation generally and the insolvency service. . . The Under-Secretary is supported by four officers at Assistant Secretary level, one of whom is exclusively concerned with insurance work and carries the title ' Head of Insurance Branch '. Primary responsibility for the Department's work on insurance rests with this Assistant Secretary. . . In the event of a

conflict of views between a junior and senior officer it is normal practice for them to discuss the subject to see if the conflict can be resolved by agreement, and in the event of agreement any minute would record the agreed view. If disagreement persisted the senior officer could either make the decision or, if the subject was of sufficient importance, refer the matter higher.

70. In contrast to the filtering upwards of day to day work, matters of policy within the Division are decided at the senior officer level and laid down for the benefit of the junior staff. It is an inherent and important part of the duties of an Under-Secretary, when the nature of the work requires the formulation of a policy or practice, to prescribe the policy or practice to be followed. Even where he does not involve himself in detail, a senior officer has a responsibility for supervising the work of his juniors, and for seeing that the work of his section, Branch or Division as a whole is well organised and proceeding efficiently. The responsibility of a senior officer does not end with matters of policy and organisation. He must exercise initiative and be prepared to enforce action when the work of junior staff has failed to produce a satisfactory result, or failed to resolve persisting doubts; and he must have a nose for trouble.

71. The question of informing (as distinct from consulting) officers above Under-Secretary level and Ministers raises different issues. Here again there are no hard and fast rules. The broad concept is that Ministers and senior officers should be warned of any problem that may have to engage the attention of the higher echelons of the Department in the immediate future. . .

328. We have reached the conclusion that responsibility for the failure of the Department to take action lies with three persons: with Mr Homewood, who was the Assistant Secretary until he left the Branch in June 1969; from that date onwards with Mr Steel who succeeded him in that post; and with Mr Jardine from the time of his appointment to the Division as Under-Secretary in July 1964 throughout the whole period. . .

333. Since responsibility for the failure of the Department to take action lay with Mr Homewood, Mr Steel and Mr Jardine it is necessary to state our conclusions whether their conduct in relation to the Company and its subsidiaries was negligent. . .

341. When we look at the totality of the evidence relating to the events of the Department's supervision of the Company from 1964 onwards when Mr Jardine became Under-Secretary, we are reluctantly driven to the conclusion that his performance as a whole fell so far below the standard which could reasonably be expected from someone in his position and with his experience (or opportunity to acquire experience) that it cannot escape the description of

'negligence' within our terms of reference – though we would call it incompetence in relation to this particular duty...

342. There remains the question whether any servant of the Crown (including Ministers) above the level of Mr Jardine acted negligently in connection with the Department's failure to exercise its powers under the 1967 Act as summarised in paragraph 324. No such allegation was made at the Inquiry and we find that the answer is clearly 'no'.

344. In our view it would not be right to criticise anyone above Mr Jardine's level for the failure to exercise any statutory power in relation to the Company before February 1971. As we have seen in paragraph 62 [4] it is the normal practice in the Department, and one which is found to be desirable in the light of experience, that almost all the work allocated to a Division is dealt with finally at the level of Under-Secretary and below. There is a grave risk in a large Department that the level of decision-making will creep upwards, and the Permanent Secretary told us in evidence that when the Department of Trade and Industry was formed he had made his view clear that it was particularly important that Under-Secretaries should maintain their position in the Department. The responsibility for deciding whether or not to exercise the Department's powers lay with Mr Jardine as the Under-Secretary in charge of the Insurance and Companies Division. If he was in doubt about anything concerning action to be taken within the Division, it was his right and duty to refer the problem to a Second Secretary or to the Permanent Secretary for guidance or decision; it might then be referred to a Minister if the matter was sufficiently important (see paragraphs 61 and 71), but no question concerning the Company was ever referred by him for guidance or decision to anyone above his level. In the absence of such a reference, we consider that Mr Jardine's superiors were entitled to assume that he did not feel in doubt as to the course of action to be pursued and to rely on him to take the appropriate decisions.

[Report of the Tribunal of Inquiry into the Cessation of Trading of the Vehicle and General Insurance Co. H.C. 133, H.L. 80 of 1971–2, 15 February 1972.]

The Prime Minister made a statement on 16 February 1972. This was followed by a debate on 1 May 1972.

THE PRIME MINISTER (MR EDWARD HEATH): ... The principal findings of the tribunal are as follows... [T]here was negligence on the part of the Under-Secretary who was in charge of the Insurance

[4] See above p. 167.

and Companies Division from 1964 until the end of last year when he left the post after reaching the natural retiring age. Two other senior members of staff of the division are criticised in certain respects but not found negligent. . . [T]he tribunal considered whether there was any negligence by anyone more senior, including Ministers. It observes that no such allegation was made during the inquiry, and it finds that there was no negligence at these levels. . .

MR CARTER: Does the Prime Minister not accept that the statement he has just made is a complete rejection of any question of Ministerial resonsibility?. . .

THE PRIME MINISTER: . . . [T]he tribunal . . . has taken the view that there was a level of responsibility on each of those concerned with the operation of the Acts, and it indicated its conclusions as to where the responsibilities lay. On the question of responsibility for the failure of the company, at the end of paragraph 350 the tribunal says that the Department cannot be held liable for losses attributable to the deficiencies of the company. . .

MR PARDOE: Does not the Prime Minister agree that, although the tribunal has made it clear that there was no direct Ministerial responsibility, nevertheless 30 years ago a report of this sort would undoubtedly have led to the resignation of the Minister? Is this the burial of the doctrine of Ministerial responsibility?. . .

THE PRIME MINISTER: I do not accept what the hon. Gentleman says about the doctrine of Ministerial responsibility, but I accept that this has always been a controversial and debatable matter. The tribunal points out that if there were Ministerial responsibility it could have existed from July, 1967, onwards in respect of all Ministers who were involved. The tribunal also came to the conclusion that there was not Ministerial negligence in this sense of ' responsibility '.

After very long and thorough examination of all the details of this case the tribunal has tried to evaluate where responsibility lies for dealing with matters of this kind in the Government service and then fairly to apportion its criticism. . .

[831 H.C.Deb. 5s. c. 419. 16 February 1972]

THE SECRETARY OF STATE FOR THE HOME DEPARTMENT (MR REGINALD MAUDLING): . . . Ministers are responsible not only for their personal decisions but also for seeing that there is a system in their Departments by which they are informed of important matters which arise. They are also responsible for minimising the dangers of errors and mistakes so far as possible, and, clearly, they are responsible for the general efficiency of their Department. . .

One must look at this classic doctrine in the light of modern reality. In my own Department we get 1½ million letters a year, any one of which may lead to disaster. No Home Secretary could be expected to supervise all those 1½ million letters. It is no minimising of the responsibility of Ministers to Parliament to say that a Minister cannot be blamed for a mistake made if he did not make it himself and if he has not failed to ensure that that sort of mistake ought not to be made. In other words, this is where the blame of Ministers should arise. If a Minister gets it wrong or fails to ensure that the other chap has not got it wrong, that Minister is to blame. That does not stop Ministers being responsible to Parliament for what their Departments do.

In the case of this tribunal a different state of affairs arises. The tribunal was told by Parliament to look into what happened and to ascribe the blame in individual cases. If we appoint a tribunal of this kind, we are bound to get ascription of responsibility to individual civil servants, which would not happen in the case of a parliamentary inquiry into the conduct of a Department. Therefore, the naming of civil servants in the case of this tribunal does not set any precedent for the naming of civil servants in the general responsibility of the Government, which still rests squarely upon the shoulders of Ministers...

Mr George Cunningham: I think that the Minister should make it clear that the terms of reference of the tribunal were whether there was negligence by persons in the service of the Crown. There is nothing there which suggests that the tribunal would find in respect of individuals as against findings in respect of the Department collectively.

Mr Maudling: The terms of reference refer to persons, individuals. They are the same. I thought that the tribunal carried out its responsibility of ascribing to persons individual responsibility of a kind which would not be ascribed to them in the general criticism within Parliament about the conduct of a Department. This is a different matter and should be treated as such... I suggest that if right hon. and hon. Gentlemen look at what I have said they will see that it combines what I believe to be the tradition of full ministerial responsibility in modern circumstances with the reality of administration of a Department. Ministers will remain responsible for what their Departments do. If their Departments get things wrong, they are to be blamed in this House because their Departments get them wrong. This is the fundamental point... If the Department fails to protect the motorist, clearly the Minister carries the responsibility in this House. When inquiry is made into what happened and what individuals did, that is done by the tribunal. In those circumstances the actions of individuals become known to the public. That is quite a different thing. . .

[836 H.C.Deb. 5s. c. 33. 1 May 1972]

III. THE PARLIAMENTARY COMMISSIONER FOR ADMINISTRATION

Following the Crichel Down case the Government appointed the Franks Committee on Tribunals and Inquiries but gave it terms of reference which excluded considerations of the kind of situation that had arisen there. It was left to Justice, the British section of the International Commission of Jurists, to make a reasoned case in favour of the appointment of a permanent Commissioner on the lines of the Scandinavian Ombudsman to look into allegations of maladministration. Thus it did in its 1961 report ' The citizen and the Administration '.

In his preface to the report Lord Shawcross wrote:
' The study embodied in the Report which is here published may well form the basis of . . . a real Charter for the little man. . . [W]ith the existence of a great bureaucracy there are inevitably occasions, not insignificant in number, when through error or indifference, injustice is done – or appears to be done. The man of substance can deal with these situations. He is near to the establishment; he enjoys the status or possesses the influence which will ensure him the ear of those in authority. He can afford to pursue such legal remedies as may be available. He knows his way around. But too often the little man, the ordinary humble citizen, is incapable of asserting himself. The little farmer with four acres and a cow would never have attempted to force the battlements of Crichel Down. The little man has become too used to being pushed around; it rarely occurs to him that there is any appeal from what " they have decided ".'

After some delay the Conservative Government rejected the proposal on the grounds that it could not be reconciled with the principle of Ministerial responsibility to Parliament and would seriously interfere with the prompt and efficient despatch of business [666 H.C.Deb. 5s. c. 1123. 8 November 1962]. The Labour Government in October 1965 published a White Paper [Cmnd. 2767] in which they accepted the idea and a Parliamentary Commissioner was appointed. His appointment was subsequently confirmed and his jurisdiction set out in the Parliamentary Commissioner Act, 1965.

Parliamentary Commissioner Bill, 1966

THE LORD PRESIDENT OF THE COUNCIL AND LEADER OF THE HOUSE (MR RICHARD CROSSMAN): . . . I want to start by repudiating a notion which has got about, that in this Bill we are borrowing from other countries and trying to force into our British constitutional mould the notion of the Ombudsman which has been the pride of Sweden for 150 years.

In a country where Ministers are not responsible for the administration of their Departments, and where civil servants, therefore, are
not answerable to them, it was obvious that the citizen was in des-
perate need of protection against the bureaucracy. These were the
peculiar conditions out of which the Swedish office of Ombudsman
grew, and it is these conditions which explain why the Swedish
Ombudsman – and also the Danish and Norwegian Ombudsmen...
– have such a strong legal flavour and are usually manned by judges

The Office of Parliamentary Commissioner, which it is the object
of this Bill to create, resembles the office of Ombudsman in the one
particular that it is designed to protect the individual citizen against
bureaucratic maladministration. But because the constitutional
structure of our democracy is quite different from the Scandinavian
pattern, the institution we are trying to evolve to achieve this object
is different, too. The Swedish Ombudsman, though ultimately
responsible to Parliament, is an independent investigator and judge
who, within his defined functions, chooses his own cases to examine
and has his own independent relationship with the Press and the
public. It has been his task to provide outside Parliament that
defence of the individual against Executive excesses which our Parliamentary Questions, Adjournment debates and tribunals of inquiry
provide.

In contrast, the investigations of our Parliamentary Commissioner
will in no way replace Question Time or the Adjournment debate.
On the contrary, they will provide the back bench Member, once he
knows how to use it aright, with a new and powerful weapon which,
up till now, neither he individually nor we collectively as a House
has ever possessed – the possibility of impartial investigation into
alleged maladministration...

Question Time, Mr Speaker, under your guidance, is changing its
tempo and therewith its character. To some extent... the letter in
the hands of the skilful back bench Member which extracts lengthy
correspondence with a departmental Minister has become a more
potent instrument for helping the individual citizen with a grievance
than the Question itself.

But in both cases, the Question and the letter, there is one built-in
defect. All they can elicit from the Minister is an investigation which
is usually far from impartial and far from complete. Of course, very
occasionally, where something seriously amiss is uncovered or where
passion has been worked up, a Minister will call for a Departmental
inquiry, and, even more occasionally, he will ask for a tribunal under
the Tribunals of Inquiry (Evidence) Act, 1921, to be set up. Departmental inquiries, conducted often as not by a Q.C. selected by the
Minister, can... fulfil a vital and very useful purpose. About the

tribunal of inquiry as a method of dealing with maladministration, all I can say is that it is a very large hammer with which to crush a nut. Indeed... since these tribunals were established 45 years ago, only nine have been set up to deal with what we could possibly call maladministration.

So I am not exaggerating when I say that, when it comes to investigating maladministration, our Parliamentary system of Questions, followed by letters where the Answer is unsatisfactory, an Adjournment Debate and, very occasionally, in the last resort a Departmental inquiry or tribunal, is often deficient in one particular, and in this respect makes things far too easy for the Executive. What it lacks is the cutting edge of a really impartial and really searching investigation into the workings of Whitehall – an investigation designed primarily to deal not with great scandals but with those secondary acts of injustice against the individual which, if permitted to fester, arouse what is often a grossly unfair prejudice against the Civil Service...

[Second Reading. 734 H.C.Deb. 5s. c. 43. 18 October 1966]

THE PARLIAMENTARY COMMISSIONER ACT, 1967
[Ch. 13]

1. (1) For the purpose of conducting investigations in accordance with the following provisions of this Act there shall be appointed a Commissioner, to be known as the Parliamentary Commissioner for Administration...

(2) Her Majesty may by Letters Patent appoint a person to be the Commissioner, and any person so appointed shall (subject to subsection (3) of this section) hold office during good behaviour.

(3) A person appointed to be the Commissioner... may be removed from office by Her Majesty in consequence of Addresses by both Houses of Parliament, and shall in any case vacate office on completing the year of service in which he attains the age of sixty-five years.

(4) The Commissioner shall not be a Member of the House of Commons...

Investigation by the Commissioner

4. (1) Subject to the provisions of this section and to the notes contained in Schedule 2 to this Act, this Act applies to the government departments and other authorities listed in that Schedule.[5]

(2) Her Majesty may by Order in Council amend the said

[5] Schedule 2 lists all the Central Government Departments.

Schedule 2 . . . but nothing in this subsection authorises the inclusion in that Schedule of any body or authority not being a department or other body or authority whose functions are exercised on behalf of the Crown.

(3) Any statutory instrument made by virtue of subsection (2) of this section shall be subject to annulment in pursuance of a resolution of either House of Parliament.

(4) Any reference in this Act to a government department or other authority to which this Act applies includes a reference to the Ministers, members or officers of that department or authority.

5. (1) Subject to the provisions of this section, the Commissioner may investigate any action taken by or on behalf of a government department or other authority to which this Act applies, being action taken in the exercise of administrative functions of that department or authority, in any case where—

(*a*) a written complaint is duly made to a member of the House of Commons by a member of the public who claims to have sustained injustice in consequence of maladministration in connection with the action so taken; and

(*b*) the complaint is referred to the Commissioner, with the consent of the person who made it, by a member of that House with a request to conduct an investigation thereon.

(2) Except as hereinafter provided, the Commissioner shall not conduct an investigation under this Act in respect of any of the following matters, that is to say—

(*a*) any action in respect of which the person aggrieved has or had a right of appeal, reference or review to or before a tribunal constituted by or under any enactment or by virtue of Her Majesty's prerogative;

(*b*) any action in respect of which the person aggrieved has or had a remedy by way of proceedings in any court of law:

Provided that the Commissioner may conduct an investigation notwithstanding that the person aggrieved has or had such a right or remedy if satisfied that in the particular circumstances it is not reasonable to expect him to resort or have resorted to it.

(3) Without prejudice to subsection (2) of this section, the Commissioner shall not conduct an investigation under this Act in respect of any such action or matter as is described in Schedule 3 to this Act.

(4) Her Majesty may by Order in Council amend the said Schedule 3 so as to exclude from the provisions of that Schedule such actions or matters as may be described in the Order; and any statutory instrument made by virtue of this subsection shall be sub-

ject to annulment in pursuance of a resolution of either House of Parliament.

(5) In determining whether to initiate, continue or discontinue an investigation under this Act, the Commissioner shall, subject to the foregoing provisions of this section, act in accordance with his own discretion; and any question whether a complaint is duly made under this Act shall be determined by the Commissioner.

6. (1) A complaint under this Act may be made by any individual, or by any body of persons whether incorporated or not, not being—

(a) a local authority or other authority or body constituted for purposes of the public service or of local government or for the purposes of carrying on under national ownership any industry or undertaking or part of an industry or undertaking;

(b) any other authority or body whose members are appointed by Her Majesty or any Minister of the Crown or government department, or whose revenues consist wholly or mainly of moneys provided by Parliament.

(2) Where the person by whom a complaint might have been made under the foregoing provisions of this Act has died or is for any reason unable to act for himself, the complaint may be made by his personal representative or by a member of his family or other individual suitable to represent him; but except as aforesaid a complaint shall not be entertained under this Act unless made by the person aggrieved himself.

(3) A complaint shall not be entertained under this Act unless it is made to a member of the House of Commons not later than twelve months from the day on which the person aggrieved first had notice of the matters alleged in the complaint; but the Commissioner may conduct an investigation pursuant to a complaint not made within that period if he considers that there are special circumstances which make it proper to do so.

(4) A complaint shall not be entertained under this Act unless the person aggrieved is resident in the United Kingdom (or, if he is dead, was so resident at the time of his death) or the complaint relates to action taken in relation to him while he was present in the United Kingdom or on an installation in a designated area within the meaning of the Continental Shelf Act 1964 or on a ship registered in the United Kingdom or an aircraft so registered, or in relation to rights or obligations which accrued or arose in the United Kingdom or on such an installation, ship or aircraft.

7. (1) Where the Commissioner proposes to conduct an investigation pursuant to a complaint under this Act, he shall afford to the principal officer of the department or authority concerned, and to any other person who is alleged in the complaint to have taken or

authorised the action complained of, an opportunity to comment on any allegations contained in the complaint.

(2) Every such investigation shall be conducted in private, but except as aforesaid the procedure for conducting an investigation shall be such as the Commissioner considers appropriate in the circumstances of the case; and without prejudice to the generality of the foregoing provision the Commissioner may obtain information from such persons and in such manner, and make such inquiries, as he thinks fit, and may determine whether any person may be represented, by counsel or solicitor or otherwise, in the investigation.

(3) The Commissioner may, if he thinks fit, pay to the person by whom the complaint was made and to any other person who attends or furnishes information for the purposes of an investigation under this Act—

(*a*) sums in respect of expenses properly incurred by them;

(*b*) allowances by way of compensation for the loss of their time, in accordance with such scales and subject to such conditions as may be determined by the Treasury.

(4) The conduct of an investigation under this Act shall not affect any action taken by the department or authority concerned, or any power or duty of that department or authority to take further action with respect to any matters subject to the investigation...

8. (1) For the purposes of an investigation under this Act the Commissioner may require any Minister, officer or member of the department or authority concerned or any other person who in his opinion is able to furnish information or produce documents relevant to the investigation to furnish any such information or produce any such document.

(2) For the purposes of any such investigation the Commissioner shall have the same powers as the Court in respect of the attendance and examination of witnesses (including the administration of oaths or affirmations and the examination of witnesses abroad) and in respect of the production of documents.

(3) No obligation to maintain secrecy or other restriction upon the disclosure of information obtained by or furnished to persons in Her Majesty's service, whether imposed by any enactment or by any rule of law, shall apply to the disclosure of information for the purposes of an investigation under this Act; and the Crown shall not be entitled in relation to any such investigation to any such privilege in respect of the production of documents or the giving of evidence as is allowed by law in legal proceedings.

(4) No person shall be required or authorised by virtue of this Act to furnish any information or answer any question relating to proceedings of the Cabinet or of any committee of the Cabinet or

to produce so much of any document as relates to such proceedings; and for the purposes of this subsection a certificate issued by the Secretary of the Cabinet with the approval of the Prime Minister and certifying that any information, question, document or part of a document so relates shall be conclusive.

(5) Subject to subsection (3) of this section, no person shall be compelled for the purposes of an investigation under this Act to give any evidence or produce any document which he could not be compelled to give or produce in civil proceedings before the Court.

9. (1) If any person without lawful excuse obstructs the Commissioner or any officer of the Commissioner in the performance of his functions under this Act, or is guilty of any act or omission in relation to an investigation under this Act which, if that investigation were a proceeding in the Court, would constitute contempt of court, the Commissioner may certify the offence to the Court . . .

10. (1) In any case where the Commissioner conducts an investigation under this Act or decides not to conduct such an investigation, he shall send to the member of the House of Commons by whom the request for investigation was made (or if he is no longer a member of that House, to such member of that House as the Commissioner thinks appropriate) a report of the results of the investigation or, as the case may be, a statement of his reasons for not conducting an investigation.

(2) In any case where the Commissioner conducts an investigation under this Act, he shall also send a report of the results of the investigation to the principal officer of the department or authority concerned and to any other person who is alleged in the relevant complaint to have taken or authorised the action complained of.

(3) If, after conducting an investigation under this Act, it appears to the Commissioner that injustice has been caused to the person aggrieved in consequence of maladministration and that the injustice has not been, or will not be, remedied, he may, if he thinks fit, lay before each House of Parliament a special report upon the case.

(4) The Commissioner shall annually lay before each House of Parliament a general report on the performance of his functions under this Act and may from time to time lay before each House of Parliament such other reports with respect to those functions as he thinks fit . . .

11. . . . (2) Information obtained by the Commissioner or his officers in the course of or for the purposes of an investigation under this Act shall not be disclosed except—

    (a) for the purposes of the investigation and of any report to be made thereon under this Act . . .

and the Commissioner and his officers shall not be called upon to give evidence in any proceedings (other than such proceedings as aforesaid) of matters coming to his or their knowledge in the course of an investigation under this Act.

(3) A Minister of the Crown may give notice in writing to the Commissioner, with respect to any document or information specified in the notice, or any class of documents or information so specified, that in the opinion of the Minister the disclosure of that document or information, or of documents or information of that class, would be prejudicial to the safety of the State or otherwise contrary to the public interest; and where such a notice is given nothing in this Act shall be construed as authorising or requiring the Commissioner or any officer of the Commissioner to communicate to any person or for any purpose any document or information specified in the notice, or any document or information of a class so specified.

(4) The references in this section to a Minister of the Crown include references to the Commissioners of Customs and Excise and the Commissioners of Inland Revenue.

12. ... (3) It is hereby declared that nothing in this Act authorises or requires the Commissioner to question the merits of a decision taken without maladministration by a government department or other authority in the exercise of a discretion vested in that department or authority...

SCHEDULE 3

Matters not subject to Investigation

1. Action taken in matters certified by a Secretary of State or other Minister of the Crown to affect relations or dealings between the Government of the United Kingdom and any other Government or any international organisation of States or Governments.

2. Action taken, in any country or territory outside the United Kingdom, by or on behalf of any officer representing or acting under the authority of Her Majesty in respect of the United Kingdom, or any other officer of the Government of the United Kingdom.

3. Action taken in connection with the administration of the government of any country or territory outside the United Kingdom which forms part of Her Majesty's dominions or in which Her Majesty has jurisdiction.

4. Action taken by the Secretary of State under the Extradition Act 1870 or the Fugitive Offenders Act 1967.

5. Action taken by or with the authority of the Secretary of State

for the purposes of investigating crime or of protecting the security of the State, including action so taken with respect to passports.

6. The commencement or conduct of civil or criminal proceedings before any court of law in the United Kingdom, of proceedings at any place under the Naval Discipline Act 1957, the Army Act 1955 or the Air Force Act 1955, or of proceedings before any international court or tribunal.

7. Any exercise of the prerogative of mercy or of the power of a Secretary of State to make a reference in respect of any person to the Court of Appeal, the High Court of Justiciary or the Courts-Martial Appeal Court.

8. Action taken on behalf of the Minister of Health or the Secretary of State by a Regional Hospital Board, Board of Governors of a Teaching Hospital, Hospital Management Committee or Board of Management, or by the Public Health Laboratory Service Board.

9. Action taken in matters relating to contractual or other commercial transactions, whether within the United Kingdom or elsewhere, being transactions of a government department or authority to which this Act applies or of any such authority or body as is mentioned in paragraph (*a*) or (*b*) of subsection (1) of section 6 of this Act and not being transactions for or relating to—

(*a*) the acquisition of land compulsorily or in circumstances in which it could be acquired compulsorily;

(*b*) the disposal as surplus of land acquired compulsorily or in such circumstances as aforesaid.

10. Action taken in respect of appointments or removals, pay, discipline, superannuation or other personnel matters, in relation to—

(*a*) service in any of the armed forces of the Crown ...

(*b*) service in any office or employment under the Crown ...

11. The grant of honours, awards or privileges within the gift of the Crown, including the grant of Royal Charters.

Maladministration

In each session since the appointment of the Parliamentary Commissioner the House of Commons has appointed a Select Committee ' to examine the reports laid before this House by the Parliamentary Commissioner for Administration, and matters in connection therewith'. The following extracts are taken from its reports and those of the Parliamentary Commissioner and set out some of the principles according to which he operates. In addition to his annual reports the Commissioner publishes summaries of cases dealt with by him, arranged by Departments.

31. The Act does not define maladministration. I have to identify instances of it in the course of my casework . . .

32. . . . [T]he casework has clearly brought out the distinction between maladministration connected with the executive actions of Government, and maladministration connected with the discretionary decisions of Government.

33. By maladministration in executive actions of Government, I mean defects or failings on the part of the departmental operator or in the procedures he has to operate. Ascertainment of the facts in such cases can mean a long and difficult investigation. But the nature of the maladministration (if any) in the departmental action is relatively easy to establish: and, if the maladministration caused injustice, the appropriate remedy to the aggrieved person is usually apparent.

34. For example, I found that the Inland Revenue had lost the file relating to one complainant's affairs: they apologised to him and arranged for an officer of the Department to call on him and obtain information as would enable the Tax Office to set up adequate records to put his tax affairs on a satisfactory basis for the future. In another case, when a misapplication of rules had been found, the Ministry of Social Security paid the allowance which would have been paid if the rules had been correctly applied.

35. . . . The more difficult area of definition is that of maladministration attendant on a discretionary decision in Government. What the complainant usually wants, and the Member for that matter, is a review of the decision. Section 12 (3) of the Act prevents this from being done if the decision was taken without maladministration. Often I am asked to question a discretionary decision because the Minister's finding in that decision is alleged by the complainant to be 'biased' or 'perverse', and bias and perversity were listed as types of maladministration in the debates on the Bill. My practice so far is to regard the area for my investigation to be the administrative processes attendant on the discretionary decision: collection of the evidence on which the decision was taken, the presentation of the case to the Minister, and so on. If I find there has been a defect in these processes, detrimental to the complainant, then I do enquire into the prospects of a remedy by way of review of the decision. But if I find no such defect, then I do not regard myself as competent to question the quality of the decision, even if, in an extreme case, it has resulted in manifest hardship to the complainant . . .

38. I need not add that these distinctions (between the quality of the procedures attending the decision, and the quality of the decision

itself) are difficult to draw in my case work and give dissatisfaction to complainants and their Members, so that I shall welcome any guidance that the Select Committee can give me in the application of these, the central provisions of the Act.

[First Report of the Parliamentary Commissioner for Administration. H.C. 6 of 1967–8, 2 November 1967]

10. ... [Your Committee] think that within the terms of the Act the Commissioner can concern himself with two matters that so far he has regarded as outside his scope; the bad decision and the bad rule.

The Bad Decision

11. Your Committee agree that, in the absence of a legal definition, there is no alternative to the practical course adopted by the Commissioner of proceeding by example, i.e. identifying instances which appear to him to partake of the nature of maladministration in the course of his casework, and building up the definition from those cases. In doing so he presumably has regard to the types of administrative action which were mentioned in debate in Parliament as instances of maladministration – particularly the so called ' Crossman catalogue' (Hansard 18 October, 1966, Col. 51).[6]

12. ... [F]or the most part the administrative defects actually found and reported to members by the Commissioner ... have so far been relatively trivial in relation to the types of maladministration described in the House and elsewhere as the likely subject matter of investigation by a Parliamentary Commissioner.

13. ... Your Committee ... feel that instances of maladministration found by the Commissioner might have been more in number and less trivial in content if he had allowed himself to find on occasion that a decision had been taken with maladministration because it was a bad decision.

14. Your Committee are fully seized of the importance of section 12 (3) of the Act... Your Committee ... suggest, however, that if he finds a decision which, judged by its effect upon the aggrieved person, appears to him to be thoroughly bad in quality, he might infer from the quality of the decision itself that there had been an element of maladministration in the taking of it and ask for its review. In such cases the distinction ... between the quality of the procedures attending the decision and the quality of the decision itself, would tend to be blurred. Your Committee think that the

[6] During the Second Reading debate Mr Crossman had mentioned ' bias, neglect, inattention, delay, incompetence, ineptitude, perversity, turpitude, arbitrariness, and so on '.

Commissioner will then be able to act in some types of case where, judging by the legislative history, it was clearly the intention of Parliament that he should operate: in particular, decisions alleged by the complainant and found by the Commissioner to be biased or perverse, for bias and perversity were listed as types of maladministration in the debates on the Bill. . .

The Bad Rule

15. The other area in which Your Committee wish to encourage the Commissioner to extend his scope is the class of case where the aggrieved person is found to sustain hardship and indeed injustice through the correct application in his case of an administrative rule. . .

[A] . . . striking instance was provided by the ' Butler rules ' in the Commissioner's Third Report on Sachsenhausen.[7]

16. . . . [T]he Commissioner decided that he was not authorised to call the rule in question. He recorded as fact the result to the complainant of applying the rule, but did not go on to consider whether there was maladministration on the part of the Department in continuing to operate a rule which the aggrieved person, judging by the result for him, claimed to be defective. . . Having now given the matter further consideration, Your Committee have concluded that it would be appropriate and consistent with the provisions of the Act for the Commissioner to extend his authority in such cases.

17. Clearly the extension must be defined with care. For just as it is not for the Commissioner to substitute his administrative decisions for the Government's, so also it is not for the Commissioner to rewrite the Government's administrative rules. Nor is it for the Commissioner to judge a rule only on the strength of its result in the particular case that he has investigated. The fact that a rule causes hardship to an individual complainant does not necessarily prove that the rule is defective. For example, there may be grounds of public need which in the judgment of the Department override the hardship to the individual. But in the opinion of Your Committee it would be proper for the Commissioner to enquire whether, given the effect of the rule in the case under his investigation, the Department had taken any action to review the rule. If found defective and revised, what action had been taken to remedy the hardship sustained by the complainant? If not revised, whether there had been due consideration by the Department of the grounds for maintaining the rule? It would then be open to the Commissioner to find that the complainant had sustained injustice in consequence of

[7] See below p. 188.

maladministration, if these enquiries showed that there had been deficiencies in the departmental process of reviewing the rule.

[Second Report of the Select Committee on the Parliamentary Commissioner 1967–8. H.C. 350, 17 July 1968]

5. ... The Commissioner ... recalled that with the encouragement of Your Committee, he had widened his jurisdiction so that he put departments under inquiry whether they had reviewed rules which had caused hardship in cases which he had investigated. His view was that he was limited to satisfying himself that the department had properly reviewed the rules, but suggested that Your Committee were not so limited and might question a department whether they were right or wrong in their decision about the change of a rule.

6. Your Committee ... endorse the view that he is limited to testing the process of review of a rule, but that the Committee can add to the effectiveness of his work by testing the resulting decision, as they may do in cases where no question of review of rules, as such, arises. Your Committee so proceeded on the basis of the material set out in the Commissioner's casework in his Report and the examples given in evidence by the Commissioner, with the results set out in paragraphs 13 to 21 of this Report. . .

Rules for disposal of surplus agricultural land

13. Your Committee considered the application of the rules for disposal of surplus agricultural land, which were originally established following the Crichel Down Inquiry in 1954, in a case investigated by the Parliamentary Commissioner and included in his Annual Report for 1969. . .

15. The Commissioner, in his report on the case and in evidence before Your Committee, emphasised that there had been changes in the 1954 rules. . . The main change, which operated from February 1966 and was promulgated to departments by circular in January 1967, introduced a new factor by excluding from the ' offer back ' procedure land which carries planning permission or approval (actual or indicated) other than for agricultural purposes. The Commissioner informed Your Committee that the Ministry of Defence had correctly applied the revised rule and that he had not asked for it to be reviewed, partly because it had not necessarily caused hardship and partly because it was not the Ministry's rule. . .

17. The Treasury . . . confirmed that the instructions were determined centrally by the Government and conveyed to departments in the form of Treasury Circulars. . .

18. In evidence before Your Committee the Treasury official . . . stressed that this Circular . . . was in essence a guidance provided to

departments for the exercise of discretion in relation to the general principles which were laid down in 1954... [H]e informed Your Committee that the necessity for publicising the changes in rules was a matter of opinion.

19. Your Committee... are concerned, however, that a significant change... was introduced without any publicity. Your Committee accept that with the large number of administrative rules formulated by government every year, the extent to which changes should be made public must be a matter of judgment. But in the particular case, they note that the change was one which affected the public deeply, particularly as anyone can apply for planning permission and does not need to have an interest in the land. The Ministry of Defence evidence showed that since 1966 there were 70 sales of land by the Ministry where the land would have been offered back to the previous owners under the rules as they stood before 1966...

20. The change only came to light because two of the 70 complained, one being the case investigated by the Parliamentary Commissioner...

21. For the future Your Committee trust that consideration will be given to the need for immediate publicity where significant changes affecting the public are made in administrative rules. In the field of land disposal, Your Committee draw particular attention to the publicity attendant on the original statement of the rules in Parliament by the then Minister of Agriculture following the Crichel Down Inquiry in 1954, and suggest that when, as in this case, an administrative rule has been announced in Parliament subsequent changes of significance in that rule should also be announced in Parliament.

[First Report of the Select Committee on the Parliamentary Commissioner 1970–1. H.C. 240, 21 January 1971]

Statutory orders

7. The Speaker's Counsel submitted a paper on the subject of statutory orders which drew a distinction between Statutory Orders which are Statutory Instruments, and are, therefore, subject to the scrutiny of the Select Committee on Statutory Instruments, and those which are not... In evidence before the Committee the Speaker's Counsel stated that Statutory Instruments were mostly the exercise of legislative functions but that other Statutory Orders (not Statutory Instruments) were executive ones which could come within the administrative functions of Departments, although it was very difficult to draw the line...

10. The Attorney General endorsed the distinction drawn by the

Speaker's Counsel between Statutory Instruments and Statutory Orders which were not Statutory Instruments. In his view the whole process leading to the making of the Statutory Instrument was a legislative process and accordingly the Commissioner had no power to examine its form, its content or its merits. The question of whether or not there had been a review of the Instrument was within the jurisdiction of the Commissioner but the decision of the Minister or the department whether or not to make an amending order involved legislative processes and was not therefore for the Commissioner. He informed the Committee that in the processes leading up to the making of a Statutory Order which is not a Statutory Instrument, and in the reviewing processes subsequent to its making, a department was exercising an administrative function; and is his opinion the Commissioner had jurisdiction to investigate any complaints of maladministration in these processes . . .

11. . . . Your Committee think it is now open to the Commissioner to act in relation to the administrative processes attendant on the making and reviewing of Statutory Orders as identified by the Attorney General. This would mean that it would be proper for the Commissioner to investigate any complaint of maladministration in the administrative processes leading to the making and subsequent reviewing of Orders which are not Statutory Instruments. As regards Statutory Instruments, it would also be proper for the Commissioner to take account of the effect of an Instrument in a case under investigation and to enquire into the action taken by the Department concerned to review the operation of that Instrument.

[Report of the Select Committee on the Parliamentary Commissioner. H.C. 385 of 1968–9]

The Parliamentary Commissioner said that he would act on this recommendation [1st Report 1969–70 H.C. 13].

Conduct of Investigations

13. Stage 1 Investigation. Once a complaint has passed the ' screen ' for jurisdiction, and I propose to conduct an investigation, Section 7 (1) of the Act requires me as my first step to give to the principal officer of the department concerned an opportunity to comment on any allegations contained in the complaint. (The ' principal officer ' is the Permanent Secretary of the department or his equivalent.) The principal officer's comments to me usually contain a full statement of the facts known to the department and of the department's view of the case, often with supporting evidence. Sometimes this reply shows that I may proceed no further with my investigation. For example, it may emerge that the complainant has exercised his right of appeal to a tribunal and the complaint is thus

excluded from my jurisdiction by Section 5 (2) (a) of the Act... But if there is scope for further investigation I proceed to 'Stage 2 Investigation'.

14. Stage 2 Investigation. At this point members of my staff go to the department, availing themselves of my right of access to the files, and get further evidence from the files and through discussion with the officials who have handled the case. If it seems to me appropriate, they also take further evidence from the complainant and from any particular individual who has been named in the complaint. On occasion, e.g. the Sachsenhausen case, I have personally taken evidence from the departmental officials and also from the complainants, but usually my staff collect the evidence and present it to me with their recommendations on which I arrive at my personal conclusion as to the result of the investigation. This I embody in a results report which I render to the Member who referred the complaint to me, with a copy to the principal officer of the department. Before issuing the report I check with the department the correctness and presentation of the facts concerning them as embodied in the report. This procedure also gives the department the opportunity to consider if there is any information obtained from the department and proposed to be included in the report which, in the public interest, they would ask me not to disclose. (I cannot be denied access to information, but, under Section 11 (3) of the Act, a Minister has power to prevent me from disclosing information. The power has not so far been used.) The conclusions and findings in my results report are my personal responsibility.

15. Protection of persons complained against. The Act makes provision to ensure that any person against whom a complaint is made is not himself denied the rights of natural justice, but is given a fair opportunity to defend himself. Thus, at the same time as I send to the principal officer details of the complaint, I send a copy also to any individual named in the complaint, together with a memorandum explaining how he may comment to me on the allegations. At the time that I send my results report to the Member and to the principal officer concerned, the Act also requires me to send a copy to the person complained against, and this I do.

[Fourth Report of the Parliamentary Commissioner, 1967–8. H.C. 134, 28 February 1968]

17. It has been represented to me that, since Members take an active interest in complaints which they refer to me, I ought to afford them the opportunity of being present at any interview between a member of my staff and the complainant. The position which I have adopted is that, in the case of such an interview, I am content

for the complainant to decide whether he wishes to be accompanied by a friend or adviser; and if he wishes the Member to be present, I would not object.

18. Different considerations arise when a Member suggests, as has also been done, that I should afford him the opportunity of commenting on information and evidence given to me by the department during my investigation. This is a procedure that I cannot adopt. The reason is that in all complaints I investigate, the material I obtain from the department comes from my unrestricted inspection of their files and the evidence given to me by their officials during my investigation conducted, as the Act requires, in private. I do not think it would be compatible with my investigation procedure, or indeed with the terms on which Parliament has given me unrestricted access to departments, that I should impart the information so obtained to the Member in advance of reporting my findings to him.

[Second Report of the Parliamentary Commissioner, 1969–70. H.C. 138, 19 February 1970]

3. The Commissioner drew attention to some criticism that had been made of his procedures, particularly that he only saw the department concerned and did not give the complainant the chance to cross-examine the people against whom he complained. The Commissioner informed Your Committee that the criticism stemmed from the idea that he should operate like a judge in court, arriving at a finding on the basis of argument and counter-argument in front of him by both parties. He considered this to be incorrect. His function was to ascertain by inquiry inside the department what the departmental actions were which had given rise to the complaint of maladministration. In appropriate cases he and his staff saw, and took evidence from, the complainant and this in fact had happened in hundreds of cases.

4. Your Committee were glad to learn that it is the practice of the Commissioner to see the complainant in a significant number of cases and trust that he will continue to do so where appropriate. They endorse his procedures and his interpretation of his functions in this regard.

[First Report from the Select Committee on the Parliamentary Commissioner, 1970–1. H.C. 240, 21 January 1971]

Ministerial responsibility and the anonymity of the civil service
The Sachsenhausen case, 1967

Twelve persons who had been held in either Sonderlager A or the Zellenbau at Sachsenhausen in Germany during the 1939–45 war claimed a share of the compensation received by the British Government for the benefit of victims of Nazi persecution under the Anglo-German agreement of 1964. The Foreign Office, which was responsible for administering the fund, rejected their claims. In doing so they applied the so-called ' Butler rules ' laid down by R. A. Butler when he was Foreign Secretary. These provided that compensation was only to be paid to those who had been detained in concentration camps or in institutions in which the conditions were comparable. The Foreign Office decided that the Zellenbau and Sonderlager A were not part of the Sachsenhausen concentration camp and that the conditions in them were not comparable. The Foreign Secretary, Mr George Brown, wrote to Mr Airey Neave, M.P., on 30 December 1966: 'I cannot accept, on the basis of the evidence which has been assembled from various sources, including the officers' own statements, that they suffered treatment in any way comparable to that endured by the inmates of the main camp at Sachsenhausen or of any other concentration camp, about which I need hardly say we have abundant evidence.' A complaint was made to the Parliamentary Commissioner that in reaching this decision the Foreign Office had been guilty of maladministration which had caused an injustice. The Parliamentary Commissioner took the view that there had been maladministration in that the Foreign Office had given insufficient weight to some of the evidence, attached too much weight to other evidence, and had relied on some evidence that was irrelevant. He noted:

' 66. Summarising my conclusions:

(i) I criticise the process by which the Foreign Office decided against Sonderlager A and Zellenbau being part of Sachsenhausen Concentration Camp, because in my view the original decision was based on partial and largely irrelevant information, and the decision was maintained in disregard of additional information and evidence, particularly as regards Zellenbau.

(ii) I may not question the merits of the general ruling as applied throughout the compensation scheme that claimants judged not to have been held in a concentration camp had to establish detention in conditions comparable with those in a concentration camp " as generally understood ", meaning severe forms of Nazi persecution treatment. I record that this ruling could mean that a non-camp claimant had to pass a more severe test than a camp claimant, and that this actually happened at Sachsenhausen.

(iii) I criticise the treatment by the Foreign Office of the evidence submitted by the complainants in support of their claims as regards their own conditions under detention in Zellenbau and as regards conditions in the main compound of Sachsenhausen.'

He recommended that the Foreign Office should review the evidence and take a fresh decision on the claims [Third Report of the Parliamentary Commissioner 1967–8]. His report was debated on 5 February 1968.

THE SECRETARY OF STATE FOR FOREIGN AFFAIRS (MR GEORGE BROWN) . . . The case could not begin with me. I came to it . . . predisposed towards the views of the claimants. I wished to be generous and I questioned at that point whether the Foreign Office was being over-legalistic, but, having started from that position, I am prepared to accept the responsibility for being satisfied that all the information I need was supplied to me. This is one of the grounds on which I disagree with the Parliamentary Commissioner... [A]nd I came to my conclusions by my own processes of judgment...

I do not believe that I was misled by officials. I regard it as a Minister's job to see that he has all the necessary information. If he does not have it, that is a very severe mark against him... [W]e will breach a very serious constitutional position if we start holding officials responsible for things that are done wrong. In this country, Ministers are Members of Parliament... Ministers are responsible to Parliament. If things are wrongly done, then they are wrongly done by Ministers... It is Ministers who must be attacked, not officials. The office of Parliamentary Commissioner was intended to strengthen our form of democratic government, but... if that Office were to lead to changing this constitutional position so that officials got attacked and Ministers escaped, then I think that the whole practice of Ministers being accountable to Parliament would be undermined. I think that the morale of the Civil and Department Services would be undermined... Ministers must ... remain responsible to Parliament... Officials must remain responsible to their Minister...

Having established the office of Parliamentary Commissioner, whether I think his judgment is right or wrong, I am certain that it would be wrong to reject his view. I think that public opinion would be outraged if I rejected his view on an issue which affects personally a few very gallant men...

Newspapers talk about bungling and blundering... [N]o-one has blundered or bungled. This was an issue of judgment. The Parliamentary Commissioner's view is that our judgment was wrong. I am willing to accept that. I have therefore reviewed and revised my decision...

[H.C.Deb. 5s. c. 108. 5 February 1968]

The Select Committee took up the question of the Sachsenhausen case in their First and Second Reports of 1967–8. They were particularly concerned with what they regarded as the Foreign Minister's refusal to accept that there had been maladministration and the refusal of the Foreign Office to identify or to allow them to examine the foreign office official whom they believed to be responsible.[8] In the light of this refusal

---

[8] In the course of the Select Committee's examination of the Permanent Head of the Foreign Office, Sir Paul Gore-Booth, Mr Lyon asked which Foreign Office official was in fact dealing with the question [Minutes of evidence First Report, H.C. 258, 1967–8, Q. 315]. Sir Paul replied: 'This

they examined the Attorney-General on the general question of Ministerial responsibility and their powers in this context before making their
Second Report.

6. ... On the facts made available by the Commissioner and confirmed in evidence given to them, Your Committee endorse the
conclusion that the original decision of August 1965 was based on
information that was partial (in the sense of incomplete) and, as it
later turned out, largely irrelevant. Given the magnitude of the
officials' task (there were about 4,000 claimants...), and the lack
of time for detailed enquiries if distribution were not to be held up
Your Committee cannot blame the officials for acting on the information at their disposal without seeking to obtain the additional
evidence that later became available from the claimants themselves
and from other sources. They note, however, that the original
decision was taken in August 1965 and could have been reviewed
before the extended closing date for applications of 31st March 1966.
In their judgment the more serious criticism relates to the defective
processes by which ' the decision was maintained in disregard of
additional information and evidence, particularly as regards
Zellenbau '...

8. ... By this time the exclusion of these claims had become a
matter of Parliamentary controversy, and Foreign Office Ministers
were concerned in the details of each case. The silence of Ministers
on the subject of the Zellenbau location makes it clear that there
were defects in the information and advice provided by officials, and
Your Committee do not accept the inference that is to be drawn
from the view expressed to the House on 5th February by the
Foreign Secretary, that all the blame for such defects should fall on
Ministers because it is ' a Minister's job to see that he has all the
necessary information ' (Hansard, 5th February, c. 111). This was,
however, a case where the important facts about location ... were
twice conveyed personally to Ministers, in November 1965 and again
in December 1966. Your Committee cannot absolve the Ministers
concerned from a share of the blame for ignoring this evidence, for
not verifying it and for not providing themselves with the means to

---

is perhaps where I have to draw the line in answering questions under the
authority which I have. I can answer for the Department. I think I must
not get into the question of individual people working on the file.' In
reply to a question by Dame Irene Ward as to the grade at which it was
considered in the Foreign Office [Q. 317] he replied: ' It was being done
in a department, which is like any other, and it is then submitted up to
the Minister through an Under-Secretary. A Minister, if not satisfied, calls
for more papers, which the Minister, on a number of occasions in this
matter, did.'

tell the claimants and the Members of Parliament concerned what significance if any the Foreign Office attached to it.

[First Report of the Select Committee on the Parliamentary Commissioner, 1967–8. H.C. 258, 16 May 1968]

RT. HON. SIR ELWYN JONES, Q.C., ATTORNEY-GENERAL and a Member of the House examined. 1 May 1968.

546. (SIR ELWYN JONES) . . . [A]s I see it . . . two issues arise for consideration. . . The first is whether the Committee should publish with its Report to the House of Commons evidence disclosing the name of a certain Foreign [Office] Official, and secondly the propriety of the Foreign Secretary's refusal to permit the official to comment on that evidence. My broad submission is that to publish the name of the official would do him an injustice, would be to act contrary to the spirit of the Parliamentary Commissioner Act, would be to damage the standing and future work of the Parliamentary Commissioner himself, and possibly would undermine further than was contemplated by the setting up of the office of the Parliamentary Commissioner the doctrine of Ministerial responsibility. As to the second issue, namely the Foreign Secretary's refusal to permit the official to comment on the evidence that had been given by Mr Neave, my submission is that the Foreign Secretary's acquiescence in the Committee's request that the named official should be allowed to comment on the evidence given to the Select Committee would imply acceptance of the doctrine that it would be proper for this Committee to single out and place particular responsibility on a single civil servant, in this case, incidentally, not of senior rank, and might also have far-reaching consequences so far as the success of the Parliamentary Commissioner in carrying out the duties Parliament has imposed upon him is concerned. The Committee will appreciate that the official in question had already given evidence to the Parliamentary Commissioner who had acted strictly in accordance with his statutory responsibilities. The Parliamentary Commissioner has told the Committee the safeguards which fall to him to apply in respect of a case where an individual civil servant is named in a complaint which was not the case here. . .

The function . . . of conducting investigations into alleged maladministration was expressly laid by Parliament on the Parliamentary Commissioner and not on any Committee of the House of Commons. The Act also expressly provides that the investigations, as I have already read from section 1 (1), shall be conducted in accordance with the provisions of the Act and not otherwise. In view of the important inroad that the whole of this machinery makes into the traditional doctrine of Ministerial responsibility, Parliament must have had very much in mind that its new machinery should be very clearly described and its limitations clearly indicated... The task which is laid on the Select Committee by its terms of reference is not to investigate complaints against Departments, which is the function of the Parliamentary Commissioner, but to examine reports laid before the House by the Parliamentary Commissioner and, it is an admittedly wide phrase which follows, ' matters in connection therewith '. The Parliamentary Commissioner has in certain circumstances power to identify individual civil servants involved in the matters he is investigating. In this particular case, however, he decided that it would not be right to do so. I venture to submit that in a case like this, in which it is known that the Parliamentary Commissioner has received the full co-operation of the department, including the officials concerned, and has himself decided not to publish the name of the officials, the Select Committee should respect his decision and not depart from what was, in his view, the proper course. This aspect of the matter was referred to by the Financial Secretary who was in charge of the Bill as it went through the House. In the debate on Lords Amendments on the 15th March, 1967, Volume 743, No. 164, he said in column 635, ' My hon. Friend the Member for Nottingham, West... asked whether with the amended wording it will be possible for the Parliamentary Commissioner in making his report to identify who had made the decision, and I think that my hon. Friend was more particularly concerned at the level at which the decision had been made. It would certainly be within the Commissioner's power but, as a matter of practice, as has been stated before, one would hope that only in exceptional circumstances would he want to identify by name particular civil servants. We want to preserve the anonymity of the Civil Service. But he might think it important to draw attention to the level at which the decision had been taken, particularly if he thought the matter was of such importance that it should have been referred to a higher level. That would be within the scope of the Commissioner's powers '...

MR FLETCHER-COOKE. 549. In order to find out whether grievances have been put right, whether a proper system of administration has now been put into effect where there was none before, it is necessary for us to inquire not merely of Ministers and principal officers but of the officials who are administering whether they are administering according to the recommendations of the Parliamentary Commissioner? – I wonder whether you are not putting it a little wide in thinking that you have a roving Commission to examine the whole of the administration of a Department. Is it not rather your function to examine whether the particular maladministration has been remedied to the benefit of the individual citizen who complained and to examine whether steps have been taken to prevent a recurrence of that sort of maladministration?... I cannot see how to demand the presence of a junior civil servant and particularly to identify him by name furthers that exercise. The appropriate person to answer that kind of query is the Under-Secretary who is the senior civil servant in the Department, assisted by whomsoever he may think most informed about the problem... It is one thing to invite senior officials such as the Permanent Under-Secretary, assisted perhaps by the Legal Adviser of the Department, to answer questions on behalf of the Department. In my submission it is quite another matter for this Committee to probe again into ground already covered by the Parliamentary Commissioner by seeking to obtain evidence concerning individual junior officials and by inviting them to comment on evidence so obtained. This looks more like repeating the investigation which the Parliamentary Commissioner is authorised by the Act to conduct than an examination of the report laid before the House of Commons, and also under conditions highly disadvantageous to the individual civil servant who might be concerned... The matter was put by the Financial Secretary in the debate on the Third Reading of the Bill, column 1448 of *Hansard* for the 25th January, 1967, Vol. 739, No. 129, in this way, and I do not recollect that it was departed from by the House... 'I conceive that by and large the Select Committee will not be concerned with the investigations or the reports on particular individual cases. What it will be concerned with is in helping to work out the procedures and, in particular, the conventions which we must devise among ourselves as hon. Members in handling complaints which are to be referred to the Commissioner and, secondly, in receiving his reports and seeing what kind of action we need to take as Members of Parliament to put right situations which are brought to light by his investigations'... There is one further aspect of this matter which the Committee may think of no little importance. It is that, as I see it, there is a danger that if junior officials are called before the Committee and responsibility is laid at their door for any maladministration in the Department, the doctrine of Ministerial responsibility could be undermined more than it was intended that it should be undermined by Parliament. Traditionally, and I submit for very good reason, it is the Minister in charge of the Department who is answerable to Parliament for the workings of the Department. The individual civil servant is, of course, not so responsible... I submit that to attach blame to the individual civil servant, save in certain exceptional cases which might arise where the civil servant had himself affronted a member of the public or something of that kind by his conduct, would run counter to this long established tradition.

MR LYON. 553. . . . Is there only between us a difference of judgment about whether it is desirable for any purpose that we have in this Committee to call a junior civil servant? If that is the issue, then it is a judgment which is best reserved, is it not, for this Committee and not for the government? – I think it is a judgment which in the last resort is best reserved for the House of Commons. I respectfully agree that you are charged by the House of Commons with the responsibility, and you will have to evolve your procedures and conventions and decide how far you think you ought to go. . . If . . . you contemplate doing what is proposed, I submit . . . it is a matter upon which you may think it would be suitable to take the views of the House of Commons. . .

555. . . . – It is not the duty of this Committee to smoke out an individual junior civil servant who has slipped up. That is the Parliamentary Commissioner's job. . .

MR FLETCHER-COOKE. 557. You must surely conceive of a situation in which a principal officer who is being asked questions does give us unsatisfactory or incomplete answers . . . – Yes. . .

558. Is it your view that we should drop the investigation at that point? – No. My view of that situation is that you should report back to the House of Commons that in your investigation of this matter you have found a senior civil servant who was lacking in frankness or who failed to do whatever you criticised him in your question to me for failing to do. You would identify the situation. You could tell the House of Commons that you could not say whether in that department this maladministration had been put right but that you had heard an official who seemed to you to be thoroughly unsatisfactory. Then the Minister has got to answer for that.

[Second Report from the Select Committee on the Parliamentary Commissioner, 1967–8. H.C. 350, 19 July 1968]

24. Your Committee note that the recent report of the Fulton Committee on the Civil Service (Cmnd. 3638) recommended that the convention of anonymity should be modified and civil servants should be able to go further than now in explaining what their Departments are doing.

25. Your Committee recognise that, by setting up the Office of the Parliamentary Commissioner for Administration, Parliament has undermined the doctrine to some extent, in that the power of the Commissioner to carry out an independent investigation within the

Department, and publish what he finds, is an encroachment upon the Minister's responsibility. The anonymity of civil servants may be infringed by the findings of the Commissioner, either because the complaint under investigation is directed against a specific official or because the Commissioner may identify an official in the course of his investigation . . .

28. In his evidence the Attorney General recognised that under their Order of Reference there is no limitation upon the persons on whom Your Committee can call for evidence in discharge of their function of supporting the activities of the Parliamentary Commissioner. On the other hand, he suggested that the Committee should organise their proceedings so as to maintain the balance between this function and the protection of Ministerial responsibility upon which the efficiency of democratic Government depends.

29. Your Committee fully recognise that they have a responsibility for maintaining this balance. They also wish to state that it is a misapprehension to suppose that they regard it as their function to 'retry' cases reported by the Commissioner, or to review his findings by going over ground already covered by his investigations. If a case should occur where his adverse report identifies an official, and that report is examined by Your Committee, it will not be possible for them to avoid concerning themselves with that official, e.g. where they are considering remedial action. But in such a case the official concerned will already have received the protection provided by the Parliamentary Commissioner Act. Your Committee feel confident that they will regulate their procedure so as to avoid the impression that they are in any way seeking to identify or blame individual officials where the finding of the Commissioner is that an administrative defect is the collective responsibility of the Department or of officials in that Department.

30. On the other hand, Your Committee do not agree with the suggestion that they should confine themselves to taking evidence from the Principal Officer of a Department where they are considering what the Department should do to remedy administrative defects disclosed by the Commissioner's investigation. As the Attorney General acknowledged, they have an undoubted right under their Order of Reference to call for evidence from any persons who they think can assist them in their enquiry. They agree that generally the appropriate witness will be the Principal Officer, in view of his responsibility and authority for the administrative systems of the Department with which they are concerned. On the other hand, there may well be infrequent occasions when Your Committee will judge it necessary to inform themselves about the nature of the defect in the system as well as the measures taken to remedy that

defect. For that and other purposes they may need to obtain the evidence of those officials who are concerned at first hand with the actions in question. Your Committee are satisfied that they will be able to take evidence from subordinate officials for this purpose without exposing them to unfair publicity or criticism, and they feel that they can rely on Departments to indicate the appropriate witnesses. Your Committee note with interest that the Fulton Report (paragraph 281), in commenting on the relations between the Civil Service and Parliament, envisaged a greater involvement of civil servants below the level of Permanent Secretary (i.e. Principal Officer).[9]

[Second Report of the Select Committee on the Parliamentary Commissioner, 1967–8. H.C. 350, 19 July 1968]

IV. NATIONALISED INDUSTRIES

The History of Ministerial Control

43. The formal powers of Ministers to control the nationalised industries are laid down in the statutes... These are fundamental because even the more informal, but potent, influence of Ministers derives eventually from their possession of certain statutory powers...

45. The precise powers given in the statutes vary considerably in detail to match the particular histories and circumstances of each industry, and even the standard powers are not uniformly expressed... But the content of the main powers given to Ministers is common. These principal powers are to appoint the members of Boards, to give the Boards general directions ' in the national interest ', and to approve investment programmes (the wording varies – the usual references are to ' act on lines ' or ' in accordance with a general programme ' approved by the Minister in respect of ' substantial outlay on capital account ')...

46. Other important powers include the power to control the industry's borrowing (mainly from the Minister himself) subject to ceilings authorised by Parliament, the right to approve the forms of accounts, and the right (in several cases) to approve programmes of research and development and of training and education. In addition, Ministers have strictly limited powers to give Boards specific

---

[9] ' We have noted the potential significance of the development of the new specialised Parliamentary Committees... We hope that these will enable Members of Parliament to be more closely associated with the major business of government and administration, both national and local... we hope, too, that their consultations with departments will increasingly include civil servants below the level of Permanent Secretary.'

directions, for example following a recommendation by a Consumers' Council.

47. Ministers also have certain powers or duties in respect of the nationalised industries under legislation other than the Acts specifically concerned with the industries. Examples include the responsibilities of the Minister of Power to develop fuel policies under the Ministry of Fuel and Power Act 1945, his powers in relation to the construction of power stations under the Electric Lighting Act 1909, and the powers given to Ministers under recent prices and incomes legislation.

Wider Aspects

48. However, as has been clearly demonstrated by earlier Reports of the Committee, Ministerial control of the nationalised industries is not confined within the boundaries prescribed in the statutes. With varying degrees of formality or informality, Ministers have come to exercise power, authority or influence in certain fields – particularly regarding broad policy, prices and in some cases salaries, wages and staff relations – that is every bit as real a part of their control over the industries as that exercised under their statutory powers...

50. Ministerial control ... is something that has grown up in a somewhat haphazard way. It has been distorted by the troubles of individual industries and has not been planned with foresight, prescribed with clarity or applied with consistency...

51. The industries' responsibilities and the Ministers' statutory powers, and the extent to which they justify, or can be used to lend weight to, extra-statutory control, have been subject to greatly varied interpretations. One broad characteristic is worth emphasising. Both from the statutes and in the twenty-one years of practical application some demarcation of interest and responsibility have become plain between the Boards and Ministers. Broadly, apart from the appointment of Board members and a marginal interest in research and development and training and education, active Ministerial control has been predominantly concerned with financial and economic matters, especially investment programmes, prices, financial objectives, and surpluses, deficits and subsidies. But these do not touch on a great many factors which bear on the efficiency of the industries. Such matters as commercial policies and marketing machinery, personnel policies, labour relations, recruitment and promotion methods and internal organisation have usually been regarded as lying within the nationalised industries' own sphere of decision... Furthermore, the Committee have received surprisingly little evidence that even the quality of services and consumer relations – matters in which Ministers might have been expected to take

a great interest because of their political and public sensitivity – are the subject of Ministerial intervention, except when Ministers are pressured by parliamentary questions... Not surprisingly, though not necessarily correctly, the concern of Ministers has been almost exclusively confined to those matters in which money is directly involved...

The Theory of Ministerial Control

60. It was clearly intended by Parliament that Ministers should, to some extent or other, exercise control over the nationalised industries: for this was one of the major purposes of nationalising them. On the other hand it was equally clearly intended that the industries should benefit from some degree of managerial autonomy, and that some limits should thus be set to Ministerial control: otherwise there would be no point in establishing public corporations, with ' high-powered chairmen ' and their own independent staff – they could have been placed, like the Post Office in the past, under the direct responsibility of Ministers. Hence the statutes imply a role for Ministers, but not one that extends to what has come to be called ' day-to-day management '. They also imply a limited degree of Parliamentary control; for example the industries' expenditure is not borne on the Estimates, and if the activities of Ministers are limited the extent of their Parliamentary accountability must be limited to a similar extent.

61. The statutes imply that the industries have two types of obligation. The first of these is that they must be responsive to the public interest...

63. The second type of obligation for the industries, implied by the statutes, is to operate as efficient commercial bodies...

67. Although the obligations to be responsive to the public interest and to operate as efficient undertakings rest with the industries, the fulfilment of these obligations cannot be left to the industries alone. Ministers have responsibilities under both heads. The Chief Secretary to the Treasury argued that the function of Government in relation to the industries is, above all, to see that the economic advantage of the nation as a whole is secured by the individual industries. This meant seeing that the industries are as efficient as possible, and seeing that financial and economic policies are pursued which ensure that a proper balance is maintained between the public and private sectors...

68. [But] Ministers are, to some extent, concerned with using their control over the industries to secure wider public interests...

69. These ends vary greatly... but they have included the broader management of the economy, for example regulating the level of

investment in the public sector, ensuring conformity with prices and incomes policies by deferring price increases, and preserving industrial peace by urging a settlement of an industrial dispute. There has frequently been emphasis on securing the provision of socially desirable services such as air services to the Highlands and Islands of Scotland, the supply of electricity to rural areas, the preservation in service of branch railway lines, and assistance for the coal industry. Another conception of the public interest has shown itself in the assumption by Ministers of the responsibilities for formulating long-term policies for the industries, such as the decision to maintain a certain size of railway system. The maintenance of good employment practices – 'fair wages' for example – may involve the public interest and hence that of Ministers. And finally Ministers may wish to use their powers in response to political or Parliamentary pressures – so long, of course, as they find them in accord with the public interest.

The Nature of Ministerial Control

82. Control can be formal or informal. Formal controls are primarily those exercised under powers contained in Acts or other legislative instruments. Even if not automatically subject to Parliamentary procedures, they can, of course, be questioned in Parliament and hence made public. Informal controls range from those now well recognised extra-statutory powers, such as control over prices (although Ministers now have a formal status in this field under the prices and incomes legislation) where responsibility is publicly recognised and for which Ministers are accountable to Parliament, to the completely informal, and usually unpublicised, exercise of influence through what has been called the 'lunch-table directive'. Examples of the use of informal controls include, in addition to pricing control, influence exercised over wage questions; control of advertising by the electricity and gas industries; pressures on the National Coal Board regarding their programme for pit closures; and the pressure on the Gas Council regarding their first contract for North Sea gas...

83. Although the industries sometimes complained about its application, most of their witnesses made little criticism of the way control is often exercised informally. On the whole they accepted that this was inevitable. The Chairman of the Electricity Council said that there had been very few occasions when they had been pressed hard to accept something privately for which Ministers were not prepared to accept public responsibility... They had never 'subordinated' themselves 'to the wishes of a Minister'. Where they had complied with a Minister's wishes, this had been referred

to in their Annual Reports. The Chairman of the London Transport Board said that his relations with the Minister had always been quite open, and he had never been subject to an ' unofficial, hinted, covert, non-accountable directive '.

84. The Ministers, not surprisingly, were happy with these informal arrangements. They thought the dangers of the ' lunch-table directive ' were exaggerated. Exchanges of information, ideas and pressures were two-way. And in any event informality was inevitable. On this last point they were strongly supported by Professor Hanson, who argued that informality is inevitable since neither the Ministers nor Boards would normally wish to expose their disagreements to public comment, nor could they be compelled to do so, for ' no power on earth apart from actual physical separation and interruption of postal and telephone communications can prevent the Minister from *consulting* with the Board members whom he has appointed and whom he is able to dismiss '. Such consultations would normally end in compromise.

85. The Committee have argued in the past that where Ministers exercise control they should have statutory powers to do so, particularly in relation to financial policies and pricing.[10] And proposals for a more formal set of financial controls were included in their 1967 Report on the Post Office (Report of the Committee of 1967 on the Post Office, paragraphs XVII 20–33). The one industry that was specifically in favour of greater formalisation of controls – the National Coal Board – welcomed these proposals... But Professor Hanson was so doubtful of the possibilities of enforcing any formal demarcation of responsibilities between Ministers and Boards that he proposed that the statutory requirements should be relaxed to bring them into line with the informal conventions, rather than vice-versa. Ministers should accept a broad responsibility to Parliament for the policies and major activities of their industries.

Parliamentary Accountability

86. ... Ministerial control must be seen against the background of the responsibility of Ministers to Parliament. As the Board of Trade evidence put it, ' The Corporations recognise that the President is responsible for answering for them in Parliament on matters of Parliamentary concern, and that he must therefore be well informed on their activities and take a particular interest in their financial results, their reputation and general efficiency '...

87. ... Ministers are responsible to the House, i.e. they may be

[10] See, for example, the Report of the Committee of 1958 on the National Coal Board, paragraph 89; and the Report of the Committee on the Gas Industry, paragraphs 74–81.

questioned about, or asked to justify in debate any action they have taken in relation to the industries, whether under statutes or informally, provided, of course – and this is important – that such informal activities have become known to Members. They may also be asked to exercise their statutory powers or informal powers for which they have clearly accepted responsibility, or asked about their non-exercise. In other words Ministers are liable to account to Parliament for all the actual exercise of their control over the industries, and also for the possible or potential exercise of their formal and better-known informal powers. In addition they may, on some occasions, be required to explain and even defend matters which fall wholly within the responsibilities of the industries themselves. Ministers are not only required to answer for themselves; they may also have to act as advocates for the Boards.

[First Report of the Select Committee on the Nationalised Industries, 1967–8. H.C. 371, 24 July 1968]

V. THE BANK OF ENGLAND

BANK OF ENGLAND ACT, 1946   [9 & 10 Geo. 6 ch. 27]

2. (1)... [O]n and after... [the appointed] day there shall be a Governor, a Deputy Governor and sixteen directors of the Bank, who shall be the court of directors.

(2) The Governor, Deputy Governor and other members of the court of directors shall be appointed by His Majesty.

(3) The provisions of the Second Schedule to this Act shall have effect as respects the tenure of office, qualifications and employment of members of the court of directors and meetings of the court...[11]

4. (1) The Treasury may from time to time give such directions to the Bank as, after consultation with the Governor of the Bank, they think necessary in the public interest.

(2) Subject to any such directions, the affairs of the Bank shall be managed by the court of directors in accordance with such provisions (if any) in that behalf as may be contained in any charter of the Bank for the time being in force and any byelaws made thereunder.

(3) The Bank, if they think it necessary in the public interest, may request information from and make recommendations to bankers, and may, if so authorised by the Treasury, issue directions to

---

[11] These provide *inter alia* that the Governor and Deputy-Governor are to be appointed for terms of five years at a time, and that Members of Parliament, Ministers and civil servants may not hold the offices of Governor, Deputy-Governor or Director.

any banker for the purpose of securing that effect is given to any such request or recommendation:

Provided that: —

> (a) no such request or recommendations shall be made with respect to the affairs of any particular customer of a banker; and

> (b) before authorising the issue of any such directions the Treasury shall give the banker concerned, or such person as appears to them to represent him, an opportunity of making representations with respect thereto.

(4) If, at any time before any recommendations or directions are made or given in writing to a banker under the last foregoing sub-section, the Treasury certify that it is necessary in the public interest that the recommendations or directions should be kept secret, and the certificate is transmitted to the banker together with the recommendations or directions, the recommendations or directions shall be deemed, for the purpose of section two of the Official Secrets Act, 1911, as amended by any subsequent enactment, to be a document entrusted in confidence to the banker by a person holding office under His Majesty; and the provisions of the Official Secrets Acts, 1911 to 1939, shall apply accordingly.

(5) Save as provided in the last foregoing subsection, nothing in the Official Secrets Acts, 1911 to 1939, shall apply to any request, recommendations or directions made or given to a banker under subsection (3) of this section.

(6) In this section the expression ' banker ' means any such person carrying on a banking undertaking as may be declared by order of the Treasury to be a banker for the purposes of this section...

The Bank's relationship with the Central Government

761. ... [T]he practice of collaboration with the central government and of deference to its requirements on any critical issue of monetary policy developed by a process of practical accommodation over a considerable period of time without formal record or statutory intervention. The practice was ... established long before the nationalisation Act of 1946. ... In the new circumstances of the post-war years, in particular since the revival of a positive monetary policy after 1951, both parties have been trying to evolve and practise an allocation of their respective functions which, while recognising the clear implications of the 1946 Act that the will of the Government, formally expressed in the form of a direction, is paramount ... accepts the advantages of retaining in the Bank a separate organisation with a life of its own, capable of generating

advice, views and proposals that are something more than a mere implementation of its superior's instructions. . .

766. We do not think it likely that the complete constitutional structure of the central bank of the United Kingdom . . . can ever be built up out of a series of statutory forms and prescriptions. . . What is much more important . . . is that there should be a clear public understanding of the purposes which a central bank exists to serve. . .

767. The central bank . . . is one of the principal authorities concerned with the framing and operation of monetary policy. The controls which can be exercised in the fields of its activities are not . . . the only controls which . . . influence . . . the monetary system. It follows that . . . to plan and implement . . . monetary policy . . . requires . . . cooperation . . . between the central bank . . . and those responsible for alternative or supplementary . . . measures, essentially the Treasury and the Board of Trade. . . More than that, monetary policy . . . is a part of the country's economic policy as a whole. . . [T]his policy . . . must include the general planning of monetary policy and . . . operations. . .

768. . . . We are . . . disassociating ourselves from a view . . . that . . . the central bank should be assured complete independence from political influence . . . because it . . . assumes that the true objective of a central bank is one single and unvarying purpose, the stability of the currency and the exchanges. . . [This objective] . . . is too limited in scope and . . . incapable of achievement without concurrent action on the part of the central government. . .

770. This . . . does not lead us to advocate the view that the Bank's position should be regarded as that of a rather exceptional Government department. Such a view . . . takes too little account of the Bank's special relationship with the market, in which it is at once an operator and to some extent a controller . . . [and] the peculiar status the Bank enjoys in its overseas connections with the rest of the sterling area, overseas central banks and international agencies.

771. The present system involves continuous and confidential exchanges between the Bank and the Treasury. . . [B]ut because they are . . . to a large extent confidential they tend to obscure the . . . division of responsibility. . . The fixing of Bank Rate has presented itself to us as an instance. . . In form the Bank Rate change appears as a decision of the Court; in practice, by an understanding which long precedes 1946, no change . . . is announced without the prior approval of the Chancellor of the Exchequer. In form a change . . . is proposed to the Chancellor by the Governor on behalf of the Bank; in fact all decisions . . . are decisions of significant importance to the Government's general economic policy. . . [T]he true respon-

sibility . . . lies with the Chancellor of the Exchequer, not the Bank; and it would be better that this should be made explicit by the announcement being made in the name of the Chancellor and on his authority.

[Report of the Committee on the Working of the Monetary System. Cmnd. 827 (August 1959)]

The functions of the Bank

21. The functions performed by the Bank vary widely and are carried out by the Bank acting in a variety of different capacities:

as the direct agent of Government (e.g. exchange control);

as adviser to the Government (principally in the provision of economic and monetary advice, based in part on the Bank's economic intelligence work);

as the arm of the Government (in the implementation, for instance, of credit control or in operating in the gilt-edged and foreign exchange markets);

as a banker (in relation to its customers, be they the clearing banks, other central banks or its comparatively few private customers);

and as the background to all its work, simply as the central bank with international obligations and with a sense of responsibility for the good order of the financial system in this country.

It is not always easy to separate the different capacities. . .

Contacts between the Bank and Government

213. As the Treasury indicated to Your Committee, control is not the essence of the relationship between the Treasury and the Bank. What matters is the working relationship built up over very long periods of time. 'Co-operation' is the key word. . .

214. The relationship between the Treasury and the Bank may, as Lord Balogh suggested, depend very much on the personalities of the Chancellor and of the Governor of the time. There is no doubt that the key relationship between the Chancellor and the Governor has plenty of opportunity of developing. 'The Chancellor has a regular meeting with the Governor about once a week'. The Chancellor himself, discussing the significance of the Act of 1946 took the view that it had speeded up the evolution of the relationship between the Chancellor and the Bank. There is a contrast to be drawn between the present situation and the more distant relationships and indeed differences between Lord Cunliffe as Governor and successive Chancellors at the time of the First World War. Your

Committee regard the close contacts which now exist as being wholly desirable.

215. The Permanent Secretary to the Treasury also has 'a separate meeting with the Governor about once a week ', and there is a whole range of regular contacts between officials at lower levels ... Most of these contacts clearly have to do with market operations. It would seem clear from the evidence that the domestic affairs of the Bank are not discussed.

216. Another regular source of contact between Government and the Bank is through the various Whitehall committees on which the Bank sits. 'Somebody from the Bank is on nearly every economic committee.' Although it is against normal practice to disclose details of the machinery of inter-departmental discussion, the Bank did explain that most of the committees were probably ad hoc committees, and that 'the Bank participated in upwards of twenty official committees and that in addition there is a very much greater degree of participation in other less formalised groups and the like '. The Governor doubted whether ' any day passes without the Bank at one level or another attending meetings in Whitehall '.

217. Lord Balogh, commenting on the Bank's representation on many Whitehall committees, pointed out that there was no reciprocity ... by which he meant that no Government officials sat on Bank Committees. This point answered by the Treasury who made it clear that the Bank sat on certain inter-departmental committees whose function was to produce policy advice for the Government. The function of the Bank committees was to deal with the Bank's internal affairs; the Bank did not sit on any committees dealing with the organisation of the Treasury or the Civil Service. Your Committee accept the Treasury answer ...

218. Apart from contact, through inter-departmental committees, with Government departments other than the Treasury, the Bank also has direct contacts with the Board of Trade ' on things affecting companies legislation ' and on statistics. In the latter connection there is also close liaison with the Central Statistical Office.

The principle of public accountability
... 271. In its operations in the markets, in its implementation of monetary policy, and particularly in its giving of advice to the Government the Bank acts very much as an arm of Government. It is not, however, constituted like a Government department. It would seem to Your Committee that if the Bank is to be publicly accountable for its work in these directions it should be so primarily through the Treasury or to the same extent as the Treasury. And it would seem to them entirely proper that accountability for the

Bank's actions as agent for the Government in all spheres of monetary and economic affairs should have increased since 1946 and be
increasing all the time.

272. This opens up the question of whether sufficient light is
shed on the whole process of economic management by monetary
and fiscal means. All the journalists who gave evidence drew attention to the secrecy which surrounds this process in this country...
It was argued that perhaps the best way in which to combat this
excessive secrecy was to consider the possibility of having a Select
Committee on Economic Affairs [12]... It has not been within Your
Committee's brief to consider policy matters, but rather the way in
which the Bank carries out its functions including the implementation of policy decisions. Nevertheless it does seem to Your Committee that a strong case can be made for some closer form of parliamentary scrutiny, if not of policy, at least of the implications of
policy...

273. The way in which the Bank advises the Government may be
one of its most important functions, but Your Committee are not
qualified to comment on that advice. If a Select Committee were
ever ordered to consider general questions of economic policy (involving the Bank) it would clearly be a very different committee
from the Nationalised Industries Committee. The interest of that
Committee in the public accountability of the Bank is limited to a
narrower area, to the efficiency of the Bank of England in performing those functions which the Act of 1946 calls the ' affairs of the
Bank ' and which do not involve day-to-day liaison with Government
– that is, those functions which it performs in a way most clearly
analogous to the working of any other nationalised industry.

[First Report from the Select Committee on Nationalised Industries,
1969–70. H.C. 258, 5 May 1970]

VI. THE GOVERNMENT AND PRIVATE INDUSTRY

The Industrial Reorganisation Corporation, 1966–71

2. The need for more concentration and rationalisation to promote
the greater efficiency and international competitiveness of British
industry, which was emphasised in the National Plan, is now widely
recognised. With the cooperation of financial institutions, many
industries have already substantially altered their structure and
organisation through mergers, acquisitions and regroupings. This
process has been accelerating in recent years and may be expected

[12] See below p. 342.

to continue. Nevertheless, the pace and scale of change do not yet match the needs of the national economy.

4. There is no evidence that we can rely on market forces alone to produce the necessary structural changes at the pace required . . .

5. Although there is now a large number of institutions which can provide specialist services to meet the financial and other needs of industry, there is no organisation whose special function is to search for opportunities to promote rationalisation schemes which could yield substantial benefits to the national economy. . . The Government consider that this gap in the institutional framework needs to be filled and they propose to set up a new statutory body for the purpose, to be called the Industrial Reorganisation Corporation. The necessary legislation will be introduced as soon as possible.

6. The Corporation will seek the fullest co-operation from industry and existing financial institutions, and schemes which it initiates will, when ever possible, be put into effect either through the normal machinery of the market or in close collaboration with the market. It will be able to acquire a stake in the ownership of new groupings or enterprises it helps to create or to expand. It will not, however, act as a general holding company and will be able to dispose of its investments when the profits of rationalisation have been assured and it can do so to advantage . . .

7. The Corporation will give priority to schemes of rationalisation and modernisation which offer good prospects of early returns in terms of increased exports or reduced import requirements, and will have regard to the regional aspects of the Government's policies for economic development. It will not support ventures which have no prospect of achieving eventual viability.

8. In identifying the sectors where early action is needed, the Corporation will look for advice and suggestions from industry and the City, from Government departments and the Economic Development Committees. It will effect rationalisation and reorganisation by whatever method best suits the circumstances of the particular case. In many instances its role will be to act as catalyst, providing initiative and ideas, helping the companies concerned and their advisers to work out practical schemes and arranging for any necessary expert services to be made available. It will pay particular attention to the management needs of new groupings.

9. In order that the Corporation may be able to operate on an effective scale and to promote a number of schemes simultaneously, it must have large financial resources at its disposal. It will need funds to help put together new groupings on a sound economic basis. It may also need to provide capital for new projects or expansions of special importance to the economy. . . [I]t will be em-

powered to hold physical assets, so that in appropriate cases it will be able to purchase machines and make them available to new groupings, by leasing them or by making other suitable arrangements. The Corporation will co-operate with the Ministry of Technology and the National Research Development Corporation, which may be able to help it to make rationalisation more effective in industries which are passing through a period of rapid technological change. It will also co-operate with the Ministry of Public Building and Works in matters affecting the construction industry.

[The Industrial Reorganisation Corporation. Cmnd. 2889 (January 1966)] 1966)]

INDUSTRIAL REORGANISATION CORPORATION ACT, 1966 [Ch. 50]

1. (1) There shall be a body to be called the Industrial Reorganisation Corporation...

(2) The Corporation shall consist of a chairman and not less than seven nor more than fourteen other members.

(3) The chairman shall be appointed by the Secretary of State and the other members shall be appointed by the Secretary of State after consultation with the chairman.

(4) The members of the Corporation shall be appointed from among persons who appear to the Secretary of State to have had experience of, and to have shown capacity in, industry, technology, commercial or financial matters, administration or the organisation of workers...

(6) It is hereby declared that the Corporation is not to be regarded as the servant or agent of the Crown or as enjoying any status, immunity or privilege of the Crown, or as exempt from any tax, duty, rate, levy or other charge whatsoever, whether general or local, and that its property is not to be regarded as the property of, or property held on behalf of, the Crown...

2. (1) The Corporation may, for the purpose of promoting industrial efficiency and profitability and assisting the economy of the United Kingdom or any part of the United Kingdom,—

(a) promote or assist the reorganisation or development of any industry; or

(b) if requested so to do by the Secretary of State, establish or develop, or promote or assist the establishment or development of, any industrial enterprise.

(2) In determining how to exercise its functions under paragraph (a) of the foregoing subsection it shall be the duty of the Corporation

to consider which industries it would be expedient to reorganise or develop for the said purpose and to seek to promote or assist the reorganisation or development of those industries which in the opinion of the Corporation it would be most expedient to reorganise or develop for that purpose.

(3) The Corporation shall have power to do anything, whether in the United Kingdom or elsewhere, which is calculated to facilitate the discharge of its functions under the foregoing provisions of this section or is incidental or conductive to their discharge, including—

(*a*) the acquisition, holding and disposal of securities;

(*b*) the formation of bodies corporate;

(*c*) the making of loans and the giving of guarantees with respect to loans made by others;

(*d*) the acquisition and placing at the disposal of others of premises and plant, machinery and other equipment.

(4) The aggregate of the amounts outstanding in respect of the principal of any loans in respect of which guarantees have been given by the Corporation shall not exceed such limit as the Secretary of State may for the time being have imposed on the Corporation for the purposes of this subsection by a direction given to the Corporation with the approval of the Treasury.

(5) The Secretary of State may, after consultation with the Corporation, give to the Corporation directions of a general character as to the exercise and performance by the Corporation of its functions, and it shall be the duty of the Corporation to give effect to any such directions. . .

9. (1) The Corporation shall, within a period of four months after the end of each accounting year and as soon as possible within that period, make to the Secretary of State a report on the performance of its functions during that year.

(2) The report for any accounting year—

(*a*) shall set out any request made by the Secretary of State during that year under section 2 (1) (*b*) of this Act;

(*b*) shall set out any directions given to the Corporation under section 2 (5) of this Act during that year;

(*c*) shall set out any recommendation made under section 5 (4) of this Act as respects a period ending after the beginning of that year [13];

---

[13] Sections 3 and 4 of the Act authorised the Corporation to borrow money. S. 5 provided that the Secretary of State, with the approval of the Treasury, could also authorise payments to the Corporation of sums of money not exceeding in the aggregate £50 millions, or such greater sum as he might from time to time specify by order. It was then up to the Corporation in the first instance to decide on the annual payments to be paid to the

(*d*) shall specify the securities acquired and disposed of by the Corporation during that year, the securities held by it at the end of that year and the period for which it has held each of the securities so held; and

(*e*) shall include all relevant information relating to the Corporation's projects, past and present activities and financial position and, without prejudice to the foregoing, such information relating to those matters as the Secretary of State may from time to time direct.

(3) There shall be attached to the report for each accounting year a copy of the statement of accounts in respect of that year and a copy of any report made on the statement by the auditors.

(4) The Secretary of State shall lay a copy of each report made to him under the foregoing provisions of this section, and of the statements attached thereto, before each House of Parliament.

Para-Governmental agencies – general arguments

173. An important part of our inquiry was taken up with the subject of 'para-Governmental agencies'. By this we mean agencies that act under the general direction of the Government and are provided with public funds, but are at arm's length from Whitehall departments and exercise a degree of independence in their day-to-day actions. Two questions arose:

(1) Should Government assistance to private industries, firms or projects be handled directly by a Government department? Or alternatively should such assistance, or any parts of it, be channelled through a part-Governmental agency or agencies?

(2) If an agency is set up, what should be its form, scope and functions? E.g. should the funds at its disposal be entirely public or should private money also be involved? What should be the degree of executive independence from Government? Should it be staffed by businessmen, civil servants or whom? Should it be merely a vehicle for injecting finance, or should it try to improve the structure of an industry or the management of a firm? Should it be on the lines of (for example) the I.R.C., or should it be a State Holding Company? Should its role be wide enough to include the execution of Government regional or national economic policies?...

The general case for an agency

175. The majority of our witnesses, outside Government departments, saw merit in the principle of an agency, although there was

---

Secretary of State in return. S. 5 (4) provided that the Secretary of State could make recommendations to the Corporation as to what those payments should be for any future period.

much disagreement on its form and scope. The arguments presented to us fell mainly under three headings: (1) businessmen are better able than civil servants to judge and handle the problems that arise; (2) a certain measure of independence of Government is a distinct advantage; (3) at the same time, the ultimate sanction of Government authority gives the agency advantages over any privately-created institution.

181. Witnesses stressed the importance to an agency of being para-Governmental, i.e. relatively independent of Government although subject to its broad direction. Lord Stokes said that I.R.C. benefited from being slightly at arm's length from Government; after industrialists had got over a certain suspicion of I.R.C. in the early days it was remarkable how many came to consult I.R.C. with the feeling that they were talking to fellow industrialists.

182. Sir Joseph Lockwood and Mr Villiers said that companies were prepared to give much information to I.R.C. on condition that it was not passed on to Government. Sir Joseph told us that Rolls-Royce had given a lot of information to I.R.C. on such an understanding; and Mr Villiers said that both I.R.C. and the Government had accepted this. The same principle of confidentiality has applied in L.E.A.F.A.C.[14] (an agency with a specialist role), whose memorandum says that care is taken to preserve both the substance and the appearance of the Committee's independence; all information given to L.E.A.F.A.C. is confidential and no reasons are given either to D.T.I. or to the applicants for L.E.A.F.A.C.'s recommendations.

183. Witnesses said that an agency was less subject to changing political pressures than were Government departments. Sir Joseph Lockwood put great importance on I.R.C.'s degree of independence from pressures by politicians, trade unions and local political parties. Lord Beeching said that the merit of I.R.C. in practice was that they allowed commercial considerations to predominate; if it were left to a Minister he would be far more prone to have a non-commercial motive and results were more likely to be disappointing. Sir Frank Schon felt that the I.R.C. type of organisation could fulfil an important and possibly necessary function, but only if it had basic support from the parties and was taken out of the political field; continuity was essential. Mr Villiers said that the vital distinction lay in whether the agency was advisory or executive. Being advisory raised no great problems – the Government was surrounded by advisory bodies of businessmen; it was in the taking of executive decisions on investment that an agency needed independence.

[14] I.e. the Local Employment Acts Financial Advisory Committee, under the aegis of D.T.I.

184. Sir Joseph Lockwood and others also made the point that it was useful for the Government itself to be able to turn to a body of outside experts. Business advisers within the civil service machine were subject to the political pressures mentioned above. To be able to say that an independent body or group had recommended a particular course of action, apart from other advantages, reduced these pressures. Sir Ronald Edwards said that, independently of the question whether an agency could do the job better or worse than the civil service, it could be useful to Ministers faced by politically sensitive issues to be able to fall back on an organisation a little outside the public service...

The general case against an agency

187. Witnesses from Government departments and a few from outside opposed the idea of a para-Governmental agency, primarily because they thought it unnecessary; others criticised particular aspects of the I.R.C. or S.I.B. (the Shipbuilding Industry Board)...

192. Asked to play devil's advocate and say what was wrong with I.R.C., Sir Joseph Lockwood thought that the Corporation's powers and independence had caused political unease. Some restriction in these powers would have made I.R.C. more acceptable without seriously harming it. I.R.C. had bought equity in companies, not as a form of back-door nationalisation, but in order to put money into the companies without overloading them with fixed-interest debt. He thought it would have been quite possible to lay down that Ministerial approval were required for any purchase of equity.

193. Finally, D.T.I., while agreeing that there might be truth in the claim that an agency's partial independence of Government had some advantages, made the point that it also removed the operations further from the ambit of Parliament. Because of its relationship with Government, Parliament had a more direct view of what was going on if it were handled by a Department rather than some other body, even if that body were subject to some measure of direct supervision by Parliament...

Regional agencies

230. Hitherto in this report we have considered the nation-wide categories of agency; the first involved in industry as a whole, such as I.R.C. and the second concerned with a particular sector of industry, such as S.I.B. A third kind of agency is the agency with special regional functions. Two of the existing para-Governmental agencies in the United Kingdom, the Highlands and Islands Development Board (H.I.D.B.) and the Northern Ireland Finance Corporation (N.I.F.C.) are each confined to a single region L.E.A.F.A.C.,

which has para-regional characteristics, has been primarily concerned with administration of regional incentives. The new Industrial Development Executive, though national in scope, is intended to have strong regional responsibilities. . .

[Sixth Report from the Select Committee on Expenditure, 1971–2. H.C. 347, 6 July 1972]

In its Observations on this report the Conservative Government, in noting that they had decided to set up an Industrial Development Executive within the Department of Trade and Industry, said: 'They believe that there are real advantages in giving these functions to a body which reports direct to Ministers and is directly accountable to Parliament, and which is in a better position to co-ordinate its activities with other related Government activities' [Cmnd. 5186. December 1972]. The Industrial Reorganisation Corporation Act, 1966, was repealed by s. 1 of the Industry Act, 1971.

The National Enterprise Board

In August 1974 the Labour Government again proposed the establishment of a semi-independent body, the National Enterprise Board, which *inter alia* would have some of the functions previously performed by the Industrial Reorganisation Corporation. It also proposed a new system of 'planning agreements' between the Government and private industry. The proposals were set out in a White Paper, 'The regeneration of British industry'. The problems of Ministerial responsibility and parliamentary supervision (there called 'control') are briefly discussed in paragraphs 39 and 40.

6. ... [T]he Government propose in this White Paper the creation of two new instruments: a system of Planning Agreements with major firms in key sectors of industry, and a National Enterprise Board to provide the means for direct public initiatives in particular key sectors of industry. . .

8. ... For many of its activities the Board will be able to follow the pattern and build on the experience of the former Industrial Reorganisation Corporation.

9. These proposals will be presented to Parliament in a new Industry Bill. . .

Planning Agreements

11. ... There will ... be no statutory requirements upon a company to conclude an Agreement.

12. The heart of this system will be a series of consultations between the Government and companies, leading to an agreement about plans for the following three years; these will be reviewed and rolled forward annually. In the course of these consultations, the

Government will assess with the company its needs for assistance to support and reinforce agreed company plans, with special reference to selective assistance for new employment projects in the regions. In particular, if in the course of these discussions it becomes clear that in order to align the company's plans with national needs some financial assistance is required beyond that which would in any case be available to the company by way of capital allowances, regional development aid and regional employment premium, the Government will be ready to provide the kind of discretionary financial assistance by way of grants and loans for which the Industry Act 1972 now provides. . . Moreover these discussions could help to identify requirements for investment funds for consideration by the National Enterprise Board, if necessary by means of joint ventures with the companies. More generally, the intention is that the outcome of discussions with companies will have an important bearing on the formulation of the Government's own plans; in this way the needs of companies and the economy will be better served.

13. Financial assistance under the Industry Act 1972, including regional development grants, will of course continue to be available for companies not covered by Planning Agreements. . . The payment of regional employment premium and capital allowances will not be affected by any of these proposals . . .

15. In their discussions with companies, the Government will be concerned only with strategic issues . . . The Government would welcome the views of firms on the issues that principally concern them. Clearly they might well vary from company to company but matters of obvious concern to the Government would include:

Investment, with particular reference to its timing and location;
Prices policy;
Productivity;
Employment, with special reference to its regional balance;
Exports and import saving, and investment directed to these ends;
Product development;
Implications of company plans for industrial relations and arrangements for negotiation and consultation;
Interests of consumers and the community. . .
will also fall within the scope of the Planning Agreements system,

Companies to be Covered

17. The new arrangements will apply to major and strategic firms in key sectors of manufacturing industry, and in selected industries other than manufacturing of particular importance to the economy. Multinational companies will be included only in respect of their British holdings. . .

18. The major nationalised industries and publicly-owned firms which for them will be administered through the sponsoring Departments. . .

The Interests of Employees

19. Employees and their representatives will have a major interest in the issues covered by Planning Agreements. The Government intend that the plans to be covered by an Agreement will be drawn up by management in close consultation with trade union representatives from the firm. . .

The Government envisage that union representatives from companies, while not formally parties to Planning Agreements, would also take part where they so wished in consultations on Agreements with the Government.

20. If consultation is to be effective, union representatives must be provided with all the necessary information relevant to the contents of Planning Agreements. The Government will therefore require employers to disclose information of this kind, except where disclosure could seriously prejudice the company's commercial interests or would be contrary to the interests of national security.

Consultation

21. The Government propose to enter into immediate discussions with both sides of industry, and with the National Economic Development Council, about the best means of implementing the new system and the sectors of industry in which it might most usefully be first employed. . .

National Enterprise Board

23. The Government propose to create a new instrument to secure where necessary large-scale sustained investment to offset the effects of the short-term pull of market forces. These new powers of initiative are better exercised through a new agency than dealt with direct by Government, and for this purpose it is proposed to set up a National Enterprise Board (NEB).

24. One of the functions of this new agency will be to build on and enlarge the activities previously discharged by the Industrial Reorganisation Corporation (IRC). It will in addition be an industrial holding company with subsidiary companies in manufacturing industry. A number of existing Government shareholdings in companies will be transferred to the Board immediately on its establishment. Adequate funds will be made available to enable the Board, subject to Governmental and Parliamentary control as set out in paragraphs 38–40, to expand its activities vigorously to discharge the responsibilities set out below:

(a) It will be a new source of investment capital for manufacturing industry; in providing finance it will normally take a corresponding share in the equity capital. In this it will set out to supplement and not to displace the supply of investment from existing financial institutions and from companies' own resources (see paragraph 27).

(b) It will have the former Industrial Reorganisation Corporation's entrepreneurial role in promoting industrial efficiency and profitability by promoting or assisting the reorganisation or development of an industry but, unlike the IRC, the NEB will in general retain the shareholdings it acquires. In discharging these functions it may take financial interests in companies or act in a purely advisory role (see paragraph 28).

(c) It will act as a holding company to control and exercise central management of:
    (i) certain existing Government shareholdings vested in it;
    (ii) interest taken into public ownership under powers in the Industry Act 1972, which it is proposed to consolidate and extend;
    (iii) new acquisitions under the arrangements described in paragraphs 30–33.

(d) It will be a channel through which the Government will assist sound companies which are in short-term financial or managerial difficulties (see paragraph 32).

(e) It will be an instrument through which the Government operate directly to create employment in areas of high unemployment (see paragraph 35).

(f) Government Departments, the nationalised industries and private firms will be able to seek the advice of the NEB on financial and managerial issues.

(g) Its main strength in manufacturing will come through the extension of public ownership into profitable manufacturing industry by acquisitions of individual firms in accordance with paragraphs 30–33 below.

(h) It will have power to start new ventures and participate in joint ventures with companies in the private sector.

25. The Board will be responsible for securing the efficient management of the companies and assets vested in it. It will compete with companies in the private sector and be expected to operate in accordance with suitable financial objectives. Its guiding financial objective will be to secure an adequate return on that part of the nation's capital for which it is responsible. When the Government require the NEB to depart from this objective on social grounds, the subsidies will be administered by the NEB, and will be separately

accounted for. The Board's financial arrangements will have to be carefully worked out to safeguard against uneconomic allocation of the nation's resources.

26. The Government envisage a major development of industrial democracy throughout industry in the years ahead. Within that framework, the NEB will play its part in ensuring that enterprises under its control provide for the full involvement of employees in decision-making at all levels.

Provision of Investment Capital

27. Within the framework of Governmental control outlined below (see paragraph 38), the NEB will have powers to make loans and to take shareholdings in companies where it considers that such action is in the public interest and in particular when in its judgment lack of finance is prejudicing worthwhile industrial development. In deciding which projects to support within its financial allocation, it will be expected to give priority to the promotion of industrial efficiency; to the creation of employment opportunities in assisted areas; to increasing exports or reducing undue dependence on imports; to co-operation with the Offshore Supplies Office in promoting development in the offshore oil supplies industry; and to sponsoring investment that will offset the effect of monopoly.

Restructuring Industries

28. In exercising its powers to promote or assist in the reorganisation or development of an industry the Board may take a share in the equity capital of existing companies or take part in the establishment of new enterprises. When it is involved in restructuring programmes, its overriding purpose will be to promote the effectiveness and efficiency of the industry. It will work closely with the Department of Industry which will be able to complement initiatives by the NEB through the use of its powers of selective financial assistance under the Industry Act 1972.

Vesting Existing Government Shareholdings

29. The Government have a number of existing shareholdings in industry. Their acquisition over a large number of years has been in response to a diverse range of policy objectives. Some of these holdings may not be appropriate for vesting in the NEB, e.g., the holdings in shipbuilding companies or in companies whose activities are largely overseas (the British Petroleum Co. Ltd., Cable and Wireless Ltd. and the Suez Finance Company). It is however intended that the Government shareholdings in the following companies should be vested in the NEB:

Rolls-Royce (1971) Ltd.

International Computers (Holdings) Ltd.

George Kent Ltd.
Nuclear Enterprises Ltd.
Dunford and Elliott Ltd.
Kearney and Trecker Marwin Ltd.
Norton Villiers Triumph Ltd.

Future Acquisitions

30. The NEB will be the instrument by which the Government ensure that the nation's resources are deployed to the benefit of all, by extending public ownership into profitable manufacturing industry in accordance with the policies defined in paragraphs 31–33 below.

31. Acquisitions by, or on behalf of, the NEB may take place in a number of ways. The intention is that all holdings in companies, whether 100 per cent or in part, should be acquired by agreement. Where part holdings in companies may be acquired in future in return for assistance from the Government under the Industry Act 1972 they will normally be held by the NEB. The Board may also acquire part holdings in companies through joint ventures or through its participation in a reorganisation. But to act decisively in its role of creating employment and creating new industrial capacity, the Board will need a number of companies where it holds 100 per cent of the equity capital, in order to avoid conflict between its objectives and the interests of private shareholders. The Government consider that suitable criteria for the acquisition of a company should include the following: danger of its passing into unacceptable foreign control; and stimulation of competition in a sector where that is weak.

32. Although the NEB will be principally concerned with profitable companies, it may on occasion be called on to take over an ailing company which is in danger of collapse but needs to be maintained and restored to a sound economic basis for reasons of regional employment or industrial policy. This responsibility of the NEB will be distinct from its other functions, and it will be separated in such a way from them that the NEB will be compensated specifically for this rescue activity, to ensure that its overall financial discipline and viability are not undermined. The Board may also be asked to act in support of financial measures by the Secretary of State for Industry to assist a company in temporary difficulty, for example by providing managerial reinforcement.

33. ... If in any case compulsory acquisition proved to be necessary, this would normally be authorised by a specific Act of Parliament. If unforeseeable developments of compelling urgency were to arise – for example, the imminent failure or loss to unacceptable foreign control of an important company in a key sector

of manufacturing industry – the Government would bring the issue before Parliament, and any action would require specific parliamentary approval. Compulsory acquisitions would be subject to prompt and fair compensation to existing shareholders...

Creating Jobs

35. ... [T]he National Enterprise Board will... have a responsibility... to create employment through commercially sound enterprises and joint ventures with private enterprise in the areas of high unemployment. Its subsidiary companies will qualify for financial assistance under the Industry Act 1972 on the same terms as comparable companies in the private sector.

Financial Arrangements

36. The National Enterprise Board will be funded by the Government and the Secretary of State for Industry will be empowered, with the approval of the Treasury, to make funds available by way of loans or in the form of public dividend capital. This is capital which does not bear a fixed rate of interest, but on which a public corporation is expected to pay a dividend similar to dividends on equity shares in private companies. Since the NEB will be competing with the private sector and is intended primarily to operate within profitable sectors of manufacturing industry, it is appropriate that part of its funds should have the character of equity rather than of fixed interest finance.

37. As envisaged in paragraph 27 the Board will be a source of finance for the companies in which it holds shares, and for any new public enterprise which it establishes. The NEB's internal financial relationships with its subsidiary companies will be for it to settle with them. The NEB will be given financial obligations which reflect its duty of securing the efficient management in the public interest of the companies vested in it. Detailed financial guidelines for this purpose will be prescribed by the Government.

Relations with the Government

38. Within the framework of its constitution and the funds made available to it, the NEB will be free to exercise its commercial judgment in carrying out the functions described in paragraph 24 above. It will however require the prior agreement of the Government before it takes a controlling interest in any enterprise or a minority interest exceeding £5 million. There will also be occasions when the Government will wish to influence the activities of the Board and its constituent companies in the national interest. The Government will therefore need a power to give general and specific directions to the Board. The Government will not however inter-

fere in detailed issues of day-to-day management. Directions to the NEB will have to be given in writing by the Government and will be published in due course in the Board's annual report.

Parliamentary Control

39. The NEB will be set up under a new Industry Bill which will consolidate and develop existing legislation to promote national industrial expansion. The Board will be accountable for its actions to the Government who, in turn, will be fully accountable to Parliament for the funds which it makes available to the Board. In addition, the Board will produce an annual report and accounts which will be laid before Parliament and its activities, like those of any other major public sector body, will come under review by the appropriate Parliamentary Committee.

40. The Government already have powers under Sections 7 and 8 of the Industry Act 1972 to provide financial assistance to a company by taking share capital. These powers of agreed share purchase will be widened and made permanent. The Government propose that parliamentary control of this extended power should be on the lines of Section 8 of the Industry Act, i.e. expenditure on a single acquisition in excess of £5 million should be authorised by Resolution of the House of Commons under main legislation which provides the means by which this is to be done. . .

[Regeneration of British Industry 1974. Cmnd. 5710]

The political consequences of economic planning

It is commonplace that developments in national economic planning are likely to have important consequences for the political system. What the consequences are, however, is not so widely understood, and whether they are to be welcomed or deplored is not at all agreed. . . [T]here is [for example] the establishment of new machinery for the settlement of economic issues, notably the National Economic Development Council and the National Board for Prices and Incomes. There is nothing remarkable in the creation of institutions aside from the traditional government departments – the growth of such institutions has been the outstanding feature of British administration in the last forty years. Moreover, some of these independent institutions have been used for decision-making (as distinct from management and administration) in fields where the Government wishes to devolve responsibility. The role of the University Grants Committee is a well-known example of this principle; in fact every public corporation, council, or tribunal with its own sphere of authority, however limited, involves some transfer of power.

Nevertheless, the adoption of this device for economic planning is a development of some significance. Although taken together the earlier independent institutions wielded a large share of executive authority, they tended to be subordinate, or peripheral, or specialised, bodies. Economic planning, however, and the policies which underlie it, are matters of the greatest importance, central to the whole range of government activity. Clearly if a key role in the planning process is to be played by machinery not part of the Ministerial and Parliamentary system, then something new is afoot. . .

In the British political system, the power of the Government (the executive) has traditionally been great. This is made acceptable by the existence of democratic principles of ' representative and responsible government '. The Government derives its legitimacy from the electoral process, and its vulnerability in this process makes it pay close attention to public opinion.

To make the suppositions of the system anything like reality it is necessary that the politicians in office should have effective direction of the machinery of government. Policy decisions should be their decisions. The doctrine of ministerial responsibility is often supposed to embody this. In fact the doctrine presupposes political control, and where there is no control there is no responsibility. There have been from time to time struggles to assert this control – the nineteenth century effort to make sure of full civilian control over the armed forces is an example.

The position of the original National Economic Development Council of 1961–64 was a striking indication of the relevance of this matter to economic planning. The Council consisted originally of some 20 members. Of these only three were members of the Government. The major interest groups, the employers and the unions had six members each. The chairman was the Chancellor of the Exchequer, but the Council controlled its own agenda, and determined the work of the National Economic Development Office. The Council had no powers, and controlled no funds for investment or other purposes. Nevertheless it was the focus for a number of Economic Development Committees; it produced an indicative plan *Growth of the United Kingdom Economy to 1966* in 1963 and a survey of *Conditions Favourable to Faster Growth* in the same year; and other publications followed. By demonstration, consultation and suggestion the Council was supposed to bring about faster growth in the economy. In spite of the chairmanship of the Chancellor of the

Exchequer, the Government appeared to be no more than a partner in the process. Indeed, one of the main virtues claimed for the system was that it was voluntary; growth would come about because the main interests were *involved* in the preparation of plans to that end. But how much notice was the Government expected to take of the work of the Office? And how far could it be impelled on policy lines indicated by any consensus that appeared on the Council? Clearly, only if it took a great deal of notice of what the Council wanted would it be reasonable to expect the industrialists and the trade unionists to do the same. If the Government was selective, treated the Council as advisory, and only accepted its views when it found them congenial, then the other elements on the Council would be selective too. (In practice, the Government could hardly fail to be selective, since it was getting rival expert advice from Treasury and was under pressure from its political supporters.) On the other hand, if the Council had developed into a real policy-making forum, with the Government accepting whatever lines emerged from its research and its discussions as determinants of its own action, then the other participants might have done likewise. But would this not have been to deny the validity of the electoral process as the decisive force in the democratic polity? The attempt of the Government to play the partner, while retaining inherent powers and decision-taking responsibilities, was an invitation to misunderstand in the short-run and probably untenable in the long run . . .

[T]he Economic Development Committees . . . appointed by the Government and containing representatives of the D.E.A. and the N.E.D.C. as well as industrialists, trade unionists and independents, will, according to Sir Eric [Roll]:

> . . . examine in detail the opportunities for growth and efficiency in their industries and promote action to grasp them.[15]

Sir Robert Shone, former director-general of the National Economic Development Office, has pointed out that on the Economic Development Committees:

> The members, because of the positions they hold, have considerable influence over the organized channels of communication in their industries. This influence is particularly important when it is brought to bear on attitudes and practices which are recognized to be holding back progress.[16]

---

[15] Sir Eric Roll, ' The Department of Economic Affairs ' in *Public Administration*, Spring 1966, p. 8.

[16] Sir Robert Shone, 'The National Economic Development Council', in *Public Administration*, Spring 1966, p. 19.

The policy pursued by the Government, therefore, is one of *ad hoc* intervention, and of seeking methods of persuading enterprises to act in ways which seem desirable. The channels of contact work both ways, and Government attitudes must themselves depend in part on this process. In general these procedures constitute ' jollying along ', ' wheeling and dealing ', ' ear-stroking ', ' planning by consent ', or government by persuasion.[17]

Now, it is very difficult to see what the Government can be made to answer for in this process. It seems impossible that Ministers or their civil servants should be pinned down to particular actions or inactions in the parts of the economy involved. No doubt politicians will claim credit if things go well and blame others if they do not. The crux of the matter is that there is no way of determining the truth – partly because the process is private, but more essentially because it is a process of give and take anyway, between autonomous decision-makers.

The absence of clarity, however, does not mean that the influence of the Government is not substantial. The situation which has arisen in relation to the nationalized industries is in some ways comparable. The informal contacts between Ministers and Board chairmen have led to a system of influence which evades scrutiny because it is indeterminate; and by this means the effective power of Ministers has come to exceed their acknowledged responsibilities. In the promotion of economic growth, similar techniques are in use, and a similar incoherence is emerging.[18]

[Leonard Tivey, ' The political consequences of economic planning ', *20 Parliamentary Affairs* (1966–7), pp. 297–314.]

---

[17] Or ' planning by mutual agreement between public (or autonomous) authorities ' according to Joan Mitchell, *Groundwork to Economic Planning* (Secker and Warburg, 1966) p. 290.
[18] For the development of these methods at the Ministry of Technology, see William Plowden, ' Mintech moves on ', *New Society*, 12 January 1967, p. 51.

CHAPTER VI

THE SOVEREIGNTY OF PARLIAMENT

The 'sovereignty of Parliament' is a phrase used to describe two essential features of the United Kingdom constitution. In a narrow legal sense it describes the legislative powers of the 'Queen-in-Parliament' i.e. the House of Commons, the House of Lords and the Queen, combining to make a statute. In a broader constitutional sense it describes the constitutional position of Parliament, and in particular the House of Commons. In the first sense the 'sovereignty of Parliament', has come to describe the doctrine that so far as the courts are concerned there is no legal limit to what the 'Queen-in-Parliament' can enact in a statute; that there is no other body inside or outside the state that can make law which will be enforced by the courts without statutory authority, other than the courts themselves, or which can alter or repeal laws laid down by the 'Queen-in-Parliament' in a statute. The courts can make law to a limited extent, and they interpret statutes once they are made. But any law they make, or interpretation they put upon a statute, can be changed, even retrospectively, and even in the course of litigation, by means of a statute or by someone with statutory authority. So far as the courts are concerned statutes prevail over conflicting rules of international law or the United Kingdom's treaty obligations. The Government has the power to make treaties without the authority of Parliament but these treaties do not give rise directly to rights and obligations which can be directly enforced in the United Kingdom courts.

The sovereignty of the 'Queen-in-Parliament' is however the sovereignty of the 'Queen-in-Parliament for the time being' and any 'Queen-in-Parliament' can repeal a statute made by one of its predecessors. The traditional doctrine asserts that there is no way under the existing constitution by which the 'Queen-in-Parliament' can make an unrepealable statute or even impose some special condition or clog on a repeal that the courts will enforce, e.g. by requiring a special majority, or the passage of a certain amount of time, or a referendum. Although *prima facie* it might appear that a statutory requirement of this kind might be enforced by way of injunction restraining the presentation of a Bill to Parliament if it were not observed, there are technical problems involved in issuing injunctions against Ministers of the Crown, and the courts in the past have shown a strong preference towards leaving such matters, which they regard as matters of political controversy touching on the privileges of Parliament, to be dealt with by Parliament (see e.g. *Harper* v. *Home Secretary*, above p. 119; *Merricks* v. *Heathcoat-Amory*, below p. 267; *Bilston Corporation* v. *Wolverhampton Corporation*, below p. 265; and Lord Simon of Glaisdale in *Pickin* v. *British Railways Board*, below p. 244).

In spite, however, of the frequent repetition of statements about the unlimited legislative powers of the ' Queen-in-Parliament ' and the courts' unwillingness to be involved in the procedural aspects of legislation, it is perhaps worth adding a few words of caution. Nearly all the cases in which strong statements of this kind have been made have been about relatively trivial issues. The courts have never been asked, for example, to enforce provisions in statutes of the kind mentioned by Leslie Stephen to illustrate the sovereignty of the ' Queen-in-Parliament ', that all blue-eyed babies should be killed, or been called upon to share in a deliberate attempt to make a change in the methods of amending particular statutes, or to adjudicate on an attempt to enact a ' fundamental ' Bill of Rights. It is difficult, for example, to imagine the strong reaffirmations of the traditional doctrine by the Privy Council in *Madzimbamuto* v. *Lardner-Burke* (below p. 254) which were made in the context of the assertion of the authority of the United Kingdom Government and Parliament in Southern Rhodesia, being made in the context of blue-eyed baby legislation. Even in the recent procedural case of *Pickin* v. *British Railways Board*, in which the House of Lords reasserted the traditional position, the Court of Appeal, no mean court, thought fit to cast doubt on some of the received doctrine. Moreover, useful as quotations from past cases are in illustrating the attitudes and rhetoric of particular judges and particular courts, they do not *establish* the present constitutional position or provide a conclusive answer as to how judges in the future in different and more important circumstances ought to behave. There can in a strict sense be no legal authority for the doctrine. It is an example of what is traditionally called a constitutional convention. That it is regarded as a basic convention by the present generation of judges does not make it any more immune to change than any other part of the unwritten constitution. It is a convention which is the product of historical development and of a view of the constitution which has for some time now been handed down without serious questioning from textbook to textbook, but its real strength lies in the principles underlying it and the views and values which those principles express. Should they change the doctrine may well turn out to be less sacrosanct than the authorities would have us believe.

The second, or more broadly constitutional sense of the phrase ' the sovereignty of Parliament ' which tends to have been neglected by lawyers in the past has to do with its general position in the constitution. In spite of the fact that it is recognised that, because of the growth of large nationally-organised disciplined parties, Parliament does not play an independent political role in the government of the country, its constitutional role remains important. It would for example be consistent with the legal doctrine of the sovereignty of the ' Queen-in-Parliament ' for Parliament to delegate unlimited powers of making law to the government and allow the government to govern the country by means of delegated powers. But this would not be consistent with the present constitutional position of Parliament, and while being an expression of Parliamentary sovereignty in the first sense would be a derogation from it in the second. The principle of Parliamentary sovereignty in this second sense requires that Parliament should be given the opportunity to play a part in the important affairs of the state. It goes along with the doctrine of Ministerial responsibility, the existence and the rights of Her Majesty's Opposition, the rules of Parliamentary procedure, the regular request for a grant of supplies and authorisation of expenditure, which are then given for a limited duration. It is to safeguard this principle of Parliamentary sovereignty that Parliamentarians have been concerned, for example, to limit the scope of delegated legislation and to secure adequate and effective means of supervising it, to improve Parliament's methods of scrutinising public expenditure and administration, and to devise new methods for dealing with the problems and the challenge to the principle which have resulted from the entry of the United Kingdom into the European Economic Community. It is a principle which is much less clearly defined than the legal doctrine of the sovereignty of the ' Queen-in-Parliament' and more obviously rooted in convention. In the details of its application, and indeed as regards some of its basic features, it is frequently the subject of dispute between Government and Opposition. But, though it is often bound up with questions of purely party political controversy it remains as basic an element of the present constitution as the narrower legal doctrine of the ' Queen-in-Parliament' itself.

Although Britain's entry into the European Economic Community has been conducted in accordance with the traditional constitutional doctrine it nonetheless raises problems in relation to Parliamentary sovereignty in both its legal and its broader constitutional sense. So far as the latter is concerned there has in the past been a recognisable distinction between the Government's accountability to Parliament in foreign affairs and its accountability in domestic affairs, the Government being allowed a greater freedom of action in the former, subject always to the rule that any change in the domestic law resulting from the Government's activities in the foreign field needed authorisation by statute and was therefore subject to the normal processes for the enactment of legislation. Parliament's position in the constitution has in fact in the past been defined principally in relation to domestic affairs and the legislative process has been the context in which the constitutional proprieties of that relationship have been most fully developed (for recent efforts to develop further the principles and procedures in relation to administration and to up-date those relating to finance and public expenditure see below pp. 314 ff.). It is the legislative processes too which have provided the closest link between the two senses of the sovereignty of Parliament as well as the measure of the gap between them at their closest point, and the principles relating to the grant of delegated legislative powers and their subsequent supervision and control have hitherto set the limits to any extension of that gap. The powers granted by the European Communities Act, 1972, are in form delegated powers to legislate, but their scope, their indefiniteness, and the fact that they are not granted to the Government or to a body subject to Government control put them in a different category from existing delegated legislative powers. They have therefore widened the gap which had hitherto been regarded as the widest tolerable gap between Parliament's legal and Parliament's constitutional sovereignty.

Parliament is therefore faced with two problems. The first is the readjustment of the traditional leeway given to the Government in relation to foreign affairs so far as its activities within the Community are concerned, because of the scope of the direct impact these activities may have on the domestic scene in the United Kingdom. Secondly is the need to devise methods which will give Parliament the same kind of say in relation to Community legislation, which has the status previously enjoyed only by statutes in the United Kingdom, as it has in relation to United Kingdom statutes, and the same kind of say that it would have in relation to delegated legislation as regards those Community instruments which would correspond to what has hitherto been regarded as normal delegated legislation in the United Kingdom. These matters are discussed with the general question of the position of Parliament in the Constitution in the next chapter.

Britain's entry into the European Economic Community does not provide a direct challenge to the doctrine of the legal sovereignty of the ' Queen-in-Parliament ' because the powers of the Community institutions to make law having direct effect in the United Kingdom derives, so far as the United Kingdom courts are concerned, from the European Communities Act; and no doubt so far as the courts are concerned that statute can be repealed as easily as any other statute and their powers would then disappear. Yet even here the scope of those powers and the fact that in the last resort Community law is interpreted by the European Court makes the development an unprecedented one. It seems clear that something has happened that may well have affected the doctrine of the legal sovereignty of Parliament though it is too soon to say what, and it would certainly be premature to frame a definition of legal sovereignty to take account of these developments.

The doctrine of the legal sovereignty of the ' Queen-in-Parliament ' is illustrated in the present chapter; that of the constitutional position of Parliament in the next.

I. THE PREROGATIVE

THE ZAMORA   [1916] A.C. 201

House of Lords

LORD PARKER OF WADDINGTON . . . The idea that the King in Council or indeed any branch of the Executive has power to prescribe or alter the law to be administered by Courts of law in this country is out of harmony with the principles of our Constitution. It is true that under a number of modern statutes, various branches of the executive have power to make rules having the force of statutes, but all such rules derive their validity from the statute which creates the power, and not from the executive body by which they are made.

No one would contend that the prerogative involves any power to prescribe or alter the law administered in courts of common law or equity. . .

POST OFFICE v. *ESTUARY RADIO*   [1968] 2 Q.B. 740

Court of Appeal

DIPLOCK L.J. . . . It still lies within the prerogative power of the Crown to extend its sovereignty and jurisdiction to areas of land or sea over which it has not previously claimed or exercised sovereignty or jurisdiction. For such extension the authority of Parliament is not required. The Queen's courts, upon being informed by Order in Council or by the appropriate Minister or Law Officer of the Crown's claim to sovereignty or jurisdiction over any place, must give effect to it and are bound by it: see *The Fagernes.*[1] And so, when any Act of Parliament refers to the United Kingdom or to the territorial waters adjacent thereto those expressions must prima facie be construed as referring to such area of land or sea as may from time to time be formally declared by the Crown to be subject to its sovereignty and jurisdiction as part of the United Kingdom or the territorial waters of the United Kingdom, and not as confined to the precise geographical area of the United Kingdom or its territorial waters at the precise moment at which the Act received the Royal Assent. The area comprised within the United Kingdom and its territorial waters varies in any event from time to time by natural processes as parts of the coastline change by erosion or accretion. The accreting shingle bank at Dungeness is no Alsatia in which a citizen enjoys immunity from the law of the land. The area to which an Act of Parliament of the United Kingdom applies may vary too as the Crown, in the exercise of its prerogative, extends its claim to areas adjacent to the coast of the United Kingdom in which it did not previously assert its sovereignty. . .

ATTORNEY-GENERAL FOR CANADA v. *ATTORNEY-GENERAL FOR ONTARIO*   [1937] A.C. 326

Privy Council (Lord Atkin, Lord Thankerton, Lord MacMillan, Lord Wright M.R. and Sir Sidney Rowlatt)

LORD ATKIN [delivered the judgment of their Lordships] . . . Their Lordships, having stated the circumstances leading up to the reference in this case, are now in a position to discuss the contentions of the parties. . . It will be essential to keep in mind the distinction between (1) the formation, and (2) the performance, of the

[1] [1927] P. 311; 43 T.L.R. 746. C.A.

obligations constituted by a treaty, using that word as comprising any agreement between two or more sovereign States. Within the British Empire there is a well-established rule that the making of a treaty is an executive act, while the performance of its obligations, if they entail alteration of the existing domestic law, requires legislative action. Unlike some other countries, the stipulations of a treaty duly ratified do not within the Empire, by virtue of the treaty alone, have the force of law. If the national executive, the government of the day, decide to incur the obligations of a treaty which involve alteration of law they have to run the risk of obtaining the assent of Parliament to the necessary statute or statutes. To make themselves as secure as possible they will often in such cases before final ratification seek to obtain from Parliament an expression of approval. But it has never been suggested, and it is not the law, that such an expression of approval operates as law, or that in law it precludes the assenting Parliament, or any subsequent Parliament, from refusing to give its sanction to any legislative proposals that may subsequently be brought before it. Parliament, no doubt . . . has a constitutional control over the executive: but it cannot be disputed that the creation of the obligations undertaken in treaties and the assent to their form and quality are the function of the executive alone. Once they are created, while they bind the State as against the other contracting parties, Parliament may refuse to perform them and so leave the State in default. . .

RUSTOMJEE v. *THE QUEEN*   (1876) 1 Q.B.D. 487

Queen's Bench Division

The facts as set out by Cockburn C.J. were as follows:

'English merchants, who were English subjects in Hong Kong, were authorised by the existing law of China to trade only with merchants belonging to a particular guild, called the Cohong. If individual members of the guild became indebted to such English subjects, the remedy was against the guild, or Cohong, itself. A debt was incurred by one of the members of that guild to the present suppliant, and his ordinary remedy to get this paid would have been by the proceedings established by the existing law of China against the Cohong. War broke out between this country and China; the Cohong was abolished; and the remedy which the British subjects, the present suppliant among them, would have had under the former state of things was swept away. Under these circumstances, when peace was restored and a treaty of peace was entered into between the Queen and the Emperor of China, provision was made for doing justice to British subjects who had been deprived of their remedy to enforce their claims against members of the Cohong; but the terms of the treaty were that the money given by the Emperor of China to make good these claims should be given, not to the individual merchants who had claims or debts against members of the Cohong, but should be paid to her Majesty.'

The plaintiff brought this petition of right against the Crown claiming that the Queen had received this money as agent or trustee for the creditors or that it was money had and received for their use.

LUSH J. . . . A treaty is an act of prerogative. In making, and negotiating, and perfecting that treaty the Crown acts of its own inherent authority, not by the authority, actual or supposed, of any subject; and I think all that is done under that treaty is as much beyond the domain of municipal law as the negotiation of the treaty itself; and when this money was received, it was received by the sovereign in her sovereign character, not at all, in any view of it, actual or constructive, as the agent of any subject whatever.

It seems to me that the relation which is pressed upon us here never existed in this case between the Crown and the subject, and is one which cannot exist in any state like ours between the sovereign and the subject. No doubt a duty arose as soon as the money was received to distribute that money amongst the persons towards whose losses it was paid by the Emperor of China; but then the distribution when made would be, not the act of an agent accounting to a principal, but the act of the sovereign in dispensing justice to her subjects. For any omission of that duty the sovereign cannot be held responsible. The responsibility would rest with the advisers of the Crown, and they are responsible to Parliament, and to Parliament alone. In no view whatever can an individual subject have any such claim as the suppliant pretends to have by this petition, namely, a claim to coerce the sovereign by judicial proceedings into the payment over of a part of the indemnity received in her sovereign character from the Emperor of China. . .

COCKBURN C.J. and BLACKBURN J. delivered concurring judgments.

Judgment for the Crown

CIVILIAN WAR CLAIMANTS ASSOCIATION LTD. v. THE KING [1932] A.C. 14

House of Lords

This case was similar to the previous one. Here again the petitioners claimed that money received by the Crown from a foreign state to compensate them for the damage they had suffered was received by the Crown as agent or trustee or was money had and received to their use. During the First World War the Government had on several occasions stated that those British subjects who had suffered damage as a result of enemy attacks by sea and air would be compensated from Imperial funds, and in September 1916 the Government called upon those who had suffered to register their claims. Article 232 of the Peace Treaty with Germany provided: '... The Allied and Associated Governments... require and Germany undertakes that she will make compensation for all damage done to the civilian population of the Allied and Associated Powers and to their property during the period of the belligerency... by such aggression by land, by sea and from the air and in general all damage as defined in Annex I hereto.' The petitioners were claiming that this money had been received on their behalf and brought this petition claiming the compensation which they said was due to them.

LORD BUCKMASTER... I can see no evidence whatever of an acceptance of trusteeship on the part of the Government, or assertion of trusteeship on the part of the people who suffered damage, nor anything up to the time when the money was received to show that the conception of trusteeship was in the minds of anyone in any form whatever. Indeed, the original statements that were made were made of the readiness to compensate out of the national funds at home, and nobody suggests that the Government were trustees of those funds for this purpose.

Finally, when the moneys were received, it is said that from and after that moment the Crown became a trustee. I have pointed out in the course of the argument, and I repeat, that if that were the case, unless you are going to limit the rights which the beneficiaries enjoy, those rights must include, among the other things, a claim for an account of the moneys that were received, of the expenses incurred, and the way in which the moneys have been distributed. Such a claim presented against the Crown in circumstances such as these would certainly have no precedent, and would, as it appears to me, invade an area which is properly that belonging to the House of Commons.

That the money was received by the Crown as agent seems to me can no more be established than that the money was received by it as trustee. In fact, the trusteeship is the agency stated in other words. If the Crown was not a trustee, neither was it an agent; nor can I see that in any sense the Crown received these moneys as money had and received to the use of the people whose claims were made. The people whose claims were made were not considered by Germany on making the payment at all. The terms of the treaty were that Germany should pay the sum necessary to satisfy the claims of various people who had suffered, and it was left to the Governments themselves, as between them and their nationals, to determine how that money was to be distributed. Therefore, my Lords, on general principle, I should have thought that the petition must fail; but the general principle is immensely strengthened by the case of *Rustomjee* v. *The Queen*...[2]

[2] [Above, p. 230].

Attempts were made to distinguish that authority both on the ground of difference in the circumstances which led to the case coming before the Court, and on the ground, which I found it more difficult to apprehend, that something had happened since the decision of that case that had in some way changed the constitutional relationship of the Sovereign and the subject. I can find nothing to support such a view and I can see no reason why such a change should have taken place...

LORD ATKIN. My Lords, I concur ... [I]t appears to me, for the reasons that have been stated by the noble Lord on the Woolsack, that the petition does not in fact disclose a cause of action, for it discloses the action taken by the Crown in receiving this sum of money in circumstances which make it impossible to impute to the Crown the position either of a trustee or of an agent. In other words, when the Crown is negotiating with another Sovereign a treaty, it is inconsistent with its sovereign position that it should be acting as agent for the nationals of the sovereign State, unless indeed the Crown chooses expressly to declare that it is acting as agent. There is nothing, so far as I know, to prevent the Crown acting as agent or trustee if it chooses deliberately to do so...

LORD WARRINGTON OF CLYFFE, LORD TOMLIN, and LORD MACMILLAN concurred. *Appeal dismissed*

BLACKBURN v. ATTORNEY-GENERAL
[1971] 1 W.L.R. 1037

Court of Appeal

The plaintiff applied for declarations that the Government would be acting in breach of the law if they signed the Treaty of Rome because they would, in doing so, be surrendering for ever a part of the sovereignty of the ' Queen-in-Parliament '. Both the Master and the judge struck out the claims on the grounds that they disclosed no reasonable cause of action. He appealed.

LORD DENNING M.R. .... Much of what Mr Blackburn says is quite correct. It does appear that if this country should go into the Common Market and sign the Treaty of Rome, it means that we will have taken a step which is irreversible. The sovereignty of these islands will thenceforward be limited. It will not be ours alone but will be shared with others. Mr Blackburn referred us to a decision by the Court of Justice of the European Communities, *Costa* v. *Ente Nazionale Per L'Energia Elettrica* (*ENEL*) [1964] C.M.L.R. 425 in February 1964, in which the European court in its judgment said, at p. 455:

' ... the member-states, albeit within limited spheres, have restricted their sovereign rights and created a body of law applicable both to their nationals and to themselves '.

Mr Blackburn points out that many regulations made by the European Economic Community will become automatically binding on the people of this country: and that all the courts of this country, including the House of Lords, will have to follow the decisions of the European court in certain defined respects, such as the construction of the treaty.

I will assume that Mr Blackburn is right in what he says on those matters. Nevertheless, I do not think these courts can entertain these actions. Negotiations are still in progress for us to join the Common Market. No agreement has been reached. No treaty has been signed. Even if a treaty is signed, it is elementary that these courts take no notice of treaties as such. We take no notice of treaties until they are embodied in laws enacted by Parliament, and then only to the extent that Parliament tells us. That was settled in *Rustomjee* v. *The Queen* [above p. 230]. . .

Mr Blackburn acknowledged the general principle, but he urged that this proposed treaty is in a category by itself, in that it diminishes the sovereignty of Parliament over the people of this country. I cannot accept the distinction. The general principle applies to this treaty as to any other. The treaty-making power of this country rests not in the courts, but in the Crown; that is, Her Majesty acting upon the advice of her Ministers. When her Ministers negotiate and sign a treaty, even a treaty of such paramount importance as this proposed one, they act on behalf of the country as a whole. They exercise the prerogative of the Crown. Their action in so doing cannot be challenged or questioned in these courts.

Mr Blackburn takes a second point. He says that, if Parliament should implement the treaty by passing an Act of Parliament for this purpose, it will seek to do the impossible. It will seek to bind its successors. According to the treaty, once it is signed, we are committed to it irrevocably. Once in the Common Market, we cannot withdraw from it. No Parliament can commit us, says Mr Blackburn, to that extent. He prays in aid the principle that no Parliament can bind its successors, and that any Parliament can reverse any previous enactment. He refers to what Professor Maitland said about the Act of Union between England and Scotland. Professor Maitland in his *Constitutional History of England* (1908) said, at p. 332:

' We have no irrepealable laws; all laws may be repealed by the ordinary legislature, even the conditions under which the English and Scottish Parliaments agreed to merge themselves in the Parliament of Great Britain.'

We have all been brought up to believe that, in legal theory, one Parliament cannot bind another and that no Act is irreversible. But legal theory does not always march alongside political reality. Take the Statute of Westminster 1931, which takes away the power of Parliament to legislate for the Dominions. Can any one imagine that Parliament could or would reverse that Statute? Take the Acts which have granted independence to the Dominions and territories overseas. Can anyone imagine that Parliament could or would reverse those laws and take away their independence? Most clearly not. Freedom once given cannot be taken away. Legal theory must give way to practical politics. It is as well to remember the remark of Viscount Sankey L.C. in *British Coal Corporation* v. *The King* [1935] A.C. 500, 520:

'... the Imperial Parliament could, as matter of abstract law, repeal or disregard section 4 of the Statute of Westminster. But that is theory and has no relation to realities'.

What are the realities here? If Her Majesty's Ministers sign this treaty and Parliament enacts provisions to implement it, I do not envisage that Parliament would afterwards go back on it and try to withdraw from it. But, if Parliament should do so, then I say we will consider that event when it happens. We will then say whether Parliament can lawfully do it or not.

Both sides referred us to the valuable article by Professor H. W. R. Wade ('The Basis of Legal Sovereignty') in the *Cambridge Law Journal*, 1955, at p. 196, in which he said that 'sovereignty is a political fact for which no purely legal authority can be constituted...' That is true. We must wait to see what happens before we pronounce on sovereignty in the Common Market.

So, whilst in theory Mr Blackburn is quite right in saying that no Parliament can bind another, and that any Parliament can reverse what a previous Parliament has done, nevertheless so far as this court is concerned, I think we will wait till that day comes. We will not pronounce upon it today...

I think the statements or claim disclose no cause of action, and I would dismiss the appeal.

SALMON L.J. . . . I deprecate litigation the purpose of which is to influence political decisions. Such decisions have nothing to do with these courts... Nor have the courts any power to interfere with the treaty-making power of the Sovereign. As to Parliament, in the present state of the law, it can enact, amend and repeal any legislation it pleases. The sole power of the courts is to decide and enforce what is the law and not what it should be – now, or in the future.

STAMP L.J. agreed that the appeal should be dismissed.

SALOMON v. *COMMISSIONERS OF CUSTOMS AND EXCISE* [1967] 2 Q.B. 116

Court of Appeal

In 1950 the United Kingdom signed a Convention on the Valuation of Goods for Customs Purposes. It ratified it in 1952. The Convention required each contracting party to introduce into its domestic law the definition of value of imported goods set out in the Convention. This the United Kingdom purported to do in s. 258 of and Schedule 6 to the Customs and Excise Act, 1952. A dispute arose as to the meaning of the words used. To what extent was it possible to refer to the Convention to see what was intended?

DIPLOCK L.J. . . . Where, by a treaty, Her Majesty's Government undertakes either to introduce domestic legislation to achieve a specified result in the United Kingdom or to secure a specified result which can only be achieved by legislation, the treaty, since in English law it is not self-operating, remains irrelevant to any issue in the English courts until Her Majesty's Government has taken steps by way of legislation to fulfil its treaty obligations. Once the Government has legislated, which it may do in anticipation of the coming into effect of the treaty, as it did in this case, the court must in the first instance construe the legislation, for that is what the court has to apply. If the terms of the legislation are clear and unambiguous, they must be given effect to, whether or not they carry out Her Majesty's treaty obligations, for the sovereign power of the Queen in Parliament extends to breaking treaties (see *Ellerman Lines* v. *Murray; White Star Line and U.S. Mail Steamers Oceanic Steam Navigation Co. Ltd.* v. *Comerford* [3]), and any remedy for such a breach of an international obligation lies in a forum other than Her Majesty's own courts. But if the terms of the legislation are not clear but are reasonably capable of more than one meaning, the treaty itself becomes relevant, for there is a prima facie presumption that Parliament does not intend to act in breach of international law, including therein specific treaty obligations; and if one of the meanings which can reasonably be ascribed to the legislation is consonant with the treaty obligations and another or others are not, the meaning which is consonant is to be preferred. Thus, in case of lack of clarity in the words used in the legislation, the terms of the treaty are relevant to enable the court to make its choice between the possible meanings of these words by applying this presumption.

[3] [1931] A.C. 126; sub nom. *The Croxteth Hall; The Celtic*, 47 T.L.R. 147, H.L.(E.).

It has been argued that the terms of an international convention cannot be consulted to resolve ambiguities or obscurities in a statute unless the statute itself contains either in the enacting part or in the preamble an express reference to the international convention which it is the purpose of the statute to implement. The judge seems to have been persuaded that *Ellerman Lines etc.* v. *Murray etc.* was authority for this proposition. But, with respect, it is not. The statute with which that case was concerned did refer to the convention. The case is authority only for the proposition for which I have already cited it. Maugham J. in *Hogg* v. *Toye & Co. Ltd.,*[4] clearly took the view that it was unnecessary that there should be an express reference to the convention in the statute itself if it was apparent from a comparison of the subject-matter of the statutory provision and the convention that the former was enacted to carry out Her Majesty's Government's obligations in international law under the convention. I can see no reason in comity or common sense for imposing such a limitation upon the right and duty of the court to consult an international convention to resolve ambiguities and obscurities in a statutory enactment. If from extrinsic evidence it is plain that the enactment was intended to fulfil Her Majesty's Government's obligations under a particular convention, it matters not that there is no express reference to the convention in the statute. One must not presume that Parliament intends to break an international convention merely because it does not say expressly that it is intending to observe it. Of course the court must not merely guess that the statute was intended to give effect to a particular international convention. The extrinsic evidence of the connection must be cogent. But here we have a convention dealing specifically and exclusively with one narrow topic, the method of valuation of imported goods for the purpose of assessing ad valorem customs duties. Section 258 of and Schedule 6 to the Customs and Excise Act, 1952, deal specifically and exclusively with the same narrow topic. The terms of the statute and convention are nearly identical, save that the statute omits the ' Interpretative Notes to the Definition of Value ' which appear in the convention. The inference that the statute was intended to embody the convention is irresistible, even without reference to its legislative history, to which Russell L.J. will refer. In my view we can refer to the convention to resolve ambiguities or obscurities of language in the section of and the Schedule to the statute.

LORD DENNING M.R. and RUSSELL L.J. delivered concurring judgments.

[4] [1935] Ch. 497, 520; 51 T.L.R. 301 C.A.

II. THE RESOLUTIONS OF THE HOUSE OF COMMONS

STOCKDALE v. *HANSARD*

(1839) 9 Ad. & E. 1; 112 E.R. 1112

Court of Queen's Bench

Stockdale complained that in a report published by Hansard on the authority of the House of Commons a book published by him had been described as ' of the most disgusting nature, and the plates ... obscene and indecent in the extreme '. He sued Hansard in an action for defamation but lost his case because the jury decided that the statements were true. In the course of his judgment, however, Lord Denman cast doubt on a second defence raised by Hansard, that they had published the report on the authority of Parliament. Hansard subsequently repeated the libel in another publication. Before the action was brought to trial the House of Commons resolved:

' That the power of publishing such of its Reports, Votes and Proceedings as it shall deem necessary or conducive to the public interest, is an essential incident of the constitutional functions of Parliament, more especially to this House, as the representative portion of it. . .That by the law and privilege of Parliament, this House has the sole and exclusive jurisdiction to determine upon the existence and extent of its privileges, and that the institution or prosecution of any action, suit or other proceeding, for the purpose of bringing them into discussion or decision before any court or tribunal elsewhere than in Parliament, is a high breach of such privilege, and renders all parties concerned therein amenable to its just displeasure, and to the punishment consequent thereon. . .

That for any court or tribunal to assume to decide upon matters of Privilege inconsistent with the determination of either House of Parliament thereon, is contrary to the law of Parliament, and is a breach and contempt of the Privileges of Parliament.[5]

In response to their request for directions, the House of Commons instructed Messrs Hansard to defend the action but to rely solely on the defence that the statements were published on the authority of the House of Commons, and not to raise the defence that they were true.'

The court held that the House of Commons was not the sole judge of the existence and extent of its privileges and that in fact no such privilege as was claimed existed. Lord Denman had the following to say about the status of the Resolutions passed by the House.

LORD DENMAN C.J. . . . The grievance complained of appears to be an act done by order of the House of Commons, a Court superior to any Court of Law, and none of whose proceedings are to be questioned in any way . . . The supremacy of Parliament, the foundation on which the claim is made to rest, appears to me completely to overturn it, because the House of Commons is not the Parliament, but only a co-ordinate and component part of the Parliament. That

[5] 92 H.C.Jo., p. 419, 31 May 1837.

sovereign power can make and unmake the laws; but the concurrence of the three legislative estates is necessary; the resolution of any one of them cannot alter the law, or place any one beyond its control. The proposition is therefore wholly untenable, and abhorrent to the first principles of the Constitution of England. . .

Parliament subsequently passed the Parliamentary Papers Act, 1840, which gave statutory protection to publications of this kind. For a similar decision see *Bowles* v. *Bank of England* [1913] 1 Ch. 57.

Cp. the importance of Resolutions in relation to delegated legislation below p. 369 ff.

III. THE HOUSE OF LORDS

Since 1911 it has been possible to pass an Act of Parliament without the consent of the House of Lords by virtue of the Parliament Acts, 1911 and 1949.

PARLIAMENT ACT, 1911   [1 & 2 Geo. 5. ch. 13] [6]

Whereas it is expedient that provision should be made for regulating the relations between the two Houses of Parliament:

And whereas it is intended to substitute for the House of Lords as it at present exists a Second Chamber constituted on a popular instead of hereditary basis, but such substitution cannot be immediately brought into operation:

And whereas provision will require hereafter to be made by Parliament in a measure effecting such substitution for limiting and defining the powers of the new Second Chamber but it is expedient to make such provision as in this Act appears for restricting the existing powers of the House of Lords:

Be it therefore enacted by the King's most Excellent Majesty, by and with the advice and consent of the Lords Spiritual and Temporal, and Commons, in this present Parliament assembled, and by the authority of the same, as follows:

1. (1) If a Money Bill, having been passed by the House of Commons, and sent up to the House of Lords at least one month before the end of the session, is not passed by the House of Lords without amendment within one month after it is so sent up to that House, the Bill shall, unless the House of Commons direct to the contrary, be presented to His Majesty and become an Act of Parliament on the Royal Assent being signified, notwithstanding that the House of Lords have not consented to the Bill.

(2) A Money Bill means a Public Bill which in the opinion of the Speaker of the House of Commons contains only provisions dealing with all or any of the following subjects, namely, the imposition,

[6] As amended by the Parliament Act, 1949 [12, 13 and 14 Geo. 6. ch. 103].

repeal, remission, alteration, or regulation of taxation; the imposition for the payment of debt or other financial purposes of charges on the Consolidated Fund, or on money provided by Parliament, or the variation or repeal of any such charges; supply; the appropriation, receipt, custody, issue or audit of accounts of public money; the raising or guarantee of any loan or the repayment thereof; or subordinate matters incidental to those subjects or any of them. In this subsection the expressions ' taxation,' ' public money,' and ' loan ' respectively do not include any taxation, money, or loan raised by local authorities or bodies for local purposes.

(3) There shall be endorsed on every Money Bill when it is sent up to the House of Lords and when it is presented to His Majesty for assent the certificate of the Speaker of the House of Commons signed by him that it is a Money Bill. Before giving his certificate, the Speaker shall consult, if practicable, two members to be appointed from the Chairmen's Panel at the beginning of each Session by the Committee of Selection.

2. (1) If any Public Bill (other than a Money Bill or a Bill containing any provision to extend the maximum duration of Parliament beyond five years) is passed by the House of Commons in two successive sessions (whether of the same Parliament or not), and, having been sent up to the House of Lords at least one month before the end of the session, is rejected by the House of Lords in each of those sessions, that Bill shall, on its rejection for the second time by the House of Lords, unless the House of Commons direct to the contrary, be presented to His Majesty and become an Act of Parliament on the Royal Assent being signified thereto, notwithstanding that the House of Lords have not consented to the Bill: Provided that this provision shall not take effect unless one year has elapsed between the date of the second reading in the first of those sessions of the Bill in the House of Commons and the date on which it passes the House of Commons in the second of those sessions.

(2) When a Bill is presented to His Majesty for assent in pursuance of the provisions of this section, there shall be endorsed on the Bill the certificate of the Speaker of the House of Commons signed by him that the provisions of this section have been duly complied with.

(3) A Bill shall be deemed to be rejected by the House of Lords if it is not passed by the House of Lords either without amendment or with such amendments only as may be agreed to by both Houses.

(4) A Bill shall be deemed to be the same Bill as a former Bill sent up to the House of Lords in the preceding session if, when it is sent up to the House of Lords, it is identical with the former Bill or contains only such alterations as are certified by the Speaker of the

House of Commons to be necessary owing to the time which has elapsed since the date of the former Bill, or to represent any amendments which have been made by the House of Lords in the former Bill in the preceding session, and any amendments which are certified by the Speaker to have been made by the House of Lords in the second session and agreed to by the House of Commons shall be inserted in the Bill as presented for Royal Assent in pursuance of this section:

Provided that the House of Commons may, if they think fit, on the passage of such a Bill through the House in the second session, suggest any further amendments without inserting the amendments in the Bill, and any such suggested amendments shall be considered by the House of Lords, and, if agreed to by that House, shall be treated as amendments made by the House of Lords and agreed to by the House of Commons; but the exercise of this power by the House of Commons shall not affect the operation of this section in the event of the Bill being rejected by the House of Lords.

3. Any certificate of the Speaker of the House of Commons given under this Act shall be conclusive for all purposes, and shall not be questioned in any court of law.

4. (1) In every Bill presented to His Majesty under the preceding provisions of this Act, the words of enactment shall be as follows, that is to say:

' Be it enacted by the King's most Excellent Majesty, by and with the advice and consent of the Commons in this present Parliament assembled, in accordance with the provisions of the Parliament Acts, 1911 and 1949, and by authority of the same, as follows.'

(2) Any alteration of a Bill necessary to give effect to this section shall not be deemed to be an amendment of the Bill.

5. In this Act the expression ' Public Bill ' does not include any Bill for confirming a Provisional Order.

6. Nothing in this Act shall diminish or qualify the existing rights and privileges of the House of Commons.

7. Five years shall be substituted for seven years as the time fixed for the maximum duration of Parliament under the Septennial Act, 1715.

IV. THE TRADITIONAL DOCTRINE

LEE AND ANOTHER v. *BUDE AND TORRINGTON JUNCTION RAILWAY COMPANY*

(1871) L.R. 6 C.P. 576

Court of Common Pleas

In his report of *Dr Bonham's Case* (1610),[7] Coke noted: ' And it appears

[7] Co.Rep. at 118a; 77 E.R. at 652.

in our books, that in many cases, the common law will controul Acts of Parliament, and sometimes adjudge them to be utterly void: for when an Act of Parliament is against common right and reason, or repugnant, or impossible to be performed, the common law will controul it, and adjudge such Act to be void.' Coke's successor as Lord Chief Justice, Hobart, also said, in *Day* v. *Savadge* (1615),[8] that ' even an Act of Parliament, made against natural equity, as to make a man Judge in his own case, is void in it self, for *jura naturae sunt immutabilia*, and they are *leges legum* '. Nearly a century later Holt C.J. is reported to have made a similar statement in *City of London* v. *Wood* (1702) [9] and there are traces of the doctrine in rhetorical passages in Blackstone's *Commentaries*.[10] There is no example of a statute having been declared void on these grounds even by those who have expressed support for the view that it was possible to do so, and the judgment of Willes J. in the present case is generally regarded as expressing the modern position.

The plaintiffs in the case were solicitors who had been instrumental in obtaining the passage of two private Acts of Parliament by virtue of which the Bude and Torrington Junction Railway Company had been established. Both Acts provided that the costs incurred in obtaining the Acts were to be borne by the company. As the company had no assets, the plaintiffs applied for writs of execution against two of its shareholders. The latter, however, argued that the company was a sham and had never built any of the railway or even acquired land for the purpose. The Acts, they said, were simply part of a scheme by which the plaintiffs heaped up costs against the company and no effect should be given to them. In effect they raised a point similar to that raised by the plaintiff in the *Edinburgh and Dalkeith Railway* case (below, p. 243) but the judgment of Willes J. goes further.

WILLES J. . . . It is further urged that the company was a mere non-entity, and there never were any shares or shareholders. That resolves itself into this, that parliament was induced by fraudulent recitals (introduced, it is said, by the plaintiffs) to pass the Act

---

[8] Hob. at 87; 80 E.R. at 237.

[9] ' And what my Lord Coke says in *Dr Bonham's case* in his 8 Co. is far from any extravagancy, for it is a very reasonable and true saying, that if an Act of Parliament should ordain that the same person should be party and Judge, or, which is the same thing, Judge in his own cause, it would be a void Act of Parliament; for it is impossible that one should be Judge and party, for the Judge is to determine between party and party, or between the Government and the party; and an Act of Parliament can do no wrong, though it may do several things that look pretty odd; for it may discharge one from his allegiance to the Government he lives under, and restore him to the state of nature; but it cannot make one that lives under a Government Judge and party. An Act of Parliament may not make adultery lawful, that is, it cannot make it lawful for A. to lie with the wife of B. but it may make the wife of A. to be the wife of B. and dissolve her marriage with A.' (12 Mod. at 687; 88 E.R. at 1602).

[10] For example, vol. 1 at p. 41. Elsewhere, e.g. at p. 160, he expresses the modern view.

which formed the company. I would observe, as to these Acts of Parliament, that they are the law of this land; and we do not sit here as a court of appeal from parliament. It was once said, – I think in Hobart,[11] – that, if an Act of Parliament were to create a man judge in his own case, the Court might disregard it. That dictum, however, stands as a warning, rather than an authority to be followed. We sit here as servants of the Queen and the legislature. Are we to act as regents over what is done by parliament with the consent of the Queen, lords and commons? I deny that any such authority exists. If an Act of Parliament has been obtained improperly, it is for the legislature to correct it by repealing it; but, so long as it exists as law the Courts are bound to obey it. The proceedings here are judicial, not autocratic, which they would be if we could make laws instead of administering them. The Act of Parliament makes these persons shareholders, or it does not. If it does, there is an end of the question. If it does not, that is a matter which may be raised by plea to the sci. fa. Having neglected to take the proper steps at the proper time to prevent the Act from passing into a law, it is too late now to raise any objections to it.

As far as regards the suggestions impugning the conduct of the plaintiffs themselves, I have assumed that there is foundation for them; but I have done so merely for argument sake. If they can be sustained, recourse may be had to the proper proceedings for calling them in question: but we cannot discuss them upon this motion. I think the rule must be made absolute.

BYLES and KEATING JJ. delivered concurring judgments, the latter saying he based his opinion especially on the impossibility of giving effect to the argument that Parliament had been imposed upon.

EDINBURGH AND DALKEITH RAILWAY v. *WAUCHOPE*   (1842) 8 Cl. & F. 710; 8 E.R. 279

House of Lords (Lord Cottenham, Lord Brougham and Lord Campbell)
The respondent was here claiming that under the private Act of Parliament incorporating the company he was entitled to payment for every carriage loaded with passengers which passed over his land. The company denied that he was entitled to this tonnage under the Act but also argued that that Act had been repealed by a later private Act. To this Wauchope replied that he could not be affected by the later Act because it had been introduced into the House of Commons without his having been given proper notice as required by the Standing Orders of the House relating to the introduction of private Bills. It could not therefore affect his vested rights.

[11] In *Day* v. *Savadge* (Hob. 87). [Quoted above.]

Although he had abandoned this argument by the time that the case had reached the House of Lords, as this argument had found some support in the lower court, all their Lordships referred to it, and rejected it.

LORD CAMPBELL ... My Lords, I think it right to say a word or two upon the point that has been raised with regard to an Act of Parliament being held inoperative by a Court of Justice because the forms prescribed by the two Houses to be observed in the passing of a bill have not been exactly followed. There seems great reason to believe that an idea to that effect has prevailed to some extent in Scotland, for it is brought forward in these papers as a substantive ground of objection to the applicability of the later Act of Parliament; the objection being, that this Act being a private Act, it is inoperative as to the pursuer because he had not proper notice of the intention to apply to Parliament to pass such an Act. This defence was entered into in the Court below ... and the Lord Ordinary ... gave great weight to this objection. He said, ' he is by no means satisfied that due Parliamentary notice was given to the pursuer previous to the introduction of this last Act: undoubtedly no notice was given to him personally, nor did the public notices announce any intention to take away his existing rights. If, as the Lord Ordinary is disposed to think, these defects imply a failure to intimate the real design in view, he should be strongly inclined to hold, in conformity with the principles of Donald (27th of November 1832), that rights previously established could not be taken away by a private Act, of which due notice was not given to the party meant to be injured ' ... I cannot but express my surprise that such a notion should ever have prevailed. There is no foundation whatever for it. All that a Court of Justice can do is look to the Parliamentary roll: [12] if from that it should appear that a bill has passed both Houses and received the Royal assent, no Court of Justice can inquire into the mode in which it was introduced into Parliament, nor into what was done previous to its introduction, or what passed in Parliament during its progress in its various stages through both Houses. I trust, therefore, that no such inquiry will again be entered upon in any Court in Scotland, but that due effect will be given to every Act of Parliament, private as well as public, upon what appears to be the proper construction of its existing provisions.

Appeal dismissed

PICKIN v. BRITISH RAILWAYS BOARD

House of Lords [1974] 2 A.C. 765

The statute which provided for the setting up of the Bristol and Exeter Railway Act in 1836 provided that if the line was ever abandoned the

[12] [On this point see R. V. F. Heuston, *Essays in Constitutional Law* (1964), p. 18.]

land should revert to the ownership of the landowners on either side of the track. The British Railways Board in 1968 secured the passage of a private Act of Parliament, the British Railways Act, 1968, s. 18 of which took away the owners' rights. Mr Pickin, who objected to the closing of a branch line, bought some land on the side of the track and then claimed a declaration that he was entitled to the stretch of land adjoining it. The defendants relied on the 1968 Act but Mr Pickin claimed that that Act had been obtained fraudulently. Its preamble recited that plans and lists of the owners of the lands affected by the 1968 Act had been deposited, at, amongst other places, the Somersetshire County Council offices. He said that no plans or lists had been prepared or deposited and no notice was in fact given. He claimed, therefore, that the Board could not rely on the Act.

The Board applied to the court to have the paragraphs claiming that the Act had been fraudulently obtained and could not be relied on struck out as being frivolous and vexatious. Chapman J. granted their application. ' The position is ' he said, ' as set out in *Halsbury's Laws of England*, vol. 36 (3rd edn) p. 378 and by Willes J. in *Lee* v. *Bude and Torrington Junction Ry. Co.* (1871) L.R. 6 C.P. 576, 582. One must accept section 18 and one cannot go behind it. Otherwise there would be a head-on collision between Parliament and the courts in the Strand. It would raise a quite impossible situation to go behind the statute and seek to stultify its effect by reason of alleged failure in procedure or inaccuracy of recitals. The preamble has to be proved before Parliament. Parliament alone decides whether the preamble is true. Once accepted by Parliament and the following sections enacted, an Act must be accepted by the courts and construed by them, rather than their going behind the Act and saying it has no effect... It is not the function of the court to embark on the process of repealing rather than interpreting.'

Mr Pickin appealed to the Court of Appeal which unanimously reversed the decision of Chapman J. [[1973] Q.B. 219].

LORD DENNING M.R. . . . The master and the judge . . . have applied a supposed principle of English law, which was stated by Willes J. in 1871 in *Lee* v. *Bude and Torrington Junction Railway Co.* [above p. 241. Lord Denning quoted the passage beginning ' I would observe ' to ' bound to obey it '] . . . That passage has been repeatedly quoted in books on constitutional law. Mr Tackaberry says that that statement – and others like it in the Privy Council – was made without full argument. In particular he says that in all those cases there was no reference to an authority of the House of Lords. It is no doubt an old authority, but it says in terms that if a private Act of Parliament is obtained by fraud, the courts can investigate it. It is *M'Kenzie* v. *Stewart*. It was decided in 1752. It came from Scotland. It is fully set out in 9 Mor.Dic. 7443. The Court of Session had by a majority refused to entertain the suggestion that a private Act of Parliament was obtained by fraud. That decision was reversed in the House of Lords by seven to six. There were no reports in those days of the reasons of the House of Lords. But a note was taken of what Lord Hardwicke L.C. said, at p. 7445:

'The Lord Chancellor, in delivering his opinion, expressed a good deal of indignation at the fraudulent means of obtaining the act; and said, that he never would have consented to such private acts, had he ever entertained a notion that they could be used to cover fraud.'

A few years later, Sir William Blackstone in his *Commentaries*, 14th ed. (1803), Book II, p. 346, speaking of private Acts of Parliament, said:

'A law, thus made, though it binds all parties to the bill, is yet looked upon rather as a private conveyance, than as the solemn act of the legislature. It is not therefore allowed to be a *publick*, but a mere *private* statute; it is not printed or published among the other laws of the session; it hath been relieved against, when obtained upon fraudulent suggestions;'

Blackstone refers for that proposition to *M'Kenzie* v. *Stewart*.

Counsel for the board submitted to us that those authorities are so old and so out of date that we should not regard them any more. He invited us to give the words of Willes J. their full scope and strike out these two paragraphs in the reply.

I do not think we should pronounce on this point finally or conclusively today. But I must say that there is sufficient material from the 18th century for us to allow this plea to remain upon the record. It is quite plain that this action has to go to trial on the issue whether or not this branch line was abandoned before July 26, 1968. We should let it go for trial on the further issue whether this Act of Parliament was improperly obtained. That is a triable issue. It is deserving of investigation by the court. As I have said in the course of the argument, suppose the court were satisfied that this private Act was improperly obtained, it might well be the duty of the court to report that finding to Parliament, so that Parliament itself could take cognisance of it. Parliament could put the matter right, if it thought fit, by passing another Act. In my opinion it is the function of the court to see that the procedure of Parliament itself is not abused and that undue advantage is not taken of it. In so doing the court is not trespassing on the jurisdiction of Parliament itself. It is acting in aid of Parliament, and, I might add, in aid of justice. If it is proved that Parliament was misled, the court can, and should draw it to the attention of Parliament... I would allow the appeal accordingly.

EDMUND DAVIES L.J. I agree. It needs to be stressed that we are here concerned with a private Act of Parliament, the British Rail-

ways Act 1968. There is an abundance of authority for the proposition that in relation to public statutes the court has no alternative
but to apply them and cannot go behind them by investigating the
legislative process which preceded their receiving the royal assent. . .
But there is ancient authority of the highest court in the land lending
some support to the view that a different approach may be properly
and indeed possibly ought to be adopted by the court in relation to
private Acts of Parliament such as the one we are concerned with,
and particularly *M'Kenzie* v. *Stewart* in 1752. The curious thing is
that the assertion of Lord Hardwicke L.C. in that case, expressed
in the trenchant and powerful words already quoted by Lord
Denning M.R., seems to have disappeared largely from the judicial
landscape, for in no case thereafter, as far as we have been apprised,
was it even referred to, still less considered. The question that
accordingly looms large is, what should this court in the present
case now do? Are we to say that Lord Hardwicke must be brushed
aside, and that counsel for the appellant is not entitled to claim that
on any view there is here a difficult question which ought to be
investigated further and which can properly be investigated only by
ascertaining all the facts? In *Craies*, p. 587, it is pointed out that in
the old cases (*M'Kenzie* v. *Stewart* and *Biddulph* v. *Biddulph* (1790)
5 Cru.Dig 34 decided by the House of Lords in 1790) there was no
discussion of the proposition there acted upon that the court may go
behind private statutes and, if satisfied that they were obtained by
fraud, decline to act upon them. The editor then adds, at p. 587:
' The question has never been seriously discussed in any modern
case '.

For my part, I think it is now high time that the matter should be
discussed. Furthermore, there are features of this present case which
appear to me to make it highly desirable in the public interest that
they should be. . .

STEPHENSON J. delivered a concurring judgment.

The British Railways Board appealed. The decision of the Court of
Appeal was reversed by the House of Lords in a unanimous decision.

LORD REID . . . The idea that a court is entitled to disregard a
provision in an Act of Parliament on any ground must seem strange
and startling to anyone with any knowledge of the history and law
of our constitution, but a detailed argument has been submitted to
your Lordships and I must deal with it.

I must make it plain that there has been no attempt to question
the general supremacy of Parliament. In earlier times many learned
lawyers seem to have believed that an Act of Parliament could be
disregarded in so far as it was contrary to the law of God or the

law of nature or natural justice, but since the supremacy of Parliament was finally demonstrated by the Revolution of 1688 any such idea has become obsolete.

The respondent's contention is that there is a difference between a public and a private Act. There are of course great differences between the methods and procedures followed in dealing with public and private Bills, and there may be some differences in the methods of construing their provisions. But the respondent argues for a much more fundamental difference. There is little in modern authority that he can rely on. The mainstay of his argument is a decision of this House, *Mackenzie* v. *Stewart* in 1754. . .

At that period there were no contemporary reports of Scots appeals in this House. It would seem that quite often no other peer with legal experience sat with the Lord Chancellor and it seems to me to be probable that frequently no formal speech giving reasons was made at the conclusion of the argument. In comparatively few cases there have been preserved observations made in the House : sometimes these appear to have been observations made in the courts of the argument. In the present case we have a note made by Lord Kames in his Select Decisions reported in Morison at p. 7445 (1 Pat.App. 578, 583):

‘ The Lord Chancellor, in delivering his opinion, expressed a good deal of indignation at the fraudulent means of obtaining the act; and said, that he never would have consented to such private acts, had he ever entertained a notion that they could be used to cover fraud ’.

Lord Kames’ Select Decisions cover the earlier period of his long tenure of office as a judge. We do not know how he came to add this passage at the end of his report of the case in the Court of Session. He must have got it, perhaps at second hand, from someone present during the arguments: so these observations may have been made during the argument or in a speech. Lord Hardwicke was Lord Chancellor both in 1754 and in 1739 when the Act was passed, so he may have had some part in passing the Act. In any case I do not read his observations as indicating the ground of decision but rather as a comment on what took place when the Act was passed. . .

It appears to me that far the most probable explanation of the decision is that it was a decision as to the true construction of the Act. . .

If the decision was only as to the construction of a statutory provision that would explain why the case has received little attention in later cases. I do not think it necessary to refer to the few later references to the case which have been unearthed by the researches of counsel. . . If *Mackenzie* v. *Stewart* is found to afford no support to the respondent's argument the rest of the authorities are negligible.

In my judgment the law is correctly stated by Lord Campbell in *Edinburgh and Dalkeith Railway Co.* v. *Wauchope* (1842) 8 Cl. & F. 710; 1 Bell 252 . . . No doubt this was obiter but, so far as I am aware, no one since 1842 has doubted that it is a correct statement of the constitutional position.

The function of the court is to construe and apply the enactments of Parliament. The court has no concern with the manner in which Parliament or its officers carrying out its Standing Orders perform these functions. Any attempt to prove that they were misled by fraud or otherwise would necessarily involve an inquiry into the manner in which they had performed their functions in dealing with the Bill which became the British Railways Act 1968.

In whatever form the respondent's case is pleaded he must prove not only that the appellants acted fraudulently but also that their fraud caused damage to him by causing the enactment of section 18. He could not prove that without an examination of the manner in which the officers of Parliament dealt with the matter. So the court would, or at least might, have to adjudicate upon that.

For a century or more both Parliament and the courts have been careful not to act so as to cause conflict between them. Any such investigations as the respondent seeks could easily lead to such a conflict, and I would only support it if compelled to do so by clear authority. But it appears to me that the whole trend of authority for over a century is clearly against permitting any such investigation. . . I am therefore clearly of opinion that this appeal should be allowed and the judgment of Chapman J. restored.

LORD MORRIS OF BORTH-Y-GEST . . . The question of fundamental importance which arises is whether the court should entertain the proposition that an Act of Parliament can so be assailed in the courts that matters should proceed as though the Act or some part of it had never been passed. I consider that such doctrine would be dangerous and impermissible. It is the function of the courts to administer the laws which Parliament has enacted. In the processes of Parliament there will be much consideration whether a Bill should or should not in one form or another become an enactment. When an enactment is passed there is finality unless and until it is amended or repealed by Parliament. In the courts there may be argument as to the correct interpretation of the enactment: there must be none as to whether it should be on the Statute Book at all. . .

The conclusion which I have reached results, in my view, not only from a settled and sustained line of authority which I see no reason to question and which I think should be endorsed but also from the view that any other conclusion would be constitutionally undesirable and impracticable. It must surely be for Parliament to lay down the procedures which are to be followed before a Bill can become an Act. It must be for Parliament to decide whether its decreed procedures have in fact been followed. It must be for Parliament to lay down and to construe its Standing Orders and further to decide whether they have been obeyed; it must be for Parliament to decide whether in any particular case to dispense with compliance with such orders. It must be for Parliament to decide whether it is satisfied that an Act should be passed in the form and with the wording set out in the Act. It must be for Parliament to decide what documentary material or testimony it requires and the extent to which Parliamentary privilege should attach. It would be impracticable and undesirable for the High Court of Justice to embark upon an inquiry concerning the effect or the effectiveness of the internal procedures in the High Court of Parliament or an inquiry whether in any particular case those procedures were effectively followed.

Clear pronouncements on the law are to be found in a stream of authorities in the 19th century [13]. . .

I would allow the appeal and restore the order made by the learned judge.

LORD WILBERFORCE . . . [T]he Act of 1968 . . . was a private Bill promoted by the British Railways Board and enacted through private Bill procedure. Private Bills have a long history: in early times they were more numerous than public Acts. They represented the response of the King in Parliament to petitions of his subjects, either for relief against some general law, or for the authorisation to dispose of property by tenants in chief under the feudal system (these categories are not exhaustive . . . Because of the pressure on Parliamentary time, a number of modern private Bills, promoted by public undertakings, are not confined to provisions of local application, such as the execution of specified works, or the acquisition of specified lands, but contain legislation of general application: for example, railway Bills have been passed dealing generally with level crossings. The present Act is of this character; it contains much of a local character, but in addition it presents, in section 18, an enactment in general terms dealing with a large number of pre-existing Acts and affecting railway lines all over the country. It may be

---

[13] Lord Morris here cited *Edinburgh and Dalkeith Railway* v. *Wauchope*, *Lee* v. *Bude and Torrington Junction Railway Co.* (1871) L.R. 6 C.P. 576, *Labrador Co.* v. *The Queen* [1895] A.C. 104, and *Hoani Te Heuheu* v. *Aotea District Maori Land Board* [1941] A.C. 308.

questioned whether the procedure of putting such a clause into a private Bill is desirable or whether, on the contrary, such a provision ought to be brought in through a public Bill, and so exposed to debate and amendment on the floor of either House. The courts cannot enter into this debate. But it is open to them to notice that, even though the private Bill procedure may, in principle, be inappropriate, the procedure laid down in Standing Orders of both Houses embodies extensive safeguards, which, if properly used, can prevent any use of that procedure which may be detrimental to the interest of individuals or of the public.

Whether in any particular case, or in this case, these safeguards were made use of, whether the attention of Parliament, its committees or officers, was called to the provision in question, or what decisions (right or wrong) were taken, are not matters into which the courts can inquire. Private Acts, such as the Act of 1968, as the authorities already cited show, are as fully Acts of Parliament as public Acts, and compel acceptance by the courts...

LORD SIMON OF GLAISDALE ... The system by which, in this country, those liable to be affected by general political decisions have some control over the decision-making is parliamentary democracy. Its peculiar feature in constitutional law is the sovereignty of Parliament. This involves that, contrary to what was sometimes asserted before the 18th century, and in contradistinction to some other democratic systems, the courts in this country have no power to declare enacted law to be invalid. It was conceded before your Lordships (contrary to what seems to have been accepted in the Court of Appeal) that the courts cannot directly declare enacted law to be invalid. That being so, it would be odd if the same thing could be done indirectly, through frustration of the enacted law by the application of some alleged doctrine of equity.

A second concomitant of the sovereignty of Parliament is that the Houses of Parliament enjoy certain privileges. These are vouchsafed so that Parliament can fulfil its key function in our system of democratic government. To adapt the words of Lord Ellenborough C.J. in *Burdett* v. *Abbott* (1811) 14 East 1, 152: ' they [the Houses] would sink into utter contempt and inefficiency without [them] '. Parliamentary privilege is part of the law of the land (see *Erskine May's Parliamentary Practice*, 18th ed. (1971), ch. v). Among the privileges of the Houses of Parliament is the exclusive right to determine the regularity of their own internal proceedings (*Erskine May*, pp. 176, 195, 197).

' What is said or done within the walls of Parliament cannot be enquired into in a court of law. On this point all the judges in the two great cases which exhaust the learning on the subject, *Burdett* v. *Abbott* (1811) 14 East 1 and *Stockdale* v. *Hansard* (1839) 9 Ad. & El. 1 :—are agreed, and are emphatic.'

(Lord Coleridge C.J. in *Bradlaugh* v. *Gossett* (1884) 12 Q.B.D. 271, 275). The rule, indeed, is reflected in the Bill of Rights, 1688, art. 9, s. 1, of which I italicise the words which are relevant to this appeal:

' That the freedom of speech, and debates or *proceedings in Parliament, ought not to be impeached or questioned in any court or place out of Parliament.*'

I have no doubt that the respondent in paragraphs 3 and 4 of his reply (even as sought to be amended) is seeking to impeach proceedings in Parliament, and that the issues raised by those paragraphs cannot be tried without questioning proceedings in Parliament.

It is well known that in the past there have been dangerous strains between the law courts and Parliament – dangerous because each institution has its own particular role to play in our constitution, and because collision between the two institutions is likely to impair their power to vouchsafe those constitutional rights for which citizens depend on them. So for many years Parliament and the courts have each been astute to respect the sphere of action and the privileges of the other – Parliament, for example, by its sub judice rule, the courts by taking care to exclude evidence which might amount to infringement of parliamentary privilege (for a recent example, see *Dingle* v. *Associated Newspapers Ltd.* [1960] 2 Q.B. 405). The respondent to the instant appeal claimed that he could discharge the onus of proving the allegations in paragraphs 3 and 4 of the reply merely by reliance on presumptions, so that proceedings in Parliament need not, so far as he was concerned, be forensically questioned. Even if this were so, it would still leave unanswered how the appellant could proceed in rebuttal without calling parliamentary proceedings in question. I am quite clear that the issues would not be fairly tried without infringement of the Bill of Rights and of that general parliamentary privilege which is part of the law of the land.

The respondent claims, however, that, whatever may be the position as regards a public Act of Parliament, it is open to a litigant to impugn the validity (or, at least, by invoking jurisdiction in equity, nullify the operation) of an enactment in a private Act of Parliament. But the considerations of parliamentary privilege to which I have referred would undoubtedly seem to extend to private Bill procedure; and the authorities to which my noble and learned friends have adverted are clearly contrary to the respondent's submissions. What was said in *Edinburgh and Dalkeith Railway Co.* v. *Wauchope*, 8 Cl. & F. 710 seems to me to be particularly apposite and authoritative. . .

Moreover, the distinction that the respondent sought to draw between public and private Acts of Parliament breaks down when one considers that there is a third, intermediate, class of proceedings in Parliament between public and private Bills – namely, hybrid Bills. These are public Bills some provisions of which affect private rights. Those particular provisions are subject to, the procedure of private Bill legislation; though the Bills finally emerge as public Acts. For the purpose of his argument counsel for the respondent sought to distinguish a hybrid Bill from a private Bill on the ground that only the latter had a promoter on whom a constructive trust could be imposed arising from his having misled Parliament. But it is difficult to see how the position of a Minister in relation to the private Bill procedures applicable to a hybrid Bill differs from that of the ordinary promoter of a private Bill.

A further practical consideration is that if there is evidence that Parliament may have been misled into an enactment. Parliament might well – indeed, would be likely to – wish to conduct its own inquiry. It would be unthinkable that two inquiries – one parliamentary and the other forensic – should proceed concurrently, conceivably arriving at different conclusions; and a parliamentary examination of parliamentary procedures and of the actions and understandings of officers of Parliament would seem to be clearly more satisfactory than one conducted in a court of law – quite apart from considerations of Parliamentary privilege.

For the foregoing reasons, as well as for those set out in the speeches of my noble and learned friends, I would allow the appeal. If the respondent thinks that Parliament has been misled into an enactment inimical to his interests, his remedy lies with Parliament itself, and nowhere else.

LORD CROSS delivered a concurring judgment.

The War Damage Act, 1965

In the case of *Burmah Oil* v. *Lord Advocate* [1965] A.C. 75 the House of Lords held that the company was entitled to compensation from the Government for the destruction of their oil installations in Burma in 1942, to prevent them falling into the hands of the Japanese. After the war Burma itself had refused to contribute anything by way of compensation, The United Kingdom Government had given a sum of £10 million. This was however to compensate for damage assessed at £67

million. Burmah Oil in fact put their overall loss at £31 million. The
Government, on the advice of an independent committee put it at £17
million. The company received £4,600,000.

While the case was pending in the lower court the Deputy Treasury
Solicitor wrote to the company saying:

' I have been instructed to inform you that Her Majesty's Government,
having carefully considered the action now pending in the Court of Session
at the instance of your Company against the Crown, have been advised
that the claim in this action is wholly unfounded in law and that it is
likely to be rejected by the courts. Her Majesty's Government are moreover satisfied that the claim made is not in any event one which ought to
be met by the British taxpayer.

' Her Majesty's Government have accordingly decided that, in the unlikely event of your company succeeding, legislation would be introduced
to indemnify the Crown and its officers, servants and agents against your
company's claim. If your company should decide to abandon its claim at
this stage, Her Majesty's Government are prepared to consider the
question of contributing towards the expenses which your company has
incurred up to this date in the course of the present legislation.'

After the House of Lords decision the Government introduced the War
Damage Bill to nullify its effect.

WAR DAMAGE ACT, 1965   Ch. 18

1. (1) No person shall be entitled at common law to receive from
the Crown compensation, in respect of damage to, or destruction of,
property caused (whether before or after the passing of this Act,
within or outside the United Kingdom) by acts lawfully done by, or
on the authority of, the Crown during, or in contemplation of the
outbreak of, a war in which the Sovereign was, or is, engaged.

(2) Where any proceedings to recover at common law compensation in respect of such damage or destruction have been instituted
before this Act, the court shall, on the application of any party,
forthwith set aside or dismiss the proceedings, subject only to the
determination of any question arising as to costs or expenses.

MADZIMBAMUTO v. LARDNER-BURKE

[1969] 1 A.C. 645

Privy Council

Southern Rhodesia was annexed by the Crown by Order in Council in
1923. In 1960 it was granted a Constitution, again by Order in Council.
On 5 November 1965 the Governor declared a state of emergency.
Emergency regulations were enacted under which Madzimbamuto was
detained. On 11 November the Rhodesian Prime Minister and his
colleagues made their Declaration of Independence and were dismissed
by the Governor. On 16 November the United Kingdom Parliament

passed the Southern Rhodesia Act which declared that Rhodesia was still part of Her Majesty's Dominions and that the United Kingdom Government and Parliament still had responsibility for and jurisdiction over it. The Southern Rhodesia (Constitution) Order, 1965, which was made under that Act, declared invalid any attempt to enact a new constitution in Rhodesia and suspended the powers of the Legislative Assembly there. Nonetheless the new regime in Rhodesia adopted a new Constitution and continued to detain Madzimbamuto by virtue of regulations made under it, after the original regulations which had authorised his detention had lapsed. His wife asked the Rhodesian courts for a declaration that the new detention was unlawful. The Rhodesian courts held that although the new regime was unlawful it was necessary to give effect to its acts as it was the only effective Government in Rhodesia. Mrs Madzimbamuto appealed to the Privy Council.

LORD REID ... If the Queen in the Parliament of the United Kingdom was Sovereign in Southern Rhodesia in 1965, there can be no doubt that the Southern Rhodesia Act, 1965, and the Order in Council made under it were of full legal effect there ... [W]hen a colony is acquired or annexed, following on conquest or settlement, the Sovereignty of the United Kingdom Parliament extends to that colony, and its powers over that colony are the same as its powers in the United Kingdom. So, in 1923, full Sovereignty over the annexed territory of Southern Rhodesia was acquired. That Sovereignty was not diminished by the limited grant of self government which was then made. It was necessary to pass the Statute of Westminster, 1931, in order to confer independence and Sovereignty on the six Dominions therein mentioned, but Southern Rhodesia was not included. Section 4 of that Act provides

' No Act of Parliament of the United Kingdom passed after the commencement of this Act shall extend, or be deemed to extend, to a Dominion as part of the law of that Dominion, unless it is expressly declared in that Act that that Dominion has requested, and consented to, the enactment thereof.'

No similar provision has been enacted with regard to Southern Rhodesia ...

The learned judges [14] refer to the statement of the United Kingdom Government in 1961 ... setting out the convention that the Parliament of the United Kingdom does not legislate without the consent of the Government of Southern Rhodesia on matters within the competence of the Legislative Assembly. That was a very important convention but it had no legal effect in limiting the legal power of Parliament.

[14] I.e. in Rhodesia.

It is often said that it would be unconstitutional for the United Kingdom Parliament to do certain things, meaning that the moral political and other reasons against doing them are so strong that most people would regard it as highly improper if Parliament did these things. But that does not mean that it is beyond the power of Parliament to do such things. If Parliament chose to do any of them the courts could not hold the Act of Parliament invalid. It may be that it would have been thought, before 1965, that it would be unconstitutional to disregard this convention. But it may also be that the unilateral Declaration of Independence released the United Kingdom from any obligation to observe the convention. Their Lordships in declaring the law are not concerned with these matters. They are only concerned with the legal powers of Parliament... They are therefore of opinion that the Act and Order in Council of 1965 had full legal effect in Southern Rhodesia.

It is an historical fact that in many countries – and indeed in many countries which are or have been under British Sovereignty – there are now régimes which are universally recognised as lawful but which derive their origins from revolutions or coups d'état. The law must take account of that fact. So there may be a question how or at what stage the new régime became lawful.

A recent example occurs in *Uganda* v. *Commissioner of Prisons, Ex parte Matovu.*[15] On February 22, 1966, the Prime Minister of Uganda issued a statement declaring that in the interests of national stability and public security and tranquillity he had taken over all powers of the Government of Uganda. He was completely successful, and the High Court had to consider the legal effect. In an elaborate judgment Sir Udo Udoma C.J. said:[16]

' we hold, that the series of events, which took place in Uganda from February 22 to April, 1966, when the 1962 Constitution was abolished in the National Assembly and the 1966 Constitution adopted in its place, as a result of which the then Prime Minister was installed as Executive President with power to appoint a Vice-President could only appropriately be described in law as a revolution. These changes had occurred not in accordance with the principle of legitimacy. But deliberately contrary to it. There were no pretentions on the part of the Prime Minister to follow the procedure prescribed in the 1962 Constitution in particular for the removal of the President and the Vice-President from office. Power was seized by force from both the President and the Vice-President on the grounds mentioned in the early part of this judgment.'

[15] [1966] E.A. 514. [16] Ibid. 535.

Later he said:[17]

' . . . our deliberate and considered view is that the 1966 Constitution is a legally valid constitution and the supreme law of Uganda;
and that the 1962 Constitution having been abolished as a result
of a victorious revolution in law does no longer exist nor does it
now form part of the Laws of Uganda, it having been deprived of
its de facto and de jure validity '.

Pakistan affords another recent example. In *The State* v. *Dosso* [18]
the President had issued a proclamation annulling the existing
Constitution. This was held to amount to a revolution. Muhammed
Munir C.J. said:[19]

' It sometimes happens, however, that a Constitution and the
national legal order under it is disrupted by an abrupt political
change not within the contemplation of the Constitution. Any
such change is called a revolution, and its legal effect is not only
the destruction of the existing Constitution but also the validity of
the national legal order.'

Their Lordships would not accept all the reasoning in these
judgments but they see no reason to disagree with the results. The
Chief Justice of Uganda (Sir Udo Udoma C.J.) said: [20] ' The
Government of Uganda is well established and has no rival.'
The court accepted the new Constitution and regarded itself as sitting
under it. The Chief Justice of Pakistan (Sir Muhammed Munir C.J.)
said:[21] ' Thus the essential condition to determine whether a Constitution has been annulled is the efficacy of the change.' It would
be very different if there had been still two rivals contending for
power. If the legitimate Government had been driven out but was
trying to regain control it would be impossible to hold that the
usurper who is in control is the lawful ruler, because that would
mean that by striving to assert its lawful right the ousted legitimate
Government was opposing the lawful ruler.

In their Lordships' judgment that is the present position in
Southern Rhodesia. The British Government acting for the lawful
Sovereign is taking steps to regain control and it is impossible to
predict with certainty whether or not it will succeed. Both the judges
in the General Division and the majority in the Appellate Division
rightly still regard the ' revolution ' as illegal and consider themselves sitting as courts of the lawful Sovereign and not under the
revolutionary Constitution of 1965. Their Lordships are therefore of

---

[17] Ibid. 539.
[18] [1958] 2 P.S.C.R. 180; (1958) P.L.D. 1 S.C. (PAK) 533.
[19] [1958] 2 P.S.C.R. 180, 184.
[20] [1966] E.A. 514. 533.   [21] [1958] 2 P.S.C.R. 180, 185.

opinion that the usurping Government now in control of Southern Rhodesia cannot be regarded as a lawful government. . .

The last question involves the doctrine of 'necessity' and requires more detailed consideration. The argument is that, when a usurper is in control of a territory, loyal subjects of the lawful Sovereign who reside in that territory should recognise, obey and give effort to commands of the usurper in so far as that is necessary in order to preserve law and order and the fabric of civilised society. . .

It may be that there is a general principle, depending on implied mandate from the lawful Sovereign, which recognises the need to preserve law and order in territory controlled by a usurper. But it is unnecessary to decide that question because no such principle could override the legal right of the Parliament of the United Kingdom to make such laws as it may think proper for territory under the Sovereignty of Her Majesty in the Parliament of the United Kingdom. Parliament did pass the Southern Rhodesia Act, 1965, and thereby authorise the Southern Rhodesia (Constitution) Order in Council, 1965. There is no legal vacuum in Southern Rhodesia. Apart from the provisions of this legislation and its effect upon subsequent 'enactments' the whole of the existing law remains in force. . .

The provisions of the Order in Council are drastic and unqualified. . . [S]ection 3 (1) (*a*) provides that no laws may be made by the Legislature of Southern Rhodesia and no business may be transacted by the Legislative Assembly: then section 3 (1) (*c*) authorises Her Majesty in Council to make laws for the peace, order and good government of Southern Rhodesia: and section 6 declares that any law made in contravention of any prohibition imposed by the Order is void and of no effect. This can only mean that the power to make laws is transferred to Her Majesty in Council with the result that no purported law made by any person or body in Southern Rhodesia can have any legal effect, no matter how necessary that purported law may be for the purpose of preserving law and order or for any other purpose. . .

Their Lordships were informed that, since the making of the 1965 Order in Council, 38 Orders in Council have been made which affect Southern Rhodesian affairs but that none of these has been made under section 3 (1) (*c*) as a law for the peace, order and good government of the colony.

The position with regard to administrative acts is similar. It has not been argued that the dismissal from office of Mr Smith and his colleagues was invalid. So when the Order in Council was made there were no Ministers in Southern Rhodesia. Section 4 (1) (*b*) by providing that sections 43, 44, 45 and 46 of the Constitution shall not have effect prevented any lawful appointment of new Ministers. Section 4 (1) (*a*) provided that the executive authority of Southern Rhodesia may be exercised on Her Majesty's behalf by a Secretary of State, and section 4 (1) (*d*) authorised a Secretary of State to exercise any function vested by the Constitution or any other law in force in Southern Rhodesia in a Minister or Deputy Minister or Parliamentary Secretary. And section 6 declared that any function exercised in contravention of any prohibition or restriction imposed by or under the Order is void and of no effect.

Their Lordships have been informed that no executive action has been taken by a Secretary of State under section 4 (1) (*a*) or section 4 (1) (*d*). . .

Importance has been attached to the Governor's statement of November 11, 1965. . . That statement was made before the making of the Order in Council and in any event it could not prevail over the Order in Council. So when it was said—

> ' it is the duty of all citizens to maintain law and order in this country and to carry on with their normal tasks. This applies equally to the judiciary, the armed services, the police and the public service.'

—that must be taken with the qualification that it can only apply in so far as they can do so without acting or supporting action in contravention of the Order in Council.

It may be that at first there was little difficulty in complying with this direction and it may be that after two-and-a-half years that has become more difficult. But it is not for their Lordships to consider how loyal citizens can now carry on with their normal tasks, particularly when those tasks bring them into contact with the usurping régime. Their Lordships are only concerned in this case with the position of Her Majesty's judges.

Her Majesty's judges have been put in an extremely difficult position. But the fact that the judges among others have been put in a very difficult position cannot justify disregard of legislation passed or authorised by the United Kingdom Parliament, by the introduction of a doctrine of necessity which in their Lordships' judgment cannot be reconciled with the terms of the Order in Council. It is for Parliament and Parliament alone to determine whether the maintenance of law and order would justify giving effect to laws made by the usurping Government, to such extent as may be necessary for that purpose.

LORD PEARCE delivered a dissenting judgment.

ELLEN STREET ESTATES LTD. v.
MINISTER OF HEALTH   [1934] 1 K.B. 590

Court of Appeal

SCRUTTON L.J. ... The second point advanced by Mr Hill seems to
me even more impossible. It is. this: the Acquisition of Land
(Assessment of Compensation) Act, 1919, lays down certain principles on which compensation for land taken is to be assessed. Section
7, subs. 1, says this: ' The provisions of the Act or order by which
the land is authorised to be acquired, or of any Act incorporated
therewith, shall, in relation to the matters dealt with in this Act,
have effect subject to this Act, and so far as inconsistent with this
Act those provisions shall cease to have or shall not have effect.' Mr
Hill's contention is that if in a later Act provisions are found as to
the compensation to be paid for land which are inconsistent with
those contained in the Act of 1919, the later provisions are to have
no effect. Such a contention involves this proposition, that no subsequent Parliament by enacting a provision inconsistent with the
Act of 1919 can give any effect to the words it uses. Section 46, subs.
1, of the Housing Act, 1925, says this: ' Where land included in any
improvement or reconstruction scheme . . . is acquired compulsorily,' certain provisions as to compensation shall apply. These are
inconsistent with those contained in the Acquisition of Land (Assessment of Compensation) Act, 1919, and then s. 46, subs. 2, of the Act
of 1925 provides: ' Subject as aforesaid, the compensation to be
paid for such land shall be assessed in accordance with the Acquisition of Land (Assessment of Compensation) Act, 1919.' I asked Mr
Hill what these last quoted words mean, and he replied they mean
nothing. That is absolutely contrary to the constitutional position
that Parliament can alter an Act previously passed, and it can do so
by repealing in terms the previous Act – Mr Hill agrees that it may
do so – and it can do it also in another way – namely, by enacting a
provision which is clearly inconsistent with the previous Act. In
Maxwell's Interpretation of Statutes I find three or four pages devoted
to cases in which Parliament, without using the word ' repeal,' has
effected the same result by enacting a section inconsistent with an
earlier provision. It is impossible to say that these words that compensation shall be assessed in a particular way and, subject as aforesaid, shall be assessed in accordance with the provisions of the Act
of 1919 have no effect. This point was not dealt with before Swift J.,
because in *Vauxhall Estates Ltd.* v. *Liverpool Corporation* [22] a Divi-

---

[22] [1932] 1 K.B. 733. [There Avory J. said: ' We are asked to say that by a
provision of this Act of 1919 the hands of Parliament were tied in such a

sional Court rejected Mr Hill's argument and held that the provisions of the Act of 1925, so far as they were inconsistent with, must prevail over, those of the Act of 1919. In the present case the matter is carried a step further, because s. 12 of the Housing Act, 1930, says in effect that compensation shall be assessed in accordance with the provisions of the Act of 1919 except as altered in a series of matters which the Act of 1930 prescribed. In my opinion *Vauxhall Estates Ltd.* v. *Liverpool Corporation* was rightly decided, and Mr Hill's point fails and the appeal must be dismissed.

MAUGHAM L.J. and TALBOT J. delivered concurring judgments.

Appeal dismissed

MACCORMICK v. *LORD ADVOCATE*   1053 S.C. 396

Court of Session

The chairman and secretary of the Scottish Covenant Association petitioned the court for a declaration that the Government was not entitled to publish a proclamation describing the Queen as ' Elizabeth the Second of the United Kingdom of Great Britain ', on the grounds that so far as Scotland was concerned there had never been an Elizabeth the First. On the assumption that the use of the title was authorised by the Royal Titles Act, 1953, they argued that this statute was of no effect as it conflicted with Article I of the Treaty of Union between England and Scotland of 1707 [23] the legislation passed to give effect to it.[24] The Lord Ordinary (Lord Guthrie) rejected their petition on the grounds that no Act of Parliament could be challenged in the courts; that the Treaty of Union in any event did not prohibit the use of the title; and that the peti-

---

way that it could not by any subsequent Act enact anything which was inconsistent with the provisions of the Act of 1919. It must be admitted that such a suggestion as that is inconsistent with the principle of the constitution of this country. Speaking for myself, I should certainly hold, until the contrary were decided, that no Act of Parliament can effectively provide that no future Act shall interfere with its provisions.'

Note, however, the Ireland Act, 1949, s. 1 (2): ' It is hereby declared that Northern Ireland remains part of His Majesty's dominions and of the United Kingdom and it is hereby affirmed that in no event will Northern Ireland or any part thereof cease to be part of His Majesty's dominions and of the United Kingdom without the consent of the Parliament of Northern Ireland.']

[23] Article 1 of the Treaty of Union provides: ' That the Two Kingdoms of Scotland and England shall upon the first day of May next ensuing the date hereof and forever after be united into one Kingdom by the name of Great Britain and that the ensigns armorial of the said United Kingdom be such as Her Majesty shall appoint and the crosses of St Andrew and St George be conjoined in such manner as Her Majesty shall think fit and used in all flags, banners, standards and ensigns both at sea and land.'

[24] Act of 1707 ch. 7 and the Union with Scotland Act, 1707 [6 Anne ch. 11].

tioners had no standing to sue. On appeal both the Lord President (Lord Cooper) and Lord Russell agreed that the Treaty did not prohibit the use of the title and was also of the opinion that the 1953 Act was probably not relevant as the Queen had been proclaimed 'Elizabeth the Second' at her Accession Council, before the Act was passed. They nevertheless had something to say about the notion of the unchallengeability of an Act of Parliament.

THE LORD PRESIDENT (LORD COOPER)... The principle of the unlimited sovereignty of Parliament is a distinctively English principle which has no counterpart in Scottish constitutional law. It derives its origin from Coke and Blackstone, and was widely popularised during the nineteenth century by Bagehot and Dicey, the latter having stated the doctrine in its classic form in his Law of the Constitution. Considering that the Union legislation extinguished the Parliaments of Scotland and England and replaced them by a new Parliament, I have difficulty in seeing why it should have been supposed that the new Parliament of Great Britain must inherit all the peculiar characteristics of the English Parliament but none of the Scottish Parliament, as if all that happened in 1707 was that Scottish representatives were admitted to the Parliament of England. That is not what was done. Further, the Treaty and the associated legislation, by which the Parliament of Great Britain was brought into being as the successor of the separate Parliaments of Scotland and England, contain some clauses which expressly reserve to the Parliament of Great Britain powers of subsequent modification, and other clauses which either contain no such power or emphatically exclude subsequent alteration by declarations that the provision shall be fundamental and unalterable in all time coming, or declarations of a like effect. I have never been able to understand how it is possible to reconcile with elementary canons of construction the adoption by the English constitutional theorists of the same attitude to these markedly different types of provisions.

The Lord Advocate conceded this point by admitting that the Parliament of Great Britain 'could not' repeal or alter such 'fundamental and essential' conditions. He was doubtless influenced in making this concession by the modified views expressed by Dicey in his later work entitled Thoughts on the Scottish Union, from which I take this passage (pp. 252–253): — 'The statesmen of 1707, though giving full sovereign power to the Parliament of Great Britain, clearly believed in the possibility of creating an absolutely sovereign Legislature which should yet be bound by unalterable laws.' After instancing the provisions as to Presbyterian Church government in Scotland with their emphatic prohibition against alteration, the author proceeds:— ' It represents the conviction of the Parliament which passed the Act of Union that the Act for the security of the Church of Scotland ought to be morally or constitutionally unchangeable, even by the British Parliament. . . A sovereign Parliament, in short, though it cannot be logically bound to abstain from changing any given law, may, by the fact that an Act when it was passed had been declared to be unchangeable, receive a warning that it cannot be changed without grave danger to the Constitution of the country.' I have not found in the Union legislation any provision that the Parliament of Great Britain should be ' absolutely sovereign ' in the sense that that Parliament should be free to alter the Treaty at will. However that may be, these passages provide a necessary corrective to the extreme formulations adopted by the Lord Ordinary, and not now supported. In the latest editions of the Law of the Constitution the editor uneasily describes Dicey's theories as ' purely lawyer's conceptions ', and demonstrates how deeply later events, such as the Statute of Westminster, have encroached upon the earlier dogmas. As is well known, the conflict between academic logic and political reality has been emphasised by the recent South African decision as to the effect of the Statute of Westminster – *Harris* v. *Minister of Interior.*[25]

But the petitioners still have a grave difficulty to overcome on this branch of their argument. Accepting it that there are provisions in the Treaty of Union and associated legislation which are ' fundamental law ', and assuming for the moment that something is alleged to have been done – it matters not whether with legislative authority or not – in breach of that fundamental law, the question remains whether such a question is determinable as a justiciable issue in the Courts of either Scotland or England, in the same fashion as an issue of constitutional *vires* would be cognisable by the Supreme Courts of the United States, or of South Africa or Australia. I reserve my opinion with regard to the provisions relating expressly to this Court and to the laws ' which concern private right ' which are administered here. This is not such a question, but a matter of ' public right ' (articles 18 and 19). To put the matter in another way, it is of little avail to ask whether the Parliament of Great Britain ' can ' do this thing or that, without going on to inquire who can stop them if they do. Any person ' can ' repudiate his solemn engagement but he cannot normally do so with impunity. Only two answers have been suggested to this corollary to the main question. The first is the exceedingly cynical answer implied by Dicey (Law of the Constitution (9th ed.) p. 82) in the statement that ' it would be

[25] [1952] 1 T.L.R. 1245.

rash of the Imperial Parliament to abolish the Scotch law courts, and assimilate the law of Scotland to that of England. But no one can feel sure at what point Scottish resistance to such a change would become serious.' The other answer was that nowadays there may be room for the invocation of an ' advisory opinion ' from the International Court of Justice. On these matters I express no view. This at least is plain, that there is neither precedent nor authority of any kind for the view that the domestic Courts of either Scotland or England have jurisdiction to determine whether a governmental act of the type here in controversy is or is not conform to the provisions of a Treaty, least of all when that Treaty is one under which both Scotland and England ceased to be independent states and merged their identity in an incorporating union. From the standpoint both of constitutional law and of international law the position appears to me to be unique, and I am constrained to hold that the action as laid is incompetent in respect that it has not been shown that the Court of Session has authority to entertain the issue sought to be raised. . .

LORD RUSSELL: . . . At the highest I consider that the 1953 Act does no more than give an indirect sort of confirmation by Parliament of the style ' Elizabeth II ', but I agree that it has very little, if any, bearing on the present issue before us. In that situation it is unnecessary to determine whether the Lord Ordinary's opinion affirming in absolute terms the unchallengeable sovereignty of the United Kingdom Parliament, and the absence of any right or power of the judicature to nullify or treat as null any Act of Parliament, is or is not well founded. But I concur generally with the comments of your Lordship in the chair regarding the authority to be attributed by a Scottish Court to the opinions expressed by such writers as Professor Dicey on this topic. . .

LORD CARMONT concurred.[26]

[26] ' There is at least one clear case in which a government has altered its policy in response to critical pressure and demands for conformity with the terms of the Union. When in 1872 the Liberal Lord Chancellor Hatherley first introduced the proposal to abolish the appellate jurisdiction of the House of Lords and Privy Council, and to create instead an " imperial " Court of Appeal, Lord Cairns raised the objection (among others) that it was inconsistent with the terms of the several unions to create an English court which would hear appeals from the Scots and Irish courts. " By our Treaty of Union with Scotland we expressly contracted that under no circumstances were appeals from the Scotch courts to be sent to any of the courts in Westminster Hall " (H.L.Deb., Vol. 210, col. 1990; April 30, 1872).

In the following year, when Lord Chancellor Selborne introduced in the House of Lords the Supreme Court of Judicature Bill, he justified the facts

BILSTON CORPORATION v. WOLVERHAMPTON CORPORATION [1942] 1 Ch. 391

Chancery Division

In an agreement made between the parties in November 1892, it was provided that Wolverhampton Corporation 'shall not at any time oppose any application by the [Bilston Water] commissioners to Parliament ... for the purpose of enabling the commissioners to obtain a supply of water. Provided that no such supply or any part thereof is obtained within the water district for the time being of the corporation.' This agreement was confirmed and made binding upon the parties by s. 6 of the Bilston Commissioners (Water) Act, 1893 (a Private Act of Parliament). In 1941 Bilston Corporation, who had taken over the functions of the commissioners, introduced a Bill into Parliament to authorise them to develop additional sources of water supply. Although none of these were within the water district of Wolverhampton Corporation, the latter lodged a petition opposing the Bill. Bilston Corporation therefore applied to the court to restrain Wolverhampton Corporation from acting in breach of the agreement.

SIMONDS J. [having held that Wolverhampton were acting in breach of the agreement continued:] The question then arises whether this is a matter with which the court ought to interfere by injunction. The court clearly has power to enforce a contractual obligation entered into by a person or a corporation that he or it will not apply to Parliament or will not oppose an application to Parliament by another person. That jurisdiction was asserted over and over again by Lord Chancellors in the middle of the last century, but it is significant that the assertion was always accompanied by the statement that it was difficult to conceive a case in which such a jurisdiction should be exercised, and that when, in *Heathcote* v. *North*

---

that the new Court of Appeal was to have no jurisdiction over Scottish and Irish appeals, and that the Lords were to retain their Scottish and Irish appellate jurisdiction, by pointing to the " constitutional objections " to the course formerly proposed. " The Act of Union with Scotland expressly provides that no appeal from that country should be heard by an English court " (H.L.Deb., Vol. 214, col. 1738; March 11, 1873). It would be " dangerous " to propose a transfer of Scots appeals to the new court " without first ascertaining that such a transfer would be approved by the people of Scotland " (*ibid.*). Lord Cairns expressed satisfaction that the constitutional point had been accepted. (The 1873 Act, by section 5, provided for the possible future appointment of Scottish and Irish judges to the Court of Appeal, but the option was never taken up, being indeed pointless after 1876.) ' [Review by D. N. MacCormick of Professor Stanley de Smith's *Constitutional and Administrative Law*; *Public Law* (1972), p. 174.]

Staffordshire Ry. Co.,[27] Shadwell V.-C. did grant such an injunction, it was dissolved by Lord Cottenham L.C. In no other case which has been brought to my notice has such an injunction been granted. I do not propose to grant an injunction of this kind for the first time. I do not think it is necessary for me to add to the reasons so clearly stated by Lord Chancellors in such cases as *Att.-Gen* v. *Manchester and Leeds Ry. Co.*[28]; *Heathcote* v. *North Staffordshire Ry. Co.*[29]; *Steele* v. *North Metropolitan Ry. Co.*[30]; and *In re London, Chatham and Dover Ry. Arrangement Act.*[31]

Perhaps, however, I may add these words of my own as explaining why, in my view, it is difficult to conceive a case in which this jurisdiction, although it undoubtedly exists, can properly be exercised. It is the function of a court of law to ascertain the facts and to apply to those facts as ascertained the established principles of law. I do not mean law in a narrow sense. I include also rules of equity and those rules of public policy which have become part of the substantive law. The function of Parliament is wholly different. It is to consider public interest, and on that basis to give statutory powers to individuals or authorities. Where, as here, the conflict is between two local authorities, each seeking in the public interest to perform the duties confided to it by Parliament, considerations which are wholly inappropriate to be discussed by this court will have to be taken into account by Parliament. Questions of policy in the broadest sense which have no place in the consideration of a case in this court are, if not the only matters, the substantial matters which Parliament has to take into account. Accordingly, it would, in my view, be improper for the court to intervene to prevent those matters being put before Parliament in order that, on the broad questions of public policy, it may be determined whether or not a party should be released from some contractual obligation. That is a matter falling properly within the purview of Parliament which is informed of what has taken place and is competent to determine whether an obligation heretofore imposed on a person or corporation ought to remain binding on him. I can see no difference in this regard between a case where the contractual obligation is not to apply to Parliament and one where it is not to oppose the application by another party.

This further observation I should make. It is true that the contractual obligation created by the agreement of 1892 obtained additional force by reason of the fact that it was confirmed by the

[27] 2 Mac. & G. 100; 42 E.R. 39.   [28] 3 Jur. 379.
[29] 2 Mac. & G. 100; 42 E.R. 39.
[30] L.R. 2 Ch. 237.   [31] L.R. 5 Ch. 671.

Act of 1893 so that what was theretofore no more than a contractual
obligation became also a statutory obligation. I am unable, however,
to see any distinction for the present purpose between a contractual
and a statutory obligation. A party may petition Parliament equally
for release from a contractual obligation as from a statutory obligation. In either case the matter is one appropriate to be considered by
Parliament itself and not by this court. Accordingly, on the assumption which I make that Wolverhampton Corporation are acting in
breach of their contractual obligation in seeking to oppose in Parliament the bill promoted by Bilston Corporation. I hold that the case
is not one in which this court ought to intervene by injunction to
restrain them from doing so. . . .

Judgment for defendants [32]

MERRICKS v. HEATHCOAT-AMORY AND THE MINISTER OF AGRICULTURE, FISHERIES AND FOOD [1955] 1 Ch. 567

Chancery Division

The plaintiff here moved for a mandatory injunction against the defendant to compel him to withdraw the draft of a scheme for the marketing
of potatoes laid before each House of Parliament on 6 April 1955 and to
restrain him from seeking approval of the scheme by each House and
from making an order under s. 1 (8) of the Agricultural Marketing Act,
1931, on the ground that the draft scheme was *ultra vires*.

The Attorney-General argued *inter alia* that the court was being asked
to affect the conduct of a Member of Parliament in Parliament and that
this was clearly a breach of privilege and punishable as a contempt.
There were cases where the courts had rightly interfered before a scheme

---

[32] Cp. Dixon J. in *Attorney-General for New South Wales* v. *Trethowan*
[1931] 44 C.L.R. 394 in the High Court of Australia: ' An Act of the
British Parliament which contained a provision that no Bill repealing any
part of the Act including the part so restraining its own repeal should be
presented for the royal assent unless the Bill were first approved by the
electors, would have the force of law until the Sovereign actually did
assent to a Bill for its repeal. In strictness it would be an unlawful proceeding to present such a Bill for the royal assent before it had been
approved by the electors. If, before the Bill received the assent of the
Crown, it was found possible, as appears to have been done in this appeal,
to raise for judicial decision the question whether it was lawful to present
the Bill for that assent, the Courts would be bound to pronounce it unlawful to do so. Moreover, if it happened that, notwithstanding the statutory inhibition, the Bill did receive the royal assent although it was not
submitted to the electors, the Courts might be called upon to consider
whether the supreme legislative power in respect of the matter had in truth
been exercised in the manner required for its authentic expression and by
the elements in which it had come to reside.'

was laid before Parliament but here the court was being asked to prevent Parliament from considering a scheme that had already been laid before it. To do so might amount to a breach of privilege. It was many years since Parliament and the courts had been in conflict. Even if the injunctions were granted there would be no means of enforcing them. The jurisdiction of the House over its own proceedings was exclusive.

UPJOHN J. ... It is conceded by Mr Walker-Smith that, having regard to section 2 of the Crown Proceedings Act, 1947, he cannot succeed against the Minister if he is acting as representative of the Crown for two reasons. First, because the right defendant under section 17 of the Crown Proceedings Act, 1947, should have been the Ministry of Agriculture, and that body is not before the court. Secondly, that even if that body were before the court, section 21 would preclude him from obtaining any injunction; although, no doubt, if this action proceeds, he may be able to obtain some declaratory order [33]. ...

Mr Walker-Smith's submission is that this action is not against the Minister in his representative capacity at all: it is against the Minister in another capacity. He submits that the Minister has two other capacities: first, he may have an official capacity, not as representing the Crown but as a person designated to carry out certain functions prescribed by Act of Parliament, that is to say, a person designated to carry out the function of laying before each House of Parliament a draft of the scheme, and, if the scheme be approved, to make an order. That, he submits, is done as a person designated and not as a person representing the Crown.

Alternatively, he submits that the functions of the defendant are purely personal and not in any official capacity at all.

In support of those submissions Mr Walker-Smith relies upon the observations of Roxburgh J. in *Harper* v. *Secretary of State for the Home Department*. . .[34]

Roxburgh J. said: ' Secondly, it appears to me that the Secretary of State, if and when he submits a draft order to Her Majesty in Council, is not doing it in his general capacity as Secretary of State, but is doing it as a person to whom the duty of so doing is expressly delegated by the provisions of this Act which contains the machinery which is to be used. I do not as at present advised think that the Crown Proceedings Act has any bearing on the present case.'

It is material to notice that that conclusion was reached on an application by the plaintiff ex parte, the judge not having heard arguments on the part of the defendant. Roxburgh J. granted an

[33] [See below, p. 626].
[34] *The Times*, 18 December 1954.

injunction ex parte; but when the matter went to the Court of Appeal,[35] this point was left open by Evershed M.R. . . . .

I have heard full arguments from Mr Walker-Smith and from the Attorney-General, and I think in those circumstances that I can properly express my own views as to the capacity in which the Minister acts in carrying out or proposing to carry out the relevant functions under section 1 of the Agricultural Marketing Act, 1931. It seems to me clear that in carrying out his functions under that section he is acting as a representative or as an officer of the Crown. He is the Minister of Agriculture, who is responsible for the conduct of agricultural matters in this country; as part of his general responsibility, he was the person who would naturally be designated in the Agricultural Marketing Act as the person to carry out the functions, purposes and policy of that Act. It was no doubt for that reason that it was the Minister who was to approve any scheme under section 1 (1). It was his duty, not merely as a delegated person but as a person acting in his capacity as Minister of Agriculture, to consider the scheme, to hear objections and representations, and to hold inquiries, and he had the power and duty of making such modifications as he thought fit.

It was his duty in his capacity as Minister of Agriculture and not merely as a delegated person, if he was satisfied – with the satisfaction which he had to feel in his capacity as Minister of Agriculture and an official of the Crown – that the scheme would conduce to the more efficient production and marketing of the regulated product, to lay a draft scheme before the Houses of Parliament, and ultimately in the same capacity to make an order bringing the scheme into effect.

It seems to me that from start to finish he was acting in his capacity as an officer representing the Crown. That being so, it is conceded that no injunction can be obtained against him, and therefore the motion fails in limine.

I am not satisfied that it is possible to have the three categories which were suggested. Of course there can be an official representing the Crown, that is plainly this case. But if he were not, it was said that he was a person designated in an official capacity but not representing the Crown. The third suggestion was that his capacity was purely that of an individual. I understand the conception of the first and the third categories, but I confess to finding it difficult to see how the second category can fit into any ordinary scheme. It is possible that there may be special Acts where named persons have special duties to perform which would not be duties normally ful-

[35] [Above, p. 119].

filled by them in their official capacity; but in the normal case where the relevant or appropriate Minister is directed to carry out some function or policy of some Act, he is either acting in his capacity as a Minister of the Crown representing the Crown, or is acting in his personal capacity, usually the former. I find it very difficult to conceive of a middle classification.

A number of other points of great interest have been argued. Among them was the question whether the court had any jurisdiction and, if so, whether it would be proper in any event to interfere with the proceedings now before Parliament by making an order on the Minister to withdraw the draft scheme or restraining him by order from seeking approval of the scheme. I say no more than this, that I see much force in the arguments put forward by the Attorney-General; but in this delicate and difficult branch of the law it is much better not to express an opinion on any matter which does not directly arise for decision. As I have come to the clear conclusion that the Minister throughout is acting as a Minister of the Crown, when it is conceded that no injunction can be granted, it is much better that I should say no more. . .

Motion dismissed

V. EUROPEAN COMMUNITY LAW

THE LORD CHANCELLOR (LORD GARDINER) . . . There has also been some doubt expressed in the past about the impact of accepting the Treaty of Rome on our sovereignty, on our procedures, and upon the role of Parliament. . . In the first place, membership of the European Communities involves the acceptance of a body of law derived from the Treaties. Some of its provisions are required to be given effect to in the Member States by national legislation or other appropriate means. Much of it, however, takes effect directly as law within the Member States. . .

Perhaps the most notable features of the Treaties are these. First, they provide powers for the Community institutions themselves to issue instruments either binding upon the Member States or taking effect as law directly within them; secondly, the Community institutions have powers to enforce and adjudicate upon the provisions of the Community Law. Thus, membership of the Communities involves a transfer of legislative and judicial powers in certain fields to the Community institutions and an acceptance of a corresponding limitation of the exercise of national powers in these fields. The powers of the Communities to create new Community law are, however, limited to the purposes set out in the Treaties, and these purposes cannot be enlarged without a unanimous decision of all the members of the Community.

Apart from the impact of Community law on our present and future national law, adherence to the Treaties would, broadly speaking, have the effect of transferring to Community institutions our power of concluding treaties on tariff and commercial matters. Adherence to the Treaties would involve a considerable body of implementing legislation. This legislation would include an enactment applying as law in the United Kingdom so much of the provisions of the Treaties and of the instruments made under them as then had direct internal effect as law within the Member States and providing that future instruments similarly took effect as law here. A number of our existing Acts of Parliament would require to be amended.

This United Kingdom legislation would be an exercise of Parliamentary sovereignty and Community law, existing and future, would derive its force as law in this country from it. The Community law so applied would override our national law so far as it was inconsistent with it. Under the British constitutional doctrine of Parliamentary sovereignty no Parliament can preclude its successors from changing the law. It is, however, implicit in acceptance of the Treaties that the United Kingdom would not only accept existing Community law but would also refrain from enacting future legislation inconsistent with Community law. Such a restraint on our legislative system would not be unprecedented. Our legislation often takes account – has to take account – of treaty obligations... Further, several Acts of Parliament have reduced for all time vast territorial areas of our sovereignty – the Statute of Westminster and the various Acts of Independence granted to India and other countries. It is the continuing incidence of legislation emanating from the Community institutions that would be without precedent.

There is in theory no constitutional means available to us to make it certain that no future Parliament would enact legislation in conflict with Community law. It would, however, be unprofitable to speculate upon the academic possibility of a future Parliament enacting legislation expressly designed to have that effect. Some risk of inadvertent contradiction between United Kingdom legislation and Community law could not be ruled out; but, of course, we must remember that if we joined the Community we should be taking part in the preparation and enactment of all future Community law and our participation would reduce the likelihood of incompatibility... In the task of applying Community law, the United Kingdom courts would be assisted by the European Court to whom it falls (except in the case of the European Coal and Steel Community Treaty) to give authoritative rulings on the interpretation of the Treaties on references from national courts. If we acceded to the Treaties, we should expect to be represented on the Bench of the European Court.

Community law has little direct effect on the ordinary life of private citizens. In so far as it imposes obligations, it does so mostly in relation to industrial and commercial activities and does not touch citizens in their private capacities. By far the greater part of our domestic law would remain entirely unchanged. Nothing in the Treaties would, for example, touch our criminal law, the onus of proof or the presumption of innocence, matrimonial law, law of inheritance, land law, law of tort or its Scottish equivalent, law of contract (save in relation to restrictive practices), the relations of landlord and tenant, housing, or town and country planning. Nor would there be any reason to expect the creation of future Community law in these fields without the agreement of the United Kingdom, since any enlargement of the powers of the Community to create new law would need an extension of the empowering provisions contained in the Treaties which can be affected only by unanimous consent of all the members.

The main impact of Community law would be in the realms of commerce, Customs and restrictive practices. It would also affect the operation of the steel, coal, and nuclear energy industries. So far as the Community law imposes obligations, the sanctions are usually monetary penalties and proceedings for their enforcement are of a civil rather than a criminal nature. An important safeguard for the protection of those affected is that all decisions imposing penalties are subject to a right of appeal to the European Court. Even more important is the fact that the validity of any executive or legislative act of a Community institution is itself justiciable in the European Court.

Finally, may I say that I entirely agree with an observation made by the noble and learned Viscount, Lord Dilhorne, in the Common Market debate in this House on August 2, 1962, at column 420, when he said:

> ' I venture to suggest that the vast majority of men and women in this country will never directly feel the impact of the Community-made law at all. In the conduct of their daily affairs they will have no need to have regard to any of the provisions of that law; nor are they at all likely ever to be affected by an administrative action of one of the Community institutions.'

[H.L.Deb. 5s. c. 1197. 8 May 1967]

EUROPEAN COMMUNITIES ACT, 1972 (Ch. 68)

1. (1) This Act may be cited as the European Communities Act 1972.

(2) In this Act and, except in so far as the context otherwise requires, in any other Act (including any Act of the Parliament of Northern Ireland)—

'the Communities' means the European Economic Community, the European Coal and Steel Community and the European Atomic Energy Community;

'the Treaties' or 'the Community Treaties' means, subject to subsection (3) below, the pre-accession treaties, that is to say, those described in Part I of Schedule 1 to this Act, taken with—

(*a*) the treaty relating to the accession of the United Kingdom to the European Economic Community and to the European Atomic Energy Community, signed at Brussels on the 22nd January 1972; and

(*b*) the decision, of the same date, of the Council of the European Communities relating to the accession of the United Kingdom to the European Coal and Steel Community;

and any other treaty entered into by any of the Communities, with or without any of the member States, or entered into, as a treaty ancillary to any of the Treaties, by the United Kingdom; and any expression defined in Schedule 1 to this Act has the meaning there given to it.

(3) If Her Majesty by Order in Council declares that a treaty specified in the Order is to be regarded as one of the Community Treaties as herein defined, the Order shall be conclusive that it is to be so regarded; but a treaty entered into by the United Kingdom after the 22nd January 1972, other than a pre-accession treaty to which the United Kingdom accedes on terms settled on or before that date, shall not be so regarded unless it is so specified, nor be so specified unless a draft of the Order in Council has been approved by resolution of each House of Parliament.

(4) For purposes of subsections (2) and (3) above, 'treaty' includes any international agreement, and any protocol or annex to a treaty or international agreement.

2. (1) All such rights, powers, liabilities, obligations and restrictions from time to time created or arising by or under the Treaties, and all such remedies and procedures from time to time provided for by or under the Treaties, as in accordance with the Treaties are without further enactment to be given legal effect or used in the

United Kingdom shall be recognised and available in law, and be enforced, allowed and followed accordingly; and the expression 'enforceable Community right' and similar expressions shall be read as referring to one to which this subsection applies.

(2) Subject to Schedule 2 to this Act, at any time after its passing Her Majesty may by Order in Council, and any designated Minister or department may by regulations, make provision—

(a) for the purpose of implementing any Community obligation of the United Kingdom, or enabling any such obligation to be implemented, or of enabling any rights enjoyed or to be enjoyed by the United Kingdom under or by virtue of the Treaties to be exercised; or

(b) for the purpose of dealing with matters arising out of or related to any such obligation or rights or the coming into force, or the operation from time to time, of subsection (1) above;

and in the exercise of any statutory power or duty, including any power to give directions or to legislate by means of orders, rules, regulations or other subordinate instrument, the person entrusted with the power or duty may have regard to the objects of the Communities and to any such obligation or rights as aforesaid.

In this subsection 'designated Minister or department' means, such Minister of the Crown or government department as may from time to time be designated by Order in Council in relation to any matter or for any purpose, but subject to such restrictions or conditions (if any) as may be specified by the Order in Council.

(3) There shall be charged on and issued out of the Consolidated Fund or, if so determined by the Treasury, the National Loans Fund the amounts required to meet any Community obligation to make payments to any of the Communities or member States, or any Community obligation in respect of contributions to the capital or reserves of the European Investment Bank or in respect of loans, to the Bank, or to redeem any notes or obligations issued or created in respect of any such Community obligation; and, except as otherwise provided by or under any enactment,—

(a) any other expenses incurred under or by virtue of the Treaties or this Act by any Minister of the Crown or government department may be paid out of money provided by Parliament; and

(b) any sums received under or by virtue of the Treaties or this Act by any Minister of the Crown or government department, save for such sums as may be required for disbursements permitted by any other enactment, shall be paid into the Consolidated Fund or, if so determined by the Treasury, the National Loans Fund.

(4) The provision that may be made under subsection (2) above includes, subject to Schedule 2 to this Act, any such provision (of any such extent) as might be made by Act of Parliament, and any enactment passed or to be passed, other than one contained in this Part of this Act, shall be construed and have effect subject to the foregoing provisions of this section; but, except as may be provided by any Act passed after this Act, Schedule 2 shall have effect in connection with the powers conferred by this and the following sections of this Act to make Orders in Council and regulations. . .

3. (1) For the purposes of all legal proceedings any question as to the meaning or effect of any of the Treaties, or as to the validity, meaning or effect of any Community instrument, shall be treated as a question of law (and, if not referred to the European Court, be for determination as such in accordance with the principles laid down by and any relevant decision of the European Court).

(2) Judicial notice shall be taken of the Treaties, of the Official Journal of the Communities and of any decision of, or expression of opinion by, the European Court on any such question as aforesaid; and the Official Journal shall be admissible as evidence of any instrument or other act thereby communicated of any of the Communities or of any Community institution.

SCHEDULE 1

PART I

THE PRE-ACCESSION TREATIES

1. The ' E.C.S.C. Treaty ', that is to say, the Treaty establishing the European Coal and Steel Community, signed at Paris on the 18th April 1951.

2. The ' E.E.C. Treaty ', that is to say, the Treaty establishing the European Economic Community, signed at Rome on the 25th March 1957.

3. The ' Euratom Treaty ', that is to say, the Treaty establishing the European Atomic Energy Community, signed at Rome on the 25th March 1957.

4. The Convention on certain Institutions common to the European Communities, signed at Rome on the 25th March 1957.

5. The Treaty establishing a single Council and a single Commission of the European Communities, signed at Brussels on the 8th April 1965.

6. The Treaty amending certain Budgetary Provisions of the

Treaties establishing the European Communities and of the Treaty establishing a single Council and a single Commission of the European Communities, signed at Luxembourg on the 22nd April 1970.

7. Any treaty entered into before the 22nd January 1972 by any of the Communities (with or without any of the member States) or, as a treaty ancillary to any treaty included in this Part of this Schedule, by the member States (with or without any other country).

SCHEDULE 2
PROVISIONS AS TO SUBORDINATE LEGISLATION

1. (1) The powers conferred by section 2 (2) of this Act to make provision for the purposes mentioned in section 2 (2) (*a*) and (*b*) shall not include power—

   (*a*) to make any provision imposing or increasing taxation; or
   (*b*) to make any provision taking effect from a date earlier than that of the making of the instrument containing the provision; or
   (*c*) to confer any power to legislate by means of orders, rules, regulations or other subordinate instrument, other than rules of procedure for any court of tribunal; or
   (*d*) to create any new criminal offence punishable with imprisonment for more than two years or punishable on summary conviction with imprisonment for more than three months or with a fine of more than £400 (if not calculated on a daily basis) or with a fine of more than £5 a day.

(2) Sub-paragraph (1) (*c*) above shall not be taken to preclude the modification of a power to legislate conferred otherwise than under section 2 (2), or the extension of any such power to purposes of the like nature as those for which it was conferred; and a power to give directions as to matters of administration is not to be regarded as a power to legislate within the meaning of sub-paragraph (1) (*c*).

2. (1) Subject to paragraph 3 below, where a provision contained in any section of this Act confers power to make regulations (otherwise than by modification or extension of an existing power), the power shall be exercisable by statutory instrument.

(2) Any statutory instrument containing an Order in Council or regulations made in the exercise of a power so conferred, if made without a draft having been approved by resolution of each House of Parliament, shall be subject to annulment in pursuance of a resolution of either House. . .

H. P. BULMER LTD. v. *J. BOLLINGER S.A.*
[1974] 3 W.L.R. 202

Court of Appeal

Article 177 of the Treaty of Rome provides:

' The Court of Justice shall have jurisdiction to give preliminary rulings concerning: (a) the interpretation of this Treaty; (b) the validity and interpretation of acts of the institutions of the community; (c) the interpretation of the statutes of bodies established by an act of the Council, where those statutes so provide.

Where such a question is raised before any court or tribunal of a member state, that court or tribunal may, if it considers that a decision on the question is necessary to enable it to give judgment, request the Court of Justice to give a ruling thereon.

Where any such question is raised in a case pending before a court or tribunal of a member state, against whose decisions there is no judicial remedy under national law, that court or tribunal shall bring the matter before the Court of Justice.'

The plaintiffs applied to the High Court for declarations that they were entitled to use the terms ' champagne cider ' and ' champagne perry ' in connexion with their products. French champagne producers in a counterclaim asked the court for declarations that the use of those descriptions to describe any beverage was contrary to Regulations 816 and 817 of 1970, made by the European Commission under the Treaty of Rome. They also requested the trial judge to refer the question of the proper interpretation of those Regulations and the circumstances in which trial judges should refer questions of interpretation to the European Court of Justice to that court. The trial judge refused to refer either question on the ground that it was not necessary to do so.

LORD DENNING M.R. . . . It seems that three points of principle arise:

First: *by which court* should these Regulations be interpreted? By the European Court at Luxembourg? or by the national courts of England?

Second: *at what stage* should the task of interpretation be done? Should it be done now *before* the case is tried out in the English court or at a later stage *after* the other issues have been determined?

Third: in any case, whichever be the court to interpret them, *what are the principles* to be applied in the interpretation of the Regulations? . . .

To make the discussion easier to understand, I will speak only of the interpretation of ' the Treaty ', but this must be regarded as including the Regulations and directives under it. . .

5. *The impact of the Treaty on English law*

Parliament has decreed that the Treaty is henceforward to be part of our law. It is equal in force to any statute. The governing provision is section 2 (1) of the European Communities Act 1972 [above p. 274]. Any rights or obligations created by the Treaty are to be given legal effect in England without more ado. Any remedies or procedures provided by the Treaty are to be made available here without being open to question. In future, in transactions which cross the frontiers, we must no longer speak or think of English law as something on its own. We must speak and think of community law, of community rights and obligations, and we must give effect to them... We have to learn a new system. The Treaty, with the regulations and directives, covers many volumes. The case law is contained in hundreds of reported cases both in the European Court of Justice and in the national courts of the nine. Many must be studied before the right result can be reached. We must get down to it.

6. *By what courts is the treaty to be interpreted?*

It is important to distinguish between the task of interpreting the Treaty – to see what it means – and the task of *applying* it – to apply its provisions to the case in hand. Let me put on one side the task of *applying* the Treaty. On this matter in our courts, the English judges have the final word. They are the only judges who are empowered to decide the case itself. They have to find the facts, to state the issues, to give judgment for one side or the other, and to see that the judgment is enforced... In the task of *interpreting* the Treaty, the English judges are no longer the final authority... The supreme tribunal for *interpreting* the Treaty is the European Court of Justice, at Luxembourg. Our Parliament has so decreed [in] section 3 of the European Communities Act 1972...

Coupled with that section, we must read article 177 of the Treaty. It says:

(1) ' The Court of Justice ' (i.e. the European Court of Justice) ' shall have jurisdiction to give preliminary rulings concerning: (*a*) the interpretation of this Treaty; (*b*) the validity and interpretation of acts of the institutions of the community; (*c*) the interpretation of the statutes of bodies established by an act of the Council, where those statutes so provide '.

(2) ' Where such a question is raised before any court or tribunal of a member state, that court or tribunal may, if it considers that a decision on the question is necessary to enable it to give judgment, request the Court of Justice to give a ruling thereon.'

(3) ' Where any such question is raised in a case pending before a court or tribunal of a member state, against whose decisions there is no judicial remedy under national law, that court or tribunal shall bring the matter before the Court of Justice.'

... If a question is raised before the House of Lords on the interpretation of the Treaty – on which it is necessary to give a ruling – the House of Lords is bound to refer it to the European court. Article 177 (3) uses that emphatic word ' shall '. The House has no option. It must refer the matter to the European court, and, having done so, it is bound to follow the ruling in that *particular* case in which the point arises. But the ruling in that case does not bind *other* cases. The European court is not absolutely bound by its previous decisions: see *Da Costa en Schaake N.V.* v. *Nederlandse Belastings-administratie* [1963] C.M.L.R. 224... Its decisions are much influenced by considerations of policy and economics: and, as these change, so may their rulings change. It follows from this that, if the House of Lords in a *subsequent* case thinks that a previous ruling of the European court was wrong – or should not be followed – it can refer the point again to the European court: and the European court can reconsider it. On reconsideration it can make a ruling which will bind that *particular* case. But not subsequent cases. And so on.

7. *The discretion to refer or not to refer*

But short of the House of Lords, no other English court is bound to refer a question to the European court at Luxembourg... Article 177 (2) uses the permissive word ' may ' in contrast to ' shall ' in article 177 (3). In England the trial judge has complete *discretion*. If a question arises on the interpretation of the Treaty, an English judge ... need not refer it to the court at Luxembourg unless he wishes... If he does decide it himself, the European court cannot interfere...

The European court take the view that the trial judge has a complete discretion to refer or not to refer: see *Rheinmühlen, Düsseldorf, Düsseldorf-Holthausen (Firma)* v. *Einfuhr und Vorratsstelle für Getreide und Futtermittel, Frankfurt-am-Main*, January 16, 1974 – with which they cannot interfere: see *Milchwerke Heinz Wöhrmann & Sohn K.G.* v. *Commission of the European Economic Community* [1963] C.M.L.R. 152. If a party wishes to challenge the decision of the trial judge in England – to refer or not to refer – he must appeal to the Court of Appeal in England...

... The judges of the Court of Appeal, in their turn, have complete discretion... If a party wishes to challenge the decision of the Court of Appeal – to refer or not to refer – he must get leave to go to the House of Lords and go there. It is only in that august place that there is no discretion. If the point of interpretation is one which is ' necessary ' to give a ruling, the House must refer it to the European court at Luxembourg. The reason behind this imperative is this: the cases which get to the House of Lords are substantial cases of the first importance. If a point of interpretation arises there, it is assumed to be worthy of reference to the European court at Luxembourg. Whereas the points in the lower courts may not be worth troubling the European court about: see the judgment of the German Court of Appeal at Frankfurt in *In re Export of Oat Flakes* [1969] C.M.L.R. 85, 97.

8. *The condition precedent to a reference. It must be ' necessary '*

Whenever any English court thinks it would be helpful to get the view of the European court – on the interpretation of the Treaty – there is a *condition precedent* to be fulfilled. It is a condition which applies to the House of Lords as well as to the lower courts. It is contained in the same paragraph of article 177 (2) and applies in article 177 (3) as well. It is this: an English court can only refer the matter to the European court ' *if it considers* that a decision on the question is necessary to enable it to give judgment '. . .

If the English judge considers it *necessary* to refer the matter, no one can gainsay it save the Court of Appeal. The European court will accept his opinion. It will not go into the grounds on which he based it. The European court so held in *Algemene Transport en Expeditie Onderneming van Gend en Loos, N.V.* v. *Nederlandse Tariefcommissie* [1963] C.M.L.R. 105, 128, 129 and *Albatros S.A.R.L* v. *Société des Petroles et des Combustibles Liquides (SOPECO)* [1965] C.M.L.R. 159, 177. It will accept the question as he formulates it: *Fratelli Grassi* v. *Amministrazione delle Finanze* [1973] C.M.L.R. 332, 335. It will not alter it or send it back. Even if it is faulty question, it will do the best it can with it: see *Deutsche Grammophon Gesellschaft m.b.H.* v. *Metro-S.B.-Grossmärkte G.m.b.H. & Co. K.G.* [1971] C.M.L.R. 631, 656. The European court treats it as a matter between the English courts and themselves – to be dealt with in a spirit of co-operation – in which the parties have no place save that they are invited to be heard. It was so held in *Hessische Knappschaft* v. *Maison Singer et Fils* [1966] C.M.L.R. 82, 94. . . If the English judge considers it ' *not necessary* ' to refer a question of interpretation to the European court – but instead decides it itself [*sic*] – that is the end of the matter. It is no good a party going off to the European court. . . They are conscious that the Treaty gives the final word in this respect to the English courts. From all I have read of their cases, they are very careful not to exceed their jurisdiction. They never do anything to trespass on any ground which is properly the province of the national courts.

9. *The guide lines*

Seeing that these matters of ' necessary ' and ' discretion ' are the concern of the English courts, it will fall to the English judges to rule upon them... It may not be out of place, therefore, to draw attention to the way in which other national courts have dealt with them.

(1) *Guide lines as to whether a decision is necessary*

(i) *The point must be conclusive.*

The English court has to consider whether ' a decision on the question is *necessary* to enable it to give *judgment* '... The judge must have got to the stage when he says to himself: ' This clause of the Treaty is capable of two or more meanings. If it means *this*, I give judgment for the plaintiff. If it means *that*, I give judgment for the defendant '. In short, the point must be such that, whichever way the point is decided, it is conclusive of the case. Nothing more remains but to give judgment. The Hamburg court stressed the necessity in *In re Adjustment Tax on Petrol* [1966] C.M.L.R. 409, 416. In *Van Duyn* v. *Home Office* [1974] 1 W.L.R. 1107, in England Pennycuick V.-C. said: ' it would be quite impossible to give judgment without such a decision '.

(ii) *Previous ruling.*

In some cases, however, it may be found that the same point – or substantially the same point – has already been decided by the European court in a previous case. In that event... the English court... can follow the previous decision without troubling the European court. But, as I have said, the European court is *not* bound by its previous decisions. So if the English court thinks that a previous decision of the European court may have been wrong – or if there are new factors which ought to be brought to the notice of the European court – the English court may consider it *necessary* to re-submit the point to the European court. In that event, the European court will consider the point again. It was so held by the European court itself in the *Da Costa* case [1963] C.M.L.R. 224; in Holland in *Vereniging van Fabrikanten en Importeurs van Verbruiksartikelen (F.I.V.A.)* v. *Mertens* [1963] C.M.L.R. 141, and in Germany in *In re Import of Powdered Milk (No. 3)* [1967] C.M.L.R. 326, 336.

(iii) *Acte claire.*

In other cases the English court may consider the point is reasonably clear and free from doubt. In that event there is no need to interpret the Treaty but only to apply it: and that is the task of the English court. It was so submitted by the Advocate-General to the European Court of Justice in the *Da Costa* case [1963] C.M.L.R. 224, 234. It has been so held by the highest courts in France. By the Conseil d'Etat in *In re Société des Petroles Shell-Berre* [1964] C.M.L.R. 462, 481, and by the Cour de Cassation in *State* v. *Cornet* [1967] C.M.L.R. 351 and *Lapeyre* v. *Administration des Douanes* [1967] C.M.L.R. 362, 368. Also by a superior court in Germany in *In re French Widow's Pension Settlement* [1971] C.M.L.R. 530.

(iv) *Decide the facts first.*

It is to be noticed, too, that the word is ' necessary '. This is much stronger than ' desirable ' or ' convenient '. There are some cases where the point if decided one way, would shorten the trial greatly. But, if decided the other way, it would mean that the trial would have to go its full length. In such a case it might be ' convenient ' or ' desirable ' to take it as a preliminary point because it might save much time and expense. But it would not be ' necessary ' at that stage ... As a rule you cannot tell whether it is necessary to decide a point until all the facts are ascertained. So in general it is best to decide the facts first.

(2) *Guide lines as to the exercise of discretion*

Assuming that the condition about ' necessary ' is fulfilled, there remains the matter of discretion. This only applies to the trial judge or the Court of Appeal, not to the House of Lords ...

The national courts of the various member countries have taken into account such matters as the following:

(i) *The time to get a ruling.*

The length of time which may elapse before a ruling can be obtained from the European court ... The average length of time at present seems to be between six and nine months. Meanwhile, the whole action in the English court is stayed until the ruling is obtained ... This was very much in the mind of the German Court of Appeal of Frankfurt in *In re Export of Oat Flakes* [1969] C.M.L.R. 85, 97. It said that it was important ' to prevent undue protraction of both the proceedings before the European court and trial before the national courts '. On that ground it decided a point of interpretation itself, rather than submit it to the European court.

(ii) *Do not overload the court.*

The importance of not overwhelming the European court by references to it ... There are nine judges of that court. All nine must sit in plenary sessions on these cases, as well as many other important cases: see article 165 ... The Court of Appeal in Frankfurt took this view pointedly in *In re Import Licence for Oats* [1968] C.M.L.R. 103, 117:

' the European court must not be overwhelmed by requests for rulings ... This viewpoint should induce courts to exercise their right sparingly. A reference to the European court must not become an automatic reaction, and ought only to be made if serious difficulties of interpretation occur . . .'

(iii) *Formulate the question clearly.*

The need to formulate the question clearly. It must be a question of *interpretation only* of the Treaty. It must not be mixed up with the facts. It is the task of the national courts to find the facts and apply the Treaty... That appears from *Salgoil S.p.A.* v. *Foreign Trade Ministry of the Italian Republic* [1969] C.M.L.R. 181, 193 and *Sirena S.R.L.* v. *EDA S.R.L.* [1971] C.M.L.R. 260, 263 . . .

(iv) *Difficulty and importance.*

. . . Unless the point is really difficult and important, it would seem better for the English judge to decide it himself . . . English judges have . . . decided several points of interpretation on the Treaty . . . I refer to the decision of Whitford J. in *Leorose Ltd.* v. *Hawick Jersey International Ltd.* [1973] C.M.L.R. 83; Graham J. in *Minnesota Mining & Manufacturing Co.* v. *Geerpress Europe Ltd.* [1973] C.M.L.R. 259; Bridge J. in *Esso Petroleum* v. *Kingswood Motors (Addlestone) Ltd.* [1974] Q.B. 142; [1973] C.M.L.R. 665; Graham J. in *Löwenbrau München* v. *Gruhalle Lager International Ltd.* [1974] C.M.L.R. 1 and Mr Suenson-Taylor Q.C. in *Processed Vegetable Growers Association Ltd.* v. *Customs and Excise Commissioners* [1974] C.M.L.R. 113.

(v) *Expense.*

. . . That influenced a Nuremberg court *In re Potato Flour Tax* [1964] 3 C.M.L.R. 96, 106. On a request for interpretation, the European court does not as a rule award costs, and for a simple reason. It does not decide the case. It only gives advice on the meaning of the Treaty. If either party wishes to get the costs of the reference, he must get it from the English court, when it eventually decides the case: see *Sociale Verzekeringsbank* v. *H. J. Van der Vecht* [1968] C.M.L.R. 151, 167.

(vi) *Wishes of the parties.*

. . . If both parties want the point to be referred to the European court, the English court should have regard to their wishes, but it should not give them undue weight. The English court should hesitate before making a reference against the wishes of one of the parties, seeing the expense and delay which it involves.

10. *The principles of interpretation*

In view of these considerations, it is apparent that in very many cases the English courts will interpret the Treaty themselves...

What then are the principles of interpretation to be applied? Beyond doubt the English courts must follow the same principles as the European court. Otherwise there would be differences between the countries of the nine ... It is enjoined on the English courts by section 3 of the European Community Act 1972... The Treaty is quite unlike any of the enactments to which we have become accustomed. The draftsmen of our statutes have striven to express themselves with the utmost exactness. They have tried to foresee all possible circumstances that may arise and to provide for them ... They have become long and involved. In consequence, the judges have followed suit. They interpret a statute as applying only to the circumstances covered by the very words. They give them a literal interpretation. If the words of the statute do not cover a new situation – which was not foreseen – the judges hold that they have no power to fill the gap. To do so would be a ' naked usurpation of the legislative function': see *Magor and St. Mellons Rural District Council* v. *Newport Borough Council* [1952] A.C. 189, 191. The gap must remain open until Parliament finds time to fill it.

How different is this Treaty? It lays down general principles. It expresses its aims and purposes. All in sentences of moderate length and commendable style. But it lacks precision. It uses words and phrases without defining what they mean. An English lawyer would look for an interpretation clause, but he would look in vain ... All the way through the Treaty there are gaps and lacunae. These have to be filled in by the judges, or by Regulations or directives ... That appears from the decision of the Hamburg court in *In re Tax on Imported Lemons* [1968] C.M.L.R. 1.

Likewise the Regulations and directives ... They are quite unlike our statutory instruments. They have to give the reasons on which they are based: article 190. So they start off with pages of preambles, ' whereas ' and ' whereas ' and ' whereas '. These show the purpose and intent of the Regulations and directives. Then follow the provisions which are to be obeyed. Here again words and phrases are used without defining their import. Such as ' personal conduct ' in the Directive 64/221, article 3 (E.E.C.) which was considered by Pennycuick V.-C. in *Van Duyn* v. *Home Office* [1974] 1 W.L.R. 1107. In the case of difficulty, recourse is had to the preambles ... But much is left to the judges. The enactments give only an outline plan. The details are to be filled in by the judges.

Seeing these differences, what are the English courts to do when they are faced with a problem of interpretation? ... No longer must they examine the words in meticulous detail. No longer must they argue about the precise grammatical sense. They must look to the purpose or intent. To quote the words of the European court in the

Da Costa case [1963] C.M.L.R. 224, 237, they must deduce 'from the wording and the spirit of the Treaty the meaning of the community rules'. They must not confine themselves to the English text. They must consider, if need be, all the authentic texts, of which there are now eight: see *Sociale Verzekeringsbank* v. *Van der Vecht* [1968] C.M.L.R. 151. They must divine the spirit of the Treaty and gain inspiration from it. If they find a gap, they must fill it as best they can. They must do what the framers of the instrument would have done if they had thought about it. So we must do the same...

Lord Denning then considered the particular issues before the court and decided that it was neither necessary nor desirable to refer the interpretation of the Regulations to the European court. He also held that it was not necessary to refer the question as to the circumstances in which a court should refer a matter to the European court. 'I am quite clear that it is unnecessary to ask this question. The answer is clear. It is not the province of the European court to give any guidance or advice to the national court as to when it should, or should not, refer a question. That is a matter for the national court itself. It is no concern of the European court.'

STEPHENSON J. delivered a concurring judgment. STAMP L.J. agreed.

CHAPTER VII

THE ROLE OF PARLIAMENT

I. PARLIAMENTARY PROCEDURE

The importance of Parliamentary procedure and institutions

... The political development of our own day has laid bare – in the first instance in England, and then in nearly all the constitutional states of Europe – the *conventional* foundation of parliamentary government. Parliamentary conventions appear above all in the forms of parliamentary action, in the limitations to party strategy imposed by the inviolable bounds of the rules and in the tacit agreement among all who take part in parliamentary life to handle these rules in a reasonable way... Except within these rules, conventions and forms parliamentary work is impossible...

There may... be political feelings of such depth as to threaten the allegiance of an individual to the state in which he lives; his political views may have deeper and firmer roots than his patriotism; they may spring from religious emotion, or from a feeling of nationality; in the future, perhaps, a craving for social or economic equality may produce the same effect: in all such cases the *majority principle*, a fundamental convention upon which all parliamentary government is built, must needs begin to lose its moral force. At the same time and to the same degree the principle of protection for the minority begins to suffer from decay. There is a total collapse of the system of ideas of representative government, based as it is on understandings and a common loyalty, which find in the principles and forms of parliamentary procedure their most refined and sublimated expression.

From this point of view we may assign to the order of business in a national representative assembly its special significance in regard to the general constitutional and political situation. It is, as it were, *a political pressure-gauge, indicating the tension in the parliamentary machine and thence in the whole organism of the state*... Many of its rules and principles express the general requisites for the existence of representative government and summarise the conditions necessary for the action of a national representative assembly which exercises, or at least shares in, the supreme functions of the state: these rules belong therefore, theoretically

286

speaking, to constitutional law, whether they are embodied in the fundamental laws of the state or not... Parliamentary government as a system of law is intimately connected with parliamentary government regarded as a political system determined by history and by national and social characteristics. As the nature of the political functions of a parliament is determined, primarily, by such considerations, so also, though secondarily, are the corresponding functions of the law of its procedure.

[Redlich, *The Procedure of the House of Commons* (1908), vol. III, p. 196]

If we take a rapid glance back over the developments in the procedure of the House of Commons during the last quarter of a century, we shall find little difficulty in recognising from the course of events, the chief results which have been effected. Three tendencies stand out in bold relief; the strengthening of the disciplinary and administrative powers of the Speaker, the continuous extension of the rights of the Government over the direction of all parliamentary action in the House, and, lastly, the complete suppression of the private member, both as to his legislative initiative and as to the scope of action allowed to him by the rules. Not one of the three is the consequence of any intentional effort; they have all arisen out of the hard necessity of political requirements.

The reasons for entrusting greater power to the Speaker in the conduct of the proceedings can be clearly seen. The Irish policy of obstruction... had the simple result of calling into full activity the powers latent in the historic office of the Speaker...[1] No less obvious is the connection between practical politics and the new law of procedure in the matter of the position of authority given to the Government... The British constitution, as it is understood and worked at the present day... has done away with the possi-

---

[1] [The Ballot Act, 1872, made possible the return of 59 Irish Home Rulers. In 1875 Parnell, with their support, began a policy of systematic obstruction in the House of Commons, not merely with the object of defeating the passage of particular Bills, but of bringing the machinery of Parliament to a standstill. In 1882, Parliament introduced into its Standing Orders the motion for closure which enables the Government to put an end to a debate provided not less than 100 Members vote in the majority and provided the Speaker does not regard the motion as an abuse of the rules of the House or an infringement of the rights of the minority. This is now used by Governments as a time-saving device and not simply to defeat obstruction. Other time-saving devices include the power of the Speaker and Chairmen of Committees to select the new clauses and amendments to be proposed at the committee and report stages of Bills, and Allocation of Time Orders. In the latter, the House fixes dates by which the stages of a Bill are to be completed.]

bility of a political conflict between the majority of the House of Commons and the Ministry ... It was then a simple dictate of political logic that the metamorphosis in the attitude of Government towards Parliament should receive outward formulation in parliamentary procedure ...

The third tendency which we have named, the depreciation of the position of the individual member on the floor of the House, is closely connected with the second. It is a necessary corollary to the development of the parliamentary system of government. The assumption on which the system rests, the existence of two great parties alternately obtaining power and place, involves the maintenance of an elaborate discipline among the supporters of the Government. The establishment of the system whereby party cabinets of opposite views succeed one another leads to the further consequence that the Opposition is regarded as an indispensable component in the machine of the state. There follows a necessity for party discipline among the members of the Opposition also ... Each Cabinet which attains to power is more than its predecessor a direct mandatory of the electorate, having, with the majority given to it, received instructions and authority to carry out a definite political or legislative programme. The extension of the suffrage has operated in two directions – it has enormously strengthened the Government, who are supported by the votes of the majority of the nation, and it has deprived the single member, and with him the House of Commons as a whole, of importance and initiative.

[Redlich, *op. cit.* vol. I, p. 206]

THE LEADER OF THE HOUSE AND LORD PRESIDENT OF THE COUNCIL (MR RICHARD CROSSMAN): ... Let me describe the central problem as I see it. The physical conditions under which we work and many of our main procedures are survivals from a period when parties were weak, when the making and unmaking of Ministries still rested with the House of Commons, not with an electorate based on universal suffrage, and when the Cabinet was merely the executive committee of the Commons. Procedurally, we still behave as though we were a sovereign body which really shared with the Government in the initiation of legislation, which exercised a real control not only of finance, but of the administration of the Departments. But, today, not only the House of Lords has been shorn of most of its authority. The House of Commons, too, has surrendered most of its effective powers to the Executive and has become in the main the passive forum in which the struggle is fought between the modern usurpers of parliamentary power, the great political machines. In this transformation of the Parliamentary scene, the House of Commons has largely lost the three functions for which its procedures were evolved and to which they are relevant, the making of Ministries, initiation of legislation shared with the Cabinet, and the watchdog control of finance and administration. The question the reformer has to ask is whether we should look backwards in an attempt to restore the pristine powers of this House to which our procedures are relevant or whether we should accept our present limited functions largely as they are and adapt our procedures to them. I know that there are some of my hon. Friends who dream of a time when the secret negotiations of the Government with outside interests which precede all modern legislation and the secret decisions in the Committee Room upstairs which largely determine party attitudes will be rendered insignificant because the House of Commons will once again become sovereign and make decisions for itself. I think they are crying for the moon.

It is no good trying to reform ourselves by harking back to ancient days. An effective reform must be an adaptation of obsolete procedures to modern conditions and to the functions we should fulfil in a modern highly industrialised society. Today, for example, it must be the electorate, not the Commons, who normally make and unmake Governments. It must be the Cabinet that runs the Executive and initiates and controls legislation, and it must be the party machines that manage most of our business, through the usual channels, as well as organising what was once a congeries of independent back-benchers into two disciplined armies. Since this is the structure of modern political power, the task of the reformer is to adapt our institutions and procedures to make them efficient.

I believe that there are three questions by which the working of the House of Commons can be tested, both today and for future change. First, is the legislative process designed to enable policies to be translated into law at the speed required by the tempo of modern industrial change? Secondly, can our timetable leave room for debating the great issues and especially for the topical debates on matters of current controversy which provide the main political education of a democracy? Thirdly, while accepting that legislation and administration must be firmly in the hands of the Government, does the House of Commons provide a continuous and detailed check on the work of the Executive and an effective defence of the individual against bureaucratic injustice and incompetence? It is by these three tests, I suggest, that we should try out both our existing procedures and the proposals for modifying them put forward by the various schools of parliamentary reform.

Here I would call attention to one confusion which is always recurring in our discussions of parliamentary reform. There is a great deal of talk about the need for modernisation, for equipping the House with a more efficient voting system, for improving our libraries, for improving our physical accommodation – even on occasion, for television. I would not decry for one moment modernisation of this kind... But there is a difference between modernisation and parliamentary reform. One can, for example, be in favour of introducing loudspeakers into the House of Commons, or improving the Library system, and yet be opposed to every proposal for adapting our procedures to modern conditions.

[738 H.C.Deb. 5s. c. 479. 14 December 1966]

In referring to this speech a year later [754 H.C.Deb. 5s. c. 242. 14 November 1967] Mr Crossman noted: 'I said then that the Parliamentary reformer must keep three aims firmly in mind... It seems to me obvious that these aims are, to a large extent, inconsistent with each other and that, if ever one of them is pushed to excess, another essential function of Parliament is endangered. That is why Parliamentary reform does not simply consist of discovering a number of useful changes and stringing them together. What the reformer must try to achieve is a balanced set of changes, a harmonious combination of measures designed to make public Bill procedure more efficient, to restore the Floor of this Chamber as the forum of the nation's political debate and, simultaneously, to strengthen Parliamentary control of the Executive...'

Cp. the comments of Mr Selwyn Lloyd in the same debate: 'There is a sort of mystical belief about that the position of the House of Commons today compares unfavourably with its stature in 1867, a hundred years ago, that the House of Commons then was supreme, that Ministers shook with fright when back benchers spoke to them, and that the Executive was cowed, timid and subservient.

In fact, that is a lot of nonsense. The House of Commons is much more powerful today than it was then. I do not believe that Mr Gladstone or Mr Disraeli were in any way terrified by their back benchers. The Executive at that time – for example, the War Office – was a law unto itself. The only difference was that there was less of the Executive then...'

II. LEGISLATION

(i) Origins and preparation

1. Most legislative proposals are integral parts of the policy of the Government which is for the time being in power... Although

Parliament is commonly called 'the Legislature' it has to be recognised that legislative initiative lies mainly with the Executive and that in such cases the function of Parliament is limited to examining and criticising those proposals, requiring the Government to justify them, and accepting them with or without modification or rejecting them.

[Memorandum of the Study of Parliament Group to the Select Committee on Procedure, Fourth Report (H.C. 303 of 1964–5)]

5. The origin of Bills and the manner of their preparation are as diverse as the Bills themselves. Some Bills derive directly from a political decision or a commitment in a manifesto, as for example this Session's Industrial Relations Bill. Others grow naturally out of the ordinary work of Government Departments; in such cases the start of preparation for a new Bill may be hardly distinguishable from the continuing process of administering the existing law. Departments maintain close contact with local authorities and others concerned in the administration of the various services and many proposals for amendment of the law come to notice in this way. Memoranda from professional and trade associations, academic studies, articles in the Press, letters from Members and the public all contribute suggestions for legislation. It would often be impossible to disentangle the threads and say with confidence where a particular provision in a Bill originated. Special considerations apply in the case of particular categories of Bills, such as Bills to authorise the ratification of international agreements, consolidation Bills and law reform Bills prepared by the Law Commission or the Criminal Law Revision Committee.

6. The extent of the consultation with outside interests during the preparatory stages of Bills and the forms which it takes also vary greatly; in some few cases there is no consultation at all. Where local authorities are concerned in the administration of a service, it is normal practice to consult their associations, more particularly on the practical provisions needed to give effect to the broad policy decisions. Similar consultations take place with representative bodies in other fields, sometimes on the initiative of those bodies. In some cases there is an extended process of public consultation, as when legislation is based on the published report of a Royal Commission or Departmental Committee which has taken evidence from the public. Many Bills are founded on White Papers which, even when not debated, provide interested persons with the opportunity to comment during the formative stage. Reports of the Law Commission, including the text of a draft Bill, are published

in advance of legislation and are themselves produced after consultation with interested bodies.

[Memorandum by the Lord President of the Council and the Chief Whip to the Select Committee on Procedure. Second Report. H.C. 538 of 1970–1]

15. ... [I]t may assist the Committee if we briefly outline the present arrangements for the formulation of taxation policy within Government... A decision in principle to introduce a new tax, or to make major structural changes in an existing one is political. It will sometimes be taken as part of the continuing process of Government, after a period of preparation and study undertaken by officials, or it may stem from a commitment in the election manifesto of an incoming Government. Consideration will be given to the economic and social implications, both in relation to the decision in principle, and thereafter, in settling the framework of the tax. The task of working out the details, and of having draft legislation prepared is primarily a job for the relevant revenue department, which will instruct Parliamentary Counsel and consult other Government departments as appropriate. Ministers require to be consulted on any major points which arise in drafting, and to be kept in touch with the drafting process. Ministerial approval for a particular detail of the proposals will sometimes be conditional on the securing of a satisfactory draft. If time allows, Ministers may wish to publish an outline of the proposals. In any case there will frequently be at least informal consultations, on a confidential basis, with the appropriate professions and other representative bodies, except where special problems would arise from consultations before the Chancellor's intention to take action is announced. It will be appreciated, however, that such consultations, where they take place, are essentially about ways and means, and not about the overall desirability or otherwise of the measures which the Government is contemplating.

16. New taxes and major changes apart, proposals for legislation may originate either in the Department concerned, or in recommendations made by representative bodies, or in Parliament, e.g. in debate on an earlier Finance Bill or in suggestions made by members of the public. Ministerial decisions are sought as early as possible; and, once the decision has been given, instructions for drafting are prepared and sent to Parliamentary Counsel, and the drafting process begins. Representative bodies are consulted to an increasing degree both when proposals are under consideration and during the drafting stage which can disclose points of detail which may not have been apparent earlier. Once the Finance Bill is published it is

of course open for public comment, including articles in the Press and the learned journals. Members of Parliament may table formal amendments to the Bill after it has had its Second Reading, and it is also standard practice in the interval between publication and the Committee Stage for representative bodies to make written representations, or to bring deputations (which may include MPs) either to Ministers or to officials to discuss aspects of the legislation. Some comments may lead to Government amendments at the Committee or Report Stages; others may inspire Opposition amendments. There is extensive opportunity for outside comment on Finance Bills, limited only by the Parliamentary timetable.

25. ... It may sometimes be possible to publish proposals in the form of a White or Green Paper,[1] ahead of their presentation in legislative form: a recent example was the publication in February 1970 of proposals for the recasting of tax provisions affecting superannuation, some weeks ahead of the appearance of the Finance Bill in which the relevant legislation was included...

[Memorandum by the Treasury to the Select Committee on Procedure, First Report. H.C. 276 of 1970–1]

Prior discussion of proposals for legislation

11. Your Committee believe that the House should be brought in at an earlier point in the legislative process so as to allow discussion by Parliament of subjects and details of potential legislation before the Government finally prepare a Bill. As the Opposition Chief Whip told Your Committee: 'Everyone knows that a Minister preparing a Bill is consulting all sorts of outside organisations, and indeed must do so inevitably. The one lot of people he never consults in any way before he prepares it are the Members of the House of Commons ... All too often the Bill is produced in a form agreed outside and is then given to the House on a much more "take it or leave it" basis than sometimes Members would wish it to be'... Your Committee recognise that responsibility for the form in which their Bills are presented must rest with the Government of the day but Parliament is entitled to have its views taken into consideration, whenever possible, at a sufficiently early stage in the formulation of those decisions... There are several improvements in procedure that could be made to this end, both by debates in the House and by the work of Committees.

12. *Debates in the House.* It is already the practice, on some occasions, for the Government to test the opinion of the House by publishing a White Paper and arranging a debate before a Bill is

[1] For Green Papers generally see below p. 481.

published and before the Government have become publicly committed to details. In recent years this has been done on complex and contentious issues such as steel nationalisation, leasehold reform and town and country planning. Your Committee recommend that there should be more general debates of this kind...

13. *Specialist Committees.* With the growth of the use of Select Committees which concern themselves with particular subjects (such as Science and Technology) or particular Departments of State (such as Agriculture, Fisheries and Food) it will become increasingly possible for such Committees to consider ideas for legislation referred to them, or for them to propose legislation themselves as a result of their enquiries. The Select Committee on Nationalised Industries, for instance, have already considered the form the proposed Corporation for the Post Office might take... Your Committee recommend that this aspect of the work of the specialised Committees should be developed as more of these Committees are set up.

14. *Ad hoc Committees to consider future legislation.* In his evidence, the Leader of the House also envisaged Committees which would convert into practical terms ideas for legislation either in social or technical fields which had perhaps already been considered by experts (e.g. divorce laws; the termination of pregnancy; decimal coinage). There are many precedents for the appointment of Committees (including Joint Committees) to consider the desirability of legislation in particular fields. An example of such a Committee is that of the present Session ' to review the law and practice relating to the censorship of stage plays '. Your Committee consider that there is considerable scope for the increased use of *ad hoc* Committees for this purpose, and they agree with the Leader of the House that such a development would be of assistance in the field of social and moral questions that are often left to Private Members' Bills, but sometimes prove too heavy a burden for one Member to carry. There is no need to limit their use to such matters, however. Although questions of party political controversy, subjects that have to be kept secret until legislation is introduced and matters that need urgent Government action will usually be outside the scope of such Committees, matters of policy such as the Regional Employment Premium, and the rating system, are ones that could very usefully be canvassed before a Committee of Members. They would be able to hear the views of interested parties – views that frequently at present are only presented to the Departments and not directly to Parliament at all. Your Committee recommend that regular use should in future be made of such *ad hoc* Committees to study and report on

the specific topics of possible legislation referred to them. It would be for the Government to find time for legislation introduced in the light of the Committees' recommendations.

[Sixth Report from the Select Committee on Procedure. H.C. 539 of 1966–7. Public Bill Procedure]

4. In 1967 the Procedure Committee . . . recommended that Members should be able, by the medium of general debates on, for example, White Papers and Reports of Royal Commissions and Committees of Enquiry, to indicate their opinions at a sufficiently early stage to enable the Government to take account of them. In the event, the House between 1966 and 1970 spent an average of 69 hours per session on general debates on Government policy, White Papers, etc. compared with an average of 90 hours between 1960 and 1964. The average length of sessions, respectively, was 177 and 161 days. . . Information supplied by the Civil Service Department showed that in 1967–68, of 48 public bills (excluding financial, consolidation and private Members' Bills) 11 were based on a White Paper, six on a published report and 15 on a public statement. But of these important sources of legislation, the House debated only one White Paper, one report and four Statements. The corresponding figures for session 1968–69 were 44 public bills, of which eight were based on a White Paper, eight on a published report and eleven on a public statement. Only three White Papers, three reports and five statements were debated. . .

Pre-legislation Committees

8. . . . In arguing the case for the establishment of such Committees Your Committee emphasise that the subject of the enquiry should be at the discretion of the Government and that the Select Committee would be considering specific matters which might subsequently form the basis of legislation. . . It is not suggested that the work of a Select Committee would be a substitute for the appointment in suitable cases of a Departmental Committee or a Royal Commission. The appointment of these Committees need therefore not result in any delay in the legislative programme of the Government, since their work would be done before a draft Bill was in contemplation and perhaps one or two years before any legislation based on their report was introduced. Again, if the Government were unwilling to introduce legislation following the recommendations of the Report of a pre-legislation committee, yet were not hostile to their general implication, if would be open to a private Member to introduce a bill founded on the recommendations. Pre-legislation com-

mittees would provide an invaluable opportunity to inform Members on the subjects of future legislation and enable them to deploy the special knowledge thus gained in the service of the House.

9. ... The report of the joint committee of 1966–67 on the censorship of stage plays resulted in the passage in the next session of the Theatres Act 1968. Since 1900 'nearly half of the pre-legislation committees have given rise to identifiable legislation '; committees from 1900 to 1939 ' appear in the main to have dealt with narrow issues, though these issues were of considerable complexity within their narrow scope '. Your Committee therefore recommend that regular use should in future be made of pre-legislation committees, when appropriate in the form of joint committees, to consider matters with a view to consequent legislation.

Post-legislation Committees

10. Pressure of Government business in each session often reduces the chance of securing a place in the legislative programme for a Bill to amend an Act passed within recent years. For this reason, years may pass before Parliament has an opportunity to consider legislation embodying amendments to a recent Act, the need for which has become imperative following, for example, a judgment in the Courts, difficulties of interpretation, impracticability in everyday use, or the nature of the delegated legislation made under its authority. A proposal has been made that, should a need arise, a select committee should be appointed ad hoc to examine the working of a statute within a short period after its enactment. The kernel of such a committee, which has been described as a ' post-legislation ' committee, might be formed by some members of the standing committee on the Bill, or by Members who took a special interest in the Bill during its passage through Parliament. The post-legislation committee would be empowered to take evidence from officials and outside witnesses, including possibly those practitioners who had experienced difficulty in interpreting and applying the Act. The committee might then make recommendations for amending the Act or possibly consider the draft of an amending Bill produced by the Government. An example of a field in which a post-legislation committee might have fulfilled a useful function is that of conducting an enquiry into the working of the Abortion Act 1967, which task was recently entrusted to a committee appointed by the Government.

11. ... The proposal for post-legislation committees was supported by the Leaders of both Houses and by the Opposition Chief Whip in the House of Commons. Your Committee accordingly recommend that post-legislation committees should be appointed where necessary to enquire into difficulties in the application or interpretation of

statutes and consequent delegated legislation within a short period of their enactment, and that, where appropriate, such committees should be appointed as joint committees of both Houses of Parliament. . .

Specialist Departmental Committees

30. A former Opposition Chief Whip and another Opposition Member put forward comprehensive proposals for the establishment of a system of specialist Departmental committees, which would work in close relationship with Departments in the preparation of legislation and its subsequent progress through Parliament. Each Committee would deal with the legislation in the sphere of the Department over whose activities it exercised oversight. Your Committee note the view of the Leader of the House that the select committee structure established earlier in this session should be allowed to develop ' before introducing further major innovations '. A problem exists also of manning new select committees in addition to those already recommended by Your Committee. For these reasons, they see no likelihood in the immediate future of this proposal being adopted.

[Second Report of the Select Committee on Procedure. H.C. 538 of 1970–1. The Process of Legislation]

The Government accepted in principle the proposals for pre- and post-legislation committees but thought that there would be little scope for them [825 H.C.Deb. 5s. c. 649. 8 November 1971].

(ii) The stages of a Bill in the House of Commons

Second Reading

2. The second reading debate provides the only opportunity for the House to consider the bill as a whole and the wider implications of the problems with which it is concerned, and although the *decision* of the House at this stage on a Government bill is normally a foregone conclusion, the *debate* enables the Government, the official Opposition and back-bench Members (whether acting independently or on behalf of interested bodies) to state publicly the main arguments. The second reading debate is an important stage in the progress of legislation; it is the only occasion on which not only the bill but the whole problem it seeks to deal with can be discussed. All other stages are restricted to the actual proposals contained in the bill or alternative specific proposals put forward by Government, Opposition or back-benchers.

[Memorandum of the Study of Parliament Group. H.C. 303 of 1964–5]

The Committee stage

The Select Committee on Procedure noted in their Second Report of 1970–1 that ' in the course of their inquiry into the origin and course of legislation Your Committee would have desired to have made a comprehensive examination of the whole process of recent legislation and to have been able to identify not only the source of the legislative proposal but also the initiative for amendment that was made in the consequent course of proceedings on the particular Bill. They have been prevented from so doing by the constitutional prohibition against disclosure by civil servants of what has occurred during the period of office of a preceding administration, and by lack of time in which to make studies in sufficient detail. None the less they have been provided with two detailed studies of Standing Committee proceedings submitted to them in evidence.'

One of these was by Professor John Griffith of the London School of Economics.[2]

22. As outsiders attending meetings of committees and talking to Parliamentarians, we are struck by two facts. The first is that what happens in one committee room may be totally unlike what happens next door. To move from the discussion on the Immigration bill ... to the discussion on the Water Resources bill, for example, is to exchange heated party political argument on a great social issue for technical low-toned chat on a matter which is unlikely to stir the blood. What each side is trying to achieve in one committee room is hardly comparable with what it is trying to achieve in the other. The second fact is that, on any bill which has some matters which are controversial ... two kinds of discussion take place. One kind is concerned with questions of principle and the other kind is concerned with questions of detail...

25. We have looked in some detail at the Town and Country Planning bill of 1968 when in standing committee...

26. ... [O]n the Government side, backbenchers made 117 speeches, moved 16 amendments or new clauses and achieved one success.

27. ... [T]he burden of Opposition fell principally on two members who spoke a total of 112 times ... They were chiefly supported by two other members who spoke a total of 112 times ... other Opposition members spoke a total of 65 times. These speeches resulted in five successes.

28. ... We realise that the number of amendments successfully moved by Opposition spokesmen and by Government backbenchers is not a true indication of the purpose or value of debate. Of the 174 new clauses and amendments moved by members other than

[2] The other was by Mr Edward Rowlands on the Leasehold Reform Bill.

Ministers, 111 were withdrawn after debate and, of these, 31 extracted from Ministers promises ' to look again ' and, in a further 19, Ministers indicated a more favourable attitude. And in several instances, Government amendments on Report met these points.

29. Backbench activity is most strikingly manifested by a member voting on a division against his own front bench. During the 24 sittings and 49 divisions of the Town and Country Planning bill in Standing Committee, one Government backbencher cross-voted on three occasions, two cross-voted twice and one cross-voted once; no Opposition backbencher cross-voted on any occasion.

30. We have also made a detailed study of the Race Relations bill which was in Standing Committee for 13 sessions in 1968. The number of speeches made was:

Ministers	94	
Government backbench ...	86	
	——	180
Opposition frontbench ...	75	
Opposition backbench ...	129	
	——	204
		——
		384

31. Of the 59 amendments moved by members other than Ministers, 34 were withdrawn after debate and, of these, 10 extracted from Ministers promises ' to look again ' and, on a further 6, Ministers indicated a more favourable attitude.

32. The Race Relations bill differed markedly from the Town and Country Planning bill not only in being more contentious between the parties but also by being far more contentious within the parties...

36. The purpose of committee stage on a bill is not, however, only to give an opportunity to the Opposition to seek modifications in Governmental policy as expressed in the bill. It is also to expose the Government and individual Ministers to public criticism, and to require them to explain and defend not only the details of their particular legislative proposals but also their more general political positions. And, for this latter purpose, opportunity is given to other committee members both on Clause Stand Part and by chairmen traditionally not being overstrict in their control. The right of backbenchers to participate in the criticism must be protected.

37. It is also important to emphasise that backbenchers on both sides have opportunities to urge on their own leaders changes which they (or outside interests) would like to see made in the bill.

[Memorandum by Professor John Griffith and Miss Norma Percy to the Select Committee on Procedure, Second Report. H.C. 538 of 1970–1]

The Report stage

The Report Stage is not unimportant:

   (a) The Bill as it emerges from Committee is often a much modified Bill, and the Opposition may now have a new attitude to parts of it.

   (b) The Report Stage offers to the Opposition the last chance to secure what they think are important changes in the Bill.

   (c) The deliberations of the Committee, even those which have not resulted in amendments to the Bill, have often been of considerable effect on the thinking of both sides. This reveals itself at the Report Stage.

   (d) In most important Bills, undertakings have been given by the Government during discussions – at the Report Stage these undertakings are honoured,

       (i) by Government concessions.

       (ii) by discussing the Government's decision that after further consideration it accepts a point – or goes halfway to meet it – or rejects it.

[Memorandum by Mr Speaker to the Select Committee on Procedure, Sixth Report. H.C. 539 of 1966–7]

(iii) European Community legislation

The problem of Parliamentary participation in Community affairs

MR RIPPON: ... The Government [3] are deeply concerned that Parliament, as well as United Kingdom Ministers, should play its full part when future Community policies are being formulated, and in particular that Parliament should be informed about and have an opportunity to consider at the formative stage those Community instruments which, when made by the Council, will be binding in this country.

Her Majesty's Ministers will at all times be responsible to Parliament for the action they take within the Community machine and the House will be able to bring its influence to bear by all the traditional parliamentary procedures, such as Questions, Adjournment debates and Supply Days. No Government would proceed on a matter of major policy in the Council unless they knew that they had the approval of the House.

MR WILLIAM BAXTER (*West Stirlingshire*): On the question of the role of Parliament, if when the Minister reports back and a debate takes place, the decision of Parliament is against the decision of

---

[3] i.e. the Conservative Government which negotiated the United Kingdom's entry into the European Economic Community.

the Common Market Communities, how would we resolve that situation?

MR RIPPON: That would be in breach of the treaty. When the Government come to Parliament with proposals they will have to carry them through the House. But in addition to the traditional procedures there is a need, in the Government's view, for the House to have special arrangements under which it would be apprised of draft regulations and directives before they go to the Council of Ministers for decision.

[831 H.C.Deb. 5s. c. 268. 15 February 172]

The reports and proposals of the Select Committee on European Community Secondary Legislation
Why is anything new and special required?

33. ... As the inevitable consequence of the entry of the U.K. into the Community substantial and important parts of [the law of the United Kingdom] are now and will be made in new and different ways with new and different consequences, e.g.[4]

(*a*) by way of Council Regulations which take effect immediately as part of the law of the U.K. and prevail over any law of the U.K. which is inconsistent with them; and

(*b*) by way of Council Directives which place upon Parliament an obligation to make or change the law of the U.K. in all such respects as is necessary to give legal effect in the U.K. to the provision of the Directives.

34. The outstanding difference between these and the existing processes for making or amending the law are of course that in (*a*) the Executive itself by agreeing with the other member Governments to a proposal for legislation makes the law i.e. has assumed the constitutional function and power of Parliament, and that in case (*b*) whilst the semblance of Parliamentary control remains it would in practice be extremely difficult to assert (much more difficult even than in the case of domestic delegated legislation).

35. It is further to be observed (i) that so long as unanimity is required in the Council such laws can be either rescinded or amended by, but only by, a further unanimous decision of all member Governments, and (ii) that if and when such decisions come to be taken by a majority vote the United Kingdom could then secure rescission or amendment by obtaining the support of a bare majority of member Governments, but it follows equally that such laws might then be made or amended or rescinded by a bare majority of the

---

[4] The same consequences flow of course from Commission regulations and directives.

other member Governments and without the assent of even the Executive, or any other institution, of the United Kingdom.

36. Nevertheless it remains central to the United Kingdom concept and structure of Parliamentary Democracy that control of the law making processes lies with Parliament – and ultimately with the elected members of it. It follows therefore that new and special procedures are necessary to make good so far as may be done the inroads made into that concept and structure by these new methods of making law.

What is it desired to achieve?

37. The objective must be to restore to Parliament responsibilities for, and opportunities to exercise its constitutional rights in respect of, the making of these laws – involving as that must acceptance:—

> (a) by the Government that it necessarily follows that that must be at the expense of some of the freedom of action enjoyed by the Executive since U.K. entry into the E.E.C.; and
>
> (b) by Parliament that the scope, means and degree of scrutiny and control must all be attuned to the fact that it is dealing with a new way of making laws which is very different from that to which it is accustomed...

The freedom of the Executive

39. Your Committee are aware that there are those who lay great stress on the fact that as the working of the Council is essentially a matter of negotiation it could be a great deal easier for a negotiator to obtain a successful outcome if he is not hedged in by any restrictions and indeed that he may be positively hampered if so restricted; and accept that that will sometimes be so (though not always, for on occasion such limitations must surely strengthen rather than weaken the negotiator's position); but reject entirely any suggestion that the Executive should, for that or any other reason, have an unfettered right to make or alter any part of the law it may choose, subject only to securing the agreement of other Governments to those changes.

40. Constitutionally that would seem wholly unacceptable. In practice it would seem neither necessary nor desirable, for (a) if the Government of the day has the support of the House, and in particular of its own elected supporters *from whose election springs its very mandate to govern*, it will surely secure from the House the specific mandate it requires, and (b) if it does not enjoy that support for the specific change of law involved it must surely be better that it should discover that fact before committing itself rather than after...

51. ... It seems plain that there is no possibility of exercising in

this field anything like the same degree of detailed control as is available to the House of Commons under the present process of enacting a Statute. However, so long as the weighted majority rule in the E.E.C. Treaty is in abeyance and so long as the practice of unanimity is required, it should be possible to exert at least as much control over this legislation as is currently available in respect of delegated legislation in the United Kingdom. And some means must be provided for bringing such parts of it as merit the attention of the whole House before the House in such a way that the House may by resolution express such views as it wishes in respect of them.

52. Questions have been raised in Your Committee as to the legal and constitutional effects of a resolution forbidding the Government to agree to a proposed change in the law. But Your Committee consider it inconceivable that any Government would act contrary to such a resolution even if, which is doubted, it were legally and constitutionally entitled to do so and accordingly unnecessary to consider this area of the law and the constitution further at this stage.

[Second Report of the Select Committee on European Secondary Legislation, 1972–3. H.C. 463, 25 October 1973]

3. ... The secondary legislation of the Communities consists of: —
   (1) regulations, made by the Council or the Commission, which are of general application, binding in their entirety and directly applicable in all Member states;
   (2) directives, issued by the Council or the Commission, which are binding as to the result to be achieved but which leave the choice of form and methods to the Member states;
   (3) decisions, taken by the Council or the Commission, which are binding in their entirety upon those to whom they are addressed;
   (4) the general budget, a preliminary draft of which must be submitted to the Commission to the Council by 1st September each year, and which must thereafter be sent to the European Assembly [5] by 5th October, and returned to the Council for final decision before 31st December;
   (5) instruments, made by the Council, concluding Treaties negotiated by the Community institutions, for example Treaties between the E.E.C. and third parties (this excludes Treaties to which the Member states of the E.E.C. are signatories as individual states).

[5] So termed in this Report, although commonly called the European Parliament.

Recommendations are also made and opinions delivered by the Council or the Commission, but have no binding force.

This Community legislation takes effect in U.K. law either directly as part of the law of the European Communities Act 1972, section 2 (1) (in the case of regulations and, sometimes, decisions), or indirectly in the case of directives in so far as they require an alteration of previous United Kingdom law, under section 2 (2) of the Act. Provisions of Community Treaties may be directly applicable or they may be only indirectly applicable in much the same way as directives. Council legislation, which, as regulations, is effective immediately under United Kingdom law or, as directives, requires legislative enactment in the United Kingdom, may be expected to number some 300 instruments a year on average. For example, from 1st January to 9th October 1972 (the cut-off period in preparation for the accession of new Members of the European Economic Community) there were 155 Council regulations and 25 Council directives. Commission regulations, which come into force in United Kingdom law automatically, form the bulk of the Community legislation, and accounted for 90 per cent. of it in 1971. These Community instruments are usually of less importance and are often ephemeral in effect. The Commission is open to suggestions by governments on them and Her Majesty's Government's technical representatives participate on various Committees concerned with the policies leading up to them. There is no point of time at which Commission instruments are published as drafts, and their treatment is one of the matters that Your Committee are leaving for further consideration.

[First Report of the Select Committee on European Secondary Legislation, 1972–3. H.C. 143]

5. In their First Report Your Committee listed the secondary legislation of the Communities [6], i.e. regulations, directives, decisions, the general budget, and instruments concluding treaties with third parties. The first three of these may be made, issued or taken, respectively, by the Council of Ministers or, in limited circumstances, by the Commission alone; the last two normally [7] require final decision by the Council.

6. Your Committee recognise that this secondary legislation stems from: —

    1. primary legislation, which is defined as the basic Treaties of the Community and any amendments to them,

---

[6] In this Report often referred to as secondary legislation, or, where appropriate, as ' instrument ', ' proposal ' or ' legislative proposal '.

[7] Exceptionally the Commission has power to make cooperation agreements under Articles 229–231 of the E.E.C. Treaty.

2. Summit meetings of heads of state or of government. and the communiqués issued at them,
3. recommendations made by the Council or the Commission,
4. opinions delivered by the Council or the Commission,
5. resolutions agreed to by the Council [8],
6. communications made by the Council or the Commission [9],
7. consultative documents issued by the Commission [10],

and that these items, which may be of far greater significance than individual proposals for secondary legislation, could, time permitting, be debated or questioned in Parliament under existing procedures. . .

[Second Report of the Select Committee on European Community Secondary Legislation, 1972–3]

Proposals and new procedures
The Select Committee's First Report, 1973

7. . . . Your Committee have the following recommendation to make which have as their object to give Members early information as to the scope and importance of proposed European secondary legislation:

For each of the 300 or so legislative proposals from the Commission to the Council of Ministers each year there should be issued by Her Majesty's Government a statement in writing bearing the reference number of the Community proposal. This statement should include: —

(1) The general effect of the document, and its title.
(2) The U.K. ministry which takes primary responsibility, indicating where appropriate what other ministries have substantial but subsidiary responsibility.
(3) The effect which the proposed instrument would have on U.K. law and what supplementary and/or additional legislation would be introduced if the instrument were made; Your Committee is of opinion that responsibility for this part of the statement should be placed on the Law Officers.
(4) The policy implications of the document, including the effects on existing governmental practice.
(5) Whether the proposal awaits consideration by any other Community body (in particular the European Assembly or the Economic and Social Committee), and the date on which it is likely to be considered by the Council of Ministers, to any extent that this is known.

[8] e.g., the ' snake in the tunnel' resolution, which has no binding force.
[9] e.g., Com. (73) 1000, on strengthening of the budgetary powers of the European Parliament. [10] e.g., the Commission document on regional policy.

(6) Any other information which Her Majesty's Government may wish to add.

As regards sub-paragraph (5) in the proposed statement :—

(A) There should be published well in advance a monthly list giving the possible agenda of forthcoming meetings of the Councils of Ministers, or if this is impossible, at least a monthly list of subjects likely to be dealt with at the next meeting of the Council. It is true that the formal agenda of the Council of Ministers is not known even to the participants themselves until a day or two before they meet, but Your Committee feel that such a list each month would be, even if only provisional, of great assistance to Members.

(B) A monthly statement in the House should be made by the Chancellor of the Duchy to accompany the list in (A), on which he could then be questioned. The statement would give Members the opportunity of eliciting what the forthcoming events in the Council would entail.

(C) The Chancellor of the Duchy, or if the subject warrants it a particular Minister, should make a regular report to the House after each month's meeting of the Council of Ministers, similar to the statements made on a regular basis during the course of the pre-Accession negotiations.

(D) Ministers engaged in negotiations at Community institutions should report regularly to the House of Commons, if their negotiations are of sufficient importance.

[First Report of the Select Committee on European Community Secondary Legislation, 1972–3]

The Conservative Government of the day accepted the proposals for the provision of explanatory memoranda, monthly lists of subjects likely to be dealt with at the next meeting of the Council and for oral statements to be made after Council meetings provided that the nature of the matters discussed warranted this. They did not accept the proposal that an oral statement should accompany the monthly list. The Leader of the House of Commons, Mr Prior, said: ' First, such statements would cover such a wide area, covering many other issues besides the consideration of Community legislation, that one Minister could not possibly hope to deal, or could deal only superficially, with many of the issues raised, except on the basis of undertaking to bring the points raised to the notice of his appropriate colleague.

' Secondly, these forecasts of Council business cannot be other than tentative and incomplete, to some extent because of the confidential, negotiating character of much of the business transacted in the Council. Formal Ministerial statements would give an unjustified status and certainty to these provisional forecasts.

' Thirdly, such public questioning of Ministers, perhaps just a few days in advance of a meeting of the Council, on, say, currency matters, would, we believe, either put at risk the interests of effective negotiation on the country's behalf or result in a series of such guarded replies as would not be a worthwhile use of the time of the House. Surely it would be better for questions arising on forthcoming business in the Council to be put down in the normal way to the responsible Minister who could then give a considered reply.

' In my view, therefore, it would be more realistic and appropriate for the House to use the written estimates of Council business that are to be placed in the Vote Office as the basis of scrutiny by the traditional methods of the putting of Questions to the appropriate Minister and, if necessary, by pressure for debate on particular topics. The House will wish to bear in mind, however, that many of the draft instruments will have been available to hon. Members for many months before the meetings of the Council of Ministers announced in the written estimates of Council business.

' It will generally be better for hon. Members to raise issues of concern to them at an earlier stage rather than wait until shortly before the meetings of the Council of Ministers which are to approve them.' [855 H.C.Deb. 5s. c. 550. 18 April 1973]

The Select Committee's Second Report, 1973

53. ... Your Committee believe that Parliament must both

    (a) receive the fullest and most accurate information about all proposals for European Community Secondary Legislation at the earliest possible stage and thereafter whenever new facts emerge or changes occur, and

    (b) provide for itself special facilities for reaching and expressing a conclusion on proposals before they are brought to decision in the Council of Ministers, ...

Information

55. Your Committee are glad that the Government has accepted the duty to supply information about European Community Secondary Legislation to the House and has implemented some of the recommendations in the first Report ...

Facilities for Reaching and Expressing a Conclusion

60. Assuming at least 300–400 proposals a year [11] it would obviously be necessary to have a sifting process to select the more important proposals for consideration by the House.

61. The first process necessary will be to identify and isolate proposals of political importance and every proposal which if adopted

---

[11] See, e.g., Evidence, p. 142, Q. 606.

would effect a change in or require Parliament to effect a change in the law of the U.K.

62. ... [I]n the first instance a committee of officials, drawn, say, from the Office of the Chancellor of the Duchy, the Foreign and Commonwealth Office, the Department of Trade and Industry, and the Ministry of Agriculture, should isolate all those proposals which it considers to be *un*important and report to those two Ministers and to the Committee which Your Committee now recommend. (Though officials are politically neutral they would have the instinct to mark those proposals which appeared to have a political content and not to include them amongst the *un*important.)

63. The Minister and the Law Officer concerned would then lay the results of their sifting before a new Committee composed of Members of the House of Commons.

64. This will be a new and different type of Committee, for its function and duties are of a new and different kind. It will not be similar to a Standing Committee. Nor will it be similar in nature or functions to a Select Committee, for its essential role is participation in legislation in this new way ... Its working procedures will be as determined by it, and as varied by it as considered necessary to deal with each situation, and could therefore be at all times as formal or informal as the Committee considered appropriate to the occasion.

65. This Committee should have not less than 9 and not more than 15 members. In view of the importance of its work it should have a quorum of one-third of its membership, plus one i.e. 4 out of 9 or 6 out of 15...

67. The meetings of the Committee should always be attended by the Minister with overall responsibility for E.E.C. affairs and the Law Officer, who as indicated in para. 63 above would lay their views before the Committee and be subject to questioning by the Committee. Your Committee are also of opinion that, where a matter is obviously complicated or important, each of these two Ministers should furnish a report on the proposals in question and preferably at least 48 hours in advance of the meeting if possible (and in appropriate cases the Minister with special responsibility might furnish in advance a report in addition to or in place of a report by the Minister with overall responsibility).

68. ... In addition to examining legislative proposals the Committee should be on the lookout for proposals which embody matters of importance even before the stage where such proposals have been formally transmitted from the Commission to the Council. It is essential that the Committee (and through it the House) should receive as much early warning as possible of major proposals so that

appropriate action can be taken to consider their probable impact on the constitution, law and practice in the U.K.

69. The object of the Committee will be to inform the House as to any proposals of legal or political importance and to make recommendations as to their further consideration. Its task would not be to debate the reasons for or against a proposal but to give the House the fullest information as to why it considered the particular proposal of importance and to point out the matter of principle or policy which it affects and the changes in U.K. law involved. . .

72. The Committee should have power to report at any time. Those proposals which it reported to be only of lesser importance would require no special procedure for their further consideration by the House, i.e. it would be open to any Member to table a motion rejecting or amending them. But a proposal reported by the Committee to be of major importance should be referred to the House for consideration and debate well before the expected decision of the Council of Ministers upon the proposal. And a proposal reported by the Committee to be of extreme urgency and importance should be debated by the House within two weeks of the report, unless an earlier debate in normal business includes the subject matter of the proposal, or is necessary in order to ensure that the matter does come before the House before it comes before the Council. . .

Implementation

80. It may be considered desirable, perhaps even in some instances necessary, to make some additions to or changes in Standing Orders or otherwise to secure the effective implementation of these recommendations. It seems to Your Committee, however, to be entirely within the power of a government to give full effect to the recommendations without any such changes, e.g., by undertaking to provide, and providing, time as required by the recommendations of the new Committee (para. 72) and by accepting, as any Government must, that it will not cause or permit the law of the U.K. to be changed contrary to a resolution of the House. Further, if a matter were found to be of importance by the scrutiny Committee, and if it was urgent but the Government had not yet found time for it, there would obviously be a case for a debate under the existing S.O. No. 9 procedure.

[Second Report of the Select Committee on European Community Secondary Legislation, 1972–3]

The Committee also recommended that the Government should make a report to Parliament each six months on E.E.C. matters generally, and that two days should be provided in each session to debate these reports.

The Conservative Government accepted the proposal for a sifting committee but not the suggestion that a committee of officials should be associated with it. The Lord President of the Council Mr Prior said: 'I doubt whether it would be possible for a body of departmental officials to be formally linked with a House committee in the way proposed by the Select Committee. To do so would cause problems of divided loyalties and could cut across the accepted principle of ministerial responsibility.

I suggest to the House that a better approach would be for the committee to call upon Ministers and their officials to give evidence to it. Ministers would take responsibility for the Government's view as to the importance of the instrument and the Committee would then make up its own mind. That would give the Select Committee what it requires in a slightly different way' [867 H.C.Deb. 5s. c. 1906. 31 January 1974].

The Government also agreed to provide time for debate and also to provide a twice yearly report. On the question of the Government's not allowing the law to be changed contrary to a Resolution of the House, Mr Davies as Chancellor of the Duchy of Lancaster said: '[I]n the exceptional cases where there had been a specific resolution of Parliament on a given issue, which was a precise issue arising in the case of a Council debate, a Minister who defied that would defy it at his risk and also at the risk of the Government of which he was a member' [*ibid.*].

The Labour Government which came to power in February 1974 also announced that it accepted the recommendation of the Committee on European Community Secondary Legislation that a 'sifting committee' should be established, that more time should be found for the discussion of Community matters in the House and that regular ministerial oral statements should be made on forthcoming business of the Council of Ministers [870 H.C.Deb. 5s. c. 796. 18 March 1974]. A further statement was made by the Lord President of the Council, Mr Short in a written answer on 2 May 1974.

MR ADAM HUNTER asked the Lord President of the Council whether he is now able to make a statement about the Government's proposals with regard to the implementation of the recommendations made in the Second Report from the Select Committee on European Community Secondary Legislation (Session 1972–73).

MR EDWARD SHORT: The Government tabled on 29th April a motion to set up the House scrutiny committee proposed last November in the Second Report of the Select Committee on European Community Secondary Legislation (the Foster Committee).

The principal purpose of this committee, in accordance with the recommendations of the report, is to assist the House to identify those proposals for Community secondary legislation which are of particular importance to the House and to the country. This is an essential basis for the effective involvement of Parliament in the consideration of such proposals before decisions are taken in the Council of Ministers. I hope this committee can begin its important work in the very near future.

Ministers and Departments will do all they can to assist the new committee and will, of course, be available to appear before the committee and to give evidence about Community proposals, as required. A new senior House official is to be appointed, as proposed in the report, to assist the committee in dealing with the legal implications of proposals, and the Government will provide further staffing support, including research assistance, to the committee, as the need shows itself.

I have already indicated to the House, on 18th March, the Government's acceptance of the other main recommendations made in the report. In particular, the Government accept that in future ministerial oral statements should accompany the monthly written forecasts of Council business; that Government reports should be made twice a year to Parliament on EEC matters generally; that these reports should be debated on two allotted days; that, in addition, four further days should be allocated to general EEC matters; and that a place for Questions relating to EEC matters should be specifically allocated in the Question rota.

Discussions will take place through the usual channels regarding the apportionment between Government and Opposition time of these further days for the debate of Community matters, and the most convenient way of providing an appropriate slot in the Question rota.

Whilst departmental Ministers will continue to be answerable to the House in respect of the substance of particular proposals for European Community secondary legislation, the Minister with overall responsibility for the supply of information to the House about such proposals will be my right hon. Friend the Secretary of State for Foreign and Commonwealth Affairs. It is not considered that the appointment of an additional Law Officer specifically concerned with these matters would be justified, but this proposal will be kept under review. The present Law Officers will be available to advise the committee on the legal implications of particular proposals.

Besides this further allotted time for the debate of Community matters there will be the normal opportunities for debate and, if necessary, the use of the provisions of the Standing Order No. 9 procedure. I do not think a special SO9 procedure for Community matters is needed. Provided the scrutiny committee makes its views known in sufficient time, I can assure the House that it is the Government's firm intention that the debate of any proposal which the committee reports as being of extreme urgency and importance should take place before a final decision is taken in the Council of Ministers.

The establishment of this committee represents a further important step in the construction of an effective system of parliamentary scrutiny over proposals for Community secondary legislation. The measures taken, following the Foster Committee's First Report, for the notification of the House, were the first step. The new scrutiny committee and the implementation of the other recommendations to which I have referred will be a further step. But this does not rule out in any way the consideration of further measures which experience may show are necessary in order to secure a proper degree of parliamentary control in these matters.

[872 H.C.Deb. 5s. (Written Answers) c. 523. 2 May 1974]. On 7 May 1974 the House of Commons appointed a sifting committee ' to consider draft proposals by the Commission of the European Economic Community for secondary legislation and other documents published by the Commission for submission to the Council of Ministers, and to report their opinion as to whether such proposals or other documents raise questions of legal or political importance, to give their reasons for their opinion, to report what matters of principle or policy may be affected thereby, and to what extent they may affect the law of the United Kingdom, and to make recommendations for the further consideration of such proposals or other documents by the House '. A similar committee was appointed in the House of Lords on 5th June 1974.

(iv) Private Bills

1. Private Bills are bills of a special kind for conferring particular powers or benefits on any person or body of persons – including individuals, local authorities, statutory companies, or private corporations – sometimes in excess of or in conflict with the general law. They are therefore bills for the particular interest or benefit of the person or persons concerned and are clearly distinguished from Public Bills which are applicable to the general community. The parliamentary procedure concerning them differs in many respects from that relating to Public Bills.

2. A Private Bill is promoted by those parties interested and is founded upon a Petition to the House of Commons, which has to be deposited in accordance with standing order. As a bill for the particular benefit of certain persons may be injurious to others, provision is made by standing order for the due notification to everyone who may be affected by the bill of the provisions contained therein, so that all concerned know how their interests may be affected and can take the appropriate steps to protect them. Parliament thereupon has not only to exercise its legislative function, that is to decide whether it is in the public interest to grant the promoter's petition, but also to act in a judicial capacity, in deciding between the claims of the various

parties. Both these functions are for the most part delegated to Private Bill Committees before whom the parties may appear and may be represented by Counsel and to whom reports from departments of State are referred. By Standing Orders, Committees are required to inform the House how such reports have been dealt with.

3. In both Houses Private Bills have to go through the same stages as do Public Bills although in the House of Commons special times are allotted for their discussion.

4. Those persons or bodies entitled to promote Private Bills are many and various but they can be grouped into certain broad categories. First, all local authorities can, and often must, promote private legislation in order to carry on the good government of their localities. They often need powers in excess of the general law in respect of such things as the acquisition of land, street works, regulation of public entertainments, public health and the like. Secondly, water undertakings, whether in the form of public boards or private companies may have to come to Parliament for any extension to their powers. Before nationalisation Gas and Electricity Boards and Companies also frequently promoted Bills. Thirdly, the railways, now of course all represented by the British Transport Commission, have to promote a bill every year to authorise various works, etc. In this category can also be included Docks and Harbour Boards, other than those controlled by the British Transport Commission. Fourthly, statutory companies have to come to Parliament for the alteration or extension of their statutory powers, and companies, registered under the Companies Act, have to obtain Parliamentary approval to do any act not authorised by their memorandum and articles of association. Fifthly, a number of societies, church bodies, charities, etc. promote bills for such objects as extending their original powers, the conversion or provision of burial grounds, etc.

5. During the last 40 years since the end of the First World War, some 2,300 Private Bills have been introduced into Parliament. Between the wars, except for three exceptional years, 1920, 1929 and 1930, the average number was about 71 per Session, but since the last war the number has dropped to about 37. This is largely due to the passing of the Public Health Act of 1936 and to alternative methods of obtaining powers by means of Orders, under the Statutory Orders (Special Procedure) Act, 1945, but the nationalisation of the railways, gas and electricity industries has also had some effect.

[Memorandum submitted by the Clerk of the House of Commons, Sir Edward Fellowes, and the Clerk of Private Bills, Mr M. Farmer, to the Joint Committee on the Promotion of Private Bills. H.L. 176, H.C. 262 of 1958–9]

LOCAL GOVERNMENT ACT, 1972   [Ch. 70]

239. (1) Subject to the provisions of this Act, where a local authority other than a parish or community council, are satisfied that it is expedient to promote, or any local authority are satisfied that it is expedient to oppose, any local or personal Bill in Parliament, the local authority may... promote or oppose the Bill accordingly, and may defray the expenses incurred in relation thereto.

(2) A resolution of a local authority to promote or oppose a Bill under subsection (1) above shall be—

(a) passed by a majority of the whole number of the members of the authority at a meeting of the authority held after the requisite notice of the meeting and of its purpose has been given by advertisement in one or more local newspapers circulating in the area of the authority, such notice being given in addition to the ordinary notice required to be given for the convening of a meeting of the authority; and

(b) in the case of the promotion of a Bill, confirmed by a like majority at a further such meeting convened in accordance with paragraph (a) above and held as soon as may be after the expiration of fourteen days after the Bill has been deposited in Parliament and, if the resolution is not confirmed, the local authority shall take all necessary steps to withdraw the Bill.

(3) For the purposes of subsection (2) above the requisite notice is thirty clear days' notice in the case of promotion of a Bill and ten clear days' notice in the case of opposition to a Bill.

(4) The power conferred on a local authority by subsection (1) above shall be in substitution for any power conferred on that authority by a local Act...

III. EXPENDITURE, ADMINISTRATION AND THE ECONOMY

Control of finance formed the subject of some of the leading cases of the seventeenth century constitutional disputes which were finally settled in 1689.

One of the most important provisions of the Bill of Rights so far as Parliament's position in the Constitution was concerned was that which provided that ' the levying money for or to the use of the Crown by pretence of prerogative without grant of Parliament for longer time or in other manner then the same is or shall be granted is illegal '. It was this principle together with the requirement of its consent to legislation which formed the basis of its political power. During the eighteenth and nineteenth centuries Parliament consolidated its position and extended its control over the expenditure of the money it had granted. It made a distinction between the money granted to the King for the expenses of Government and those to meet his personal expenses, and granted him a fixed sum, known as the Civil List, in return for the surrender of his hereditary revenues, to meet the latter. It extended the practice of appropriation by which in granting money it allocated it to the particular purposes for which it had been requested. It set up the Consolidated Fund at the Bank of England and in 1866 established a Comptroller and Auditor-General to control outgoings from this account and also to conduct a continuous audit of Government accounts to see not only that the money granted was being spent for the purposes for which it had been granted but also that it was not being wasted. It also set up an all party Public Accounts Committee to whom the Comptroller and Auditor General reported. In 1912 it added an Estimates Committee to examine the estimates of departmental expenditure laid before Parliament each year and to make recommendations as to economies that might be achieved in the execution of the policies embodied in them. By the beginning of the twentieth century, therefore, Parliament could point to a developed system of supervision and control of public expenditure, going well beyond the limited control of taxation set out in the Bill of Rights.

The extracts which follow illustrate the challenge of the twentieth century and in particular the post war years to the assumptions behind these developments and the adequacy of the procedures and institutions which they generated. The challenge has arisen largely because of the increasing assumption by Governments of both major parties of responsibility for the management of the economy, and in the field of taxation and expenditure of the practice of making decisions on taxation and expenditure on a broader basis than what is actually needed for the provision of services, or their financing, complicated as even these narrower decisions have become. The traditional concerns of the constitutional lawyer about taxation and expenditure have been swallowed up in the larger concern about decisions relating to the economy as a whole. It is not difficult to see that the value of what is left in one's pocket is as important as the amount, which was the major concern about taxation, or that the prospect of employment which will produce an income is as important as the amount of that income which will be taken by way of taxation. If this is the case it is the process of reaching decisions on these matters which should form the focus of a constitutional lawyer's attention as much as those directly affecting taxation and expenditure. Nor is the broadening of the focus limited to moving out from questions of taxation and expenditure to problems of the economy as a whole. As the discussions leading up to the establishment of 'specialist' committees and the Select Committee on Expenditure show, there is a close parallel between the problems of Parliamentary supervision of taxation, expenditure and the economy, and the problems Parliament has in relation to supervision of governmental activities as a whole. The issues raised therefore lie at the heart of the problem of the role of Parliament in relation to Government in general.

(i) Public Expenditure

The Plowden Report, 1961

6. ... The level of Government expenditure, and thus the level of taxation, are ultimately the consequence of basic Government policies, and the crucial point is the system by which policies affecting public expenditure are made and by which decisions about public expenditure are taken. This includes both the responsibilities of Ministers and the duties of officials, and the procedures by which matters are prepared for Ministers, and then decided: it includes the impact of Parliament and public opinion on these decisions.

7. This is the matter to which we have devoted most attention, and we have reached a definite conclusion on it, viz., that decisions involving substantial future expenditure should always be taken in the light of surveys of public expenditure as a whole, over a period of years, and in relation to prospective resources. Public expenditure decisions ... should never be taken without consideration of (a) what the country can afford over a period of years having regard to prospective resources and (b) the relative importance of one kind of expenditure against another ...

8. In the traditional system in this country, as it developed in the 19th century ... the tendency is for expenditure decisions to be taken piecemeal. ..

... Discussion among Ministers is likely to centre on the merits of the particular proposal in relation at most to a general background of the financial situation, rather than upon the competing claims on the present and future resources of the country which are represented by the aggregate of the spending policies of the Government. ..

9. The system of control of public expenditure depends upon the attitude to public spending both of Parliament and of public opinion. In former times there were strong external pressures on the Government to reduce both expenditure and taxes, and every Minister who wanted to spend had to run the gauntlet of severe criticism from his Cabinet colleagues, from Parliament and from the public. The system was then effective in keeping expenditure down. ..

10. In our judgment, the social, political and economic changes of the last 20 years have created a new situation. First, the scale of public expenditure is far greater. .. The total of public expenditure of all kinds including that of the Government above and below the line, that of local authorities, of national insurance funds, and the capital expediture of nationalised industries, represents about 42% of the gross national product. Second, public expenditure has become more complex including as it does the cost of the most advanced technological projects and of scientific research; the financing of commercial

risks that the private sector cannot take; aid of many different kinds to a variety of under-developed countries; and social insurance schemes of unprecedented scope. All of these involve commitments, contractual or moral, extending several years ahead. Third, there has taken place a great change in economic thought: the Keynsian revolution in the role of public finance and its relationship to the national economy as a whole. The Budget is seen, not as a simple balancing of tax receipts against expenditure, but as a sophisticated process in which the instruments of taxation and expenditure are used to influence the course of the economy.

11. These ... have created a situation in which, in our opinion, the traditional system can no longer be expected to be effective in containing the growth of expenditure within whatever limit the Government have set.

Principles of reconstruction

12. We would favour a reconstruction based on four elements: —

A. Regular surveys should be made of public expenditure as a whole, over a period of years ahead, and in relation to prospective resources; decisions involving substantial future expenditure should be taken in the light of these surveys.

B. There should be the greatest practicable stability of decisions on public expenditure when taken, so that long-term economy and efficiency throughout the public sector have the best possible opportunity to develop.

C. Improvements should be made in the tools for measuring and handling public expenditure problems, including in particular major simplifications of the form of the Estimates, modernisation and clarification of the Exchequer Accounts, and more widespread use of quantitative methods in dealing with these problems throughout the public service. These should serve both to improve the work inside the governmental machine, and to contribute to a better understanding by Parliament and by the public.

D. There should be more effective machinery for the taking of collective responsibility by Ministers on matters of public expenditure...

13. The development and use by Government of long-term surveys of expenditure and resources is the core of our proposals. This involves techniques of management and measurement that are in their infancy... However, the Treasury has been actively developing these techniques in recent years; and it should now be possible to make substantial progress, provided that the practical considerations are kept fully in mind, and that no more weight is put on this work than it can technically bear...

16. ... [T]he prospective development of income or economic resources... is susceptible to prediction five years ahead only within broad limits ... Nevertheless, we think that it should be possible to form worthwhile judgments about whether a certain size and pattern of public expenditure is likely to stimulate or to retard the growth of gross national product, and is likely to outrun prospective resources available to finance it.

17. In our view therefore it is technically practical and administratively necessary to develop long-term surveys on these lines. But... this work is in its early stages ... It will not provide automatic criteria, or create a substitute for the application of judgment. It is therefore doubtful whether any Government will feel able to place these surveys before Parliament and the public. To do this would involve disclosing the Government's long-term intentions for a wide range of public expenditure; and also explaining the survey's assumptions about employment, wages, prices and all the other main elements in the national economy.

Parliamentary control
The annual basis of Supply

61. ... [W]e considered whether we should recommend a change in the system of annual cash provision on which the Estimates and Exchequer Accounts and the Parliamentary Supply procedures are based. We decided not to do so...

62. A period of one year for the purpose of Governmental accounting, as for private enterprise, is surely right. It is suggested from time to time that one year is too short a time for expenditure control, and that the period should be extended to eighteen months or two years. The year would then cease to be the unit of Government Accounts: there would be one Budget, one Finance Act, and one Appropriation Act every eighteen months or two years, and no longer one of each in every year. We were advised, and it seems to us reasonable, that neither in expenditure nor in revenue is it possible to look ahead for two years with anything approaching the necessary precision for budgeting and that the out-turn at the end of the two years would vary greatly from the original provision. The various factors in the national economy – production, investment, wages, prices, balance-of-payments, gross national product – which determine the general nature of the Budget, cannot be seriously predicted in the sense required for the determination of short-term fiscal policy for periods of more than one year. Indeed, the pressure in recent years has been the other way in the direction of more frequent Budgets, or their equivalents, to take the action required to keep the economy stable.

Parliamentary Control of Commitments

72. The suggestion is sometimes made that Parliament should in future authorise commitments. This is inspired by the apprehension that the bulk of expenditure cannot be effectively controlled by a system of annual Estimates alone. . .

73. We found formidable difficulties. It would be essential in any event for Parliament to retain control over the amount to be spent in each year; so there would have to be a double system, authorising both spending in the year and commitments to be undertaken in the year. Commitments are of many different types, and often span a number of years. Some means would have to be found of organising this complex of varying periods and projects into a workable system; and we must bear in mind that every major long-term project, whether it is the development of a guided missile or the expansion of technical education, goes in the course of time through a continuous series of modifications, for each of which new Parliamentary authority would presumably have to be sought. This is not the kind of work for which the Parliamentary machine is equipped.

74. Moreover, the considerations which led us to conclude that the Government should not approve commitments without examining expenditure as a whole, over a period of time, and in relation to prospective resources, would apply equally to Parliament. Thus, Parliament if it were to authorise commitments as well as cash provision, would need just the same kind of long-term expenditure surveys as we propose that the Government should make and use; otherwise its decisions could not but be ill-informed and possibly damaging to the national interests. The Government could hardly make its own surveys fully available, since limits are quickly reached in the practicable disclosure of the Government's judgment of future uncertainties and intentions in detail for several years ahead in defence, major economic policy, and of course in social policy and in legislation.

75. We have therefore advised the Government firmly against this kind of proposal. In our view, it would be impossible to work efficiently any system of Parliamentary control of commitments which went beyond what is already implied in the present processes of Supply and legislation. This view does not however alter our opinion that it would be desirable for the Government to develop means of informing Parliament and enabling it to consider and approve the broad issues of policy involving public expenditure for some years ahead at the time when the effective decisions are taken. No Government will be able to do this to any substantial extent until much more experience has been gained of long-term expenditure surveying. Nevertheless, we hope that this will be every Government's aim, to be

furthered as fast as reasonably practicable. Unless the issues of long-term expenditure priorities and policies can be discussed in Parliament and becomes the subject of public controversy, it will be difficult for Governments to carry public opinion with them.

The Parliamentary Committees

83. In considering how the deployment of the Public Accounts Committee's work, and the investigations of the Comptroller and Auditor General and his staff, could bear most effectively upon the problems of public expenditure, we have been impressed by the change that has in fact taken place in recent years. The original purpose of the Committee nearly a hundred years ago was to ensure that expenditure conformed as closely as possible to annual Estimates and to ensure that the Government in fact spent the money on the things for which Parliament had voted it. The emphasis of its Reports was upon instances of expenditure without proper or adequate authority; on questions of financial impropriety in the narrower sense; on questions about the charging of particular items to particular Votes or Subheads or to one year rather than another; and on questions about the procedure on contracts. Topics of this kind recur from time to time, but the emphasis has come to be placed more and more on the efficiency of the financial administration of Departments, as reflected for example in the costs of capital works, stores or supplies purchased on Government account, the maximisation of receipts due to the Government, the incidence of losses or waste of various kinds, the standards of store keeping, the accuracy of estimating, and so on...

Concluding observations

91. ... We have considered many subjects, but although in doing so we had the advantage of the complete cooperation of the Treasury and the Departments, we found great difficulty in getting to grips with the problem... This is partly because of sheer size. The Supply Estimates for the current year total £5,187 million; National Debt interest and other expenditure from the Consolidated Fund, above and below the line, and from the national insurance funds, bring the total up to around £7,500 million; the capital and current expenditure of local authorities, and the capital expenditure of nationalised industries make the aggregate of public expenditure well over £10,000 million. But the difficulty is not only of size, but of comprehending and relating together such diverse subjects as defence, economic aid, pensions, education, roads, agriculture, hospitals, power, each with its own special circumstances. It is this diversity that has led to the traditional piece-meal treatment of public expenditure which we wish to see changed.

92. Despite the large aggregates, much of the work of Government

is carried out in small organisational units... This diffuseness is even more striking in local authorities and in the units of the hospital service...

93. It is not easy to generalise about this breadth and diversity of activity or to develop a strategy of approach to the problem of public expenditure which avoids immersion in a sea of detail on the one hand and superficiality on the other. But everyone in a position of responsibility in these matters – the Permanent Secretary and Principal Finance Officer in respect of each Department's expenditure, the Treasury in respect of the whole of Government expenditure, the Parliamentary Committees in respect of their functions – must devise a procedure and technique for handling and examining and probing the expenditures within their purview...

97. ... Looking at public expenditure as a whole tends to bring to the surface the universal factors that are influencing all of it, such as the problems of pay determination, of the relationship of capital expenditure to the future growth of current expenditure, of the way in which population movements are influencing public expenditure and are likely to do so in the future, and so on...

106. This Report is concerned mainly with systems and techniques in the Departments, in the Treasury, in the Cabinet, in Parliament. But we are aware that the issues go further. The best system and the most up-to-date techniques will succeed only if public opinion is actively stimulated and enabled to take a balanced view of the alternative uses of national resources that are posed...

[The control of public expenditure. Cmnd. 1432 (July 1961)]

The planning and control of public expenditure. A Treasury view
11. ... [T]he Plowden Report shifted the debate to a new plane by recognising that the problem of public expenditure extended over a wide area, covering not only the expenditure of central government (and *a fortiori* not only that part of that expenditure which happened to be authorised annually by the House of Commons through Votes) but also all expenditure by local authorities, however financed, the gross outgoings of the National Insurance Funds, and the whole of the investment of the nationalised industries and other public corporations; and by placing public sector expenditure in the context of an assessment of the real resources likely to be available to meet these demands – that is to say, not merely the effect upon taxation (although that obviously has its own importance), but the relationship of this demand by the public sector for real resources to the total resources of the whole community – the national product – and to the other demands which would be made on that product by exports and the

private sector. The Report thus envisaged public expenditure being set in a context suitable for rational decisions to be taken about the aggregate demand upon resources which the public sector should make, and for the whole structure of expenditure decisions in the public sector to be related to this base.

The implementation of Plowden

14. From 1961 onwards the system was adopted of conducting annual Public Expenditure Surveys. A number of features of these surveys, some of which were set out in the White Paper 'Public Expenditure in 1963–64 and 1967–68' [Cmnd. 2235] published in December, 1963, should be noted:

(*a*) They covered all expenditure by the public sector regardless of the way in which the expenditure was financed. . .

(*b*) The figures were analysed by function, that is to say by reference to the object of the expenditure. This enabled comprehensive figures to be drawn up showing the relative amounts spent or proposed to be spent on, e.g. defence, health, education, social security, assistance to industry and so on. These were the figures on which major decisions by Ministers on the size and pattern of future expenditure were taken.

(*c*) The figures were also analysed by economic category (current expenditure on goods and services, gross domestic fixed capital formation, grants to persons and so on). This was essential if the figures were to be integrated into the forecasts of the development of the economy referred to below (paragraph 15).

(*d*) The figures in each Survey covered a period of five years – that is to say, the 1961 Survey covered the period up to and including the financial year 1965–66 and each following Survey rolled the figures forward a year. . .

15. The annual Surveys of expenditure were, from the start, linked with the developing annual forward assessments of prospective movements in the economy. . . The value of this proceeding is to expose for the Government's consideration any unacceptable consequences which may be implicit in the interaction of the Government's expenditure policies and the other probable movements in the economy, and to do this over a time scale sufficiently long to allow of adjustment of public sector spending programmes should this be necessary or desirable. . .

Allocation within the public sector

23. . . . [P]ublic expenditure will not only be an important element in the total economic scene in the years ahead, it will also in part determine what that scene will be; and it will in turn be affected by

other elements in the economy. Decisions about the future course of aggregate public expenditure should therefore be taken with full regard to the best assessment possible of future prospects of the economy as a whole; but another powerful influence on those decisions will be the shape of the individual public expenditure programmes themselves which go to make up that aggregate; and their shape is to a large extent determined by their chosen objectives, the extent of advance commitments, and the extent to which, under the existing policies, the level of expenditure would depend on external factors. Conversely, the view taken by the Government on the aggregate of public expenditure can itself affect the levels of individual programmes. As the result of this process, aggregates for the public sector and the individual programmes eventually represent the particular balance which the Government, with its own view of social and economic priorities, desires to see. . .

24. The object of projecting the individual services goes far beyond providing a realistic assessment of the aggregate of the claims the public sector will be making. It provides also the basis for reasonably firm planning and execution of policy in the services. This gives the ground for confidence in forward planning, although of course no system can insulate services from the effects of major events, national or international, which alter the broad economic assessment.

25. Governments are always operating with programmes inherited from previous years, the product of a series of decisions taken at earlier points of time. These have a certain momentum of their own and they can only be changed gradually. Even over a five year period any major change in the presently planned rate of growth of the aggregate, or in the pattern of allocation within the aggregate, could be achieved by major changes of policy. . .

26. The effects of some public expenditure decisions may be felt for decades ahead – for example, on social security payments, where changes in the demographic pattern may have a strong effect upon costs. Again, some major capital programmes – power stations, major roads, hospitals – require a total planning and construction period running over five to ten years or more. Adjustments in present plans, therefore, assuming that expenditure to date on projects currently under construction is not to be written off as abortive, is only possible over a considerable period of time. The expansion of a major service, such as education, cannot be carried out more rapidly than, e.g. the supply of teachers can be increased, and this in turn may entail an expansion in the building programme for teacher training colleges, which could mean a period of five or six years before any significant change of policy could begin to show up in terms of more teachers in

classrooms, although expenditure would arise at an earlier stage. The research, development and production cycle for major items of defence equipment is frequently of the order of ten years and in this field too, unless major changes in commitments of the kind made in the last few years are to be made, adjustments in expenditure cannot be made quickly.

27. It is important to apprehend public expenditure as consisting of spending in a variety of fields few of which are susceptible to short-term adjustment without serious damage to policy aims, not all of which are under direct central Government control, and major changes in which can only be brought about over a period of time. Furthermore, the very nature of some policies (agricultural support and investment grants are good examples) is such that, once the policy has been settled, the Government commitment is open-ended in the sense that payments have to be made to all who qualify under the conditions laid down. . .

28. When, therefore, Ministers consider the allocation of public expenditure each year, the choices before them relate to marginal changes. Even the important post-devaluation decisions [12] involved reducing projected rates of increase over the next two years, and affected the projected levels only by $1\frac{3}{4}$ and $2\frac{1}{2}$ per cent. The annual decisions on the allocation to individual programmes are subject to similar constraints.

Parliamentary Estimates

29. It will be seen that Government decisions about public expenditure are taken on figures which, as far as possible, cover the whole of the public sector. It is necessary to explain the relationship and the difference between these and the Parliamentary Supply Estimates.

30. The Supply Estimates consist of that part of central Government expenditure which requires to be voted annually by Parliament. . . [T]here is some central Government expenditure – the Consolidated Fund Standing Services, and the loans made from the National Loans Fund to, e.g. nationalised industries and local authorities – which is authorised once for all by statute, and which does not require annual voting. In 1968–69 these non-voted expenditures were estimated to total nearly £4,000 million, while the original Supply Estimates for 1968–69 were some £10,500 million. . . Even this £10,500 million cannot be regarded as simply part of the public sector expenditure total upon which, as has been explained above, decisions are based. There are some items on Votes which are pay-

[12] Public Expenditure in 1968–69 and 1969–70 (Cmnd. 3515).

ments from the central Government to another part of the public sector (e.g. grants to local authorities) and these have to be netted out in compiling total public sector figures because they will appear as part of the expenditure by the recipient authority. Again, there are some expenditures on Votes which, for the purposes of the annual Public Expenditure Survey, rank as offsets to taxation receipts rather than as expenditure, e.g. refunds of Selective Employment Tax. The Supply Estimates are thus neither the whole nor simply a part of the central Government share of total public expenditure. . .

32. . . . The form of the Estimates, which go into considerable detail, is different from that of the Survey figures, since the latter are analysed functionally while the former are essentially Departmental documents. A functional heading in the Survey may span the expenditure of more than one Department, although one Department may have several Estimates.

[Memorandum of the Treasury to the Select Committee on Procedure, First Report. H.C. 410 of 1968–9]

The Select Committee on Procedure, 1969

7. . . . Government decisions, both about the level of public expenditure as a whole, and about the way in which the total amount of public expenditure is allocated between its various components, are among the most important which Ministers take. It is desirable that decisions of such importance should be taken, so far as possible, in the light of public discussion of the issues involved, and that the grounds on which they are taken should be made known to the public.

8. Hitherto, the House of Commons has exercised nominal control over part of this expenditure, in the main that part authorised annually under the Supply procedure to be spent by the Crown in the ensuing year and constituting less than two-thirds of the total. The expansion of Government activity into many fields, and the extension of the time-scale on which plans for public spending now have to be made, have not been matched by corresponding developments in the financial procedures of Parliament. Parliament has lacked the information on which to base its examination of these matters; and the Government have not been required to seek Parliament's formal authorisation before proceeding with their plans.

9. For example . . . much progress has been made in the forward planning of Government expenditure since the Report of the Plowden Committee, but the procedure of the House has never been adapted to it. The House still considers expenditure on an annual

cash basis. But Government planning of expenditure now covers total real public (and not simply Supply) expenditure several years ahead. Priorities will be increasingly chosen after analysis by function or objectives – that is to say, by reference to the real object of the expenditure – and after consideration of the possible alternative priorities and the benefits to be expected, of the resources likely to be available and of the phasing of the expenditure over years. This 'forward look' is necessary because many expenditure proposals, particularly capital projects, require lengthy planning in advance, involve relatively small expenditure in the first year or two and build up to larger sums later. The House has no machinery for scrutinising this complicated process and has had little opportunity to debate the forward projections of expenditure produced during recent years. As a result, discussions of the annual cash expenditures are not adequately based on knowledge of prior commitments under the forward planning, of the limitations on adjustment in any one year, and of the choices made or foregone in the use of the community's resources. Moreover, Ministers have to take their decisions without the benefit of an informed public debate on the issues.

10. The House has recently made two changes which affect its examination of Government policy without, however, improving its check on the expenditure process. Changes in Supply procedure have finally ended the procedural fiction that the House itself makes a detailed examination of all the Estimates: Supply Days have become 'Opposition days', used for debates, sometimes at short notice, on aspects of policy and only rarely on details of spending. A further change has been the establishment of a series of specialist Select Committees in addition to the Nationalised Industries Committee, the Public Accounts Committee and the Estimates Committee. But the new Committees, on Agriculture, Education and Science, Overseas Aid and Science and Technology, whilst they conduct extensive enquiries into the Department or subject, do not appear to have attempted to scrutinise the process of Government expenditure... At the same time, the introduction of these Committees has depleted the membership of the Estimates Committee and reduced the scope of its examination of Departmental spending.

A System of Scrutiny

11. With the creation, one hundred years ago, of the Public Accounts Committee and the Exchequer and Audit Department, Mr Gladstone was able to say that the 'last portion of the circle' of parliamentary control of expenditure was complete. This involved discussion and prior approval of the financial implications of Government decisions (as reflected in the annual Supply Estimates),

and examination of the outturn afterwards as reflected in the Appropriation Accounts. The economic thinking of the time insisted that Government was a mere consumer of wealth and should be limited accordingly; the notion that public spending could be productively and efficiently planned and managed, and that this was the concern of Parliament, did not arise. The Estimates Committee was added in 1912, being temporarily replaced in the 1939–45 war by the National Expenditure Committee. It has undoubtedly become more effective in the years since 1945. The House, however, has not made changes in procedure that would allow it to consider systematically the merits of proposed expenditures compared with alternatives and with resources likely to be available, nor to consider the effectiveness with which they are managed.

12. Your Committee believe that the House should now develop its procedures further, and formally establish a system of expenditure scrutiny, containing not two elements but three:

First, discussion of the Government's expenditure strategy and policies, as set out in projections of public expenditure several years ahead;

Second, examination of the means (including new methods of management) being adopted to implement strategy and to execute policies, as reflected in annual estimates of expenditure;

Third, retrospective scrutiny of the results achieved and the value for money obtained on the basis of annual accounts and related information from departments on the progress of their activities.

These three tasks are closely related to one another.

The arrangements for scrutiny by the House must recognise that fact and provide an effective ' link between the system for allocating resources and the system for getting value for money '.

Consideration of Projections

13. In evidence to Your Committee, published as a Green Paper,[13] the Government have announced their intention to publish annually a White Paper on projected public expenditure over five years... Your Committee believe that the annual discussion of public expenditure foreshadowed in these proposals could and should come to occupy as important a place in parliamentary and public discussion of economic affairs as that now occupied by the annual Budget debate...

14. The chief proposals in the Green Paper are that figures of expenditure will be shown in the Expenditure White Paper annually

[13] Cmnd. 4017. Public Expenditure: A New Presentation.

for ' the year preceding publication, the year of publication (year 1) and each of the four following years (years 2 to 5) '.[14] Years 1 to 3 will be the period for which the Government will have taken decisions; ' the figures for years 4 and 5 will represent projections of the cost of present policies, not decisions '.[15] Capital expenditure of the nationalised industries will be included as public expenditure. Projections will be given of receipts from taxation, contributions, and all other receipts in the public sector; existing taxes at existing rates of taxation will be assumed. ' An assessment will be given of the prospects for the growth of national production in the period ahead '.[16]

16. In debating the projections of expenditure, the House should be able to take account of the assessment made by the Government of the development of the economy in the ensuing three years, in other words, the assumptions on which these projections are based. This medium-term economic assessment is made each Spring in conjunction with the preparation of the report to the Government of the Public Expenditure Survey Committee. Material from the assessment was published in the form of a Green Paper, ' The Task Ahead ', in February, 1969.[17] No commitment has yet been made by the Government to publish an Economic Assessment annually. However, for informed debate ... the House of Commons will require the Government's range of assessments of the probable development in the economy in the medium term ...

17. ' The Task Ahead ' did not contain forecasts of movements of prices and earnings in the three succeeding years (or estimates of the effect of deviations from these forecasts), although these are produced in the annual medium term economic assessment made by the Department of Economic Affairs... The disadvantages of publishing such forecasts would be that the forecast figures would be accepted as a minimum in bargaining on earnings and in determining prices and that this would cause serious economic difficulties... Your Committee take the view that the balance of advantage is in favour of publication of these forecasts.

18. Your Committee believe that it will also be of the greatest importance to set out the assumptions and methods used in determining the expenditure projections presented to the House of Commons. The House can then, in a way that has not been possible hitherto, debate priorities in the light of the various relevant criteria. For example, it should be able as far as possible, to judge projected ex-

[14] Ibid., paragraph 27.
[15] Ibid., paragraph 28.
[16] Ibid., paragraph 40.
[17] The Task Ahead: Economic Assessment to 1972.

penditure by its costs in real resources. It should be informed of the results of analyses undertaken by the Government to show their view of the costs and benefits to individuals and the community of particular programmees or projects such as raising the school leaving age, or constructing the Channel Tunnel or the third London Airport – and it should know what assumptions have been made in these ' cost/ benefit' studies. Again, on public investment, the House should increasingly have information so that, in addition to other considerations, it can weigh the value of benefits expected to arise in the more or less distant future – against the alternative of higher consumption and a higher standard of living now. In other words, it should be able to consider such matters as the ' discount rate' applied in drawing up public investment plans. This matter was considered recently by the Select Committee on Nationalised Industries.

Execution of Policy

19. The Government's dispositions for executing its longer term policies ... are reflected in the annual Estimates of expenditure. Although the House of Commons still approves these, it no longer discusses them in substance or in detail during the Supply debates. The Estimates provide a basis for the House to authorise the use of certain classes of resources (such as staff), by the Government, and a basis on which the Comptroller and Auditor General can audit Government spending ... But in their present form they are not designed to provide information for judgment of the efficiency of action in pursuit of defined objectives. . .

22. In particular, Your Committee consider that the House should encourage the use of what is known as ' output budgeting'. An output budgeting system ' analyses expenditure by the purpose for which it is to be spent and relates it as far as possible to the results it is hoped to achieve'. . . . Output budgeting is of great significance to the House of Commons for two reasons. First, by setting out the activities of Departments in the form of costed programmes over a number of years, directed towards stated objectives, it will enable the House to weigh the objectives selected by Departments against possible alternatives. Second, the development of output budgeting will increase the possibilities of assessing Departments' efficiency in setting objectives and their measure of success in realising them; and the information derived from costed programmes of objectives will be complementary to the projections of expenditure. . . Your Committee realise that it may take some years before output budgeting is extensively introduced, and that it may not be suitable for some branches of expenditure; but they recommend that, as output budgeting is introduced in Departments, information derived from

it and necessary for scrutiny of their objectives and achievements should be published to Parliament with the annual Estimates.

23. Your Committee are not suggesting that the existing system of cash appropriation and cash accounting can immediately be discontinued as the formal basis for the House's prior authorisation and retrospective scrutiny of government spending year by year. But they... recommend that the Treasury should review the basis on which the departmental Estimates are presented to the House, with a view to presenting them as far as possible in functional form.

Retrospective Scrutiny

24. Retrospective examination of expenditure is the third element in the proposed new system of scrutiny, and the accounts provide the information on which it is based. Over the years the Public Accounts Committee has become as interested in value for money as in propriety and regularity, and is already 'more concerned with the efficiency of the financial mechanism and the control of departments than with the individual cases' which have already happened before they come to be examined...

The public expenditure projections and greater emphasis in Whitehall on the achievement of objectives will... provide better yardsticks for scrutinising the results of public spending... These developments... may raise questions about accountability to the House of Commons... which will require consideration by the Government, Parliament and the Comptroller and Auditor General.

Scrutiny of Policy and Administration

30. The existing system of select committees for scrutinising policy and its execution is at present inadequate for the functions set out in earlier paragraphs. The range and the terms of reference of the Estimates Committee are not wide enough: the recommendations of the Fourth Report of the 1964–65 Procedure Committee [18] ... were never implemented. The manner in which specialist select committees have developed has given rise to problems to which attention has been drawn by two of these committees and in debate in the House.[19] A committee investigating the activities of a particular Department is inhibited from pursuing enquiries into activities of Departments other than that to which its Order of reference restricts it. A further difficulty has been uncertainty as to the length of life of

[18] See below, p. 333.
[19] Special Report from the Select Committee on Agriculture, 1968–69, H.C. 138. Third Special Report from the Select Committee on Education and Science, 1968–69, H.C. 103. 1967–68: H.C.Deb. 756, cols. 1491–6, H.C.Deb. 759, cols. 777–98, H.C.Deb. 764, cols. 1117–74; 1968–69: H.C.Deb. 773, cols. 827–38.

specialist select committees, which has restricted their effectiveness. . .

32. Your Committee recommend that the Estimates Committee should be changed to a Select Committee on Expenditure. The Order of reference of the Committee should be: ' To consider public expenditure, and to examine the form of the papers relating to public expenditure presented to this House '. The Committee should be appointed from Members willing to serve on a series of ' functional ' Sub-Committees and on a General Sub-Committee. . .

34. The Order of reference of each Sub-Committee of the Select Committee on Expenditure should be:

' To consider the activities of Departments of State concerned with [naming a functional field of administration] and the Estimates of their expenditure presented to this House; and to examine the efficiency with which they are administered.'

The eight Sub-Committees would be neither ' subject ' nor ' departmental ', but ' functional '. They would neither be limited to considering the activities of one Department, as was the recent Select Committee on Agriculture, nor at liberty simply to investigate a ' subject ' such as Science and Technology. . .

35. The task of each Sub-Committee would be threefold: —

(*a*) It should, first, study the expenditure projections for the Department or Departments in its field, compare them with those of previous years, and report on any major variations or important changes of policy and on the progress made by the Departments towards clarifying their general objectives and priorities.

(*b*) It should examine in as much detail as possible the implications in terms of public expenditure of the policy objectives chosen by Ministers and assess the success of the Departments in attaining them.

(*c*) It should enquire, on the lines of the present Estimates Sub-Committees, into Departmental administration, including effectiveness of management. . .

37. Your Committee also recommend a General Sub-Committee of the Expenditure Committee. . . Two main reasons have led Your Committee to this recommendation: Firstly, scrutiny will be needed of the projections of public sector expenditure as a whole after the annual debate on the Expenditure White Paper and, in the light of points made in the debate or elsewhere, consideration will be needed of the adequacy of the material presented. Secondly, one of the weaknesses of present practice has been that time is rarely provided for debates on the reports of Select Committees. Your Committee believe that the General Sub-Committee is needed to give an

account to the House of the work of the Sub-Committees and also to act on behalf of the whole Committee in discussions with the Government on matters concerning the work of the Committee, particularly opportunities for debate. Furthermore, whilst leaving to the Sub-Committees the final decisions on particular enquiries they wish to undertake, the General Sub-Committee should guide the work of the Committee as a whole, including the main lines of investigation, and co-ordinate the enquiries undertaken with the work of other Select Committees, for example the Public Accounts Committee... Finally, the General Sub-Committee should scrutinise the Supplementary Estimates and report, as a Sub-Committee of the Estimates Committee does at present, on any shortcomings of administration revealed.

38. Your Committee recommend that the Public Accounts Committee and the Select Committee on Nationalised Industries should be retained and should continue to fulfil their present functions. With regard to the remaining Select Committees, for example those on Science and Technology, Education and Science, Overseas Aid and Scottish Affairs, Your Committee recommend that the House should decide on their future in the light of this Report and as the occasion arises...

42. The aim of Your Committee's enquiry has been to seek the provision of information for the House on the present-day system of planning public expenditure and to propose means by which the House can scrutinise Government decisions on plans and priorities and can check on their execution by Departments of State. Their Report necessarily contains proposals covering difficult detailed issues... Your Committee believe that the main outlines of the proposed changes in procedure should be embarked on without delay if the House is to develop its proper influence in these fields...

[First Report of the Select Committee on Procedure, 1968–9. H.C. 410, 23 July 1969. Scrutiny of Public Expenditure and Administration]

(ii) Specialist committees and the Select Committee on Expenditure

At the same time as the Select Committee on Procedure was considering the ways in which Parliament could play a more effective role in relation to public expenditure consideration was also being given to the problem of Parliamentary scrutiny of administration in general. So far as specific complaints were concerned one result of this consideration was the establishment of the Parliamentary Commissioner (above p. 172). But Parliament was also concerned with the way in which the Executive was carrying out its responsibilities generally and not merely with complaints about injustices in particular cases. In this the Select Committee on Estimates had paved the way. Although primarily concerned with an examination of the estimates and proposals for expenditure on particular services, and barred by its terms of reference from considering matters of policy, it began to investigate the administration of policy in specific areas falling within the responsibilities of a department, not merely with a view to seeing whether the money spent could be spent more economically, which was its original brief, but to see how the Executive was dealing with particular problems, in much the same way as the Select Committee on Nationalised Industries looked at the whole range of the activities of the nationalised industries and the problems they faced. It was partly as a result of this development that the Select Committee on Procedure suggested in 1964 that it was time that this function was more specifically recognised and that the Estimates Committee should be deliberately developed in such a way as to provide information about the way in which Government departments were carrying out their responsibilities, without being confined to questions of economy and without being barred from considering questions of policy (below p. 334). The Government did not accept this suggestion but did support the establishment of two new 'specialist' committees in December, 1966, one to consider the activities of the Ministry of Agriculture and Fisheries, the other to consider the subject generally of Science and Technology (the former becoming known as a 'departmental', the latter, as a 'subject' committee).

The Select Committee on Agriculture was reappointed in the 1967–8 session and again in the 1968–9 session but then only to finish work it had in hand. In the 1967–8 session a new departmental committee was appointed to consider the activities of the Department of Education and Science. By then the Government had made it clear that the departmental committees were not intended to be permanent but were expected to consider a particular department for a session or two and then be replaced. A second subject committee was appointed to consider Race Relations and Immigration in the 1968–9 session, and select committees on Scottish Affairs and the Ministry of Overseas Development were appointed in the same session. The Government had made it clear that they regarded these committees as experimental and 'the whole question of specialist committees was the subject of a Green Paper in 1970. By then the Select Committee on Procedure had brought forward its proposals for an Expenditure Committee in its report on the scrutiny of expenditure and administration. From this point on, therefore, the question of the way in which Parliament organised itself to consider administration again became bound up with the way in which it dealt with the problems of public expenditure. The result was the establishment of a Select Committee on Expenditure with functional sub-committees, one of which specialised in pure expenditure matters, the others being concerned generally with a particular area, covering policy, expenditure and administration.

The Select Committee on Procedure, 1964

3. Your Committee are convinced that a main purpose of Parliamentary reform must be to increase the efficiency of the House of

Commons as a debating chamber. At the same time no change should ... absolve them [the Commons] from their duty to examine Government expenditure and administration. In order to achieve this latter purpose Your Committee have come to the conclusion that more information should be made available to Members of the way government departments carry out their responsibilities, so that, when taking part in major debates on controversial issues, they may be armed with the necessary background of knowledge. This requires that the House should possess a more efficient system of scrutiny of administration. Your Committee are aware that the 'responsibilities' of government departments are in fact the responsibilities of Ministers. They refer to the departments rather than the Ministers in this Report as a way of distinguishing between responsibility for the 'administrative policy' of day-to-day departmental administration, with which the Report is concerned, and responsibility for policy questions of political significance...

5. In accepting the need to improve the House's sources of information, Your Committee have turned their attention to the Select Committee system as the means of achieving this end. In doing so they have sought to avoid disturbing the relationship of Ministers to Parliament, and also the creation or extension of procedures which might drain away interest from the proceedings of the House as a whole. Their object is to provide all Members with the means to carry out their responsibilities, rather than to elevate any Committees of the House to new positions of influence.

6. ... [T]he Estimates Committee already provide a wide review of the field of Government administration...

7. The principal duty of the Estimates Committee is ' to examine such of the estimates presented to this House as may seem fit to the Committee and report how, if at all, the policy implied in those estimates may be carried out more economically ' (S.O. No. 80). The Committee can thus range over the whole field of ministerial administrative responsibility and have been able, within those terms of reference, to ask the question ' are the managerial arrangements under which expenditure takes place fully effective? ', as well as the more limited question of what specific economies might be made. In addition to ' value for money ', and the investigation of variations between current and past estimates and the form of the estimates, which the Estimates Committee carry out, there is a need for investigation of the long-term proposals and prospects for expenditure in the various fields (such as the ' forward looks ') and an examination of the administrative policy of Government Departments, freed from the considerations of economy alone. The Clerk Assistant proposed to Your Committee that the principal order of reference

of a revised investigating Committee might be ' to examine how the departments of state carry out their responsibilities ', and it appears to Your Committee that such an order of reference would provide a good basis for the type of work they have in mind.

8. It is not the wish of Your Committee that ' specialist ' committees should become involved in matters of political controversy. Many witnesses emphasised the dangers, both for the relations of the House with Ministers, and for the effectiveness of the Committees' work, if the range of investigation got beyond that which could properly be replied to by civil servants...

9. Your Committee do not pretend that the distinction between what are policy questions and what are not is an easy one to make... They do believe, however, that the example of the Nationalised Industries Committee, in producing informative and objective Reports in what is politically a highly sensitive field is one that could profitably be followed by Committees specialising in the activities of Government Departments.

10. ... Your Committee... accordingly recommend that a new Select Committee should be developed from the Estimates Committee, which would work through Sub-Committees each named according to its special subject, such as, for example, ' The Sub-Committee on the Social Services '. In addition to these Sub-Committees, there would be a steering Sub-Committee and at least one other Sub-Committee to consider supplementary estimates and the form of the estimates and carry out investigations ' across the board ' of Government expenditure and control. The order of reference of the new Committee would be ' to examine how the departments of state carry out their responsibilities and to consider their Estimates of Expenditure and Reports '...

12. Your Committee were told in evidence that the power to send for persons, papers and records has proved adequate in the past. They accordingly make no recommendation on this subject, but they wish to emphasise the importance they attach to a close working relationship between the Committee and the Departments. In the event of a serious clash, the Government of the day can always use its majority to refuse information to a Committee. Your Committee consider that such a clash can be avoided, without impairing the effectiveness of the proposed Committee. If useful results are to be achieved, however, Your Committee believe that a close liaison between the Committee and the Departments will have to be attained, which may call for day-to-day relationships between officers of the Committee and civil servants...

13. Your Committee... wish to associate themselves with the

recommendation of the Estimates Committee [20] that investigating Sub-Committees should be empowered to hold sittings abroad for the purposes of their enquiries. It is clearly unsatisfactory that Sub-Committees are at present conducting their investigations as the guests of the Departments under examination. . .

14. Your Committee have given close attention to the question of the staff appropriate to the proposed Select Committee, and the assistance now available to the Estimates Committee has been described to them. One witness compared the sort of assistance an investigating committee should employ to that needed by a Royal Commission; another thought that there should be a much larger staff, sufficient to give ' countervailing help ' to Members on a scale comparable with that given to Ministers by the Civil Service. . . The Nationalised Industries Committee employ two Clerks, who serve no other Committees, and this has worked well. Your Committee consider that in the first instance there should be two Clerks supervising the work of the new Committee and one full-time Clerk to each Sub-Committee. . .

15. Your Committee have, further, considered the question of specialist assistance for Committees conducting enquiries into technical matters. They accept the evidence of the Chairman of the Estimates Committee, that there is no question of Committees of the House setting themselves up as rival technical experts to Government Departments. They note the conclusions of the Nationalised Industries Committee [21] and the Estimates Committee [22] that much technical information can be obtained in the form of evidence, and that both the employment of permanent specialists, and the use of civil servants on temporary loan, create serious problems. Your Committee understand that there would be no obstacle to the payment of professional fees to technical advisers, were the power to employ them on a temporary basis granted, and they accordingly recommend that the proposed new Select Committee have power to employ temporary technical and scientific assistance.

[Fourth Report from the Select Committee on Procedure, 1964–5. H.C. 303]

Specialist Committees. The views of the Select Committee on Agriculture

3. In our view, these Committees should have the following main functions. First, they should elicit information and thereby open

[20] Sixth Special Report, 1964–65, H.C. 162.
[21] Special Report, July 1959 (H.C. 1958–59, 276).
[22] Fifth Special Report, April 1965 (H.C. 1964–65, 161).

up the processes of Government to parliamentary scrutiny. Second, through a continuing dialogue with government and outside interests, they should identify and pose the questions to be asked before policy decisions are made. Third, they should enable a body of members to acquire within a particular field a greater breadth of knowledge and experience. This knowledge is of use not merely in debates on reports of the Committee, but in general debates on topics covered by the Committee and it produces more informed participation, as, for instance, at Question time. . . Later these Committees may enable Standing Committees for legislation to become more specialised bodies by using the Specialist Committee Members as the core of the Standing Committee to which an agricultural bill is committed. The Committees might also play a role in examining the background both to proposed new legislation and delegated legislation. . .[23]

12. In the formation of policy, interested bodies outside Parliament are consulted as a matter of course, some members of the Committee being in the curious position that they might be asked to give their opinions by the Ministry in their capacity as office-bearers in such bodies but not in their capacity as Members of Parliament. The Specialist Committee was set up, in part, to extract information so that a group of members would be in a position to express views on matters which were being examined by the Ministry and which were the subject of negotiations with the external interests concerned. Yet there is no evidence that the Government did consider the opinions of the Committee or that it recognised that there were other points of view than those of the Ministry, the producers' organisations and other interested groups which might be relevant to the formation of policy. This is particularly significant when consumers and taxpayers are not so effectively organised. The Committee were never able to find spokesmen for these more generalised interests. This refusal to consider the Committee's views was demonstrated when the Report of our Sub-Committee on Fisheries had been made to the House and was in the printer's hands, and when the Ministry were concurrently reviewing their policy with regard to deep sea subsidies. They announced their decisions the day before the Report was published, without any enquiry as to when the Report would be available or whether the Committee had any observations to make relevant to these subsidies. . .

Legislative function

18. . . . With the evolution of Parliament, the nature of the legislative process has changed radically. Before a major agricultural bill

[23] And see above, pp. 294ff.

is presented to Parliament, vital and prolonged discussions take place between the Ministry and various interested bodies, such as the unions and trade associations. The bill presented for second reading in the House has gone through these processes and Ministers are loath to contemplate any drastic changes which might upset the consensus achieved. But in these processes, back-bench Members of Parliament are not consulted ... [T]hey are unlikely to influence the Bill as much as people who were consulted before the Bill was finally drafted. This defect could be remedied by the use of the Select Committee. The Minister and his Civil Servants could come to the Committee and, either in public or private, be questioned and made aware of the considered views of elected representatives who have specialised knowledge of their subject. We consider that this pre-legislative function of Specialist Committees should be developed.

[Special Report of the Select Committee on Agriculture. H.C. 138 of 1968–9, 12 February 1969]

The Conservative Government's Green Paper, 1970

12. Some assessment of what the Specialist Committees have achieved is necessary as a preliminary to considering what should be done for the future. This is not to pass judgment on the work of individual Committees, but rather to ask whether this form of Parliamentary scrutiny has been so far justified by results as to warrant its continuance and whether there are any changes which experience suggests to be desirable. It must be borne in mind that it is less than 4 years since the first of the Committees was appointed; given the novelty of the task it was not to be expected that the full potential of this form of proceeding could be realised in so short a period...

13. Considering first the contribution which the Committees have made to the functioning of the House, it must be conceded that when – too rarely – their reports have been debated, the degree of interest shown by other Members has sometimes been disappointingly small... The indirect contribution which the Committees have made to the quality of debate and of Questions by making Members better informed cannot be measured, but it is beyond dispute that they have acquired a growing body of expertise and have brought together in their reports, for the benefit of the House and the public generally, a valuable body of fact and opinion on some important issues. Further than that the Committees have, in the course of their enquiries, opened up new channels of communication between Parliament and interested bodies and individuals throughout the

country. To take an example, the Select Committee on Science and Technology took evidence from a wide variety of people and representative bodies including Government Departments, nationalised boards, public corporations, public companies, learned societies, universities and the Confederation of British Industry; they met representatives of local authorities and of the Services, and others directly concerned. Members of the Committee travelled in Europe and the United States of America, and visited many places in the United Kingdom in order to make on the spot assessments.

14. It is as yet too soon to assess the contribution which the Committees have made to the formation of outside opinion and their influence on Government policy. But there is no doubt that reports of Committees have attracted widespread publicity in the Press and other media and have done much to stimulate discussion of current problems. The influence of the Committees on the formation of new policies is more subtle and in many cases will not be visible for some time to come.

15. This represents a considerable achievement, the more so when account is taken of the difficulties under which the Committees have laboured. New institutions of this sort need time to find the most appropriate style and the Committees have been hampered in the planning of their work by the fact that they were appointed only for a session at a time and did not know what their expectation of life was. In some cases also, particularly in the case of more technical inquiries, the work of Committees has suffered from shortage of supporting staff.

Proposals for the Future

16. ... Although the Select Committee on Procedure [in its First Report of 1968–9, above p. 332] recommended the retention of the Select Committee on Nationalised Industries and expressed no view on the future of the Specialist Committees, the Government believe that these Committees could not continue to exist as they are now alongside the proposed comprehensive Expenditure Committee because the combined demand on the time of Members would be much too heavy and the overlap between their fields of inquiry too great.

17. ... [A]ssuming that no member served on more than one functional Sub-Committee and that half the members of the General Sub-Committee sat on a functional Sub-Committee, a total of some 80 members would be required, compared with the 33 of the Estimates Committee. Attention has already been drawn ... to the growing demands made by Committee work on Members in recent years; and there is a danger that this will have an adverse effect on

the proceedings in the Chamber itself, which must remain the centre of Parliament. In the Government's view therefore the burden should not be further increased and efforts should be made to reduce it...

18. The recommendations of the Select Committee on Procedure would provide a clean cut and comprehensive solution... But although almost all policies find expression in expenditure at some point, it does not follow that their examination is always best approached from this angle; under such a system subjects with small expenditure implications may not receive the attention that they deserve. Moreover the functional structure of Sub-Committees proposed by the Select Committee on Procedure could not well provide for the consideration of subjects such as Scottish Affairs and Race Relations which cut across this whole basis of classification. And a Select Committee on Nationalised Industries, able to range over the whole of their activities, would seem a more effective instrument for scrutinising the public corporations than Sub-Committees of an Expenditure Committee, which would be directly concerned only with the corporations' capital investment; it also better reflects the constitutional relationship between the industries and Ministers.

19. These considerations suggest that there would be advantage in a dual system which provided for the retention of the Select Committee on Nationalised Industries and some Specialist Select Committees alongside an Estimates Committee somewhat enlarged in numbers and transformed into an Expenditure Committee. It appears to be the general view that 'subject' Committees are to be preferred to 'departmental', because their inquiries are not inhibited by the artificial limits of departmental responsibility, and the Government do not intend to recommend to the House the appointment of any more departmental Committees. Both education and overseas aid involve substantial public expenditure and could for the future appropriately be studied by the new Expenditure Committee...

20. The Estimates Committee would be restyled the Expenditure Committee, with suitable amended terms of reference and a membership of, say, 45. These changes would enable the Committee to focus its attention on public expenditure rather than on the Supply Estimates and to examine a wider selection of the issues arising in this field. Because the new Committee, unlike the Estimates Committee, would not be barred from considering the policies behind the figures, there would be occasions when it would be appropriate for Ministers to give evidence before it, as they have before the Specialist Select Committees.

21. The new Expenditure Committee should presumably have the

same permanent status under the Standing Orders of the House as the Estimates Committee now enjoys; but it would introduce an undesirable rigidity into the structure to afford the same status to the Specialist Committees. It is, however, important for the effective working of the Committees that they should know over what period to plan their work and the Government would propose to make clear on moving for their first appointment that they envisaged the Committees on Science and Technology, on Race Relations and Immigration and on Scottish Affairs as continuing for the remainder of this Parliament, subject in the case of the last named to any reconsideration made necessary by constitutional developments. . .

25. Any system of Select Committees must make additional work for Ministers, their Departments and, of course, for Select Committee members themselves. It increases the pressure on the parliamentary timetable and the risk of controversy over the proper limits to the confidentiality of the decision-making process. But this is the inevitable price to be paid for the significant strengthening of the parliamentary system to which the proposals in this paper are addressed.

[Select Committees of the House of Commons. Cmnd. 4507 (October 1970)]

Standing Order 87 of the House of Commons now provides:

' 87. (1) There shall be a select committee, to be called the Expenditure Committee, to consider any papers on public expenditure presented to this House and such of the estimates as may seem fit to the committee and in particular to consider how, if at all, the policies implied in the figures of expenditure and in the estimates may be carried out more economically, and to examine the form of the papers and of the estimates presented to this House; to consist of forty-nine Members, who shall be nominated at the commencement of every session, and of whom nine shall be a quorum.

(2) The committee shall have power to send for persons, papers and records, to sit notwithstanding any adjournment of the House, to adjourn from place to place, and to report from time to time.

(3) The committee shall have power to appoint persons with technical knowledge either to supply information which is not readily available or to elucidate matters of complexity within the committee's order of reference.

(4) The committee shall have power to appoint sub-committees and to refer to such sub-committees any of the matters referred to the committee; three shall be the quorum of every such sub-committee.

(5) Every such sub-committee shall have power to send for persons, papers and records, to sit notwithstanding any adjournment of the House, and to adjourn from place to place.

(6) The committee shall have power to report from time to time the minutes of evidence taken before sub-committees.

(7) The committee and any sub-committee appointed by the committee shall have power to admit strangers during the examination of witnesses unless they otherwise order.'

(iii) Proposals for a Select Committee on Economic Affairs

Much of the discussion about the problems of public expenditure make it clear that these questions are intimately bound up with questions relating to the economy as a whole. This has led to proposals for a further development, beyond the existing Expenditure Committee, to the establishment of a Select Committee on Economic Affairs. Although the proposal was rejected by the Select Committee on Procedure some of the considerations on which it was based provide a useful supplement to the discussion of ministerial responsibility in relation to the economy in Chapter V and the problems of openness and participation in the formulation of economic policy touched on in Chapter X below. This applies in particular to the emphasis on the way in which the Government's increased responsibility for providing a satisfactory framework within which the economy of the country can be carried on, and the creation of non-Parliamentary institutions which do not fit easily into the traditional pattern of ministerial responsibility, have led to a demand for some new Parliamentary device which will take these developments more fully into account. References to other grounds for proposing a Select Committee on Economic Affairs have therefore been omitted in the extract which follows.

The Brittan-Jay proposals, 1970

24. ...[T]he standing of Parliament requires that Parliament itself should not surrender to the unelected National Economic Development Council and the rest of the official network for consulting interest groups its fundamental duty of scrutinising and questioning Government policy in the vital area of economic affairs – indeed, the problem of 'industrial interference in Government' through the operation of official non-elected bodies and committees is, we believe, one that should soon receive Parliament's particular attention... A S.C.E.A. would be uniquely well placed to open up to rational public inquiry new areas of possible economic policy, to marshal facts and arguments and to promote wider public discussion before Government has made up its mind... [M]ore generally, a S.C.E.A. would be well placed to serve as a focus of public discussion at a high professional level on the major unsolved questions of how economic systems work, thereby drawing into a single dialogue the official, industrial and academic arguments which at present confront each other too seldom...

36. The [first] argument raises a fundamental question of Parliament's constitutional role in relation to the growing network of

consultation between Government and interest groups at the formative stage before legislation is presented, often 'cut and dried', to Parliament...

37. ... Examples of major strategic developments in economic policy which received very little prior discussion in Parliament, or indeed in any disciplined environment, include: —

(a) the heavy reliance on Bank rate between 1951 and 1955;

(b) the Thorneycroft experiment in 1957;

(c) the enshrinement of growth as the prime goal (at least in theory) of economic policy from about 1962;

(d) the development of the growing disequilibrium in the U.K.'s balance of payments during the 1960s, which culminated in devaluation; and

(e) the resurrection of monetary policy, with especial emphasis on the money supply, after devaluation.

38. All might have gone better if they had been first subjected to the weight of informed public discussion and analysis. At this present time, the whole question of international monetary reform, including more active international use of exchange rates, cries out for Parliamentary examination and discussion. Then there is trade policy. And again there are questions of regional economic arrangements, such as the European Economic Community, which concern themselves with agriculture. There is the wider question of European monetary arrangements. In a different sphere there is the effectiveness of different weapons of regional policy within the U.K. Few Members of Parliament have, for example, been able to scrutinise critically the theory of the Regional Employment Premium.

39. Fundamental changes are in the air in the vital area where social security and taxation meet... Poverty economics is little understood at the political level. It is likely that the choice between charges, contributions, levies and taxation in financing necessary public programmes will be a major issue of political controversy over the next five or more years. Almost no preparatory work has been done to make Parliament and the public ready for this.

40. In all these areas a S.C.E.A. could play a vital role and at the same time shed great credit on itself and Parliament as the natural and proper focus of public debate at all levels on matters of public policy. Thus, much more than by the proliferation of unsystematically chosen specialist committees, a S.C.E.A. could help to reverse the long and debilitating trend away from Parliament as the chief forum of national self-determination. This would be in addition to its regular work in monitoring the quarter to quarter progress of the economy and in examining the income side of the annual public expenditure review...

51. The main purpose [of the Committee] would be ... to facilitate Parliamentary debate; and if the S.C.E.A. simply led Governments to a fuller disclosure of the material supporting their policies ... the result would be amply justified...

52. The S.C.E.A. would, if successful, be a rival, not to the Executive, but to the Royal Commissions and numerous *ad hoc* committees (such as Richardson on the value added tax) set up to advise Ministers on specific problems. Parliamentary Committees were normally used in the first half of the nineteenth century for such work; and the resulting Blue Books, for example on factory conditions, became part of the history of the age. Royal Commissions and Parliamentary Committees continued side by side in the second half of the nineteenth century; and it was only in the twentieth century that the independent committee finally triumphed.[24] One reason for this development was the possibility of including non-partisan experts on independent bodies of enquiry. A S.C.E.A. with an adequate expert staff would retain this advantage, while helping Parliament to recapture an essential part of a role which has since passed to other bodies...

61. ... Special considerations are ... often alleged to apply to tax policy because of the need to avoid jeopardising the security of the Budget speech... Even on an entirely conventional view of the latter, the distinction is now recognised between the tax structure and tax rates. The involvement of a major tax reform in the Budget security mechanism will often mean that it will have been inadequately discussed, even in Whitehall, before it is announced... Governments have themselves recognised ... this by introducing the Green Paper device notably in the case of the Regional Employment Premium in 1967... The natural complement to the Green Paper is an adequately staffed Parliamentary Committee to probe it; the absence of such a body leaves the field entirely free to producer and regional pressure groups with their own access to the Government machine. The kind of information which Treasury and Revenue officials would be called upon to supply would be no different from that supplied in the past to such bodies as the Richardson Committee or the Royal Commission on Taxation; and it is hardly improper that officials should supply Parliament with information they already furnish to such non-Parliamentary bodies...

69. The one area where embarrassment could arise would be overseas financial or trade negotiations. Here common sense and case law could achieve a great deal. The basic demarcation would

[24] See Ronald Butt, *The Power of Parliament* (1967), p. 81.

be between currency negotiations on which the Government was engaged, or the appropriateness of a particular parity, on the one hand, and the examination of goals or mechanisms on the other. A S.C.E.A. would not for example interfere in the course of negotiations with the E.E.C.; but it might well carry out an expert examination both of the recent White Paper and of any agreement that emerged from negotiations. The S.C.E.A. would not discuss issues such as devaluation. But it might well investigate alternative methods of international adjustment. It would not have concerned itself with the negotiations which led up to the Basle sterling area arrangements. But it might well have examined the resulting arrangements and analysed the alternative next steps, preferably well in advance, and without getting involved in negotiating tactics.

70. There are two kinds of question which could put officials in an embarrassing situation. These would relate either to confidential information or to the actual advice given to Ministers. Officials would be protected from these questions by existing conventions. Their main job would be to explain and analyse the vast mass of available information of a non-confidential kind.

71. Far more information is already disclosed in the quarterly balance of payments statistics or publications such as *Economic Trends, Financial Statistics* or *The Bank of England Bulletins* than is generally realised. . . [B]ut there is a danger of much of these hard-earned labours going to waste through lack of an informed dialogue about their implications. . . If official advisers are able to write of their work in *Economic Trends* or *The Bank of England Bulletin*, it is surely reasonable that they should answer questions about it to a S.C.E.A.

[Evidence of Mr Samuel Brittan and Mr Peter Jay to the Select Committee on Procedure, Second Special Report, 1969–70. H.C. 302]

In rejecting the proposal the Select Committee said that it did not believe that the time was yet ripe for the appointment of such a committee but they ' accepted the possibility that many of the matters referred to in the evidence given by Messrs. Brittan and Jay could be investigated by another Select Committee.' Instead the Committee went on to support a narrower proposal, namely that the Expenditure Committee should be increased in size to enable it to have a sub-committee on the more limited subject of Taxation and Finance, and in this way to complement that committee's concern with the expenditure side of the equation. The terms of reference which it suggested for such a sub-committee were ' to consider the existing system of taxation, proposals for major changes in the structure of existing taxes and proposals for new forms of taxation and to consider the economic implications of different forms of taxation ', and it added: 'Your Committee ... foresee that the Sub-Committee may, in the course of its enquiries into the economic implications of taxation, and in response to a growing demand in the House, be led to examine wider economic issues. Such enquiries would enable the Sub-Committee to build up, for themselves and for the House, a more balanced and comprehensive picture of the economic background to taxation and the financing of public expenditure. If the work of the Sub-Committee were to develop along these lines, Your Committee consider that a strong argument might then exist for the development of the Sub-Committee into an independent Select Committee on Taxation and Economic Affairs.' [First Report 1970–1, 'The scrutiny of taxation'. H.C. 276]

IV. SOME PROBLEMS FACING SELECT COMMITTEES OF THE HOUSE OF COMMONS

(i) Access to information

The trials and tribulations of the Select Committee on Agriculture, 1967

13. ... [T]wo particular difficulties which Your Committee wish to mention in detail concerned the Foreign Office...

14. The first of these was a request by the Committee for copies of some official correspondence about the staffing of the British delegation to the E.E.C. at Brussels... Sir James Marjoribanks, its head ... revealed that he had, some six months previously, applied for an assistant to help the agricultural attaché, but because of shortage of staff at home his request had not been granted... [H]is evidence on the matter seemed to be at variance with that of the Ministry of Agriculture ... to the effect that they were quite satisfied that the staffing on agricultural questions of the Delegation was adequate...

15. The Committee considered that this matter was important and should be cleared up. Accordingly they asked to be supplied with copies of the correspondence concerning the application and its refusal. This was on 26 April... On 26 June ... the Foreign Secretary wrote formally to the Chairman ... saying that the submission of the correspondence raised constitutional issues and that he could not give his consent to the Committee being given the documents... The Committee ... again requested that the original correspondence should be submitted to them, but that if this was not possible, an explanation of the reasons for withholding it should be given to the Committee... [A] further letter arrived from the Foreign Office on 26 July. In this the Foreign Secretary again refused to permit the Committee to see the correspondence which,

the letter said, contained confidential matter relating to the internal administration of the Department.

16. The issue of confidentiality had already been discussed informally with a Minister of State at the Foreign Office and it was accepted that such material might not have been suitable for publication, but this difficulty could have been overcome quite easily by a request that the paper be treated as strictly for the use of the Committee only (as was done in the case of some other documents submitted by the Ministry of Agriculture . . .) or even by ' blanking out ' names and details by which they could be identified. There are many precedents for arrangements of this sort being amicably arrived at between Committees of the House and Government Departments. . .

17. Apparent nervousness about the activities of the Committee was displayed by the Foreign Office to a much more marked extent . . . in considering a proposal that they should visit Brussels. . .

18. The Foreign Office were informed of the Committee's intentions in March, and the Commission of the E.E.C. were asked by letter on 22 March if they would be prepared to receive a visit by the Committee. Two months later, no reply having been received to this letter and the Foreign Office having not indicated their willingness to make arrangements for the visit, the Committee had an informal discussion with a Minister of State of the Foreign Office. At this meeting, on 31 May, it was indicated to the Committee that, while there was no objection to their visiting the British Embassy at Brussels to take further evidence on staffing from the Delegation, a formal visit by the Committee to the E.E.C. Commission would be embarrassing to the Government. The Committee was most anxious to avoid this, and to get round the difficulty it was agreed that the Foreign Office should explore the possibility of a compromise by which the Committee's official visit should be only to the British Delegation, but that while in Brussels Members should take the opportunity of holding informal discussions with the staff of the Commission.

19. Two weeks elapsed and a second meeting took place with a different Minister of State. Again no objection was raised to the compromise . . . and arrangements for implementing it were discussed. However, a week later, on 21 June, at a third informal meeting, the Committee were informed that the Government had strong objections to the visit being made and would not permit it to take place.

20. . . . The Committee . . . gratefully accepted an offer by the Leader of the House to discuss the matter with them and, at the meeting, it proved at last possible to clear up some misunderstandings. In the event, a motion was finally tabled, by agreement with the Govern-

ment, requesting the House that the Committee should be given leave to hold sittings in Brussels...[25]

[Report from the Select Committee of Agriculture, 1966–7. H.C. 378]

The Select Committee on Science and Technology and the Docksey Report, 1972

During a debate in which the activities of the specialist committees were considered on 21 December 1967 Mr Crossman said [756 H.C.Deb. 5s. c. 1493] that the Select Committee on Agriculture had been given the same powers as any other Select Committee to call for persons and papers and added: 'How Committees use them vary enormously, and their success in using them depends largely on their skill and experience.' In 1971 the Select Committee on Science and Technology settled a dispute over the publication of a report submitted to a Minister by publishing it itself. The Secretary of State for Trade and Industry, Mr Davies, had announced in February 1971 that he had commissioned Mr P. Docksey, formerly General Manager of the Research and Technical Development Department of British Petroleum Ltd., to advise him on the exploitation of inventions resulting from public research and on the support by the National Research Development Corporation for the development of inventions from other sources. He received the report in December. In spite of a number of requests he refused to publish it. The Select Committee therefore published it itself. It then published its justification in a special report.

1. The purpose of this Report is to consider questions of principle which arise when Ministers withhold from Parliament reports prepared for Government which have an important bearing on future policy decisions...

   4. Mr Docksey's enquiry was first announced in a Written Answer by the Secretary of State for Trade and Industry on 17th February

[25] During the negotiations over the visit the Leader of the House of Commons had written to the chairman of the Committee : 'It is the Foreign Secretary's considered view that an official visit by your full committee to Brussels would be inopportune at this juncture in the relations between Britain and the Common Market countries... The Government would, however, have no objection whatsoever if the Chairman and Vice-Chairman and one or two others were to visit the Delegation in Brussels in order to complete the investigations... When members of a Select Committee travel abroad it inevitably puts itself in a position where its presence at a particular time in a particular place may prejudice the Government's negotiations... Of course there is nothing in the constitution of the Committee which would prevent it disregarding the Government's advice. But I would hope that it would be the aim of every one of us, whether in Government or on the backbenches, to prevent such an overt clash between the Executive and a Committee of the House of Commons, and to resolve such differences as must inevitably arise by discussion and understanding.'

1971 (H.C.Deb. (1971) 811, *c. 498*). Throughout last Session the Committee pressed for the publication of Mr Docksey's report.

5. We tried to persuade the Secretary of State to agree to publication when he gave evidence to us on 10th May last (H.C. 375, page 439, Q. 1749). As Mr Davies remained reluctant, the Committee invited Mr Docksey himself to give evidence in public on 19th July 1972. At that meeting Mr Docksey said that he saw no reason why his report should not be published in an edited form (H.C. 399, Q. 87) – and it is precisely in this form that we publish it. On 24th July the Committee made a formal request for the production of the report. On 9th August the Minister for Aerospace wrote, offering to send the report to the Committee; copies were received on the 13th September.

6. We consider that the Government should have published the report early this year. We were concerned at the reason given for non-publication by Mr Davies when he gave evidence in May. He said: ' I think the Government needs to consider very carefully how far the recommendations of that report are compatible with its broad approach to research and development generally speaking. I think that the Government will not wish to publish the report until they have finished that consideration, and perhaps not to publish it at all if they were to reach the conclusion that it was incompatible with the Government's broad approach to research and development '.

7. We do not take this view. Too often Governments seek to avoid being questioned on aspects of policy by appointing an enquiry, then refusing to make any comment on the subject until the enquiry has reported. This device is made doubly objectionable if the Government then decide not to publish the report.

8. We consider it essential that Select Committees should be given unobstructed access to reports which have a direct bearing on their work. It is inevitable that Ministers receive much confidential advice – and we accept that this should be so – but we think that reports of enquiries commissioned by the Government should be made available unless there are unusually compelling reasons to prevent it. It is only in this way that advice given to the Government can be subject to critical evaluation by the House, and ' open government ' made a reality.

[First Special Report from the Select Committee of Science and Technology, 1972–3. H.C. 43]

On 12 June 1973 the Leader of the House wrote to the Chairman of the Committee: ' [T]he Government accepts the general principle that as much information as is available to the Government should be available to Select Committees, but that in the last resort the Government must be able to retain the right to withhold information on security and other grounds which it considers to be in the public interest ... I do not think, however, that it would be practicable, or desirable, to narrow the discretion of individual Ministers to judge where they consider the public interest to lie in the detailed circumstances of a particular case in which the disclosure to a Select Committee of confidential information is under consideration. This being so, and whilst the Government will continue to do all they can to meet the wishes of Select Committees in this field, it would seem that there must inevitably arise occasional instances where the views of Ministers and Select Committees regarding the disclosure of information available to the Government are at variance. Ultimately, of course, Ministers are answerable to Parliament for their decisions...

It is ... already standard practice for Departments to make it known to Select Committees if they have information which might be useful to them but which could only be made available in confidence. In such cases the Clerk of the Committee is informed of the existence of the material and of the reasons why the information can only be made available on a confidential basis.

The " side-lining " procedure, previously confined to the Public Accounts Committee, is also now applicable in Select Committees generally, and provides a further means whereby information which a Department does not consider suitable for publication is sometimes made available to the members of a Select Committee and, in addition to these standard procedures, Departments are always ready to consider requests from Select Committees for confidential information to be made available in other ways on an informal basis. I am sure that Ministers will do all they can to assist the Select Committee in this matter.'

The Chairman replied on 2 July 1973: ' We particularly welcome your statement that the Government accepts the general principle that as much information as is available to the Government should be available to Select Committees. We have had some reason recently to doubt whether Departments or Ministers are fully aware that this is Government policy. You might, perhaps, consider whether it would be not untimely to remind them. We hope, too, that we could count on your assistance in supporting the relevant Motion if at some future time the Committee is forced to report to the House the failure of a Department to produce papers directly relevant to an enquiry.

We were a little surprised to hear that it was already standard practice for Departments to make it known to Select Committees if they have information which might be useful to them but which could only be made available in confidence. We wish this were so. Although the Departments have occasionally offered such advice it is far from being the universal practice. Perhaps you might consider circulating a reminder to Ministers and Departments on this subject also.' [Second Special Report from the Select Committee on Science and Technology, 1972–3. H.C. 376]

Problems of security and commercial confidentiality

1248. ... There are three main areas we have to keep a watch on. One naturally, is what information, if published, would be of value to the enemy... Secondly, there is the whole question of our financial relations with firms... [W]e add on certain contingencies because we think this is what will happen, but we do not tell the firm that because it would reduce the financial discipline in the firm... Thirdly, there is a category not as important as the other two, but we have to have regard in collaborative projects to the likely attitude of our friends with whom we collaborate. So an international aspect does come into the business on occasion...

[Evidence of Sir James Dunnett, G.C.B., C.M.G., Permanent Under-Secretary of State, Ministry of Defence, to the Select Committee on Expenditure. Ninth Report, 1971–2. H.C. 516]

6. Security rests on deterrence. The deterrent value of a military effort on the scale of the American may well be enhanced by the publication of information about forces and equipment emphasising the country's power. For a country such as the United Kingdom, however, an important element in deterrence is to keep potential enemies in a state of uncertainty about our capabilities; with our limited forces and defence budget, the disclosure of relatively few facts and figures would reveal significant indications of overall strengths and weaknesses...

[Memorandum of the Ministry of Defence to the Select Committee on Expenditure, Eighth Report, 1973–4. H.C. 169]

6. During the course of the last Session the Ministry of Defence agreed to submit classified information up to and including the classi-fication level of ' Secret ' on certain conditions, one of which was that such information would not be published... The Sub-Committee are well aware that they have received more classified information on defence matters than any Committee of the House hitherto... The Sub-Committee feel, however, that the existing security classification procedure is unnecessarily restrictive and they recommend that the Permanent Under-Secretary to the Ministry of Defence should review the existing procedure particularly in relation to the First Report. The Sub-Committee feel that they should not be restricted in making their own value judgments on the factual information they have received (for example they should be free to say ' serious increase in cost ' even if they cannot give the actual percentage figure). They also feel that diplomatic considerations involving other countries should

not be so strictly governed by security classifications. The Sub-Committee questions whether cost escalations expressed in percentage terms should be classified information, and believe that they should be freer to inform the House of the unit costs of major equipment items where they judge this as necessary to highlight important defence expenditure options. In general, the Sub-Committee are convinced that the Ministry of Defence has nothing to fear from a freer discussion over Defence Expenditure and that greater disclosure would lead to a more informed debate. They recognise that national security considerations must be the final arbiter, but since these decisions in effect limit the effectiveness of Parliamentary control over the Executive, the Sub-Committee believe they should be taken on a consistent basis and at Permanent Under-Secretary level within the Ministry of Defence...

[Second Report from the Expenditure Committee, 1971–2. H.C. 141]

Consider the following extract from the Second Report of the Select Committee on Expenditure 1971–2 [H.C. 141] as an example of restricted reporting:

' 41. In oral examination, witnesses from the Ministry of Defence were questioned about cost and contingency allowances. The Sub-committee were informed that increased costs were a matter of xxx to xxx per cent. The original contingency allowance was about xxx and it has now been reduced to xxx at 1970 prices but if research and development costs are taken into account it rises to xxx. The heaviest expenditure will come between 1977 and 1984, when it should be between xxx and xxx a year at 1970 prices, or xxx per cent of the whole defence budget (Evidence not reported).'

271. Before we finally turn to the question of Parliamentary control, we need to comment on one underlying factor which recurred frequently in evidence. The need to safeguard commercial confidence was invoked to cover three somewhat different situations. The first is that of the firm prepared to disclose information to I.R.C., L.E.A.F.A.C. or other para-Governmental agency on condition that it is not passed on to Government itself... Secondly, there is the information which Government departments receive in confidence from firms. D.T.I. told us that if this were automatically made available to Parliament the source would often dry up, because such information would then be equally available to the firms' competitors. Thirdly, there is the reverse situation illustrated by Concorde where D.T.I. said that they were unwilling to disclose the estimated development costs of the Olympus 593 engine because this would involve revealing to the manufacturers the Department's built-in contingency

reserve, knowledge of which might weaken a firm's discipline of trying to complete the programme within estimated costs.

272. There are two dangers in these arguments. The first is that Government Departments, Ministers and beneficiary companies may be tempted to invoke commercial confidentiality as an excuse for avoiding proper financial control and responsible criticism. The second is the danger that the authentic private interest of a firm may override a large public financial interest. While it may be justifiable that a small public interest should sometimes take second place, where it is large it should be dominant...

273. The strongest argument for preserving confidentiality is that it may increase the firm or project's chances of viability by safeguarding its competitiveness and thus in turn protect the public interest. While we recognise this important argument, there is a risk of its abuse, and there may be a case for expecting firms in receipt of Government assistance to accept some loss of confidentiality in the interests of full Parliamentary scrutiny.

[Sixth Report from the Select Committee on Expenditure, 1971–2. H.C. 347, 6 July 1972. Public Money in the Private Sector]

(ii) Civil Servants and Select Committees

A proposed Select Committee on taxation

5. ... Under the British system, Ministers who are themselves members of one or other of the Houses of Parliament have the initiative in the formulation of policy and are responsible and answerable to Parliament for their actions. At the same time, Parliament expects that important Ministerial decisions or new proposals in policy matters will be brought initially to the floor of the House of Commons and discussed there...

9. ... Following the report of the Fulton Committee, it is generally accepted that officials should be encouraged to join more readily in public exposition and explanation of Government policies. But it may be doubted whether a point has been reached at which officials should be drawn into public discussion of matters which are central to the conflict between the political parties, and which would involve them in defence of Government policies. This is particularly important in the field of taxation: as the experience of recent years amply illustrates, proposals for new taxes and proposals for major development or modification of existing taxes are frequently the subject of acute controversy between the parties... Some witnesses have suggested that officials in such a case should deal with a controversial issue in a non-controversial way, but it seems to us inevitable that under critical questioning officials would find themselves being put in

the position of defending the Government's particular policy. The difficulty is increased by the fact that a full transcript of evidence is taken and published. This has an inhibiting effect, particularly upon official witnesses who must allow for the possibility that off-the-cuff remarks may subsequently be taken as, in effect, a Departmental commitment.

10. Moreover the difficulty for officials would not be confined to matters of overt party political concern. It is assumed in much of the evidence that a distinction can be drawn in the tax field between questions of policy, which may or may not be politically sensitive, and technical matters. But there is very little, however technical it may look on the surface, which does not contain some elements of policy, and many of the matters about which there has been most ' technical ' argument in recent years and which have figured in the annual representations which professional bodies put to the Chancellor or the Revenue Departments either before the Budget or by way of comment on the Finance Bill provisions, have depended directly upon an underlying decision of policy taken by the Chancellor of the day. Officials, if they were questioned on such points, could only rest upon Ministerial decisions. Some witnesses have suggested that a Select Committee would find in purely technical matters a sufficient area of inquiry. The Committee will wish to consider whether this is likely to be the case, given the close inter-relationship of technical and policy considerations over much of the field. In this connection, some of those giving evidence have assumed that the relationship of the Revenue Boards and their officials with Treasury Ministers is such that their position, in giving evidence or other assistance to a Select Committee, would be easier than that of Treasury or other officials. But ... there are the closest working links between the departments advising the Chancellor and in policy matters the Revenue Boards stand to Treasury Ministers in the same relationships as other departments to their Ministers.

[Memorandum of the Treasury to the Select Committee on Procedure, First Report, 1970–71. H.C. 276]

(iii) Sitting in public

10. We recognise that visits by Select Committees have frequently taken place in the past and are likely to continue to do so in view of the wide terms of reference of the Select Committees which have recently been set up. But when they take place, it should be emphasised that the duty of maintaining order at such meetings is laid on those responsible for the premises in which the Committee meets. In general, we consider that meetings of Select Committees ought to

be held at Westminster. It is only in circumstances where it is for the greater convenience of all concerned, and it is apparent that more satisfactory evidence will be obtained that Committees should take evidence outside the precincts of the House. Where, however, it is anticipated that disorderly conduct may impede the work of a Select Committee meeting outside the precincts, its proceedings should not be in public. In our view Members, when acting as representatives of the House, should not expose themselves to situations which they are unable to control and which could reflect upon the authority of Parliament. Otherwise circumstances may arise from time to time where a contempt of the House may be committed but where it would be inappropriate to invoke its penal jurisdiction.

[Report of the Select Committee of Privileges into the Events Attending the Visit of Sub-Committee B appointed by the Select Committee on Education and Science to the University of Essex. H.C. 308 of 1968–9]

(iv) Debates in Parliament

In its report on the Scrutiny of Expenditure and Administration the Select Committee on Procedure said [para. 13 p. 327 above] that the annual discussion of public expenditure 'could and should come to occupy as important a place in parliamentary and public discussion of economic affairs as that now occupied by the annual Budget debate'.

Since then there have been three such debates on the three Papers issued so far, leaving aside special occasions like the debate on the government's major policy document, *New policies for public spending*, in October 1970. No one, however generously inclined, could describe them as other than disappointing... Why... has the response of Parliament... been so modest?... To some extent the range and complexity of the White Paper inhibits understanding and thus dampens debate and controversy. Elaboration in the White Paper itself, in part, as I have shown, a response to demands of the Select Committee on Expenditure, is a factor. Excessive concentration on technicalities by speakers in the debate of December 1971 provoked Mr Douglas Houghton to describe it in terms that justify repetition: ' It has not been a political debate but a discussion between practioners, craftsmen, accountants, quantity surveyors and forecasters. It was described to me as being like a gathering of bridge enthusiasts. It has been a debate between those who have become more or less accomplished in the art of financial prediction, a highly sophisticated financial edition of Old Moore's Almanack.' There may be some exaggeration here but it is difficult to withold sympathy entirely from Mr Houghton.

It can be argued that too great an effort is required from ordinary

Members to grasp in its entirety a subject so large and complex involving more than £25,000 million of expenditure and over twenty major programmes. It has also been claimed that the issues raised are not sufficiently controversial or not presented in a sufficiently controversial or provocative manner. They are too much based on fact. Thus it is difficult to attack the government's policy on education if figures show that this is going ahead at a rate of 4·5 per cent per annum, or even the Defence Budget (if generally one is in favour of limiting defence spending) if the figures show that this is increasing at a rate of only 1·4 per cent per annum.

It is also hard for Members to answer the question: ' If you want more of this what are you willing to give up; and if you will not give it up in the public sector are you willing to abandon it in the private sector by accepting an increase in taxation? ' This sort of approach tends to dampen emotion and defuse controversy. It would thus fail to attract the large mass of Members, leaving only the specialists to whom Mr Houghton referred.

[Sir Samuel Goldman, *The Developing System of Public Expenditure, Management and Control*, Civil Service College Studies, II (1973), p. 19.]

CHAPTER VIII

DELEGATED LEGISLATION

Definition

6. In his memorandum of evidence to Your Committee, Counsel to Mr Speaker (Sir Robert Speed) has defined delegated legislation thus: —

(1) Delegated legislation covers every exercise of a power to legislate conferred by or under an Act of Parliament or which is given the force of law by virtue of an Act of Parliament. It can be expressed in a variety of forms: —

> (*a*) Measures passed by the General Synod of the Church of England.
> (*b*) Provisional orders confirmed by a Provisional Order Confirmation Act ...
> (*c*) Orders in Council and regulations, orders, rules, schemes or other instruments made by a Minister or Government Department or Rule Committee or similar authority.
> (*d*) Orders, bye-laws or other instruments, made by public or local authorities (in some cases confirmed by the Privy Council, a Minister or a Government Department).

(2) In some cases the power to legislate may be conferred by legislation which is itself a piece of delegated legislation, e.g. an Order in Council.

(3) The documents by which a power of delegated legislation is exercised are, in the main, statutory instruments ...

Special Procedure Orders:

9. There is an entirely separate type of order in the nature of a private Bill which is subject to the procedure under the Statutory Orders (Special Procedure) Acts 1945 and 1965, commonly described as Special Parliamentary Procedure.

[Report of the Joint Committee on Delegated Legislation. H.L. 184, H.C. 475 of 1971–2]

I. REPORT OF THE COMMITTEE ON MINISTERS' POWERS, 1932

It is customary to-day for Parliament to delegate minor legislative powers to subordinate authorities and bodies. Ministers of the Crown are the chief repositories of such powers; but they are conferred also, in differing degrees, upon Local Authorities, statutory corporations and companies, Universities, and representative bodies of solicitors, doctors and other professions. Some people hold the view that this practice of delegating legislative powers is unwise, and might be dispensed with altogether. A similar view is held with regard to the delegation to Ministers by Statutory authority of judicial and quasi-judicial functions. It has even been suggested that the practice of passing such legislation is wholly bad, and should be forthwith abandoned. We do not think that this is the considered view of most of those who have investigated the problem, but many of them would like the practice curtailed as much as possible. . . We do not agree with those critics who think that the practice is wholly bad. We see in it definite advantages, provided that the statutory powers are exercised and the statutory functions performed in the right way. But risks of abuse are incidental to it, and we believe that safeguards are required. . .

It is difficult to find and it may be misleading to look for any clear and conscious purpose in the historical development of the process. But it is possible to distinguish between two types of delegated legislation, and to say that one of them represents the *normal* and the other the *exceptional* practice of Parliament. The *normal* type of delegated legislation has two distinguishing characteristics: — one positive and the other negative. The positive characteristic is that the limits of the delegated power are defined so clearly by the enabling Act as to be made plainly known to Parliament, to the Executive and to the Public, and to be readily enforceable by the Judiciary. The negative characteristic is that powers delegated do not include power to do certain things, namely—

(i) to legislate on matters of principle or to impose taxation;

(ii) to amend Acts of Parliament, either the Act by which the powers are delegated, or other Acts. There are, however, to be found on the Statute Book certain *exceptional* instances of delegated legislative powers, which may be conveniently classified as follows: —

(i) Instances of powers to legislate on matters of principle, and even to impose taxation;

(ii) Instances of powers to amend Acts of Parliament, either the Act by which the powers are delegated, or other Acts;

(iii) Instances of powers conferring so wide a discretion on a Minister, that it is almost impossible to know what limit Parliament did intend to impose;

(iv) Instances where Parliament, without formally abandoning its normal practice of limiting delegated powers, has in effect done so by forbidding control by the Courts.

... When Parliament has resorted to any of them, it has generally been on account of the special nature of the subject matter and without the intention of establishing a precedent...

Necessity for Delegation

We have already expressed the view that the system of delegated legislation is both legitimate and constitutionally desirable for certain purposes, within certain limits, and under certain safeguards. We proceed to set out briefly – mostly by way of recapitulation – the reasons which have led us to this conclusion: —

(1) Pressure upon Parliamentary time is great. The more procedure and subordinate matters can be withdrawn from detailed Parliamentary discussion, the greater will be the time which Parliament can devote to the consideration of essential principles in legislation.

(2) The subject matter of modern legislation is very often of a technical nature. Apart from the broad principles involved, technical matters are difficult to include in a Bill, since they cannot be effectively discussed in Parliament...

(3) If large and complex schemes of reform are to be given technical shape, it is difficult to work out the administrative machinery in time to insert in the Bill all the provisions required; it is impossible to foresee all the contingencies and local conditions for which provision must eventually be made...

(4) The practice, further, is valuable because it provides for a power of constant adaptation to unknown future conditions without the necessity of amending legislation. Flexibility is essential. The method of delegated legislation permits of the rapid utilisation of experience, and enables the results of consultation with interests affected by the operation of new Acts to be translated into practice...

(5) The practice, again, permits of experiment being made and thus affords an opportunity, otherwise difficult to ensure, of utilising the lessons of experience. The advantage of this in matters, for instance, like town planning, is ... obvious...

(6) In a modern State there are many occasions when there is a sudden need of legislative action. For many such needs delegated legislation is the only convenient or even possible remedy. No doubt, where there is time, on legislative issues of great magnitude, it is right that Parliament itself should either decide what the broad outlines of the legislation shall be, or at least indicate the general scope of the delegated powers which it considers are called for by the occasion.

But emergency and urgency are matters of degree; and the type of need may be of greater or less national importance. It may be not only prudent but vital for Parliament to arm the executive Government in advance with almost plenary power to meet occasions of emergency, which affect the whole nation – as in the extreme case of the Defence of the Realm Acts in the Great War, where the exigency had arisen; or in the less extreme case of the Emergency Powers Act, 1920, where the exigency had not arisen but power was conferred to meet emergencies that might arise in future...

But the measure of the need should be the measure alike of the power and of its limitation. It is of the essence of constitutional Government that the normal control of Parliament should not be suspended either to a greater degree, or for a longer time, than the exigency demands...

For these reasons a system of delegated legislation is indispensable. Indeed the critics of the system do not seek to deny its necessity in some form. Their complaint lies rather against the volume and character of delegated legislation than against the practice of delegation itself... We agree with them in thinking that there are real dangers incidental to delegated legislation; and we think it may be convenient to summarize the main criticisms, although we do not thereby commit ourselves to complete concurrence with the critics...

(1) Acts of Parliament may be passed only in skeleton form and contain only the barest general principles. Other matters of principle, transcending procedure and the details of administration, matters which closely affect the rights and property of the subject, may be left to be worked out in the Departments, with the result that laws are promulgated which have not been made by, and get little supervision from Parliament...

(2) The facilities afforded to Parliament to scrutinise and control the exercise of powers delegated to Ministers are inadequate...

(3) Delegated powers may be so wide as to deprive the citizen of protection by the Courts against action by the Executive which is harsh, or unreasonable.

(4) The delegated power may be so loosely defined that the area it is intended to cover cannot be clearly known, and it is said that uncertainty of this kind is unfair to those affected.

(5) While provision is usually made
    (*a*) for reasonable public notice, and
    (*b*) for consultation in advance with the interests affected,
       where they are organized,
this is not always practicable, particularly where the public affected is general and not special and organized.

(6) The privileged position of the Crown as against the subject in legal proceedings places the latter at a definite disadvantage in obtaining redress in the Courts for illegal actions committed under the authority of delegated legislation.[1]

Each of these criticisms is important, but they do not destroy the case for delegated legislation. Their true bearing is rather that there are dangers in the practice; that it is liable to abuse; and that safeguards are required. . .

We are . . . convinced that at the present time Parliamentary control over delegated legislation is defective in two respects: —

    (i) Legislative powers are freely delegated by Parliament without the members of the two Houses fully realising what is being done;

    (ii) although many of the regulations made in pursuance of those powers are required to be laid before both Houses and in fact are so laid, there is no automatic machinery for their effective scrutiny on behalf of Parliament as a whole; and their quantity and complexity are such that it is no longer possible to rely for such scrutiny on the vigilance of private Members acting as individuals. A system dependent on human initiative is liable to break down, and the best security for the effective working of any system is machinery which is automatic in its action.

We have, therefore, arrived at the conclusion that the time has come to establish in each House a Standing Committee charged with the duty of scrutinising—

    (i) every Bill, containing any proposal for conferring legislative powers on Ministers, as and when it is introduced;

    (ii) every regulation, made in the exercise of such powers and required to be laid before Parliament, as and when it is laid.

We desire to make it clear that in no case do we contemplate that the Committee should go into the merits of either the Bill or the regulation.

The sole object of the Committee as conceived by us would be to inform the House in the one case of the nature of the legislative powers which it was proposed to delegate and of the general characteristics of the regulation in the other.

In other words the task of the Committee would not be to act as critic or censor of the substantive proposals in either case, but to supply the private Member with knowledge which he lacks at present, and thus enable him to exercise an informed discretion whether to object or criticise himself.

---

[1] Note that the report was published before the Crown Proceedings Act, 1947.

There would, therefore, be no question in the case of a regulation of doing the work of the Government Department responsible for the regulation over again or of rehearing interested parties...

Recommendations in regard to delegated legislation

15. We desire to make the following recommendations: —

I. The expressions 'regulation', 'rule' and 'order' should not be used indiscriminately in statutes to describe the instrument by which the law-making power conferred on Ministers by Parliament is exercised...

II. The precise limits of the law-making power which Parliament intends to confer on a Minister should always be expressly defined in clear language by the statute which confers it: when discretion is conferred, its limits should be defined with equal clearness.

III. The use of the so-called 'Henry VIII Clause', conferring power on a Minister to modify the provisions of Acts of Parliament (hitherto limited to such amendments as may appear to him to be necessary for the purpose of bringing the statute into operation) should be abandoned in all but the most exceptional cases, and should not be permitted by Parliament except upon special grounds stated in the Ministerial Memorandum attached to the Bill (see Recommendation No. XIII).

IV. The 'Henry VIII Clause' should (a) never be used except for the sole purpose of bringing an Act into operation; (b) be subject to a time limit of one year from the passing of the Act.

V. The use of clauses designed to exclude the jurisdiction of the Courts to enquire into the legality of a regulation or order should be abandoned in all but the most exceptional cases, and should not be permitted by Parliament except upon special grounds stated in the Ministerial Memorandum attached to the Bill (see Recommendation No. XIII).

VI. Whenever Parliament determines that it is necessary to take the exceptional course mentioned in the last recommendation and to confer on a Minister the power to make a regulation whose validity is not to be open to challenge in the Courts—(a) Parliament should state plainly in the statute that this is its intention; (b) a period of challenge of at least three months and preferably six months should be allowed. Apart from emergency legislation, we doubt if there are any cases where it would be right to forbid challenge absolutely.

VII. Except where immunity from challenge is intentionally conferred, there should not be anything in the language of the statute even to suggest a doubt as to the right and duty of the Courts of Law to decide in any particular case whether the Minister has acted within the limits of his power.

VIII. The Rules Publication Act, 1893, should be amended in the following respects: —

(a) the anomalous exceptions to Section 1 (in regard to antecedent publicity) should be removed, so that the section will apply to every exercise of a law-making power conferred by Parliament of so substantial a character that Parliament has required the rule or regulation to be laid before it, whoever may be the rule-making authority concerned and whether the rule or regulation comes into operation before being laid, or not. . .

IX. Except in a very special case no future statute should provide for the exclusion of regulations made thereunder from the ambit of the new Rules Publication Act. . .

X. The system of the Department consulting particular interests specially affected by a proposed exercise of law-making power should be extended so as to ensure that such consultation takes place whenever practicable.

XI. The Departmental practice of appending to a regulation or a rule in certain cases a note explaining the changes made thereby in the law etc., should be extended.

XII. Except when Parliament expressly requires an affirmative resolution, there should be uniform procedure in regard to all regulations required to be laid before Parliament, namely that they should be open to annulment – not modification – by resolution of either House within 28 days on which the House has sat, such annulment to be without prejudice to the validity of any action already taken under the regulation which is annulled. The resolution itself should *ipso facto* annul.

XIII. Standing Orders of both Houses should require that every Bill presented by a Minister which proposes to confer law-making power on that or any other Minister should be accompanied by a Memorandum drawing attention to the power, explaining why it is needed and how it would be exercised if it were conferred, and stating what safeguards there would be against its abuse.

XIV. Standing Orders of both Houses should require that a small Standing Committee should be set up in each House of Parliament at the beginning of each Session for the purpose of—

(A) considering and reporting on every Bill containing a proposal to confer law-making power on a Minister:

(B) considering and reporting on every regulation and rule made in the exercise of delegated legislative power, and laid before the House in pursuance of statutory requirement . . .

[Report of the Committee on Ministers' Powers. Cmd. 4060 (1932)]

II. STATUTORY INSTRUMENTS

The Select Committee on Delegated Legislation, 1953

33. We asked for information from 22 Departments on two points, namely: —

(1) the procedure followed in the Department in connection with drafting a clause in a Bill giving power to make regulations, and,

(2) the procedure followed in the Department in making the regulations. . . .

36. In broad outline, the methods followed in all the Departments are the same.

37. The procedure in connection with the preparation of a bill is as follows: —

(1) All important matters of policy and principle are dealt with directly in the Bill itself and the general practice is to limit regulation-making powers to:

(*a*) matters too detailed, e.g. procedural points or technical issues;

(*b*) matters in which elasticity is desirable to enable alterations to be made in the light of changed circumstances;

(*c*) matters in which new Statutory powers are being created and in which the line of future developments cannot be fully foreseen.

(2) The Minister throughout is responsible. He settles the general line of the proposed legislation. The clause giving power to make regulations is carefully considered from the outset and the Minister decides its form and the extent of the powers which he will recommend to Parliament.

38. Then with regard to the instrument, made in pursuance of the power given by the enabling Act, the practice is to follow the instructions of the Minister. Wherever practicable, outside interests which may be affected (e.g. local authorities, trade interests, professional organisations and so on), are consulted informally. The document is then drafted by the Legal Staff of the Department. In some Departments there is a regular Committee of senior officials of the Department who go through all draft instruments in detail and report thereon to the Minister before he signifies his final approval.

39. All regulations which are subject to Parliamentary procedure and all other regulations of importance are signed by the Secretary of State or other Minister responsible. In minor cases such as those relating to purely local matters, the instrument may be signed on behalf of the Minister, provided, even in those cases, that the approval of the Minister has first been obtained.

40. In certain cases subordinate legislation is submitted for approval to the Legislation Committee of the Cabinet whose terms of reference leave it to the discretion of the Minister concerned to decide whether a particular instrument should be submitted in draft to the Committee. The Committee must, however, have an opportunity of examining: —

(*a*) all Orders in Council under emergency or transitional legislation.

(*b*) all statutory instruments likely to affect a large number of Departments whose interests cannot conveniently be ascertained by direct consultation.

(*c*) all statutory instruments likely to give rise to criticism by the Scrutiny Committee. . .[2]

(*d*) all statutory instruments involving any departure from precedent; e.g. in the type of penalties imposed, in the procedure relating to such matters as appeals, or in encroachments on the liberty of the subject.

The Legislation Committee is presided over by a Senior Cabinet Minister and normally includes the Lord Chancellor, the Leaders of the two Houses, and Law Officers and the Chief Whip. The Department concerned with the proposed instrument prepares and sends to the Committee a memorandum explaining why the Order is required and the Minister has to obtain the approval of his colleagues.

[Report of the Select Committee on Delegated Legislation. H.C. 310 of 1953]

STATUTORY INSTRUMENTS ACT, 1946
[9 & 10 Geo. 6. ch. 36]

1. (1) Where by this Act or any Act passed after the commencement of this Act power to make, confirm or approve orders, rules, regulations or other subordinate legislation is conferred on His Majesty in Council or on any Minister of the Crown then, if the power is expressed—

(*a*) in the case of a power conferred on His Majesty, to be exercisable by Order in Council;

(*b*) in the case of a power conferred on a Minister of the Crown, to be exercisable by statutory instrument,

any document by which that power is exercised shall be known as a ' statutory instrument ' and the provisions of this Act shall apply thereto accordingly.

[2] See below p. 377.

(2) Where by any Act passed before the commencement of this Act power to make statutory rules within the meaning of the Rules Publication Act, 1893, was conferred on any rule-making authority within the meaning of that Act,[3] any document by which that power is exercised after the commencement of this Act shall, save as is otherwise provided by regulations made under this Act, be known as a 'statutory instrument' and the provisions of this Act shall apply thereto accordingly.

2. (1) Immediately after the making of any statutory instrument, it shall be sent to the King's printer of Acts of Parliament and numbered in accordance with regulations made under this Act, and except in such cases as may be provided by any Act passed after the commencement of this Act or prescribed by regulations made under this Act, copies thereof shall as soon as possible be printed and sold by the King's printer of Acts of Parliament.

3. (1) Regulations made for the purposes of this Act shall make provision for the publication by His Majesty's Stationery Office of lists showing the date upon which every statutory instrument printed and sold by the King's printer of Acts of Parliament was first issued by that office; and in any legal proceedings a copy of any list so published purporting to bear the imprint of the King's printer shall be received in evidence as a true copy, and an entry therein shall be conclusive evidence of the date on which any statutory instrument was first issued by His Majesty's Stationery Office.

(2) In any proceedings against any person for an offence consisting of a contravention of any such statutory instrument, it shall be a defence to prove that the instrument had not been issued by His Majesty's Stationery Office at the date of the alleged contravention unless it is proved that at that date reasonable steps had been taken for the purpose of bringing the purport of the instrument to the notice of the public, or of persons likely to be affected by it, or of the person charged.

(3) Save as therein otherwise expressly provided, nothing in this section shall affect any enactment or rule of law relating to the time at which any statutory instrument comes into operation...

8. (1) The Treasury may, with the concurrence of the Lord Chancellor and the Speaker of the House of Commons, by statutory instrument make regulations for the purposes of this Act, and such regulations may, in particular:—

(*a*) provide for the different treatment of instruments which are of the nature of a public Act, and of those which are of the nature of a local and personal or private Act;

---

[3] This covers e.g. statutory Orders in Council and instruments made by Ministers.

(*b*) make provision as to the numbering, printing, and publication of statutory instruments including provision for postponing the numbering of any such instrument which does not take effect until it has been approved by Parliament, or by the House of Commons, until the instrument has been so approved;

(*c*) provide with respect to any classes or descriptions of statutory instrument that they shall be exempt, either altogether or to such extent as may be determined by or under the regulations, from the requirement of being printed and of being sold by the King's printer of Acts of Parliament, or from either of those requirements;

(*d*) determine the classes of cases in which the exercise of a statutory power by any rule-making authority constitutes or does not constitute the making of such a statutory rule as is referred to in subsection (2) of section one of this Act, and provide for the exclusion from that subsection of any such classes;

(*e*) provide for the determination by a person or persons nominated by the Lord Chancellor and the Speaker of the House of Commons of any question—

(i) as to the numbering, printing, or publication of any statutory instrument or class or description of such instruments:

(ii) whether or to what extent any statutory instrument or class or description of such instruments is, under the regulations, exempt from any such requirement as is mentioned in paragraph (*c*) of this subsection:

(iii) whether any statutory instrument or class or description of such instruments is in the nature of a public Act or of a local and personal or private Act:

(iv) whether the exercise of any power conferred by an Act passed before the commencement of this Act is or is not the exercise of a power to make a statutory rule.

(2) Every statutory instrument made under this section shall be subject to annulment in pursuance of a resolution of either House of Parliament.

REGINA v. *SHEER METALCRAFT LTD. AND*
ANOTHER   [1954] 1 Q.B. 586

Kingston-upon-Thames Assizes

Sheer Metalcraft Ltd. and their managing director were charged on an indictment containing fourteen counts of infringements of the Iron and

Steel Prices Order, 1951 (S.I. 1951, No. 252). It was contended on their behalf that the Order was not a valid statutory instrument because the Schedules to it, which were an integral part of it and which set out the maximum prices, had not been published with the instrument when it was printed by the Queen's printer, as required by s. 2 (1) of the Statutory Instruments Act, 1946, although the Minister had not certified under regulation 7 of the Statutory Instruments Regulations, 1947, that the printing was unnecessary.[4] It was argued for the Crown that this omission did not invalidate the instrument but merely made it necessary for the Crown, in accordance with s. 3 (2), to prove that the purport of the instrument had been brought to the notice of the public of those likely to be affected by it or the persons charged.

STREATFEILD J. [quoted section 3 (2) of the Act, and continued]: It seems to follow from the wording of this subsection that the making of an instrument is one thing and the issue of it is another. If it is made it can be contravened; if it has not been issued then that provides a defence to a person charged with its contravention. It is then upon the Crown to prove that, although it has not been issued, reasonable steps have been taken for the purpose of bringing the instrument to the notice of the public or persons likely to be affected by it.

I do not think that it can be said that to make a valid statutory instrument it is required that all of these stages should be gone through; namely, the making, the laying before Parliament, the printing and the certification of that part of it which it might be unnecessary to have printed. In my judgment the making of an instrument is complete when it is first of all made by the Minister concerned and after it has been laid before Parliament. When that has been done it then becomes a valid statutory instrument, totally made under the provisions of the Act.

The remaining provisions to which my attention has been drawn, in my view, are purely procedure for the issue of an instrument validly made – namely, that in the first instance it must be printed by the Queen's Printer unless it is certified to be unnecessary to

---

[4] Regulation 7 of the Statutory Instruments Regulations, 1947, made under s. 8 (1) of the Act, provides: 'If the responsible authority considers that the printing and sale in accordance with the requirements of subsection (1) of section 2 of the principal Act of any Schedule or other document which is identified by or referred to in a statutory instrument ... is unnecessary or undesirable having regard to the nature or bulk of the document and to any other steps taken or to be taken for bringing its substance to the notice of the public, he may, on sending it to the King's printer of Acts of Parliament, certify accordingly; and any instrument so certified shall, unless the Reference Committee otherwise direct under these regulations, be exempt from the requirements aforesaid so far as concerns the document specified in the certificate.'

print it; it must then be included in a list published by Her Majesty's Stationery Office showing the dates when it is issued and it may be issued by the Queen's Printer of Acts of Parliament. Those matters, in my judgment, are matters of procedure. If they were not and if they were stages in the perfection of a valid statutory instrument, I cannot see that section 3 (2) would be necessary, because if each one of those stages were necessary to make a statutory instrument valid, it would follow that there could be no infringement of an unissued instrument and therefore it would be quite unnecessary to provide a defence to a contravention of any such instrument. In my view the very fact that subsection (2) of section 3 refers to a defence that the instrument has not been issued postulates that the instrument must have been validly made in the first place otherwise it could never have been contravened.

In those circumstances I hold that this instrument was validly made and approved and that it was made by or signed on behalf of the Minister on its being laid before Parliament; that so appears on the face of the instrument itself. In my view, the fact that the Minister failed to certify under regulation 7 does not invalidate the instrument as an instrument but lays the burden upon the Crown to prove that at the date of the alleged contraventions reasonable steps had been taken for bringing the instrument to the notice of the public or persons likely to be affected by it. I, therefore, rule that this is admissible.

[When the evidence of the steps taken to bring the instrument to the notice of the public and of the contravention of it by the accused had been given, His Lordship summed up and the jury, after a retirement of two minutes, found both the accused guilty on all counts.]

Verdict : Guilty on all counts

III. PROVISIONS FOR PARLIAMENTARY SUPERVISION

The categories of Parliamentary control

12. Delegated legislation may be divided into categories according to the kind of Parliamentary control which is applied to it. The category into which an instrument falls is determined by its parent Act. The Act may provide that—

(1) the instrument shall expire or shall not come into effect unless it, or a draft of it, is approved by a resolution of both Houses of Parliament (or in certain cases, usually if finance is involved, of the House of Commons only); an instrument of this type is referred to in this Report as an ' affirmative instrument '. . .

(2) the instrument shall come into effect automatically, but shall be subject to annulment in pursuance of a resolution of either House of Parliament (or the House of Commons only), thus attracting section 5 of the Statutory Instruments Act 1946; or shall come into effect only if no annulling resolution is passed while it is laid in draft, thus attracting section 6 of the Act; an instrument of either of these types is referred to as a ' negative instrument ', and a motion to annul such an instrument is commonly known as a ' prayer ':

(3) the instrument shall be laid before both Houses of Parliament (or the House of Commons only) with no provision for Parliament to take any action upon it:

(4) the instrument shall be a statutory instrument, with no provision that it shall be laid before either House.

[Report from the Joint Select Committee on Delegated Legislation, 1971–2. H.L. 184, H.C. 475]

Selection *as between the affirmative, negative or informative procedures*

2. The question whether the exercise of a given power of delegated legislation is to be subject to the Affirmative, Negative, or Informative procedure is decided in the course of preparation of the enabling Bill in the same way as are other questions of policy arising on a Bill, that is to say, on the responsibility of the Minister in charge of the Bill subject to the ordinary processes of consultation with his colleagues. The level of the Government organisation at which the question is decided on any particular Bill varies as in the case of other questions of policy; it can, however, be said that the question is one on which the draftsman regularly receives express instructions from the Department or asks for them if he does not.

3. No express rules for the decision of this question are in existence. It is submitted that this is right. Rules for the settlement of questions such as this, which must arise in circumstances of infinite variety, are nothing but an embarrassment, tending to encumber the task of arriving at the right answer in any particular case. The matter is, however, regulated in large measure by precedent, the sense of which can be deduced from an examination of the relevant provisions of statutes now in force.

4. Such an examination shows, of course, that *as between the Affirmative and the Negative procedures* the latter is normal. Analysis of provisions for the Affirmative procedure indicates a classification of powers in relation to which it is required into three particular classes and a fourth miscellaneous or general class. The first particular class consists of powers the exercise of which will

substantially affect provisions in Acts of Parliament, whether by alteration of their effect, or by increase or limitation of the extent or duration of their effect, or otherwise; the word 'substantially' is used because powers to modify statutory provisions merely by way of consequential adaptation and the like are not infrequently subjected only to the Negative procedure. The second particular class consists of powers to impose financial charges (e.g. to purchase tax) or to make other forms of financial provision. The third particular class consists of what may be called skeleton powers, that is to say, powers to make schemes and so on where only the purpose is fixed by the enabling Act and the whole substance of the matter will be in the delegated legislation... These three classes may be estimated to comprise at least three-quarters of the powers in relation to which the Affirmative procedure is required... The remaining such powers, which fall into the miscellaneous or general class, are powers the exercise of which has for a variety of reasons been thought to involve considerations of some special importance.

5. I am not sure that the difference in effect between the Affirmative and the Negative procedures has ever been fully considered. Formally, of course, there is the big psychological difference between expressly assenting and merely refraining from dissenting. But perhaps the practical differences are not so great as the formal difference might suggest. The Affirmative procedure imposes on the Government the necessity to draw attention to the exercise of the power by putting a notice on the Paper, to take account of it in the allocation of time for Government business, and to keep a House at the time when it is to be dealt with; the Affirmative procedure further gives more liberty for criticism, in as much as criticism can be by way of comment rather than of opposition. It may perhaps be doubted whether these practical differences are very significant in the case of a matter which is notorious and controversial, though no doubt they are important in the case of a matter which, if it were subject to the Negative procedure only, might not attract attention. It may be hazarded that it is rather respect for the formal difference than deliberate consideration of the practical differences which has usually been the reason for the selection of the Affirmative procedure.

[Memorandum of Sir Alan Ellis to the Select Committee on Delegated Legislation, 1953]

The Immigration Bill, 1971

The Opposition moved amendments designed to make the rules made under the Act subject to the affirmative resolution procedure instead of the negative.

Mr JOHN SILKIN: ... This is a matter which invariably comes up for debate. The Government of the day most frequently seek to provide that the rules, regulations, or whatever they may be, should be subject to the negative procedure, while the Opposition very often take the opposite view. That is true irrespective of which party is in Government. In this case there are two factors that one has to bear in mind in relation to the rules. The rules are described as dealing with administration and control, but the draft rules that we have seen go a great deal further than that. They give substantive rights. Throughout the debates in Committee the Government relied upon the rules. Whenever we sought to introduce certain provisions into the Bill to give specific rights by means of legislation, the Government said that it was not necessary because all that we wanted was provided for in the rules. It follows that it may be necessary to amend the rules from time to time, and to legislate not merely in respect of immigration control but in respect of rights of people coming into this country, or the rights of those who are already here... It seems to us inadequate that these matters should be dealt with by way of negative control, which means having to take a chance on the ability to put down a Prayer and debate it. Our view is that instead of adopting that procedure, the Government ought to bring their proposals before the House formally and ask for approval for them... At the moment it is extremely difficult to find time to debate matters which are subject to the negative procedure. These particular rules are so closely akin to legislation that they must be regarded as of very great moment and much more important than many of the matters at present dealt with by the negative procedure. Although we must accept with some gratitude the rt. hon. Gentleman's concession in an Amendment to provide that the House shall have some say during the passage of these rules into law – the Act originally gave the Home Secretary complete discretion, apart from having to lay the rules before Parliament – it is inadequate. He should go the whole way and enable Parliament to approve the rules affirmatively...

Mr MAUDLING (SECRETARY OF STATE FOR THE HOME DEPARTMENT): ... I had hoped that I had gone a good way towards meeting the views of the House... I do not think that I can go further, for good reasons. If there is to be a system of immigration rules, it must be continuous and flexible, and should have no gaps. If there is a loophole, it may be necessary to act very quickly... It was generally accepted in 1962 that the rules should not be subject to Parliamentary control but merely laid before Parliament. That was the position, satisfactorily, for aliens before this Bill. But it was argued strongly in Committee that, because we were taking from

Commonwealth citizens a statutory right and incorporating them in the rules, there was a case for making them subject to Parliamentary control. I accept that argument... It must be by negative procedure, because otherwise there might be considerable periods when Parliament was not sitting, when we had to act quickly and could not... That is why we have drafted the Amendments as we have, providing for a statement to be made about any new rules and that if it is annulled, we shall have to return with a proposal which is more likely to meet the wishes of the House. I accept that important points could arise, but I feel confidence... that, if we introduced new rules or amendments of rules which raised important matters, the House could arrange to debate them urgently on a negative motion...

[Report Stage, 819 H.C.Deb. 5s. c. 482. 26 June 1971]

Immigration Rules made under the Act were in fact negatived when they were first introduced into the House of Commons on 22 November 1972.

The Joint Select Committee on Delegated Legislation, 1973

35. In his memorandum to the House of Commons Select Committee of 1953 Sir Alan Ellis... wrote: —' No express rules for the decision of this question [i.e. whether delegated legislation should be subject to affirmative or negative resolution] are in existence... Rules for the settlement of questions such as this... are nothing but an embarrassment '... [T]he Civil Service Department confirms that this is still the official view.

36. ... Your Committee... nevertheless thought it right to invite their Specialist Advisers in their examination of the Statute Book during the past six years to consider whether any consistent pattern or practice emerged which might serve as a guide for the future... With few exceptions no such consistent pattern was discoverable...

38. ... [I]t is contended that the selection of the appropriate procedure depends on the political judgment of Ministers and Parliament, and therefore can only be decided *ad hoc*. Against this it is argued that the establishment of guidelines, however loosely defined, would be of value in enabling Parliament... to make a considered choice of its means of control...

39. On balance Your Committee... are not in favour of trying to formulate precise rules. But they consider that if a classification can be devised of the cases in which each type of procedure is normally appropriate, this may be some help to Parliament in checking whether powers proposed to be delegated by Bills fit into the normal pattern of control, or whether they should, as regards

Parliamentary control, be treated exceptionally. Accordingly, Your Committee think it desirable to indicate in the following paragraphs some of the main features which normally attach to each of the three broad categories of instruments.

Instruments subject to affirmative procedure

40. This procedure provides the most stringent form of Parliamentary control, as the instrument must receive positive approval. It would therefore seem the appropriate procedure for cases which raise a substantial question of principle where Parliament considers that the Government should be bound positively to justify the action taken (e.g. orders under the Monopolies and Mergers Act 1965 s. 3), or where the Government thinks that Parliament should be seen to share legislative responsibility for each instrument (e.g. Southern Rhodesia Act 1965 s. 2)...

43. In the memorandum referred to above, Sir Alan Ellis went on to analyse the precedents for the use of affirmative procedures...

44. The research confirms this analysis in the sense that most of the powers subjected to affirmative procedures fall within one or more of the four classes [mentioned by Sir Alan Ellis] – indeed the description of the fourth class is such that a power can hardly fail to fall within it if it misses the others. On the other hand, for every one power within these general classes which is subject to affirmative procedures there are two or more which are not. The only classes within which affirmative procedures predominate are sub-species of classes (1) and (2) namely—

(i) Orders imposing or increasing taxation or other financial burdens on the subject;

(ii) Orders raising statutory limits on the amounts which may be borrowed by or lent or granted to public bodies...

New formulae

48. One new feature has emerged from the research. This is the use of a new formula giving the Government an option between the affirmative and negative procedures. The parent Act may specify that an order is subject to annulment unless it has been made after receiving Parliamentary approval in draft.[5] Since different orders made under the same power may differ in political impact, there are obvious advantages in this type of provision which may well gain ground as legislation proceeds. Indeed it is possible that further useful variants may emerge in the future.

49. But Your Committee consider that the option conferred by the new formula is too wide if it is conferred in respect of instru-

[5] European Communities Act 1972, Sch. 2, para. 2 (2).

ments of a class which would normally be subject to the affirmative procedure. In such a case Parliamentary control would be diminished, because there would be a standing temptation for Governments to leave matters to the negative procedure in order to ease the congestion of business, in cases where the affirmative procedure would have been appropriate. The formula would have been useful in the Hovercraft Act 1968, where, instead of making two instruments one of which is subject to the negative procedure and one to the affirmative, it would have been helpful to have been able to merge the negative instrument into the affirmative. For these reasons Your Committee are of opinion that a provision of this kind is useful, but that it should be restricted to a power to adopt the affirmative procedure in respect of instruments of a class which would normally be subject to the negative procedure.

50. Your Committee recommend that the Statutory Instruments Act 1946 should be amended to confer such an option in respect of all negative instruments made under powers in future Acts...

Explanatory Memoranda

53. In order to assist Parliament to check that the instruments proposed are made subject to the appropriate procedure Your Committee recommend that there should be included in the Explanatory Memorandum which is normally attached to every Public Bill a section headed ' Delegated Legislation ', containing a list of all delegated powers to be conferred by the Bill, with an indication of the category into which each power falls. This section would not be argumentative or justificatory; it would follow the normal form of Explanatory Memoranda in being purely factual.

[Second Report from the Joint Select Committee on Delegated Legislation, 1972–3. H.L. 204, H.C. 468, 24 October 1973]

The effect of the provisions for Parliamentary supervision

STATUTORY INSTRUMENTS ACT, 1946
[9 & 10 Geo. 6. ch. 36]

4. (1) Where by this Act or any Act passed after the commencement of this Act any statutory instrument is required to be laid before Parliament after being made, a copy of the instrument shall be laid before each House of Parliament and, subject as hereinafter provided, shall be so laid before the instrument comes into operation:

Provided that if it is essential that any such instrument should come into operation before copies thereof can be so laid as aforesaid, the instrument may be made so as to come into operation before it has been so laid; and where any statutory instrument comes into operation before it is laid before Parliament, notification shall forthwith be sent to the Lord Chancellor and to the Speaker of the House of Commons drawing attention to the fact that copies of the instrument have yet to be laid before Parliament and explaining why such copies were not so laid before the instrument came into operation. . .[6]

5. (1) Where by this Act or any Act passed after the commencement of this Act, it is provided that any statutory instrument shall be subject to annulment in pursuance of resolution of either House of Parliament, the instrument shall be laid before Parliament after being made and the provisions of the last foregoing section shall apply thereto accordingly, and if either House, within the period of forty days beginning with the day on which a copy thereof is laid before it, resolves that an Address be presented to His Majesty praying that the instrument be annulled, no further proceedings shall be taken thereunder after the date of the resolution, and His Majesty may by Order in Council revoke the instrument, so, however, that any such resolution and revocation shall be without prejudice to the validity of anything previously done under the instrument or to the making of a new statutory instrument.[7]

6. (1) Where by this Act or any Act passed after the commencement of this Act it is provided that a draft of any statutory instrument shall be laid before Parliament, but the Act does not prohibit the making of the instrument without the approval of Parliament, then, in the case of an Order in Council, the draft shall not be submitted to His Majesty in Council, and in any other case the statutory instrument shall not be made, until after the expiration of a period of forty days beginning with the day on which a copy of the draft is laid before each House of Parliament, or, if such copies are laid on different days, with the later of the two days, and if within that period either House resolves that the draft be not submitted to His Majesty or that the statutory instrument be not made, as the case may be, no further proceedings shall be taken thereon, but without prejudice to the laying before Parliament of a new draft.[8]

---

[6] [S. 4 (3) applies the same rule to Orders in Council and other documents required by any Act passed before 1 January 1948 to be laid before Parliament after being made.]

[7] [S. 5 (2) applies the same rule to statutory instruments made subject to an annulling resolution by Acts passed before 1 January 1948.]

[8] [S. 6 (2) applies the same rule to draft Orders in Council or other documents required by Acts passed before 1 January 1948 to be laid before Parliament for a specified period before being submitted to His Majesty in Council or made.]

7. (1) In reckoning for the purposes of either of the last two fore-going sections any period of forty days, no account shall be taken of any time during which Parliament is dissolved or prorogued or during which both Houses are adjourned for more than four days.

(2) In relation to any instrument required by any Act, whether passed before or after the commencement of this Act, to be laid before the House of Commons only, the provisions of the last three foregoing sections shall have effect as if references to that House were therein substituted for references to Parliament and for references to either House and each House thereof.

(3) The provisions of sections four and five of this Act shall not apply to any statutory instrument being an order which is subject to special Parliamentary procedure, or to any other instrument which is required to be laid before Parliament, or before the House of Commons, for any period before it comes into operation.

The Joint Scrutiny Committee

Recommendation XIV of the Ministers' Powers Committee (above p. 363) had recommended the establishment of a Standing Committee in each House to consider all bills delegating legislative powers and all regulations made under them, and to report anything exceptional about them. So far as the House of Commons was concerned nothing was done until 1944, when the Statutory Instruments Committee was set up for the first time. Its terms of reference limited it however to the consideration of the delegated legislation itself and not extend to the bills authorising it. The corresponding committee in the House of Lords was the Special Orders Committee. Its terms of reference were limited to instruments subject to the affirmative procedure. Neither was concerned with the merits of the instruments. In the debate preceding the setting up of the Committee in 1944 the Lord President of the Council, Mr Herbert Morrison said: ' [T]he Committee is dealing with legislation which the Executive is authorised to make pursuant to an Act of Parliament. There would clearly be an impossible situation if the merits of an Act of Parliament were to be re-debated in the Select Committee because it would then become an instrument of the party game and perhaps of obstruction against the Executive...' [400 H.C.Deb. 5s. c. 258. 17 May 1944]

Following a recommendation to this effect by the Joint Committee on Delegated Legislation the two committees were combined in 1973 into a Joint Scrutiny Committee.

STATUTORY INSTRUMENTS (JOINT COMMITTEE)

Ordered, That a Select Committee be appointed to join with a Committee to be appointed by the Lords to consider:

(1) Every instrument which is laid before each House of Parliament and upon which proceedings may be or might have been

taken in either House of Parliament, in pursuance of an Act of Parliament; being

(*a*) a statutory instrument, or a draft of a statutory instrument;

(*b*) a scheme, or an amendment of a scheme, or draft thereof, requiring approval by statutory instrument;

(*c*) any other instrument (whether or not in draft) where the proceedings in pursuance of an Act of Parliament are proceedings by way of an affirmative resolution;

(*d*) or an order subject to special parliamentary procedure.

(2) Every general statutory instrument not within the foregoing classes, and not required to be laid before or to be subject to proceedings in this House only, but not including Measures under the Church of England Assembly (Powers) Act 1919 and instruments made under such Measures,

with a view to determining whether the special attention of the House should be drawn to it on any of the following grounds—

(i) that it imposes a charge on the public revenues or contains provisions requiring payments to be made to the Exchequer or any Government department or to any local or public authority in consideration of any licence or consent or of any services to be rendered, or prescribes the amount of any such charge or payments;

(ii) that it is made in pursuance of any enactment containing specific provisions excluding it from challenge in the courts, either at all times or after the expiration of a specific period;

(iii) that it purports to have retrospective effect where the parent Statute confers no express authority so to provide;

(iv) that there appears to have been unjustifiable delay in the publication or in the laying of it before Parliament;

(v) that there appears to have been unjustifiable delay in sending a notification under the proviso to subsection (1) of section four of the Statutory Instruments Act, 1946, where an instrument has come into operation before it has been laid before Parliament;

(vi) that there appears to be a doubt whether it is intra vires or that it appears to make some unusual or unexpected use of the powers conferred by the Statute under which it is made;

(vii) that for any special reason its form or purport call for elucidation;

(viii) that its drafting appears to be defective; or

on any other ground which does not impinge on its merits or on the

policy behind it; and to report their decision with the reasons thereof
in any particular case...

That the Committee and any Sub-Committee appointed by them
have power to require any Government department concerned to
submit a memorandum explaining any instrument which may be
under their consideration or to depute a representative to appear
before them as a Witness for the purpose of explaining any such
instrument...

That the Committee have power to report to the House from
time to time any Memorandum submitted to them or other evidence
taken before them or any Sub-Committee appointed by them from
any Government department in explanation of any instrument.

That it be an Instruction to the Committee that before reporting
that the special attention of the House be drawn to any instrument
the Committee do afford to any Government department concerned
therewith an opportunity of furnishing orally or in writing to them
or to any Sub-Committee appointed by them such explanations as
the department think fit.

That it be an Instruction to the Committee that they do consider any instrument which is directed by Act of Parliament to be
laid before and to be subject to proceedings in this House only,
being—

(*a*) a statutory instrument, or draft of a statutory instrument;

(*b*) a scheme, or an amendment of a scheme, or a draft thereof,
requiring approval by statutory instrument; or

(*c*) any other instrument (whether or not in draft), where the
proceedings in pursuance of an Act of Parliament are proceedings by way of an affirmative resolution;

and that they have power to draw such instruments to the special
attention of the House on any of the grounds on which the Joint
Committee are empowered so to draw the special attention of the
House; and that in considering any such instrument the Committee
do not join with the Committee appointed by the Lords.—(*Mr
Humphrey Atkins*)

[850 H.C.Deb. 5s. c. 1217. 13 February 1973]

IV. THE JOINT SELECT COMMITTEE ON DELEGATED LEGISLATION, 1972

The effectiveness of technical scrutiny

55. ...[T]he Department responsible for an instrument is given an
opportunity to deal with any criticisms, before the [Statutory Instru-
ments] Committee take their decision whether or not to draw the
special attention of the House to it.

56. The effect of this consultation is that defects are in many cases corrected by withdrawal of the offending instrument or (as is more usual) by agreement to ensure that such defects are not repeated in subsequent instruments. The Statutory Publications Office issues detailed procedural guidance to Departments in the Statutory Instruments Handbook, and the Civil Service Department issues circulars from time to time drawing attention to criticisms made by the Committee and to any consequential changes in procedure required. These are, where appropriate, incorporated as amendments to the Statutory Instruments Handbook.

57. The outcome of the present procedure is that the majority of points taken by the Committee are dealt with satisfactorily, but there remains a minority of cases where nothing remedial is done, even in the face of a critical report...

61. The Statutory Instruments Committee in their Special Report of the 1970–71 session pointed out the unsatisfactory position regarding negative instruments on which that Committee have reported to the House. The function of the Statutory Instruments Committee is completed as soon as it has made a report to the House, and it is then up to a Member of the House (whether a member of the Committee or not) to raise the matter in the House. In the case of negative instruments there is great difficulty in finding opportunity to do this. It is hard enough to find time in the House of Commons for prayers against negative instruments on their merits... It is still more difficult to find time for a prayer on technical grounds, even where it is backed by a report of the Statutory Instruments Committee...

65. ... [T]he Statutory Instruments Committee made the following proposal, which was repeated in recommendation 19 of the Commons Procedure Committee Report of the 1970–71 Session: ' Once the Statutory Instruments Committee have drawn the special attention of the House to any negative instrument it should, unless debated within the 40-day period, automatically become subject to the affirmative procedure.'

In their written evidence to the Committee, the Leaders of the two Houses say that this ... proposal seems open to the objection that the reasons leading to a report by the Statutory Instruments Committee, which are by definition of a technical kind, are not necessarily matters which are most appropriately discussed on the Floor of the House: furthermore, it would cause potentially serious administrative problems, both in Government and to the general public and industry, if the bringing into operation of an instrument was affected because of changes in the category of the instrument after its laying...

102. ... Your Committee have carefully considered this forthright proposal which would force the Government to find time for debate on orders which the Statutory Instruments Committee had thought right to bring to the special attention of the House... While Your Committee might not rule out so drastic a measure if no other remedy could be devised, they believe that the recommendations they make below should provide an effective remedy, which would not be open to the same objections.[9]

[Report of the Joint Select Committee on Delegated Legislation, H.L. 184, H.C. 475, 1971–2]

The effectiveness of scrutiny of the merits of delegated legislation
Affirmative instruments
94. The Government finds the time to debate affirmative instruments because otherwise they will not come into force... The number of motions to approve affirmative instruments varies widely from one session to another, but averages about a hundred per session...

Negative instruments
95. About 500 negative instruments are laid before Parliament each session. Adequate opportunity for the debating of prayers against these orders has been denied in recent years...[10]
97. In 1954, following the recommendation of the Clement Davies Committee,[11] a Sessional Order was passed establishing the 11.30 rule.[12] This Sessional Order was replaced in the 1957–58 Session by Standing Order...
98. After 1954 the 11.30 rule made it increasingly difficult to be certain that a prayer would be taken on the day for which notice was given, because it was becoming more common for Government business to continue after 10 p.m.; and indeed debates on a Bill which is subject to a guillotine motion regularly continue until 11 p.m. ...

[9] See below p. 383.
[10] Cp. the Second Report of the Select Committee on Procedure 1970–1 (H.C. 538): '42.... The failure of Governments of both parties to find time to debate prayers has led to a breakdown of part of the process of legislation, as Parliament is not being given the opportunity to consider negative instruments made under the Acts which were passed on the understanding that such an opportunity would in every case exist... Your Committee believe it to be of cardinal importance that the House should appreciate the gravity of the inroads into its power of control of legislation.'
[11] I.e. the Select Committee on Delegated Legislation, 1953.
[12] The rule provided that debates on prayers should not continue after 11.30 p.m. It followed occasions when the Opposition had used the previous freedom to keep Government supporters in the House late into the night.

100. The result ... has been that time is only found nowadays for 'major' prayers, that is to say, prayers in respect of which there is strong pressure by the Opposition Whips. But the volume of business is becoming such that the Opposition Whips are unable to obtain time even for all those prayers which they would like to sponsor officially...

101. Since it is in the nature of delegated legislation that it often may effect only a small number of people or a small segment of industry, it is common for backbenchers to be unable to exert sufficient pressure to get a prayer debated. The opportunity for an Opposition backbench prayer is remote enough, but ' a Government backbench prayer stands considerably less chance of being given time than an Opposition prayer '...

110. Your Committee accordingly have examined a scheme under which all instruments which were the subject of prayers would be referred to a Standing Committee for debate, unless in a particular case it were agreed otherwise through the usual channels, or unless 20 or more Members rose in their places to object (the same procedure as now applies to motions to commit a Bill, after First Reading, to a Second Reading Committee).

111. The Government also, if the subject of an affirmative instrument seemed too technical or narrow to require debate on the Floor of the House, could move that it be referred to the Standing Committee, a motion which could be blocked in the same way if a sufficient number of Members thought otherwise...

112. Further, those negative instruments to which the Joint Scrutiny Committee had seen fit to draw the special attention of the House could be referred to the same Standing Committee. The points at issue, being concerned with technicalities and not with policy are intrinsically more suited to debate in Committee than on the Floor of the House; and, if these instruments were automatically given precedence on the Committee's order paper, that would guarantee their being debated without delay and thus fill a serious gap in the present efficacy of Parliamentary control...

113. Your Committee agree with the suggestion in the Second Clerk Assistant's evidence that it should be the instrument itself which is referred for consideration to the Standing Committee, rather than the motion, prayer or affirmative resolution relating to that instrument...

127. ... Your Committee's ... intent is to make recommendations which will close the present gaps in the efficiency of Parliamentary control over delegated legislation...

128. ... If Ministers can make law by way of statutory instruments and Members of Parliament find they are without any opportunity to

debate some of these instruments, Parliamentary control over delegated legislation is illusory.

143. In recommending the establishment of a new Standing Committee, Your Committee would not wish to rule out . . . additional proposals for securing additional time to debate negative instruments on the Floor of the House . . . [e.g. a] modification of the 11.30 rule so that a negative instrument could be debated on a ' take note ' motion at any hour, however late, subject to not more than one such debate being permitted on any one night and a time limit of 1½ hours. . .

[Report from the Joint Select Committee on Delegated Legislation, 1971–2]

The Government accepted the proposal for the establishment of Standing Committees to consider the merits of delegated legislation but rejected the suggestion that negative instruments to which the Joint Scrutiny Committee had drawn the attention of the House should be referred to it, on the grounds that there was no reason why a committee set up to consider the merits of delegated legislation should also consider technical improprieties. It also rejected a further proposal of the Committee that no affirmative resolution should be moved until the Joint Scrutiny Committee had reported on the instrument it was confirming. It accepted the suggestion that the 11.30 rule might be modified to make possible a one and half hour ' take note ' debate on a negative instrument after 11.30 p.m. [848 H.C.Deb. 5s. c. 991. 18 December 1972]

STATUTORY INSTRUMENTS (STANDING COMMITTEES)

Ordered, That during the remainder of the present Session—

(1) There shall be one or more standing committees, to be called Standing Committees on Statutory Instruments, for the consideration of statutory instruments or draft statutory instruments referred to them.

(2) Any Member, not being a member of such a Standing Committee, may take part in the deliberations of the Committee, but shall not vote or make any motion or move any Amendment or be counted in the quorum.

(3) Where—

(i) a Member has given notice of a motion for an humble address to Her Majesty praying that a statutory instrument be annulled, or of a motion that a draft of an order in Council be not submitted to Her Majesty in Council, or that a statutory instrument be not made, or

(ii) a Minister of the Crown has given notice of a motion that a statutory instrument or draft statutory instrument be approved,

a motion may be made by a Minister of the Crown at the commencement of public business, that the said instrument or draft instrument be referred to such a Committee, and the question thereupon shall be put forthwith; and if, on the question being put, not less than twenty Members rise in their places and signify their objection thereto, Mr Speaker shall declare that the noes have it.

(4) Each Committee shall consider each instrument or draft instrument referred to it on a motion, ' That the Committee has considered the instrument (or draft instrument) '; and the chairman shall put any question necessary to dispose of the proceedings on such a motion, if not previously concluded, one and a half hours after the commencement of those proceedings; and the Committee shall thereupon report the instrument or draft instrument to the House without any further question being put.

(5) If any motion is made in the House of the kind specified in paragraph 3 (i) or 3 (ii) of this Order, in relation to any instrument or draft instrument reported to the House in accordance with paragraph (4) of this Order, Mr Speaker shall put forthwith the question thereon; and proceedings in pursuance of this paragraph, though opposed, may be decided after the expiration of the time for opposed business.

[853 H.C.Deb. 5s. c. 680. 3 March 1973]

V. DELEGATED LEGISLATION AND THE EUROPEAN ECONOMIC COMMUNITY

The Joint Select Committee on Delegated Legislation, 1972

130. Clause 2 of the [European Communities] Bill makes general provision for rights and obligations arising under ' the Treaties ' as defined in the Bill... On the Second Reading of the Bill the Chancellor of the Duchy of Lancaster, Mr Rippon, described these rights and obligations thus: — ' They have effect in two quite different ways... First there are the provisions which are to take direct effect in Member States... secondly there are " non-direct " provisions where the obligation rests on the Member State to take the necessary action for implementation.' Provisions of the first type are generally made by the Community Institutions in the form of instruments called ' Regulations '... Provisions of the second type are made by instruments called ' Directives ' or ' Decisions ' addressed to the United Kingdom Government (though Directives may, exceptionally, contain prohibitory provisions which take direct effect)...

133. ... [O]nce Regulations, Directives or Decisions have been made by the appropriate Community Institution, domestic legislation may be required to give legal effect to them in the United Kingdom. Much of this is likely to take the form of delegated legislation...

134. Under Clause 2 (1) of the Bill, Regulations, whether made by the Council or the Commission, and those exceptional provisions of Directives which have direct effect, have the force of law in this country *ipso jure*. . .

135. But it is common for Regulations to contain a provision that Member States shall take all necessary measures to make the Regulations effective. Thus even in the case of Regulations, domestic legislation may be needed in order to set up the machinery for implementation and enforcement of the Regulation. In addition to this, consequential legislation may be needed to supplement the Regulation or to clarify its effect. . .

136. In contrast to Regulations, Directives (subject to the rare exceptions mentioned above) and Decisions do not take effect directly in the United Kingdom. The Government is required to take all necessary steps to apply them here. In some cases administrative action may suffice, but many of them will call for domestic legislation. In some cases the necessary legislation may take the form of delegated legislation made under powers in existing Acts of Parliament. Some of it the Government may decide can most suitably be enacted by primary legislation; but the time limit within which effect must be given to Directives and Decisions in Member States will probably make it necessary for the great majority of these instruments to be dealt with by delegated legislation made under powers contained in the European Communities Bill itself, rather than by a fresh Act of Parliament. Where this is so, they will fall to be dealt with under Clause 2 (2) and (4) of the Bill, which incorporates powers to repeal or to amend existing Acts of Parliament.

137. Where delegated legislation arising from Community membership is made under existing Acts of Parliament, it will be, so far as Parliamentary scrutiny is concerned, no different from any other ordinary delegated legislation and automatically will be subject to the ordinary technical scrutiny. This will also be the position as respects delegated legislation made under the powers contained in the European Communities Bill itself, since paragraph 2 (2) of Schedule 2 of the Bill provides that any delegated legislation under the Bill ' made without a draft having been approved by resolution of each House of Parliament shall be subject to annulment in pursuance of a resolution of either House '.

138. Delegated legislation made under the powers contained in the European Communities Bill will, however, differ radically from ordinary delegated legislation subject to negative resolution, in that it may repeal and amend existing Acts of Parliament. Exceptionally an Act of Parliament does delegate to a Minister or other appropriate authority a limited power to repeal or amend by statutory instrument

provisions of previous enactments dealing with a particular subject matter. But the power of repeal and amendment of Acts of Parliament by statutory instrument which is conferred by the European Communities Bill is much more far-reaching. It is subject to no other limitation than that the repeal or amendment must be for the purpose of dealing with some matter arising out of or related to a Directive or Decision or the coming into force or the operation from time to time of a Regulation. These are very wide powers. The extent of such repeal and amendment which would have been involved if the United Kingdom had been a member of the European Community since its inception on 1st January 1958 may be judged by the amendments of existing law which are set out in Part II of and Schedules 3 and 4 to the Bill...

141. Your Committee do not underrate the exceptional importance which may attach to some of the delegated legislation likely to come before Parliament as a consequence of Britain's adherence to the Communities. But... the quantity, as distinct from the nature and quality, of such instruments is unlikely, on the best information at present obtainable, to make more than a relatively small addition to the number of instruments, approaching one thousand a year, which already are scrutinised by the Statutory Instruments Committee of the House of Commons.

142. Accordingly, provided that the improvements in procedure recommended in this Report are adopted, Your Committee believe that it should become possible for Parliament to maintain a watch over delegated legislation stemming from a decision to join the European Communities, without over-straining the Parliamentary machinery.

[Report of the Joint Select Committee on Delegated Legislation, 1971–2]

VI. THE COURTS AND DELEGATED LEGISLATION

5. The power to legislate, when delegated by Parliament, differs from Parliament's own power to legislate: Parliament is supreme and the power of the Queen in Parliament to legislate is unlimited. On the other hand, the power of legislation granted by Parliament to another body or persons is limited by the exact extent of the delegated power so granted; the purported exercise of power beyond the extent so granted will be *ultra vires* and ineffective.

6. The legality of an Act of Parliament cannot be challenged in or by the Courts of Law, but the question whether subordinate legislation is within the power delegated by Parliament can be and is challenged in and by the Courts of Law.

7. Frequently, subordinate legislation is issued in the form of an Order in Council, that is an Order expressed to be made by Her Majesty by and with the advice of Her Privy Council and signed by the Clerk of the Council.

But not every instrument so issued is an enactment of subordinate legislation under a power delegated by Act of Parliament.

Orders in Council are of two kinds and they differ fundamentally in constitutional principle. The two kinds are: —

(*a*) those made in virtue of the Royal Prerogative, and

(*b*) those which are authorised by Act of Parliament.

The Royal Prerogative is that which remains of the original sovereign power of the Crown to legislate without the authority of Parliament, e.g. power to declare a rigid blockade of enemy territory in time of war.

This power is in no sense delegated and Orders in Council issued in exercise of this power are not subordinate: they are original legislation. Your Committee are not concerned with them in this report. Your Committee have to consider (*inter alia*) those Orders in Council made under the authority of an Act of Parliament.

[Report of the Select Committee on Delegated Legislation, 1953]

CHESTER v. *BATESON*   [1920] 1 K.B. 829

Divisional Court

The Defence of the Realm Consolidation Act, 1914 [5 & 6 Geo. 5. ch. 8], provided: ' 1. (1) His Majesty in Council has power during the continuance of the present war to issue regulations for securing the public safety and defence of the realm ... and may by such regulations authorise the trial ... and punishment of persons committing offences against the regulations and in particular against any of the provisions of such regulations designed ... (*e*) to prevent ... the successful prosecution of the war being endangered.'

One of the regulations made, Regulation 2A, provided: ' If as respects any area in which the work of manufacturing ... war material is being carried on, the Minister of Munitions is of opinion that the ejectment from their dwellings of workmen employed in that work is calculated to impede, delay or restrict that work, he may by order declare the area to be a special area for the purpose of this regulation. Whilst the order remains in force no person shall, without the consent of the Minister of Munitions, take, or cause to be taken, any proceedings for the purpose of obtaining an order or decree for the recovery of possession of, or for the ejectment of a tenant of, any dwelling-house or other premises situate in the special area, being a house or premises in which any workman so employed is living, so long as the tenant continues duly to pay the rent and to observe the other conditions of the tenancy, other than any condition for the delivery up of possession. If any person acts in contravention of this regulation he shall be guilty of a summary offence against these regulations.'

Chester let a dwelling house to Bateson who was a munitions worker. When the tenancy expired Bateson refused to give up the property. Chester therefore preferred the complaint against him in the local court of summary jurisdiction under the Small Tenements Recovery Act, 1838. It was argued for the defendant that the justices had no jurisdiction. The Minister had made an order under Regulation 2A, applying it to the area in which the dwelling house was situated, and Chester had not obtained the consent of the Minister to the initiation of proceedings. Chester argued *inter alia* that Regulation 2A was *ultra vires* and not authorised by s. 1 (1) of the Defence of the Realm Act.

The justices, having heard evidence that Bateson was employed as a munitions worker, held that they had no jurisdiction until the Minister's consent had been given. Chester appealed to the Divisional Court.

DARLING J. ... Mr Langdon has contended that this regulation violates Magna Carta, where the King declares: ' To no one will we sell, to no one will we refuse or delay right or justice.' I could not hold the regulation to be bad on that ground, were there sufficient authority given by a statute of the realm to those by whom the regulation was made. Magna Carta has not remained untouched; and, like every other law of England, it is not condemned to that immunity from development or improvement which was attributed to the laws of the Medes and Persians. I found my judgment rather on the passage in *Rex* v. *Halliday* [13] where Lord Finlay says that Parliament may entrust great powers to His Majesty in Council, feeling certain that such powers will be reasonably exercised; and, further, on these words of Lord Atkinson in the same case [14]: ' It by no means follows, however, that if on the face of a regulation it enjoined or required something to be done which could not in any reasonable way aid in securing the public safety and the defence of the realm it would not be ultra vires and void. It is not necessary to decide this precise point on the present occasion, but I desire to hold myself free to deal with it when it arises.' Here I think it does at last arise; and I ask myself whether it is a necessary, or even reasonable, way to aid in securing the public safety and the defence of the realm to give power to a Minister to forbid any person to institute any proceedings to recover possession of a house so long as a war worker is living in it.

The main question to be decided is whether the occupant is a workman so employed, and the regulation might have been so framed as to make this a good answer to the application for possession, still leaving that question to be decided by a Court of law. But the regulation as framed forbids the owner of the property access to all legal

[13] [1917] A.C. 268.   [14] [1917] A.C. 272.

tribunals in regard to this matter. This might, of course, legally be done by Act of Parliament; but I think this extreme disability can be inflicted only by direct enactment of the Legislature itself, and that so grave an invasion of the rights of all subjects was not intended by the Legislature to be accomplished by a departmental order such as this one of the Minister of Munitions.

... It is to be observed that this regulation not only deprives the subject of his ordinary right to seek justice in the Courts of law, but provides that merely to resort there without the permission of the Minister of Munitions first had and obtained shall of itself be a summary offence, and so render the seeker after justice liable to imprisonment and fine. I allow that in stress of war we may rightly be obliged, as we should be ready, to forgo much of our liberty, but I hold that this elemental right of the subjects of the British Crown cannot be thus easily taken from them. Should we hold that the permit of a departmental official is a necessary condition precedent for a subject of the realm who would demand justice at the seat of judgment the people would be in that unhappy condition indicated, but not anticipated, by Montesquieu, in De l'Esprit des Lois, where he writes: ' Les Anglais pour favoriser la liberté ont ôté toutes les puissances intermédiaires qui formoient leur monarchie. Ils ont bien raison de conserver cette liberté; s'ils venoient à la perdre, ils seroient un des peuples les plus esclaves de la terre.' (Livre 2, c. 4.)

AVORY and SANKEY JJ. delivered concurring judgments.

Appeal allowed; case remitted to justices

ATTORNEY-GENERAL v. WILTS UNITED DAIRIES LTD.   (1921) 37 T.L.R. 884

Court of Appeal

S. 3 of the New Ministers and Secretaries Act, 1916, established a Food Controller. S. 4 provided: ' It shall be the duty of the Food Controller to regulate the supply and consumption of food in such manner as he thinks best for encouraging the production of food.' Regulation 2F of the Defence Regulations, made under the Defence of the Realm (Consolidation) Act, 1914, provided that he might ' make orders regulating ... the production, manufacture, treatment, use, consumption, transport, storage, distribution, supply, sale or purchase of, or other dealing in, or measures to be taken in relation to any article (including orders providing for the fixing of maximum and minimum prices) where it appears to him necessary or expedient to make any such order for the purpose of encouraging or maintaining the food supply of the country '. In April 1919 the Food Controller made the Milk Summer Prices Order, 1919. Instead of fixing a uniform maximum price for the whole country he fixed a lower maximum, 1*s*. 4*d*. a gallon instead of 1*s*. 6*d*., for the more highly productive areas such as Cornwall, Devon, Dorset and Somerset, but provided that where milk was taken from these areas to the areas with a higher maximum price, 2*d*. a gallon should be paid to the Food Controller. The defendants had applied for licences to purchase milk in the four counties and had agreed in consideration of the issue of the licences to pay the 2*d*. per gallon. They subsequently refused to pay and the Attorney-General brought this action to recover the sum due. The company argued that the Food Controller had no power to impose the condition of payment in granting a licence and that the condition amounted to a tax, which could not be imposed upon the subject without clear and distinct legal authority.

ATKIN L.J. . . . The present charge is in respect of money claimed on behalf of the Crown by the Food Controller as a condition of a grant of a licence. It could not be disputed that the Food Controller could only acquire the right to make such a charge by statutory authority. No power to make a charge upon the subject for the use of the Crown could arise except by virtue of the prerogative or by statute, and the alleged right under the prerogative was disposed of finally by the Bill of Rights [15]. . . Though the attention of our ancestors was directed especially to abuses of the prerogative, there can be no doubt that this statute declares the law that no money shall be levied for or to the use of the Crown except by grant of Parliament. We know how strictly Parliament has maintained this right – and, in particular, how jealously the House of Commons has asserted its predominance in the power of raising money. An elaborate custom of Parliament has prevailed by which money for the service of the Crown is only granted at the request of the Crown made by a responsible Minister and assented to by a resolution of the House in Committee. By constitutional usage no money proposal can be altered by the Second Chamber, whose powers are confined to acceptance or rejection. Similar elaborate checks exist in respect to authority for expenditure of the public revenue, both in respect to obtaining the statutory authority to expend money and to obtaining the executive acts necessary to place the money at the disposal of the spending authority.

In these circumstances, if an officer of the executive seeks to justify a charge upon the subject made for the use of the Crown (which includes all the purposes of the public revenue), he must show, in clear terms, that Parliament has authorized the particular charge. The intention of the Legislature is to be inferred from the language used, and the grant of powers may, though not expressed, have to be implied as necessarily arising from the words of a statute; but in view of the historic struggle of the Legislature to secure for itself the

[15] [Above, p. 2].

sole power to levy money upon the subject, its complete success in that struggle, the elaborate means adopted by the Representative House to control the amount, the conditions and the purposes of the levy, the circumstances would be remarkable indeed which would induce the Court to believe that the Legislature had sacrificed all the well-known checks and precautions, and, not in express words, but merely by implication, had entrusted a Minister of the Crown with undefined and unlimited powers of imposing charges upon the subject for purposes connected with his department.

I am clearly of opinion that no such powers, and indeed no powers at all, of imposing any such charge are given to the Minister of Food by the statutory provisions on which he relies. I will express no opinion upon the Defence of the Realm Consolidation Act, 1914, itself, whether the provisions of the statute should be construed as authorizing regulations to be made giving the executive power to impose charges upon the subject. But I am satisfied that the powers given by regulation 2F include no such powers. There are clearly no express words, and all the powers given appear capable of perform- ance without any power to levy money. It is indeed significant that it was thought necessary to give expressly even such a power as that of fixing maximum and minimum prices... If this power existed, there has been hardly any article of any description in connexion with the production or distribution of which charges might not have been made by some one or more of the executive officers of State. Naturally, counsel for the Food Minister disclaimed any wide powers. But no limit was suggested which appeared to afford any logical basis. There seems no reason why the Food Controller should have limited his charge to 2d. He might have directly prohibited transactions by making the charge 3d. or more; he might have put a duty on milk transferred from one county to another to be collected at the county boundary; he might have imposed a duty on the profits of those licensed, either on the profits derived from the licensed dealings or generally. In none of these matters would Parliament have had any voice in the time or manner of the levy of the money; and for that reason, in my opinion, all such imposts would have been illegal...

It makes no difference that the obligation to pay the money is expressed in the form of an agreement. It was illegal for the Food Controller to require such an agreement as a condition of any licence. It was illegal for him to enter into such an agreement. The agreement itself is not enforceable against the other contracting party; and if he had paid under it he could, having paid under protest, recover back the sums paid, as money had and received to his use... I have no doubt whatever as to the good faith of the Food Controller. His inten- tions in making this charge may have been excellent, but he adopted methods which, in my opinion, are unconstitutional and contrary to law, and his agreements cannot be enforced.

I agree, therefore, that the appeal should be allowed, and judgment on the information entered for the defendants.

BANKES and SCRUTTON L.JJ. delivered concurring judgments.

Appeal allowed [16]

COMMISSIONERS OF CUSTOMS AND EXCISE v. CURE & DEELEY LTD. [1962] 1 Q.B. 340

Queen's Bench Division

The Finance (No. 2) Act, 1940, provided: ' 33 (1) The Commissioners may make regulations providing for any matter for which provision appears to them to be necessary for the purpose of giving effect to the provisions of this Part of this Act and of enabling them to discharge their functions thereunder...' The Commissioners made the following regulation, Regulation 12 of the Purchase Tax Regulations, 1945: 'If any person fails to furnish a return as required by these Regulations or furnishes an incomplete return the Commissioners may, without prejudice to any penalties which may be incurred by such person, determine the amount of the tax appearing to them to be due from such person, and demand payment thereof, which amount shall be deemed to be the proper tax due from such person and shall be paid within seven days of such demand unless within that time it is shown to the satisfaction of the Commissioners that some other amount is the proper tax due which other amount shall immediately be paid to the Commissioners.'

The Commissioners made a determination and a demand for payment and now brought this action for the sum demanded. The defendants argued that Regulation 12 was *ultra vires* and not authorised by s. 33 (1) of the Finance Act. They cited, *inter alia*, *Chester* v. *Bateson* (above, p. 387) and Viscount Simonds in *Pyx Granite Co. Ltd.* v. *Ministry of Housing and Local Government.*[17]

SACHS J. .... In the first place I reject the view that the words ' appear to them to be necessary ' when used in a statute conferring powers on a competent authority, necessarily make that authority the sole

---

[16] The decision of the Court of Appeal was subsequently confirmed by the House of Lords (38 T.L.R. 781). At the beginning of the Second World War, s. 2 (1) of the Emergency Powers (Defence) Act, 1939, expressly authorised the Treasury to provide by order for the imposition and recovery, in connexion with any scheme of control contained in or authorised by Defence Regulations, of such charges as might be specified in the order.

For a case where the court held that the Crown could validly make a charge for services although it was not expressly authorised to do so by statute, see *China Navigation Co.* v. *Attorney-General* [1932] 2 K.B. 197.

[17] [1960] A.C. at 286. ' It is a principle not by any means to be whittled down that the subject's recourse to Her Majesty's courts for the determination of his rights is not to be excluded except by clear words.'

judge of what are its powers as well as the sole judge of the way in which it can exercise such powers as it may have. It is axiomatic that, to follow the words used by Lord Radcliffe in the Canadian case,[18] ' the paramount rule remains that every statute is to be expounded according to its manifest or expressed intention '. It is no less axiomatic that the application of that rule may result in phrases identical in wording or in substance receiving quite different interpretations according to the tenor of the legislation under consideration. As an apt illustration of such a result it is not necessary to go further than *Liversidge* v. *Anderson* [19] and *Nakkuda Ali* v. *Jayaratne*,[20] in which cases the words ' reasonable cause to believe ' and ' reasonable grounds to believe ' received quite different interpretations.

To my mind a court is bound before reaching a decision on the question whether a regulation is intra vires to examine the nature, objects, and scheme of the piece of legislation as a whole, and in the light of that examination to consider exactly what is the area over which powers are given by the section under which the competent authority is purporting to act. . .

Having reached the above conclusion I now turn to the legislation under consideration in the present case . . . [U]ntil one reaches regulation 12 one finds a quite normal set of provisions which define the goods and transactions which attract tax and leave it to the courts to decide disputes between the executive and the subject in a normal way. . .

[S]ection 31 (2) in particular provides that the tax shall be recoverable as a debt and enables the subject thus to obtain decisions on points in dispute. It is in relation to this general scheme that the functions of the commissioners are by section 30 provided to be as follows:

' (1) The tax shall be under the care and management of the commissioners.

(2) The commissioners may do all such acts as may be deemed necessary or expedient for raising, collecting, receiving, and accounting for the tax in the like and as full and ample a manner as they are authorised to do with relation to any duties under their care and management.'

It is next to be observed that it is fully practicable to draft a regulation which enables the commissioners to assess tax where there has been no return or an incomplete return without in that regulation providing that the assessment cannot be made the subject of an appeal. Indeed, no parallel provision of any Act was cited to me which excluded all right of appeal to an independent tribunal. Whilst the

---

[18] *Attorney-General for Canada* v. *Hallett & Carey Ltd.* [1952] A.C. 427, 449.
[19] [1942] A.C. 206.
[20] [1951] A.C. 66.

present case relates to an incomplete return, it is pertinent that regulation 12 equally applies whenever any person fails to furnish a return ' as required by these regulations '. That is a phrase of wide implications which are by no means reduced by the instruction on P.T. ɪɪ that the return must comply with the directions given in the various notices. . .

It is against the background of the above examination of the relevant legislation that the court has to interpret the words ' for the purpose of giving effect to the provisions of this Part of the Act and of enabling them to discharge their functions thereunder ' to see what is the area over which the power of the commissioners to make regulations extends. . .

On the above footing it is, to my mind, clear that regulation 12 is ultra vires on at any rate three grounds, which, to my mind, are distinct in law though they overlap in so far as they may be different ways of expressing the result of certain facts. First, it is no part of the functions assigned to the commissioners to take upon themselves the powers of a High Court judge and decide issues of fact and law as between the Crown and the subject. Secondly, it renders the subject liable to pay such tax as the commissioners believe to be due, whereas the charging sections impose a liability to pay such tax as in law is due. Thirdly, it is capable of excluding the subject from access to the courts and of defeating pending proceedings. This last is a distinct ground that needs to be stated separately, not least because there is nothing in the regulation to preclude the commissioners from making a determination on a transaction whilst proceedings are pending in the High Court either for a declaration or for the determination of a case stated on a section 21 arbitration. The regulation thus enables the commissioners to oust the subject's right to have issues determined in the courts not only before relevant proceedings are commenced but whilst they are pending.

The first ground derives from the proper construction of the word ' functions ' in section 33; the second from the fundamental repugnance of regulation 12 to the charging provisions of the relevant legislation; and the third from a general examination of the nature, objects and scheme of the legislation.

There also exists, parallel to the third ground, a subsidiary repugnance between the regulation and that part of section 21 which makes obligatory the reference of certain disputes to arbitration.

In the result this attempt to substitute in one segment of the taxpayer's affairs the rule of tax collectors for the rule of law fails. . .

Judgment for the defendants [21]

[21] See also below 577.

McELDOWNEY v. *FORDE* [1971] A.C. 632

House of Lords

The Civil Authorities (Special Powers) Act (Northern Ireland) 1922 provided:

' 1. (1) The civil authority shall have power, in respect of persons, matters and things within the jurisdiction of the Government of Northern Ireland, to take all such steps and issue all such orders as may be necessary for preserving the peace and maintaining order, according to and in the execution of this Act (which regulations, whether contained in the said Schedule or made as aforesaid, are in this Act referred to as " the regulations "):

Provided that the ordinary course of law and avocations of life and the enjoyment of property shall be interfered with as little as may be permitted by the exigencies of the steps required to be taken under this Act...

(3) The Minister of Home Affairs shall have power to make regulations—(*a*) for making further provision for the preservation of the peace and maintenance of order, and (*b*) for varying or revoking any provision of the regulations; and any regulations made as aforesaid shall, subject to the provisions of this Act, have effect and be enforced in like manner as regulations contained in the Schedule to this Act...'

Regulation 24A, made in 1922, provided:

' Any person who becomes or remains a member of an unlawful association or who does any act with a view to promoting or calculated to promote the objects of an unlawful association or seditious conspiracy shall be guilty of an offence against these regulations...

The following organisations shall for the purposes of this regulation be deemed to be unlawful associations: —

The Irish Republican Brotherhood,
The Irish Republican Army,
The Irish Volunteers,
The Cumann na m'Ban,
The Fianna na h'Eireann.'

Regulations in the 1930s added Saor Eire, The National Guard and Cumann Problachta na h'Eireann.

The Civil Authorities (Special Powers) Acts (Amending) (No. 1) Regulations (Northern Ireland), 1967 provided:

' Regulation 24A of the principal regulations shall have effect as if the following organisations were added to the list of organisations which for the purpose of that regulation are deemed to be unlawful associations: " The organisations at the date of this regulation or at any time thereafter describing themselves as ' republican clubs ' or any like organisation howsoever described ".'

McEldowney was charged with being a member of a Republican club contrary to Regulation 24A. The local magistrates dismissed the charge They stated:

' Bearing in mind the contents and purposes of " the Act " that the regulations thereunder are " Regulations for Peace and Order in Northern Ireland " and noting the words " or any like organisation howsoever described " in the said Statutory Rule and Order of 1967 and that no definition of the term " republican club " was shown to us, we came to the conclusion that the only reasonable interpretation and the true meaning of the portion of paragraph 1 of the said Statutory Rule and Order within the inverted commas in the context in which it has to be considered is " The organisations at the date of this regulation or at any time hereafter describing themselves as ' republican clubs ' – being clubs which have as their object the absorption of Northern Ireland in the Republic of Ireland the activities of whose members in seeking to further that object constitute a threat to peace and order in Northern Ireland – or any like organisation howsoever described." '

They noted that no evidence had been given that the club to which McEldowney belonged was a threat to peace, law and order and that witnesses for the prosecution had admitted that as far as the police were aware there was nothing seditious in the activities of the club or its members. It had therefore not been shown that the club was an unlawful association within Regulation 24A. The Court of Appeal in Northern Ireland reversed this decision and McEldowney appealed to the House of Lords. There he did not base his case on the grounds relied on by the magistrates but on the wider grounds that the 1967 amendment was *ultra vires*, that the 1967 Amendment was void for uncertainty and unreasonableness, and because it was not necessary for the peace, order and good government of Northern Ireland.

LORD GUEST ... There is no doubt that it is open to the courts to hold that a regulation made under a statute is ultra vires of the empowering Act. Such an argument was advanced in *Rex* v. *Halliday* [1917] A.C. 260, but unsuccessfully... Since that case I have been unable to discover any case in which a regulation made under an Act of Parliament in the form of a statutory instrument has ever been challenged... There are a multitude of statutes in which powers are given to Ministers by order to make regulations and indeed in some cases to alter the terms of the statute by regulation. In the absence of any such challenges of the validity of regulations made in virtue of statutory power it must be plain that the task of a subject who endeavours to challenge the validity of such a regulation is a heavy one...

In such a case as this the discretion entrusted to the Minister to make regulations for the preservation of peace and the maintenance of order in Northern Ireland is a very wide power and his discretion will not lightly be interfered with. The court will only interfere if the Minister is shown to have gone outside the four corners of the Act or has acted in bad faith (see Lord Greene M.R. in *Carltona Ltd.* v. *Works Commissioners* [1943] 2 All E.R. 560). Lord Radcliffe in

Attorney-General for Canada v. *Hallet & Carey Ltd.* [1952] A.C. 427, 450 said that the executive act, to be valid, must be ' capable of being related to one of the prescribed purposes ' of the empowering Act.

Approaching the present regulations with these principles in view, I turn to the argument for the appellant which was that as there was no evidence that there was anything sinister about the word ' republican ' which could be a threat to peace and order the regulation was ultra vires. My answer to that argument is that I do not know what significance the word ' republican ' has in Northern Ireland. It may well be that it will bear a different construction in Northern Ireland from what it might bear in another context. These, however, are matters for the Minister. It is important to observe that the inclusion of republican clubs eo nomine is an additional category to a list of organisations in regulation 24A, all of which, according to the Lord Chief Justice, were notoriously of a militant type and were unlawful organisations. Three of these organisations bear the name ' republican.' No challenge was made of the validity of regulation 24A as originally made which was admittedly intra vires. In these circumstances I am not able to say that a Minister acting in good faith – as it is conceded he did – under section 1 (3) of the Act was exceeding his powers in adding to the category of organisations deemed to be unlawful organisations described as ' republican clubs.' In my view, in the words of Lord Greene, the regulation was ' within the four corners of the Act ' or, in the words of Lord Radcliffe, was ' capable of being related to the powers ' conferred by the Act. In these circumstances the court cannot, in my view, interfere with the exercise of the Minister's discretion.

There is a long line of authorities dealing with executive orders made by Ministers under powers conferred on them by the Defence (General) Regulations 1939 of which *Carltona Ltd.* v. *Works Commissioners* [1943] 2 All E.R. 560 and *Point of Ayr Collieries Ltd.* v. *Lloyd-George* [1943] 2 All E.R. 546 are only examples. In the latter case the Minister was given power under the Defence (General) Regulations, 1939, ' if it appeared to ' him ' that in the interests of the public safety, the defence of the realm, or the efficient prosecution of the war ... it ' was ' necessary to take control ' of property. It was held that there was no jurisdiction to interfere with the exercise of an executive power within his delegated authority... The fact that in the cases above referred to there was a provision in the regulations to the effect that if it appeared to the Minister to be necessary for the specified purposes does not, in my view, distinguish these cases from the present. In the regulation in question the expediency is stated in the regulation and in the absence of any charge of bad faith expediency is presumed, provided that the exercise of the power is capable of being related to the specified purposes.

The final argument for the appellant related to the third category of organisations which it is said the regulation covered, namely, ' or any like organisation howsoever described '. It was submitted that this would cover any club whatever its name and whatever its objects and that such an exercise of the Minister's power was unreasonable, arbitrary and capricious. In my view this argument is not well founded. The regulation first of all embraces republican clubs eo nomine and they are caught by their very description. If they do not bear the name ' republican ', it would be a question of interpretation after evidence whether any particular club was covered by the words ' any like organisation howsoever described '. It is indeed not necessary for the purposes of this case where the organisation bore the name ' republican club ' to examine this question in any great detail. But my provisional view is that the regulation would cover any organisation having similar objects to those of a republican club or of any of the named organisations or of any organisation whose objects included the absorption of Northern Ireland in the Republic of Ireland.

Having regard to all these matters I cannot say that the class of ' like organisations ' is either ambiguous or arbitrary so as to invalidate the regulation. In my view this ground of attack also fails. . .

LORD HODSON . . . The proscription of present and future ' republican clubs ' including ' any like organisations howsoever described ' is said to be something outside the scope and meaning of the Act and so incapable of being related to the prescribed purposes of the Act. Accepting that the word ' republican ' is an innocent word and need not connote anything contrary to law, I cannot escape the conclusion that in its context, added to the list of admittedly unlawful organisations of a militant type, the word ' republican ' is capable of fitting the description of a club which in the opinion of the Minister should be proscribed as a subversive organisation of a type akin to those previously named in the list of admittedly unlawful organisations. The context in which the word is used shows the type of club which the Minister had in mind and there is no doubt that the mischief aimed at is an association which had subversive objects. On this matter, in my opinion, the court should not substitute its judgment for that of the Minister, on the ground that the banning of ' republican clubs ' is too remote. I agree that the use of the words ' any like organisation howsoever described ' lends some support to the contention that the regulation is vague and for that reason invalid, but on consideration I do not accept the argument based on vagueness. It is not difficult to see why the Minister, in order to avoid subterfuge, was not anxious to restrict himself to the description ' republican ' seeing that there might be similar clubs which he might seek to proscribe whatever they called themselves. If and when any case based on the words ' any like organisation ' arises it will have to be decided, but I do not, by reason of the use of those words, condemn the regulation as being too vague or uncertain to be supported. I would dismiss the appeal.

LORD PEARSON ... A republican club in Northern Ireland is presumably one whose members believe in a republican form of government, and wish to have such a form of government introduced into Northern Ireland, which would naturally be effected by Northern Ireland being severed from the United Kingdom and incorporated in the Irish Republic. Did such clubs in Northern Ireland at the time when the regulation was made have a tendency to become militant, causing disturbances and perhaps committing acts of violence, or did they not? I could not answer that question, not having the relevant information. But presumably the Minister of Home Affairs in Northern Ireland did at that time have relevant information and on the basis of that information did form the opinion that the continued existence of those clubs would be a threat to the preservation of the peace and maintenance of order. In saying that, I am applying the presumption of regularity. At any rate there is not in the provisions of the regulation any evidence that it was made otherwise than for the specified purposes. . .

There is one further argument against the validity of this regulation, and it is the most formidable one. It is that the regulation is too vague, because it includes the words ' or any like organisation howsoever described '. I have had doubts on this point, but in the end I think the argument against the validity of the regulation ought not to prevail. The Minister's intention evidently was (if I may use a convenient short phrase) to ban republican clubs. He had to exclude in advance two subterfuges which might defeat his intention. First, an existing republican club might be dissolved, and a new one created. The words ' or at any time thereafter ' would exclude that subterfuge as well as applying to new republican clubs generally. Secondly, a new club, having the characteristic object of a republican club, might be created with some other title such as ' New Constitution Group ' or ' Society for the alteration of the Constitution '. The words ' or any like organisation however described ' would exclude that subterfuge.

In construing this regulation one has to bear in mind that it authorises very drastic interference with freedom of association, freedom of speech and in some circumstances the liberty of the subject. Therefore it should be narrowly interpreted. Also it should if possible be so construed as to have sufficient certainty to be valid – ut res magis valeat quam pereat.

The Northern Ireland Parliament must have intended that somebody should decide whether or not the making of some proposed regulation would be conducive to the ' preservation of the peace and maintenance of order.' Obviously it must have been intended that the Minister of Home Affairs should decide that question. Who else could? He might consult other Ministers before making the decision, but it would be his decision. The courts cannot have been intended to decide such a question, because they do not have the necessary information, and the decision is in the sphere of politics, which is not their sphere.

When the Minister has made a regulation, and purports to have made it under section 1 (3) of the Act, the presumption of regularity (omnia praesumuntur rite esse acta) applies and the regulation is assumed prima facie to be intra vires. But if the validity of the regulation is challenged, and it is contended that the regulation was made otherwise than for the specified purposes, the courts will have to decide this issue, however difficult the task may be for them in some circumstances.

The ways in which an instrument may be shown to be ultra vires have been discussed in many cases, and I do not find it necessary to enter into such a discussion in this case. I shall assume that the regulation might be shown prima facie to be ultra vires (made otherwise than for the specified purposes) either by internal evidence from the provisions of the regulation itself – e.g., if it purported to render all chess clubs unlawful – or by external evidence of the factual situation existing at the time when the regulation was made...

In my opinion the proper construction of the regulation is that the organisations to be deemed unlawful are—

(i) any organisation describing itself as a ' republican club ', whatever its actual objects may be, and

(ii) any organisation which has the characteristic object of a republican club – namely, to introduce republican government into Northern Ireland – whatever its name may be.

I would dismiss the appeal.

LORD DIPLOCK (dissenting)... The regulations... are purported to be made under the powers conferred in paragraph (a) of [subsection (3) of section 1]... To be valid they must comply with the description contained in that paragraph of the kind of regulation which the Minister is empowered to make.

The relevant characteristic of regulations to which that description refers is the effect to be achieved by them. To be valid their effect must be to promote the preservation of the peace and the maintenance of order. I use the expression ' effect' rather than ' purpose', for purpose connotes an intention formed by the maker of the regulation to achieve a particular object, and substitutes for the objective test of the effect which the regulation is in fact likely to achieve, the subjective test of what effect the Minister himself whether rightly or mistakenly believes that the regulation is likely to achieve. It is to be observed that in contrast to the words of delegation of legislative powers used in modern statutes the description in section 1 (3) of the kind of regulations which the Minister is empowered to make contains no reference to the Minister's own opinion as to the necessity or expediency of the regulation for achieving the effect defined. He is not empowered to make such further provision as he may think or deem fit or necessary or expedient or advisable for the preservation of the peace or the maintenance of order.

It was words of delegation of this latter kind which were under consideration in the authorities relied upon by the majority of the Court of Appeal. The relevant characteristic of subordinate legislation so described in the words of delegation is the belief of the person empowered to make it that it will achieve the effect described. If he does so believe it is valid. It is only if he does not that it is ultra vires and void. . .

But where, as in the present case, the subordinate legislation which the Minister is empowered to make is described in the statute by reference to the effect to be achieved and not by reference to the Minister's own belief in the effect which it will achieve, the relevant inquiry which the court has to make if the subordinate legislation is challenged is not in my view the same. Omnia praesumuntur rite esse acta and the onus lies upon the party challenging the subordinate legislation to establish its invalidity. The Minister's belief in its necessity or expediency is cogent evidence of its validity but it is not conclusive, and the ultimate decision whether or not the likelihood that it will achieve the effect described in the statute is sufficient to bring it within the words of delegation and whether or not it will have any effects which may be prohibited by those words is one for the court itself to make upon the facts proved in evidence before it, or of such general public notoriety that the court may take judicial notice of them without further proof. . .

In *Rex* v. *Halliday* [1917] A.C. 260 the words of delegation in the Defence of the Realm Consolidation Act, 1914, were in a form comparable to that employed in the Special Powers Act. Your Lordships' House by a majority upheld the challenged regulation, but did so by forming its own opinion based upon matters of which it was entitled to take judicial notice that the regulation was reasonably likely to achieve the effect described in the words of delegation . . . In my view the words used by the Minister in the regulation are either too wide to fall within the description of the regulations which he is empowered to make under section 1 (3) of the Special Powers Act or are too vague and uncertain in their meaning to be enforceable.

I would allow this appeal.

CHAPTER IX

LOCAL GOVERNMENT

I. THE PURPOSE AND SCOPE OF LOCAL GOVERNMENT

The Royal Commission on Local Government in England, 1969

27. ... What is, and what ought to be, the purpose which local government serves; and, what at the present day, is its scope? ... [I]ts existing functions ... are of immense scope and significance, covering as they do responsibility for the police, for the fire service, for almost all education other than university, for the health and welfare of mothers and infants, the old and the sick, for children in need of care, for public health, for housing, for sport and recreation, for museums, art galleries and libraries, for the physical environment and the use of land, for highways, traffic and transport, and for many other matters. . . But in considering the structure which will best enable local authorities to discharge these responsibilities, we have kept in mind the whole potential of local government, given the existing functions as the substance of what it does. This substance we see as an all-round responsibility for the safety, health and well-being, both material, and cultural, of people in different localities, in so far as these objectives can be achieved by local action and local initiative, within a framework of national policies. . .

28. ... Local government is not to be seen merely as a provider of services. . . The importance of local government lies in the fact that it is the means by which people can provide services for themselves; can take an active and constructive part in the business of government; and can decide for themselves, within the limits of what national policies and local resources allow, what kind of services they want and what kind of environment they prefer. More than this, through their local representatives people throughout the country can, and in practice do, build up the policies which national government adopts – by focusing attention on local problems, by their various ideas of what government should seek to do, by local initiatives and local reactions. Many of the powers and responsibilities which local authorities now possess, many of the methods now in general use, owe their existence to pioneering by individual local authorities. . . Local government is the only representative political institution in the country outside Parliament; and being,

by its nature, in closer touch than Parliament or Ministers can be with local conditions, local needs, local opinions, it is an essential part of the fabric of government. Central government tends, by its nature, to be bureaucratic... It is only by the combination of local representative institutions with the central institutions of Parliament, Ministers and Departments, that a genuine national democracy can be sustained.

29. We recognise that some services are best provided by the national government; where the provision is or ought to be standardised throughout the country, or where the decisions involved can be taken only at the national level, or where a service requires an exceptional degree of technical expertise and allows little scope for local choice. Even here, however, there is a role for local government in assessing the impact of national policies on places and on people, and in bringing pressure to bear on the national government for changes in policy or in administration, or for particular decisions. And wherever local choice, local opinion and intimate knowledge of the effects of government action or inaction are important, a service is best provided by local government, however much it may have to be influenced by national decisions about the level of service to be provided and the order of priorities to be observed...

32. During this century, and notably since the end of the last war, there have been revolutionary changes in our society – in the means of organising it, in the dangers that threaten it, and in the nature of government. One change that has radically affected the position of local government has been the revolution in communications. This has not only altered the scale on which it is now rational to organise local government... It also means that it is now technically possible to direct far more of government activity from the centre than it was 60 or 70 years ago, and that, for all the clamour against increasing centralisation, there is constant pressure for this to be done. The centre has become more aware of local problems and more susceptible to local pressures, and so less willing to leave local problems to local solution. The individual can nowadays more easily make his grievances heard at the centre, and so is more prone, failing local satisfaction, to appeal to the centre for redress. If local government, however reorganised, is to achieve its full potential it will need a deliberate determination by Ministers and Parliament, supported by the press, radio and television, both to make local authorities responsible for any services which ought to be provided locally and to allow local authorities to settle local issues for themselves.

33. It has to be recognised, however, that the case for a stronger and more interventionist system of central government has increased... For one thing, a demand for greater equality of oppor-

tunity has emerged and been accepted. This entails action at the national level, both in insistence on minimum standards in certain local services and in increased financial assistance to poorer areas. For another, Britain is now more vulnerable than ever before both to economic forces and to military aggression. The relative safety in which the British developed their self-governing institutions and their individual liberties has sensibly diminished. In the relations between central and local government the most obvious example of unavoidably increased intervention by central government lies in the economic sphere. Since the end of the last war, central government has had to assume far more direct responsibility for the management of the economy. This involves, among other things, control over the rate of capital expenditure by public authorities. Public expenditure is, in any event, now running at a level unprecedented in time of peace. Local authorities are responsible for 31 per cent of it [1] – 15 per cent of the gross national product. In 1966–67, English and Welsh local authorities spent £3,621 million on current account and £1,412 million on capital account. Each year the figures rise. Of a total working force in England of 21,400,000 local authorities were employing, in 1968, over 1,360,000 people full-time and nearly 587,000 part-time.[2] Measures designed to protect the economy are bound to have local government in mind and sometimes to be directly aimed at it.

34. The immediate effect on local government of the control exercised by central government over its capital expenditure is severely to limit the freedom of local authorities to determine the rate at which they will develop their various services. . .

35. Local government is caught between two conflicting forces: national insistence on a high level of services and national restriction of the level of capital expenditure. Inevitably this raises the question what scope there is for independent local government.

36. The close involvement of the national government in the affairs of local government is, today, inescapable. We believe, however, that this only increases the need for strong and independent-minded local authorities, speaking with a voice to which the national government must listen, capable of injecting their ideas into national policies, competent to implement the policies in whatever way is best suited to local conditions, and without the need for any detailed supervision. . . [C]entral government has become increasingly dependent on local authorities. Ministers cannot secure the results they want . . . except by means of fully competent authorities, able both to play their part, from their local knowledge, in the development of policies, and to exercise an independent judgment in deciding how the policies can

---

[1] Fin. Statement 1968–9, H.M.S.O., 1968.
[2] *Employment and Productivity Gazette*, October 1968, H.M.S.O.

best be applied, and social needs can best be met, in their particular conditions. . .

[Report of the Royal Commission on Local Government in England, 1966–9. Cmnd. 4040 (June 1969)]

II. THE STATUS OF LOCAL AUTHORITIES

The Committee on the Management of Local Government, 1967

250. . . . Although local authorities are elected bodies they have to operate within the framework of the constitution in which sovereignty lies in Parliament. . .

252. Local authorities occupy a wide range of subsidiary or dependent positions in relation to Parliament and the central government. Even where a local authority has legal independence of action, it owes it to statute, and in any case is likely to be dependent on the central government for finance. . .

256. Local authorities are dependent on Parliament for the basic legal powers to tax, that is to raise money by the rates, and to interfere with individual and public rights. . . [T]heir freedom is limited by the doctrine of *ultra vires*, in that they must be able to point to statutory sanction, in general enabling legislation, in specific legislation or in private acts for every action taken by them. It is not sufficient that a course of action should seem to a local authority to be in the public interest; it cannot embark on it without the authority of an Act of Parliament. . .

257. . . . In the past local authorities enjoyed considerable freedom in the exercise of powers conferred or of obligations imposed on them; more recently when powers have been given to local authorities, at the same time new responsibilities have also been given to ministers. The autonomy of local authorities has thus been sensibly diminished.

258. The powers conferred on ministers vary in the extent to which they confine those of local authorities. On the one hand a minister may have powers of guidance, supervision or even approval. . . On the other hand, a minister may be statutorily responsible for a service with local authorities as his instruments. . .

259. Local authorities do not deal with a single department of state, and the attitude of central government varies not only with the relevant legislation, but also according to the practices of the department and the nature of the service. . .

261. Apart from the statutory responsibilities of ministers and apart from their guiding, supervisory and approving functions laid down in legislation, there are many other methods by which the central government influences and controls the work of local authorities. Circulars are issued to obtain information, to explain

new legislation, to introduce departmental publications and to give policy or technical guidance to local authorities. Ministers have appellate and confirmatory functions in the approval of general plans, proposals and schemes relating to certain services and for compulsory purchase and slum clearance orders. Ministers act in quasi-judicial capacity in, for example, disputes between local education authorities and governors of schools and hear appeals by parents against the refusal of local education authorities to amend or revoke a school attendance order. There are government inspectors for the children, fire and police services and for schools. Their duties are both inspectorial and advisory. Other inspectors conduct enquiries into compulsory purchase and slum clearance orders, and into development plans and planning appeals. Under legislation ministers have powers to act in default of a local authority as for instance in the case of libraries, housing and planning...

[Report of the Committee on the Management of Local Government, vol. I, ch. 4, p. 69]

Cp. the following passages from the Report of the Royal Commission on Local Government in Greater London, 1957–60 [Cmnd. 1164]:

' 708. Already central government has large powers of control over local government. The power to give or withhold sanction to loans for the purpose of financing capital works vitally affects not only the timing of work by local authorities but also the policy they shall pursue. The power to make or withhold grants and subsidies works in the same direction. Where local authorities have permissive powers, there are numerous ways in which central government can and does make its influence felt. Where power is accompanied by duties, it often happens that a Minister, through his powers to call for and approve some scheme of operation, can and does control to some considerable extent the way in which the local authority discharges its functions. Local authorities are subjected to a stream of circulars from government departments, advising, exhorting, cajoling, and occasionally directing them as to how they should conduct their business...

709. Intervention by central government appears to be inevitable also in three other ways. First, no local authority (with a few exceptions) has power to spend its ratepayers' money except for purposes within its statutory powers. These powers are conferred by Parliament, or by some Minister acting under parliamentary powers. Thus there are arrangements for auditing. Here Parliament has acted to protect the ratepayer against expenditure *ultra vires* by local authorities. Secondly, in various branches of local authority work specific powers for the protection of the citizen against possible oppression are given to central government. For example, there is a right of appeal from a decision in town and country planning which a citizen may consider unjust or injurious to him; and orders for the compulsory acquisition of land require confirmation... Thirdly, Ministers are often given powers to approve or disapprove

actions of local authorities in order to ensure that the total effect of the actions of the local authorities concerned may be in accordance with national policy. It is, no doubt, for this reason for example that local authorities' development plans and their revision need ministerial approval.'

III. THE SIZE OF UNITS

The Royal Commission on Local Government in England, 1969

272. ... We do not believe that democratic control of services calls necessarily for a small functional unit...

273. When the size of an authority goes beyond a certain point, however, the more difficult becomes the problem of reconciling the management of increasingly complicated services by able and powerful officials with democratic control by the elected representatives. For democratic control to be a reality, the size of the unit must be such that the elected representatives can comprehend the problems of the area, determining priorities and taking decisions on policy in full understanding of the issues at stake.

274. It is also essential that they should maintain contact with their constituents. We agree with the Committee on Management in Local Government that Councils should not be too big if they are to manage their business with efficiency and establish sound relations between council members and their officers (the committee suggested that 75 members should be the maximum). But if the size of councils must ... be limited, then the larger the authority's area, the greater will be the number of citizens each councillor represents...

275. Moreover, the bigger the unit, the more doubtful it becomes whether the individual citizen can have a real sense of belonging to it... People should be able to feel that they are included in a particular unit for purposes of government because they share a common interest with other inhabitants in the efficient administration of the public services provided. But when an authority is very large there is less chance that they will be willing to regard it as the only authority that ought to provide all their local government services. The distance between the people and their authority, therefore, must not be too great. This is particularly important for the personal services.

276. There can be no firm rule about the maximum size of an authority. But we concluded that the range of population, from about 250,000 to not much above 1,000,000, which we considered most suitable on functional and organisational grounds for authorities administering all local government services, was also appropriate on democratic grounds. Within this range the size of each particular unit should be determined by reference to all the local circumstances – the social, economic and geographic facts, the areas most appropriate for organising services, the accessibility of a suitable headquarters,

the existing pattern of local government and other relevant considerations...

[Report of the Royal Commission on Local Government, 1966–9. Cmnd. 4040].

IV. LOCAL AUTHORITIES AND THE COURTS

ASSOCIATED PROVINCIAL PICTURE HOUSES, LTD. v. *WEDNESBURY CORPORATION* [1948] 1 K.B. 223

Court of Appeal

The Sunday Entertainments Act, 1932, provided:

' 1. (1) The authority having power, in any area to which this section extends, to grant licences under the Cinematograph Act, 1909, may, notwithstanding anything in any enactment relating to Sunday observance, allow places in that area licensed under the said Act to be opened and used on Sundays for the purpose of cinematograph entertainments, subject to such conditions as the authority think fit to impose...'

In granting a licence, the defendants imposed a condition that no children under the age of fifteen were to be admitted. The plaintiffs asked the court for a declaration that the condition was *ultra vires*.

LORD GREENE M.R. ... Mr Gallop, for the plaintiffs, argued that it was not competent for the Wednesbury Corporation to impose any such condition and he said that if they were entitled to impose a condition prohibiting the admission of children, they should at least have limited it to cases where the children were not accompanied by their parents or a guardian or some adult. His argument was that the imposition of that condition was unreasonable and that in consequence it was ultra vires the corporation. The plaintiffs' contention is based, in my opinion, on a misconception as to the effect of this Act in granting this discretionary power to local authorities. The courts must always, I think, remember this: first, we are dealing with not a judicial act, but an executive act; secondly, the conditions which, under the exercise of that executive act, may be imposed are in terms, so far as language goes, put within the discretion of the local authority without limitation. Thirdly, the statute provides no appeal from the decision of the local authority.

What, then, is the power of the courts? They can only interfere with an act of executive authority if it be shown that the authority has contravened the law. It is for those who assert that the local authority has contravened the law to establish that proposition. On the face of it, a condition of the kind imposed in this case is perfectly lawful. It is not to be assumed prima facie that responsible bodies like the local authority in this case will exceed their powers; but the court, whenever it is alleged that the local authority have contravened the law, must not substitute itself for that authority. It is only concerned with seeing whether or not the proposition is made good. When an executive discretion is entrusted by Parliament to a body such as the local authority in this case, what appears to be an exercise of that discretion can only be challenged in the courts in a strictly limited class of case. As I have said, it must always be remembered that the court is not a court of appeal. When discretion of this kind is granted the law recognizes certain principles upon which that discretion must be exercised, but within the four corners of those principles the discretion, in my opinion, is an absolute one and cannot be questioned in any court of law. What then are those principles? They are well understood. They are principles which the court looks to in considering any question of discretion of this kind. The exercise of such a discretion must be a real exercise of the discretion. If, in the statute conferring the discretion, there are to be found expressly or by implication matters which the authority exercising the discretion ought to have regard to, then in exercising the discretion it must have regard to those matters. Conversely, if the nature of the subject-matter and the general interpretation of the Act make it clear that certain matters would not be germane to the matter in question, the authority must disregard those irrelevant collateral matters. There have been in the cases expressions used relating to the sort of things that authorities must not do, not merely in cases under the Cinematograph Act but, generally speaking, under other cases where the powers of local authorities came to be considered. I am not sure myself whether the permissible grounds of attack cannot be defined under a single head. It has been perhaps a little bit confusing to find a series of grounds set out. Bad faith, dishonesty – those of course, stand by themselves – unreasonableness, attention given to extraneous circumstances, disregard of public policy and things like that have all been referred to, according to the facts of individual cases, as being matters which are relevant to the question. If they cannot all be confined under one head, they at any rate, I think, overlap to a very great extent. For instance, we have heard in this case a great deal about the meaning of the word ' unreasonable '.

It is true the discretion must be exercised reasonably. Now what does that mean? Lawyers familiar with the phraseology commonly used in relation to exercise of statutory discretions often use the word ' unreasonable ' in a rather comprehensive sense. It has frequently been used and is frequently used as a general description of the things that must not be done. For instance, a person entrusted with a discretion must, so to speak, direct himself properly in law. He must call his own attention to the matters which he is bound to consider. He must exclude from his consideration matters which are irrelevant to what he has to consider. If he does not obey those rules, he may truly be said, and often is said, to be acting ' unreasonably '. Similarly, there may be something so absurd that no sensible person could ever dream that it lay within the powers of the authority. Warrington L.J. in *Short* v. *Poole Corporation*[3] gave the example of the red-haired teacher, dismissed because she had red hair. That is unreasonable in one sense. In another sense it is taking into consideration extraneous matters. It is so unreasonable that it might almost be described as being done in bad faith; and, in fact, all these things run into one another.

In the present case, it is said by Mr Gallop that the authority acted unreasonably in imposing this condition. It appears to me quite clear that the matter dealt with by this condition was a matter which a reasonable authority would be justified in considering when they were making up their minds what condition should be attached to the grant of this licence. Nobody, at this time of day, could say that the well-being and the physical and moral health of children is not a matter which a local authority, in exercising their powers, can properly have in mind when those questions are germane to what they have to consider. Here Mr Gallop did not, I think, suggest that the council were directing their mind to a purely extraneous and irrelevant matter, but he based his argument on the word ' unreasonable ', which he treated as an independent ground for attacking the decision of the authority; but once it is conceded, as it must be conceded in this case, that the particular subject-matter dealt with by this condition was one which it was competent for the authority to consider, there, in my opinion, is an end of the case. Once that is granted, Mr Gallop is bound to say that the decision of the authority is wrong because it is unreasonable, and in saying that he is really saying that the ultimate arbiter of what is and is not reasonable is the court and not the local authority. It is just there, it seems to me, that the argument breaks down. It is clear that the local authority are entrusted by Parliament with the decision on a matter which the knowledge and experience of that authority can best be trusted to deal with. The subject-matter with which the condition deals is one relevant for its consideration. They have considered it and come to a decision upon it. It is true to say that, if a decision on a competent matter is so unreasonable that no reasonable authority could ever have come to it, then the courts can interfere. That, I think, is quite right; but to prove a case of that kind would require something overwhelming, and, in this case, the facts do not come anywhere near anything of that kind. I think Mr

[3] [1926] Ch. 66, 90, 91.

Gallop in the end agreed that his proposition that the decision of the local authority can be upset if it is proved to be unreasonable, really meant that it must be proved to be unreasonable in the sense that the court considers it to be a decision that no reasonable body could have come to. It is not what the court considers unreasonable, a different thing altogether. If it is what the court considers unreasonable, the court may very well have different views to that of a local authority on matters of high public policy of this kind. Some courts might think that no children ought to be admitted on Sundays at all, some courts might think the reverse, and all over the country I have no doubt on a thing of that sort honest and sincere people hold different views. The effect of the legislation is not to set up the court as an arbiter of the correctness of one view over another. It is the local authority that are set in that position and, provided they act, as they have acted, within the four corners of their jurisdiction, this court, in my opinion, cannot interfere.

... The appeal must be dismissed with costs.

SOMERVELL L.J. and SINGLETON J. concurred. *Appeal dismissed*

ROBERTS v. *HOPWOOD* [1925] A.C. 578

House of Lords

Under s. 62 of the Metropolis Management Act, 1855, the Poplar Borough Council was authorised to employ such servants as might be necessary and to allow them 'such ... wages as the [Council] may think fit '. In the exercise of this power the Council fixed the minimum wage for its lowest grade of employees, whether men or women, at £4 per week. This was the same rate that it had fixed for the previous year even though the cost of living had fallen from 176 per cent to 82 per cent above the pre-war level. In its view this was the minimum wage that a local authority ought, as a model employer, to pay its employees, and it had stated at the last election that this would be its policy if it were elected. The accounts of the Council were subject to audit by the District Auditor who was required by s. 247 (7) of the Public Health Act, 1875, to disallow any item contrary to law and to surcharge it on the person making or authorising the payment. He decided that the wages were so excessive as to be illegal and were not wages but gifts. Using the pre-war wages paid by the Council as a starting point he added an increase proportionate to the increase in the cost of living and a further £1 by way of margin and surcharged the excess, amounting to £5000, on the councillors responsible.[4]

S. 247 (8) of the Public Health Act provided that councillors aggrieved

---

[4] This was not the first time that Poplar Borough Council had been in trouble with the courts. In 1921 they had refused to pay Poplar's rate contribution to the London County Council and the Metropolitan Asylums

by an auditor's decision could apply by way of certiorari to the Divisional Court. This they did. The Divisional Court (Lord Hewart C.J., Sankey and Salter JJ.) upheld the auditor. Their decision was reversed by the Court of Appeal (Scrutton and Atkin L.JJ., Bankes L.J. dissenting).

LORD SUMNER. . . . I can find nothing in the Acts empowering bodies, to which the Metropolis Management Act, 1855, applies, which authorizes them to be guided by their personal opinions on political, economic or social questions in administering the funds which they derive from levying rates . . . To my mind a council acts for a collateral purpose, if it fixes by standards of its own on social grounds a minimum wage for all adults, and is not in so doing acting for the benefit of the whole community.

Much was said at the Bar about the wide discretion conferred by the Local Government Acts on local authorities. In a sense this is true, but the meaning of the term needs careful examination. What has been said in cases, which lie outside the provisions as to audit altogether, is not necessarily applicable to matters, which are concerned with the expenditure of public money. There are many matters, which the Courts are indisposed to question. Though they are the ultimate judges of what is lawful and what is unlawful to borough councils, they often accept the decisions of the local authority simply because they are themselves ill-equipped to weigh the merits of one solution of a practical question as against another. This, however, is not a recognition of the absolute character of the

---

Board, on the ground that the assessments imposed a far greater burden on the poorer boroughs than was proper, and had refused to obey an order of *mandamus* addressed to them, ordering them to pay. On the day that their refusal was to be considered by the court, thirty of the fifty councillors assembled outside the Town Hall and marched to court accompanied by an official carrying the mace and headed by a banner bearing the words ' Poplar Borough Council march to the High Court, and possibly to prison, to secure equalisation of rates for the borough '. The court ordered them to levy the rates within 14 days or go to prison. The Lord Chief Justice on this occasion had noted: ' The Court was much impressed by the sincerity and honesty of those men . . . Their motives were amiable, and perhaps laudable. Their mistake lay in looking through a microscope at the distress around them in Poplar, forgetting that they were part of a community of five million people, and that such conduct as theirs ended in complete anarchy. Mr Lansbury admitted that this action was of the nature of propaganda. He (his Lordship) was sorry that this course had been taken, for the question of equalization of rates was a political one of great difficulty, and that Court was not the place to discuss it. They had simply to consider whether the council had done its duty; they had admitted that they had consciously failed to do it. The result must be that these writs must go and lie in the office for 14 days, and if in the meantime the rate was not levied these persons must go to prison, with the exception of the minority who had committed no contempt ' (*The Times*, 30 July 1921).

local authority's discretion, but of the limits within which it is practicable to question it. There is nothing about a borough council that corresponds to autonomy. It has great responsibilities, but the limits of its powers and of its independence are such as the law, mostly statutory, may have laid down, and there is no presumption against the accountability of the authority. Everything depends on the construction of the sections applicable. In the present case, I think that the auditor was entitled to inquire into all the items of expenditure in question, to ask whether in incurring them the council had been guided by aims and objects not open to them or had disregarded considerations by which they should have been guided, and to the extent to which they had in consequence exceeded a reasonable expenditure, it was his duty to disallow the items.

The material facts are as follows: The year under review is 1921–22, and in that year both men and women in Grade A, which, it seems, is the lowest grade, received a wage of £4 a week. There are two tests by which these payments can be criticised. One is the rise or fall in the cost of living, according to the index figures published monthly by the Ministry of Labour in the Labour Gazette, the other is the publication every three months of the rates of wages fixed for various grades of work-people by the Joint Industrial Council for local authorities' employees in the London district. Neither has any binding authority over the Poplar Council, and no doubt exception can be taken to both. The first is based on careful and extensive statistical inquiries, and has been widely relied on for many years past. The second represents what numbers of employers and employees have been content to pay and to take, following the agreed opinion of representatives on both sides assembled for the purpose. The respondents have not criticised any of these figures in detail, or pointed out any errors in them, or put forward any preferable materials. They say simply that they did not think fit to adopt them . . .

Their reason the respondents give as follows: ' The council did not and does not take the view that wages paid should be exclusively related to the cost of living. They have from time to time carefully considered the question of the wages and are of the opinion as a matter of policy that a public authority should be a model employer and that a minimum rate of £4 is the least wage which ought to be paid to an adult having regard to the efficiency of their workpeople, the duty of a public authority both to the ratepayers and to its employees, the purchasing power of the wages and other considerations which are relevant to their decision as to wages.'

From this carefully considered answer I think it is plain that the respondents have deliberately decided not to be guided by ordinary economic (and economical) considerations. The first sentence above quoted means that, when the cost of living passes £4 a week, the rate of wages paid will follow it upwards, but, however it may fall, the £4 rate will be stabilised and will stand. There is nothing definite about the statement that a public authority should be a model employer. To whom is it to be a model? If to other public authorities, the council's resolution is vox clamantis in deserto, for other authorities, with rare exceptions, turn a deaf ear to it. If to other private employers, the example of the council is necessarily thrown away on concerns, which must make both ends meet and have not the ratepayers' purse to draw on. Whatever ' having regard to the efficiency of their workpeople ' may mean, it is not proved or suggested that the workpeople employed in Poplar are in any way exceptional in their powers of work, or that the cost of maintaining a workman's efficiency is higher in Poplar than elsewhere. The one definite thing is that the respondents contend that no adult employee should in any circumstances have less than £4 a week, whether young or old, male or female, married or single, skilled or unskilled. It is not shown that the women's work is the same as, or is comparable with, the men's, or that the women inter se or the men inter se are engaged in equivalent tasks. I express no opinion as to the merits of this view, that the dignity of adult labour requires at least a £4 wage, nor has the honesty of those who entertain it been questioned, but I think it is plain that such a course, whether it be ideal or social or political or all three, forms no part of the conduct, as ordinarily understood, of such practical enterprises as borough councils are by statute authorized to engage in. No authority and no statutory provision was cited to your Lordships, which enables a borough council to give practical effect, at the ratepayers' expense, to such an abstract resolution, nor am I for my own part aware of any. I am, therefore, of opinion that on their own showing the respondents have exercised such discretion as the Metropolis Management Act gives to the council in the matter of wages upon principles which are not open to the council, and for objects which are beyond their powers. Their exercise of those powers was examinable by the auditor, and on the above grounds the excess expenditure was liable to be disallowed by him as contrary to law. . .

LORD ATKINSON. . . . In paragraph 9 of Mr Scurr's affidavit he . . . said that they [i.e. the council] . . . were of opinion that a public authority should be a model employer, and that a minimum rate of £4 per week (i.e., £208 per annum) is the least wage which ought to be paid to an adult. . . This . . . might possibly be admirably philanthropic if the funds of the council at the time they were thus administered belonged to the existing members of that body. These members would then be generous at their own expense. . . The indulgence of philanthropic enthusiasm at the expense of persons other than the philanthropists is an entirely different thing from the indulgence of it at the expense of the philanthropists themselves. . . A body charged with the administration for definite purposes of funds contributed in whole or in part by persons other than the members of that body, owes, in my view, a duty to those latter persons to conduct that administration in a fairly businesslike manner with reasonable care, skill and caution, and with a due and alert regard to the interest of those contributors who are not members of the body. Towards these latter persons the body stands somewhat in the position of trustees or managers of the property of others. This duty is, I think, a legal duty, as well as a moral one. . .[5]

At the meeting on May 31, 1923, at which a large number of rate-payers attended and objected to the allowance of such large sums for wages, it was apparently put forward that the council were only responsible to their constituents; that the scale of wages had been before the electors at the election in the previous November, and also at two recent bye-elections, and had been approved of by them; that the council should do their duty towards these electors, and not their duty towards the large ratepayers who lived outside the district and were not ' in ' (i.e., parties to, I presume) this matter at all. A gentleman named L. W. Key, one of the applicants in the present suit, appears from the auditor's affidavit to have put the council's case pithily and plainly in the following few words : ' We do not say we have no discretion, but we say a mandate from the electorate was not to be despised.' These observations do not appear to have been disapproved of by any of the members of the council present. . . It was strongly pressed in argument that the auditor believed the council acted bona fide; but what in this connection do the words ' bona fide ' mean? Do they mean, as apparently this gentleman thought, that no matter how excessive or illegal their scale of wages might be, they were bound to put it into force because their constituents gave them a mandate so to do, or again, do the words mean that as the payment of wages was

---

[5] Cp. the statement of Jenkins L.J. in *Prescott* v. *Birmingham Corporation* [1955] 1 Ch. 210, where Birmingham Corporation was proposing to subsidise a scheme for free travel for old age pensioners from the rates: ' Local authorities are not, of course, trustees for their ratepayers, but they do, we think owe an analogous fiduciary duty to their ratepayers in relation to the application of funds contributed by the latter. Thus local authorities running an omnibus undertaking at the risk of their ratepayers, in the sense that any deficiencies must be met by an addition to the rates, are not, in our view, entitled, merely on the strength of a general power, to charge different fares to different passengers or classes of passengers, to make a gift to a particular class of persons of rights of free travel on their vehicles, simply because the local authority concerned are of opinion that the favoured class of person, ought on benevolent or philanthropic grounds, to be accorded that benefit '

a subject with which they had legally power to deal, the amount of their funds which they devoted to that purpose was their own concern which no auditor had jurisdiction to revise, or in reference to which he could surcharge anything? The whole system of audit to which the Legislature has subjected every municipal corporation or council is a most emphatic protest against such opinions as these...

... [A]s wages are remuneration for services, the words ' think fit ' must, I think, be construed to mean ' as the employer shall think fitting and proper ' for the services rendered. It cannot, in my view, mean that the employer, especially an employer dealing with moneys not entirely his own, may pay to his employee wages of any amount he pleases. Still less does it mean that he can pay gratuities or gifts to his employees disguised under the name of wages... What is a reasonable wage at any time must depend, of course, on the circumstances which then exist in the labour market. I do not say there must be any cheeseparing or that the datum line, as I have called it, must never be exceeded to any extent, or that employees may not be generously treated. But it does not appear to me that there is any rational proportion between the rates of wages at which the labour of these women is paid and the rate at which they would be reasonably remunerated for their services to the council...

I think the appeal suceeds.

LORD BUCKMASTER, LORD WRENBURY and LORD CARSON delivered concurring judgments.

Order of the Court of Appeal reversed and order of the King's Bench Division restored

SAGNATA LTD. v. NORWICH CORPORATION
[1971] 2 Q.B. 614

Court of Appeal

The Betting, Gaming and Lotteries Act 1963 provided that licences to provide amusements with prizes were to be ' at the discretion of the local authority ' but that in the case of a refusal an applicant could appeal to the court of Quarter Sessions. Having found a site which was approved for the purpose by the Town Planning Committee the applicants had their application for a licence refused by the Fire and Licensing Committee of the Council. The grounds of the refusal were (a) the use of these premises as an amusement place would be likely to have undesirable effects on the young people expected to frequent them and (b) that the making available of gaming facilities in Norwich which could be used by children was something which the committee were not prepared to permit. In coming to their decision the committee had taken into account the prior decision of the General Purposes Committee of the Council that there should be no amusement arcades in Norwich.

The applicants appealed to Quarter Sessions and the Recorder granted them permission. The Council appealed to the Court of Appeal.

PHILLIMORE L.J. No doubt, speaking broadly, local decisions are best taken by local people, but if the local authority are to be free from any form of check, justice and fair dealing can suffer... Now there is no need for authority for the proposition that a council and its committees are entitled to agree on a policy provided always that they do not impose it inflexibly. In this case, however, we were told that the chairman of the committee – a former Mayor of Norwich – gave evidence before the recorder to the effect that they had rejected the application solely on the basis of the policy decision taken by the General Purposes Committee. The recorder giving judgment before the Gaming Act, 1968, had come into force, said:

'... In my view (and Mr Marriage virtually conceded this), the licensing committee have decided that they will not grant a permit for any amusement place with prizes in the City of Norwich and the reasons they gave for this refusal would apply to any application.'

And after referring to the *Torquay* case [1951] 2 K.B. 784 he recited the words of Lord Goddard C.J., at p. 790, as follows:

' " They must, of course, apply their minds properly to the circumstances of each particular case," which again shows that there is nothing wrong in justices laying down a line of policy for themselves, provided that they consider whether a particular case before them calls for the application of that policy.'

He went on to say:

' I am forced to the conclusion that in this case, where the application met with all the ordinary requirements as to suitability of site, premises and management, the general policy must have been applied. In other words, no application to the local authority, however suitable, would succeed.'

In other words the council had *not* exercised any form of discretion. They had simply dismissed this application after going through the necessary motions without regard to its individual merits or demerits. I take this to be a finding of fact with which this court is in no position to interfere.

Incidentally, I cannot see that the recorder could avoid this decision. Apparently no evidence was called to support either ground (a) or ground (b). Nobody came forward to say that this sort of arcade had resulted in disastrous damage to the morality of the young in Great Yarmouth or any other seaside place or was likely to prove particularly harmful to the young of Norwich. Indeed, as I think, the

Act of 1964 by section 3 tends to suggest that in regard to premises such as this it is wrong to refuse a licence on the ground that some particular class such as young persons may be injuriously affected.

I am bound to say that I entirely agree with the judgment of Lord Parker C.J. with which the other members of the Divisional Court agreed. I think that the recorder was clearly right and that his judgment should not be disturbed. This is a case where he was satisfied that the council's committee had failed to keep an open mind and had applied their policy without regard to the facts of the individual case.

I must, however, turn for a moment to the question of the appeal to quarter sessions. What sort of appeal is it? Is the recorder to look at the reasons of the committee and to give effect to them *unless* they are so lacking in grammar or so obviously wrong on the face of them that certiorari would lie?

The position seems to me to be so well established that it is not susceptible of legal subtlety. The hearing of an appeal at quarter sessions is a rehearing. It cannot be less so if the decision from which the appeal is brought is an administrative decision by the committee of a local authority which heard no evidence, before which no one took an oath, or was cross-examined. . .

What is the recorder to do? Is he to read the reasons given by the licensing committee and to say: ' Well, they sound very sensible and after all they are the local authority, so I must support them, or is he to listen to the appellant who says that he has not had justice and would like to call evidence to prove it? . . . I think the recorder must hear evidence . . . I think he must give effect to that evidence and reach what he regards as a just conclusion. Of course, he will bear in mind the views expressed by the local authority and will be slow to disagree; but if he is satisfied, as he was in this case, that they regarded themselves as tied hand and foot by a policy decision without liberty to look at the facts of the particular case, I should hope that he would do as the recorder did in this case and allow the appeal of the citizen. . .

EDMUND DAVIES L.J. delivered a concurring judgment.

LORD DENNING M.R. [dissenting]. . . . In this case the local authority formed the opinion that it was socially undesirable to have amusement arcades in Norwich. That is why they laid down their general policy. But the recorder put their views on one side. He was not prepared, he said, to act on ' unproved general principles of social undesirability and potential danger to young people,' but wanted evidence on it.

I think that, in so holding, the recorder misdirected himself in law.

Seeing that Parliament has entrusted the discretion to the local authority, it must intend then that their views should carry great weight. They are elected by the people to do all things proper to be done for the good administration of their city. They know their locality. They know its needs. They respond to the feelings of the citizens. If they think that an amusement arcade is socially undesirable, they are entitled to say so. They do not require evidence for the purpose. It is a matter of opinion on which their views are worth as much as those of any other person: and, indeed, worth more than those of a stranger. In any case, their views coincide with those of the Churches' Committee on Gambling: and that goes a long way. Their views should not be pushed on one side by the courts as worth nothing. Just as with their power to make by-laws, so also with their power to grant licences for amusement arcades. Their decision ' ought to be supported if possible ': see *Kruse* v. *Johnson* [1898] 2 Q.B. 91, 99, *per* Lord Russell C.J. In rejecting their views, the recorder was in error.

My brethren disagree. Together with the recorder, and all the other judges, they hold that the views of the citizens of Norwich must be overruled. They must grant the freedom of their city to this amusement arcade, even though they believe it to be socially undesirable. I do not think this is right. This, in my opinion, is a matter for local self-government. Parliament intentionally made this a matter for the discretion of the local authority and there is no good reason for overruling their decision.

REGINA v. BARNET AND CAMDEN RENT TRIBUNAL, Ex Parte FREY INVESTMENTS LTD. [1972] 2 Q.B. 342

Court of Appeal

The Rent Act, 1968, provided: ' 72 (1) Either the lessor or the lessee under a Part VI contract or the local authority may refer the contract to the rent tribunal for the district in question.' In this case the local authority had made 22 references of contracts of tenants of the appellants to the local tribunal. The appellants applied to the court for an order of prohibition to prevent the tribunal hearing the cases on the grounds that the references were invalid as they had been motivated by malice and on improper considerations.

SALMON L.J. . . .

I consider it of the utmost importance to uphold the right, and indeed the duty, of the courts to ensure that powers shall not be exercised unlawfully which have been conferred on a local authority or the executive, or indeed anyone else, when the exercise of such powers affects the basic rights of an individual. The court should be alert to see that such powers conferred by statute are not exceeded or abused, and I hope that nothing that I say in this judgment will be construed as in any way casting doubt upon the principle which I have just enunciated.

Mr Bernstein, in the course of his most interesting argument, has referred us to a number of authorities on this topic and he cites in particular the judgment of Lord Greene M.R. in *Associated Provincial Picture Houses Ltd.* v. *Wednesbury Corporation* [1948] 1 K.B. 223. The passage upon which he relies sums up Lord Greene M.R.'s opinion, at p. 233 :

' The court is entitled to investigate the action of the local authority with a view to seeing whether they have taken into account matters which they ought not to take into account, or, conversely, have refused to take into account or neglected to take into account matters which they ought to take into account. Once that question is answered in favour of the local authority, it may be still possible to say that, although the local authority have kept within the four corners of the matters which they ought to consider, they have nevertheless come to a conclusion so unreasonable that no reasonable authority could ever come to it . . .'

There have been a number of other cases to which we have been referred such as *Hanks* v. *Minister of Housing and Local Government* [1963] 1 Q.B. 999 and *Hall & Co. Ltd.* v. *Shoreham-by-Sea Urban District Council* [1964] 1 W.L.R. 240. Cases such as these in which a licence is being sought for the purpose of enabling the applicant to carry on his business and earn his living, or in which town planning permission is sought, or a compulsory purchase order is being challenged, vitally affect the basic rights of the persons concerned and seem to me to differ very substantially from the case which we are now considering. In a case such as the present, no decision is taken by the authority invested with a power which vitally affects the basic rights of the individual. The only decision taken by the local authority is to refer the matter to the rent tribunal so that the tribunal may consider whether or not the rent is too high. The party concerned (that is to say, the landlords) have every opportunity of appearing before the tribunal, and it is the decision of that tribunal which affects their basic rights.

For my part I doubt whether the principle laid down by Lord Greene M.R. applies, or was intended to apply, to cases of the present kind. For example, I think it would be difficult to suppose that if the local authorities referred the matter to the rent tribunal without having considered some material matter, that would necessarily vitiate the reference. I say that particularly because under the Rent Act 1968 the local authority, in contradistinction to the tribunal, have no powers to demand information in relation to the tenancy agreement and necessarily may be in a position where all the material facts cannot be known to them. It is, of course, conceded that the local authority must act bona fide. It is not here suggested that there has been any mala fides on the part of the local authority. Moreover, I consider that it is implicit in the Rent Act 1968 that when the local authority make a reference to the tribunal they shall not act frivolously or vexatiously. In my judgment, unless the landlords can show either mala fides or that the local authority acted frivolously or vexatiously it is impossible to say that the local authority in referring the matter to the rent tribunal was acting ultra vires . . .

The object of the legislature in giving the local authority the power to refer the tenancy agreements to the rent tribunal was clearly conferred so as to take care of cases in which tenants, perhaps of working class dwellings, were not in a position to look after themselves, or were afraid of making a reference to the tribunal. There are many districts – and Camden is apparently one – where there is a great shortage of reasonably priced working class dwellings, and a tenant who applied to the tribunal might well consider that if he offended the landlord by so doing he might find himself in the street or compelled to go and live in a district which was inconvenient for his purposes.

In Camden there exists a body which calls itself Camden Housing Action. . . In the summer of 1970 they were urging the local authority to exercise their powers in relation to property belonging to the landlords and let to tenants. The local authority attempted to obtain information in relation to a number of properties belonging to the landlords by sending their valuation officers to make such inquiries as they could about the tenancy agreements and the premises to which they referred. The valuation officers succeeded in interviewing 22 tenants. These officers reported that they felt that the rents were a little high.

The matter, I think, was first considered by the local authority or their housing committee on July 2, 1970. It came before the same committee on September 15 . . . The town clerk reported what he had learned from the valuation officers. . .

At that meeting – which apparently lasted some time – the local authority adjourned the matter so that the opinion of counsel might be taken. Counsel advised, or expressed the hope, that the local authority should take action. The committee met on October 27 and further considered the matter, and on December 1 when it again met it had a resumé of counsel's opinion before it. The committee then decided to exercise their powers under section 72 and that decision of the committee was ratified by the local authority on January 6.

It is quite obvious that the local authority did not act precipitously. Indeed, it is plain that they went into this matter with the most meticulous care ... It is said that they did not take into account the tenants' views, but an affidavit has been sworn by Mr Coskie, the chief legal officer to the local authority, and according to his evidence he stated:

> 'At the meeting of September 15 I summed up the feelings of the tenants as conveyed to the valuation officers that the local authority would receive a measure of support from the tenants if it referred their contracts to the rent tribunal, although some of them were against this and others who would support the action were not prepared to attend at the rent tribunal to say so. I knew these facts from seeing the valuation officers' notes of their interviews with the tenants.'

... [T]here has been no application to cross-examine the legal adviser and no reason to suppose that what he stated in his affidavit is other than accurate...

... I do not think, however, that the powers of the local authority to refer can conceivably be inhibited by the fact that the tenants themselves do not want references to be made ... No doubt the wishes of the tenants are something which the local authority should bear in mind, but even if the tenants are against references being made, there is nothing to prevent the local authority from taking a different view...

As far as the argument that the local authority did not consider whether there was any likelihood of the rents being reduced is concerned, in my judgment there is equally little substance in that contention. They had the opinion of their officers that the rents were a little too high, that is to say that they were a little higher than what would have been the reasonable rent. It would be for the tribunal to decide whether or not the rents in those circumstances should be reduced, and there would be nothing to prevent the tribunal from coming to a decision that they should be reduced. On the material before this court it seems to me that there was ample material upon which the local authority could reasonably come to the conclusion that there was something for the tribunal to consider and a reasonable likelihood that they might reduce the rents.

As to the allegation that they wrongly took into account the landlords' refusal to allow inspection of certain premises of the landlords, I am afraid that, in spite of the argument that has been addressed to us, I consider that this contention also is ill-founded . . . I should have thought that the local authority was perfectly entitled to take the view that that might have been because the landlords were most unwilling for the local authority to be fully informed about the tenancies. It is a factor which might justifiably have strengthened the impression of those members of the local authority who thought there was something to refer to the tribunal. . . I naturally agree that if the landlord could show, for example, that the local authority were referring the tenancy agreements to the tribunal out of spite because they disliked the landlords and did not genuinely believe that there was anything of substance in the information that the rents were too high, then that would have been an excess of power. It would also have been capricious and vexatious, and might well have come within the classification of being mala fides. But there is not any ground that I can discern on which the Divisional Court could have come to such a conclusion, and they clearly did not do so. Nor do I.

I recognise that when a reference is made by the local authority to the tribunal, although it is true that no decision has been taken against the landlords which affects their basic rights in the sense that I have indicated, it follows that they may be put to expense and inconvenience. Nevertheless, in my judgment, the landlords are given all the protection which is reasonably necessary, if the Act of 1968 requires, as in my view it does require, only that the local authority shall act bona fide and not make a decision capriciously or vexatiously. The assumption must be, until the contrary is proved – and the onus of proving the contrary is upon the landlords – that the local authority did act properly. I cannot discern any evidence from which it would be possible to draw the inference that the local authority in this case acted other than properly. . .

Before I part with the case it is important that I should refer to *Rex* v. *Paddington and St. Marylebone Rent Tribunal, Ex parte Bell London and Provincial Properties Ltd.* [1949] 1 K.B. 666. This was a decision on its own very special facts. If, as has been suggested, this decision has inhibited local authorities from referring cases in which they considered that there was a reasonable prospect of the tribunal reducing the rent, then it can only be because *Bell's* case has been misunderstood. That case concerned a large block of flats of which Lord Goddard C.J. said that the tenants enjoyed all the amenities usually afforded in high-class blocks of flats in the West End of London and were people well able to look after themselves. A very different class of accommodation and a very different type of tenant from the accommodation and the tenants with which we are concerned. In that case the local authority in question had referred 302 tenancy agreements to the rent tribunal merely because the rent tribunal had reduced the rents of two flats in this block. The decision is correctly set out in the headnote, at p. 666:

'... the method of reference adopted by the local authority indicating, as it did, that no investigation or inquiry could have been made by them into the nature of the contracts of tenancy referred by them to the tribunal, did not constitute a valid and bona fide exercise by the local authority of the powers conferred on them by Parliament. It was never intended by the Act that a local authority should refer cases of contracts in respect of which they had neither received a complaint from the tenant, nor had themselves made any inquiry to see whether there was a prima facie case or anything to indicate that there was any unfairness in the rent charged.'

The present case is entirely different, not only because we are dealing with a different class of property and a different type of tenant, but because in this case there was an investigation, and a careful investigation, and inquiry by the local authority into the relevant facts. ... Lord Goddard C.J. said, at p. 680:

'No doubt, the reason why it was provided that cases might be referred by a local authority was because it was recognised that there might be tenants who would hesitate, themselves, to refer the case for fear of the consequences that might befall them, but it could never have been intended that local authorities could refer cases respecting which they had neither received complaint from the tenant, nor had made any inquiry as to whether there was a prima facie case... The borough council in question have decided as a matter of policy that in the case of any property in respect of which two or more reductions in rent had been made, all the contracts of letting to which the Act applied relating to such property should be referred to the tribunal.'

Then he said this, which points the difference – or one of the many differences – between that case and the present: 'This may be a perfectly proper course to take in respect of certain cases, as for instance one or two houses ' – and he might have said even seven – ' in the same ownership all of which are let out in separate tenements to poor or working class persons, but to apply this policy to 550 flats without any inquiry or indeed knowledge as to whether the Act applies or not, is an entirely different matter,' and he goes on to point out that any other view might lead to the conclusion that the local authority, without any information or inquiry as to the tenancies in question, could refer all the flats within their jurisdiction to the rent tribunal, which would clearly be highly inconvenient for the landlords and equally inconvenient for the tribunal. Lord Goddard C.J. said, at p. 681:

' In our opinion the action of the borough council in referring the whole of these flats in the manner they have done is not a genuine exercise of the powers conferred on them by the Act, and we cannot refrain from saying that it is regrettable that in the form of reference, information purports to be given to the tribunal which is quite inaccurate, and which has been given without the slightest attempt to see that it was accurate.'

In the present case the fullest information was given to the tribunal. The size of the rooms let – and they were all very small – the number of persons occupying each room, the rent, and the condition of the premises, the standard of furnishing and the facilities were all given. In the great majority of cases, these were assessed as fair to poor. . . It is not suggested that any of the information contained in the references is wrong. This case is entirely different from *Bell's* case.

There are two sentences at p. 680 in the judgment of Lord Goddard C.J. that have been seized upon. The first sentence is: ' It was never intended that this Act should be used as a general rent-fixing tribunal throughout a district.' That, of course, is correct, and if all the flats in a district could be referred to the rent tribunal by the local authority without making any inquiry, it might be said that the Act was being used as a general rent fixing tribunal, but nothing of the kind happened here. The second sentence is: ' It is to deal with individual cases where hardship exists or may be reasonably supposed to exist.' Those words could, perhaps, be given a very wide meaning. I think, however, that all that Lord Goddard C.J. intended to lay down was that if the local authority referred tenancy agreements to the tribunal in circumstances in which no reasonable local authority could have done so, then the local authority were acting ultra vires. In that particular case no reasonable local authority could have properly referred the tenancy agreements to the tribunal, having made no inquiry about them. . .

For these reasons, I would dismiss the appeal.

EDMUND-DAVIES L.J. It is generally agreed that the vast majority of members of local authorities perform without fear or favour tasks in the public service, yet experience shows that they receive as a result more brick-bats than bouquets. It is frequently insufficiently recognised that without their voluntary service local government as we know it in this country would be impossible. That is but one of the many reasons why, as I think, adopting the words of Lord Reading C.J. in *Rex* v. *Brighton Corporation, Ex parte Thomas Tilling Ltd.* (1916) 85 L.J.K.B. 1552, 1555, the court ought to be very slow in interfering with their decisions. . .

The question has been canvassed as to whether the test enunciated in *Associated Provincial Picture Houses Ltd.* v. *Wednesbury Corporation* [1948] 1 K.B. 223, 233 by Lord Greene M.R. is appropriate to cases such as the present...

The reason I think that the strict *Wednesbury* approach would be a hardship is that, while the local authority have to do the best they can to glean information relating to furnished lettings, their ability to gain it is limited and quite unassisted by the statute... It may come from a variety of sources. It may come from the tenants themselves, and, indeed, as Lord Goddard C.J. said in the *Bell* case [1949] 1 K.B. 666, the wishes of the tenants surely ought at least to be taken into account. They may gain some information from outside bodies. They must, of course, be careful not to act upon gossip or rumour which may be maliciously inspired or honestly mistaken. In most cases one would hope that a landlord, on being approached, would co-operate with them in his own interest and give the information they were seeking, though there is no shadow of doubt he is under no obligation to co-operate in any way.

Like Salmon L.J., I think that the proper test to apply is whether or not in resolving to refer a Part VI contract to the rent tribunal there are grounds for concluding that the local authority was actuated by mala fides or was acting capriciously or vexatiously...

[Mr Bernstein] said that the local authority failed in two respects: it failed to take into account the views of the tenants... I do not think that the first ground of complaint urged by Mr Bernstein is established...

The second factor which it was urged should have been taken into consideration by the local authority and was in fact ignored was that in the circumstances obtaining it was unlikely, to put it at its highest, that any of these 22 references to the rent tribunal would result in a reduction in the rent... Certainly that is a relevant factor in considering whether a local authority acted capriciously or vexatiously, but there may still be circumstances where the public weal requires that when, for example, rumours are going about, the air should be clarified by a reference to a tribunal which can establish in an authoritative manner where the truth lies...

It is lastly said by Mr Bernstein that the local authority wrongly allowed themselves to be influenced by the persistent and sustained pressure of the small body of, I think, six persons known as the Camden Housing Action, who had expressed quite strongly worded views critical of the Part VI contracts in respect of which the landlords were the lessors. That the housing committee was impressed by the activities of that group Lord Widgery C.J. thought beyond question, for in the course of his judgment he said, ante, p. 346D: 'As a result of this pressure – and it seems to me there is no doubt it was as a result – the housing committee of Camden decided to make investigations of the terms of letting in the houses with which Messrs. Frey were associated.'

For my part I am quite prepared to accept this view expressed by Lord Widgery C.J., but who is to say that it is wrong for a local authority to allow its determination to be affected by the view expressed – it may be persistently and vociferously and strongly – by a pressure group? Is that enough of itself to indicate that the local authority is allowing itself to be overborne and persuaded to make a decision which is mala fide or vexatious or capricious? I would have thought it must depend upon what the action group say and how they say it, and, in so far as their assertion could be tested, the extent to which it appeared to have some foundation? If it was manifestly baseless, if there were suspicion of some ulterior motive, be it financial or political or inspired solely by personal aggrandisement, then of course the local authority should dismiss it from their minds. But if what was said by the action group provided food for thought, and if it appeared to have at least some reasonable degree of support, for my part I reject the idea that it would be improper to be influenced by what the action group said. In this particular case and in relation to this particular pressure group, I am not satisfied that the local authority, when (as I am prepared to accept) they were impressed by what they said, were doing something which they ought not to do. . .

STAMP L.J. . . . I would have thought it wrong in principle for the High Court, on an application for an order of prohibition to prevent the local authority referring a rent or rents to the appropriate statutory tribunal, to go into the merits of the decision to refer: for if the reference is without merit it must be assumed that the rent tribunal will take no action on it. In determining whether or not to invoke the section the local authority is in no sense exercising a judicial function and it is not even, as I see it, exercising such a discretion as a licensing authority exercises, or as a local authority exercises in relation to Acts such as the Town and Country Planning Act 1962 or which has to be exercised in determining whether to make a compulsory acquisition. . .

If, therefore, the matter was res integra, I would myself take the view that in the absence of any allegation that the local authority had been acting ultra vires or mala fide, the present proceedings were misconceived and failed in limine. Reliance, however, was placed on the decision of the Divisional Court in *Rex* v. *Paddington and St. Marylebone Rent Tribunal, Ex parte Bell London and Provincial Properties Ltd.* [1949] 1 K.B. 666 which has already been referred to by Salmon and Edmund-Davies L.JJ. So far as the decision in that case rested upon the view that the local authority there was not acting bona fide, it is, so I will assume without expressing an opinion, perhaps not open to criticism; but I cannot accept, as appears to be suggested in a part of the judgment heavily relied upon by the landlords, that the court has a general power to examine the proceedings of local authorities to see whether in coming to a purely administrative decision not affecting rights they have taken into account all those factors which ought to be taken into account in order to arrive at a wise or correct decision... As is pointed out in ' *Smith's Judicial*' *Review of Administrative Action*, 2nd ed. (1968), p. 3 : ' The administrative process is not, and cannot be, a succession of justiciable controversies. Public authorities are set up to govern and administer, and if their every act or decision were to be reviewable on unrestricted grounds by an independent judicial body the business of administration could be brought to a standstill.'

V. BY-LAWS

LOCAL GOVERNMENT ACT, 1972 [Ch. 70]

235. (1) The council of a district and the council of a London borough may make byelaws for the good rule and government of the whole or any part of the district or borough, as the case may be, and for the prevention and suppression of nuisances therein.

(2) The confirming authority in relation to byelaws made under this section shall be the Secretary of State.

(3) Byelaws shall not be made under this section for any purpose as respects any area if provision for that purpose as respects that area is made by, or is or may be made under, any other enactment.

236. (1) Subject to subsection (2) below, the following provisions of this section shall apply to byelaws to be made by a local authority under this Act or any other enactment... for which specific provision is not otherwise made.

(2) This section shall not apply to byelaws made by statutory water undertakers under section 17 or 18 of the Water Act 1945 or by the Civil Aviation Authority under section 31 of the Civil Aviation Act 1971.

(3) The byelaws... shall not have effect until they are confirmed by the confirming authority.

(4) At least one month before application for confirmation of the byelaws is made, notice of the intention to apply for confirmation shall be given in one or more local newspapers circulating in the area to which the byelaws are to apply.

(5) For at least one month before application for confirmation is

made, a copy of the byelaws shall be deposited at the offices of the authority by whom the byelaws are made, and shall at all reasonable hours be open to public inspection without payment.

(6) The authority by whom the byelaws are made shall, on application, furnish to any person a copy of the byelaws, or of any part thereof on payment of such sum, not exceeding 10p for every hundred words contained in the copy, as the authority may determine.

(7) The confirming authority may confirm, or refuse to confirm any byelaw submitted under this section for confirmation. . .

(11) In this section the expression ' the confirming authority ' means the authority or person, if any, specified in the enactment (including any enactment in this Act) under which the byelaws are made, or in any enactment incorporated therein or applied thereby, as the authority or person by whom the byelaws are to be confirmed, or if no authority or person is so specified, means the Secretary of State.

237. Byelaws to which section 236 above applies may provide that persons contravening the byelaws shall be liable on summary conviction to a fine not exceeding such sum as may be fixed by the enactment conferring the power to make the byelaws, or, if no sum is so fixed, the sum of £20, and in the case of a continuing offence a further fine not exceeding such sum as may be fixed as aforesaid, or, if no sum is so fixed, the sum of £5 for each day during which the offence continues after conviction thereof.

KRUSE v. *JOHNSON* [1898] 2 Q.B. 91

Divisional Court

Kent County Council made a by-law under s. 16 of the Local Government Act, 1888, which provided: ' No person shall sound or play upon any musical or noisy instrument or sing in any public place or highway within fifty yards of any dwelling-house after being required by any constable, or by an inmate of such house personally, or by his or her servant, to desist.'

The appellant, Kruse, had been conducting an open-air religious service and had continued to sing a hymn after a constable had required him to stop. He was convicted under the by-law. On appeal to the Divisional Court, Lord Russell C.J. and Mathew J. had disagreed and the case was referred to the full court, consisting of Lord Russell, Sir F. H. Jeune, Chitty L.J., and Wright, Darling, Channell and Mathew JJ.

Counsel for Kruse argued that the by-law was invalid because it was unreasonable. He argued that under it an inhabitant could object to and stop the singing of a hymn not because he really objected to the hymn or the singing but because he objected to the propaganda of the singer. He noted that the power was given to a constable in his absolute discretion and was likely to be abused. Constables were not to be trusted to refrain from an unnecessary exercise of the power.

LORD RUSSELL OF KILLOWEN C.J. . . . The question reserved for this Court is whether the by-law is valid. . . It is necessary, therefore, to see what is the authority under which the by-law in question has been made, and what are the relations between its framers and those affected by it . . . Parliament has thought fit to delegate to representative public bodies in towns and cities, and also in counties, the power of exercising their own judgment as to what are the by-laws which to them seem proper to be made for good rule and government in their own localities. But that power is accompanied by certain safeguards. There must be antecedent publication of the by-law with a view, I presume, of eliciting the public opinion of the locality upon it, and such by-laws shall have no force until after they have been forwarded to the Secretary of State. Further, the Queen, with the advice of her Privy Council, may disallow the by-law wholly or in part, and may enlarge the suspensory period before it comes into operation. I agree that the presence of these safeguards in no way relieves the Court of the responsibility of inquiring into the validity of by-laws where they are brought in question, or in any way affects the authority of the Court in the determination of their validity or invalidity . . . In this class of case it is right that the Courts should jealously watch the exercise of these powers, and guard against their unnecessary or unreasonable exercise to the public disadvantage. But . . . looking to the character of the body legislating under the delegated authority of Parliament, to the subject-matter of such legislation, and to the nature and extent of the authority given to deal with matters which concern them, and in the manner which to them shall seem meet, I think courts of justice ought to be slow to condemn as invalid any by-law, so made under such conditions, on the ground of supposed unreasonableness. Notwithstanding what Cockburn C.J. said in *Bailey* v. *Williamson*,[6] an analogous case, I do not mean to say that there may not be cases in which it would be the duty of the Court to condemn by-laws, made under such authority as these were made, as invalid because unreasonable. But unreasonable in what sense? If, for instance, they were found to be partial and unequal in their operation as between different classes; if they were manifestly unjust; if they disclosed bad faith; if they involved such oppressive or gratuitous interference with the rights of those subject to them as could find no justification in the minds of reasonable men, the Court might well say, ' Parliament never intended to give authority to make such rules; they are unreasonable and ultra vires.' But it is in this sense, and in this sense only, as I conceive, that the question of unreasonableness can properly be regarded. A by-law is not unreasonable merely because particular

6 (1873) L.R. 8 Q.B. 118, at p. 124.

judges may think that it goes further than is prudent or necessary or convenient, or because it is not accompanied by a qualification or an exception which some judges may think ought to be there. Surely it is not too much to say that in matters which directly and mainly concern the people of the county, who have the right to choose those whom they think best fitted to represent them in their local government bodies, such representatives may be trusted to understand their own requirements better than judges. Indeed, if the question of the validity of by-laws were to be determined by the opinion of judges as to what was reasonable in the narrow sense of that word, the cases in the books on this subject are no guide; for they reveal, as indeed one would expect, a wide diversity of judicial opinion, and they lay down no principle or definite standard by which reasonableness or unreasonableness may be tested.

So much for the general considerations which, it seems to me, ought to be borne in mind in considering by-laws of this class. I now come to the by-law in question.

[Having rejected the objection that the by-law was bad because it was not confined to cases where the playing or singing was causing annoyance, Lord Russell continued:]

As to the second objection – namely, that the policeman has the power of putting the by-law into operation by requiring the player or singer to desist ... In support of this objection pictures have, in argument, been drawn – more or less highly coloured – of policemen who without rhyme or reason would or might gratuitously interfere with what might be a source of enjoyment to many. In answer, I say a policeman is not an irresponsible person without check or control. If he acts capriciously or vexatiously, he can be checked by his immediate superiors, or he can be taught a lesson by the magistrates should he prefer vexatious charges. If the policeman persisted in saying that the musician should desist when the people in the neighbourhood desired his music, his gratuitous interference would promptly come to an end. Nor is it correct to say, as has been erroneously stated in some of the cases cited, that the magistrate would be bound in every case to convict where the musician did not desist when called upon. It is clear that under s. 16 of the Summary Jurisdiction Act 1879, the magistrate, if he thinks the case of so trifling a nature that it is inexpedient to inflict any punishment, may, without proceeding to conviction, dismiss the information ... In my opinion, judged by the test of reasonableness, even in its narrower sense, this is a reasonable by-law; but, whether I am right or wrong in this view, I am clearly of opinion that no Court of law can properly say that it is invalid ...

Sir F. H. Jeune, President of the P.D. and A. Division. ... [T]he by-law ... was made by the county council of Kent – that is to say, a public representative body to which Parliament has confided the duty of making by-laws for the good rule and government of the inhabitants of Kent and the prevention of nuisances in that county. Three considerations appear to me to apply with especial force to such an authority, dealing with such subject-matter. First, the case is wholly different from that of manorial authorities, or of trading corporations such as dock or railway companies, who often have a pecuniary interest in their by-laws, or even of such a municipal corporation as might be supposed to have trade interests involved. Secondly, such an authority as a county council must be credited with adequate knowledge of the locality, its wants and wishes. Thirdly, the opportunity afforded by legislation for a request for reconsideration, and an appeal to higher authorities, by members of the public shews that any by-law which comes into force has secured at least the acquiescence of those whom it affects. Cases may be imagined in which, in spite of these considerations, this Court, acting in the discharge of its undoubted powers and duty, might feel compelled to hold a by-law made by a county council invalid on the ground that it was unreasonable. But, when a question of the requirements and wishes of the locality is involved, this Court should, I think, be very slow to set aside the conclusions of the local authority...

MATHEW J. [dissenting] ... For the respondent it was argued that the by-law was well enough. It had been framed by a representative body, created under recent legislation, whose regulations should be indulgently treated. It must be taken, it was said, that Parliament intended that local authorities should be upheld, and to this end that new canons of construction should be adopted by the Courts to preserve their by-laws from being declared invalid. It was no longer enough to point out that a by-law according to its terms was unreasonable; it should be upheld if it might be reasonably enforced, and it was no longer an objection that it might be unreasonably enforced. It was urged that there were adequate safeguards for the public which, though not expressed, ought to be implied. It was true that any policeman might prohibit acts of which no reasonable man ought to complain; but it was said that confidence might be reposed in the discretion of a policeman, and that he would not be likely to interfere unreasonably. This seems to me too generous a view of the qualifications of the ordinary constable. There was, it was said, a further safeguard, namely, that the county council would not sanction interference by the police unless there was some good cause. But a by-law once made could not be, and ought not to be, controlled in its operation by the members of the council. Further, the policeman who interfered without good cause would, it was argued, be reprimanded by his superiors, or a magistrate would probably refuse to issue a summons. These suggestions imply that there would be cases in which a constable ought not to have the power to prohibit or to prosecute. It seems to me that the public ought to be informed in clear language what these cases were. It would not be satisfactory to a person, who was innocent of any real offence and was summoned as a criminal, to have an apology offered to him on the ground that the policeman had been wanting in discretion. Again, it was said that the magistrate would have the power to refuse to convict, in a trifling case, under s. 16 of the Summary Jurisdiction Act; but the by-law affords no security that this power would be exercised. A magistrate might reasonably consider that he was bound to convict; for a by-law once duly published becomes part of the law of the land in the locality to which it applies. It should be remembered that this by-law has been made for the purpose of securing the good rule and government of the district. It would appear not to be well calculated in its present form to secure any such result. The interference of a policeman, which the by-law permits, would not be unlikely, it seems to me, to produce angry altercation, and to lead to a breach of the peace. . .

In my judgment this by-law should be amended. It came into operation on May 19, 1897, and the offence with which it deals is therefore of very recent creation. As it stands, any constable may prohibit any singing on any highway within fifty yards of a dwelling-house in any parts of the county of Kent, except such as are within any municipal borough. It has been suggested that the real intent of the council was to prevent noisy demonstrations which would be offensive to residents within their jurisdiction. If this were so, it becomes difficult to understand why this intention was not stated in plain terms, and why the language should be so wide of the mark. It seems to me of special importance, where the aid of constables is invoked to maintain order, that the duties of the police on the one hand, and the obligations of the public on the other, should be stated with reasonable clearness. Laxity in the preparation of local enactments is not to be encouraged. . .

I am of opinion that this conviction should be quashed.

CHITTY L.J., WRIGHT, DARLING and CHANNELL JJ. concurred in the judgment of LORD RUSSELL.

Judgment for the respondent

POWELL v. *MAY*   [1946] 1 KB 330

Divisional Court (Lord Goddard C.J., Humphreys and Henn Collins JJ.)
LORD GODDARD C.J. [delivered the judgment of the court.] . . . The objection taken by the appellant to this by-law is that it is ultra vires the county council because it is repugnant to the general law of the

land. By-laws in form indistinguishable from the present have been before the courts on more than one occasion and upheld, but all those cases were before the Street Betting Act, 1906, and therefore also before the Betting and Lotteries Act, 1934, and the question that has to be decided in the present case is whether this by-law can be regarded as valid although it goes beyond the provisions of those general Acts and makes something unlawful which is expressly exempted from the provisions of those Acts and which it is accordingly argued is at least inferentially permitted by them. There is no question but that a by-law which is repugnant to the general law is invalid, but it is not so easy to determine what is covered by the word ' repugnant ', and under what circumstances a by-law is to be held invalid on that ground. Obviously, it cannot permit that which a statute expressly forbids nor forbid that which a statute expressly permits, though it can, of course, forbid that which otherwise would be lawful at common law, otherwise no prohibitory by-law could be valid. It is but seldom that a statute expressly enacts that something shall be lawful, unless indeed it is dealing with the conferment of powers upon some body or person, but it is by no means unusual to find a statute which, while making some particular thing unlawful, goes on to provide that the thing prohibited may be done or at least not be prohibited if certain conditions are observed. If Parliament prohibits a certain thing from being done and imposes a penalty for doing it and in the same Act says the prohibition is not to apply, or that no penalty is to be incurred, if the very same thing is done in a certain way or under certain conditions, it seems almost pedantic to say that Parliament has not at least impliedly authorized the doing of that thing subject to the conditions laid down. . .

CHAPTER X

OPENNESS AND PARTICIPATION IN GOVERNMENT

I. OPENNESS

The Fulton Committee on the Civil Service, 1968

277. We think that the administrative process is surrounded by too much secrecy... The increasingly wide range of problems handled by government, and their far-reaching effects upon the community as a whole, demand the widest possible consultation with its different parts and interests. We believe that such consultation is not only necessary in itself but will also improve the quality of the ultimate decisions and increase the general understanding of their purpose.

278. We welcome the trends in recent years towards wider and more open consultation before decisions are taken; and we welcome, too, the increasing provision of the detailed information on which decisions are made. Both should be carried much further... There are still too many occasions where information is unnecessarily withheld and consultation merely perfunctory. Since government decisions affect all of us in so many aspects of our lives, consultation ... should form part of the normal processes of decision-making. It is an abuse of consultation when it is turned into a belated attempt to prepare the ground for decisions that have in reality been taken already.

279. We recognise that there must always be an element of secrecy (not simply on grounds of national security) in administration and policy-making. At the formative stages of policy-making, civil servants no less than Ministers should be able to discuss and disagree among themselves about possible courses of action, without danger of their individual views becoming a matter of public knowledge; it is difficult to see how on any other basis there can be mutual trust between colleagues and proper critical discussion of different hypotheses. But the material, and some of the analyses, on which these policy discussions are going forward, fall into a different category; unless there are overriding considerations to the contrary (e.g. on grounds of national security, the confidential nature of information supplied by individual firms, or to prevent improper financial gain), there would be positive advantages all round if such information were made available to the public at the formative stage of policy-making.

280. Civil servants, and perhaps also Ministers, are apt to give great and sometimes excessive weight to the difficulties and problems which

435

would undoubtedly arise from more open processes of administration and policy-making... Some restrictions on the objective of 'open decisions openly arrived at' will doubtless remain necessary; but a mature democracy rightly demands that they should be kept to the absolute minimum. The fuller the information, the closer the links between government (both Ministers and civil servants) and the community; and the smaller the gap of frustration and misunderstanding between 'them' and 'us'.

[Report of the Committee on the Civil Service, 1966–8]

(i) The convention of Cabinet secrecy

Cabinet discussions as distinct from Cabinet decisions must, from their nature, be kept secret. Members of the Cabinet, as party leaders, cannot differ from one another in public unless the whole Cabinet system is altered. During discussions leading up to a decision, the members of a Cabinet ought often to differ. Official disclosure of Cabinet discussions would not only reveal these differences but tend to draw Ministers into public participation in them. A point of a quite different kind is that Cabinet discussions often depend upon confidential advice from civil servants or reports from Ambassadors. If those were disclosed and thus became subject to public attack, it would be extremely difficult for the Cabinet to secure free and frank advice.

Somewhat the same considerations apply to consultations between the Cabinet and outside interests – such as the T.U.C. and the C.B.I. Cabinet discussions might well involve the secrets of these bodies as well as those of the Cabinet. In any case, if Cabinet discussions were disclosed, there would be no possibility of confidential advice from interested bodies; it would always have to be given in public and out loud...

The main effective change towards less secrecy would be for the Cabinet to share with Parliament and public more of the factual information on which the Government make some of their decisions. Moves in this direction have begun to be taken...

[Patrick Gordon-Walker, *The Cabinet* (1970), p. 167]

Cabinet documents

Mr Shinwell asked the Prime Minister why permission had been given to Sir Anthony Eden to publish Cabinet minutes and documents relating to Middle East affairs when he was Prime Minister, in view of the general rule prohibiting publication.

THE PRIME MINISTER (MR HAROLD MACMILLAN): I have not recognised, in the serialised extracts from Sir Anthony Eden's book, direct quotations from Cabinet minutes or Cabinet memoranda relating to Middle East affairs during the period when he was Prime Minister. There are general references to the subject matter of Cabinet discussions and there are extracts from other official documents relating to Middle East affairs during this period. Sir Anthony Eden submitted the text of his book to me, through the Secretary of the Cabinet. I did not regard the publication of these references and extracts as open to objection. . . The only actual quotations from the Cabinet memoranda, for which, of course, approval has to be given by the Queen, were on a matter when Sir Anthony Eden was Foreign Secretary, dealing with Far Eastern affairs. . . We have always had a procedure by which a Minister of a past Administration has been able to consult the files and it has been done normally through the Cabinet Secretary. I think that it will be found that exactly the same precedent was followed by Lord Attlee in relation to the series of volumes published by my right hon. Friend the Member for Woodford (Sir W. Churchill).

MR GAITSKELL: . . . May I ask the Prime Minister whether he is aware that many of us feel that the way in which these conventions have been administered recently has become increasingly lax and that we would not accept the parallel with the memoirs of the right hon. Member for Woodford (Sir W. Churchill) as being something which should always be followed? There was something special about that particular case. . .

THE PRIME MINISTER: What the right hon. Gentleman is saying is something which I am bound to say has occurred to me. Perhaps we ought to treat the war and immediate post-war as something different. It would be a novel procedure, but it was that kind of thing I had in mind when I said that we ought perhaps to consider establishing new conventions for what one might call different times. I have just followed the ordinary conventions up to now. . . There is a difference between ex-Ministers having a look at documents and what is published. When there is a question of publication, what is laid down is that a person must receive not only the authority of the Prime Minister, but the Queen's authority, advised by him. . . The general reading of old papers and so forth is another question.

[618 H.C.Deb. 5s. c. 571. 25 February 1960]

VISCOUNT HAILSHAM: . . .

If a matter arises which concerns some previous Administration the practice is to communicate with the Prime Minister who was then responsible to find out whether he has any objection to publication, and if he has no objection then the duty falls upon the Prime Minister of the day to advise His Majesty as to whether or not it is proper, in the particular circumstances, to make a disclosure. A common instance which occurs to all of us when such a disclosure is possible and is invariably permitted, is when a Cabinet Minister feels it incumbent upon himself to resign his office because of his disagreement on some high matter of policy with his colleagues. In such a case it is the invariable practice to permit the resigning Minister, if he so desires, to state the circumstances which led to his resignation and the reasons why he was unable to remain a member of the Cabinet from which he has resigned. But that privilege is granted to that particular Minister on his application by His Majesty on the advice of the Prime Minister, and without that previous consent it would be improper, even in that case, for the resigning Minister to make any statement at all. The permission is always given, but the permission has to be obtained in order to absolve the Minister from the duty, which is otherwise an imperative and absolute duty, of keeping silence. . .

[86 H.L.Deb. 5s. c. 527. 21 December 1932]

(ii) Legal restrictions on the disclosure and dissemination of information

(a) *The Public Records Act, 1958*

PUBLIC RECORDS ACT, 1958 [Ch. 51] [1]

5. (1) Public records in the Public Record Office, other than those to which members of the public had access before their transfer to the Public Record Office, shall not be available for public inspection until the expiration of the period of thirty years beginning with the first day of January in the year next after that in which they were created, or such other period either longer or shorter, as the Lord Chancellor may, with the approval, or at the request, of the Minister or other person, if any, who appears to him to be primarily concerned, for the time being prescribe as respects any particular class of public records.

(2) Without prejudice to the generality of the foregoing subsection, if it appears to the person responsible for any public records . . . that they contain information which was obtained from members of the public under such conditions that the opening of those records to the public after the period determined under the foregoing subsection would or might constitute a breach of good faith on the part of the Government or on the part of the persons who obtained the information, he shall inform the Lord Chancellor accordingly and those records shall not be available in the Public Record Office for public inspection even after the expiration of the said period except in such circumstances and subject to such conditions, if any, as the Lord Chancellor and that

[1] As amended by the Public Records Act, 1967.

person may approve, or, if the Lord Chancellor and that person think fit, after the expiration of such further period as they may approve.

(3) Subject to the foregoing provisions of this section, subject to the enactments set out in the Second Schedule to this Act (which prohibit the disclosure of certain information obtained from the public except for certain limited purposes) and subject to any other Act or instrument whether passed or made before or after this Act which contains a similar prohibition, it shall be the duty of the Keeper of Public Records to arrange that reasonable facilities are available to the public for inspecting and obtaining copies of public records in the Public Record Office.

(4) Subsection (1) of this section shall not make it unlawful for the Keeper of Public Records to permit a person to inspect any records if he has obtained special authority in that behalf given by an officer of a government department or other body, being an officer accepted by the Lord Chancellor as qualified to give such an authority.

(5) The Lord Chancellor shall as respects all public records in places of deposit appointed by him under this Act outside the Public Record Office require arrangements to be made for their inspection by the public comparable to those made for public records in the Public Record Office, and subject to restrictions corresponding with those contained in the foregoing provisions of this section...

Public Records Bill, 1967

THE ATTORNEY-GENERAL (SIR ELWYN JONES): ... This Bill reduces the period from 50 years to 30 years for which public records, subject to certain exceptions, are closed to public inspection... Those for which longer periods have been prescribed fall into the following categories: Firstly, those containing information about individuals whose disclosure would cause distress or embarrassment to living persons or their immediate descendants, such as criminal or prison records, records of courts-martial, records of suspected persons and certain police records; secondly, those containing information obtained with a pledge of confidence, for example, the census returns; thirdly, certain papers relating to Irish affairs; fourthly, certain exceptionally sensitive papers, which affected the security of the State... In these matters the Lord Chancellor is advised by the Advisory Council on public records.

MR MICHAEL FOOT (*Ebbw Vale*): Could my right hon. and learned Friend explain to the House why it is there is this special provision about Irish affairs?

THE ATTORNEY-GENERAL: There is a sensitive area in regard to Irish affairs which remains, and I do not think it would be prudent for me to pursue it on the Floor of the House. But there are papers

which it would not be in the interests of this country to disclose ...
The same principle will apply to prescribing periods longer than 30
years as have applied for the prescription periods longer than 50 years.
The Lord Chancellor in another place has told us of the kind of cases
that he has in mind – confidential correspondence with or about British
firms abroad, the disclosure of which might be harmful to our trade;
comments by Ministers and officials on officials and persons abroad
which could be exploited by hostile propagandists or used to make
trouble for us, and foreign rulers or statesmen whose public careers
have spanned a 30-year period...

MR MICHAEL FOOT: ... I recognise that there are strong arguments
for preventing the adoption of the American system. I do not think
that it is a good idea that every discussion in the Cabinet should be
open to immediate or very early investigation by the Press and students,
because that would make the processes of government almost impossible. Therefore, there have to be limitations, but they must be
exercised with great care... I cannot understand why a special restriction should apply presumably to discussions on Irish affairs which went
on in the Foreign Office and other quarters of the Government in the
1920s and 1930s. I should have thought that exactly the same principle
should apply to any decisions made on important matters in Ireland as
would apply to affairs in this country...

THE ATTORNEY-GENERAL: ... Documents relating to Irish affairs
are not generally restricted. The only ones which are restricted are
certain records dealing with what are commonly called 'the
troubles'...

[Second Reading. 749 H.C.Deb. 5s. c. 25. 26 June 1967]

(b) *The Official Secrets Acts, 1911–34*

Although many of the provisions of these Acts are directly concerned
with espionage they are drafted in terms wide enough to cover other
activities as well. Members of the Committee of 100, for example, were
prosecuted under the Act for attempting to immobilise an air base as
part of their campaign against nuclear weapons (*Chandler* v. *D.P.P.*
below p. 713). More important from the point of view of openness in
Government, however, is the catch-all provision relating to the communication of official information in s. 2 of the Act of 1911, and the
discussions of principle relating to it contained in the report of the
Committee set up to consider it in 1972.

THE OFFICIAL SECRETS ACT, 1911

[1 & 2 Geo. 5. ch. 28]

2. (1) If any person having in his possession or control any sketch,
plan, model, article, note, document, or information which relates to

or is used in a prohibited place or anything in such a place . . . or which has been entrusted in confidence to him by any person holding office under His Majesty or which he has obtained owing to his position as a person who holds office under His Majesty, or as a person who holds or has held a contract made on behalf of His Majesty, or as a person who is or has been employed under a person who holds or has held such an office or contract,—

(a) communicates the sketch, plan, model, article, note, document, or information to any person, other than a person to whom he is authorised to communicate it, or a person to whom it is in the interests of the State his duty to communicate it, or

(b) retains the sketch, plan, model, article, note, or document in his possession or control when he has no right to retain it or when it is contrary to his duty to retain it:

that person shall be guilty of a misdemeanour.

(2) If any person receives any sketch, plan, model, article, note, document, or information, knowing, or having reasonable ground to believe, that the sketch, plan, model, article, note, document, or information is communicated to him in contravention of this Act, he shall be guilty of a misdemeanour, unless he proves that the communication . . . was contrary to his desire. . .

(4) Any person who attempts to commit any offence under this Act, or incites, or counsels, or attempt to procure another person to commit an offence under this Act, shall be guilty of felony or of a misdemeanour according as the offence is felony of misdemeanour, and on conviction shall be liable to the same punishment, and to be proceeded against in the same manner, as if he had committed the offence.

(8) A prosecution for an offence under this Act shall not be instituted except by or with the consent of the Attorney-General:

Provided that a person charged with such an offence may be arrested, or a warrant for his arrest may be issued and executed, and any such person may be remanded in custody or on bail, notwithstanding that the consent of the Attorney-General to the institution of a prosecution for the offence has not been obtained, but no further or other proceedings shall be taken until that consent has been obtained.

(12) In this Act, unless the context otherwise requires,—

. . . Expressions referring to communicating or receiving include any communicating or receiving . . . whether the sketch, plan, model, article, note, document, or information itself or the substance, effect, or description thereof only be communicated or received; expressions referring to obtaining or retaining . . . include the copying or causing to be copied. . .

THE OFFICIAL SECRETS ACT, 1920

[10 & 11 Geo. 5. ch. 75]

1. (2) If any person—

(a) retains for any purpose prejudicial to the safety or interests of the State any official document . . . when he has no right to retain it, or when it is contrary to his duty to retain it, or fails to comply with any directions issued by any Government Department or any person authorised by such department with regard to the return or disposal thereof; or

(b) allows any other person to have possession of any official document issued for his use alone . . . or, without lawful authority or excuse, has in his possession any official document . . . issued for the use of some person other than himself, or on obtaining possession of any official document by finding or otherwise, neglects or fails to restore it to the person or authority by whom or for whose use it was issued, or to a police constable . . .

he shall be guilty of a misdemeanour.

(3) In the case of any prosecution under this section involving the proof of a purpose prejudicial to the safety or interests of the State, subsection (2) of section one of the principal Act shall apply in like manner as it applies to prosecutions under that section.[2]

6.[3] (1) Where a chief officer of police is satisfied that there is reasonable ground for suspecting that an offence under section one of the principal Act has been committed and for believing that any person is able to furnish information as to the offence or suspected offence, he may apply to a Secretary of State for permission to exercise the powers conferred by this subsection and, if such permission is granted, he may authorise a superintendent of police, or any police officer not below the rank of inspector, to require the person believed to be able to furnish information to give any information in his power relating to the offence or suspected offence, and, if so required and on tender of his reasonable

---

[2] S. 1 (2) of the 1911 Act provides: 'On a prosecution under this section, it shall not be necessary to show that the accused person was guilty of any particular act tending to show a purpose prejudicial to the safety or interests of the state, and, notwithstanding that no such act is proved against him, he may be convicted if, from the circumstances of the case, or his conduct, or his known character as proved, it appears that his purpose was a purpose prejudicial to the safety or interests of the state; and if any sketch, plan, model, article, note, document, or information relating to or used in any prohibited place within the meaning of this Act, or anything in such a place, is made, obtained, or communicated by any person other than a person acting under lawful authority, it shall be deemed to have been made, obtained, or communicated for a purpose prejudicial to the safety or interests of the state, unless the contrary is proved.'

[3] This section was substituted for the original section by s. 1 of the Official Secrets Act, 1939.

expenses, to attend at such reasonable time and place as may be specified by the superintendent or other officer; and if a person required in pursuance of such an authorisation to give information, or to attend as aforesaid, fails to comply with any such requirement or knowingly gives false information, he shall be guilty of a misdemeanour.

(2) Where a chief officer of police has reasonable grounds to believe that the case is one of great emergency and that in the interest of the State immediate action is necessary, he may exercise the powers conferred by the last foregoing subsection without applying for or being granted the permission of a Secretary of State, but if he does so shall forthwith report the circumstances to the Secretary of State.

(3) References in this section to a chief officer of police shall be construed as including references to any other officer of police expressly authorised by a chief officer of police to act on his behalf for the purposes of this section when by reason of illness, absence, or other cause he is unable to do so.

Information and the Public Interest, 1969

32. No business organisation allows its employees to make unrestricted use of information about its internal deliberations, policies and processes. In the case of information about the work of Government, special and even stronger considerations apply. Ministers are responsible to Parliament and to the public for the protection of national security, for the privacy of information supplied by citizens for Government purposes only, and for the fair and effective conduct of Government business generally. The Government's view is therefore that any person who has access to official information should not be allowed to publish it at will. In the course of their day to day work departments do, in practice, authorise the release of much official information, but the ultimate responsibility for policy in this matter must rest with Ministers themselves.

33. A sanction is needed to ensure the protection of some official material; and the Official Secrets Acts provide it. It has sometimes been suggested that the scope of these Acts ought to be limited, so that it would not be an offence to disclose official information without authority unless national security or some other major public interest were directly involved. There would, however, be the greatest difficulty in defining satisfactorily what categories of information should qualify for this special protection and what should not, because the range of information which may need this protection is so varied.

34. To meet this difficulty, the Official Secrets Acts were drafted in wide terms; and (as in other statutes in which it is not possible to define an offence in narrow terms) a provision was added that there could be no prosecution without the consent of the Attorney General or, in

Scotland, the Lord Advocate. That provision is a valuable and effective safeguard, because it ensures that there shall be no prosecution unless the Attorney General or the Lord Advocate is satisfied that the disclosure has, or might have, damaged national security or some other major public interest, and that it is in the public interest to proceed: as a result, prosecutions under the Official Secrets Acts are infrequent.

35. It needs to be stressed, however, that in any event the Official Secrets Acts in themselves are not in any way a barrier to greater openness in Government business. They are concerned only with *unauthorised* disclosures of information, and not with the extent to which the amount of *authorised* disclosure may be increased. They do not inhibit the authorised release of information in any way; they affect only disclosures of official information made without authority. What the Fulton Committee commended, and what the Government propose to expand in every way possible, is the practice of widening the range of information whose release is authorised. The Official Secrets Acts in no way conflict with this practice.

[Information and the public interest. Cmnd. 4089 (June 1969)]

The Franks Committee, 1972

18. ... A Crown servant who discloses official information commits an offence ... only if the information is disclosed to someone ' other than a person to whom it is in the interest of the State his duty to communicate it.' ... Actual practice within Government rests heavily on a doctrine of implied authorisation, flowing from the nature of each Crown servant's job...

Ministers are – in effect – self-authorising. They decide for themselves what to reveal.[4] Senior civil servants exercise a considerable degree of personal judgment in deciding what disclosures of official information they may properly make, and to whom. More junior civil servants, and those whose duties do not involve contact with members of the public, may have a very limited discretion, or none at all...

32. Official information is disseminated, in a properly authorised manner, in a variety of ways. Ministerial statements in Parliament and elsewhere, Government publications, and written and oral statements by Government Public Relations Officers, are by no means the only ways in which this is done. A great deal of information is given by Ministers and by civil servants (mainly senior ones) by less formal means. Much of this is given by word of mouth, often on social or informal occasions when the Crown servant concerned is not obviously on

---

[4] But if they make a mistake they may suffer from it, as Mr Dalton did in 1947 when he carelessly revealed the contents of his Budget speech to a journalist, and resigned.

duty. Some of this information is given openly and may be published by its recipients as coming from a Government source. Some is given on a ' non-attributable ' basis, which means that it may be published by its recipients provided they do not identify its source. Some is given as ' background ', which means that the recipient may take account of it (e.g. it might affect the interpretation of events made by a journalist) but the information itself may not be used directly. Some is given in confidence, for instance in the case of consultations between the Government and outside interests, and such information is not intended for general disclosure. . .

33. . . . It is part of the job of Ministers and senior civil servants to communicate information in these ways. They are ' authorised ' to do so in terms of Section 2. . .

56. The way in which our constitution works (i.e. in general, quite apart from the Official Secrets Acts) determines both the degree of openness in government and the role and behaviour of the Civil Service. In this country Ministers take decisions and lay down policy. Ministers are held responsible for their decisions and are accountable to Parliament for them. It is the function of Ministers to explain and defend their decisions and their policies and to decide what official information shall be revealed. The function of the Civil Service is to advise Ministers, and to carry out their decisions and their policies. Owing to the wide range of governmental functions today, and the sheer size of the Government machine, senior civil servants in practice take many decisions within the ambit of Ministerial policies, and have a substantial role in explaining official policies and disclosing official information. Senior civil servants also engage in consultations, soundings and discussions, both formal and informal, to enable them to formulate advice to Ministers. In doing so they inevitably give information and views as well as receiving them. Junior civil servants are more circumscribed, but those whose work involves contact with the public may also have a function of explaining policy and giving information.

57. There is no direct connexion between these constitutional arrangements and Section 2. The section does not fetter Ministers in any way in deciding what to disclose and what to withhold. Their decisions are influenced mainly by the normal operation of the system of Parliamentary government, by the attentions of the media and by public pressure of all kinds. Senior civil servants who disclose official information do so on behalf of Ministers, and in accordance with their express or implied wishes. Junior civil servants act in accordance with their instructions. . .

[Report of the Committee on Section 2 of the Official Secrets Act, 1911. Cmnd. 5104 (1972)]

Ministers and official information
The Bank Rate leakage, 1957

Following rumours that there had been prior knowledge of a change in the Bank Rate and consequent speculation on the Stock Exchange, a Tribunal of Inquiry was set up under the Act of 1921 (below p. 551) to look into the matter. It appeared that the Chancellor of the Exchequer had, prior to the announcement, seen a number of journalists, party officials, and the Director-General of the Confederation of British Industries, and told them about some of the economic measures he was intending to announce, though he did not mention the Bank Rate. The propriety of these kinds of interviews was discussed in the debate on the Tribunal's report.

THE SECRETARY OF STATE FOR THE HOME DEPARTMENT (MR R. A. BUTLER): ... The Report ... says, in paragraph 5: ' The ... question whether, and if so, in what circumstances prior disclosure of intended Government measures to persons outside the Government and Civil Service may properly be made is, of course, a question for Parliament alone '. ... The fact is that it is entirely within the authority of any Chancellor of the Exchequer or, indeed, any other Ministers to disclose information in the interests of his policy to anybody in whom he reposes trust. Of course, this must be done deliberately and with discretion; he must be certain that they will not use their advance information for private ends. ... The Report describes the steps which the Government thought it right to take to ensure that the measures which were to be announced on 19th September were seen in their proper context and were given maximum support by the various organs of responsible opinion.

The Chancellor of the Exchequer had talks with seven representatives of the Press, with the Director-General of the F.B.I., the Deputy-Chairman of the Conservative Party and two of his officials. More or less simultaneously, the Minister of Power and the Minister of Labour had similar talks with the chairmen of the main nationalised industries, the representatives of the T.U.C. and the B.E.C.

I will take, first, the Press. I should be surprised if any hon. Member in this debate seriously advanced the view that in no circumstances can it be right to give advance information about Government announcements or actions to members of the Press on a confidential basis. I think that everyone in this House must be well aware that for many years this has been a clearly established practice, which has been followed by Ministers of all political parties. ... The right hon. Member for Battersea, North (Mr Jay) is reported to have said recently on television: ' The blunder the Chancellor made was not in seeing the clearing bankers and the journalists but in seeing them the day before the announcement and not the day after it . . . Does he really think that a Chancellor of the Exchequer, in making a request to the clearing bankers to limit the level of their advances to the level of the previous twelve months, without consultation beforehand, lets them read it in their financial papers and then asks them along to discuss it with him on the following day? Does he really think that this is the way to enlist their co-operation, or, what is more important, to ensure the effective character of his measures? . . .

[I]t has been said that . . . it was wrong to see only selected journalists or representatives of the Press. I wish to make only two points on this. First, it has been perfectly normal practice in the exchanges between Ministers of all parties and the Press for many years. Secondly, it would be absurd to say that all newspapers have an inherent right to exactly equal treatment in all circumstances, that if a Minister was going to talk to one journalist he should open his door to all journalists. . .

Besides, there was no question of giving an unfair advantage to selected journalists. . . Because well before any daily newspapers could go to press about the announcement my right hon. Friend held a conference at which representatives of all the Press were present. . .

. . . I have not heard any complaints that the Minister of Power saw representatives of the nationalised industries and that the Minister of Labour saw representatives of the T.U.C. and the B.E.C. In such a matter as restricting the level of investment, it is of the utmost importance to carry those representatives of our industrial life with us. There are the most respectable precedents for so doing. . .

Then there is the question of interviews with the party officials. . . The discretion of a Minister is really exactly the same in respect of and in regard to officials of his party's organisation as it is to other persons whom he may feel it desirable to consult.

. . . [I]t has been publicly stated that the Labour Government not only informed but consulted their party organisation in advance of announcing economic and financial decisions of the highest importance.

I will take the most reputable and strict of almost all Chancellors of the Exchequer, namely, Lord Snowden. He describes the following events, in his autobiography. He says: ' On the suggestion of Mr Henderson, the Cabinet Economy Committee met the General Council of the Trade Union Congress, the Executive of the Labour Party, and the Consultative Committee of the Parliamentary Labour Party on the afternoon of 20th August.'

That was in 1931. He adds that the meeting was on the subject of the cuts proposed by the Cabinet. He adds . . . ' I went with great reluctance. I had never recognised the right of the Trades Union Congress Committee to be consulted in matters of Cabinet policy.' He says: ' I went to this meeting, however, because, in addition to the Trade Union

Congress Committee, there were present representatives of the Labour Party Executive and of the Parliamentary Labour Party ' . . .

[I]n the case of the right hon. Member for Monmouth there is no question of his having consulted the party or any of its executive. What he did was to hand to Mr Poole [the Deputy-Chairman of the Conservative party] . . . and to a member of the Conservative Research Department, the documents about the restrictive financial measures other than the Bank Rate . . . to enable the party to have a little time to prepare its part in the public presentation of the policy.

Those who have served in any Government . . . will realise that the right relationship between Whitehall and the party organisation is important. The Government in power obviously depend upon a party and its organisation. Indeed, it is and should be strengthened by contacts with its own party whether through the organisation or through any research department that it may have.

We are in agreement that the utmost care must be exercised in a Government in giving information to party organisations, but, on the closest examination, my colleagues and I have found that this practice has been very carefully watched under our Administration . . .

MR HAROLD WILSON (*Huyton*): . . . [N]o one . . . would wish to fetter the rights of Ministers to consult industrial interests who may be concerned . . . in decisions such as cuts in investment programmes of publicly or privately owned industry . . . Propriety in such matters . . . must be a matter of judgment in each case. . . But the issue raised here . . . is the former Chancellor's wisdom and sense of the fitness of things in seeing certain selected newspapers and Mr Poole and other officials of the Conservative Central Office the day before the Bank Rate went up. . . The general rule should be wherever possible to see the Lobby correspondents, because I do not believe that there is any recorded case of a Minister who has done so who has been let down. In a special case he could see City editors, but, if there is anything secret involved, not before the event, nor on a selective basis, nor individually.

It was certainly a risky decision to see them. . .

MR GORDON WALKER (*Smethwick*): . . . Of course, it is often right for a Chancellor, or for any Minister, to see journalists and party officials, but not on such occasions as these, when great and high secrets are at stake. Our Amendment does not say that it is always wrong for Ministers to see such people; that they should never see them. It says it was wrong on that particular occasion. . . Our Amendment picks out, particularly, the decision . . . to see party officials. . .

. . . Our whole party democracy depends on a clear and precise distinction between the State and party machines. It is because our Governments depend on parties that they have to take immense pains not to transgress in the slightest degree the line that must be rigorously drawn between the Government machine and the party machine. . .[5]

[581 H.C.Deb. 5s. c. 815. 3 February 1958]

Lobby journalists

1. For about 63 years, journalists have been permitted to ' enter and remain in ' the Members' Lobby of the House of Commons. The journalists granted that privilege are placed on a ' List ' which is compiled by the Serjeant-at-Arms, under the authority of Mr Speaker . . .

2. Journalists on the ' List ' are admitted to the Lobby for the purpose of making and maintaining contact with Members of all Parties, Ministers and officials, with a view to recording events and generally explaining the political scene. They have always been accepted by the House on terms of mutual confidence and trust. . .

4. Contacts between Honourable and Right Honourable Members and the Lobby Journalists take two forms : —(a) Individual contacts between Members and Journalists. Members normally maintain close touch with the representatives of the newspapers in their own Divisions, for instance, on matters of national and local importance, and on their own activities. (b) Collective contacts, in which Members are given facilities for meeting the Lobby Journalists as a body.

5. *Individual contacts* . . . Any Honourable Member is, of course, free to give or withhold information at his own discretion, but the Journalist has always been free to use his own skill and ingenuity and general knowledge of political and public matters, in order to gain information on matters of national or local importance, so long as the privileges of the House are not infringed.

6. The practice has always been that no Honourable Member or other informant is to be quoted textually or mentioned by name without express permission. But any information gained may be used by the Lobby Journalist in his own words and on his own responsibility. It has always been the practice for a Lobby Journalist to accept full responsibility for what he writes and never to quote an informant should any complaint or criticism arise. The publication of such information rests on the discretion of the Lobby Journalist, and the closeness of his relations with the Member concerned. It is on this that the tradition of mutual confidence and trust has been established. The degree of confidence between a Journalist and a Member naturally depends to some extent on the closeness of their personal relationship.

7. *Collective contacts.* These are arranged, for mutual convenience, between Honourable Members and the Lobby Journalists as a body, when some information of general interest is to be imparted. The meet-

[5] Cp. above p. 78.

ings are arranged so that an Honourable Member may address all the Lobby Journalists together, as a means of saving time and trouble.

At these meetings, the same practice applies, as for individual Lobby contacts – no quotation without permission, the Lobby Journalist to take full responsibility for anything written, and anything said to be available for publication unless specifically put ' off the record '.[6]

8. In both individual and collective contacts the assumption is that any facts given or views expressed are intended for publication unless the contrary is stated. . .

9. It has always been a tradition among Lobby Journalists that anything which an Honourable Member might ask to be ' off the record ' is regarded as strictly confidential and not for publication.

11. Sanctions against the abuse of the privilege of entry into the Members' Lobby lie entirely and exclusively in the hands of Mr Speaker. He may, at will, exclude any Journalist from the Lobby, and there is no appeal against that decision. The only other person who can exercise any authority over a Lobby Journalist in this connection is his own Editor, who can recall him from the Lobby, even if he is still acceptable to Mr Speaker.

The Lobby Journalists as a body therefore have no voice in the selection or admission of any of their number, or of their retention, exclusion or withdrawal from the Lobby.

[Memorandum of Mr Guy Eden to the Select Committee on the Budget Disclosure. H.C. 20 of 1947–8]

Cp. the statement of Mr Watkinson, Minister of Defence, 28 May 1962: ' I am not prepared to disclose the detailed record of a conference which gave background briefing to the press on a non-attributable or off-the-record basis. This would set a completely new precedent, and would not be fair to the correspondents who took part. . . [I]t is the tradition of this House that right hon. or hon. Members who say things to Press correspondents on an agreed basis do not break the bargain afterwards.' [660 H.C.Deb. 5s. c. 978]

Members of Parliament and the Official Secrets Acts
Duncan Sandys' case

On 17 June 1938 Mr Duncan Sandys sent to the Secretary of State for War, Mr Hore-Belisha, the draft of a Parliamentary Question in which he drew attention to the grave shortage of anti-aircraft guns and other equipment. He quoted figures which, in the view of the War Office,

---

[6] The Lobby rules laid down by the Lobby journalists provide that members of the Lobby are under an obligation to keep secret even the fact of such meetings. A resolution was, however, passed by the Lobby in 1955 which gave members of the Lobby authority to tell their editors the sources of their information ' on the rare occasions that this may be vital '. [See Jeremy Tunstall, *The Westminster Lobby Correspondents* (1970)]

could only have been obtained by him as the result of a breach of the Official Secrets Acts, 1911–20. Following an interview with the Attorney-General, Sir Donald Somervell, Mr Sandys complained that he had been threatened with prosecution under the Acts for refusing to reveal the source of his information. A Select Committee was appointed to consider, *inter alia*, the question of the applicability of the Official Secrets Acts to members in the discharge of their parliamentary duties.

2. The privilege to which Your Committee were directed by the order of reference to have due regard is that usually referred to as the privilege of freedom of speech. This privilege is declared by the Bill of Rights in the following terms: — ' That the freedom of speech and debates or proceedings in parliament ought not to be impeached or questioned in any court or place out of parliament.'

3. The article in the Bill of Rights is not necessarily an exhaustive definition of the cognate privileges. But even assuming that it is, the privilege is not confined to words spoken in debate or to spoken words, but extends to all proceedings in parliament. While the term ' proceedings in parliament ' has never been construed by the courts, it covers both the asking of a question and the giving written notice of such question, and includes everything said or done by a member in the exercise of his functions as a member in a committee of either House, as well as everything said or done in either House in the trans-action of parliamentary business.

4. The privilege of freedom of speech being confined to words spoken or things done in the course of parliamentary proceedings, words spoken or things done by a member beyond the walls of parliament will generally not be protected. Cases may, however, easily be imagined of communications between one member and another, or between a member and a minister, so closely related to some matter pending in, or expected to be brought before, the House, that though they do not take place in the chamber or a committee room they form part of the business of the House, as, for example, where a member sends to a minister the draft of a question he is thinking of putting down or shows it to another member with a view to obtaining advice as to the propriety of putting it down or as to the manner in which it should be framed. The Attorney-General said that, should such a case come before the courts, he could not but think that they would give a broad construction to the term ' proceedings in parliament ' having regard to the great fundamental purpose which the privilege of freedom of speech served, and that he could ' see a possible construction of " proceedings " which would extend to matters outside the precincts if they were related to what is to happen in the House '.[7]

---

[7] [These paragraphs were quoted with approval by the Committee of Privileges in 1957, when it was considering whether a threat by the London

10. Your Committee are of opinion that disclosures by members in the course of debate or proceedings in Parliament cannot be made the subject of proceedings under the Official Secrets Acts. They think that a disclosure made by a member to a minister or by one member to another directly relating to some act to be done or some proceedings in the House, even though it did not take place in the House, might be held to form part of the business of the House and consequently to be similarly protected. On the other hand, a casual conversation in the House cannot be said to be a proceeding in Parliament, and a member who discloses information in the course of such a conversation would not, in their view, be protected by privilege, though it might be a question whether the evidence necessary to secure his conviction could be given without the permission of the House. . .

15. A member who discloses information of the kind in question in a speech in his constituency or anywhere beyond the walls of parliament would clearly not be protected by parliamentary privilege from proceedings under the Acts.

16. Your Committee are of opinion that the soliciting or receipt of information is not a proceeding in parliament, and that neither the privilege of freedom of speech nor any of the cognate privileges would afford a defence to a member of parliament charged with soliciting, inciting or endeavouring to persuade a person holding office under the Crown to disclose information which such person was not authorised to disclose, or with receiving information knowing, or having reasonable grounds to believe, that the information was communicated to him in contravention of the Official Secrets Acts. It might well be that what the

---

Electricity Board to bring an action for libel against Mr G. R. Strauss was 'calculated to impede him as a Member in the performance of his parliamentary duties' and constituted a breach of privilege. Mr Strauss had written to the Paymaster-General to complain about the way in which the London Electricity Board disposed of its scrap. The Paymaster-General replied that the disposal of scrap was a matter of day-to-day administration and was therefore the responsibility of the Board and not of the Minister of Power, whom the Paymaster-General represented in the House of Commons. A copy of Mr Strauss's letter was sent to the chairman of the Board. He objected to some of the statements in it and after Mr Strauss had refused to withdraw them, the Board's solicitor wrote to him and threatened to institute proceedings for libel. The Committee of Privileges took the view that writing to a Minister about the affairs of a nationalised industry was a 'proceeding in Parliament' and was therefore protected by the Bill of Rights, and the threat to institute proceedings was a breach of privilege (Fifth Report from the Committee of Privileges, H.C. 305 of 1956–7). The House of Commons refused to accept the Committee's view, and on a free vote decided by a narrow majority that the writing of a letter to a Minister was not a 'proceeding in Parliament' and that therefore the letters from the Electricity Board did not constitute a breach of privilege (591 H.C.Deb. 5s. c. 334. 8 July 1958).]

defendant had said in the House had caused the authorities to institute inquiries, but if the prosecution could prove its case without giving evidence of what he had said, the proceedings could not be regarded as a questioning of a debate or proceeding in parliament. If, however, it were necessary, in order to prove the fact charged, to produce evidence of what the defendant had said in the House, it would be in the power of the House to protect him by withholding permission for the evidence to be given.

17. As regards the reception of information, some protection is afforded to members of parliament by the fact that under the Official Secrets Acts information may lawfully be communicated to an un-authorized person provided that it is the duty in the interest of the state of the person who communicates such information to do so. But it should be clearly realized that such a defence must be founded on the express words of the proviso to the Act and is not derived in any sense from privilege. In each individual case the burden of proof would lie upon the official and the member of parliament concerned to show that the circumstances of the disclosure were such as to give rise to the duty, and such circumstances could only be shown in exceptional cases. It would be highly dangerous to give any colour to the view that the mere fact of election to the House of Commons creates a general duty towards the person elected on the part of the depositaries of official secrets to disclose those secrets without authori-zation. And in the case of such matters as, for example, the proceed-ings of the Cabinet, the provisions of the forthcoming Budget, the disposition of the Fleet on mobilization, the formula of a new gas, or the specifications of a new submarine, the circumstances that would justify disclosure must be so exceptional as to be almost unthinkable.

18. Although the legal position with regard to the solicitation of the disclosure by, or the receipt of information from, a person holding office under the Crown is as stated in paragraphs 16 and 17, official information, as the debates of the House show, is frequently obtained by members of parliament from persons who are not authorized to disclose it. Members' sense of responsibility and discretion have, your Committee believe, prevented them from making use of any informa-tion thus obtained in a manner detrimental to the interests or safety of the state. Indeed, the information, though technically confidential, often does not relate to matters affecting the safety of the State. But as the the interests or safety of the State and the solicitation or receipt of information the disclosure of which would be prejudicial to the interests or safety of the State and the solicitation or receipt of information the disclosure of which is merely unauthorized, the Acts, if strictly enforced, would make it difficult for members to obtain the information without which they cannot effectively discharge their duty.

Any action which, without actually infringing any privilege enjoyed by members of the House in their capacity as members, yet obstructs or impedes them in the discharge of their duties, or tends to produce such results, even though the act be lawful, may be held to be a contempt of the House.

19. Apart from the protection afforded by privilege there are three safeguards against the possibility of the Official Secrets Acts being used in such a way as to obstruct members in the performance of their parliamentary functions. In the first place the initiation of the consideration of proceedings would almost invariably rest with the department whose secret had been disclosed, and though the head of the department need not necessarily be a member of the House of Commons, the department would be represented in the House. Secondly, no prosecution can be instituted without the consent of the Attorney-General in England or the Lord Advocate in Scotland. . .

20. . . . [W]hile the Attorney-General told Your Committee that it would be impossible to formulate in precise form all the circumstances which would fall to be considered should such an issue be placed before the Attorney-General, it would be said, ' clearly be proper and inevitable for him to have due regard to the special position and duties of a member of parliament '. . .

21. A third safeguard is the right of a member who finds himself threatened with a prosecution under the Official Secrets Acts to bring the matter before the House as a question of privilege. Unless, therefore, the incident occurs during a recess the matter can be discussed and considered by the House before any irrevocable step is taken.

22. Your Committee think it would be inadvisable to attempt by legislation or otherwise to define with precision the extent of the immunity from prosecution under the Official Secrets Acts to which members of parliament are or ought to be entitled . . . The privileges of parliament, like many other institutions of the British constitution, are indefinite in their nature and stated in general and sometimes vague terms. The elasticity thus secured has made it possible to apply existing privileges in new circumstances from time to time. Any attempt to translate them into precise rules must deprive them of the very quality which renders them adaptable to new and varying conditions, and new or unusual combinations of circumstances, and indeed, might have the effect of restricting rather than safeguarding members' privileges, since it would imply that, save in the circumstances specified, a member could be prosecuted without any infringement of the privileges of the House. ' The dignity and independence of the two Houses,' says Sir William Blackstone with great force, ' are in great measure preserved by keeping their privileges indefinite. If all the privileges of parliament were set down and ascertained, and no privilege to be allowed but what was so

defined and determined, it were easy for the executive power to devise some new case, not within the line of privilege, and under pretence thereof to harass any refractory member and violate the freedom of parliament[8]...

24. The House of Commons has disciplinary powers over its members, and a member who abuses his privilege of speech may be punished, not merely by suspension from the service of the House, but by imprisonment or expulsion from the House, or both.[9] Expulsion at least cannot be considered a light penalty, It is not so much on penal sanctions, however, that Your Committee would desire to rely for the prevention of abuses of parliamentary privilege prejudicial to the safety of the realm, as on the good sense of members themselves, who are as much concerned as ministers to prevent such abuses...

[Report from the Select Committee on the Official Secrets Acts. H.C. 101 of 1938–9]

The Franks Committee and the Official Secrets Acts, 1972

104. ... The essence of our proposals is that the criminal law should not be invoked except where there is a specific reason for giving this special protection to the information in question ...

CHAPTER 9: *The security of the nation and the safety of the people*

116. National security is widely accepted as the prime justification for employing criminal sanctions to protect official information... Closer analysis indicates that the kinds of information coming within these categories have several characteristics in common. They all go to the fundamentals of government. They are all matters of major importance. They are all matters which affect the nation as a whole. A safe and independent life for a nation and its people requires effective defence against the threat of attack from outside. It requires the main-

---

[8] [*Commentaries*, vol. 1, p. 164.]

[9] [This applies generally. Cp. the Speaker on 7 June 1961: 'I am very anxious that nothing I should say should be thought – it would not be thought in the House, but might be thought outside – to mean that this House would not, in certain circumstances, be alert to protect the citizen against the activity of one of its Members. I am not saying that. Supposing there was a case ... where an hon. Member knowingly and deliberately put a false and defamatory allegation about a citizen into a Question, and thereby used the procedure and paper of this House to give publicity to the allegation while he himself was protected, I imagine that it might well be that the House would think that there was an abuse of procedure such as to constitute a contempt, and that the House would undoubtedly think it right to deal with it, because such a statement could only be challenged here in the House, and the House would want to look after the rights of its Member, on the one hand, and the rights of the citizen, on the other. That is what I would feel about it ' (641 H.C.Deb. 5s. c. 1090).]

tenance of the nation's relations with the rest of the world, and of its essential economic base. It requires the preservation of law and order, and the ability to cope with emergencies threatening the essentials of life... The most appropriate general description for all these matters is that they concern the security of the nation and the safety of the people.

117. It is in this context that strong measures are clearly justified in preventing serious injury to the nation. It is less clear that the criminal law must be brought in to reinforce other means of protection where the possible injury is of a less serious nature...

Section A: *General categories of official information affecting the security of the nation and the safety of the people*

Defence and internal security

124. We propose that the Official Information Act should apply to official information relating to matters which concern or affect the defence or security of the realm, including in particular those matters set out in the sub-paragraphs below. Information relating to the defence or security of allied Powers, covering matters of the kind mentioned in sub-paragraphs a to f (but not sub-paragraph g), should be included in this category. It must be remembered, in reading these sub-paragraphs, that criminal sanctions will only cover such information within this category as also comes within the second part of the definition, on the ground that its disclosure could cause serious injury:—

a. the Armed Forces of the Crown and matters relating thereto;
b. military weapons, stores and equipment of all kinds, including nuclear weapons, ships, aircraft, vehicles, communications systems and all means of warfare;
c. the research, development and production of all items covered by sub-paragraph b;
d. defence policy and strategy and other military planning, including plans and measures for the maintenance of essential supplies and services in the event of war;
e. intelligence and security services, and information obtained by them;
f. military treaties and arrangements with other Powers, and negotiations of such treaties and arrangements;
g. internal defence and security, and plans and measures relating thereto, including plans and measures for the maintenance and restoration of public order or of essential supplies and services in contingencies short of war...

Foreign relations

129. Information in the field of foreign affairs can be divided into two broad classes. First there is information shared between the United Kingdom Government and one or more other governments. Examples

are exchanges with other governments, including negotiations of all kinds, and information circulated by or within international organisations. Some international negotiations succeed in being conducted in secrecy. The frank and honest exposure of differing points of view, the exploration of possible concessions, the striking of bargains, is handicapped if conducted in the open. This is particularly so where sensitive issues of national prestige and pride are involved, and the glare of publicity would convert a negotiation into a propaganda war. . .

131. The second area of secrecy in the field of foreign affairs covers information within the United Kingdom Government which relates to our relations with other governments. Much of this information consists of or is based upon reports from our representatives overseas. The value of reports of this kind is limited if they cannot be completely frank, and in this context secrecy is an essential condition of frankness. They include information and assessments of all kinds on the situation in other countries, including, for instance, comment on leading political and other personalities. . . The information in reports from posts abroad is then a major ingredient in the assessments which form the basis of policy decisions by Ministers in London on the conduct of our relations with other countries. The conduct of these relations could be severely prejudiced by leakage.

132. The distinguishing feature of the information mentioned in paragraphs 129–131 is that it all relates to matters which concern or affect the relations of the United Kingdom Government with another government or an international body . . . and not to the wider field of trade and consular affairs when these are not being handled between governments. Once a matter reaches the inter-governmental level, it attracts a political element, and secrecy may be required for one of the reasons we have mentioned. Many matters dealt with among governments are not of sufficient importance to warrant the protection of criminal sanctions, but these cannot be distinguished on the basis of subject matter. We discuss in section B of this Chapter the method of excluding disclosures not causing serious injury. In terms of subject matter, the single characteristic which should attract the possibility of criminal sanctions is that relations between governments are involved. Other aspects of foreign affairs should be excluded. . .

134. We propose that the Official Information Act should apply to official information relating to any matters which concern or affect foreign relations or the conduct of foreign relations. By ' foreign relations ' we mean relations between the United Kingdom Government and any other Power or any international body the members of which are governments.

The currency and the reserves

137. It . . . seems clear to us that exceptionally grave injury to the economy qualifies for the protection of criminal sanctions . . . There is only one instance, it seems to us, where an unauthorised disclosure could cause economic injury of this degree of seriousness, and that is the currency. . .

139. We propose that the Official Information Act should apply to official information relating to any proposals, negotiations or decisions connected with alterations in the value of sterling, or relating to the reserves, including their extent or any movement in or threat to them. . .

Information falling outside our categories

141. Governments take particular precautions to maintain the secrecy of the Budget, of other fiscal changes, and of changes in the Bank Rate. These precautions include the rigid restriction of who may have access to such information, which is usually the most effective form of protection. These matters are traditionally included in any catalogue of secret official information . . . By the touchstone of serious injury to the nation as a whole, however, they do not qualify. Any injury resulting from premature revelation would not in our view be such as to warrant criminal sanctions in addition to the other protections available. One of the main effects of a fiscal leak is often political embarrassment, rather than injury to the economy, and this does not justify the use of the criminal law. Governments will still take appropriate measures to protect such information, without the use of criminal sanctions. There will remain the sanction of loss of career facing any Crown servant found to have leaked. But one mischief which may be caused by the leakage of impending fiscal changes is that those thereby put in the know can use their knowledge to make money. Leakages of this kind are covered by our proposal in Chapter 12 that the use or disclosure of official information for purposes of private gain should be made an offence.

142. Another kind of economic information not covered by our proposals comprises forecasts and assumptions, for instance about wage and price movements and levels of unemployment, made as part of the process of formulating economic policy. These are ordinarily never published. Such forecasts are also made by non-official bodies, but the fact that a forecast is a *Government* forecast gives it an altogether different significance. The Treasury say, in their written memorandum, that if a leak gives people cause to fear a certain turn of events, they may take action in their own interests which will produce that very turn of events; the Government's ability to meet this situation is then prejudiced, and the country suffers. Premature knowledge of impending policy changes, it is said, including tax changes, can have a

similar effect. On the other hand the Treasury stated that changes do occur in the views taken by Governments about the extent to which their planning and decision-making processes in this field should be revealed. Our proposal is not that governments should no longer protect economic and financial information of this kind. It is that those leaking such information should no longer be liable to prosecution and imprisonment, unless it is done for private gain.

143. There are other issues of domestic policy, outside our categories, which may also be important or sensitive. There may be good reasons why Governments should wish to avoid unauthorised disclosures concerning their internal discussions of such matters, or concerning negotiations or consultations about such issues with those outside the Government. But what we have to consider is the different question whether those responsible for such disclosures should be liable to the pains and penalties of the criminal law. We propose that these pains and penalties should be retained for disclosures of information within our categories, if sufficiently serious . . .

Section B : *The identification within the categories of disclosures serious enough to warrant criminal sanctions*

144. In section A of this Chapter we have identified three broad categories of official information which affect the security of the nation or the safety of the people. . . [T]he generalised descriptions of these categories . . . should be combined with a more precise method of identifying that particular information within them the unauthorised disclosure of which is likely to cause serious injury to the nation. There is only one method which in our view is capable of achieving this object satisfactorily. This is for each individual item of information to be identified and marked by the Government in a way which enables those who come into possession of it to recognise that it is covered by the provisions of the new law.

145. . . . [T]he question of injury to the nation is essentially political . . . not judicial. It is essentially a Government responsibility to assess the importance of information in our three categories . . . Any system which placed this responsibility elsewhere would detract from the responsibility of the Government to protect the security of the nation and the safety of the people. It would remove the element of constitutional accountability.

Classification and the law

150. The present criterion for classifying official information as SECRET is that its unauthorised disclosure would cause serious injury to the interests of the nation. . .

154. There are . . . some particular considerations relating to defence. The Ministry of Defence . . . said that, in their view, serious damage

could result from the disclosure of information about weapons and equipment which had properly been classified as CONFIDENTIAL. For example, many details of the performance of new military equipment are graded CONFIDENTIAL. In many cases, however, if a large number of these individual items were assembled together, e.g. on a computer tape, and this assembled information was disclosed without authority, serious injury would undoubtedly be caused to the national interests...

157. ... [W]e propose that the Official Information Act should contain the following... provisions on classification:—

    a. Information should count as 'classified' within the meaning of the Act if—

        i. in the case of a document, it is marked with the word SECRET or with words including the word SECRET, or it relates to military weapons or equipment (as defined in paragraph 124 b. and c.) and it is marked DEFENCE–CONFIDENTIAL and in either case it has been classified in accordance with the provisions of the Act and of regulations on classification made under it;

        ii. in the case of a communication by non-documentary means, the information relates to the contents of a document which is classified in accordance with i., or is information which, if it had been contained in a document, ought to have been so classified.

    b. The Secretary of State should make regulations about the classification and declassification of documents, which should include provisions on levels of authority at which decisions on classification may be taken and on arrangements for review and declassification.

    c. The unauthorised removal of a classification mark, or the making of a copy of a classified document without the mark, should not affect the classified status of that document...

Safeguards against over-classification

161. ... [W]e propose that, before a decision is taken whether to prosecute, there should be a review of the classification of the information which had allegedly been disclosed without authority... by the responsible Minister. He should be required to consider whether, at the time of the alleged disclosure that information was properly classified... If he is satisfied, he should give a certificate to that effect to the court. This certificate should be conclusive evidence of the fact that the information was classified within the meaning of the Act...

163. ... This proposal does not cover situations where a person who comes into possession of information which is classified SECRET or

above, or DEFENCE–CONFIDENTIAL thinks that it ought not to be so classified, and wishes to disclose or publish the information. . .

165. We think it would be valuable if a Committee were to be established . . . to provide a central point of reference for any person to ascertain whether information which he has received (not necessarily in documentary form) is classified, and also to question the validity of a particular classification. . .

166. We think that this Committee should be non-statutory, and should be established by agreement between the Government and the outside interests most closely concerned, which include the news media. It should . . . be appointed by and report to the Prime Minister as the Minister with overall responsibility for matters of national security. . .

CHAPTER 10: *The maintenance of law and order*

170. . . . [U]nauthorised disclosures of official information affecting the maintenance of law and order cannot appropriately be dealt with in the law by the same means as the three categories of information discussed [above]. . . The touchstone of serious damage to the security of the nation and the life of the people does not apply in quite the same way. It would be unusual for any single disclosure of official information concerning the maintenance of law and order to cause serious damage to the nation as a whole. . .

175. We propose that the Official Information Act should apply to official information (including police, prison and Post Office information) which comes within one of the three following descriptions: —

a. it is likely to be helpful in the commission of offences. Instances are information about the route and timing of the runs of vehicles carrying money or other valuable loads, or about a burglar alarm system and how to neutralise it.

b. it is likely to be helpful in facilitating an escape from legal custody or other acts prejudicial to prison security. This group includes information about the premises, security measures, organisation or routine of prisons and other places where persons are held in legal custody which might enable persons in custody to escape, or to circumvent measures of control. It does not include information about treatment and discipline in such establishments.

c. its disclosure would be likely to impede the prevention or detection of offences or the apprehension or prosecution of offenders. This group includes information about police measures and equipment for the prevention and detection of crime, criminal intelligence, the identity of informers, information about police plans for dealing with a possible serious public disturbance, and information in the hands of the police or of prosecuting authorities which might enable an offender to escape justice. . .

CHAPTER 11: *The processes of Government and the Cabinet*

176. In Chapters 9 and 10 we have discussed kinds of official information which require protection because their disclosure would have a damaging effect... An argument of a quite different kind for protecting official information... [is] the importance of Ministers and administrators being able, in some instances and at some stages, to discuss matters frankly and fully in private. This need may arise whatever the subject under discussion; it may be felt irrespective of whether an unauthorised disclosure would, by itself, be particularly damaging to the nation.[10]

179. ... The questions which we have to consider are these: would this position in fact be undermined by the amendments of the law which we propose? Is there a case for the use of criminal sanctions to give *general* protection to the internal processes of government, in addition to the *specific* protection given by the other new provisions which we propose?

180. We answer both these questions in the negative.

181. ... The leakage of information about discussions within the Civil Service cannot, as such, be regarded as sufficient justification for imposing criminal liability... The discipline of the public service is in our view an adequate means, as well as being the appropriate means, of dealing with such matters.

The Cabinet

182. It is implicit in some of the Government evidence that the considerations set out in paragraphs 176–8 apply with very special force to... the Cabinet...

184. It is of course true that a certain amount of information about matters likely to come before the Cabinet and conclusions reached on particular issues becomes known and is discussed in the press. Some but not all of this information is attributable to the briefing of accredited correspondents by Ministers or by others on their behalf. A small amount does not come from such authorised briefings, but is the natural product of a place like Westminster – or any centre of government – where Ministers and a hundred or more political correspondents work closely together. It is unreasonable to expect the silence of the monastery in a modern centre of government. Different Ministers will always interpret differently the secrecy enjoined on them. Some talk more freely than others. It is valuable to have the ear of a friendly correspondent, and he will appreciate a little guidance from time to time. Equally, when a Cabinet is under stress, it is tempting for a Minister to

[10] Cp. above p. 436 and below p. 521ff.

hint in private conversation with a lobby man where at any rate he stands. Anyone with working knowledge of the system knows that this happens. But the effect of it all, even allowing for rare indiscretions, in our view still falls a long way short of the consequences of publishing the text of Cabinet documents or disclosing the course of Cabinet proceedings. We must distinguish between the small coin of day-to-day exchanges around Westminster and disclosures about transactions within the Cabinet which could destroy its effectiveness.

185. ... We think it important that Cabinet documents should continue to receive ... the protection of criminal sanctions against unauthorised disclosure. Although the circulation of such documents within the Government is restricted, the number of civil servants with access to them is inevitably considerable. Those who have access are at all levels, from Permanent Secretaries to the typists who type the papers and the clerks who file them. Thus the possibility of leakage of a document at some point is not negligible. In any event the governing factor in considering the need for protection is the seriousness of the damage that a leak would cause rather than the likelihood of leakage.

186. ... For our purposes ' the Cabinet ' means the full Cabinet, and Cabinet committees the members of which are Ministers. The considerations we have mentioned apply equally to both; they do not apply any further.

187. We have mentioned in paragraph 184 the way in which day-to-day exchanges around Westminster include the disclosure of a certain amount of information about the business of the Cabinet. It can be very difficult to establish where this kind of disclosure came from, whether it was authorised or not, and whether it is a factual disclosure or intelligent speculation. We do not think it feasible that communications of this kind concerning the Cabinet should form the subject of criminal prosecutions. The real damage with which we are concerned would be caused by the publication of the actual documents of the Cabinet – that is, papers put to the Cabinet for consideration, and the minutes recording its discussions and its conclusions. Criminal sanctions should apply to the unauthorised communication of these papers. Such a communication need not, however, take the form of handing over a Cabinet document, or a copy or a part of such a document. The words on a document can be stored in the memory, written down, or recorded in some other way. They can then be communicated or transmitted in a way which makes it possible to reconstruct and publish the document either verbatim or in what is to all intents and purposes its original form. The law should accordingly cover both the communication of an actual Cabinet document or a substantial part of one, and the communication of information about the document which enables another person to

reproduce the document or a substantial part of it in a verbatim or virtually verbatim form. The law should not extend to the gist, or a summary, of a Cabinet document.

188. Criminal sanctions should apply only from the moment when a document assumes its status as a Cabinet document. This is the point in time when a paper bearing the appropriate heading is circulated to Cabinet Ministers. Earlier official papers on the same subject, and drafts of a Cabinet document, are not themselves Cabinet documents, however similar their contents. We are proposing criminal sanctions for the protection of Cabinet documents not on account of the contents of these documents, but to safeguard the collective responsibility of the Cabinet. This collective responsibility is not engaged before a document is circulated to the members of the Cabinet. This, therefore, is the point in time from which criminal sanctions should apply.

189. . . . It is important for the practical operation of our proposals that persons outside the Government who come into possession of Cabinet documents should be able to recognise them. The Official Information Act should therefore provide for the Secretary of the Cabinet to prescribe the markings on Cabinet documents. . .

CHAPTER 12: *Breaches of confidence and the use of official information for private gain*
. . .

The confidences of the citizen reposed in the Government

193. Information about individuals in the possession of the Government includes the following: that collected by the Registrars General in the course of the registration of births, marriages and deaths, some of which is kept confidential and is not available for public inspection or publication; census information and other similar information from surveys; information in tax returns; information acquired by social security offices in the course of dealing with claims for benefit of all kinds; information about immigrants and those seeking naturalisation; information about prisoners and other criminals, or suspected criminals; information about those seeking the exercise of the Royal Prerogative of Mercy or complaining against the police; information about National Health Service patients; information about those holding, or considered for, judicial office, a great variety of other Crown or Government appointments and honours; the personal particulars of teachers; information about qualifications, job record, etc., given to the employment services; and a variety of other similar kinds of information.

194. Information about organisations in the possession of the

Government includes the following:— information about industrial, commercial, agricultural, and fishing undertakings of all kinds relating to such things as their financial and trading position, plans, policies, new projects and mergers; share of the market, pricing policies, imports and exports; wages, conditions of work and internal relations; and products and manufacturing processes. This information may come to the Government in statutory returns, e.g. under the legislation on taxation and on statistics of trade; and in connection with the administration of Customs and Excise, applications for grants, for planning permission and for other permissions, and tenders for Government contracts. Apart from information of this kind, related directly to the execution of specific government functions, the Government also receives a considerable amount of information in the course of consultations with business and industry, which are intended to help the Government to formulate economic policy and to take specific decisions. Apart from the fact that this information is confidential, its publication or disclosure, e.g. to competitors, could in many instances be seriously damaging to the undertakings concerned.

The need to protect these confidences by criminal sanctions

197. ... We do not suppose that the withdrawal of the present legal protection would be followed by any significant number of unauthorised disclosures of this kind of information. In our view there are nevertheless proper reasons for maintaining the protection of criminal sanctions... The Government is requiring more and more information from citizens and bodies. This information is given willingly and frankly only on the assurance, implicit or explicit, that it will be kept confidential... Any breakdown of this trust between Government and people could have considerable adverse repercussions on the government of the country...[11]

199. ... Some of the information concerned is admittedly of a relatively innocuous or trivial kind, and indeed may be clearly less important than some of the government information which we believe should no longer be protected by the criminal law. But the withdrawal of the existing protection of the criminal law from information entrusted to the Government would in our view be a mistake.

200. Information entrusted to the Government by citizens and private bodies may or may not be given on the clear understanding that it is confidential. It seems to us proper, however, that the law should be drafted in terms of all information given to the Government by individuals and private bodies, and should not require proof

[11] Note however the case of *Norwich Pharmacal Co.* v. *Customs and Excise Commissioners* [1974] A.C. 133.

of an express or implied condition of confidence... We propose that the Official Information Act should apply to information given to the Government by private individuals or concerns, whether given by reason of compulsory powers or otherwise, and whether or not given on an express or implied basis of confidence.

The use of official information for private gain
...

205. We propose that the Official Information Act should contain the following provisions, which would in effect form an extension of the existing law on corruption: —

    a. It should be an offence for a Crown servant, contrary to his official duty, to use official information for the purpose of obtaining private gain for himself or any other person, or to communicate the information to any other person with a view to enabling that person or any other person to obtain private gain. ' Private gain ' means the making of a gain, or the avoidance of a loss, in money or money's worth.

    b. This offence should also cover—

        i. a Government contractor who uses or communicates official information for private gain, otherwise than for the purposes of the contract;

        ii. a person entrusted with official information in confidence, who uses or communicates that information for private gain, otherwise than for the purposes for which it was entrusted.

    c. It should be an offence for a recipient of official information, which he knows or has reasonable ground to believe has been disclosed by a Crown servant contrary to his official duty, or by a Government contractor or person entrusted with official information in confidence contrary to above, to use that information for the purpose of obtaining private gain for himself or for another.

CHAPTER 16: *Control over the institution of prosecutions...*

248. The offences we propose relating to law and order and private gain seem to us to raise no special considerations of the kind which in recent years have been regarded as pointing towards a control by the Attorney General rather than the Director of Public Prosecutions. Accordingly we propose that the Director should exercise control in England and Wales in relation to these offences...

255. We propose that the institution of prosecutions under the Official Information Act relating to information in the fields of defence and internal security, foreign relations, the currency and the reserves,

and the confidences of the citizen, and to Cabinet documents, should be controlled by the Attorney General...

[Report of the Departmental Committee on Section 2 of the Official Secrets Act, 1911. Cmnd. 5104 (September 1972)]

The reaction of the Conservative Government, 1973

THE SECRETARY OF STATE FOR THE HOME DEPARTMENT (MR ROBERT CARR): ... The Government ... accept in principle that Section 2 of the 1911 Act should be repealed and replaced by new legislation along the general lines proposed by the Franks Committee... In the Government's view there are some areas in which it will be necessary to modify some of the detailed recommendations...

Under the heading of 'Defence and Internal Security' the committee recommended that information should be protected which was classified 'secret' or above and related to intelligence and security services and information obtained by them. However, in view of the indivisible nature of the operations of the Security Service, we think that there should be protection for all information related to intelligence and security services and the information obtained by them. This is a very difficult sphere in which one cannot discuss all the difficulties openly, but we believe that the security problem is indivisible and that, in the nature of intelligence, it is the collation of lots of bits of information, some of which individually need to be marked 'Secret' and others do not, and the integration of all those pieces of information which is the essence of any intelligence system. That is why we believe that for the protection of the security services, which operate in this country under a strict charter – that is something that we must always protect – the whole of their operations should be protected by the law.

Coming to currency and the reserves, we agree with the Franks Committee that any disclosure of information which might adversely affect the Government's ability to manage the economy should be prohibited by law. We are very doubtful, however, whether the line can be drawn as sharply as the Franks Committee proposes between questions affecting currency and the reserves and other aspects of the Government's economic and budgetary policy. It does not seem right, for example, to exclude from the scope of legislation protection of matters which relate to monetary policy, including impending changes in domestic interest rates. Equally, it seems to us that information about impending Budget proposals should be protected, because there is validity in the importance we have always attached in this House and in the country to any leakage of information in this area. Premature leakage not only damages the national interest but can give great advantage, or, in some cases, disadvantage, to individual people and groups of our community.

Another area of difficulty I want to expose, on which I hope hon. Members will comment, is that of foreign relations...

I am bound to tell the House that we have some real doubts whether the committee has sufficiently taken account of the great damage which can be caused by disclosure of material which arises in the normal conduct of foreign affairs. Take, for example, dispatches from our diplomatic representatives abroad which may not merit the classification of 'secret'... We believe that many of them if disclosed, could unacceptably impair our relations with the country concerned. It is not just that they could give rise to damaging embarrassment in particular negotiating situations – I think that is fairly obvious – but more generally that they could do unacceptable damage to our relations with another country; for example, by making public our representatives' judgments of events and personalities in the countries to which they are accredited...

There is also the fact that a good deal of information in the 'confidential' category is exchanged between us and our allies on the understanding at present that it will not be divulged and is protected by the criminal law. If the criminal sanction were no longer to apply to unauthorised disclosure of this material we might find a greater reluctance on the part of our allies to share such information with us, and that, we believe, would again be unacceptable in the interests of our own country.

So for all these reasons we think that there could well be a case for extending the protection of the law to information about foreign relations somewhat more widely than the Franks Committee was prepared to recommend.

Many of the arguments with which the committee supports its recommendation for the creation of a new class of 'defence–confidential' would also apply to foreign relations...

As for the protection of Cabinet documents, there is an inevitable conflict of interest, and this is an area about which we very much want to hear what the House has to say. The fundamental principle is that our system of government depends on the collective responsibility of the Cabinet...

The difficulty is that virtually all ministerial decisions, even those taken by Ministers in their own Departments, are relevant to collective responsibility. Moreover, the publication of an advance draft of a document just before its circulation to the Cabinet would be no less harmful than publication of that same document after it had been officially stamped as a Cabinet paper...

On the principles advanced by the Franks Committee itself, it can be strongly argued that where an official committee, as opposed to a ministerial committee, is considering a subject in close conjunction with Ministers, or where Ministers have referred back to officials for further work a subject which has already gone to the Cabinet or a Cabinet committee, the papers should be accorded the same protection as Cabinet documents. It seems to us difficult to know where to draw the line here. Any decision is bound to be somewhat arbitrary...

As to the confidences of the citizen... the essence of the committee's proposal is that criminal sanctions should apply to the disclosure of information given to the Government by private individuals or concerns. But this would mean that the protection afforded to the same piece of information would vary according to whether it had been given to the Government by the persons concerned or had come into the Government's hands in some other way.

We believe that, however acquired, personal information about individuals, or, for that matter about private companies and concerns, held by a Government Department requires protection from improper disclosure by the criminal law.

[858 H.C.Deb. 5s. c. 1885. 29 June 1973]

(iii) ' D ' Notices

6. A ' D ' notice is a formal letter of warning or request, signed by the Secretary of a Committee known as the Services, Press and Broadcasting Committee, and addressed to newspaper editors, to news editors, in sound broadcasting and television, to editors of some periodicals concerned with defence information and to selected publishers concerned with biographies and historical and technical subjects. They are normally headed ' Private and Confidential ' (or ' Secret ') and are accepted by the recipients as confidential communications. Their purpose is to request a ban on the publication of certain subjects, indicated in the notices, which bear upon defence or national security. Sometimes they take the form of a simple requested suppression; sometimes they identify certain subjects as areas of danger for the purposes of security and suggest limits within which they can safely be treated.

7. The ' D ' notice system is a voluntary one. There is no compulsion behind it, and non-observance of the request contained in a notice carries no penalties. The force of its appeal arises from the fact that it is put forward by some branch of Her Majesty's Government which has reason to suppose that its request is justified by the needs of security and that a notice cannot be issued unless its form and contents have been approved by the Committee, of whose members Press representatives are more than twice as numerous as the representatives drawn from Government Departments. Breaches of

the terms of ' D ' notices do occur from time to time, but it seems to be agreed that nearly every breach that has occurred has been attributable to inadvertence, and a deliberate refusal to comply with a ' D ' notice is extremely rare.[12] If it were otherwise, the system, which has worked effectively under what are substantially its present conditions since the end of the last War, would have long since broken down: for unless ' D ' notices are to be generally observed as a matter of obligation between each newspaper and the others as well as between all newspapers and the Government, it is obvious that single newspapers cannot be expected to continue to observe them when they are ignored by other newspapers who may be in competition with them.

8. The process that brings a ' D ' notice into existence is as follows. The proposal will originate with one of the Government Departments concerned. A draft of what is required is then discussed with the Secretary of the Committee. Not all proposals for ' D ' notices survive this discussion: some are withdrawn if the Secretary considers that they could not reasonably be submitted to the Press. If one is to go forward, he advises on such detailed points as to its presentation as he thinks are likely to be of interest of his Committee. A draft is then circulated among its members for their comments and, if approved, it is issued by the Secretary in the name of the Committee as a whole. In cases of special urgency the Secretary is authorised to ... send out a notice on his own responsibility, provided that he secures the prior approval of not less than three of the Press members of the Committee, who must meet together for the purpose.

[12] In its submission to the Committee the Government stated:
' There have of course been breaches of " D " notices before and there no doubt will be again; the system is not infallible because it is not enforceable. Technical or minor infringements, not involving any real harm to security are fairly frequent. Recent examples have been the mention by name of a former Head of M.I.6, and the appearance on television of one of their former employees (the B.B.C. acknowledged and apologised for this transgression). Major infringements knowingly committed and causing or arising from disagreement between newspapers and the official side, are very much more rare. The previous Radcliffe Committee took cognisance of the difficulty over the Blake case in this connexion. Since then the only major incident, apart from the present case [the publication by the *Daily Mail* of an article on the interception of cables], arose over the arrival in England in 1963 of the Russian defector, Dolnytsin, whose whereabouts the security authorities wished to keep secret. The Secretary of the Services Press and Broadcasting Committee sent out a Private and Confidential message asking that the details should not be published but this was disregarded by the *Daily Telegraph*, apparently on the grounds that they had obtained the information from a foreign source, and also that the disclosure of Dolnytsin's name in a " D " notice circulated on the Press Association's tape removed any justification for withholding it.'

9. The Secretary's office is therefore the central point of the system. He is the servant of the Committee as a whole, and his duties are whole-time. The greater part of his daily work consists in offering advice and assistance to different members of the Press as to the interpretation and application of the ' D ' notices (of which there are to-day as many as 16 outstanding). Sometimes a ' D ' notice can only be expressed as a general guide to editors on the treatment of ' sensitive ' subjects, and we have no doubt that from time to time questions of real difficulty arise as to the application of a particular notice to some unpredictable combination of circumstances. It is on such questions in particular that the Secretary is invited to advise. It must not be thought that he is invested with any authority to give ' rulings ' or judicial interpretations. The system is not institutionalised and it operates throughout as one of free co-operation. But the evidence that we received satisfied us that, although individual editors vary from each other to some extent in their attitude on this matter, the Secretary's interpretations of the meaning and effect of the notice are regarded with very great respect and would not be departed from by a particular newspaper until at any rate the matter had been fully discussed with him and a considered decision taken in the editorial chair.

10. It may be that on special occasions the Secretary finds himself urging with respect to a particular piece of news that has suddenly broken that, whether or not it is covered by a ' D ' notice or even if it is not so covered, it is undesirable, unwise or unsafe that it should be published... But action of this kind falls outside the ' D ' notice system. The considerations that give a peculiar weight to the impact of a ' D ' notice, such as we have alluded to above, do not apply to such an appeal or request as this. It lies wholly within an editor's discretion whether he rejects it or accedes to it ...

Publication of ' D ' notices

73. We devote a section to this subject only because it was put in controversy by articles in the issues of the *Spectator* dated 3 and 10 March 1967 respectively. The first article published verbatim the relevant parts of the two ' D ' notices to which the Prime Minister had alluded in the House of Commons... The second article was entitled ' " D " Notices and the *Spectator* ', and its purport was to explain to its readers that, while the publication of ' D ' notices was ' unprecedented ', the editor considered that, having regard to the Prime Minister's criticism of the *Daily Express* in the House of Commons on 21st February, the precise wording of specific ' D ' notices had become a major public issue, and it was in the public interest that the wording should be made known ...

74. Hitherto it has never been the practice, as the article recognises, to publish ' D ' notices... The notices are clearly headed ' Private and Confidential ' or ' Secret ' and are distributed to their recipients on that understanding. It was made plain to us, on behalf of the Committee, that its members were much concerned at the *Spectator's* action, a departure of which they disapproved... [T]he publication of ' D ' notices can give away information of significance to security and the possibility of their being made public might well affect the willingness of Government Departments to resort to them, thus prejudicing the operation of the whole system...

77. ... The mere fact of the issue of a ' D ' notice, the bare circumstances that it is necessary to issue a warning, amounts in itself to a security ' pointer ' for a hostile intelligence service: and, besides that, it is virtually impossible to concoct an effective ' D ' notice that is sufficiently clear to tell a reader what is requested of him without at the same time imparting some modicum of information of security value. This is an acknowledged dilemma in all ' D ' notice questions... [W]e think that the only safe rule for everyone to proceed on ... is that all notices should be treated as confidential documents, guarded with care under editorial control and withheld from publication...

[Report of the Committee of Privy Councillors Appointed to Inquire into ' D ' Notice Matters. Cmnd. 3309 (June 1967)]

Cp. the Report of the Radcliffe Committee on Security Procedures in the Public Service, Cmnd. 1681 (1962):

' 134. It is necessary to ask what practical alternative there is to maintaining a system of this kind. One must begin with recognition of the fact that in this country the Press do acquire a very considerable volume of information on secret matters which, *prima facie*, is of interest and importance to their public. This information comes from a variety of sources, often unidentifiable at any one moment, but not by any means necessarily illegitimate or reprehensible. So far as legal sanctions go, there is nothing to restrict publication except the provisions of the Official Secrets Acts, 1911–39; and these provisions, though widely drawn are, generally speaking, confined to the protection of information about ' prohibited places ' and information obtained through some ' wrongful communication ' by or through an official. Some that comes to the Press may originate in this way, but at any rate some may not: and in any event, it must often be impossible at the critical moment of publication for the editor himself to say whether he is within or without the provisions of the Acts. While, therefore, their existence does serve as a general restraining influence at the back of editorial life and there is always the possibility that they might be resorted to in the case of gross breach of security, they do not on the other hand provide a working code of what should or should not be published on any particular subject nor is there a lively expectation in the Press that in any ordinary case of publication of matters which the Government wishes to keep secret publication will be followed by a criminal prosecution. It must be taken, therefore, that the Official Secrets Acts are not an effective instrument for controlling Press publication of that kind of 'military' information of some though perhaps no great individual importance which it is nevertheless most desirable to keep from hostile intelligence.

135. Such an instrument is provided by the D Notice system and, in the absence of compulsory Press censorship or voluntary censorship supported by *ad hoc* Defence Regulation (the system that prevailed in the last war) we see no alternative to it.'

II. PARTICIPATION

The most substantial developments in relation to participation, or at least consultation, have been in the economic field. It has long been the practice of Governments to consult the interests affected before introducing legislation and this applies as much in the economic field as elsewhere. The importance of such bodies as the Trades Union Congress and the Confederation of British Industries, however, involves them in continuous contact with the Government and Government Departments over the whole range of governmental activities, whether or not particular legislation is being planned. And although this is also true of many other bodies in relation to their spheres of interest, the importance of the problems of the economy and of the interests which these bodies represent put them into a special category. The institutionalisation of these contacts in such bodies as the National Economic Development Council, the industry-wide Economic Development Committees and the Regional Economic Planning Councils is in itself a recognition of this fact. The N.E.D.C. was established by a Conservative Government in 1962 'to examine the economic performance of the nation with particular concern for plans for the future in both the private and public sectors of industry; to consider together what are the obstacles to quicker growth, what can be done to improve efficiency and whether the best use is being made of our resources; to seek agreement upon ways of improving economic performance, competitive power and efficiency, or in other words to increase the rate of sound growth.' The Economic Development Committees followed in 1963. In 1964 the Labour Government established the Regional Economic Planning Councils '(a) to assist in the formulation of regional plans, having regard to the best use of the region's resources; (b) to advise on the steps necessary for implementing the regional plans on the basis of information and assessment provided by the Economic Planning Boards [consisting of civil servants representing the Departments active in the regions]; (c) to advise on the regional implications of national economic policies.'

One of the express intentions behind the establishment of these bodies was to give publicity to their findings and views. This was also true of the National Board for Prices and Incomes, which in the voluntary phases of prices and incomes policy depended on publicity for its effectiveness.

The National Economic Development Council, the Economic Development Committees, the Regional Economic Planning Councils and the National Board for Prices and Incomes have all been important experiments in the institutionalisation of the constitutional arrangements relating to openness and participation in a mixed economy. This needs to be emphasised because the bulk of the extracts which follow do not refer specifically to their work. They concern one particular industry, agriculture, and one particular area of government activity, planning, where the demand for 'public' participation has been most pressing.

(i) The openness of participation

[T]he necessary intimate relationship between the public authorities and private interest groups has to be made more explicit and open. The great enlargement of the sphere of public power does not make that power less sensitive to the pressures of private interests and individuals. On the contrary, the increased range and subtlety of the relationship between the public and the private sectors have made it less feasible to govern effectively by decree. The system will not function unless private organizations give their willing collaboration to the pursuit of public purposes. What is therefore required is the opposite of a bully state – rather a wheeling and dealing type of public authority constantly seeking out allies, probing and manoeuvring for the active consensus.[13] On the one hand this creates an additional force making for a new kind of political equilibrium: enhanced governmental power generates its own offset. But on the other hand the important private interest groups, on whom the government depends for active collaboration over a widening range of its activities, often play little part in the overt democratic process conducted by the officially elected representatives of the people. The essential dialogue in a country like Britain tends to take place out of earshot, between the faceless government official and the discreet emissary of some 'recognized' association with an interest in the business in hand. By the time a legislative proposal reaches the floor of parliament, many of the substantial matters for parliament will have been settled at another level.

Making Power Visible

There is nothing wrong with this dialogue at the level of interest groups – so long as its existence is full recognized. One of the advantages of the American system of 'public hearings' before Congres-

[13] An outstanding example of the mid-1960s is the devious and complicated bargaining conduct in pursuit of an 'incomes policy'. . .

sional committees, it has been pointed out by French admirers of the device, is that it forces all the lobbyists and other interested parties out into the open. By this method, ' which marries ingeniously the inquest and the petition ' [14] everyone, including the Congress, is made aware, before it is too late, of what the issues really are in any projected piece of legislation. Elsewhere the spokesmen of interest groups are sometimes given an official status inside the apparatus of government – the Planning Commissions in France and the National Economic Development Council in Britain are familiar examples – but the public's information about what they are up to is usually confined to a newspaper photograph of a backview of a man disappearing into a pompous building. At best there may be a few muttered syllables to a television camera on the way out again.

Clearly, the pursuit of visibility should not be pushed to the point of insisting that all such discussions are held in public... If there were no routine for making discussions confidential, some important questions would never be asked – or if asked, never satisfactorily answered. But while it is necessary to have a set of rules which will permit an argument over public policy to be conducted in private, the purpose of democratic control will fail to be met unless the privilege is used with conscientious reluctance...

[Andrew Shonfield, *Modern Capitalism* (1965), p. 389]

(ii) The Annual Agricultural Price Review

The Agriculture Act, 1947, provides:

1. (1) The following provisions of this Part of this Act shall have effect for the purpose of promoting and maintaining, by the provision of guaranteed prices and assured markets...a stable and efficient agricultural industry capable of producing such part of the nation's food and other agricultural produce as in the national interest it is desirable to produce in the United Kingdom, and of producing it at minimum prices consistently with proper remuneration and living conditions for farmers and workers in agriculture, and an adequate return on capital invested in the industry...

2. (1) At such date each year as the Ministers may determine, they shall review the general economic condition and the prospects of the agricultural industry...

(3) In the holding of any review under this section the Ministers shall consult all such bodies of persons as appear to them to represent the interests of producers in the agricultural industry...

[14] Club Jean Moulin, *L'Etat et le citoyen*, p. 389. Another interesting device, which the Americans use as part of their effort to make the interest groups involved in the process of government more visible is to insist on the official registration of ' lobbyists '.

The Select Committee on Agriculture, 1969. Memorandum of the Ministry of Agriculture

12. ... [T]he Annual Review is the culmination of a continuing process of consideration of agricultural policy and issues by the Government in consultation with farmers and with trade and other interests, including the statutory marketing boards, affected by the operation of the guarantee system ... [T]he Acts distinguish between the Annual Review, which must be held in consultation with representatives of producers, and the subsequent determination by the Ministers of the guarantee arrangements for the ensuing year.[15] In effect, the Annual Review provides the background of established data and informed discussions from which the Government can draw their conclusions and then reach decisions, taking into account all the relevant factors as well as national economic and other policy considerations.

13. The Annual Review and determination of the guarantee fall into five main stages:—

  (*a*) Preparation of economic and statistical data
  (*b*) Commodity considerations
  (*c*) General policy considerations
  (*d*) Consultations with farmers' representatives
  (*e*) Process of reaching Government decisions

Preparation of Statistical and Economic Data

14. The economic and statistical material ... is built up from a wide range of sources, and is examined at a series of technical meetings between economists of the Agricultural Departments and the Farmers' Unions in the weeks preceding the Annual Review. In this way, the degree of reliability of the general economic and statistical data is assessed and broadly agreed between the Government and the producers' representatives before the general discussions take place...

[15] This distinction was reinforced in evidence by the Permanent Secretary to the Minister of Agriculture. Mr Mackintosh asked him [Q. 671] what importance was attached to getting an agreed Review which the unions would accept? He replied: ' I regard this as an element which enters into the political judgment Ministers make... [T]he statutory responsibility [on Ministers] is to make determinations... [T]here is nothing in the statutes or the system as a whole which considers the question of agreement or disagreement with the National Farmers Union.' Later, he added [Q. 679]: '[T]here is a distinction between the Annual Review as required under Statute and the determination by Ministers following the Annual Review... It is absolutely vital before Ministries make their determinations that they should be as well equipped as possible with information not merely which can be produced by the Department but which can be given to them by those who represent the producers.'

Some of this information is published in the White Paper presented to Parliament at the conclusion of each Annual Review. Much more information is prepared for consideration at each Annual Review and a substantial amount is published regularly...

Commodity Considerations

16. The consideration by the Agricultural Departments of the course of production commodity by commodity and the impact of the guarantee arrangements on other sectors of the national economy is a continuing process... In this process, the need for possible change in the guarantee arrangements may be identified so that it can be considered later in the Annual Review discussions. The normal course of contacts with farmers, trade and other interests may similarly raise issues for consideration and ensure that views expressed can be taken into account in the formulation of policy...

General Policy Considerations

17. Co-ordination of issues to be raised at each Annual Review is started in the preceding autumn. Officials of the Agricultural Departments and other Departments, in particular the Central Economic Departments (Treasury, D.E.A. and Board of Trade) meet to form a general view of the economic state of the industry and to prepare advice to Ministers on the operation of the guarantees, on production objectives, and on wider considerations of national policy which may be relevant.

Consultation with representatives of farm workers and landowners

18. Immediately before the start of each Annual Review, representatives of the Agricultural Workers' Unions and of the Country Landowners' Association are invited to give their views on the state of agriculture and on changes in the guarantees.

Consultations with Farmers' Representatives

19. The discussions are normally begun around mid-February and continue for about three weeks. They are presided over by a senior official of the Ministry of Agriculture, Fisheries and Food, supported by senior officials of the other Agricultural Departments. The Farmers' Representatives include the Presidents and other chief officers and officials of the three Farmers' Unions.

20. The discussions, which are in strict confidence, start with an examination of the economic data, with the aim of agreeing, as far as possible, general conclusions on the economic conditions and prospects of the industry. A broad indication is given of the Government's assessments and of the Government's views on production policy,

which is followed by the assessments and view of the farmers' representatives.

21. Detailed discussions centre around a review of all the factors that need to be taken into account in relation to the industry as a whole as well as commodity by commodity . . .

22. During these discussions an attempt is made to establish as much common ground as possible on the weighting to be attached to the relevant factors and on any broad changes in the guarantees which appear desirable. Particular problems may be identified as requiring further examination after the Review.

23. Although broad indications of desirable changes in the guarantee arrangements may be referred to during the consultations, actual changes in guarantee prices are not discussed.

24. At the close of the consultations, officials report to Ministers on the course of the discussions, on the areas of agreement or disagreement, and on the inferences to be drawn for commodity policy and for the guarantees overall.

Process of reaching Government decisions

25. On the basis of the reports by officials Ministers decide on the conclusions to be drawn from the Review. In the light of these conclusions, the Government consider possible changes in the level of the guarantees, both in total and for each commodity, against the wider background of national and other policy considerations, including the effect on trade interests and on consumers. These possible changes in the levels, and also where necessary in the form, of the guarantees are then discussed with farmers' representatives on a strictly confidential basis either by officials under direct instructions by Ministers or by Ministers themselves, so that Ministers may be aware of the views of the farmers' representatives on them, on the broad balance they would achieve as between the various sectors of the industry and on the likely reaction of producers to them.

26. The Ministers then decide on the determinations to be made in relation to the guarantees. These determinations are announced to Parliament by a summary statement in both Houses, and by presentation of a White Paper which gives the Review determinations in detail, and explains the broad considerations of national policy which have influenced the Government in reaching their determinations. It includes a general account of the economic development of the industry over the previous twelve months, and contains detailed sections describing the factors taken into account in reaching the determinations on individual commodities and production grants. It also contains appendices giving detailed information over several years on pro-

duction, imports, yields, numbers of workers, inputs, output, net income, cost changes, and Exchequer support.

[Memorandum of the Ministry of Agriculture to the Select Committee on Agriculture. H.C. 137 of 1968-9, 12 February 1969]

Evidence to the Select Committee

683. CHAIRMAN.[16] ... Would you tell us whether there is any consultation with bodies other than the farmers' unions at a particular stage?—[Mr J. D. Mitchell] [17] The Statutes lay down that Ministers are to conduct the Annual Review in consultation with producers' representatives. These have been regarded as the three farmers' unions. There is no consultation with other outside bodies during the Review stage...

684. Does the Ministry ever get representations from outside bodies by memorandum?— ... [T]here is a regular occasion when views are received from the National Union of Agricultural Workers and from the Country Landowners' Association. There are other bodies which give us their views at this time and, indeed, throughout the year. We regard it as part of our function to be ready to receive views from any bodies who are concerned with matters of policy or indeed matters of relevant detail. It is part of our job to keep our ear to the ground in this way...

685. MR GARRETT. May such bodies include the agricultural sections of I.C.I., Fison's and other chemical firms producing fertilisers?—At the time of the Annual Review they may well make representations but they are not consulted; at other times we meet their trade associations to consult in a more positive way if there is some question of policy change under consideration.

686. Does the Chemical Association consult with the Ministry when they propose to increase prices of their products?—In that situation the prices and incomes policy comes into effect and the early warning arrangements, and apart from any consideration of the Annual Review there is a machine which is there.

687. To your Ministry?—(MR MOSS.) It is always very difficult to be specific without a background knowledge of individual associations and one has to be a little careful about saying that a particular company or organisation does come to the Ministry. Therefore I cannot answer the question precisely. But I will answer it in another way by looking at my experience when I was in another job in the Ministry. There, for example, the retail butchers, the wholesale butchers, the sausage manufacturers, the auctioneers and others were regularly in

[16] Mr Tudor Watkins.
[17] Deputy Secretary (Ministry of Agriculture).

contact with the operative Divisions of the Ministry saying they thought the shoe was pinching in a particular way, that their industry would function better if guarantees operated differently and so on. This is the kind of information fed into the Ministry which enables the Ministry to enter into the sort of discussions we were mentioning earlier in the consultative process.

688. MR MILLS. Might I just ask whether Mr Mitchell is absolutely sure that no other bodies are consulted at the Price Review such as the Milk Marketing Board or the bacon curing industry?— . . . The Government relies on the Farmers' Unions to be in touch with the boards. When there are measures affecting marketing directly, or when it is proposed to alter the method of operating the guarantee, the appropriate board is consulted. . .

689. So the Chairman of the Milk Marketing Board is not consulted on the Price Review?—This is perfectly true, but I emphasise that when one is talking about formal consultation and who is consulted and who is not one is glossing over the very important fact that a Department in this position at the centre of a whole range of interests is in touch in a less formal way and is consulting constantly with very many people. . .

[Report of the Select Committee on Agriculture. H.C. 137 of 1968–9]

The Committee's Report

28. Relying mainly on decisions of government for its level of profitability, agriculture's confidence depends overwhelmingly on its understanding and acceptance of government policy. . .

30. . . . Confidence is in our view best established where the interested parties know how the major decisions affecting their livelihood are reached, and respect the method of decision-making. The Ministry submitted to us a paper describing the mechanism of the Review, but not explaining how the levels of the various methods of support were determined. The Minister refused to throw more light on this decision-making stage. This is the stage which most attracts suspicion in the industry. There are suspicions of ' package deals ', of bargaining one part of the industry against another and of unfair treatment of the industry as a whole. In this case, we believe it is mistaken to adhere to the practice of not revealing the workings of cabinet committees. To know more about the mechanism involved, as opposed to the specific issues in any review, would increase confidence in the industry and demonstrate how decisions vitally affecting its well-being were taken. This would outweigh the inconvenience the government might suffer in reaching its decisions more openly.

Parliamentary participation

31. The Ministry of Agriculture treats the Price Review in the same way as the Treasury treats the Budget. Ministers will not discuss projected agricultural policy with Members with constituency interests. The whole review system, its confidential consultations with interested sectional bodies and its ministerial conclaves, have withdrawn these agricultural questions from effective Parliamentary review and public knowledge. This withdrawal from public scrutiny is not in the interests of Parliamentary democracy. We consider that the situation would best be redressed by a permanent Committee on Agriculture, with proper access to the Department on matters currently subject to decision and having a part in policy planning. It would participate in the dialogue leading to the Determinations and could represent to the Minister those considerations and criteria which it considered relevant. . .

35. Statutory consultation during the Review takes place only with the Farmers' Unions. Preliminary talks are held with other interested bodies in preparation for the Review and we questioned the logic of holding consultations of a special status only with producers' organisations. The N.U.A.A.W. were happier not to be formally a party to the Review. The C.L.A. wished for a formal status in the Review mechanism in their proposed triennial review. We also received representations that certain suppliers and merchants' organisations wished to have a voice in an enlarged review consultation. The essential quality of consultation is the spirit in which it is held. Whether or not it is statutory is of lesser significance. We recommend that the Ministry, in the circumstances of long term plans executed through annual reviews, consider how best they can avail themselves of the wisdom of all interests and not least of consumer interests – an area in which we ourselves have failed.

[Report of the Select Committee on Agriculture. H.C. 137 of 1968–9]

(iii) Public participation in the legislative process – Green Papers

One of the devices that Governments have used to secure wider public discussion of legislative proposals than can be had simply by consulting those organisations with whom they are in continuous contact has been the Green Paper. The first of these was published in April 1967 in connection with a proposal to pay a regional employment premium to manufacturing establishments in development areas. On 13 May 1969 Mr Sheridan asked the Prime Minister if he would define the extent of the commitment of the Government to proposals published in the form of a Green Paper.

THE PRIME MINISTER: As my rt. hon. Friend the then Secretary of State for Economic Affairs explained to the House on 5 April 1967, at the time of the publication of the first Green Paper, this is intended as a means of putting forward proposals for full consultation and public discussion, while policy is still in the formative stage [18] [744 H.C.Deb. c. 245. . .].

MR SHELDON: Does my rt. hon. Friend agree that one of the main aspects of the usefulness of a Green Paper is that Government Ministers are uncommitted and so the debate can be extremely full and thorough?

THE PRIME MINISTER: . . . A Green Paper is put forward to set out the Government's views on how the matter might be tackled, to invite views not only of hon. Members but of all experts and interests in that field all over the country. . . In the case of one Green Paper . . . as a result of consultations the Government decided not to proceed further on the lines indicated. In the case of the Green Paper on roads, it is of value that there should be discussion by economic planning councils, by local authorities and by road users. . . Clearly individual Ministers do not enter into public and contentious discussions about it, if that is what my hon. Friend was asking. . .

MR THORPE: We read in the Press that arising out of the 3 April Cabinet meeting the Prime Minister indicated that Green Papers must bind Ministers as much as White Papers. Do we take it that that was the decision that was taken in the Cabinet and also that was one of the matters to which the Cabinet agreed that publicity should be given?

THE PRIME MINISTER: The answer to the first part of the question is, ' Yes, Sir '. . . In relation to Green Papers the position is this . . . There is no collective obligation on the Government that a Green Paper put forward will be the basis of legislation. It is put out for discussion and for consultation. . . On the other hand, that public discussion should not get to the point where individual Ministers take up different sides in that discussion. . . A White Paper indicates the broad lines of the legislation the Government intend to introduce and, very often, of executive action that will be taken. Many of the details of the legislation should be a matter for consultation. . .

[783 H.C.Deb. 5s. c. 1218. 13 May 1969]

[18] This does not, however, mean that, pending discussion of a Green Paper, the Government will abstain from expressing its own views on issues arising from it. When the Select Committee on Science and Technology recommended that proposals in a Green Paper should not be impaired and public discussions prejudiced by Government statements made beforehand, the Government replied: ' [that] it did not believe that hard and fast rules should be laid down on the content of Green Papers '. It added that in the particular case ' the early endorsement of some very general points enabled the widespread discussions and consultations on the more detailed arrangements to take place in full knowledge of the Government's general approach '. [Government Observations on the First and Fourth Reports of the Select Committee, 1971–2. Cmnd. 5177 (December 1972)]

(iv) Public participation in the administrative process

When one moves from questions of general legislative policy to particular decisions it is in the field of planning that most attention has been given to the problems of public participation. This has ranged from attempts to improve the normal administrative processes for dealing with particular planning applications, e.g. by securing more publicity for planning applications which may have a significant effect on the local community, to the introduction of new procedures to deal with particular aspects of planning. Of these latter the most important have been the procedures for the preparation of local development plans and the procedure adopted for the consideration of proposals for the location of London's third airport.

(a) *Publicity and planning*

Some of the principles relating to publicity were set out in a Circular from the Department of the Environment in June 1973.

2. In the view of the Secretaries of State the basic principle should be that opinion should be enabled to declare itself before any approval is given to proposals of wide concern or substantial impact on the environment; and that this should be so whether the proposal is that of a Government Department, a local authority, statutory undertakers or a private developer. Local planning authorities will sometimes have to judge proposals by principles which may not reflect the views expressed by people in the immediate locality but it will nevertheless assist them not only in deciding those applications but also in their wider planning responsibilities to be aware of local feeling about significant proposals...

3. Planning is concerned to ensure that in the development of land the public interest is taken fully into account. Its objective is not the safeguarding of private property rights as such; nor, in particular, to protect the value of individual properties or the views to be had from them. Those who argue for a right for neighbours to be notified individually of *all* prospective development do not give sufficient weight to this. There are, however, occasions when the public interest may require that the interests of those immediately affected by even a comparatively minor proposal should be taken into account as a planning consideration...

4. It has been suggested that ... there should be a general require-ment for the display of a site notice whenever an application for plan-ning permission is made, so that those who might feel that the public interest might be involved could express a view... The Secretaries of State have carefully considered this point but have come to the con-clusion that the objections to such a move outweigh the advantages. The planning system is administered by democratically elected local

councils and the Government would not wish to impose absolute duties across the whole field of that administration. Furthermore, from a practical point of view the desire for more publicity has to be weighed against the need not to overload the planning machine. There were in 1972 over 600,000 planning applications, the majority in respect of quite minor development. This represents a 40 per cent increase in two years. The display of site notices in every case would be bound to lead to a large volume of correspondence on matters which would not be a material consideration in reaching planning decisions and would give rise to misunderstanding as well as to unwarranted delay in the handling of applications. . .

7. The Secretaries of State take the view that the selective approach is the right one and that pending legislation local authorities should ask applicants to display a site notice where permission is sought for development which, in the authority's opinion, is likely to have a substantial impact on the neighbourhood. It is impossible to lay down precise rules and it must be for authorities to decide the circumstances in which the public interest is sufficiently involved to warrant publicity. . .

11. . . . Many local authorities already undertake publicity over and above statutory requirements by making lists of applications available both in public places and in the press and to bodies such as local civic and amenity societies – a most useful practice which is commended – and by informing those who may be affected by development of neighbouring properties. The new arrangements for posting of site notices are, of course, not intended to replace these existing arrangements unless there would be obvious duplication. The Secretaries of State ask planning authorities to supplement their arrangements in appropriate cases with, for example, press and local radio handouts and notices in public libraries, clubs, evening institutes, citizens' advice bureaux, etc. The main function of site notices, and other forms of publicity is, of course, to direct attention to the fact that full details of an application can be found in the planning register. . .

12. Consideration should be given during any informal discussions prior to the submission of a planning application to the need for publicity and the manner in which it is to be secured; this will save time when the application is submitted. Arrangements for publicity in these circumstances must be primarily a matter for agreement between the developer and the local planning authority. In the case of substantial proposals, authorities may arrange for advance publicity, e.g. for meetings between applicants, the planning authority and members of

the public; and in some cases for exhibitions at which plans and models can be displayed. In such cases, the possibility of a change in the proposals before a formal application is submitted should, of course, be brought out and the desirability of avoiding unnecessary 'blighting' of property should receive careful consideration. Where there has been no opportunity for advance publicity for substantial proposals authorities will have to seek the co-operation of the applicant when the application is made and, where necessary, his agreement to an extension of time to enable adequate publicity to be given to the proposal.

20. Appeals may be dealt with either by way of a local inquiry or by written representations. Where there is any substantial local objection an inquiry will usually be necessary and there will be local publicity. The Secretaries of State rely on local planning authorities to warn them if local concern in an appeal is known to be sufficient to justify an inquiry. Where the appeal is to be the subject of a local inquiry, the authority is asked to give as much public notice of the inquiry date as possible.

21. Many appeals are now decided on written representations by the parties, even where there is some third party interest, e.g. near neighbours. Where it has been agreed that an appeal should be conducted by written representations the planning authority will be asked to notify local residents or others who may be affected as soon as possible that the Secretary of State or the person deciding the appeal will take into account any views which are put to him in writing, provided those views are disclosed to the planning authority and the appellant. The statement of case sent by the authority to the Secretary of State should be made available for inspection locally, as should the appellant's 'grounds of appeal', unless there are special reasons for withholding all or part of it, e.g. where he has given details of his personal circumstances.

Development not the subject of a planning application

22. The arrangements set out above relate in general to planning applications formally made to local planning authorities. Where proposals for development are not the subject of a formal planning application – for example because the development is to be undertaken by a Government Department, or the local planning authority or is development carried out by statutory undertakers in circumstances where they do not need to apply for permission – the general principles underlying these arrangements should still be applied in deciding whether local publicity . . . is necessary. Agreement has been reached on this following discussions with the local authority associa-

tions and with Government Departments which themselves carry out development or have responsibility for statutory undertakers . . .

[Publicity for Planning Applications, Appeals and Other Proposals for Development. D.O.E. Circular 71/73]

(b) *The community and the planning process*

Fifty Million Volunteers, 1972

(a) We have been struck by the haphazard way in which the procedures for public participation in planning seem to have grown up, without any clear formulation of the objectives or investigation of the best means of achieving them.

(b) *People and Planning* [below p. 491] was the name given to a report produced in 1969 by the Skeffington committee. In fact the name was rather misleading because the report was concerned only with one very small aspect of the involvement of people in planning. Its terms of reference were closely related to the new publicity provisions for development plans in the Town and Country Planning Act 1968 and restricted it to considering ' the participation of the public at the formative stage in the making of development plans for their area '. It was thus excluded from consideration of the machinery for everyday planning, and the many other major planning decisions in which the public will wish to be involved. . .

(c) In view of the importance which the idea of public participation has attained in the making of any decision affecting the environment, there is a real need for a comprehensive review of the multifarious systems at present in operation for achieving effective participation. This review should cover the whole range of planning procedures as well as the operation of the planning inquiry machinery as part of those procedures. Only in the context of such an overall investigation can the problem be properly resolved and the vast amount of experimental work already carried out by many local authorities be drawn together and systematised.

(d) At the same time it may not be possible to separate traditional land-use planning from all the other activities of government – local and national – which affect a person's environment and often affect it much more directly . . . Spontaneous participation will come from different types of people at different levels of the hierarchy of planning. The objective should be to provide a system which is responsive and encouraging to spontaneous reaction at all levels. The machinery for public participation in traditional planning issues should be seen simply as one part of this system.

(e) A second weakness imposed upon the Skeffington Committee by its terms of reference was the limitation to ' formative ' stages of development plans. Thus the emphasis of the report is on responsible co-operation between the various groups within the community to produce the best plan for all. ' We see the process of giving information and opportunities for participation as one which leads to greater understanding and co-operation rather than to a crescendo of dispute.'

(f) Since planning will always involve choices between irreconcilable alternatives – as to allocation of resources, etc. it would seem to us to follow that the more people there are involved in the decision and the better informed those people are, the greater will be the discord. Greater dissemination of information and expertise should lead to a better definition of the issues, but it is unlikely to lead to greater harmony.

(g) We feel strongly, therefore, that any review of the machinery of public participation must include a consideration of the machinery by which conflict is ultimately resolved and in particular the role of the public inquiry. . .

Planning procedures

(a) There is a clear need for public inquiries to be made more accessible to groups and individuals who cannot afford professional representation.

(b) A planning inquiry is generally performing two entirely distinct functions. The first function is as a protection of the property rights of individuals. Thus, a person who has been refused permission to develop his land, or whose land has been proposed for compulsory acquisition is given a right of a hearing before a quasi-judicial tribunal. This is the traditional function of the public inquiry, and for it a formal procedure may be entirely appropriate.

(c) The second function is as an outlet for the views of the public on questions affecting them, not directly as property owners, but indirectly as people concerned in the planning of their environment.

(d) The formality which is appropriate to the first function seems to us quite inappropriate for the second. The patience of Inspectors has enabled both functions to be performed with some success, but no attempt has been made to evolve a procedure to suit the dual role of the inquiry.

(e) Within the formal framework of the inquiry, provision should be made for more informal discussions and meetings under the general supervision of the Inspector or Panel presiding over the inquiry. Experiments along these lines have already been tried. For instance, at motorway inquiries objectors suggesting alternative routes are sometimes given an opportunity to discuss them informally with the Department's engineers to help to identify the basic problems to be overcome. There have also been occasions when an inquiry has included a public meeting outside office hours.

(f) There is a need for more experiments along these lines ...

(g) Similar issues arise in relation to the second point mentioned in the evidence – the artificial polarity created by the public inquiry. There seems to be a lack of any effective pre-inquiry machinery for clarifying and defining the issues. If the public inquiry itself suffers from excessive formality the pre-inquiry procedure suffers from the opposite failing. Exhortation from central government to local authorities to disclose their case in advance are no substitute for a formal machinery by which disclosures of necessary information can be compelled.

Once again, there seems to be a need for a hybrid procedure – an adaptation of the formal pre-hearing procedures of civil litigation as a framework within which informal discussions and consultations can take place.

(h) A starting point is already apparent in the Town and Country Planning (Amendment) Bill, at present before Parliament. This provides for a new form of inquiry for the consideration of structure plans, which it is hoped will be less formal in nature and more suitable for the discussion of complicated issues of strategic planning [below p. 494]. The Secretary of State will define the issues to be examined at the inquiry and will have power to restrict the right of hearing to such objections as he considers to be relevant to those issues.

(i) This development is important in the present context because the machinery which is established for defining issues and selecting objections to be heard might well be extended to cover other pre-inquiry matters, such as the disclosure of necessary information and the award of grants or legal aid in suitable cases. At other forms of inquiry, a similar procedure could be introduced, or the supervision of the Inspector over the inquiry itself could be extended to cover the pre-inquiry matters ...

[Fifty Million Volunteers. A Report on the Role of Voluntary Organisations and Youth in the Environment. H.M.S.O. 1972]

(c) *The preparation of structure plans*

The Town and Country Planning Act 1971 required local planning authorities to conduct surveys of their areas and in the light of these surveys to prepare structure plans for them. It then provided:

67. (3) The structure plan for any area shall be a written statement—
   (*a*) formulating the local planning authority's policy and general proposals in respect of the development and other use of land in that area (including measures for the improvement of the physical environment and the management of traffic);
   (*b*) stating the relationship of those proposals to general proposals for the development and other use of land in neighbouring areas which may be expected to affect that area; and

(*c*) containing such other matters as may be prescribed or as the Secretary of State may in any particular case direct.

(4) In formulating their policy and general proposals under subsection (3) (*a*) of this section, the local planning authority shall secure that the policy and proposals are justified by the results of their survey under section 6 of this Act and by any other information which they may obtain and shall have regard—

(*a*) to current policies with respect to the economic planning and development of the region as a whole;

(*b*) to the resources likely to be available for the carrying out of the proposals of the structure plan; and

(*c*) to such other matters as the Secretary of State may direct them to take into account. . .

(6) A structure plan for any area shall contain or be accompanied by such diagrams, illustrations and descriptive matter as the local planning authority think appropriate for the purpose of explaining or illustrating the proposals in the plan, or as may be prescribed, or as may in any particular case be specified in directions given by the Secretary of State; and any such diagrams, illustrations and descriptive matter shall be treated as forming part of the plan.'

In a circular of guidance issued to local authorities in July 1974 [Circular 98/74] the Department of the Environment said that structure plans had three main functions:

' a. To state and justify, to the public and to the Secretary of State, the authority's policies and general proposals for the development and other use of land in the area concerned (including measures for the improvement of the physical environment and the management of traffic), and thus provide guidance for development (including development control) on issues of structural importance. . .

b. To interpret national and regional policies in terms of physical and environmental planning for the area concerned.

National and regional policies tend to be primarily economic and social (though they also include an important physical and environmental content): structure plans represent the stage in planning at which such policies are integrated with the economic, social and environmental policies of the county and expressed in terms of their effect on land use, environmental development and the associated transportation system. (The material on economic and social policies in the written statement should therefore be limited to those policies which have implications for land use, environmental development or transportation.)

c. To provide the framework and statutory basis for local plans, which then in turn provide the necessary further guidance for development control at the more detailed, local level. . .'

In preparing their plans, the Department said, local planning authorities should concentrate on key issues. These, it suggested, were likely to be:

' a. The location and scale of employment

    b. The location and scale of housing (including new development, redevelopment and rehabilitation) and

    c. The transportation system.'

Other issues which might be of particular importance were:

    ' d. The extent of conservation of the character of the area (whether urban or rural)

    e. The extent of provision for recreation and tourism

    f. The location and scale of shopping centres and

    g. The location and scale of land reclamation.'

In summarising its advice it suggested that authorities should:

    ' a. make explicit the assumptions (and the reasons for those assumptions) on which the structure plan is based

    b. concentrate on essentials, i.e. their key issues

    c. deal with those issues in whatever depth is necessary to provide reasoned justification for the chosen policies, and

    d. in general, plan for about 15 years ahead.'

The Town and Country Planning Act, 1971, further provided:

    ' 8. (1) When preparing a structure plan for their area and before finally determining its content for submission to the Secretary of State, the local planning authority shall take such steps as will in their opinion secure—

> (*a*) that adequate publicity is given in their area to the report of the survey under section 6 of this Act and to the matters which they propose to include in the plan;
>
> (*b*) that persons who may be expected to desire an opportunity of making representations to the authority with respect to those matters are made aware that they are entitled to an opportunity of doing so; and
>
> (*c*) that such persons are given an adequate opportunity of making such representations;

and the authority shall consider any representations made to them within the prescribed period...

    (3) A structure plan submitted by the local planning authority to the Secretary of State for his approval shall be accompanied by a statement containing such particulars, if any, as may be prescribed—

> (*a*) of the steps which the authority have taken to comply with subsection (1) of this section; and
>
> (*b*) of the authority's consultations with, and consideration of the views of, other persons with respect to those matters.'

If the Minister was not satisfied with the steps taken by a local authority in this respect he was authorised to send the plan back and to direct them ' to take such further action as he may specify in order better to achieve ' the purposes set out in s. 8 (1).

The original requirements for structure plans and their preparation were embodied in the Town and Country Planning Act, 1968. In March 1968 a committee was appointed (the Skeffington committee) ' to consider and report on the best methods, including publicity, of securing the participation of the public at the formative stage in the making of development plans for their areas.' The report was primarily intended as a guide for local authorities, though the committee itself thought it might be of assistance in other spheres as well. It noted: ' Certainly the committee feel that this broader aspect of their work is important in a large, complex and socially advanced industrial nation like ours where the principle of public participation can improve the quality of decisions by public authorities and give personal satisfaction to those affected by the decisions.'

People and Planning. The report of the Skeffington Committee, 1969

5. We understand participation to be the act of sharing in the formulation of policies and proposals. Clearly, the giving of information by the local planning authority and of an opportunity to comment on that information is a major part in the process of participation, but it is not the whole story. Participation involves doing as well as talking and there will be full participation only where the public are able to take an active part throughout the plan-making process. There are limitations... One is that responsibility for preparing a plan, is, and must remain, that of the local planning authority. Another is that the completion of plans – the setting into statutory form of proposals and decisions – is a task demanding the highest standards of professional skill, and must be undertaken by the professional staff of the local planning authority...

7. ... There is a growing demand by many groups for more opportunity to contribute and for more say in the working out of policies which affect people, not merely at election time, but continuously as proposals are being hammered out and certainly, as they are being implemented...

8. Planning is a prime example of the need for this participation, for it affects everyone. People should be able to say what kind of community they want and how it would develop; and should be able to do so in a way that is positive and first hand ... This becomes all the more vital where the demands of a complex society occasion massive changes ... which in some areas may completely alter the character of a town, a neighbourhood or a rural area. The pace, intensity and scale of change will inevitably bring bewilderment and frustration if people affected think it is imposed without respect for their views... Some people are bound to be hurt and others will remain dissatisfied even though they are informed of proposals and are able to comment on them. Not everyone's wishes can be met. But the fact that some people may ultimately be hurt only strengthens the need for them to know of proposals early, to understand them and to be involved in shaping them...

11. Where information comes too late and without preliminary

public discussion there is the likelihood of frustration and hostility... [T]he reasons for decisions do not emerge, nor are people told why superficially attractive alternatives have been put aside...

14. ... Many authorities have recognised and voluntarily responded to the spontaneous demand for participation in their area... Several of our recommendations are based on the experience of those pioneering authorities...[19]

59. We have looked for ways in which two main groups of the country may make a constructive response. They are first, the active minority... and, second, the passive... Into the active groups fall those who normally join local organisations...

A community forum

60. Many organisations (for example, local chambers of trade) may have been set up to foster an interest that concentrates mainly on one of many topics that are brought together in a development plan...[A] local planning authority could well prepare its plan by taking into account the views of those organisations separately, or in groups of like interests, and then producing its comprehensive proposals... [B]ut we have considered whether groups might not be brought together in a community forum for corporate discussions so that there might be a cross-fertilisation of ideas and a wider realisation of the problems of an area as a whole and of the differing needs for which an authority must cater. The community forum could also provide a means of a two-way flow of information between local planning authorities and the public... Because planning involves so many interests a forum of this kind would be of particular value when plans are being prepared; but there is no reason why its discussions should not embrace with advantage issues other than physical planning.

61. We do not know whether this idea has been tried in Great Britain over a period in relation to the whole area of a local planning authority but we give at *Appendix 4* some details of a meeting called in Croydon to discuss the evidence to be sent to our own Committee... We have also noted with interest parallel experiments in Holland and America, although these have had a greater rigidity of structure than we envisage for a community forum and they have concentrated on physical planning. In Chicago, for example, Model Area Planning Councils have been established through which residents are deeply involved in planning their area as soon as the preparation of a new plan is mooted. They co-operate with the City Planning Depart-

---

[19] The Committee included in an Appendix descriptions of the way in which Coventry and Washington Development Corporation had tackled the problem.

ment, for example by preparing statements describing present conditions, problems and needs in each area as seen by area residents and groups. These statements are submitted to the authority and form the basis of a continuing dialogue about proposals and their implementation.

62. We do not suggest that a consultative committee on the pattern described above should be established but we do believe that a forum for discussion could work creatively in some areas ...

63. The initiative for convening a community forum could come from the local planning authority, in partnership with district councils where possible ...

64. Once the forum had got under way, we would not expect the authority to play a leading part in its activities. The authority would call a meeting of representatives of bodies such as local churches ... voluntary social organisations, civic and amenity societies, residents and tenants associations, trade unions, political parties, chambers of trade, youth and other organisations interested in the working of the community. There would then exist the basis for a continuing and cohesive framework maintained by the sponsoring organisations...

68. The community forum would not, and often could not, seek to reconcile ideas, although where there was a single collective view it might be expected to carry considerable weight with the authority; nor would it prevent or take the place of discussions between the authority and constituent members.

69. We think it fair to say that the concept of a community forum has not generally been well received by those with whom we have had discussions. The local authority associations thought it would serve little purpose in the form in which we presented it to them...

80. The methods of participation that we have described above are ... designed mainly to assist the involvement of organisations. But, in addition, we consider that the making of the development plan should be an opportunity for those who do not normally take part in community affairs to do so. We consider that this can best be achieved by someone working with the people concerned in the area where they live.

81. Some authorities already have such people. Often they do so in areas where there are particular problems, such as in deprived communities, or in areas of high unemployment, or to help re-settlement in a new town. Depending on the problems of the area, the type and emphasis of the role will change. For instance, it may be that in some areas, the social and welfare aspects of the role will be so strong that participation will best be achieved primarily through the personal, welfare and community services. In others, it may be concerned wholly with some aspect of planning...

82. ... We are concerned that this role should be undertaken to provide a catalyst for, local opinion. In the following paragraphs where we describe how this function might be carried out we have ... done so as if the role had been allocated to one man who undertakes ' planning participation ' only ... [W]e call him the Community Development Officer. ..

84. The work of the Community Development Officer would depend on the identification of groups within the community, whether based on neighbourhoods, industries or other interests. .. The officer's work ... would have three main facets; to give information, to receive and transmit reactions, and to be a link with existing groups or to promote new local ones which would eventually stand on their feet as independent bodies for participation. ..

87. ... Community Development Officers ... should work as much as possible through existing groups and also assist the formation of groups where none exist. These new groups would need fostering until they were firmly established and their own group leaders emerged.

88. The Community Development Officer would ... bring cooperation between organised and specialist groups and those which may have arisen mainly as a form of self protection against a proposal. He should encourage the ... members of the former groups to act as a bridge between those with special skills and knowledge and those needing an advocate to help in the expression of their views.

89. We have discussed the Community Development Officer as if he were an employee of a local authority ... but other arrangements may be possible; for example ... he might be an employee of a council of social service. ..

[People and Planning. Report of the Committee on Public Participation in Planning, 1969]

The examination in public

Once a local planning authority had submitted its structure plan to the Minister, the Town and Country Planning Act, 1971 as amended by the Town and Country Planning (Amendment) Act, 1972, then provided:

' 9. (1) The Secretary of State may, after considering a structure plan submitted ... to him, either approve it (in whole or in part with or without modifications or reservations) or reject it.

(2) In considering any such plan the Secretary of State may take into account any matters which he thinks are relevant, whether or not they were taken into account in the plan as submitted to him.

(3) Where on taking any such plan into consideration the Secretary of State does not determine then to reject it, he shall, before determining whether or not to approve it—

(a) consider any objections to the plan, so far as they are made in accordance with regulations under this Part of this Act, and (*b*) cause a person or persons appointed by him for the purpose to hold an examination in public of such matters affecting his consideration of the plan as he considers ought to be so examined.

(4) The Secretary of State may after consultation with the Lord Chancellor make regulations with respect to the procedure to be followed at any examination under subsection (3) of this section.

(5) The Secretary of State shall not be required to secure to any local planning authority or other person a right to be heard at any examination under the said subsection (3), and the bodies and persons who may take part therein shall be such only as he may, whether before or during the course of the examination, in his discretion invite to do so :

Provided that the person or persons holding the examination shall have power, exercisable either before or during the course of the examination, to invite additional bodies or persons to take part therein if it appears to him or them desirable to do so.

(6) An examination under subsection (3) (*b*) of this section shall constitute a statutory inquiry for the purposes of section 1 (1) (*c*) of the Tribunals and Inquiries Act 1971, but shall not constitute such an inquiry for any other purpose of that Act.

(7) On considering a structure plan the Secretary of State may consult with, or consider the views of, any local planning authority or other person, but shall not be under any obligation to do so.

(8) On exercising his powers under subsection (1) of this section ... the Secretary of State shall give such statement as he considers appropriate of the reasons governing his decision.'

Guidance in relation to the holding of examinations in public was in the first instance set out in a Code of Practice which also set out some of the underlying principles.

3.1. The primary purpose of the examination in public is to provide the Secretary of State with the information and arguments he needs, in addition to the material submitted with a structure plan and to the objections and representations made on it, to enable him to reach a decision on the plan. The examination will normally be conducted by a small panel, appointed by the Secretary of State ... and will take the form of a discussion, led by the panel, with selected participants, including the planning authority responsible for the plan. It will be directed to the matters which the Secretary of State considers need to be further investigated in this way...

The panel

3.7. The Chairman will be an independent chairman who has had a wide range of relevant experience (in central or local government or in the professions) in conducting investigations of this kind.

3.8. The panel will usually have two other members. One will be from the Department of the Environment, normally from the Regional Office concerned. His knowledge of the area of the plan and the issues it raises, of neighbouring areas and of the region, will enable him to promote relevant discussion at the examination; and to see that essential considerations are brought out. It will not be his role to advocate changes in the plan on behalf of the Department. The other member will be from the Department's Inspectorate, experienced in dealing with matters raised by objections and representations.

3.9. The Secretary of State may appoint assessors to the panel where expert knowledge in a specialist field is essential.

Selection of matters for examination

3.10. The Secretary of State's selection of matters will be based on the structure plan itself; on the local planning authority's statement about publicity and public participation, and consultation; and on objections and representations made on the plan as submitted. . .

3.11. . . . In his consideration of the plan as a whole, the Secretary of State will concentrate on its major issues at the level which it is the function of a structure plan to bring before him for decision. . .

3.12. Not all key issues will throw up matters which need to be selected for reference to the examination in public. The treatment of many of them in the plan will have proved to be generally acceptable. The Secretary of State will be concerned to select only those matters arising on the plan on which he needs to be more fully informed. . .

3.13. Matters which need to be examined are likely to arise, principally, from clashes between the plan and national or regional policies, or those of neighbouring planning authorities; from any conflicts between the various general proposals in the plan; or from issues involving substantial controversy which has not been resolved. . . [A]n examination will not be concerned with every provision in a plan, any more than with pursuing all comments on it, whether objections or representations.

3.15. . . . When a local planning authority submit their structure plan to the Secretary of State, they must send to him a statement about the steps they have taken to secure publicity and public participation, and about the consultations they have had. . .

3.16. This statement will help the Secretary of State to appreciate what issues have proved controversial, and do not appear to have been suitably resolved, and what alternatives have been considered, in the course of the preparation of the plan. He will be able, accordingly, to consider which of these give rise to matters which should be selected for the examination.

3.17. The selection of matters is closely linked with the effectiveness of public participation and consultation. The more constructively they are carried out, the more the matters which do need to be selected will stand out and the more effectively they can be examined... These stages will show the extent to which alternatives are opposed or supported, and make it easier to bring out... any alternative which clearly needs to be examined.

3.18. *Objections.* The Secretary of State has a statutory duty to consider all objections to a structure plan.

3.19. His consideration of objections, in their own right, and of representations will be an important part of his consideration of the plan as a whole.

3.20. Also, the content of objections will help him to appreciate which are the matters he should select for discussion at the examination...

3.22. Objections should be relevant to the plan, and have regard to the fact that a structure plan is essentially a written presentation of policy and general proposals. It will not be appropriate, or indeed possible, in the context of the examination, or even in the consideration of the structure plan, to deal with objections which are really directed to detail instead of to structural issues...

3.25. The local planning authority will be asked to put a copy of objections on deposit with the plan, so that those who want to can see what features of the plan are being commented on...

Selection of participants

3.28. ... In selecting participants, the basic criterion will be the effectiveness of the contribution which, from their knowledge or the views they have expressed, they can be expected to make to the discussion. The local planning authority responsible for the structure plan will always be invited.

3.29. As the examination is directed to discussion of the selected matters, and not to hearing objections, it is not intended that all those who have objected should be invited to the examination... The aim will be to select participants who can... reflect the objections which are significant at the structure plan level...

3.30. Individuals as well as organisations will be eligible for selection. But one aim of the arrangements... is to make it easier for those with views in common... to get together... and to secure that, where they consider specialist advice is needed, it can be obtained... In such cases, it will be easier also for the Department to identify those organisations or individuals most likely to be able to contribute effectively to the examination.

Representations

3.32. This booklet has already pointed to the importance of representations which support a plan or proposals in it or which comment on them... It will be important, for the examination and in promoting a balanced discussion, that... [the Secretary of State] should take account of representations and those making them. In this way, a broader and more representative body of opinion can be secured to pursue the structural issues raised by the plan than if the discussions at the examination were restricted to objections...

Information about selected matters and participants

3.34. The list of matters to be examined and of those to be invited to take part will be published in as short a time as practicable after the end of the period for making objections or representations...

3.35. The list will make it clear that its publication provides the opportunity for those who wish to send written comments to the Department about the selection of matters and participants to do so...

3.36. ... [W]hile ... [the Secretary of State] may add or make other changes to the list, the selection will be such that additions or changes are unlikely, in the normal case to be necessary: or, if they are, to be at all extensive.

3.37. The Act gives the chairman a discretion ... to invite additional participants... The Secretary of State ... will ... as a matter of practice associate the Chairman with the selection of both matters and participants ...

Announcement of the examination

3.40. The Department will publish an announcement, saying when and where the examination will be held, referring to the names of the Chairman and other members of the panel, and to the final list of matters and participants...

The nature of the examination

3.45. The essential feature will be that of a probing discussion, led by the Chairman and other members of the panel, with the local planning authority and the other participants ...

3.48. The Chairman and other members of the panel will take an active part in the examination. An important feature of their role will be to ensure that relevant points of view can be explored.

3.49. ... [T]he Chairman ... will allow reasonable flexibility in the way the selected matters are discussed, and have regard to the wishes of participants; but he will chair the examination so as to encourage contributions which are constructive, concise and not repetitive. It will be for him to ensure that the examination goes into the selected matters in suitable depth without lapsing into a degree of detail not appropriate to a structure plan or to the examination...

3.52. ... The panel will not normally have Counsel to assist them. It is important that participants should not feel that unless they are professionally represented they will necessarily be at a disadvantage or their contribution not effectively made. The active part which the panel will be taking means that if they consider that participants (whether a group or an individual) have a relevant point or argument worth pursuing but which the participants cannot themselves develop sufficiently, it will be for the Chairman and panel to take it up and pursue it.

3.53. It will be open to participants to be accompanied at the examination by their professional or other advisers (to whom they would have easy access); to have their contribution made on their behalf; and to arrange for those with special knowledge of a subject to speak it as part of their contribution.

3.54. ... In addition to providing for the appropriate participants and those accompanying them, provision will always be made, within the limits of the accommodation available, for the local authorities primarily concerned, members of the public and the press to hear the discussion.

Participants from government departments

3.55. A matter to be discussed may involve, in an important respect, the interests of a government department (including the Department of the Environment). Where the department concerned can make a useful contribution to the discussion, it will be invited to send a participant. He will be there primarily to explain his department's views about the policies and proposals in the plan which concern it, and give appropriate information.

Separate discussions

3.56. A more detailed, expert, analysis of certain material may be needed than could conveniently or usefully be undertaken at the examination itself. It may be necessary to examine the technical basis of conflicting views; or for participants to produce an agreed statement, or identify or clarify points of difference. If it has not been possible to deal with such points at an earlier stage, it will be open to the Chairman to ask the participants concerned, or their advisers, to pursue them in a separate room, while the main examination continues.

The report

3.57. The Chairman will send the panel's report to the Secretary of State as soon as possible after the end of the examination. Basically, the report will be an assessment of the selected matters in the light of the discussion which has taken place at the examination, and will include recommendations. It will not contain a detailed account of the arguments advanced by participants: the transcript will be available of the proceedings at the examination.

[The Examination in Public: Code of Practice. Department of the Environment, 1972]

(d) *National planning by Commission. The Roskill experiment*

The following account of the events leading up to the appointment of the Royal Commission is taken from its report.

'In July 1953 the Government of the day published a White Paper [London's Airports, Cmd. 8902, July 1953] ... The White Paper ... proposed that traffic should be concentrated at Heathrow ... A second airport should serve as the main alternative ... while a third should be used as a supplementary airport to handle aircraft which for any reason could not use the main alternative ... It was decided that Gatwick should be developed as the main alternative airport ... A public local inquiry to hear local objections ... was held in 1954 ... The Inspector reported that the evidence put before him established ... that Gatwick was a " suitable " site ... The Inspector added that the limited scope of the inquiry made it impossible to say whether or not Gatwick was the most suitable site...

[In 1960] ... the Ministry of Aviation, in a memorandum submitted to the Estimates Committee, pointed out that Stansted was ... making a loss and that most of its flying activity could be transferred elsewhere ... The Estimates Committee in its Fifth Report for the Session 1960–1 [London's Airports, H.C. 233] recommended " that the Ministry of Aviation in association with the Air Ministry and the Ministry of Transport, should undertake an immediate detailed study of the prospects of Stansted as a future third airport for London " ... Acting on the advice of the Estimates Committee, the Minister of Aviation appointed in November 1961 a committee to study the need for a third London airport and where it should be sited ... It included representatives of airlines, government departments and the National Air Traffic Control Services. On the basis of this Committee's report (commonly referred to as the Interdepartmental Committee's report) [Report of the Interdepartmental Committee on the third London airport 1964] published in 1964, the Government decided that Stansted should be developed as the third London airport.

The Ministry of Housing and Local Government subsequently appointed an Inspector to hold a public inquiry into " local objections relating to the suitability of choice of Stansted for an airport and the effect of the proposed development on local interests ". Though the inquiry was apparently intended to form part of the process of public discussion called for by the Government when it published the report of the Interdepartmental Committee. These extremely limited terms of reference virtually precluded public discussion of all but local issues. Perusal of the lengthy manuscript of the inquiry shows that much time was taken in argument whether a particular issue was within or without the ambit of the inquiry ... The Inspector stated in his report (submitted in 1966 and published in 1967) that, on the basis of the evidence put forward at the inquiry, he felt that Stansted could not be regarded as a suitable site ... In his view the objections, based on noise, traffic, regional planning, agriculture and house values, were " formidable and justified ". His conclusion was that " it would be a calamity for the neighbourhood if a major airport were placed at Stansted. Such a decision would only be justified by national necessity. Necessity was not proved by evidence at this inquiry." The Inspector went on to recommend that " a review of the whole problem should be undertaken by a Committee equally interested in traffic in the air, traffic on the ground, regional and national planning. The review should cover military as well as civil aviation." Throughout the hearing the Inspector had the assistance of a technical assessor on aviation matters of a technical nature; in his own report, the assessor stated that much of the evidence of a technical nature had appeared to be rather superficial and that he too would be very much happier to see a general examination in more depth before any firm decision was taken.

When it received the Inspector's report the Government carried out what was stated to be " a comprehensive and searching re-examination of the many complex issues. The report ... has never been published. However, a White Paper published in May 1967 claimed that Stansted had advantages over all other sites which had previously been considered. The White Paper contained a brief commentary on the advantages and disadvantages of a number of alternatives to Stansted which had been canvassed at the public inquiry ... Two representative sites were examined, in detail: Thurleigh (Bedford) and Silverstone ... The conclusion was that a new major airport should be developed at Stansted."

The White Paper was discussed by the House of Commons on 29 June 1967. By this time there was a demand for an independent committee to look into the matter. On 22 February the President of the Board of Trade announced that it was proposed to set up a new Commission of Inquiry. The announcement that the chairman would be a judge and the terms of reference followed on 20 May 1968.

THE PRESIDENT OF THE BOARD OF TRADE (MR ANTHONY CROSLAND): I will, with permission, make a statement on the Government's proposals for the inquiry into the siting of the third London airport. The form of the inquiry must meet two requirements. On the one hand, this is one of the most important investment and planning decisions which the nation must take in the next decade; this points to an expert rigorous and systematic study of the many and complex problems involved. At the same time, the decision will profoundly affect the lives of thousands of people near the chosen site; and this calls for an adequate method of representation of the local interests affected. We have sought to find a form of inquiry which will meet these two, to some extent conflicting, needs. We have had discussions with the official Opposition, and I must acknowledge the constructive help which they have given. We have reached a broad agreement.

The Government propose a non-statutory Commission with the following terms of reference:

> To inquire into the timing of the need for a four-runway airport to cater for the growth of traffic at existing airports serving the London area, to consider the various alternative sites, and to recommend which site should be selected.

In order to meet the two requirements which I mentioned earlier there will be two sides to the Commission's work. For part of the time, it will sit as a normal committee of inquiry, commissioning research and analysing its findings, sifting expert evidence, forming its own judgments, and finally preparing its report. But there will be other phases of the inquiry when interested parties can be represented by counsel and have the right to cross-examine, both at a series of local inquiries once the possible sites have been reduced to a small number and also before the main Commission itself. . .

The Hon. Mr Justice Roskill has agreed to act as Chairman . . . and I shall announce the names of the other members as soon as possible. . . [T]he kind of membership I have in mind would include perhaps a traffic engineer, an aviation expert, an economist, a businessman, and a regional planner, in addition to [a] . . . planning inspector. . .

MR KIRK: . . . Will this inquiry obviate the need for a public local inquiry at the end of it into the site chosen?

MR CROSLAND: . . . I would hope that the answer is ' Yes '; in all probability the Government will decide to give planning clearance for the selected site by means of a Special Development Order. There is no obligation to hold an inquiry in respect of such an Order and . . . I hope that no further inquiry would be considered necessary. . .

[765 H.C.Deb. 5s. c. 32. 20 May 1968]

At the same time as the announcement was made the following Note was circulated in the Official Report:

Inquiry into Siting of Third London Airport – Constitution, Terms and Reference and Procedure

Constitution of Commission

1. The Government will set up a non-statutory Commission with the following terms of reference:

To inquire into the timing of the need for a four-runway airport to cater for the growth of traffic at existing airports serving the London area, to consider the various alternative sites, and to recommend which site should be selected.

The Commission will be provided with staff and will be authorised to commission research into matters relevant to its investigation.

The Commission will have its attention directed to the following points which appear to be among the matters particularly relevant to its inquiry:

(a) General planning issues, including population and employment growth, noise, amenity, and effect on agriculture and existing property;

(b) Aviation issues, including air traffic control and safety;

(c) Surface access;

(d) Defence issues;

(e) Cost including the need for cost/benefit analysis.

Procedure

2. The Government envisage that the Commission will proceed broadly in the following manner, though they do not wish to impose an unduly rigid procedure: —

3. *Stage I.* At this first stage, the Commission will consider in a broad way the whole range of alternative sites, eliminate those which are clearly unsuitable and identify the small number which require more detailed consideration. The Commission will carry out this process of preliminary selection on the basis of general evidence that may be put to it and of information that it may itself seek. At this stage, there will be no right of representation before the Commission; though the Commission itself will be free to seek oral evidence if this is required to elucidate the matters it is considering.

4. At the end of Stage I, the Commission will announce the sites it wishes to investigate in greater detail, and will, for the purposes of that examination, define the approximate boundaries of the sites in question, and give such other general indications as may be necessary (e.g. flight paths and runway alignments) to enable those living in the localities to understand how they would be affected.

5. *Stage II* will consist of the hearing of evidence of a local character concerning the short-listed sites. This would probably be undertaken by a senior planning inspector, who would be a member of the Commission, visiting the locality and holding a public local inquiry. Subject to the general reservations mentioned in paragraphs 8–10 below, the interested parties will be entitled to be represented at this stage. As these proceedings will take some time, they will continue while Stages III and IV are going on.

6. Simultaneously, a start will be made with Stage III and the subsequent stages. *Stage III* would consist of investigation and research into matters relevant to the choice to be made between the sites (e.g. air traffic patterns, surface transport, noise, regional planning etc.). Some of this work might be undertaken by the Commission and its staff; some commissioned from consultants; and some produced in the form of written

evidence by the parties concerned or by bodies having an interest in these matters.

7. *Stage IV*. The Commission would consider the material produced during the course of Stage III. It will, if necessary, examine the experts who have produced it. If differences of opinion emerge from the expert evidence the Commission will, in the first place, invite those concerned to consult together with a view to reaching agreement.

8. *Stage V*. The purpose of this stage is to enable the interested parties to test the material produced during the earlier stages. At this stage, they may, by leave of the Commission, be represented by counsel or otherwise. Since the number of interested bodies is potentially large, it is hoped that bodies with similar interests will, wherever possible, be represented by the same counsel.

9. Counsel representing the parties may, by leave of the Commission, lead evidence on relevant matters, and cross-examine witnesses appearing on behalf of other parties or experts responsible for reports which are being taken into consideration by the commission.

10. Before giving leave, the Commission will need to be satisfied that such new evidence is useful and relevant; and that the proposed examination and cross-examination of witnesses is not repetitious.

11. *Finally*, the Commission will consider the whole of the evidence, including that produced at the local inquiries. The Commission will then prepare its report and recommendation.

Procedure after the Commission has reported:

12. The Government will decide in the light of the circumstances of the time whether formal planning clearance should be given by way of a Special Development Order or whether they should require the British Airports Authority to make a specific planning application for the recommended site which would be called in for decision by the responsible Ministers, if necessary after a statutory local inquiry.

The Report of the Commission, 1971
Methods of approach

3.1. Not the least of the tasks facing the Commission ... was the need to establish public confidence that its work would be impartial, unbiased and entirely uninfluenced by anything which had gone before. Though in some quarters its appointment was welcomed, in others it was suggested that the Committee was intended to do no more than to give a veneer of respectability to a decision already taken in Whitehall. . .

3.2. . . . [T]hese expressions of suspicion were but the manifestation of the distrust which had been aroused by the previous handling of the ' Stansted issue ', including the secrecy attaching to the decisions which had been taken, the rigid limitation of the terms of reference at the Chelmsford inquiry and the lack of public participation.

3.3. It seemed clear to us from our terms of reference and from

the procedure which it had been suggested that we should follow ...
that the need both for public participation and for the establishment
of confidence in the proposed procedure had now been accepted. ...
The five stages of the procedure seemed clearly to aim at securing the
widest degree of public criticism of material which we should from
time to time publish. ...

3.6. This brief account of the background serves to explain three
decisions which we took early in our work ...

(a) we must start afresh, unfettered by the past, drawing up our
own list of possible sites and devising our own criteria for
assessing them;

(b) so far as was possible and was compatible with considerations
of national security our work should be done in public;

(c) we should make use of cost/benefit analysis as the best available
aid to rational decision making but the results must be subject
to close public scrutiny and discussion before any final
recommendation.

We concluded that if our final recommendation were to command
respect and acceptance it had not only to be as right as the best
methods could make it but the reasons leading to our judgment had
to be as objective and as explicit as we could make them. Only by
this approach would there be any hope of persuading informed
opinion that our conclusion should be accepted whatever its degree of
popularity. We have accordingly published at all stages all the
material which we have felt able. Few commissions of inquiry can
have published so much material in advance of their final report. ...

3.7. ... We did not publish the detailed reasons for the selection
of the four short-listed sites early in 1969 and have been criticised for
our refusal so to do ... The procedure recommended by the Government did not envisage that the selection of the short list sites would be
publicly debated. On the contrary the selection was left entirely to
us. Debate would have prolonged our proceedings unduly. We decided
upon the short list on the best evidence then available. Public participation could thus be concentrated on a short list of sites and the
crucial issues debated with reference to them alone [20]. ...

The use of cost/benefit analysis

3.9. The technique of cost/benefit analysis is not widely or easily
understood but it is essential for the reasons we have already stated
that ordinary members of the public should understand the significance of its results. Problems can be analysed by statisticians, opera-

[20] The Commission described the methods used in compiling the short list and
the reasons for the choice later in its Report.

tional research workers, systems analysts, economists and other specialists. But however expert in their own fields, they cannot dictate the conclusion... The expert evidence at the final series of public hearings has made it abundantly plain that there is no one right view on these matters. Informed judgment is required at every stage... The Commission carries the responsibility for its recommendation which has been arrived at by applying its judgment to the whole of the evidence which is publicly available as well as to the public criticisms of it...

3.10. ...It seemed essential wherever possible to avoid subjective judgments upon any part of a problem which had roused such deep emotions and that our method of analysis must be devised with this primary aim in mind...

3.12. We recognised the difficulties of placing money values upon some of the factors which we would need to consider. For example, there would be major difficulties in bringing regional planning issues within the cost/benefit framework... We were alive to the problems of valuing the historic and architectural qualities of Norman or even Victorian churches, open countryside, the unique qualities of the ecology on the shores of Foulness Island and peaceful Sunday afternoons in the garden, to mention but a few of the matters which have been widely canvassed since we began our work.

3.13. In some areas we recognised that the reliability of the results would be doubtful. In others the results would be acceptable. At least an attempt would be made to measure and value factors which are external to ordinary market transactions...

3.14. ...Nothing on this scale has ever been attempted before in government or business circles in this country or, we believe, abroad... [W]e are as conscious as the authors of the cost/benefit analysis that further developments of the technique may well make even this example of it appear 'rather rudimentary' in years to come.

3.15. ...We have been well aware of the extent and nature of the human problems involved – sacrifice of homes for some, peace and quiet for others... Cost/benefit analysis does not ignore them. It seeks so far as it can to assist in bringing all problems into their proper perspective. It provides a logical framework within which to assess all the effects flowing from a particular investment or planning decision. It tries to ensure that decisions are taken on the basis of people's individual values and choices as revealed by their behaviour rather than on the basis of the decision maker's own preferences or standards or of those of vociferous and politically powerful groups. There are formidable technical difficulties in achieving these aims. Quite apart from the difficulty of quantifying certain important matters... it is rarely easy to observe and draw correct inferences from people's behaviour. In addition there is the problem... of finding the correct basis for predicting the repercussions of the alternatives being studied. Finally we have been alerted to the danger of seeing only those consequences with which our own supposed social background makes us familiar and of ignoring those to which importance is attached by the young and by people of different circumstances.

Staff

3.17. Before our first meeting, Mr John Caines, an Assistant Secretary of the Board of Trade, was seconded to us as our Secretary. We also obtained the secondment of Mr F. P. Thompson, then a Senior Economic Adviser at the Ministry of Transport, as our Director of Research... Mr Thompson, with the help of the Board of Trade and the Civil Service Department, recruited from within and without the Civil Service a full-time professional research team of nearly two dozen economists, engineers, operational research scientists, systems analysts, planners and statisticians...

3.18. No previous commission of enquiry has, we believe, ever had placed at its disposal a research team of both such size and such calibre...

3.19. ... To supplement the services of the Research Team as well as to expedite the work we commissioned at an early stage many special studies from government departments, from statutory authorities and from outside consultants...

The first stage

3.20. No rigid timetable was proposed by the Government... At the start the target at which we aimed was two years... [A]part from the time taken in considering what recommendation we would make and in writing this report the... original estimate was remarkably accurate... To have attempted a more speedy study of the problem could only have meant less thorough work and less public participation. It would of course have shortened the period of intolerable uncertainty which those affected by the four short-listed sites have endured with much patience in spite often of considerable financial and other hardships. But the disadvantages of undue speed seemed clearly to outweigh the advantages...

3.21. Following our first private meeting on 25 June 1968 and certain subsequent private meetings we published on 15 July 1968 an invitation for evidence of a general nature as well as for site suggestions. We wrote to a number of public, commercial and other organisations... asking them to submit any suggestions. These included airlines and other aviation interests, planning organisations, employers' and employees' organisations, associations and societies concerned with the problem of noise, agricultural interests, land preservation and amenity organisations, local authorities and those concerned with the possible commercial and industrial implications of the airport.

3.22. The response to this invitation was considerable... [W]e continued to hold regular private meetings, usually weekly, during the remaining part of 1968. The views then expressed to us and also revealed in the evidence submitted as a result of our invitation made it clear that it was desirable for some of the most crucial issues to be ventilated in public even at that early stage. We therefore held five public hearings during November and December 1968. The first of these on 1st November 1968 was devoted to evidence from the British Airports Authority and in particular from its Chairman, Mr Peter Masefield. Later hearings were devoted to questions of regional planning, noise, surface access and air traffic control ... The hearings were informal. There was no legal representation. The many views expressed were not subjected to any cross-examination. All the oral and written evidence obtained in this way has been published ... or made available for public inspection. At the same time the work on the selection of the short list was proceeding ... [t]he short list was decided upon in February 1969 and published on 4th March 1969 ...

The second stage – the local hearings

3.23. The local hearings ... were designed to be the first occasion upon which the public could bring its views and its criticisms to bear upon our published work. It was inevitable that the selection of the three inland sites – coupled with the impossibility of disclosing at this time the reasons which had led to their selection as well as to the exclusion of Stansted without reopening the entire controversy – would lead to the development of local opposition to each of those sites at least as intense, if not more so, as that which had developed to the Stansted proposals ...

3.24. We decided that every opportunity must be given at the local hearings to allow any opposition to make itself felt in whatever way it wished to do so. It is worth noting that in the case of Gatwick in 1954 and of Stansted in 1966 the local inquiries had been the only such opportunity. But the final series of public hearings would inevitably concentrate upon wider and possibly more complex issues than would be the case at the local hearings. These were to be the opportunity for the ordinary man and woman affected by the four site proposals to make his or her individual views felt ... We were never under any illusions as to the extent of the disruption of daily life which the selection of any inland site must cause... [H]owever, there were some voices wishing to be heard in favour of the proposals of each of those sites. These views were of a minority and they were unpopular with the local resistance associations . . . We determined that these voices too should be heard however small a group they represented.

3.25. At intervals during the first half of 1969 we published in relation to each of the four sites site information which gave in broad outline certain basic factors such as the approximate location of the airport and possible layout and alignment of its runways together with indications of the likely population to be directly dependent upon the airport. More detailed information was not possible at this early stage before detailed site investigations had been carried out. We also provided noise contours which were approximate and based on the provisional alignments. We were criticised for not providing more detail . . . for without more detail it was difficult for individuals to know whether they were affected. . . Our early publications did not and could not show whether a particular householder or a particular farmer would be just within or just without the airport site. Nor could they show whether a particular district, let alone a particular householder or a farmer, was more likely than not to be affected by noise. But had we waited with publishing this site information until we could answer every such question, the duration of our work would have been endless . . .

3.26. We have also been criticised for having subsequently altered the location, layout and alignment at the sites and we were pressed to arrange for further local hearings. It was, however, an inevitable implication of our procedure that if we were to bring local considerations to bear at an early stage upon our work there should be changes in the light of the evidence presented to us. To have embarked upon further local hearings each time an alteration was made to any of the main factors set out in the first publication would have placed an impossible burden on all concerned.

3.27. The local hearings were in no sense ordinary local planning inquiries. In the case of an ordinary local planning inquiry there is a definite proposal of a particular kind for which the promoter – be it a government department, a local authority, or an individual – seeks to obtain planning permission. This had been the case at the Chelmsford inquiry into the Stansted proposals when the then Ministry of Aviation promoted the proposals. But there would be no promoters at any of our local hearings – only objectors and possibly supporters. The Commission was not proposing an airport at any of the four sites. It was investigating the possibility that there might be an airport at one of them. It was seeking information as to local reactions should that possibility become a reality. It had always been envisaged that each local hearing would be conducted by our colleague Mr A. J. Hunt, a principal planning inspector of the Ministry of Housing and Local Government, But even his extensive experience of public inquiries did not extend to an inquiry of the kind proposed – it could not do so for there was no precise precedent.

3.28. We therefore devised the procedure for those hearings in full consultation with all interested parties. Naturally the county councils and country borough councils in each area were closely concerned. So of course were borough councils, urban and rural district councils in each area. So were many organisations. So, above all, were individuals. We welcomed the formation of resistance associations for each of the three inland sites as well as the Action Committee against Foulness Airport and the Sheppey Group. The existence of these bodies made our task easier. It also made the organisation of the opposition considerably more effective since the collective effect of a well managed organisation is necessarily greater than the isolated efforts of individuals however praiseworthy in themselves.

3.29. We would pay particular tribute in this connection to the initial work of the Nuthampstead Preservation Association whose written presentation of their case was a model of its kind. . . We are also indebted to the Wing Airport Resistance Association and to the Bedfordshire Airport Resistance Association for their help in organising the evidence given at the local hearings as well as for their major contributions at subsequent stages of our work. The Buckinghamshire County Council, however, chose, as it was entitled to do, a somewhat different method of presenting the opposition to the proposal for Cublington. It organised the submission of a large number of letters and written representations on the basis of a common form. These too were impressive.

3.30. Each of the four local hearings took place . . . during the summer of 1969. A total of twenty-four days was occupied in hearing evidence. The whole of the evidence given has been published or made available for public inspection.

The third stage – detailed investigation and research

3.31. After the announcement of the short list the Research Team carried out its detailed investigation and research into matters relevant to the choice between the four sites and to the timing of the need. . . The methodology which the Research Team devised for its work under our general direction was published in June 1969 so that it might have the benefit of constructive criticism from outside.

3.32. The results of the application of that methodology together with the advice which we received from government departments and other authorities and the results of studies which we commissioned from specialised consultants were published early in 1970. This was the material which formed the main basis of the final series of public hearings.

3.33 At the outset of this third stage we again enlisted the help of the public at large. We invited evidence likely to make a useful contribution to the detailed site investigation – and to the cost/benefit analysis – and to the timing of the need. All the evidence which we received as a result has been published or made available for inspection. It also formed part of the basis for the final series of public hearings.

3.34. Our aim in inviting fresh evidence at this stage was to give people the opportunity of bringing to our attention matters which were not within the necessarily limited ambit of the local hearings but which could contribute to the detailed appraisal of the comparative merits of the four sites. We wanted the Research Team to be able to take account of these contributions at the earliest possible moment so that the differences of view and omissions which would have to be explored at the final series of public hearings could be kept to a minimum. Many of the main parties who were subsequently represented at these hearings took the opportunity of our invitation to set out their approach to the problems. The major contribution of the Essex, Hertfordshire and Cambridgeshire and Isle of Ely County Councils was in the form of a cost/benefit appraisal of the four sites... Many of the other local authorities affected by the four sites subsequently took advantage of the lead given by these three County Councils and adopted the work of some of the consultants retained by them.

3.35. The Research Team's cost/benefit analysis showed that for those items which it had been possible to evaluate in money terms Cublington was overall the 'best' site. There was little to choose between Cublington and the other two inland sites. The gap between the inland sites and Foulness was relatively wide...

3.37. Throughout this third stage we continued to hold private meetings of the Commission at weekly intervals. At these meetings we discussed issues arising from the work of the Research Team and of our consultants. We had discussions with a number of people and organisations whose help we wished to enlist; the substance of these discussions has to a large extent been subsequently published... We also reviewed the evidence submitted in response to our invitation. Our own activities culminated ... just before Christmas 1969 ... when we gave our final agreement to the publication of the results of the Research Team's work.

3.38. Although we had been closely associated with the Research Team's work and with the work of all the consultants, we attached considerable importance to remaining uncommitted... [W]e embarked upon the final series of public hearings with an open mind... We wanted the work which we had commissioned to be fully tested in public and we intended to treat it in the same way as other evidence put before us during our work.

Visits overseas

3.39. Members of the Research Team visited Paris in the spring of 1969 for discussions with those responsible for the new Paris airport project...

3.40. In the autumn of 1969 the Commission accompanied by the Director of Research and the Secretary paid a ten-day visit to the United States to draw upon American experience...

The fourth stage – discussions between experts

3.41. The procedure recommended to us envisaged that prior to the final series of public hearings the technical experts who had produced material during the research and investigation stages should consult together in order to reach agreement on or to define precisely any differences of opinion revealed in that material ... [W]e could not expect that many major points would be conceded if the effect were to undermine the case which a particular party was proposing to make. In February and March 1970 we arranged a series of private meetings to which all those who had been given leave to appear at the hearings were invited. In addition a number of informal discussions between the Research Team and individual parties took place. While our somewhat pessimistic expectations about the success of this operation were confirmed, the meetings did give a useful indication of some of the basic technical points of difference and did permit much elucidation of both the Research Team's and the parties' views.

3.42. This process of discussion between experts did not cease with the opening of the public hearings. Throughout there was continuing contact between the Research Team and other technical experts. Under the stress of the hearings there was a much greater incentive than during the fourth stage to narrow and identify the points of difference and a considerable measure of agreement was reached on many important matters.

The fifth stage – the final series of public hearings

3.43. The final series of public hearings began on 6th April 1970 and continued on four days each week without a break until 12th August 1970. The proceedings occupied seventy-four working days. Forty-eight different organisations appeared or were represented and over 160 witnesses gave oral evidence on their behalf or in support of the material which we had published. In addition we received sixty written representations from other organisations and from individuals, including Members of Parliament, who did not wish to apply for leave to appear before us...

3.44. As for the earlier local hearings we devised the procedure for the conduct of these hearings after full consultation with the parties concerned. We insisted on all evidence being submitted in writing so that examination-in-chief could be kept to a minimum and all evidence could be taken as having been read by everybody in advance...

3.45. The majority of parties chose to have legal representation but... those who did not... did not appear to be at any disadvantage... We retained a team of counsel, who received their instructions both from us and the Research Team but they were not in the normal sense of the word representing either. We took this step... because our interest at the hearings was to have tested in public all relevant points... The experiment of having our team of counsel was a complete success. We were able to keep ourselves above the debate and observe the strengths and weaknesses of the various points as they were unfolded before us. Our ability to comprehend objectively all the evidence would have been seriously impaired if we had had to conduct our own detailed questioning of witnesses.

3.46. Following the completion of the public hearings we reviewed all the evidence and submissions which we had received throughout the two years of our work and decided upon our final recommendation. We were assisted in this task by the Research Team who continued to act as our technical advisers. As part of this task the Team revised the cost/benefit analysis in accordance with our instructions to take account of the conclusions we reached as a result of the suggestions and criticisms made during the hearings...

[Report of the Commission on the Third London Airport, 1971]

The Commission, with Professor Buchanan dissenting, recommended that Cublington should be the site of the Third London Airport. On 26 April 1971 the Conservative Government announced that it had decided not to accept this recommendation. Instead it designated Foulness on the grounds that environmental and planning considerations pointed to it rather than Cublington. [816 H.C.Deb. 5s. c. 34.]

For a comment on the use of a Commission in such circumstances see P. Self, 'Nonsense on Stilts', *Political Quarterly*, 41 (1970), p. 249.

CHAPTER XI

COURTS AND TRIBUNALS

I. THE INDEPENDENCE OF THE COURTS

PROHIBITIONS DEL ROY (1607) 12 Co.Rep. 63; 77 E.R. 1342

Note, upon Sunday the 10th of November in this same term, the King, upon complaint made to him by Bancroft, Archbishop of Canterbury, concerning prohibitions, the King was informed, that when the question was made of what matters the Ecclesiastical Judges have cognizance, either upon the exposition of the statutes concerning tithes, or any other thing ecclesiastical, or upon the statute 1 El. concerning the high commission or in any other case in which there is not express authority in law, the King himself may decide it in his Royal person; and that the Judges are but the delegates of the King, and that the King may take what causes he shall please to determine, from the determination of the Judges, and may determine them himself. And the Archbishop said, that this was clear in divinity, that such authority belongs to the King by the word of God in the Scripture. To which it was answered by me, in the presence, and with the clear consent of all the Judges of England, and Barons of the Exchequer, that the King in his own person cannot adjudge any case, either criminal, as treason, felony, &c. or betwixt party and party, concerning his inheritance, chattels, or goods, &c. but this ought to be determined and adjudged in some Court of Justice, according to the law and custom of England... And the Judges informed the King, that no King after the Conquest assumed to himself to give any judgment in any cause whatsoever, which concerned the administration of justice within this realm, but these were solely determined in the Courts of Justice... [T]hen the King said, that he thought the law was founded upon reason, and that he and others had reason, as well as the Judges: to which it was answered by me, that true it was, that God had endowed His Majesty with excellent science, and great endowments of nature; but His Majesty was not learned in the laws of his realm of England, and causes which concern the life, or inheritance, or goods, or fortunes of his subjects, are not to be decided by natural reason but by the artificial reason and judgment of law, which law is an act which requires long study and experience, before that a man can attain to the cognizance of it: that the law was the golden met-wand and measure to try the causes of the subjects; and which

514

protected His Majesty in safety and peace: with which the King was greatly offended, and said, that then he should be under the law, which was treason to affirm, as he said; to which I said, that Bracton saith, *quod Rex non debet esse sub homine, sed sub Deo et lege.*

(i) The Attorney-General and the courts

The Communist conspiracy trial, 1925

On 14 and 22 October 1925 twelve leading members of the Communist party, including Campbell and Hannington (see below, p. 660), were arrested and their homes and the party's headquarters were searched and all the copies of that week's *Workers' Weekly* seized. They were charged with conspiracy to publish and utter seditious libels, to incite others to commit breaches of the Incitement to Mutiny Act, 1797, and to seduce persons serving in the armed forces from their allegiance.

On 1 December 1925 the Leader of the Opposition, Mr Ramsay Mac-Donald, moved ' That the action of the Government in initiating the prosecution of certain members of the Communist Party is a violation of the traditional rights of freedom of speech and publication of opinion.'

During the debate Sir John Simon gave his view of the role of the Attorney-General in such cases.

SIR JOHN SIMON: ... [T]here is no greater nonsense talked about the Attorney-General's duty than the suggestion that in all cases the Attorney-General ought to prosecute merely because he thinks there is what lawyers call ' a case '. It is not true, and no one who has held that office supposes that it is.

I understand the duty of the Attorney-General to be this. He should absolutely decline to receive orders from the Prime Minister, or Cabinet or anybody else that he shall prosecute.[1] His first duty is to see that no one is prosecuted with all the majesty of the law unless the Attorney-General, as head of the Bar, is satisfied that a case for prosecution lies against him. He should receive orders from nobody. But that is very different from saying that the Attorney-General ought in all cases to ask nobody else's view, because he thinks there is a case to institute a prosecution without finding out what his colleagues or the Government think. That is a ridiculous proposition. If the Leader of the Opposition at the General Election were to make a seditious speech, does anyone mean to tell me a Conservative Attorney-General would start a prosecution against him without consulting the Cabinet? Of course, he would

---

[1] [This passage was quoted with approval by Prime Minister Macmillan on 16 February 1959 when members were pressing for an inquiry into the circumstances in which the Lord Advocate had failed to prosecute two policemen who had been charged with assaulting John Waters at Thurso. A Tribunal of Inquiry was subsequently appointed (600 H.C.Deb. 5s. c. 31).]

not.[2] I am confident that the Attorney-General would never undertake a prosecution, whatever anybody asked him to do, unless he thought the prosecution was justified, but I should regard him ... as a fool if he were to start on his own motion prosecutions which involve grave matters of public concern – treason, sedition, corruption and the like – ... if he did such a thing without knowing that, in the view of his colleagues, public policy was not offended by undertaking such prosecution.

[188 H.C.Deb. 5s. c. 2105. 1 December 1925]

Sir Hartley Shawcross, 1951

In October 1950 the Attorney-General prosecuted ten gas maintenance men for taking part in a strike in contravention of the Conditions of Employment and National Arbitration Order, 1940 (S.R. & O. 1305). This was a wartime regulation which had been continued in operation after the war. It provided, in Article 4, that no worker was to take part in a strike in connection with any trade dispute unless the dispute had been reported to the Minister of Labour and 21 days had elapsed without the dispute being referred to him for settlement. This was the first prosecution under the Order since the war and the Attorney-General was asked why he had prosecuted in this case and not in others where the Order had been contravened.

THE ATTORNEY-GENERAL (SIR HARTLEY SHAWCROSS): ... My hon. and learned Friend then asked me how I direct myself in deciding whether or not to prosecute in a particular case... [T]here is ... one consideration which is altogether excluded, and that is the repercussion of a given decision upon my personal or my party's or the Government's political fortunes... Apart from that, the Attorney-General may have to have regard to a variety of considerations, all of them leading to the final question – would a prosecution be in the public interest, including in that phrase of course, in the interests of justice? Usually it is merely a question of examining the evidence ... It is not in the public interest to put a man upon trial, whatever the suspicions may be about the matter, when the evidence is insufficient to justify his conviction, or even to call upon him for an explanation. So the ordinary case is one where one has to review the evidence, to consider whether the evidence goes beyond mere suspicion and is sufficient to justify a man being put on trial for a specific criminal offence. In other cases wider considera-

---

[2] [In an earlier passage he referred to the speeches made by the Conservative leaders at the time of the Home Rule Crisis (above p. 27) and said: ' I have no doubt ... it was a very grave question of public policy whether it was to the public interest that attempts should be made to prosecute.' For the view of Asquith, who was Prime Minister at the time, see J. A. Spender and Cyril Asquith, *Life of Lord Oxford and Asquith* (1932), vol. II, p. 22.]

tions than that are involved. It is not always in the public interest to go through the whole process of the criminal law if, at the end of the day, perhaps because of mitigating circumstances, perhaps because of what the defendant has already suffered, only a nominal penalty is likely to be imposed. And almost every day in particular cases, and where guilt has been admitted, I decide that the interests of public justice will be sufficiently served not by prosecuting, but perhaps by causing a warning to be administered instead.

Sometimes, of course, the considerations may be wider still. Prosecution may involve a question of public policy or national, or sometimes international, concern; but in cases like that, the Attorney-General has to make up his mind not as a party politician; he must in a quasi-judicial way consider the effect of prosecution upon the administration of law and of government in the abstract rather than in any party sense. Usually, making up my mind on these matters, I have the advice of the Director of Public Prosecutions and very often of Treasury Counsel as well. I have hardly ever, if ever, refused to prosecute when they have advised prosecution. I have sometimes ordered prosecution when the advice was against it.

I think the true doctrine is that it is the duty of an Attorney-General, in deciding whether or not to authorise the prosecution, to acquaint himself with all the relevant facts, including, for instance, the effect which the prosecution, successful or unsuccessful as the case may be, would have upon public morale and order, and with any other considerations affecting public policy.

In order so to inform himself, he may, although I do not think he is obliged to, consult with any of his colleagues in the Government; and indeed, as Lord Simon once said, he would in some cases be a fool if he did not. On the other hand, the assistance of his colleagues is confined to informing him of particular considerations which might affect his own decision, and does not consist, and must not consist, in telling him what that decision ought to be. The responsibility for the eventual decision rests with the Attorney-General, and he is not to be put, and is not put, under pressure by his colleagues in the matter. Nor, of course, can the Attorney-General shift his responsibility for making the decision on to the shoulders of his colleagues. If political considerations which, in the broad sense that I have indicated, affect government in the abstract arise, it is the Attorney-General, applying his judicial mind, who has to be the sole judge of those considerations. . .

The existence of this discretion and the utility of this discretion in the Attorney-General whether or not to prosecute in particular cases has been so well recognised that there has been an increasing tendency in recent years to provide that there shall be no proceedings as to particular classes of offences created by Statute without the consent of the

Attorney-General or the Director of Public Prosecutions.[3] That kind of provision has been made to ensure that there will be no automatic prosecutions and that there will be no frivolous and unnecessary prosecutions in such cases. That is a Parliamentary recognition, if any such recognition were required, that it is the duty of the Attorney-General and the Director to exercise their discretion in every case whether or not to invoke the machinery of the criminal law.

But where a provision of that kind does not exist, where it is not expressly provided that there shall not be any prosecution without the consent of the Attorney-General or the Director of Public Prosecutions, the general position in English law – I think it is different in Scotland where my right hon. and learned Friend the Lord Advocate prosecutes at his discretion in all cases – is that any private citizen can come along and set the criminal law in motion.[4] That is really the safeguard if the Attorney-General and the Director of Public Prosecutions and the police all neglect their duties and do not prosecute in cases where, manifestly, prosecutions ought to take place... In a case of murder, although a private citizen may initiate proceedings to the extent of applying for and obtaining a warrant for the arrest of some named individual, it is the statutory duty of the Director of Public Prosecutions to step in and take over the conduct of the case, no doubt because Parliament has thought that in cases of such gravity it is important that the prosecution should be conducted with all possible safeguards by an experienced official such as the Director of Public Prosecutions...

But, apart from certain particular cases where, if proceedings are started, the Director of Public Prosecutions must intervene and take them over, the general rule of law is that if the Director, the Attorney-

---

[3] E.g. s. 2 of the Official Secrets Act, 1911. In a memorandum to the Departmental Committee on s. 2 the Attorney-General stated:

' 14. The responsibility for deciding whether to consent to a prosecution under the Official Secrets Act is that of the Attorney-General alone. His decision is taken independently of the Government. The practice of including a consent provision in criminal statutes is not unusual, and is a way of ensuring that where a statute has been drawn in wide terms a prosecution will follow only when the real mischief at which the statute aims has occurred...

15. In exercising this discretion the factors which the Attorney-General of the day takes into account are (1) the strength of the evidence; (2) the degree of culpability of the potential defendant; (3) the damage to the public interest which has resulted from the disclosure; (4) the effect of prosecution on the public interest.

In considering factors relating to the public interest, I and my predecessors may consult other Ministers so that we are in a better position to assess the damage which has been caused and the effect which the prosecution may have on the public interest; but the responsibility remains that of the Attorney-General alone.' [Cmnd. 5104. September 1972]

[4] And see *R.* v. *Commissioner of the Metropolitan Police, Ex parte Blackburn* [1968] 2 Q.B. 118.

General or the police do not institute criminal proceedings themselves, then it is open to any private individual so to do.

[483 H.C.Deb. 5s. c. 681. 29 January 1951]

The Attorney-General has however the power to enter a *nolle prosequi* which will effectively stop proceedings on indictment [*The Queen* v. *Allen* (1862) 1 B. & S. 850; 121 E.R. 929] though not summary proceedings.

(ii) Statements by the Executive in matters of foreign affairs

CARL ZEISS STIFTUNG v. RAYNER AND KEELER LTD. (No. 2)   [1967] 1 A.C. 853

House of Lords

The Carl Zeiss Stiftung was established in Jena in 1891. Its constitution provided that it was to be under the direction of the same department of state as the University of Jena. At that time Jena was in the Grand Duchy of Saxe-Weimar. In 1918 it became part of the Land of Thuringia. In 1949 the German Democratic Republic was established in the Russian zone of Germany and in 1952 a decree of the German Democratic Republic divided Thuringia with Jena being put in Gera. The Council of Gera brought an action in the English courts to prevent the defendants using the words Carl Zeiss Stiftung, Carl Zeiss or Zeiss in connection with optical or glass products. The defendants argued that the Council had no standing to bring such an action as the German Democratic Republic was not recognised by the United Kingdom Government and the decrees of 1952 were therefore of no effect. The Court of Appeal asked the Foreign Office whether the Government had recognised de jure or de facto the German Democratic Republic or its Government. On 16 September 1964 the Foreign Secretary replied: ' Her Majesty's Government have not granted any recognition de jure or de facto to (a) the " German Democratic Republic " or (b) its " Government ".' In reply to a further request the Foreign Secretary replied on 6 November 1964 that since June 1945 ' Her Majesty's Government have recognised the State and Government of the Union of Soviet Socialist Republics as de jure entitled to exercise governing authority in respect of that zone [i.e. the zone of occupation allocated to the U.S.S.R. under the protocol of 12 September 1944 and the agreement of 26 July 1945, as modified by the protocol of the proceedings of the Berlin Conference of 2 August, 1945].'

LORD REID. ...

It is a firmly established principle that the question whether a foreign state ruler or government is or is not sovereign is one on which our courts accept as conclusive information provided by Her Majesty's Government: no evidence is admissible to contradict that information. ' It has for some time been the practice of our courts ... to take judicial notice of the sovereignty of a state, and for that purpose (in any case of uncertainty) to seek information from a Secretary of State; and when information is so obtained the court does not permit it to be questioned by the parties' (*per* Lord Cave in *Duff Development Co. Ltd.* v. *Government of Kelantan* [5]). ' Such information is not in the nature of evidence; it is a statement by the sovereign of this country through one of his ministers upon a matter which is peculiarly within his cognizance ' (*per* Lord Finlay [6]) . . .

The purpose of a certificate is to provide information about the status of foreign governments and states and therefore the statement that since June, 1945, ' Her Majesty's Government have recognised the state and Government of the Union of Soviet Socialist Republics as de jure entitled to exercise governing authority in respect of that zone ' cannot merely mean that Her Majesty's Government have granted this recognition so as to leave the courts of this country free to receive evidence as to whether in fact the U.S.S.R. are still entitled to exercise governing authority there. The courts of this country are no more entitled to hold that a sovereign, still recognised by our Government, has ceased in fact to be sovereign de jure, than they are entitled to hold that a government not yet recognised has acquired sovereign status. So this certificate requires that we must take it as a fact that the U.S.S.R. have been since 1945 and still are de jure entitled to exercise that governing authority. . .

The U.S.S.R. may have purported to confer independence or sovereignty on the German Democratic Republic but, in my judgment, that certificate clearly requires us to hold that, whatever the U.S.S.R. may have purported to do, they did not in fact set up the German Democratic Republic as a sovereign or independent state . . .

If we are bound to hold that the German Democratic Republic was not in fact set up as a sovereign independent state, the only other possibility is that it was set up as a dependent or subordinate organisation through which the U.S.S.R. is entitled to exercise indirect rule . . .

It appears to me to be impossible for any de jure sovereign governing authority to disclaim responsibility for acts done by subordinate bodies which it has set up and which have not attempted to usurp its sovereignty. So, in my opinion, the courts of this country cannot treat as nullities acts done by or on behalf of the German Democratic Republic . . .

We recognise them, not because they are acts of a sovereign state, but because they are acts done by a subordinate body which the U.S.S.R. set up to act on its behalf.

LORDS HODSON, GUEST, UPJOHN, and WILBERFORCE delivered concurring judgments on this point.

[5] [1924] A.C. 797, 805–806; 40 T.L.R. 566, H.L.(E.).
[6] [1924] A.C. 797, 813.

(iii) Claims by the Crown to prevent disclosure of documents and information

CONWAY v. *RIMMER*   [1968] A.C. 910

House of Lords

The plaintiff, a former police constable, had been prosecuted for theft but the charge had been dismissed. He subsequently brought this action for malicious prosecution against one of his superior officers. He asked for the disclosure of reports on his conduct as a probationary constable and also reports relating to the bringing of proceedings against him. The Home Secretary objected to the production of the reports, on the ground that it was not in the public interest that they should be disclosed.[7] The leading authority at the time was the case of *Duncan* v. *Cammell Laird and Co. Ltd.* [1942] A.C. 624. In that case in which the Government had objected to the production inter alia of the design of a new submarine that had sunk on its first trial, Viscount Simon had said that whether the claim was made on the ground of the content of the particular document or on the ground that it belonged to a class of documents which it was not in the public interest to disclose the courts should regard it as conclusive. The use of the claim and its treatment as conclusive had long been a matter of controversy. It had been strongly criticised by Devlin J. in *Ellis* v. *Home Office* [1953] 2 Q.B. 135, and on two occasions, in 1956 and 1962 the Government itself had given undertakings not to make the claim in certain situations [197 H.L.Deb. 5s. c. 741 6 June 1956 and 237 H.L.Deb. 5s. c. 1191 8 March 1962]. More recently the Court of Appeal in a number of decisions had attempted to cast doubt on the correctness of the law laid down in Duncan's case and to suggest that Viscount Simon was wrong in treating all claims by the Crown as conclusive. While holding that the Court of Appeal was not free to ignore Duncan's case the House of Lords itself exercised its new power to reconsider its own previous decisions and asserted the right of the courts to consider any claim and to reject it if it was in their view not well-founded. They also cast doubt on the validity of some of the wider claims that had been made in the past in respect of classes of documents.

LORD REID [having read out the affidavit of the Home Secretary, continued]: The question whether such a statement by a Minister of the Crown should be accepted as conclusively preventing any court from ordering production of any of the documents to which it applies

---

[7] ' I personally examined and carefully considered all the said documents and I formed the view that those numbered 38, 39, 40 and 48 fell within a class of documents comprising confidential reports by police officers to chief officers of police relating to the conduct, efficiency and fitness for employment of individual police officers under their command, and that the said document numbered 47 fell within a class of documents comprising reports by police officers to their superiors concerning investigations into the commission of crime. In my opinion the production of documents of each such class would be injurious to the public interest.'

is one of very great importance in the administration of justice. If the commonly accepted interpretation of the decision of this House in *Duncan* v. *Cammell Laird & Co. Ltd.*[8] is to remain authoritative the question admits of only one answer – the Minister's statement is final and conclusive. . .

I have no doubt that the case . . . was rightly decided. The plaintiff sought discovery of documents relating to the submarine *Thetis* including a contract for the hull and machinery and plans and specifications. The First Lord of the Admiralty had stated that ' it would be injurious to the public interest that any of the said documents should be disclosed to any person '. Any of these documents might well have given valuable information, or at least clues, to the skilled eye of an agent of a foreign power. But Lord Simon L.C. took the opportunity to deal with the whole question of the right of the Crown to prevent production of documents in a litigation. Yet a study of his speech leaves me with the strong impression that throughout he had primarily in mind cases where discovery or disclosure would involve a danger of real prejudice to the national interest. I find it difficult to believe that his speech would have been the same if the case had related, as the present case does, to discovery of routine reports on a probationer constable . . .

Lord Simon did not say very much about objections [9] ' based upon the view that the public interest requires a particular class of communications with, or within, a public department to be protected from production on the ground that the candour and completeness of such communications might be prejudiced if they were ever liable to be disclosed in subsequent litigation rather than on the contents of the particular document itself '. But at the end [10] he said that a Minister ' ought not to take the responsibility of withholding production except in cases where the public interest would otherwise be damnified, for example, where disclosure would be injurious to national defence, or to good diplomatic relations, or where the practice of keeping a class of documents secret is necessary for the proper functioning of the public service '. I find it difficult to believe that he would have put these three examples on the same level if he had intended the third to cover such minor matters as a routine report by a relatively junior officer . . .

It is universally recognised that here there are two kinds of public interest which may clash. There is the public interest that harm shall not be done to the nation or the public service by disclosure of certain documents, and there is the public interest that the administration of justice shall not be frustrated by the withholding of documents which

[8] [1942] A.C. 624; 58 T.L.R. 242; [1942] 1 All E.R. 587, H.L.
[9] [1942] A.C. 635.   [10] Ibid. 642.

must be produced if justice is to be done . . . I do not believe that Lord
Simon really meant that the smallest probability of injury to the public
service must always outweigh the gravest frustration of the administration of justice.

It is to be observed that . . . Lord Simon referred to the practice of
keeping a class of documents secret being ' *necessary* [my italics] for
the proper functioning of the public interest '. But the certificate of the
Home Secretary in the present case does not go nearly so far as that.
It merely says that the production of a document of the classes to which
it refers would be ' injurious to the public interest ': it does not say
what degree of injury is to be apprehended. It may be advantageous to
the functioning of the public service that reports of this kind should be
kept secret . . . but I would be very surprised if anyone said that that is
necessary.

There are now many large public bodies, such as British Railways
and the National Coal Board, the proper and efficient functioning of
which is very necessary for many reasons including the safety of the
public. The Attorney-General made it clear that Crown privilege is
not and cannot be invoked to prevent disclosure of similar documents
made by them or their servants even if it were said that this is required
for the proper and efficient functioning of that public service. I find it
difficult to see why it should be *necessary* to withhold whole classes of
routine ' communications with or within a public department ' but
quite unnecessary to withhold similar communications with or within a
public corporation. There the safety of the public may well depend on
the candour and completeness of reports made by subordinates whose
duty it is to draw attention to defects. But, so far as I know, no one
has ever suggested that public safety has been endangered by the candour or completeness of such reports having been inhibited by the fact
that they may have to be produced if the interests of the due administration of justice should ever require production at any time . . . [I]t
appears to me that the present position is so unsatisfactory that this
House must re-examine the whole question in light of all the
authorities . . .

A Minister's certificate may be given on one or other of two grounds :
either because it would be against the public interest to disclose the
contents of the particular document or documents in question, or
because the document belongs to a class of documents which ought to
be withheld, whether or not there is anything in the particular document
in question disclosure of which would be against the public interest. It
does not appear that any serious difficulties have arisen or are likely to
arise with regard to the first class. However wide the power of the court
may be held to be, cases would be very rare in which it could be proper
to question the view of the responsible Minister that it would be con-

trary to the public interest to make public the contents of a particular document. A question might arise whether it would be possible to separate those parts of a document of which disclosure would be innocuous from those parts which ought not to be made public, but I need not pursue that question now. In the present case your Lordships are directly concerned with the second class of document . . .

I would . . . propose that the House ought now to decide that courts have and are entitled to exercise a power and duty to hold a balance between the public interest, as expressed by a Minister, to withhold certain documents or other evidence, and the public interest in ensuring the proper administration of justice. That does not mean that a court would reject a Minister's view: full weight must be given to it in every case, and if the Minister's reasons are of a character which judicial experience is not competent to weigh, then the Minister's view must prevail. But experience has shown that reasons given for withholding whole classes of documents are often not of that character. For example a court is perfectly well able to assess the likelihood that, if the writer of a certain class of document knew that there was a chance that his report might be produced in legal proceedings, he would make a less full and candid report than he would otherwise have done.

I do not doubt that there are certain classes of documents which ought not to be disclosed whatever their content may be. Virtually everyone agrees that Cabinet minutes and the like ought not to be disclosed until such time as they are only of historical interest. But I do not think that many people would give as the reason that premature disclosure would prevent candour in the Cabinet. To my mind the most important reason is that such disclosure would create or fan ill-informed or captious public or political criticism. The business of government is difficult enough as it is, and no government could contemplate with equanimity the inner workings of the government machine being exposed to the gaze of those ready to criticise without adequate knowledge of the background and perhaps with some axe to grind. And that must, in my view, also apply to all documents concerned with policy making within departments including, it may be, minutes and the like by quite junior officials and correspondence with outside bodies. Further it may be that deliberations about a particular case require protection as much as deliberations about policy. I do not think that it is possible to limit such documents by any definition. But there seems to me to be a wide difference between such documents and routine reports. There may be special reasons for withholding some kinds of routine documents, but I think that the proper test to be applied is to ask, in the language of Lord Simon in *Duncan's* case,[11] whether

[11] [1942] A.C. 624, 642.

the withholding of a document because it belongs to a particular class is really ' necessary for the proper functioning of the public service.'

It appears to me that, if the Minister's reasons are such that a judge can properly weigh them, he must, on the other hand, consider what is the probable importance in the case before him of the documents or other evidence sought to be withheld. If he decides that on balance the documents probably ought to be produced, I think that it would generally be best that he should see them before ordering production and if he thinks that the Minister's reasons are not clearly expressed he will have to see the documents before ordering production ... If on reading the document he still thinks that it ought to be produced he will order its production.

But it is important that the Minister should have a right to appeal before the document is produced. This matter was not fully investigated in the argument before your Lordships. But it does appear that in one way or another there can be an appeal if the document is in the custody of a servant of the Crown or of a person who is willing to co-operate with the Minister. There may be difficulty if it is in the hands of a person who wishes to produce it. But that difficulty could occur today if a witness wishes to give some evidence which the Minister unsuccessfully urges the court to prevent from being given. It may be that this is a matter which deserves further investigation by the Crown authorities.

The documents in this case are in the possession of a police force. The position of the police is peculiar. They are not servants of the Crown and they do not take orders from the Government. But they are carrying out an essential function of Government, and various Crown rights, privileges and exemptions have been held to apply to them. Their position was explained in *Coomber* v. *Berkshire Justices* [12] and cases there cited. It has never been denied that they are entitled to Crown privilege with regard to documents, and it is essential that they should have it.

The police are carrying on an unending war with criminals many of whom are today highly intelligent. So it is essential that there should be no disclosure of anything which might give any useful information to those who organise criminal activities. And it would generally be wrong to require disclosure in a civil case of anything which might be material in a pending prosecution: but after a verdict has been given or it has been decided to take no proceedings there is not the same need for secrecy. With regard to other documents there seems to be no greater need for protection than in the case of departments of Government.

It appears to me to be most improbable that any harm would be done by disclosure of the probationary reports on the appellant or of the

[12] (1883) 9 App.Cas. 61, H.L.

report from the police training centre. With regard to the report which the respondent made to his chief constable with a view to the prosecution of the appellant there could be more doubt, although no suggestion was made in argument that disclosure of its contents would be harmful now that the appellant has been acquitted. And, as I have said, these documents may prove to be of vital importance in this litigation.

In my judgment, this appeal should be allowed and these documents ought now to be required to be produced for inspection. If it is then found that disclosure would not, in your Lordships' view be prejudicial to the public interest, or that any possibility of such prejudice is, in the case of each of the documents, insufficient to justify its being withheld, then disclosure should be ordered.

LORD MORRIS OF BORTH-Y-GEST. It was conceded that objection on behalf of the Crown to production of a document on the ground of injury to the public interest which was shown (a) not to have been taken in good faith or (b) to have been actuated by some irrelevant or improper consideration or (c) to have founded upon a false factual premise, would not be final or conclusive and could be overriden by the court. If, as is thus conceded, the court possesses such wide powers of overruling an objection to production, it would seem only reasonable and natural that it should also have the duty of assessing the weight of competing public interests ...

In my view, it should now be made clear that whenever an objection is made to the production of a relevant document it is for the court to decide whether or not to uphold the objection. The inherent power of the court must include a power to ask for a clarification or an amplification of an objection to production though the court will be careful not to impose a requirement which could only be met by divulging the very matters to which the objection related. The power of the court must also include a power to examine documents privately, a power, I think, which in practice should be sparingly exercised but one which could operate as a safeguard for the executive in cases where a court is inclined to make an order for production, though an objection is being pressed. I see no difference in principle between the consideration of what have been called the contents cases and the class cases. The principle which the courts will follow is that relevant documents normally liable to production will be withheld if the public interest requires that they should be withheld. In many cases it will be plain that documents are within a class of documents which by their very nature ought not to be disclosed. Indeed, in the majority of cases I apprehend that a decision as to an objection will present no difficulty. The cases of difficulty will be those in which it will appear that if there is non-disclosure some injustice may result and that if there is disclosure the public interest may to some extent be affected prejudicially. The courts can and will recognise that a view honestly put forward by a Minister as to the public interest will be based upon special knowledge and will be put forward by one who is charged with a special responsibility. As Lord Radcliffe said in the *Glasgow Corporation* case,[13] the courts will not seek on a matter which is within the sphere and knowledge of a Minister to displace his view by their own. But where there is more than one aspect of the public interest to be considered it seems to me that a court, in reference to litigation pending before it, will be in the best position to decide where the weight of public interest predominates. I am convinced that the courts, with the independence which is their strength, can safely be entrusted with the duty of weighing all aspects of public interests and of private interests and of giving protection where it is found to be due.

The objection to the production of the probationary reports has been explained as being put forward on the basis that . . . if such reports could ever be subject to production, then the future candour of future writers of such reports would be affected . . . While accepting that the view is held that some measure of prejudice to the public interest would or might result from production it may be that a greater measure of prejudice to the public interest would result from their non-production.

As to the report of the chief constable of January 13, 1965, the matter is put on a somewhat different basis. That was a report of a police officer to his superior in relation to the alleged commission of a crime. . . I think that any court must recognise the weight of the consideration that the police in their work of fighting crime, which is work that is so much in the public interest, must in no way be impeded or frustrated. Whether it would or might be is a matter which it is well within the competence of a court to assess . . .

LORD HODSON. . . . [I]t is not to be disputed that there are classes of documents which from their very character ought to be withheld from production if protection is properly claimed on grounds of state. I have in mind those enumerated by Salmon L.J. in *In re Grosvenor Hotel, London (No. 2)* [14] such as Cabinet minutes, dispatches from ambassadors abroad and minutes of discussions between head of departments. The expression ' class ', however, covers not only such documents which pass at a high level and which require absolute protection, but also those communications not readily distinguishable from those passing in the ordinary course of business conducted by commercial organisations and carrying only a qualified privilege.

Lord Lyndhurst L.C. in *Smith* v. *East India Co.* . . . said : ' [I]t is quite obvious that public policy requires . . . that the most unreserved

[13] 1956 S.C.(H.L.)1.
[14] [1965] Ch. 1210, 1258–9; [1964] 3 W.L.R. 992; [1964] 3 All E.R. 354, C.A.

communication should take place ... that it should be subject to no restraints or limitations; but it is also quite obvious that if, at the suit of a particular individual, those communications should be subject to be produced in a court of justice, the effect would be to restrain the freedom of the communications, and to render them more cautious, guarded and reserved.' ... One would have supposed that the qualified privilege which protects non-malicious communications in the ordinary case should be sufficient just as much where Government departments are concerned as where the affairs of ordinary citizens are concerned. .. It is, I think, at the present day impossible to justify the maintenance of the doctrine laid down by Lord Lyndhurst in its widest form. It is strange if civil servants alone are supposed to be unable to be candid ... without protection of an absolute privilege denied other fellow subjects. ..

LORD PEARCE. ... Any department quite naturally and reasonably wishes, as any private business or any semi-state board must also wish, that its documents or correspondence should never be seen by any outside eye. If it can obtain this result by putting forward a general vague claim for protection on the ground of candour it can hardly be blamed for doing so. ' It is not surprising ' it has been said (Professor Wade, Administrative Law, 2nd ed. at page 285) ' that the Crown, having been given a blank cheque, yielded to the temptation to over-draw '. ...

One may perhaps take police reports of accidents as an extreme example of the malaise that can be produced by a total acceptance of the theory that all documents should be protected whenever the Minister says so on the basis that candour will be injured if there is production. In *Spigelman's* case [15] counsel for the Treasury urgently intervened to prevent production of a policeman's notebook. Many authorities were cited. Finally the learned judge inspected the notebook which contained merely the usual account of a road accident. What policeman *could* be deterred from candour by the thought that a judge might read his notes?

Another unsatisfactory example is the case of *Broome* v. *Broome* [16] where an attempt was made to advance Crown privilege to quite un-reasonable limits. It was relevant in a divorce case to establish whether a husband, an army sergeant, had been pleasant or unpleasant to his wife when he met her on her arrival at Singapore, and it was desired to call a representative of S.S.A.F.A. which had taken a reconciling hand in their matrimonial troubles. This evidence, like that of a probation officer, might have had privilege as between the parties, but the Ministry of Defence intervened, in case the parties might waive the privilege, to object not only to the production of reports made to the War Office, but

[15] 150 L.T. 256.   [16] [1955] P. 190.

also to oral evidence being given by the S.S.A.F.A. representative. Sachs J. rightly refused the suggested extension of Crown privilege and innocuous evidence was given by the witness. But the fact that the privilege was sought shows that it is not easy for the department concerned to make an objective appraisal of the matter. Again, in the case of *Ellis* v. *Home Office* [17] Crown privilege claimed on a ' class ' basis was upheld but was with reason criticised at the trial and by the Court of Appeal . . .

In 1956 as a concession to discontent on this subject the Lord Chancellor announced that privilege would no longer be claimed in certain matters, e.g., reports on accidents on the road or accidents on government premises, or involving government employees; for medical reports on certain employees or when a doctor (or the Crown) is sued for negligence and for documents needed by the defence on a criminal charge. But these concessions, though valuable, left untouched the underlying defect of the present situation, its inherent rigidity, and, in many cases, its illogicality . . .

LORD UPJOHN delivered a concurring judgment.

The documents were produced. Lord Reid on behalf of the court then stated: ' My Lords, I have examined the five documents with which this case is concerned. I can find nothing in any of them the disclosure of which would, in my view, be in any way prejudicial to the proper administration of the Cheshire Constabulary or to the general public interest. I am therefore of the opinion that they must be made available in this litigation.' The court therefore agreed that the order for production should be restored.

REGINA v. *LEWES JJ., Ex parte THE HOME SECRETARY*
[1973] A.C. 388

House of Lords

The appellant in this case asked the local justices to issue a summons calling on the Gaming Board and the chief constable of Sussex to produce, inter alia, a letter alleged to have been sent by the assistant chief-constable of Sussex to the Board, about his suitability for a licence to conduct an establishment for gaming. The Attorney-General applied to the court for an order of certiorari to quash the summons on the ground that it was contrary to the public interest that the letter should be disclosed.

LORD REID. . . . The ground put forward has been said to be Crown privilege. I think that that expression is wrong and may be misleading. There is no question of any privilege in the ordinary sense of the word. The real question is whether the public interest requires that the letter

[17] [1953] 2 Q.B. 135.

shall not be produced and whether that public interest is so strong as to override the ordinary right and interest of a litigant that he shall be able to lay before a court of justice all relevant evidence. A Minister of the Crown is always an appropriate and often the most appropriate person to assert this public interest, and the evidence or advice which he gives to the court is always valuable and may sometimes be indispensable. But, in my view, it must always be open to any person interested to raise the question and there may be cases where the trial judge should himself raise the question if no one else has done so. In the present case the question of public interest was raised by both the Attorney-General and the Gaming Board. In my judgment both were entitled to raise the matter. Indeed I think that in the circumstances it was the duty of the board to do as they have done.

The claim in the present case is not based on the nature of the contents of this particular letter. It is based on the fact that the board cannot adequately perform their statutory duty unless they can preserve the confidentiality of all communications to them regarding the character, reputation or antecedents of applicants for their consent.

Claims for ' class privilege ' were fully considered by this House in *Conway* v. *Rimmer* [1968] A.C. 910. It was made clear that there is a heavy burden of proof on any authority which makes such a claim. But the possibility of establishing such a claim was not ruled out. I venture to quote what I said in that case, at p. 952:

> ' There may be special reasons for withholding some kinds of routine documents, but I think that the proper test to be applied is to ask, in the language of Lord Simon in *Duncan* v. *Cammell Laird & Co. Ltd.* [1942] A.C. 624, 642 whether the withholding of a document because it belongs to a particular class is really " necessary for the proper functioning of the public service ".'

I do not think that ' the public service ' should be construed narrowly. Here the question is whether the withholding of this class of documents is really necessary to enable the board adequately to perform its statutory duties. If it is, then we are enabling the will of Parliament to be carried out.

There are very unusual features about this case. The board require the fullest information they can get in order to identify and exclude persons of dubious character and reputation from the privilege of obtaining a licence to conduct a gaming establishment. There is no obligation on anyone to give any information to the board. No doubt many law abiding citizens would tell what they know even if there was some risk of their identity becoming known, although many perfectly honourable people do not want to be thought to be mixed up in such affairs. But it is obvious that the best source of information about dubious characters must often be persons of dubious character them-selves. It has long been recognised that the identity of police informers must in the public interest be kept secret and the same considerations must apply to those who volunteer information to the board. Indeed, it is in evidence that many refuse to speak unless assured of absolute secrecy.

The letter called for in this case came from the police. I feel sure that they would not be deterred from giving full information by any fear of consequences to themselves if there were any disclosure. But much of the information which they can give must come from sources which must be protected and they would rightly take this into account. Even if information were given without naming the source, the very nature of the information might, if it were communicated to the person concerned, at least give him a very shrewd idea from whom it had come.

It is possible that some documents coming to the board could be disclosed without fear of such consequences. But I would think it quite impracticable for the board or the court to be sure of this. So it appears to me that, if there is not to be very serious danger of the board being deprived of information essential for the proper performance of their difficult task, there must be a general rule that they are not bound to produce any document which gives information to them about an applicant.

We must then balance that fact against the public interest that the course of justice should not be impeded by the withholding of evidence. We must, I think, take into account that these documents only came into existence because the applicant is asking for a privilege and is submitting his character and reputation to scrutiny. The documents are not used to deprive him of any legal right. The board have a wide dis-cretion. Not only can they refuse his application on the ground of bad reputation although he may say that he has not deserved that reputation; it is not denied that the board can also take into account any unfavour-able impression which he has made during an interview with the board.

Natural justice requires that the board should act in good faith and that they should so far as possible tell him the gist of any grounds on which they propose to refuse his application so that he may show such grounds to be unfounded in fact. But the board must be trusted to do that; we have been referred to their practice in this matter and I see nothing wrong in it.

In the present case the board told the appellant nothing about the contents of this letter because they say that they had sufficient grounds for refusing his application without any need to rely on anything in the letter. Their good faith in this matter is not subject to any substantial challenge. If the appellant had not by someone's wrongful act obtained a copy of the letter there was no reason why he should ever have known anything about it.

In my judgment on balance the public interest clearly requires that documents of this kind should not be disclosed, and that public interest is not affected by the fact that by some wrongful means a copy of such a document has been obtained and published by some person. I would therefore dismiss the appellant's appeal.

There is a cross appeal by the Gaming Board because the Divisional Court refused to make in favour of the board an order similar to that which they made in favour of the Home Secretary. The point of law certified was:

'Whether the Divisional Court were right in refusing to make an order unholding the claim by the Gaming Board for Great Britain to privilege in respect of the production of the letters of July 7 and September 15, 1969 referred to in the said witness summons.'

For the reasons which I have given I do not think that the right to withhold the documents depends on or flows from any privilege. It arises from the public interest and the board are entitled to assert that public interest. I would therefore allow the cross appeal.

LORD PEARSON. My Lords . . . I wish to add a few words as to the procedure, on which there has been some discussion.

It seems to me that the proper procedure is that which has been followed, I think consistently, in recent times. The objection to disclosure of the document or information is taken by the Attorney-General or his representative on behalf of the appropriate Minister, that is to say, the political head of the Government department within whose sphere of responsibility the matter arises, and the objection is expressed in or supported by a certificate from the appropriate Minister. This procedure has several advantages: (1) The question whether or not the disclosure of the document or information would be detrimental to the public interest on the administrative or executive side is considered at a high level. (2) The court has the assistance of a carefully considered and authoritative opinion on that question. (3) The Attorney-General is consulted and has opportunities of promoting uniformity both in the decision of such questions and in the formulation of the grounds on which the objections are taken. The court has to balance the detriment to the public interest on the administrative or executive side, which would result from the disclosure of the document or information, against the detriment to the public interest on the judicial side, which would result from non-disclosure of a document or information which is relevant to an issue in legal proceedings. Therefore the court, though naturally giving great weight to the opinion of the appropriate Minister conveyed through the Attorney-General or his representative, must have the final responsibility of deciding whether or not the document or information is to be disclosed.

Although that established procedure is the proper procedure, it is not essential as a matter of law. It is not always practicable. If the appropriate Minister is not available, some other Minister or some highly-placed official must act in his stead. If it becomes evident in the course of a trial or in interlocutory proceedings that perhaps some document or information ought in the public interest to be protected from disclosure, it must be open to the party or witness concerned or the court itself to raise the question. If such a situation arises in the course of a trial, the court can adjourn the trial for the appropriate Minister or the Attorney-General to be consulted, but the court will be reluctant to adjourn the trial unless it is really necessary to do so, and in some cases that will be unnecessary because the court is able to give an immediate answer.

The expression ' Crown privilege ' is not accurate, though sometimes convenient. The Crown has no privilege in the matter. The appropriate Minister has the function of deciding, with the assistance of the Attorney-General, whether or not the public interest on the administrative or executive side requires that he should object to the disclosure of the document or information, but a negative decision cannot properly be described as a waiver of a privilege.

LORD SIMON OF GLAISDALE. My Lords, ' Crown privilege ' is a misnomer and apt to be misleading . . . It is not a privilege which may be waived by the Crown (see *Marks* v. *Beyfus* at p. 500) or by anyone else. The Crown has prerogatives, not privilege. The right to demand that admissible evidence be withheld from, or inadmissible evidence adduced to, the courts is not one of the prerogatives of the Crown.

Where the Crown comes into the picture is that some of the matters of public interest which demand that evidence be withheld are peculiarly within the knowledge of servants of the Crown. The evidence, for example, may be of acts of state (see A. L. Smith L.J. in *Chatterton* v. *Secretary of State for India In Council* [1895] 2 Q.B. 189, 195) or have a bearing on national security. Any litigant or witness may draw attention to the nature of the evidence with a view to its being excluded. The court will proprio motu exclude evidence the production of which it sees is contrary to public interest (see Wills J. in *Hennessy* v. *Wright* (1888) 21 Q.B.D. 509, 519; *Chatterton's* case [1895] 2 Q.B. 189; Viscount Simon L.C. in *Duncan* v. *Cammell Laird & Co. Ltd.* [1942] A.C. 624, 642) – particularly where it falls into a class the exclusion of which has already received judicial recognition, like sources of police information (*Rex* v. *Hardy*, 24 State Tr. 199, 808; *Hennessy* v. *Wright*, 21 Q.B.D. 509, 519; *Marks* v. *Beyfus*, 25 Q.B.D. 494. But the evidence may fall into a class which has not previously received judicial recognition; or it may be questionably of a previously recognised class; or it may fall outside any class of evidence which should be excluded in the public interest, yet still itself as an individual item be excluded in the public interest. In all these cases a Minister of the Crown is likely to be in a peculiarly favourable position to form a judgment as to the public prejudice of forensic publication; and the communication of his view is likely to be of assistance to the court in performing its duty of ruling on the admissibility of evidence. Moreover, for the reasons stated by my noble and learned friend, Lord Pearson, there are advantages in processing the matter through the Law Officers' Department; and the Attorney-General is traditionally the person entitled to intervene in a suit where the prerogatives of the Crown are affected (see *Adams* v. *Adams* (*Attorney-General intervening*) [1971] P. 188, 197H): although there is no prerogative in itself to exclude evidence, certain evidence may affect the prerogative (e.g. of diplomatic relations or as the fount of honour)...

LORD MORRIS OF BORTH-Y-GEST and SALMON delivered concurring judgments.

II. TRIBUNALS

(i) The Report of the Franks Committee, 1957

In November 1955, after the Crichel Down affair (above, p. 155), the Government appointed a committee under Sir Oliver Franks ' to consider and make recommendations on (*a*) The constitution and working of tribunals other than the ordinary courts of law, constituted under any Act of Parliament by a Minister of the Crown or for the purposes of a Minister's functions. (*b*) The working of such administrative procedures as include the holding of an enquiry or hearing by or on behalf of a Minister on an appeal or as the result of objections or representations, and in particular the procedure for the compulsory purchase of land.' The following extract is from that part of its report which dealt with tribunals.

37. Reflection on the general social and economic changes of recent decades convinces us that tribunals as a system for adjudication have come to stay. The tendency for issues arising from legislative schemes to be referred to special tribunals is likely to grow rather than to diminish. It is true that the Restrictive Trade Practices Act, 1956, provides for cases to be determined by a new branch of the High Court, the Restrictive Practices Court, and not by a tribunal... [R]ecent preferences for determinations by courts of law do not, however, alter our general conviction.

The choice between tribunals and courts of law

38. We agree with the Donoughmore Committee [18] that tribunals have certain characteristics which often give them advantages over the courts. These are cheapness, accessibility, freedom from technicality, expedition and expert knowledge of their particular subject. It is no doubt because of these advantages that Parliament, once it has decided that certain decisions ought not to be made by normal executive or departmental processes, often entrusts them to tribunals rather than to the ordinary courts. . .

39. Moreover, if all decisions arising from new legislation were automatically vested in the ordinary courts the judiciary would by now have been grossly overburdened. . .

Tribunals as machinery for adjudication

40. Tribunals are not ordinary courts, but neither are they appendages of Government Departments. Much of the official evidence, including that of the Joint Permanent Secretary to the Treasury, appeared to reflect the view that tribunals should properly be regarded as part of the machinery of administration, for which the Government must retain a close and continuing responsibility. Thus, for example, tribunals in the social service field would be regarded as adjuncts to the administration of the services themselves. We do not accept this view. We consider that tribunals should properly be regarded as machinery provided by Parliament for adjudication rather than as part of the machinery of administration. The essential point is that in all these cases Parliament has deliberately provided for a decision outside and independent of the Department concerned, either at first instance (for example in the case of Rent Tribunals and the Licensing Authorities for Public Service and Good Vehicles) or on appeal from a decision of a Minister or of an official in a special statutory position (for example a valuation officer or an insurance officer). Although the relevant statutes do not in all cases expressly enact that tribunals are to consist entirely of persons outside the Government service, the use of the term ' tribunal ' in legislation undoubtedly bears this connotation, and the intention of Parliament to provide for the independence of tribunals is clear and unmistakable.

The application of the principles of openness, fairness and impartiality

41. We have already expressed our belief that Parliament in deciding that certain decisions should be reached only after a special procedure must have intended that they should manifest three basic characteristics: openness, fairness and impartiality. The choice of a tribunal

[18] I.e. the Committee on Ministers Powers. Cmd. 4060. 1931.

rather than a Minister as the deciding authority is itself a considerable step towards the realisation of these objectives, particularly the third. . .

42. In the field of tribunals openness appears to us to require the publicity of proceedings and knowledge of the essential reasoning underlying the decisions; fairness to require the adoption of a clear procedure which enables parties to know their rights, to present their case fully and to know the case which they have to meet; and impartiality to require the freedom of tribunals from the influence, real or apparent, of Departments concerned with the subject matter of their decisions. . .

45. . . . This is particularly so when a Government Department is a frequent party to proceedings before a tribunal. . .

The composition of tribunals

46. A substantial volume of the evidence has advocated the appointment of all chairmen and members of tribunals by the Lord Chancellor. There is no doubt that such a change would serve to stress the independence of tribunals; it might also, by reason of the esteem in which the office of Lord Chancellor is held, enhance their status. . .

47. On the other hand . . . it was urged upon us that to require the Lord Chancellor to exercise patronage in cases so numerous that it would be obvious that he could not give personal consideration to the choice of the candidates would be to weaken his authority as an instrument of judicial patronage.

48. . . . [W]e feel that the best practical course would be for the responsibility of the Lord Chancellor for . . . appointments not to be extended beyond the chairman, though we consider that he should retain his present responsibility for appointing members of certain tribunals and that there may be scope for extending this responsibility to a few other tribunals.

49. Although we are unable to recommend that all members of tribunals should be appointed by the Lord Chancellor we are satisfied that their appointment should not rest with the Ministers concerned with the subject-matter of the adjudications. In order to enhance the independence of tribunals, both in appearance and in fact, we consider that the Council on Tribunals should make these appointments. . .

51. . . . Responsibility for the removal of a chairman or member during his term of office should, however, rest exclusively with the Lord Chancellor. . .

52. Our recommendations concerning the appointment of members of tribunals are intended to apply also to appointments to the panels from which the members of some tribunals are selected as required. In such cases the selection should be carried out not by the Minister or

the clerk of the tribunal, as is usually now the case, but by the chairman of the tribunal.

55. ... Objectivity in the treatment of cases and the proper sifting of facts are most often best secured by having a legally qualified chairman, though we recognise that suitable chairmen can be drawn from fields other than the law. We therefore recommend that chairmen of tribunals should ordinarily have legal qualifications but that the appointment of persons without legal qualifications should not be ruled out when they are particularly suitable. . .

57. ... On the question of remuneration we are agreed in rejecting any suggestion that in general, tribunal service should become whole-time or salaried. Such a change would, we think, impair many valuable features of the system. Clearly there are a few important appointments which should be salaried, for example certain appointments on the Lands Tribunal. . .

58. ... [A]ll chairmen of appellate tribunals should have legal qualifications. . .

59. The practice whereby the majority of clerks of tribunals are provided by the Government Departments concerned from their local and regional staffs seems partly to be responsible for the feeling in the minds of some people that tribunals are dependent upon and influenced by those Departments. Not only for this reason but also because there would appear to be advantages in improving the general quality of tribunal clerks we have considered the possibility of establishing under the Lord Chancellor's Department a central corps of clerks from which a service could be provided for all tribunals.

60. Though this idea has many attractions we have, after careful consideration, rejected it. . . The main objection is that it is difficult to see how any reasonable prospects of a career could be held out to the members of such a general service. It would also be difficult to arrange sittings for the various tribunals in one area in such a way that the clerks were fully occupied and the tribunals could meet when most convenient to the members. Finally, it would no longer be possible for the social service Departments to give some members of their staff a period of service as clerks of tribunals which is doubtless valuable in developing the outlook appropriate to the administration of a social service.

61. We therefore consider that the present arrangements for providing clerks of tribunals should continue. In order, however, to ensure that departmental clerks cannot exercise a departmental influence upon tribunals, we regard it as essential that their duties and conduct should be regulated on the advice of the Council on Tribunals. The general principles to be followed are that the duties of a clerk should be confined to secretarial work, the taking of such notes of evidence as may be

required and the tendering of advice, when requested, on points connected with the tribunal's functions. Like a magistrates' clerk he should be debarred from retiring with the tribunal when they consider their decision, unless he is sent for to advise on a specific point.

Procedure: general

64. There has been considerable emphasis, in much of the evidence we have received, upon the importance of preserving informality of atmosphere in hearings before tribunals, though it is generally conceded that in some tribunals, for example the Lands Tribunal, informality is not an overriding necessity. We endorse this view, but we are convinced that the attempt which has been made to secure informality in the general run of tribunals has in some instances been at the expense of an orderly procedure. Informality without rules of procedure may be positively inimical to right adjudication, since the proceedings may well assume an unordered character which makes it difficult, if not impossible, for the tribunal properly to sift the facts and weigh the evidence... The object to be aimed at in most tribunals is the combination of a formal procedure with an informal atmosphere... On the one hand it means a manifestly sympathetic attitude on the part of the tribunal and the absence of the trappings of a court, but on the other hand such prescription of procedure as makes the proceedings clear and orderly.

65. Some witnesses have criticised the arrangements under which many tribunals sit in premises of the Department concerned with the subject-matter...

66. We do not regard the location of tribunal premises as a major point of principle, but we think that the independence of tribunals from Departments would be emphasised if arrangements were made for them to sit in premises separate from any Government office.

Procedure at the tribunal hearing

77. We are in no doubt that if adjudicating bodies... are to inspire ... confidence... they should, in general, sit in public. But just as on occasion the courts are prepared to try certain types of case wholly or partly *in camera* so, in the wide field covered by tribunals, there are occasions on which we think that justice may be better done, and the interests of the citizen better served, by privacy.

78. The first type of case is where considerations of public security are involved. Such cases are not often likely to arise before tribunals...

79. The more frequent type of case in which privacy is desirable is that in which intimate personal or financial circumstances have to be disclosed. Few people would doubt the wisdom of the practice whereby hearings before the General and Special Commissioners of Income Tax

are held in private in order that details of taxpayers' affairs shall not become public knowledge. In the case of National Assistance Appeal Tribunals . . . there is a danger that public proceedings would so deter applicants that the purpose of the legislation would be frustrated. Another case in which the privacy of proceedings is justified is the hearing at which a medical examination of the applicant may take place.

80. A third type of case in which privacy is on balance desirable is that involving professional capacity and reputation, where the machinery includes provision for a preliminary and largely informal hearing before any decision is made to institute formal proceedings which may involve penalties . . .

81. Accordingly we recommend that where a tribunal is of a class which has to deal almost exclusively with any of these three types of case the hearing should continue to be in private. In the case of all other classes of tribunal, however, the hearing should be in public, subject to a discretionary power in the chairman to exclude the public should he think that a particular case involves any of these considerations.

Procedure after the tribunal hearing

99. As soon as possible after the hearing the tribunal should send to the parties a written notice of decision, which should include not only the decision itself but also a statement of the findings of fact by the tribunal and the reasons for the decision . . .

100. The notice of decision should in addition always set out clearly the rights of appeal against the decision . . .

102. Publication of reports of leading cases dealt with by final appellate tribunals would be of help, not only in satisfying the public that decisions were reasonably consistent but also as a guide to appellants and their advisers. Accordingly we recommend that all final appellate tribunals should publish selected decisions and circulate them to any lower tribunals. The selection of such cases should be the responsibility of the appellate tribunals.

Appeal and judicial review

105. The first question is the extent to which appeals should lie to the courts or to further appellate tribunals. An appeal to the courts on matters of fact would not, we think, be desirable since it would constitute an appeal from a body expert in the particular subject to a relatively inexpert body. In the absence of special considerations we consider that the ideal appeal structure for tribunals should take the form of a general appeal from a tribunal of first instance to a second or appellate tribunal. By a general appeal we mean an appeal on fact, law or merits . . . As a matter of general principle we consider that appeal should not lie from a tribunal to a Minister.

106. It is not essential to set up an appellate tribunal when the tribunal of first instance is so exceptionally strong and well qualified that an appellate tribunal would be no better qualified to review its decisions . . .

107. We are firmly of the opinion that all decisions of tribunals should be subject to review by the courts on points of law. This review could be obtained either by proceedings for certiorari or by appeal. If, as we recommend, tribunals are compelled to give full reasons for their decisions any error of law in such a decision would subject the decision to quashing by order of certiorari in England . . . [A]n application to quash a decision on this ground is quite different from an appeal on a point of law. In the former case the court can only quash the decision, while in the latter case the court may substitute, or in effect substitute, its own decision. Again, in the former case, the court must find the error, if it can, on the face of the record, for example in the notice of decision . . . it cannot look at anything else. In the latter case the court can in addition look at the notes of the evidence given before the tribunal if the point of law is whether there was evidence on which the tribunal could in law have arrived at its decision. An appeal on a point of law is therefore wider in scope. For all these reasons we recommend that review by the courts of decisions of tribunals should in general be provided by making the decisions subject to appeal on points of law. We think, however, that special considerations arise in connection with the National Insurance Commissioner, the Industrial Injuries Commissioner and National Assistance Appeal Tribunals.

108. It is no doubt true that the Commissioners often have to adjudicate on points of law of considerable complexity which could be said to warrant appeals to the courts. Parliament, however, has taken care to provide that each Commissioner and his deputies should be barristers or advocates of considerable experience, appointed by Royal Warrant, and their salaries are in excess of those of County Court judges. Moreover, in difficult cases a Commissioner sits with two deputies, thus constituting a tribunal of exceptional experience and standing. Further, it has always been recognised that the nature of the services with which the Commissioners are concerned makes it essential that final decisions should be reached with the minimum of delay. Finally, there has been little demand for a right of appeal to the courts in these cases . . . These considerations lead us to think that it would be right to make an exception and to leave any review by the courts in these cases to be exercised by certiorari.

109. . . . [W]e think that an exception to the general rule should also be made in the case of . . . [National Assistance Appeal] Tribunals, leaving any review by the courts to be exercised by certiorari . . .

114. A challenge to the jurisdiction of a tribunal should continue to be dealt with by motion for an order of certiorari. We think, however, that the present period for the making of an application (six months) is too long ...

115. There remains the question of the court to which appeals on points of law should lie ...

116. We do not necessarily intend that in every case there should be unrestricted recourse through the Supreme Court and up to the House of Lords. To permit this would in many cases be inconsistent, by reason of the expense and delay involved, with the purposes for which tribunals are established. We suggest that in each case there should be one further appeal on law, by leave, and no more.

117. Whatever may be decided as to the scope and method of appeals to the courts from tribunals we are convinced that the remedies by way of orders of certiorari, prohibition and mandamus should continue. They are clearly necessary in cases where questions of jurisdiction are involved and in cases where no provision is made for appeals on points of law. Accordingly no statute should contain words purporting to oust these remedies ...

120. Finally, we mention two special proposals put forward in evidence. First, Professor Robson advocated the establishment of a general administrative appeal tribunal ...

121. ... [This] proposal seems to us to have several disadvantages. First, a general tribunal could not have the experience and expertise in particular fields which, it is generally accepted, should be a characteristic of tribunals. Appeals would thus lie from an expert tribunal to a comparatively inexpert body, and we see little advantage in this ...

122. A second disadvantage is that the establishment of a general appellate body would seem inevitably to involve a departure from the principle whereby all adjudicating bodies in this country, whether designated as inferior courts or as tribunals, are in matters of jurisdiction subject to the control of the superior courts. This unifying control has been so long established and is of such fundamental importance in our legal system that the onus of proof must lie clearly upon the advocates of change. We are satisfied that the case for change has not been made out.

123. There is a third disadvantage. Quite apart from questions of jurisdiction, final determinations on points of law would be made by the general administrative appeal tribunal in relation to tribunals but by the superior courts in relation to matters decided by the courts. Thus two systems of law would arise, with all the evils attendant on this dichotomy ...

124. The last two objections do not apply to the second special proposal put before us. This ... was ... for the establishment of a new

division of the High Court, called the Administrative Division, which, like the general administrative appeal tribunal described above, would have general appellate jurisdiction not only over the field of our terms of reference but also over administrative decisions generally.

125. Even though this proposal avoids conflicting systems of law it is none the less open to serious objection on the ground that appeals would lie from expert tribunals to an inexpert general appellate body. Moreover, it emerged . . . that the main purpose of the proposal was to provide a forum of appeal against administrative decisions not arrived at after a special procedure, which decisions are . . . outside the scope of our enquiry. . . We are unable to support the proposal in relation to our terms of reference.

[Report of the Committee on Administrative Tribunals and Inquiries. Cmnd. 218 (1957)]

(ii) The Tribunals and Inquiries Act, 1971

The Tribunals and Inquiries Act 1958 was passed to give effect to some of the principal recommendations of the Franks Committee. It has now been replaced by the Tribunals and Inquiries Act, 1971. This Act sets out in its First Schedule the tribunals to which at any time it applies. These include the adjudicators and Immigration Appeals Tribunal under the Immigration Act, 1971, industrial tribunals, the Lands Tribunal, Mental Health Review Tribunals, local tribunals under the National Insurance Act, 1965, medical appeal tribunals, the National Insurance Commissioner, Supplementary Benefits Appeals Tribunals, rent tribunals and rent assessment committees. All these are put under the general supervision of the Council on Tribunals also set up by the 1958 Act. (The Council also has authority to consider and report on matters relating to any tribunal and to any administrative procedure which may involve a statutory inquiry.) In addition the Act makes special provision as regards some of the tribunals. S. 7 for example provides that the chairmen of certain tribunals are to be chosen from panels appointed by the Lord Chancellor. These include the local tribunals under the National Insurance Act, 1975, medical appeal tribunals and Supplementary Benefit Appeal Tribunals. S. 8 requires that the Lord Chancellor's consent be obtained before anyone can be removed from a tribunal or a panel. This applies to the great majority of the tribunals over which the Council has jurisdiction. S. 13 provides for an appeal on a point of law from a number of them to the High Court. This includes rent tribunals and rent assessment committees.

The following extract sets out some of the more important of its other provisions.

TRIBUNALS AND INQUIRIES ACT, 1971 [Ch. 62]

10. (1) No power of a Minister, the Lord President of the Court of Session or the Commissioners of Inland Revenue to make, approve,

confirm or concur in procedural rules for any such tribunal as is specified in Schedule 1 to this Act shall be exercisable except after consultation with the Council. . .

(3) In this section ' procedural rules ' includes any statutory provision relating to the procedure of the tribunal in question.

11. (1) The Lord Chancellor, after consultation with the Council, may make rules regulating the procedure to be followed in connection with statutory inquiries held by or on behalf of Ministers; and different provision may be made by any such rules in relation to different classes of such inquiries.

(2) Any rules made by the Lord Chancellor under this section shall have effect, in relation to any statutory inquiry, subject to the provisions of the enactment under which the inquiry is held, and of any rules or regulations made under that enactment.

(3) Subject to subsection (2) of this section, rules made under this section may regulate procedure in connection with matters preparatory to such statutory inquiries as are mentioned in subsection (1) of this section, and in connection with matters subsequent to such inquiries, as well as in connection with the conduct of proceedings at such inquiries. . .[19]

12. (1) Subject to the provisions of this section, where—
    (a) any such tribunal as is specified in Schedule 1 to this Act gives any decision; or
    (b) any Minister notifies any decision taken by him after the holding by him or on his behalf of a statutory inquiry, or taken by him in a case in which a person concerned could (whether by objecting or otherwise) have required the holding as aforesaid of a statutory inquiry,
it shall be the duty of the tribunal or Minister to furnish a statement, either written or oral, of the reasons for the decision if requested, on or before the giving or notification of the decision, to state the reasons.

(2) The said statement may be refused, or the specification of the reasons restricted, on grounds of national security, and the tribunal or Minister may refuse to furnish the statement to a person not primarily concerned with the decision if of opinion that to furnish it would be contrary to the interests of any person primarily concerned.

(3) Subsection (1) of this section shall not apply to any decision taken by a Minister after the holding by him or on his behalf of any inquiry or hearing which is a statutory inquiry by virtue only of an order made under section 19 (2) of this Act unless the order contains a direction that this section is to apply in relation to any inquiry or hearing to which the order applies.

(4) Subsection (1) of this section shall not apply to decisions in respect of which any statutory provision has effect, apart from this

[19] For an example, see below p. 620.

section, as to the giving of reasons, or to decisions of a Minister in connection with the preparation, making, approval, confirmation, or concurrence in regulations, rules, or byelaws, or orders or schemes of a legislative and not executive character.

(5) Any statement of the reasons for such a decision as is mentioned in paragraph (*a*) or (*b*) of subsection (1) of this section, whether given in pursuance of that subsection or of any other statutory provision, shall be taken to form part of the decision and accordingly to be incorporated in the record.

(6) If, after consultation with the Council, it appears to the Lord Chancellor and the Lord Advocate that it is expedient that decisions of any particular tribunal or any description of such decisions, or any description of decisions of a Minister, should be excluded from the operation of subsection (1) of this section on the ground that the subject-matter of such decisions, or the circumstances in which they are made, make the giving of reasons unnecessary or impracticable, the Lord Chancellor and the Lord Advocate may by order direct that subsection (1) of this section shall not apply to such decisions . . .

14. (1) As respects England and Wales . . . any provision in an Act passed before 1st August 1958 that any order or determination shall not be called into question in any court, or any provision in such an Act which by similar words excludes any of the powers of the High Court, shall not have effect so as to prevent the removal of the proceedings into the High Court by order of certiorari or to prejudice the powers of the High Court to make orders of mandamus . . .

(3) Nothing in this section shall affect section 26 of the British Nationality Act 1948 or apply to any order or determination of a court of law or where an Act makes sepcial provision for application to the High Court or the Court of Session within a time limited by the Act.

16. (1) Any power of the Lord Chancellor and the Lord Advocate or either of them to make rules or orders under this Act shall be exercisable by statutory instrument subject to annulment in pursuance of a resolution of either House of Parliament.

(2) Any power of those Ministers to make orders under any section of this Act includes power to vary or revoke any order under that section by a subsequent order but any such subsequent order under section 12 (6) of this Act shall be made only after consultation with the Council.

19. (1) In this Act, except where the context otherwise requires—
' statutory inquiry ' means—

    (*a*) an inquiry or hearing held or to be held in pursuance of a duty imposed by any statutory provision; or (*b*) an inquiry or hearing, or an inquiry or hearing of a class, designated for the purposes of this section by an order under subsection (2) of this section . . .

(2) The Lord Chancellor and the Lord Advocate may by order designate for the purposes of this section any inquiry or hearing held or to be held in pursuance of a power conferred by any statutory provision specified or described in the order, or any class of such inquiries or hearings . . .

(iii) National insurance and supplementary benefits

National insurance

SOCIAL SECURITY ACT, 1975 [Ch. 14]

Determination of claims

97. (1) Insurance officers shall be appointed by the Secretary of State, subject to the consent of the Minister for the Civil Service as to number, to act for such areas or otherwise as the Secretary of State directs, and may include officers of the Department of Employment appointed with the concurrence of the Secretary of State in charge of that Department.

(2) A local tribunal shall consist of—

(*a*) one member drawn from a panel composed of persons representing employers and persons representing earners other than employed earners;

(*b*) one member drawn from a panel of persons representing employed earners; and

(*c*) a person appointed by the Secretary of State to act as chairman.

(3) Her Majesty may from time to time appoint, from among persons who are barristers or advocates of not less than 10 years' standing, a Chief National Insurance Commissioner and such number of other National Insurance Commissioners as Her Majesty may think fit.

98. (1) There shall be submitted forthwith to an insurance officer for determination in accordance with sections 99 to 104 below—

(*a*) any claim for benefit . . .

99. (1) An insurance officer to whom a claim . . . is submitted . . . shall take it into consideration and, so far as practicable, dispose of it . . . within 14 days of its submission to him.

(2) [T]he insurance officer may in the case of any claim . . . submitted to him—

(*a*) decide it in favour of the claimant; or

(*b*) decide it adversely to the claimant; or

(*c*) refer it to a local tribunal.

(3) Where an insurance officer refers a case to a local tribunal, notice in writing of the reference shall be given to the claimant.

100. (1) ... [W]here the insurance officer has decided a claim ... adversely to the claimant, the claimant may appeal to a local tribunal.

(2) The claimant shall be notified in writing of the insurance officer's decision and the reasons for it, and of his right of appeal under this section ...

(4) An appeal under this section shall be brought by giving notice of appeal at a local office within 21 days after the date of the decision or within such further time as the chairman of the local tribunal may for good cause allow.

(5) A notice of appeal under this section shall be in writing and shall contain a statement of the grounds upon which the appeal is made. . .

101. (1) Subject to the provisions of this section, an appeal lies to a Commissioner from any decision of a local tribunal.

(2) The persons at whose instance an appeal lies under this section are—

> (*a*) an insurance officer;
> (*b*) the claimant;
> (*c*) in any of the cases mentioned in subsection (3) below, a trade union ...

(3) The following are the cases in which an appeal lies at the instance of a trade union—

> (*a*) where the claimant is a member of the union at the time of the appeal and was so immediately before the question at issue arose;
> (*b*) where that question in any way relates to a deceased person who was a member of the union at the time of his death ...

(4) Subsections (2) and (3) above, as they apply to a trade union, apply also to any other association which exists to promote the interests and welfare of its members.

(5) An appeal to a Commissioner must be brought within 3 months from the date of the decision of the local tribunal, or such further period as a Commissioner may in any case for special reasons allow; and such an appeal shall be brought by giving notice in writing in a form approved by the Secretary of State stating the grounds of the appeal—

> (*a*) in the case of an appeal by an insurance officer, to the claimant; and
> (*b*) in the case of an appeal by the claimant, or a trade union or other association mentioned above, at a local office.

(6) If it appears to a Commissioner that an appeal under this section involves a question of fact of special difficulty, the Com-

missioner may direct that in dealing with the appeal or any part of it he shall have the assistance of an assessor or assessors specially qualified and selected from a panel appointed for that purpose.

(7) A Commissioner may, if he thinks fit, refer any question arising for his decision to a medical practitioner for examination and report.

102. (1) Where a question under this Act first arises in the course of an appeal to a local tribunal or a Commissioner, the tribunal or Commissioner may, if they think fit, proceed to determine the question notwithstanding that it has not been considered by an insurance officer.

104. (1) Any decision . . . of an insurance officer, a local tribunal or a Commissioner may be reviewed at any time by an insurance officer or, on a reference from an insurance officer, by a local tribunal, if—

    (a) the officer or tribunal is satisfied and, in the case of a decision of a Commissioner, satisfied by fresh evidence, that the decision was given in ignorance of, or was based on a mistake as to, some material fact; or

    (b) there has been any relevant change of circumstances since the decision was given . . .

(2) A question may be raised with a view to a review under this section by means of an application in writing to an insurance officer, stating the grounds of the application. . .

(4) A decision given on a review under this section, and a refusal to review a decision thereunder, shall be subject to appeal in like manner as an original decision . . .

115. (1) Regulations may, for any purpose of this Part of this Act, make any such provision as is specified in Schedule 13 (procedure, evidence, hearings, forms of documents and other matters relating to adjudication). . .

(5) Procedure regulations prescribing the procedure to be followed in cases before a Commissioner shall provide that any hearing shall be in public except in so far as the Commissioner for special reasons otherwise directs.

(6) It is hereby declared that the power to prescribe procedure includes power to make provision as to the representation of one person, at any hearing of a case, by another person whether having professional qualifications or not. . .

116. (1) If it appears to the Chief National Insurance Commissioner . . . that an appeal falling to be heard by one of the Commissioners involves a question of law of special difficulty, he may direct that the appeal be dealt with, not by that Commissioner alone, but by a Tribunal consisting of any 3 of the Commissioners.

(2) If the decision of the Tribunal is not unanimous, the decision of the majority shall be the decision of the Tribunal.

117. (1) Subject to the provisions of this Part of this Act, the decision of any claim or question in accordance with those provisions shall be final . . .

(2) Subsection (1) above shall not make any finding of fact or other determination embodied in or necessary to a decision, or on which it is based, conclusive for the purpose of any further decision. . .

SCHEDULE 10

PANELS FOR APPOINTMENT TO LOCAL TRIBUNALS

1. (1) The panels referred to in section 97 (2) of this Act shall be constituted by the Secretary of State for the whole of Great Britain, and each panel shall relate to such an area as the Secretary of State thinks fit, and be composed of such persons as the Secretary of State sees fit to appoint.

(2) Before appointing members to either of the panels, the Secretary of State may take into consideration any recommendations from any local committee representing employers or employed earners or both, or from organisations concerned with the interests of employers or employed earners, including friendly societies or organisations representative of friendly societies.

(3) The members of the panels shall hold office for such period as the Secretary of State may direct:

Provided that the Secretary of State may at any time terminate the appointment of any member of a panel.

(4) So far as practicable, each member of a panel shall be summoned in turn to serve upon a local tribunal:

Provided that—

    (*a*) no member of a panel shall sit upon a local tribunal during the consideration of a case—

        (i) in which he appears as the representative of the claimant; or

        (ii) by which he is or may be directly affected; or

        (iii) in which he has taken any part as an official of an association, or as an employer, or as a witness . . .

    (*b*) where the benefit claimed is unemployment benefit, the member chosen from the first panel shall, if practicable, be a representative of employers; and

    (*c*) in any case in which the claimant is a woman, at least one of the members of the tribunal, if practicable, shall be a woman.

Tribunal chairmen

2. (1) A person appointed to act as chairman of a local tribunal shall hold and vacate office in accordance with the terms of his letter of appointment.

(2) Where several persons are appointed to act as chairmen for a particular area they shall as far as practicable be invited to preside over a tribunal in turn . . .

Supplementary benefits
The Supplementary Benefits Commission

THE MINISTER OF PENSIONS AND NATIONAL INSURANCE (MISS MARGARET HERBISON): . . . Within the [new] Ministry [of Social Security] there will be a Supplementary Benefits Commission, one of whose main tasks will be the administration, under regulations made by the Minister, of the non-contributory benefits. All the decisions, for example, as to the award of benefit and the conditions under which it is awarded, the adjustments to deal with various kinds of situation and exceptional circumstances and the kind of benefits to be paid will be made by the local officers acting under the direction of the Commission. The Commission will thus have a directing and adjudicating function. . . Responsibility for determining awards of benefit should not be vested in a Minister but in a group of independent people with an extensive knowledge of the kind of persons with whom the scheme is concerned. Such a body with its discretionary powers to deal with exceptional circumstances is the best means of ensuring that the administration is responsive to particular individual needs and to the variations of the changes in social climate. It is important in any field where questions of social policy are involved to be able to draw on the knowledge and experience of people of distinction outside the Government service. The Commission will, I hope, provide that knowledge and experience. . . The Commission will not constitute, as the [National Assistance] Board does today, a separate Government Department. Responsibility for the main lines of policy and for the standards of benefit will be the Minister's. . .

[W]e intend that the members of the Commission shall cover a wide variety of interests, that they will be a source of advice to the Minister on many social problems, and that, in particular, they will assist the Minister's programme of research into those problems. . .

[Ministry of Social Security Bill, Second Reading. 729 H.C.Deb. 5s. c. 339. 24 May 1966]

MINISTRY OF SOCIAL SECURITY ACT, 1966

[Ch. 20]

Supplementary Benefits Appeal Tribunals

3. (1) There shall be established . . . a Commission, to be known as the Supplementary Benefits Commission, which shall exercise the functions conferred on them by this Act in such manner as shall best promote the welfare of persons affected by the exercise thereof. . .

5. (1) The question whether any person is entitled to benefit and the amount of any benefit shall, subject to the provisions of this Act as to appeals, be determined by the Commission . . .

18. (1) A person claiming or in receipt of benefit may appeal to the Appeal Tribunal against any determination of the Commission, or a refusal by the Commission to review a determination . . .

(3) On an appeal . . . the Appeal Tribunal may confirm the determination appealed against (or, if the appeal is against a refusal to review a determination, confirm the refusal) or substitute therefor any determination which the Commission could have made, and any determination of the Tribunal shall be conclusive for all purposes.

SCHEDULE 3

CONSTITUTION AND PROCEEDINGS OF APPEAL TRIBUNALS

1. Each of the tribunals shall consist of a chairman and two other members.

2. Each tribunal shall have jurisdiction in respect of such district as may be assigned to them by the Minister.

3. (1) The chairman and other members of every tribunal shall be appointed by the Minister, and of those other members one shall be so appointed from among persons appearing to the Minister to represent work-people. . .

6. (1) The Minister may make rules—

   (*a*) as to the tenure of office of members of tribunals;
   (*b*) as to the procedure of tribunals and the procedure in connection with the bringing of matters before a tribunal, and as to the time within which matters may be brought before tribunals;
   (*c*) as to the payment by the Minister to persons attending proceedings before tribunals of travelling and other allowances (including compensation for loss of remunerative time);
   (*d*) for authorising proceedings notwithstanding that the members of the tribunal are not all present;

and in any case where proceedings take place in accordance with rules made in accordance with sub-paragraph (*d*) of this paragraph, the tribunal shall, notwithstanding anything in this Act, be deemed to be properly constituted, and the chairman or acting chairman shall have a second or casting vote.

(2) The power under this paragraph to make rules as to procedure includes power to make provision as to the representation of one person in any proceedings by another person.

(iv) Tribunals of Inquiry

TRIBUNALS OF INQUIRY (EVIDENCE) ACT, 1921
[11 Geo. 5. ch. 7]

1. (1) Where it has been resolved . . . by both Houses of Parliament that it is expedient that a tribunal be established for inquiring into a definite matter described in the Resolution as of urgent public importance, and in pursuance of the Resolution a tribunal is appointed for the purpose either by His Majesty or a Secretary of State, the instrument by which the tribunal is appointed or any instrument supplemental thereto may provide that this Act shall apply, and in such case the tribunal shall have all such powers, rights, and privileges as are vested in the High Court, or in Scotland the Court of Session, or a judge of either such court, on the occasion of an action in respect of the following matters : —

(*a*) The enforcing the attendance of witnesses and examining them on oath, affirmation, or otherwise;

(*b*) The compelling the production of documents . . .

(2) If any person—

(*a*) on being duly summoned as a witness before a tribunal makes default in attending; or

(*b*) being in attendance as a witness refuses to take an oath legally required by the tribunal to be taken, or to produce any document in his power or control legally required by the tribunal to be produced by him, or to answer any question to which the tribunal may legally require an answer; or

(*c*) does any other thing which would, if the tribunal had been a court of law having power to commit for contempt, have been contempt of that court;

the chairman of the tribunal may certify the offence of that person under his hand to the High Court, or in Scotland the Court of Session, and the court may thereupon inquire into the alleged offence and . . . punish or take steps for the punishment of that person in like manner as if he had been guilty of contempt of the court.

(3) A witness before any such tribunal shall be entitled to the same immunities and privileges as if he were a witness before the High Court or the Court of Session.

2. A tribunal to which this Act is so applied as aforesaid—

(*a*) shall not refuse to allow the public or any portion of the public to be present at any of the proceedings of the tribunal unless in the opinion of the tribunal it is in the public interest expedient so to do for reasons connected with the subject matter of the inquiry or the nature of the evidence to be given; and

(*b*) shall have power to authorise the representation before them of any person appearing to them to be interested to be by counsel or solicitor or otherwise, or to refuse to allow such representation. . .

The Royal Commission on Tribunals of Inquiry, 1966

27. . . . [W]e are strongly of the opinion that the inquisitorial machinery set up under the Act of 1921 should . . . always be confined to matters of vital public importance concerning which there is something in the nature of a nation-wide crisis of confidence. In such cases we consider that no other method of investigation would be adequate.

28. Normally persons cannot be brought before a tribunal and questioned save in civil or criminal proceedings. Such proceedings are hedged around by long standing and effective safeguards to protect the individual. . . There are, however, exceptional cases in which such procedures must be used to preserve the purity and integrity of our public life without which a successful democracy is impossible. It is essential that on the very rare occasions when crises of public confidence occur, the evil, if it exists, shall be exposed so that it may be rooted out; or if it does not exist, the public shall be satisfied that in reality there is no substance in the prevalent rumours and suspicions by which they have been disturbed . . .

30. . . . It is inherent in the inquisitorial procedure that there is no plaintiff or defendant, no prosecutor or accused; there are no pleadings defining issues to be tried, no charges, indictments, or depositions. The inquiry may take a fresh turn at any moment. It is therefore difficult for persons involved to know in advance of the hearing what allegations may be made against them . . .

32. The difficulty and injustice with which persons involved in an inquiry may be faced can however be largely removed if the following cardinal principles . . . are strictly observed : —

1. Before any person becomes involved in an inquiry, the Tribunal must be satisfied that there are circumstances which affect him and which the Tribunal proposes to investigate.

2. Before any person who is involved in an inquiry is called as a witness he should be informed of any allegations which are made against him and the substance of the evidence in support of them.

3. (*a*) He should be given an adequate opportunity of preparing his case and of being assisted by legal advisers.

(*b*) His legal expenses should normally be met out of public funds.

4. He should have the opportunity of being examined by his own solicitor or counsel and of stating his case in public at the inquiry.

5. Any material witnesses he wishes called at the inquiry should, if reasonably practicable, be heard.

6. He should have the opportunity of testing by cross-examination conducted by his own solicitor or counsel any evidence which may affect him. . .

Alternative Procedures

33. We will now consider methods of investigation which might be regarded as possible alternatives to the procedure set up under the Act of 1921. . .

1. *A Royal Commission*

34. In modern times Royal Commissions have not been used to carry out inquiries into the facts of a particular case. They have been used to make recommendations on matters of broad policy. It is for this alone that they are appropriate. Their members are not customarily called upon to become involved whole time and to sit on a day by day basis. The tempo of even the most expeditious Royal Commission is altogether too slow for the requirements of an investigation into matters with which the Act of 1921 is concerned. Moreover a Royal Commission has no real power to compel anyone to give evidence or produce documents . . .

2. *A Select Parliamentary Committee of Inquiry*

35. The record of such Committees appointed to investigate allegations of public misconduct is, to say the least, unfortunate . . . The Marconi scandal for this purpose sounded the death knell of this form of investigation, and because it was wholly discredited, the Act of 1921 was passed. To go back to it would, in our view, be a retrograde step. . . [T]here are many purposes for which Select Parliamentary Committees are most useful and indeed indispensable – but the investigation of allegations of public misconduct is not one of them. Such matters should be entirely removed from political influences. A Select Parliamentary Committee is constituted of members representing the relative strength of the parties in the House. Accordingly it may tend in its report to reflect the views of the party having the majority of members, or indeed, as in the Marconi case, it may produce two reports and when these are debated in the House, the House may divide along party lines. On the other hand the reports of Tribunals under the Act of 1921, no doubt because of their excellence and the standing and political impartiality

of their members, have invariably been accepted by Parliament without question. A further defect of a Select Parliamentary Committee is that it does not normally hear counsel and some if not all of its members will have had no experience of taking evidence or of cross-examining witnesses. Finally, witnesses who give evidence before a Select Parliamentary Committee may not be entitled to the same absolute privilege as they would enjoy before a Tribunal under the Act of 1921 . . .

3. *An inquiry of the type carried out by Lord Denning into the Profumo case*

37. In the chapter dealing with the history of Tribunals of Inquiry . . . we have . . . expressed the view that the measure of acceptance which the report achieved was due to the exceptional qualities and standing of Lord Denning alone, and should be regarded as a brilliant exception to what would normally occur when an investigation is carried out under such conditions. . .

39. We do not believe that it can ever be right for any inquiry of this kind to be held entirely in secret save on the grounds of security. It is true that a Tribunal does not hold a trial but only investigates and reports. Nevertheless reputations and careers may depend upon their findings, e.g., in the Budget Leak Tribunal which was held in public the Tribunal found that there had been an unauthorised disclosure by Mr J. H. Thomas to Sir Alfred Butt of information relating to the Budget and that use was made by Sir Alfred Butt of that information for private gain; thus ended both their political careers.

40. It is said that sometimes witnesses are willing to give evidence only if they are allowed to give it in private or in confidence. This is no doubt true. But such evidence in matters of this kind is treated as suspect by the general public and, in our view, rightly so. Secrecy increases the quantity of evidence but tends to debase its quality.

41. It is possible that in the future the same type of salacious rumour as some of those which were in circulation at the time of the Profumo case may circulate again. No doubt it would be wrong to investigate them in public. The point is whether they should be investigated at all. It is no part of the duty of government to satisfy idle curiosity about scandalous gossip. It does not seem to us appropriate for a tribunal of any kind to inquire into such rumours. Gossip about such matters as these is hardly likely to cause a nation-wide crisis of confidence and is best ignored. It is an entirely different matter when it is alleged that a Minister has put himself in a situation which creates a real security risk, or that colleagues have allowed a Minister to make a personal statement which they ought to have known was untrue. If in the future there is a nation-wide crisis of confidence about any matters of this kind they should in our opinion be investigated before a Tribunal appointed under the Act of 1921. . .

4. *Departmental Inquiries*

43. These are normally used to investigate matters which are causing public concern, but which are not of such importance as to justify the appointment of a Tribunal under the Act of 1921. A Departmental inquiry is usually appointed by the responsible Minister to be conducted by an eminent lawyer alone or as chairman with others. These inquiries have no power to compel the attendance of witnesses or the production of documents and are not in our view suitable for dealing with the special type of case for which the Act of 1921 was framed.

5. *Accident Inquiries*

44. These are formal inquiries into air accidents and shipping casualties and are carried out respectively under Regulation 9 of the Civil Aviation (Investigation of Accidents) Regulations, 1951 [20] and the Shipping Casualties and Appeal and Re-hearing Rules of 1923. These inquiries are highly technical and usually include something in the nature of a *lis*; there is not the same degree of urgency about them and they are certainly not concerned with a nation-wide crisis of confidence in the integrity of any public persons. They deal with wholly different matters from those dealt with by Tribunals of Inquiry and could not be any substitute for such Tribunals.

6. *The Security Commission*

45. It seems to us that an inquiry by the Security Commission could never be a suitable alternative to an inquiry by a Tribunal appointed under the Act of 1921. The respective purposes of the two forms of inquiry are wholly different. The purpose of inquiries by the Security Commission is to report to and advise the Prime Minister upon security arrangements within the public service. The subject matter of such inquiries may have caused no public concern and indeed may well be entirely unknown to the public. In the public interest these inquiries are of necessity held in private. The purpose of inquiries under the Act of 1921, as we have already pointed out, is publicly to establish the truth when there is a nation-wide crisis of confidence about matters of urgent public importance. It is of the essence of these inquiries that they should be held in public although most exceptionally some part of them may be held in private. The only way in which the two types of inquiries may overlap is that some aspect of a matter referred to a Tribunal of Inquiry might (as in the Vassall case) by itself have been appropriate for reference to the Security Commission. . .

47. Our conclusion is that, for the reasons we have indicated, it is essential in the national interest to retain the Tribunals of Inquiry (Evidence) Act, 1921, albeit with the amendments and safeguards recommended in this Report.

[20] S.I. 1951 No. 1653.

Power to compel evidence: committal for contempt

123. We have no doubt that it is necessary that some power should exist, to be exercised only in the last resort, for the purpose of compelling persons to give evidence and preventing them from defying the Tribunal. This power is contained in Section 1 (2) of the Act of 1921 . . . It has been invoked only once since the Act came into force in 1921. This was in the Vassall Tribunal when certain journalists refused to reveal the sources of their information. . .

124. It has been said that, as a general rule, journalists should not be asked to compromise the source of their information. The Press is a watchdog of our liberties. They often reveal matters which should be disclosed in the public interest, and they might be hampered in this function if they were normally obliged to disclose the source of their information. It has also been urged in evidence on their behalf that as they are usually given information in strict confidence, it is against their conscience to reveal the name of the person who gave them the information, and that rather than disclose sources which they feel in honour bound to conceal, they would prefer to suffer a prison sentence. The matter has been put more prosaically by the chairman of a large group of newspapers who said in evidence that all these reasons are moonshine. He stated that the real reason for the reticence of journalists is that . . . [I]f it were thought that there was any risk in their revealing their sources, these would dry up. We consider that the real reason for the reticence of journalists to reveal their source is . . . an amalgam of all those given in evidence. In the ultimate analysis, it is unthinkable that a great institution such as the Press would seek to defy the law. The law clearly requires that any witness before a Tribunal should, in the national interest, reveal the source of his information if the revelation of that source is vital.

125. . . . Tribunals do not insist on the disclosure of the source of information unless it is of vital importance to the inquiry to do so. In such cases the Tribunal should, so far as practicable, fully explain to the witness precisely why the answer to the question asked is of vital importance and if necessary give the witness an opportunity of referring back to his source. In the appropriate case it might be well to point out to the witness that should he still refuse to disclose his source, the public may be left with the strong suspicion that there is none and that the journalist's story is an invention or a distortion of any information which he may have received.

[Report of the Royal Commission on Tribunals of Inquiry. Cmnd. 3121 (November 1966)]

CHAPTER XII

THE RULE OF LAW AND EXECUTIVE POWERS

The Government of the country is carried on largely by virtue of statutory powers granted for limited purposes to Ministers and other public authorities. The first check therefore on the exercise of excessive or arbitrary power by the Executive is in the hands of Parliament when it grants those powers in the first place. If it clearly grants the Executive wide arbitrary power then the Executive has wide arbitrary power. And the same applies to the jurisdiction of the courts. It is within the power of Parliament to exclude or limit their jurisdiction. The existence of that jurisdiction in any particular case depends on Parliament not having effectively done this. Although therefore when one talks of the principles of administrative law one tends to think first of the principles developed by the courts in the course of their interpretation and application of the provisions of particular statutes, it is important to remember that in the United Kingdom the principles of administrative law operate at three levels. At the first level they are principles for the guidance of Parliament in granting and the Executive in exercising statutory powers. At this level they range from the most general principle of all, the principle of the rule of law itself, which prescribes that government should be carried on by virtue of limited powers, normally subject to the supervision of the courts, through narrower principles like the so-called principles of natural justice, that no one should be a judge in his own cause, and that a man should be given an opportunity to state his case before a decision affecting him adversely is taken (*nemo judex in causa sua* and *audi alteram partem*), to, for example, the detailed elaboration of the latter principle in the report of the Franks Committee on Tribunals and Inquiries (below p. 614) or a statutory instrument like that governing public local inquiries in the field of town and country planning (below, p. 620). They are all constitutional principles which form part of the framework within which it is expected that the government of the country will be carried on. At the second level they are the principles and more particularly the procedures embodied in statutes and regulations at any given time. In the United Kingdom the numerous statutes granting powers to the Executive are not simply the detailed *subject matter* of administrative law. They determine its main outlines and form an essential part of the *framework* within which the government of the country is carried on at any particular time. But they are only part of that framework. And this is where the third level comes in. It has been the practice of successive Governments and Parliaments and it is a practice which is itself supported by the principle of the rule of law, to acquiesce in the development by the courts of principles of administrative law, and, indeed of remedies as well, which they have then applied in the course of their interpretation of particular statutes and in the course of determining the validity of actions and decisions under them. These principles include principles governing the exercise of discretionary powers, principles relating to the procedures to be followed in exercising them, and principles governing the availability of particular remedies.

The three levels are closely related. It is the principle of the rule of law, for example, which justifies the principles developed by the courts that powers should only be used for the purpose for which they have been granted (below p. 559), and that they should be exercised reasonably (below p. 568 and above p. 408), and that Parliament cannot be presumed to have intended to oust the jurisdiction of the courts unless it has done so expressly or by necessary implication (below p. 631). Many of the principles which have now been accepted at the second, and even the first level, were originally developed by the courts and then taken over and elaborated by the Government, Parliament and, more recently, the Franks Committee and the Council on Tribunals. The development of principles of this kind and their acceptance at both the second and the first levels has been greatly facilitated by the establishment of the Council on Tribunals which has been expressly given the power to make recommendations at the stage when legislation is being considered, a power assumed by the courts largely by default and then ex post facto, after the legislation had been enacted. So, for example, where in the past it was the courts which had to invoke the principles of natural justice to imply into a statute the obligation of a public authority to give someone the opportunity to state his case, and to elaborate such an obligation when it had been imposed, the obligation and even its detailed application will now often be expressly set out in a statute or a regulation made under it. The extracts which follow illustrate some of the principles developed by the courts. Those relating to public inquiries go beyond a statement of the current principles to show the development from the days when the courts were left to work out the relevant principles largely unaided (though some of the leading decisions of the mid-thirties seem to have been influenced by the report of the Committee on Ministers' Powers of 1932, especially as regards the distinction it made between administrative and so-called ' quasi-judicial ' functions) through the Report of the Franks Committee, which led to the establishment of the Council on Tribunals, to a particular example of the elaboration of procedural rules in the Town and Country Planning (Inquiries Procedures) Rules, in whose formulation the Council itself played a part.

I. PRINCIPLES RELATING TO THE EXERCISE OF DISCRETIONARY POWERS

Public authorities should exercise their statutory powers in the way in which Parliament intended, i.e.

(a) The powers should be used for the purpose for which they were given.

(b) The powers should be exercised by the person or body by whom they were intended to be exercised.

(c) The authority must be free to make a genuine exercise of any discretion which has been given to it.

(d) The authority in exercising its powers should observe any procedures which have been expressly laid down in the statute or which the courts will imply into it.

(a) *A statutory power should be used for the purpose for which it was granted*

WESTMINSTER CORPORATION v. LONDON AND NORTH WESTERN RAILWAY COMPANY
[1905] A.C. 426

House of Lords

The public Health (London) Act, 1891, provided:

' 44. (1) Every sanitary authority may provide and maintain public lavatories ... in situations where they deem the same to be required ... and may defray the expense of providing such lavatories ... and of any damage occasioned to any person by the erection or construction thereof ... as if they were expenses of sewerage.'

In 1900, Westminster Corporation, purporting to act under this power, built public lavatories and conveniences under the middle of Parliament Street and provided access to them by means of a subway near the edge of the pavement opposite the entrance to the company's premises. The company applied to the court for an injunction to restrain the corporation from maintaining the subway in that position. They argued, *inter alia*, that in building a subway which could be used to cross the street the corporation had exceeded the powers given them by statute.

LORD MACNAGHTEN. ... There can be no question as to the law applicable to the case. It is well settled that a public body invested with statutory powers such as those conferred upon the corporation must take care not to exceed or abuse its powers. It must keep within the limits of the authority committed to it. It must act in good faith. And it must act reasonably. The last proposition is involved in the second, if not in the first. But in the present case I think it will be convenient to take it separately.

Now, looking merely at what has been done – at the work as designed and actually constructed – it seems to me that ... it is impossible to contend that the work is in excess of what was authorised by the Act of 1891 ... It was not suggested that there was any notice, or any intention of putting up a notice, directing the public to this subway as a means of crossing. The entrance, which was of the usual limited dimensions, did not of itself offer any invitation to the public to enter for the purpose of crossing the roadway.

Then I come to the question of want of good faith. That is a very serious charge. It is not enough to shew that the Corporation contemplated that the public might use the subway as a means of crossing the street. That was an obvious possibility... In order to make out a case of bad faith it must be shewn that the corporation constructed this subway as a means of crossing the street under colour and pretence of providing public conveniences which were not really wanted at that particular place... The learned judge who tried the case had before him the chairman of the works committee... He asserted on oath that ' the primary object of the committee was to provide these conveniences '. Why is this gentleman not to be believed? The learned judge who saw and heard him believed his statement... I entirely agree with Joyce J. that the primary object of the council was the construction of the conveniences with the requisite and proper means of approach thereto and exit therefrom...

EARL HALSBURY L.C. and LORD LINDLEY delivered concurring judgments. LORD JAMES dissented.[1]

PADFIELD v. MINISTER OF AGRICULTURE, FISHERIES AND FOOD   [1968] A.C. 997

House of Lords

Under the Milk Marketing Scheme established in 1933 milk producers were under an obligation to sell their milk to the Milk Marketing Board at prices fixed by it. The country was divided into eleven regions for the purpose and the prices varied from region to region depending on factors such as distance from the producers to the markets. For some time the producers in the South East region had been trying to secure a bigger differential between them and the other producers, but without success. Nor was success likely since the Board consisted of twelve representatives of the regions (the North West region having two representatives) together with three members elected by the producers as a whole, and three members appointed by the Minister. Any increase in the amount they would get would mean less for producers elsewhere. The Agricultural Marketing Act, 1958, provided: ' 19. (1) The Minister [of Agriculture] shall appoint two committees (hereafter in this Act referred to as a ' consumers ' committee and a ' committee of investigation ') for Great Britain, for England and Wales and for Scotland respectively... (3) A committee of investigation shall... (b) be charged with the duty, if the Minister in any case so directs, of considering and reporting to the Minister on... any complaint made to the Minister as to the operation of any scheme which, in the opinion of the Minister, could not be considered by a consumer committee... (4) On receiving the report of a

[1] Cp. *Sydney Municipal Council* v. *Campbell* [1925] A.C. 338; *R.* v. *Paddington and St Marylebone Rent Tribunal* [1949] 1 K.B. 666; and *Webb* v. *Minister of Housing and Local Government* [1965] 1 W.L.R. 755.

committee of investigation... the Minister shall forthwith publish the conclusions of the committee in such manner as he thinks fit... (6) If a committee of investigation report to the Minister that any provision of a scheme or any act or omission of a board administering a scheme is contrary to the interests of any persons affected by the scheme, and is not in the public interest, the Minister, if he thinks fit so to do after considering the report – (a) may by order make such amendments in the scheme as he considers necessary or expedient for the purpose of rectifying the matter; (b) may by order revoke the scheme; (c) in the event of the matter being one which it is within the power of the Board to rectify, may by order direct the Board to take such steps to rectify the matter as may be specified in the order... (8) Any order made under paragraph (a) of subsection (6)... [or] under paragraph (c) of that subsection... shall be subject to annulment in pursuance of a resolution of either House of Parliament, and any order made under paragraph (b)... shall not take effect unless it has been approved by a resolution of each House of Parliament.'

When the South East producers consulted the Ministry about the possibility of the Minister referring their complaint to the Committee they were given a discouraging reply. Mr J. H. Kirk, an Under-Secretary at the Ministry, on 1 May 1964 wrote: ' 3. In considering how to exercise his discretion the Minister would, among other things, address his mind to the possibility that if a complaint were referred and the committee were to uphold it, he in turn would be expected to make a statutory order to give effect to the committee's recommendations. It is this consideration, rather than the formal eligibility of the complaint as a subject for investigation, that the Minister would have in mind in determining whether your particular complaint is a suitable one for reference to the committee. We were unable to hold out any prospect that the Minister would be prepared to regard it as suitable. 4. The reasons which led us to this conclusion were explained to you as follows: (a) The guarantee given to milk producers under the Agricultural Acts is a guarantee given to the board on behalf of all producers. The Minister owes no duty to producers in any particular region, and this is a principle that would be seriously called in question by the making of an Order concerned with a regional price; (b) such action would also bring into question the status of the Milk Marketing Scheme as an instrument for the self-government of the industry and such doubt would also, by extension, affect the other Marketing Schemes as well; and (c) it is by no means clear that the Minister could make an Order pertaining to the price of milk in the South East without determining at least one of the major factors governing prices in the other regions, and he would therefore be assuming an inappropriate degree of responsibility for determining the structure of regional prices throughout England and Wales.'

The South East producers nevertheless decided to go ahead and make a formal complaint. They complained that it was contrary to the reasonable and proper interests of producers in the South-East that they should subsidise the marketing cost of producers elsewhere, and that the present situation would lead to an unreasonable alteration in the balance of production by discouraging production in the favourable areas and encouraging it in the unfavourable areas. The Minister, as expected, refused to refer the complaint. In a letter to the complainants' solicitors his private secretary wrote on 23 March 1965: 'The Minister's main duty in considering this complaint has been to decide its suitability for investigation by means of a particular procedure. He has come to the conclusion that it would not be suitable. The complaint ... raises wide issues going beyond the immediate concern of your clients, which is presumably the prices they themselves receive. It would also affect the interests of other regions and involve the regional price structure as a whole. In any event the Minister considers that the issue is of a kind that properly falls to be resolved through the arrangements available to producers and the Board within the framework of the scheme itself.'

The producers applied to the court for an order of mandamus directing the Minister to refer the complaint and directing him to deal with it only on the basis of relevant considerations. In a written statement to the court the Minister affirmed that in considering the complaint he had taken into account the letter written by Mr Kirk in May, 1964, and all the matters put before him by and on behalf of the complainants, and that he had come to his decision on the grounds that the matter would be dealt with more appropriately by the Board.

LORD REID ... The question at issue in this appeal is the nature and extent of the Minister's duty under section 19 (3) (b) of the Act of 1958 in deciding whether to refer to the committee of investigation a complaint as to the operation of any scheme made by persons adversely affected by the scheme. The respondent contends that his only duty is to consider a complaint fairly and that he is given an unfettered discretion with regard to every complaint either to refer it or not to refer it to the committee as he may think fit. The appellants contend that it is his duty to refer every genuine and substantial complaint, or alternatively that his discretion is not unfettered and that in this case he failed to exercise his discretion according to law because his refusal was caused or influenced by his having misdirected himself in law or by his having taken into account extraneous or irrelevant considerations.

In my view, the appellants' first contention goes too far. There are a number of reasons which would justify the Minister in refusing to refer a complaint. For example, he might consider it more suitable for arbitration, or he might consider that in an earlier case the committee of investigation had already rejected a substantially similar complaint, or he might think the complaint to be frivolous or vexatious. So he must have at least some measure of discretion. But is it unfettered?

It is implicit in the argument for the Minister that there are only two possible interpretations of this provision – either he must refer every complaint or he has an unfettered discretion to refuse to refer in any case. I do not think that is right. Parliament must have conferred the discretion with the intention that it should be used to promote the policy and objects of the Act; the policy and objects of the Act must be determined by construing the Act as a whole and construction is always a matter of law for the court. In a matter of this kind it is not possible to draw a hard and fast line, but if the Minister, by reason of his having misconstrued the Act or for any other reason, so uses his discretion as to thwart or run counter to the policy and objects of the Act, then our law would be very defective if persons aggrieved were not entitled to the protection of the court. So it is necessary first to construe the Act.

When these provisions were first enacted in 1931 it was unusual for Parliament to compel people to sell their commodities in a way to which they objected and it was easily foreseeable that any such scheme would cause loss to some producers. Moreover, if the operation of the scheme was put in the hands of the majority of the producers, it was obvious that they might use their power to the detriment of consumers, distributors or a minority of the producers. So it is not surprising that Parliament enacted safeguards.

The approval of Parliament shows that this scheme was thought to be in the public interest, and in so far as it necessarily involved detriment to some persons, it must have been thought to be in the public interest that they should suffer it. But in sections 19 and 20 Parliament drew a line. They provide machinery for investigating and determining whether the scheme is operating or the board is acting in a manner contrary to the public interest.

The effect of these sections is that if, but only if, the Minister and the committee of investigation concur in the view that something is being done contrary to the public interest the Minister can step in. Section 20 enables the Minister to take the initiative. Section 19 deals with complaints by individuals who are aggrieved . . . If the Minister directs that a complaint by any of them shall be referred to the committee of investigation, that committee will make a report which must be published. If they report that any provision of this scheme or any act or omission of the board is contrary to the interests of the complainers *and* is not in the public interest, then the Minister is empowered to take action, but not otherwise. He may disagree with the view of the committee as to public interest, and, if he thinks that there are other public interests which outweigh the public interest that justice should be done to the complainers, he would be not only entitled but bound to refuse to take action. Whether he takes action or not, he may be criticised and held accountable in Parliament but the court cannot interfere.

I must now examine the Minister's reasons for refusing to refer the appellants' complaint to the committee . . .

The first reason which the Minister gave in his letter of March 23,

1965, was that this complaint was unsuitable for investigation because it raised wide issues. Here it appears to me that the Minister has clearly misdirected himself. Section 19 (6) contemplates the raising of issues so wide that it may be necessary for the Minister to amend a scheme or even to revoke it. Narrower issues may be suitable for arbitration but section 19 affords the only method of investigating wide issues. In my view it is plainly the intention of the Act that even the widest issues should be investigated if the complaint is genuine and substantial, as this complaint certainly is.

Then it is said that this issue should be ' resolved through the arrangements available to producers and the board within the framework of the scheme itself.' This re-states in a condensed form the reasons given in paragraph 4 of the letter of May 1, 1964, where it is said ' the Minister owes no duty to producers in any particular region,' and reference is made to the ' status of the Milk Marketing Scheme as an instrument for the self-government of the industry,' and to the Minister ' assuming an inappropriate degree of responsibility.' But, as I have already pointed out, the Act imposes on the Minister a responsibility whenever there is a relevant and substantial complaint that the board are acting in a manner inconsistent with the public interest, and that has been relevantly alleged in this case. I can find nothing in the Act to limit this responsibility or to justify the statement that the Minister owes no duty to producers in a particular region. The Minister is, I think, correct in saying that the board is an instrument for the self-government of the industry. So long as it does not act contrary to the public interest the Minister cannot interfere. But if it does act contrary to what both the committee of investigation and the Minister hold to be the public interest the Minister has a duty to act. And if a complaint relevantly alleges that the board has so acted, as this complaint does, then it appears to me that the Act does impose a duty on the Minister to have it investigated. If he does not do that he is rendering nugatory a safeguard provided by the Act and depriving complainers of a remedy which I am satisfied that Parliament intended them to have.

Paragraph 3 of the letter of May 1, 1964, refers to the possibility that, if the complaint were referred and the committee were to uphold it, the Minister ' would be expected to make a statutory Order to give effect to the committee's recommendations.' If this means that he is entitled to refuse to refer a complaint because, if he did so, he might later find himself in an embarrassing situation, that would plainly be a bad reason. I can see an argument to the effect that if, on receipt of a complaint, the Minister can satisfy himself from information in his possession as to the merits of the complaint, and he then chooses to say that, whatever the committee might recommend, he would hold it to be contrary to the public interest to take any action, it would be a waste of time and money to refer the complaint to the committee. I do not intend to express any opinion about that because that is not this case. In the first place it appears that the Minister has come to no decision as to the merits of the appellants' case and, secondly, the Minister has carefully avoided saying what he would do if the committee were to uphold the complaint.

It was argued that the Minister is not bound to give any reasons for refusing to refer a complaint to the committee, that if he gives no reasons his decision cannot be questioned, and that it would be very unfortunate if giving reasons were to put him in a worse position. But I do not agree that a decision cannot be questioned if no reasons are given. If it is the Minister's duty not to act so as to frustrate the policy and objects of the Act, and if it were to appear from all the circumstances of the case that that has been the effect of the Minister's refusal, then it appears to me that the court must be entitled to act . . .

As the Minister's discretion has never been properly exercised according to law, I would allow this appeal. It appears to me that the case should now be remitted to the Queen's Bench Division with a direction to require the Minister to consider the complaint of the appellants according to law.

LORD PEARCE. . . . It was obvious that the scheme and the Agricultural Marketing Act, 1958, created a monopoly and imposed severe restrictions on individuals' liberty of action. With the aim of general betterment Parliament was interfering with the individual farmer's method of earning a livelihood and subjecting him to the mercies of the majority rule of the board; but (no doubt with these considerations in mind) Parliament deliberately imposed certain safeguards. Two independent committees must be appointed (s. 19) . . . [T]he independent committee of investigation . . . was a . . . a deliberate safeguard against injustices that might arise from the operation of the scheme . . .

The appellants have . . . no avenue for their complaint except through s. 19, and that section makes access to the committee of investigation dependent on a direction of the Minister to the committee of investigation. There is no provision as to what are the duties of a Minister in this respect. Has he a duty to further complaints of substance which have no other outlet? Or can he refuse them any outlet at all if he so chooses? Need he have any valid reason for doing so? Or if he refuses without any apparent justification, is he exempt from any interference by the courts provided that he either gives no reasons which are demonstrably bad or gives no reasons at all? No express answer to these questions is given in the Act. The intention, therefore, must be implied from its provisions and its structure . . .

. . . It is quite clear from the Act that the Minister is intended to have some duty in the matter. It is conceded that he must properly consider

the complaint. He cannot throw it unread into the waste paper basket.
He cannot simply say (however honestly) ' I think that in general the
investigation of complaints has a disruptive effect on the scheme and
leads to more trouble than (on balance) it is worth. I shall therefore
never refer anything to the committee of investigation.' To allow him to
do so would be to give him the power to set aside for his period as
Minister the obvious intention of Parliament, namely, that an independent committee, set up for the purpose, should investigate grievances
and that their report should be available to Parliament. This was clearly
never intended by the Act. Nor was it intended that he could silently
thwart its intention by failing to carry out its purposes. I do not regard
a Minister's failure or refusal to give any reason as a sufficient exclusion
of the court's surveillance. If all the prima facie reasons seem to point
in favour of his taking a certain course to carry out the intentions of
Parliament in respect of a power which it has given him in that regard,
and he gives no reason whatever for taking a contrary course, the court
may infer that he has no good reason, and that he is not using the power
given by Parliament to carry out its intentions. In the present case,
however, the Minister has given reasons which show that he was not
exercising his discretion in accordance with the intention of the Act.

In the present case it is clear that Parliament attached considerable
importance to the independent committee of investigation as a means
to ensure that injustices were not caused by the operation of a compulsory scheme. It provided no other means by which an injustice could
be ventilated. It was not content to leave the matter wholly in the power
of a majority of the Board. Nor was it content that the removal of
injustice should be left to the power of the Minister. It wished to have
the published views of an independent committee of investigation (with
wide power to explore the matter fully). It also wished that committee
to consider and investigate the public interest – a fact that makes it clear
that the question of public interest was not at that stage being left to
the Minister. When the report is published the Minister may and must
make up his own mind on the subject. He has power to do what he
thinks best and decide whether or not to implement the report. He is
then answerable only to Parliament, which will have the advantage of
being able to understand the pros and cons of the matter from the
published report of an independent committee. Until that is published
nobody can effectively criticise his action, since nobody will have a
balanced view of the strength of the grievance and its impact on the
public interest.

It is clear, however, as a matter of common sense that Parliament did
not intend that frivolous or repetitive or unsubstantial complaints or
those which were more appropriate for arbitration should be examined
by the committee of investigation. And, no doubt, the Minister was

intended to use his discretion not to direct the committee to investigate those. It is argued that, if he has a discretion to *that* extent, he must also have an unfettered discretion to suppress a complaint of substance involving the public interest which has no other outlet. I cannot see why this should be so. Parliament intended that certain substantial complaints (involving the public interest) under the compulsory scheme should be considered by an independent committee. It was for the Minister to use his discretion to promote Parliament's intentions. If the court had doubt as to whether the applicants' complaint was frivolous or repetitive, or not genuine, or not substantial, or unsuitable for investigation or more appropriate for arbitration, it would not interfere. But nothing which has been said in this case leads me to doubt that it is a complaint of some substance which should properly be investigated by the independent committee with a view to pronouncing on the weight of the complaint and the public interest involved. The fact that the complaint raises wide issues and affects other regions was not a good ground for denying it an investigation by the committee. It is a matter which makes it very suitable for the committee of investigation, with its duty to report on the public interest, and its capacity to hear representatives of all the regions. Moreover the Minister was mistaken in thinking that ' normal democratic machinery of the Milk Marketing Scheme ' was a ground for refusal to have the complaint investigated. It is alleged that the normal democratic machinery of the Board is acting contrary to the public interest. The investigation under s. 19 and the Minister's power under s. 20 were intended to correct, where necessary, the normal democratic machinery of the scheme. Parliament had put into the hands of the Minister and those of the committee the power and duty, where necessary, to intervene. A general abdication of that power and duty would not be in accord with Parliament's intention. . .

LORD UPJOHN. . . . My lords, I believe that the introduction of the adjective ' unfettered ' and its reliance thereon as an answer to the appellants' claim is one of the fundamental matters confounding the Minister's attitude, bona fide though it be. First, the adjective nowhere appears in s. 19, it is an unauthorised gloss by the Minister. Secondly, even if the section did contain that adjective, I doubt if it would make any difference in law to his powers, save to emphasise what he has already, namely that acting lawfully he has a power of decision which cannot be controlled by the courts; it is unfettered. But the use of that adjective, even in an Act of Parliament, can do nothing to unfetter the control which the judiciary have over the executive, namely that in exercising their powers the latter must act lawfully, and that is a matter to be determined by looking at the Act and its scope and object in conferring a discretion on the Minister rather than by the use of adjectives . . .

Mr Kirk's letter . . . contained this paragraph : ' 3. In considering how to exercise his discretion, the Minister would, amongst other things, address his mind to the possibility that if a complaint were so referred and the committee were to uphold it, he in turn would be expected to make a statutory order to give effect to the committee's recommendations. . .' This fear of parliamentary trouble (for in my opinion this must be the scarcely veiled meaning of this letter) if an inquiry were ordered and its possible results is alone sufficient to vitiate the Minister's decision which, as I have stated earlier, can never validly turn on purely political considerations; he must be prepared to face the music in Parliament if statute has cast on him an obligation in the proper exercise of a discretion conferred on him to order a reference to the committee of investigation.

LORD HODSON delivered a concurring judgment. *Appeal allowed*

FAWCETT PROPERTIES LTD v. BUCKINGHAMSHIRE COUNTY COUNCIL [1961] A.C. 636

House of Lords

The Town and Country Planning Act, 1947, provided : ' 14. (1) . . . [W]here application is made to the local planning authority for permission to develop land, that authority may grant permission either unconditionally or subject to such conditions as they think fit, or may refuse permission, and in dealing with any such application the local planning authority shall have regard to the provisions of the development plan, so far as material thereto, and to any other material considerations. (2) Without prejudice to the generality of the foregoing subsection, conditions may be imposed . . . (a) for regulating the development or use of any land under the control of the applicant. . . 36. Where . . . a local planning authority are required to have regard to the provisions of the development plan . . . then . . . during any period before such a plan has become operative . . . that authority . . . shall have regard to the provisions which in their opinion will be required to be included for securing the proper planning of the . . . area.' Buckinghamshire County Council granted the appellants' predecessors in title permission to build two cottages subject to the condition that ' the occupation of the houses shall be limited to persons whose employment or latest employment is or was . . . in agriculture as defined by s. 11 (1) of the Town and Country Planning Act, 1947, or in forestry, or in an industry mainly dependent upon agriculture, and including also the dependants of such person as aforesaid.' The appellants now applied to the court for a declaration that the condition was ultra vires and void. In holding that the conditions were not ultra vires their Lordships made the following statements of principle.

LORD JENKINS. . . . The law relating to the *ultra vires* claim is not in dispute, and may be thus summarised :

(1) Under s. 14 of the Act of 1947 the council as local planning

authority was empowered to grant permission for the proposed development either unconditionally or subject to such conditions as they
thought fit, or might refuse permission, and under s. 36 they were enjoined in the exercise of their functions to have regard to the provisions
which in their opinion would be required to be included in the development plan for securing the proper planning of the area.

(2) The power to impose conditions though expressed in language
apt to confer an absolute discretion on a local planning authority to
impose any condition of any kind they may think fit is, however, conferred as an aid to the performance of the functions assigned to them
by the Act as the local planning authority thereby constituted for the
area in question. Accordingly the power must be construed as limited
to the imposition of conditions with respect to matters relevant to the
implementation of planning policy. This accords with the concluding
passage in s. 36... As was said by Lord Denning in *Pyx Granite Co.
Ltd.* v. *Ministry of Housing and Local Government*: [2] '... Although
the planning authorities are given very wide power to impose " such
conditions as they think fit ", nevertheless the law says that those conditions, to be valid, must fairly and reasonably be related to the permitted development. The planning authority are not at liberty to use
their powers for an ulterior object, however desirable that object may
seem to them to be in the public interest.'

(3) This does not mean that the wisdom or merits of a condition
imposed in any given case can be made the subject of an appeal to the
court at the instance of a person objecting to the condition. See
Associated Provincial Picture Houses Ltd. v. *Wednesbury Corporation,*[3] the effect of which is for the present purpose sufficiently indicated
in the following passage from the headnote: 'Held, that the local
authority had not acted unreasonably or ultra vires in imposing the
condition. In considering whether an authority having so unlimited a
power has acted unreasonably, the court is only entitled to investigate
the action of the authority with a view to seeing if it has taken into
account any matters that ought not to be or disregarded any matters
that ought to be taken into account. The court cannot interfere as an
appellate authority to override a decision of such an authority, but only
as a judicial authority concerned to see whether it has contravened the
law by acting in excess of its power.'

LORD DENNING. ... The local planning authority is empowered to
grant permission to develop land ' subject to such conditions as they
think fit ' ... In exercising this discretion they must, to paraphrase Lord
Greene's words in the Wednesbury case, have regard to all relevant
considerations and disregard all improper considerations, and they

[2] [1960] A.C. 260.
[3] Above p. 408.

must produce a result which does not offend against common sense; or to repeat my own words in the Pyx case, the conditions to be valid, must fairly and reasonably relate to the permitted development; or yet again, to borrow the words of Lord Macnaghten and Lord Wrenbury in this House, a public authority which is entrusted with a discretion must act reasonably, see *Westminster Corporation* v. *L.S.W. Ry Co.* [1905] A.C. 426, 430; *Roberts* v. *Hopwood* [1925] A.C. 578, 613; and I take it that if the authority acts reasonably the result will be reasonable.

Out of these various shades of meaning I am not sure that the last is not the best: for it puts planning considerations on much the same level as by-laws made by a local authority, to which they are so closely akin. Indeed, I see no difference in principle between them. As with by-laws so with planning conditions the courts can declare them bad for unreasonableness but they must remember that they are made by a public representative body in the public interest. When planning conditions are made, as here, so as to maintain the green belt against those who would invade it, they ought to be supported if possible. And credit ought to be given to those who have to administer them that they will be reasonably administered: see *Kruse* v. *Johnson* [1898] 2 Q.B. 391, 399...

LORDS COHEN and KEITH OF AVONHOLM delivered concurring judgments.

Cp. *Mixnam Properties Ltd.* v. *Chertsey Urban District Council* [1965] A.C. 735, where the House of Lords held invalid conditions attached to a site licence under the Caravan Sites and Control of Development Act 1960, which purported to regulate the rents to be charged, and to give security of tenure to the caravan occupiers. There, Lord Reid, for example, said: 'There appears to me a fundamental difference between providing what must or not be done on a site and restricting the site owner's ordinary freedom to contract with licensees on matters which do not relate to the manner of use of the site.'

(b) *The powers should be exercised by the person or body by whom they were intended to be exercised*

LAVENDER v. MINISTER OF HOUSING AND LOCAL GOVERNMENT
[1970] 1 W.L.R. 1231

Queen's Bench Division

The Advisory Committee on Sand and Gravel which reported in 1948 and 1953 recommended that certain areas of high quality agricultural land should be protected against disturbance from gravel working and should be reserved indefinitely for agriculture. The plaintiffs made an application for planning permission to work for gravel in one of these areas. The local planning authority consulted the Ministry of Agriculture who made it clear that it was anxious to preserve these areas and that they strongly objected to the proposal. The planning authority therefore refused permission. The plaintiffs appealed and the Minister appointed an inspector to conduct an inquiry. In his report the inspector made no recommendation since he recognised that the final decision depended on whether the Minister was prepared to make an exception to his general policy in this case. Had it not been for this, he said, he would have supported the grant of permission. The Minister dismissed the appeal. In his decision letter it was stated: 'It is the Minister's present policy that land in the reservations should not be released for mineral working unless the Minister of Agriculture is not opposed to working. In the present case the agricultural objection has not been waived and the Minister therefore decided not to grant planning permission for the working of the appeal site.'

WILLIS J. . . . It is [the] . . . last two sentences in the decision letter which lie at the heart of the matter in issue; and it is submitted, first of all, by Mr Frank, for the applicants, that they show, in this case, that the Minister had so fettered his own discretion to decide the appeal by the policy which he had adopted that the decisive matter was not the exercise of his own discretion upon a consideration of the report and other material considerations, but the sustained objection of the Minister of Agriculture. In effect he says that the decision was not that of the Minister of Housing and Local Government, the authority entrusted with the duty to decide, but of the Minister of Agriculture, who had no status save perhaps in a consultative capacity and certainly no status to make the effective decision. . .

It is not, I think, suggested by Mr Slynn that the Minister of Agriculture has any status at such an inquiry as was conducted in this case, save in so far as either the applicants or the local planning authority required the attendance of a Ministerial witness, nor that there is any statutory requirement for the Minister of Agriculture to be consulted at any stage, either before or after the hearing. As a matter of practice, nevertheless, the Ministry of Agriculture is invariably consulted by the local planning authority in the case of such an application as was made in the present instance, and I would expect the Ministry of Housing and Local Government to follow a similar practice, where agricultural land is involved. . .

In general support of his main submission, Mr Frank has referred me to Professor de Smith's well known work *Judicial Review of Administrative Action*, 2nd ed. (1968), pp. 292–297, and to certain of the cases cited therein. He really puts his argument in two ways—(1) that the Minister has fettered his discretion by a self created rule of policy, and (2) that the Minister, who has a duty to exercise his own discretion in determining an appeal, has in this case delegated that duty to the Minister of Agriculture, who has no such duty and is, statutorily, a stranger to any decision.

It is, of course, common ground between Mr Frank and Mr Slynn that the Minister is entitled to have a policy and to decide an appeal in the context of that policy. He can also differ from the inspector on any question of fact, and disagree with the inspector's conclusions and recommendations. He can, and no doubt should, reject any recommendation of an inspector which runs counter to his policy, since, as Mr Slynn pointed out, it is of the very essence of the duties laid upon the Minister by section 1 of the Minister of Town and Country Planning Act, 1943, that he should secure consistency and continuity in the framing and execution of a national policy with respect to the use and development of land.

The courts have no authority to interfere with the way in which the Minister carries out his planning policy: see *per* Lord Denning M.R. in *Luke* v. *Minister of Housing and Local Government* [1968] 1 Q.B. 172, 192. There is also no question but that the Minister, before making a decision whether or not to allow an appeal, may obtain the views of other government departments: *Darlassis* v. *Minister of Education* (1954) 52 L.G.R. 304, *per* Barry J. at p. 318.

Can there, nevertheless, come a point . . . when the court can interfere with a Ministerial decision which, ex facie, proceeds upon a consideration of the inspector's report and concludes by applying Ministerial policy?

Mr Frank submits that such a point can be reached and has been reached in this case. It is reached, he says, adopting the words of Professor de Smith in his book, *Judicial Review of Administrative Action*, at p. 294, if a tribunal, entrusted with a discretion as the Minister was in the present case, disables itself from exercising that discretion in a particular case by the prior adoption of a general policy. In *Rex* v. *Port of London Authority, Ex parte Kynock Ltd.* [1919] 1 K.B. 176, Bankes L.J. said, at p. 184:

' In the present case there is another matter to be borne in mind. There are on the one hand cases where a tribunal in the honest exercise of its discretion has adopted a policy, and, without refusing to hear an applicant, intimates to him what its policy is, that, after hearing him, it will in accordance with its policy decide against him, unless there is something exceptional in his case . . . On the other hand there are cases where a tribunal has passed a rule, or come to a determination not to hear an application of a particular character by whomsoever made.'

In another licensing case, *Reg.* v. *Flintshire County Council Licensing (Stage Plays) Committee, Ex parte Barrett* [1957] 1 Q.B. 350, where the decision was given in the interests of consistency, Jenkins L.J. said, at pp. 367, 368:

'Then they went on... to conclude... that the Queen's Theatre licence must follow the fate of the Pavilion Theatre licence, because it was essential that the same rule should be applied in all cases or, in other words, that the committee should be consistent. I cannot think that that method fulfils the requirement that the matter should be heard and determined according to law... It seems to me that it wrongly pursues consistency at the expense of the merit of individual cases.'

I have referred to those two cases since they were relied on by Mr Frank, but I am inclined to agree with Mr Slynn that the considerations applicable to licensing cases are not of much assistance when considering the scope of a Minister's duties within a statutory framework... It is, of course, clear that if the Minister has prejudged any genuine consideration of the matter before him, or has failed to give genuine consideration to, inter alia, the inspector's report, he has failed to carry out his statutory duties properly. *Franklin* v. *Minister of Town and Country Planning* [1948] A.C. 87 [below p. 611].

In the present case, Mr Frank does not shrink from submitting that the decision letter shows that no genuine consideration was given to the question whether planning permission could, in the circumstances, be granted. I have carefully considered the authorities cited by counsel, but I have not found any clear guide to what my decision should be in this case. I have said enough to make it clear that I recognise that in the field of policy, and in relation to ministerial decisions coloured or dictated by policy, the courts will interfere only within a strictly circumscribed field: see *per* Lord Greene M.R. in *Associated Provincial Picture Houses Ltd.* v. *Wednesbury Corporation* [1948] 1 K.B. 223, 228. It is also clear, and is conceded by Mr Slynn, that where a Minister is entrusted by Parliament with the decision of any particular case he must keep that actual decision in the last resort in his own hands: see *Rex* v. *Minister of Transport, Ex parte Grey Coaches*, 'The Times', March 19, 1933. I return, therefore, to the words used by the Minister. It seems to me that he has said in language which admits of no doubt that his decision to refuse permission was solely in pursuance of a policy not to permit minerals in the Waters agricultural reserve to be worked unless the Minister of Agriculture was not opposed to their working. Mr Slynn submits that, read as a whole, the decision letter should be taken as implying some such words as:

'I have gone through the exercise of taking all material considerations into account, but you have not persuaded me that this is such an exceptional case as would justify me in relaxing my policy; therefore I stick to it and apply it.'

If that were the right construction perhaps Mr Slynn would be justified in saying that there was no error in law. But in my judgment the language used is not open to any such implication. There is no indication that this might be an exceptional case such as would or could induce the Minister to change his policy. It is common ground that the Minister must be open to persuasion that the land should not remain in the Waters reservation. How can his mind be open to persuasion, how can an applicant establish an ' exceptional case ' in the face of an inflexible attitude by the Minister of Agriculture? That attitude was well known before the inquiry, it was maintained during the inquiry, and presumably thereafter. The inquiry was no doubt, in a sense, into the Minister of Agriculture's objection, since, apart from that objection, it might well have been that no inquiry would have been necessary, but I do not think that the Minister after the inquiry can be said in any real sense to have given genuine consideration to whether on planning (including agricultural) grounds this land could be worked. It seems to me that by adopting and applying his stated policy he has in effect inhibited himself from exercising a proper discretion (which would of course be guided by policy considerations) in any case where the Minister of Agriculture has made and maintained an objection to mineral working in an agricultural reservation. Everything else might point to the desirability of granting permission, but by applying and acting on his stated policy I think the Minister has fettered himself in such a way that in this case it was not he who made the decision for which Parliament made him responsible. It was the decision of the Minister of Agriculture not to waive his objection which was decisive in this case, and while that might properly prove to be the decisive factor for the Minister when taking into account all material considerations, it seems to me quite wrong for a policy to be applied which in reality eliminates all the material considerations save only the consideration, when that is the case, that the Minister of Agriculture objects. That means, as I think, that the Minister has by his stated policy delegated to the Minister of Agriculture the effective decision on any appeal within the agricultural reservations where the latter objects to the working. I am quite unable to accept that in these circumstances, the public inquiry could be justified, as Mr Slynn submits, as giving the Minister of Agriculture the opportunity to hear the case and, if he thought right, to waive his objection. Unless there was a real chance that he would do so – and it seems to me clear beyond question that there was not – the inquiry was quite futile in my view, certainly as a means of providing the Minister with the material on which he could have exercised, and should have exercised, a genuine, unfettered discretion.

As Mr Frank submits, a policy which prohibited all development in a national park where there was an objection by the National Parks Commission which was not withdrawn, or to confirm all building preservation orders unless the Royal Fine Art Commission approved, would plainly vitiate a decision reached in accordance with that policy by a tribunal which is given a discretion. I think he is right, and I can find no real distinction between such hypothetical cases and the Minister's stated policy in this case [4]. . . . I think the Minister failed to exercise a proper or indeed any discretion by reason of the fetter which he imposed upon its exercise in acting solely in accordance with his stated policy; and further, that upon the true construction of the Minister's letter the decision to dismiss the appeal, while purporting to be that of the Minister, was in fact, and improperly, that of the Minister of Agriculture, Fisheries and Food . . .

Order accordingly

ELLIS v. *DUBOWSKI*　　　　　　　　　　　[1921] 3 K.B. 621

Divisional Court

The Cinematograph Act, 1909, authorised county councils to grant cinema licences 'on such terms and conditions and under such restrictions as, subject to regulations by the Secretary of State, the council may by the respective licences determine'. The Middlesex County Council granted the owners of the Gaiety Cinema, Twickenham, a licence subject to the condition that 'no film be shown . . . which has not been certified for public exhibition by the British Board of Film Censors'. The owners showed 'The auction of souls' which did not have a certificate. They appealed against a conviction on the grounds that the condition was *ultra vires*.

LAWRENCE C.J. . . . [T]he requirement . . . that a film should be certified by the British Board of Film Censors before it can be shown is bad and *ultra vires* the licensing committee. The condition sets up an authority whose ipse dixit is to control the exhibition of films. The effect is to transfer a power which belongs to the County Council and can be delegated to committees of the Council or to district councils or to justices sitting in petty sessions alone. I think that such a condition is unreasonable, and that the committee had no power to impose it . . . I am prepared to assume that the powers of the Board are exercised wisely and discreetly. But the committee have no power to create an absolute body from which no right of appeal exists. If, as was suggested by Sankey J. in the course of the argument, the condition had reserved to the committee the right to review the decisions of the Board, it would seem to be a reasonable condition . . . But that body should not be

---

[4] Cp. rules of the Town and Country Planning (Inquiry Procedure) Rules, below, p. 620.

made the final dictator, and a condition putting the matter in the hands of a third person or body not possessed of statutory or constitutional authority is *ultra vires* the committee. The committee are a responsible body as also are the justices in petty session, both being recognised as such by statute: the British Board of Film Censors have no such authority. For these reasons it appears to me that the condition is invalid and that the appeal must be allowed.

AVORY and SANKEY JJ. delivered concurring judgments.

CARLTONA LTD. v. *COMMISSIONERS OF WORKS AND OTHERS* [1943] 2 All E.R. 560

Court of Appeal

Regulation 51 (1) of the Defence (General) Regulations, 1939, provided: ' A competent authority, if it appears to that authority to be necessary or expedient so to do in the interests of the public safety, the defence of the realm, or the efficient prosecution of the war, or for maintaining supplies and services essential to the life of the country ... may take possession of any land.' The appellant, whose factory had been requisitioned under this regulation, complained that the requisitioning was invalid on the grounds that there was no evidence that the Commissioners, who were a competent authority within the meaning of the regulation, had themselves considered the matter. All that he had received was a notice on the headed letter paper of the Ministry of Works and Planning signed by a Mr Morse on behalf of the First Commissioner, which stated that ' the department have come to the conclusion that it is essential, in the national interest, to take possession of the above premises occupied by you '.

LORD GREENE M.R. ... In the administration of government in this country the functions which are given to ministers (and constitutionally properly given to ministers because they are constitutionally responsible) are functions so multifarious that no minister could ever personally attend to them. To take the example of the present case no doubt there have been thousands of requisitions in this country by individual ministries. It cannot be supposed that this regulation meant that, in each case, the minister in person should direct his mind to the matter. The duties imposed upon ministers and the powers given to ministers are normally exercised under the authority of the ministers by responsible officials of the department. Public business could not be carried on if that were not the case. Constitutionally, the decision of such an official is, of course, the decision of the minister. The minister is responsible. It is he who must answer before Parliament for anything that his officials have done under his authority, and, if for an important matter he selected an official of such junior standing that he could not be expected competently to perform the work, the minister would have to answer for that in Parliament. The whole system of departmental organisation and administration is based on the view that ministers, being responsible to Parliament, will see that important duties are committed to experienced officials. If they do not do that, Parliament is the place where complaint must be made against them. In the present case the assistant secretary, a high official of the Ministry, was the person entrusted with the work of looking after this particular matter and the question, therefore, is . . . did he direct his mind to the matters to which he was bound to direct it in order to act properly under the regulation?

GODDARD and DU PARCQ L.JJ. concurred.

Appeal dismissed with costs

Cp. *Allingham and Another* v. *Minister of Agriculture and Fisheries* [1948] 1 All E.R. 780 where the Divisional Court held that the maxim *delegatus non potest delegare* prevented a local war agricultural executive committee to whom the Minister of Agriculture had delegated some of his powers (as he was expressly authorised to do by the Defence (General) Regulations, 1939) from delegating those powers on to their executive officer. Lord Goddard C.J. said: ' I can find no provision in any order having statutory effect or any regulation which gives the executive committee power to delegate that which the Minister has to decide and which he has power to delegate to the committee to decide for him. If he has delegated, as he has, the power of making decisions to the executive committee, it is the executive committee that must make the decision, and, on the ordinary principle of *delegatus non potest delegare*, they cannot delegate their power to some other person or body.'

COMMISSIONERS OF CUSTOMS AND EXCISE v. CURE & DEELEY LTD. [1962] 1 Q.B. 340

Queen's Bench Division

S. 4 (1) of the Customs and Excise Act, 1952, provides: ' Any act or thing required or authorised by or under any enactment to be done by the Commissioners or any of them may be done – (*a*) by any one or more of the Commissioners; or (*b*) if the Commissioners so authorise, by a secretary or assistant secretary to the Commissioners; or (*c*) by any other person authorised generally or specially in that behalf in writing by the Commissioners.' [5]

Regulation 12 of the Purchase Tax Regulations, 1945, provided: ' If any person fails to furnish a return as required by these Regulations or

---

[5] Cp. s. 13 (5) of the Immigration Act, 1971: ' A person shall not be entitled to appeal against a refusal of leave to enter . . . if the Secretary of State certifies that directions have been given by the Secretary of State (and not by a person acting under his authority) for the appellant not to be given entry to the United Kingdom on the ground that his exclusion is conducive to the public good . . .'

furnishes an incomplete return the commissioners may ... determine the amount of tax appearing to be due from such person, and demand payment thereof. . .'

The defendant company had been sent two documents. The first recorded the determination by the Commissioners of the sum due. The second was a letter of demand requiring the sum determined to be paid. The determination was signed by Mr Seed, an assistant secretary who had been authorised by the Commissioners to make determinations and demands under Regulation 12. The demand was signed by Mr Piper, the chief executive officer responsible for purchase tax recovery questions. He was not authorised to make determinations or demands. He had checked both the determination and the demand and then taken the file to Mr Seed. Mr Seed having had the case explained to him and being satisfied that both documents were in order signed the determination. Mr Piper in accordance with the usual office routine then signed the letter of demand before both were sent out to the defendants.

The defendants claimed that the letter of demand was invalid.

SACHS J. [having set out these facts, continued:] In those circumstances, it is clear that the making of the demand was authorised by a person entitled to make it and was later made by a responsible officer. The point taken on behalf on the defendants is thus singularly devoid of merits. It could not have arisen if Mr Seed has signed both documents instead of only one, and it could not have arisen if Mr Piper had been given authority in writing to do that which was in practice part of his normal routine duty.

The commissioners are in a position parallel to that of the Ministers referred to in the judgment of Lord Greene in the *Carltona case* [6] in that their functions are so multifarious that they could never personally attend to them all, and the powers given to them are normally exercised under their authority by responsible officials of the department. In that situation the point now taken probably could not have arisen before section 4 (1) of the Act of 1952 came into force: for there was nothing in the earlier Acts which made it necessary for any authority given to officers other than assistant secretaries to be in writing.

It is, however, clear, as was rightly conceded for the commissioners, that now wherever an act, other than a purely ministerial act, is by relevant legislation authorised to be done by the commissioners, then that act can only be done by a person duly authorised, as set out in section 4 (1). At one stage it was submitted that any demand for payment made by virtue of regulation 12 was a purely ministerial act and thus, unlike the determination referred to in that regulation, one to which section 4 (1) did not apply: that submission, however, was not pressed because even after a determination has been made it is an

[6] [Above, p. 576.]

important matter of discretion to decide whether and when there should be issued the demand which has the effect mentioned in the regulation.

In the result the point at issue became an extremely narrow one. The defendants submitted that it was the act of demanding which had to be made by a duly authorised person, and that the relevant words ' any act ... may be done ' ought not to be construed as if it read ' any act may be authorised '. For the commissioners it was argued that in relation to a demand section 4 (1) ought not to be read as if it contained a provision that the demand must be signed by one of the persons referred to in that subsection; and that the demand in the present case was really the act of Mr Seed, so that it was not in point whether Mr Seed signed it or indeed if the document were sent off without any signature at all. The commissioners relied on the maxim qui facit per alium facit per se, the defendants on the maxim delegatus non potest delegare.

On this narrow issue my mind has fluctuated and my conclusions have been reached with hesitation.

It is to be noted that throughout the 321 sections of the Act of 1952 a careful distinction is drawn between those acts which only a commissioner can do and those which can be done by an officer or other designated persons. The acts which are reserved to the commissioners are all of importance but none the less have in practice often to be performed in various parts of the country by others than the commissioners personally. The provisions of section 4 (1) thus seem to be designed for the protection of those who may be affected by such acts.

The demand upon which the present action is founded was one which both in terms of pleading and in common parlance was made by the letter of August 16. That demand was an act which cannot be said to have been done by the commissioners personally. To have effect it must thus, having regard to section 4 (1), be an act which was in law that of Mr Seed. Having read and re-read the letter, the act to my mind was that of Mr Piper, and though authorised by Mr Seed was not the act of Mr Seed himself. On that basis it was not the act of any person nominated by section 4 (1).

On such a point it is doubtful whether authority can be of assistance, but I am inclined to think that in *Miles* v. *Bough*[7] the reasoning of Coleridge J.[8] is in point despite the fact that he was dealing with a section which related to signatures.[9]

In coming to this unsatisfactory conclusion, which depends on the special facts of this case, I draw some comfort from the fact that the commissioners can so easily provide against a recurrence of the situation, even if they have not already done so. Moreover, in a taxing statute, it is better that sections designed to give protection to the subject

---

[7] (1842) 3 Q.B. 845; 114 E.R. 732.
[8] Ibid. 868.   [9] Ibid. 849.

be construed strictly rather than that there be allowed a laxity so as to enable the merits of a case to hold sway. . .

Judgment for the defendants

(c) *The authority should genuinely exercise any discretion which has been given to it*

BRITISH OXYGEN LTD. v. BOARD OF TRADE

[1971] A.C. 610

House of Lords

The Industrial Development Act 1966 provided: ' 1 (1) Subject to the provisions of this section, the Board of Trade . . . may make to any person carrying on a business in Great Britain a grant towards approved capital expenditure incurred by that person in providing new machinery or plant . . . (a) for carrying on a qualifying industrial process in the course of that business. . .' The appellants had applied for a grant and it had been refused on the grounds that the plant for which they had applied for the grant did not qualify. Their claim was rejected by the Board both on the basis of the provisions of the statute and on the basis of a rule it had laid down itself that items costing less than twenty-five pounds should not qualify.

LORD REID. . . . Section 1 of the Act provides that the Board of Trade ' may ' make grants. It was not argued that ' may ' in this context means ' shall '; and it seems to me clear that the Board were intended to have a discretion. But how were the Board intended to operate that discretion? Does the Act read as a whole indicate any policy which the Board is to follow or even give any guidance to the Board? If it does then the Board must exercise its discretion in accordance with such a policy or guidance *Padfield* v. *Minister of Agriculture, Fisheries and Food* [above p. 560]. One generally expects to find that Parliament has given some indication as to how public money is to be distributed. In this Act Parliament has clearly laid down the conditions for eligibility for grants and it has clearly given to the Board a discretion so that the Board is not bound to pay to every person who is eligible to receive a grant. But I can find nothing to guide the Board as to the circumstances in which they should pay or the circumstances in which they should not pay grants to such persons.

The relevant part of the long title is: ' An Act to provide for the making of grants out of moneys provided by Parliament towards expenditure on the provision of new business assets.' There is no guidance there. Then section 1 (6) deals with eligibility and provides that the amount of any grant shall be 20 per cent. of the expenditure in respect of which it is made. Sections 2 to 6 deal with special cases. Section 7 is a general power to vary the rate of grant by order. None of these throws any light on this matter, nor does section 8 which deals with conditions to be imposed in making grants.

Sections 11 and 12 are perhaps more relevant. Section 11 provides for the appointment of committees to advise the Board on the administration of the Act and it could be taken as an indication that otherwise the Board's discretion is unlimited. Section 12 provides for an annual report to Parliament so that Parliament can ex post facto consider the way in which this discretion has been exercised.

Section 13 is a definition section. ' Approved capital expenditure ' is to mean ' expenditure appearing to the Board to be of a capital nature and approved by them for the purposes of the grant.' This again gives no guidance as to reasons for which approval can be given or withheld.

I cannot find that these provisions give any right to any person to get a grant. It was argued that the object of the Act is to promote the modernisation of machinery and plant and that the Board were bound to pay grants to all who are eligible unless, in their view, particular eligible expenditure would not promote that object. That might be good advice for an advisory committee to give but I find nothing in the Act to require the Board to act in that way. If the Minister who now administers the Act, acting on behalf of the Government, should decide not to give grants in respect of certain kinds of expenditure, I can find nothing to prevent him. There are two general grounds on which the exercise of an unqualified discretion can be attacked. It must not be exercised in bad faith, and it must not be so unreasonably exercised as to show that there cannot have been any real or genuine exercise of the discretion. But, apart from that, if the Minister thinks that policy or good administration requires the operation of some limiting rule, I find nothing to stop him.

It was argued on the authority of *Rex* v. *Port of London Authority, Ex parte Kynoch Ltd.* [1919] 1 K.B. 176 that the Minister is not entitled to make a rule for himself as to how he will in future exercise his discretion. In that case Kynoch owned land adjoining the Thames and wished to construct a deep water wharf. For this they had to get the permission of the authority. Permission was refused on the ground that Parliament had charged the authority with the duty of providing such facilities. It appeared that before reaching their decision the authority had fully considered the case on its merits and in relation to the public interest. So their decision was upheld.

Bankes L.J. said, at p. 184:

' There are on the one hand cases where a tribunal in the honest exercise of its discretion has adopted a policy, and, without refusing to hear an applicant, intimates to him what its policy is, and that after hearing him it will in accordance with its policy decide against him, unless there is something exceptional in his case. I think counsel for the applicants would admit that, if the policy has been adopted for reasons which the tribunal may legitimately entertain, no objection could be taken to such a course. On the other hand there are cases where a tribunal has passed a rule, or come to a determination, not to hear any application of a particular character by whomsoever made. There is a wide distinction to be drawn between these two classes.'

I see nothing wrong with that. But the circumstances in which discretions are exercised vary enormously and that passage cannot be applied literally in every case. The general rule is that anyone who has to exercise a statutory discretion must not ' shut his ears to an application ' (to adapt from Bankes L.J. on p. 183). I do not think there is any great difference between a policy and a rule. There may be cases where an officer or authority ought to listen to a substantial argument reasonably presented urging a change of policy. What the authority must not do is to refuse to listen at all. But a Ministry or large authority may have had to deal already with a multitude of similar applications and then they will almost certainly have evolved a policy so precise that it could well be called a rule. There can be no objection to that, provided the authority is always willing to listen to anyone with something new to say – of course I do not mean to say that there need be an oral hearing. In the present case the respondent's officers have carefully considered all that the appellants have had to say and I have no doubt that they will continue to do so . . .

Viscount Dilhorne. . . . [I]n this case it was not challenged that it was within the power of the Board to adopt a policy not to make a grant in respect of such an item. That policy might equally well be described as a rule. It was both reasonable and right that the Board should make known to those interested the policy it was going to follow. By doing so fruitless applications involving expense and expenditure of time might be avoided. The Board says that it has not refused to consider any application. It considered the appellants'. In these circumstances it is not necessary to decide in this case whether, if it had refused to consider an application on the ground that it related to an item costing less than £25, it would have acted wrongly.

I must confess that I feel some doubt whether the words used by Bankes L.J. in the passage cited above are really applicable to a case of this kind. It seems somewhat pointless and a waste of time that the Board should have to consider applications which are bound as a result of its policy decision to fail. Representations could of course be made that the policy should be changed.

I cannot see any ground on which it could be said that it was ultra vires of the Board to decide not to make grants on items costing less than £25 nor upon which it could be said to be ultra vires to decide not to make a grant in respect of plant used for a dual purpose, one of which qualifies, if in its opinion the main purpose of the plant was for making delivery to customers.

LORDS WILBERFORCE and DIPLOCK agreed with the judgment of LORD REID.

COMMISSIONERS OF CROWN LANDS v. PAGE
[1960] 2 Q.B. 274

Court of Appeal

In 1937 the Commissioners of Crown Lands granted a lease of premises for 25 years to the defendant. In 1945 the Minister of Works, acting under the authority of the Defence Regulations, 1939, requisitioned the property. It was not de-requisitioned until July 1955. The Commissioners now sued for the rent due under the lease for the period during which the property had been requisitioned. The lessee argued that the requisitioning amounted to an eviction by the landlord and that therefore she was not liable to pay rent during that period. It was conceded that the Crown was both lessor and the requisitioning authority, but the Crown argued *inter alia* that the requisitioning did not amount to an eviction as it had not been carried out by it in its capacity of landlord but in its capacity as the Executive responsible for the government of the country.

DEVLIN L.J. The obligation to pay rent continues so long as the tenancy lasts, and whether or not the tenant is in occupation or enjoyment of the premises, unless he is evicted by the landlord. . .

An eviction or breach that goes to the root of the covenant (and for practical purposes they are the same thing) is a defence to an action for rent. The defendant, therefore, relies, as her only defence to the claim by the Commissioners of Crown Lands for rent, upon the action of the Commissioners of Works (as they then were) in requisitioning the premises. It has been admitted that the Crown is one and indivisible, and acts as much through the Commissioners of Works as through the Commissioners of Crown Lands. There can be no doubt, therefore, that the Crown dispossessed the defendant. . .

I think that it may well be that the covenant of quiet enjoyment is limited to acts that are done by the landlord in supposed assertion of his rights as landlord, and that other trespasses, however grave, are outside the covenant. But because the landlord in this case is also the Crown, I have found it on the whole simpler to answer the question in the case not by reference to any special limitation on the covenant of quiet enjoyment affecting all landlords, but by reference to the general limitation that affects all contracts or covenants entered into by the Crown, or for that matter by any other public authority.

When the Crown, or any other person, in entrusted, whether by virtue of the prerogative or by statute, with discretionary powers to be exercised for the public good, it does not, when making a private contract in general terms, undertake (and it may be that it could not even with the use of specific language validly undertake) to fetter itself in the use of those powers, and in the exercise of its discretion. This principle has been accepted in a number of authorities: it is sufficient to mention *Ayr Harbour Trustees* v. *Oswald*;[10] *Rederiaktiebolaget Amphitrite* v. *The King*;[11] *Board of Trade* v. *Temperley Steam Shipping Co. Ltd.*[12] and *William Cory & Sons Ltd.* v. *City of London Corporation.*[13]

The covenant for quiet enjoyment in the present case is implied, and is not dissimilar to the contractual provision considered in the two cases last cited, which were both concerned with the implied obligation on one party to a contract not to interfere with the performance by the other party of his obligations under it. In *Board of Trade* v. *Temperley Steam Shipping Co. Ltd.*,[14] the Board were the charterers of the defendant's ship, and it was contended that they had prevented the defendants from making their ship efficient for her service under the charterparty because one of the Board's surveyors had refused a licence to do certain repairs. In *William Cory & Sons Ltd.* v. *City of London Corporation*,[15] the city corporation had a contract with the plaintiffs whereunder the plaintiffs undertook to remove refuse by means of lighters and barges. Some time later the city corporation passed a by-law concerning the fitment of vessels transporting refuse which it was agreed was such as to make the performance of the contract impossible. It was held by the Court of Appeal that the corporation was not in breach of the implied term.

I do not, however, rest my decision in the present case simply on the fact that the covenant for quiet enjoyment has to be implied. For reasons which I think will appear sufficiently in the next paragraph, I should reach the same conclusion if the ordinary covenant was expressed.

In some of the cases in which public authorities have been defendants, the judgments have been put on the ground that it would be ultra vires for them to bind themselves not to exercise their powers; and it has also been said that a promise to do so would be contrary to public policy. It may perhaps be difficult to apply this reasoning to the Crown, but it seems to me to be unnecessary to delve into the constitutional position. When the Crown, in dealing with one of its subjects, is dealing as if it too were a private person, and is granting leases or buying and

---

[10] (1883) 8 App.Cas. 623, H.L.   [11] [1921] 3 K.B. 500.
[12] (1926) 26 Ll.L.R. 76; affirmed (1927) 27 Ll.L.R. 230, C.A.
[13] [1951] 2 K.B. 476, C.A.
[14] 26 Ll.L.R. 76.   [15] [1951] 2 K.B. 476, C.A.

selling as ordinary persons do, it is absurd to suppose that it is making any promise about the way in which it will conduct the affairs of the nation. No one can imagine, for example, that when the Crown makes a contract which could not be fulfilled in time of war, it is pledging itself not to declare war for so long as the contract lasts. Even if, therefore, there was an express covenant for quiet enjoyment, or an express promise by the Crown that it would not do any act which might hinder the other party to the contract in the performance of his obligations, the covenant or promise must by necessary implication be read to exclude those measures affecting the nation as a whole which the Crown takes for the public good.

During the last war the Ministries of War Transport, Food and Supply were trading on a vast scale, and were also issuing orders under their statutory powers which quite frequently frustrated their own contracts, or those made by some other government department. The Minister of Supply, for example, might be found prohibiting all importation of a commodity of a sort which he had contracted to buy; or the Ministry of War Transport might fail to make cargo space available for another department's purchases. So far as I am aware, there is no case in which it has been contended that because of such action, the Crown was in breach of contract. That shows the general understanding under which such business was done. If at the time of making any such contract the ' officious bystander ' had asked whether it was clear that the Crown was not undertaking to limit the use of its general executive powers, I think that there could have been only one answer. That is the proper basis for a necessary implication. I need not examine the question whether, if the Crown sought to fetter its future action in express and specific terms, it could effectively do so. It is most unlikely that in a contract with the subject, it would ever make the attempt. For the purpose of this case it is unnecessary to go further than to say that in making a lease or other contract with its subjects, the Crown does not (at least in the absence of specific words) promise to refrain from exercising its general powers under a statute or under the prerogative, or to exercise them in any particular way. That does not mean that the Crown can escape from any contract which it finds disadvantageous by saying that it never promised to act otherwise than for the public good. The distinction was clearly put by Roche J. in *Board of Trade* v. *Temperley Steam Shipping Co. Ltd.*,[16] where he said: ' I think and I hold that in this charterparty it is to be implied that the Crown should do nothing in connection with and in relation to and in the carrying out of the contract contained in the charterparty to prevent the shipowners from keeping the vessel seaworthy and to prevent them earning their

[16] 26 Ll.L.R. 76, 78.

hire. But I am utterly unable to imply in the charterparty a term or condition that the Crown should do nothing by virtue of some general legislation or by virtue of some executive action entirely remote from the charterparty and done by persons not connected with the performance of the contract directly or indirectly to bring about the results in question.' That is a different thing from saying that the Crown can never bind itself in its dealings with the subject in case it might turn out that the fulfilment of the contract was not advantageous. The observations of Denning J. in *Robertson* v. *Minister of Pensions*[17] on the doctrine of ' executive necessity ' were, I think, directed to a case of that sort. Here we are dealing with an act done for a general executive purpose and not an act done for the purpose of achieving a particular result under the contract in question.

LORD EVERSHED M.R. and ORMEROD J. delivered concurring judgments.

Appeal dismissed

(d) *In exercising the power the authority should observe any procedure which has been expressly laid down in the statute or which the courts will imply into the statute*

The courts have long insisted that in exercising powers which affect a person's rights, and in particular his property rights, public authorities should observe the principles of natural justice, the most important of which in the context of the exercise of administrative powers is the principle *audi alteram partem*, that the person affected should be given an opportunity to state his case. This requirement has been implied in statutes where no specific procedure has been laid down and has also been used by the courts to fill out procedures which have been specifically set out in the statute, particularly in relation to public inquiries. Public inquiries have been an integral part of the administrative process ever since Parliament began to entrust to Ministers the power to make decisions affecting private rights which had hitherto been made by Parliament either in a Private Bill or by way of a Provisional Order Confirmation Act. The obligation to hold them before a final decision is reached is to be found in particular statutes relating to the compulsory acquisition of land, town and country planning and housing schemes of local authorities which affect private property. Although Parliament set

---

[17] [1949] 1 K.B. 227, 231. [In that case a serving army officer wrote to the War Office regarding a disability from which he suffered. He received a reply stating that his disability had been accepted as attributable to military service. Relying on that statement, he omitted to obtain an independent medical opinion. The Ministry of Pensions, who were in fact the department responsible for making a final decision, later decided that the disability was not attributable to war service. Denning J. held that the assurance by the War Office that it was, was intended to be binding, intended to be acted on, and was in fact acted on. He therefore held that it was binding on the Crown.]

out the bare bones, it was left to the courts to fill them out, as they did, for example, in *Errington* v. *Minister of Health, B. Johnson and Co. (Builders)* v. *Minister of Health*, and *Franklin* v. *Minister of Town and Country Planning* (below pp. 603, 606 and 611). In 1957, however, the actions of the courts were supplemented first by the Report of the Committee on Tribunals and Inquiries and then by the Council on Tribunals which has the power to make recommendations about the rules regulating procedure before, at and after public inquiries. In this field therefore what was previously left to the courts is now covered by quite detailed rules, an example of which can be seen in the Town and Country Planning (Inquiries Procedure) Rules, 1974 (below p. 620).

There are still areas in which the courts are called upon to interpret the procedural requirements laid down in a statute and even supplement them, and because of the traditional insistence by the courts on the observance of the principles of natural justice, or the duty to act fairly as it is now more often called, applications to the court to do this are not infrequent.

Some recent reactions of the courts to these applications are also illustrated in the extracts which follow.

COOPER v. *WANDSWORTH BOARD OF WORKS*
(1863) 14 C.B.(N.S.) 180; 143 E.R. 414

Court of Common Pleas

ERLE C.J. This was an action of trespass by the plaintiff against the Wandsworth district board, for pulling down and demolishing his house; and the ground of defence that has been put forward by the defendants has been under the 76th section of the Metropolis Local Management Act, 18 & 19 Vict. c. 120. By the part of that section which applies to this case, it is enacted that, before any person shall begin to build a new house, he shall give seven days' notice to the district board of his intention to build; and it provides at the end that, in default of such notice it shall be lawful for the district board to demolish the house. The district board here say that no notice was given by the plaintiff of his intention to build the house in question, wherefore they demolished it. The contention on the part of the plaintiff has been that, although the words of the statute, taken in their literal sense, without any qualification at all, would create a justification for the act which the district board has done, the powers granted by that statute are subject to a qualification which has been repeatedly recognized, that no man is to be deprived of his property without his having an opportunity of being heard. The evidence here shews that the plaintiff and the district board had not been quite on amicable terms. Be that as it may, the district board say that no notice was given, and that consequently they had a right to proceed to demolish the house without delay, and without notice to the party whose house was to be pulled down, and without giving him an opportunity of shewing any reason why the board should delay. I think that the power which is granted by the 76th section is subject to the qualification suggested. It is a power carrying with it enormous consequences. The house in question was built only to a certain extent. But the power claimed would apply to a complete house. It would apply to a house of any value, and completed to any extent; and it seems to me to be a power which may be exercised most perniciously, and that the limitation which we are going to put upon it is one which ought, according to the decided cases, to be put upon it, and one which is required by a due consideration for the public interest. I think the board ought to have given notice to the plaintiff, and to have allowed him to be heard. The default in sending notice to the board of the intention to build, is a default which may be explained. There may be a great many excuses for the apparent default. The party may have intended to conform to the law. He may have actually conformed to all the regulations which they would wish to impose, though by accident his notice may have miscarried; and, under those circumstances, if he explained how it stood, the proceeding to demolish, merely because they had ill-will against the party, is a power that the legislature never intended to confer. I cannot conceive any harm that could happen to the district board from hearing the party before they subjected him to a loss so serious as the demolition of his house; but I can conceive a great many advantages which might arise in the way of public order, in the way of doing substantial justice, and in the way of fulfilling the purposes of the statute, by the restriction which we put upon them, that they should hear the party before they inflict upon him such a heavy loss. I fully agree that the legislature intended to give the district board very large powers indeed: but the qualification I speak of is one which has been recognised to the full extent. It has been said that the principle that no man shall be deprived of his property without an opportunity of being heard, is limited to a judicial proceeding, and that a district board ordering a house to be pulled down cannot be said to be doing a judicial act. I do not quite agree with that; neither do I undertake to rest my judgment solely upon the ground that the district board is a court exercising judicial discretion upon the point, but the law, I think, has been applied to many exercises of power which in common understanding would not be at all more a judicial proceeding than would be the act of the district board in ordering a house to be pulled down. The case of the corporation of the University of Cambridge, who turned out Dr Bentley, in the exercise of their assumed power of depriving a member of the University of his rights, and a number of other cases which are collected in *The Hammersmith Rent-Charge case*, 4 Exch. 96, in the judgment of Parke B., shew that the principle has been very widely applied . . .

BYLES J. . . . It seems to me that the board are wrong whether they acted judicially or ministerially. I conceive they acted judicially, because they had to determine the offence, and they had to apportion the punishment as well as the remedy. That being so, a long course of decisions, beginning with *Dr Bentley's case*,[18] and ending with some very recent cases, establish that, although there are no positive words in a statute requiring that the party shall be heard, yet the justice of the common law will supply the omission of the legislature. The judgment of Mr Justice Fortescue, in *Dr Bentley's case*, is somewhat quaint, but it is very applicable, and has been the law from that time to the present. He says, ' The objection for want of notice can never be got over. The laws of God and man both give the party an opportunity to make his defence, if he has any. I remember to have heard it observed by a very learned man, upon such an occasion, that even God himself did not pass sentence upon Adam before he was called upon to make his defence. " Adam " (says God), " where art thou? Hast thou not eaten of the tree whereof I commanded thee that thou shouldest not eat? " And the same question was put to Eve also.' If, therefore, the board acted judicially, although there are no words in the statute to that effect, it is plain they acted wrongly. But suppose they acted ministerially, – then it may be they were not bound to give the first sort of notice, viz. the notice of the hearing; but they were clearly bound, as it seems to me, by the words of the statute, to give notice of their order before they proceeded to execute it. Section 76 contains these words : ' The vestry or district board shall make their order in relation to the matters aforesaid, and cause the same to be notified ' (observe what follows) ' to the person from whom such notice was received, within seven days after the receipt of the notice.' The plain construction of those words, as it seems to me, is this : the order is to be notified, and, in the case of a person who has given a notice, that notification is to be conveyed to him within seven days from the date of his notice. That has not been done. There has been neither notice of the one sort nor of the other; and it seems to me, therefore, that, whether the board acted judicially or ministerially, they have acted against the whole current of authorities, and have omitted to do that which justice requires, and contravened the words of the statute.

KEATING and WILLES JJ. delivered concurring judgments.[19]

18 *The King* v. *The Chancellor etc. of Cambridge* (1723) 1 Stra. 557; 93 E.R. 698.
19 Cp. *Urban Housing Co. Ltd.* v. *Oxford Corporation* [1940] Ch. 70 and *Ridge* v. *Baldwin* [1964] A.C. 40.

WISEMAN v. *BORNEMAN* [1971] A.C. 297

House of Lords

In certain circumstances set out in s. 28 of the Finance Act, 1960, the Commissioners of Inland Revenue were authorised to give notice to a taxpayer that they intended to take steps to cancel a tax advantage he had obtained as a result of share transactions. The section then provided as follows: ' (4) The Commissioners of Inland Revenue shall not give a notice ... until they have notified the person in question that they have reason to believe that this section may apply to him in respect of a transaction or transactions specified in the notification, and if within 30 days ... the said person, being of opinion that this section does not apply to him ... makes a statutory declaration to that effect stating the facts and circumstances upon which his opinion is based, and sends it to the Commissioners, then, subject to the following subsection ... this section shall not apply to him... (5) If, where a statutory declaration has been sent to the Commissioners they have reason to take further action ... (a) the Commissioners shall send to the tribunal a certificate to that effect, together with the statutory declaration, and may also send therewith a counter-statement... (6) The tribunal shall take into consideration the declaration and the certificate, and the counter-statement, if any, and shall determine whether there is or is not a prima facie case for proceeding in the matter...'

Any person to whom notice had been given under the section was given the right of appeal to the Special Commissioners of Income Tax on the grounds that the section did not apply to him, and if he or the Commissioners of Inland Revenue were dissatisfied with the decision of the special commissioners then there could be a rehearing of the appeal by the tribunal.

In the present case the Commissioners had issued notifications to the appellants under s. 28 (4). The appellants made statutory declarations. The Commissioners replied that they intended to take further action and submit the case to the tribunal. The appellants requested copies of the certificate which the Commissioners had sent to the tribunal in accordance with s. 28 (5) and of any counterstatement that had been made under the same subsection. They also asked to be represented by counsel before the tribunal. The tribunal refused all these requests. The appellants asked the court to declare that the principles of natural justice entitled them to see the relevant documents and be represented before the tribunal.

July 29, 1969. LORD REID. ... Natural justice requires that the procedure before any tribunal which is acting judicially shall be fair in all the circumstances, and I would be sorry to see this fundamental general principle degenerate into a series of hard-and-fast rules. For a long time the courts have, without objection from Parliament, supplemented procedure laid down in legislation where they have found that to be necessary for this purpose. But before this unusual kind of power is exercised it must be clear that the statutory procedure is insufficient to achieve justice and that to require additional steps would not frustrate the apparent purpose of the legislation.

In the great majority of cases which come before this tribunal all the relevant facts are known to the taxpayer and he has a full opportunity to set out in his statutory declaration all the facts which he thinks are relevant and also all arguments on which he relies. The only advantage to him of having a right to see and reply to the counter-statement of the commissioners would then be that he could reply to their arguments. If the tribunal were entitled to pronounce a final judgment against the taxpayer, justice would certainly require that he should have a right to see and reply to this statement, but all the tribunal can do is to find that there is a prima facie case against him.

It is, I think, not entirely irrelevant to have in mind that it is very unusual for there to be a judicial determination of the question whether there is a prima facie case. Every public officer who has to decide whether to prosecute or raise proceedings ought first to decide whether there is a prima facie case, but no one supposes that justice requires that he should first seek the comments of the accused or the defendant on the material before him. So there is nothing inherently unjust in reaching such a decision in the absence of the other party.

Even where the decision is to be reached by a body acting judicially there must be a balance between the need for expedition and the need to give full opportunity to the defendant to see the material against him. I do not think that a case has been made out that it is unfair to proceed as the statute directs. But I do not read the statute as preventing the tribunal from seeking farther comment from the taxpayer if in any unusual case they think that they could carry out their task more effectively in that way. If they do that, then they must allow the commissioners to reply if so advised, because any decision against the commissioners is a final decision.

LORD MORRIS OF BORTH-Y-GEST. My Lords, that the conception of natural justice should at all stages guide those who discharge judicial functions is not merely an acceptable but is an essential part of the philosophy of the law. We often speak of the rules of natural justice. But there is nothing rigid or mechanical about them. What they comprehend has been analysed and described in many authorities. But any analysis must bring into relief rather their spirit and their inspiration than any precision of definition or precision as to application. We do not search for prescriptions which will lay down exactly what must, in various divergent situations, be done. The principles and procedures are to be applied which, in any particular situation or set of circumstances, are right and just and fair. Natural justice, it has been said, is only ' fair play in action '. Nor do we wait for directions from Parliament. The common law has abundant riches: there may we find what Byles J. called ' the justice of the common law ' (*Cooper* v. *Wandsworth Board of Works* (1863) 14 C.B.N.S. 180, 194).

I approach the present case by considering whether in all the circumstances the tribunal acted unfairly. . .

It is important to have in mind exactly what the tribunal had to do. There was no question of their being required to come to a determination as to whether section 28 applied to the appellants in respect of the transactions in question. There was to be no decision comparable to that in *Rex* v. *Housing Appeal Tribunal* [1920] 3 K.B. 334. The decision or determination that the tribunal had to make was whether there was or was not a prima facie case ' for proceeding in the matter '. That was a most limited decision. A decision that there was such a case would mean that it could not be said that the commissioners must definitely not give a notice under subsection (3) because they would certainly be wrong if they gave one. The tribunal is a statutory body. There are statutory directions to it. While I have expressed the view that the statutory provisions must not be read as in any way absolving the tribunal from doing at all times what in all the circumstances is fair, even at a stage when no decision finally adverse to the taxpayer is being made, it is, I think, a positive consideration that Parliament has indicated what it is that the tribunal must do and has set out that the tribunal must take into consideration three documents (a) the declaration (b) the certificate and (c) the counter-statement, if there is one. In his statutory declaration the taxpayer, who ought to know all about his affairs, will have been able to set out fully why he considers that section 28 does not apply. If the tribunal follows the course that Parliament has defined and decides not to extend that course I do not think that by reason of that circumstance alone it should be held that they have acted unfairly.

I would dismiss the appeal.

LORDS GUEST, DONOVAN and WILBERFORCE delivered concurring judgments.

A. T. DURAYAPPAH v. W. S. FERNANDO AND OTHERS
[1967] 2 A.C. 337
Privy Council

The Ceylon Municipal Councils Ordinance provided in para. 277 (1): ' If . . . it appears to the Minister that a municipal council is not competent to perform, or persistently makes default in the performance of, any duty or duties imposed upon it, or persistently refuses or neglects to comply with any provision of law, the Minister may by Order . . . direct that the council shall be dissolved. . .' The Minister in this case sent a commissioner to investigate the affairs of a local council. Although he had access to all the minutes of the council he did not question anyone or give members of the council an opportunity to state their views. After receiving his report the Minister made an order dissolving the council on the ground that it was not competent to perform its duties. The former mayor of the council applied to the court for an order of certiorari on the grounds that the Minister had failed to observe the rules of natural justice.

LORD UPJOHN . . . Their Lordships were of course referred to the recent case of *Ridge* v. *Baldwin* [20] where this principle was very closely and carefully examined. In that case no attempt was made to give an exhaustive classification of the cases where the principle audi alteram partem should be applied. In their Lordships' opinion it would be wrong to do so. Outside well-known cases such as dismissal from office, deprivation of property and expulsion from clubs, there is a vast area where the principle can only be applied upon most general considerations. For example, as Lord Reid [21] when examining *Rex* v. *Electricity Commissioners* [22] pointed out, Bankes L.J.[23] inferred the judicial element from the nature of the power and Atkin L.J.[24] did the same. Pausing there, however, it should not be assumed that their Lordships necessarily agree with Lord Reid's analysis of that case or with his criticism of *Nakkuda Ali* v. *Jayaratne*.[25] Outside the well-known classes of cases, no general rule can be laid down as to the application of the general principle in addition to the language of the provision. In their Lordships' opinion there are three matters which must always be borne in mind when considering whether the principle should be applied or not. These three matters are: first, what is the nature of the property, the office held, status enjoyed or services to be performed by the complainant of injustice. Secondly, in what circumstances or upon what occasions is the person claiming to be entitled to exercise the measure of control entitled to intervene. Thirdly, when a right to intervene is proved, what sanctions in fact is the latter entitled to impose upon the other. It is only upon a consideration of all these matters that the question of the application of the principle can properly be determined. Their Lordships therefore proceed to examine the facts of this case upon these considerations. . .

[T]he Minister can dissolve the council on one of three grounds: that it (a) is not competent to perform any duty or duties imposed upon it (for brevity their Lordships will refer to this head as incompetence);

[20] [1964] A.C. 40; [1963] 2 W.L.R. 935; [1963] 2 All E.R. 66, H.L.(E.).
[21] [1964] A.C. 40, 76.
[22] [1924] 1 K.B. 171; 39 T.L.R. 715, C.A.
[23] [1924] 1 K.B. 171, 198.
[24] Ibid. 206–7.   [25] [1951] A.C. 66; 66 T.L.R.(Pt. 2) 214, P.C.

or (b) persistently makes default in the performance of any duty or duties imposed upon it; or (c) persistently refuses or neglects to comply with any provision of law ...

While their Lordships are only concerned with the question of incompetence, the true construction of the section must be considered as a whole and its necessary intendment in the light of the common law principles already stated. It seems clear to their Lordships that it is a most serious charge to allege that the council, entrusted with these very important duties, persistently makes default in the performance of any duty or duties imposed upon it. No authority is required to support the view that in such circumstances it is plain and obvious that the principle audi alteram partem must apply.

Equally it is clear that if a council is alleged persistently to refuse or neglect to comply with a provision of law it must be entitled (as a matter of the most elementary justice) to be heard in its defence. Again this proposition requires no authority to support it. If, therefore, it is clear that in two of the three cases, the Minister must act judicially, then it seems to their Lordships, looking at the section as a whole, that it is not possible to single out for different treatment the third case, namely, incompetence. Grammatically, too, any differentiation is impossible. Section 277 confers upon the Minister a single power to act in the event of one or more closely allied failures and he can only do so after observing the principle audi alteram partem ...

The third matter can be dealt with quite shortly. The sanction which the Minister can impose and indeed, if he is satisfied of the necessary premise, must impose upon the erring council is as complete as could be imagined; it involves the dissolution of the council and therefore the confiscation of all its properties... In their Lordships' opinion this case falls within the principle of *Cooper* v. *Wandsworth Board of Works* where it was held that no man is to be deprived of his property without having an opportunity of being heard. For the purposes of the application of the principle it seems to their Lordships that this must apply equally to a statutory body having statutory powers, authorities and duties just as it does to an individual. Accordingly on this ground too the Minister should have observed the principle.

For these reasons their Lordships have no doubt that in the circumstances of this case the Minister should have observed the principle audi alteram partem. ...

PEARLBERG v. *VARTY*　　　　　　　[1972] 1 W.L.R. 534

House of Lords

LORD HAILSHAM OF ST MARYLEBONE L.C. . . . Despite the majestic concept of natural justice on which it was argued, I do not believe that this case involves any important legal principle at all. On the contrary, it is only another example of the general principle that decisions of the courts on particular statutes should be based in the first instance on a careful, even meticulous, construction of what that statute actually means in the context in which it was passed. It is true, of course, that the courts will lean heavily against any construction of a statute which would be manifestly unfair. But they have no power to amend or supplement the language of a statute merely because on one view of the matter a subject feels himself entitled to a larger degree of say in the making of a decision than the statute accords him. Still less is it the function of the courts to form first a judgment on the fairness of an Act of Parliament and then to amend or supplement it with new provisions so as to make it conform to that judgment. The doctrine of natural justice has come in for increasing consideration in recent years, and the courts generally, and your Lordships' House in particular, have, I think rightly, advanced its frontiers considerably. But at the same time they have taken an increasingly sophisticated view of what it requires in individual cases. As Tucker L.J. observed in *Russell* v. *Duke of Norfolk* [26] in a passage repeatedly cited with approval in your Lordships' House : ' There are, in my view, no words which are of universal application to every kind of domestic tribunal. The requirements of natural justice must depend on the circumstances of the case, the nature of the inquiry, the rules under which the tribunal is acting, the subject matter that is being dealt with, and so forth. Accordingly, I do not derive much assistance from the definitions of natural justice which have been from time to time used, but whatever standard is adopted, the essential is that the person concerned should have a reasonable opportunity of presenting his case.'. . .

VISCOUNT DILHORNE. . . . [C]ounsel for the appellant relied very strongly on certain observations in *Wiseman* v. *Borneman* [above p. 590] . . . In the course of his speech, my noble and learned Friend Lord Reid said, at p. 308 : ' Natural justice requires that the procedure before any tribunal which is acting judicially shall be fair in all the circumstances. . . For a long time the courts have, without objection from Parliament, supplemented procedure laid down in legislation where they have found that to be necessary for this purpose. But before this unusual kind of power is exercised it must be clear that the statutory procedure is unsufficient to achieve justice and that to require additional steps would not frustrate the apparent purpose of the legislation. . . .' I respectfully agree. I would only emphasise that one should not start by assuming that what Parliament has done in the lengthy process of legislation is unfair. One should rather assume that

[26] [1949] 1 All E.R. 109, 118.

what has been done is fair until the contrary is shown... And Parliament thought it fair that the person affected should have the right to be heard where leave was sought under s. 51 of the Finance Act, 1960, and have the right to make representations to the tribunal under s. 28 of the Act. The omission to provide in s. 6 of the Income Tax Management Act, 1964, cannot in my opinion be regarded as anything other than deliberate, and, if deliberate, it should be assumed that Parliament did not think that the requirements of fairness made it advisable to provide any such rights to the person affected...

LORDS PEARSON and SALMON delivered concurring judgments.

REGINA v. GAMING BOARD, Ex parte BENAIM AND KHAIDA
[1970] 2 Q.B. 417

Court of Appeal

The Gaming Act, 1968, required premises used for gaming to be licensed by the licensing justices. No application however could be made for a licence without a certificate of consent from the Gaming Board. When representatives of Crockfords applied the Board refused to give them a certificate. In a letter to their solicitors the Board stated:

'As your clients are aware, the matters discussed with them at the interview on December 11, 1969, were: (a) the association of your clients with certain persons who are of unacceptable background and reputation, especially with Marcel Paul Francisci, Roland Francisci and Amende Darlay (or Attal); (b) the board's doubts as to the capacity of your clients to control the club effectively, having regard to the extent of their business interests outside Great Britain, the time they spent outside Great Britain; and their imperfect command of the English language; (c) the misgivings raised by certain transactions involving the taking abroad of cheques drawn on foreign banks. The board sought to satisfy themselves that this was not done with the object of evading exchange control; (d) the uncertainty as to the legal ownership of Crockford's. While your clients appeared to be the de facto owners, it was necessary to establish their effective and lawful ownership, and to explore the circumstances of the purchase; (e) the doubt thrown on the character of your clients by their operations as hoteliers and casino managers in Algeria during and before the civil war in that country and their subsequent expulsion.'

When the solicitors asked for further explanations the Board replied:

'The board are not obliged to give their reasons for the decisions they reach and it is not their practice to do so. They are not prepared to indicate to what extent they are still not satisfied in regard to any of the specific matters mentioned at (a) to (e) in the second paragraph of my letter of February 24. They are, however, prepared to consider further written representations of any of these matters if your clients wish to put further evidence before them.'

Benaim and Khaida thereupon applied to the court for an order of certiorari to quash the Board's decision on the grounds that it had refused to reveal to them the sources and contents of information it had received about them and had therefore failed to observe the principles of natural justice. They also asked for an order of mandamus directing the Board to reveal the information. Both orders were refused by the Divisional Court and they appealed.

LORD DENNING M.R. ... It is not possible to lay down rigid rules as to when the principles of natural justice are to apply: nor as to their scope and extent. Everything depends on the subject-matter: see what Tucker L.J. said in *Russell* v. *Norfolk* (*Duke of*) [1949] 1 All E.R. 109, 118 and Lord Upjohn in *Durayappah* v. *Fernando* [1967] 2 A.C. 337, 349. At one time it was said that the principles only apply to judicial proceedings and not to administrative proceedings. That heresy was scotched in *Ridge* v. *Baldwin* [1964] A.C. 40. At another time it was said that the principles do not apply to the grant or revocation of licences. That too is wrong. *Reg.* v. *Metropolitan Police Commissioner, Ex parte Parker* [1953] 1 W.L.R. 1150 and *Nakkuda Ali* v. *Jayaratne* [1951] A.C. 66 are no longer authority for any such proposition. See what Lord Reid and Lord Hodson said about them in *Ridge* v. *Baldwin* [1964] A.C. 40, 77–79, 133.

So let us sheer away from those distinctions and consider the task of this Gaming Board and what they should do. The best guidance is, I think, to be found by reference to the cases of immigrants. They have no right to come in, but they have a right to be heard. The principle in that regard was well laid down by Lord Parker C.J. in *In re H. K.* (*An Infant*) [1967] 2 Q.B. 617. He said, at p. 630:

' ... even if an immigration officer is not in a judicial or quasi-judicial capacity, he must at any rate give the immigrant an opportunity of satisfying him of the matters in the subsection, and for that purpose let the immigrant know what his immediate impression is so that the immigrant can disabuse him. That is not, as I see it, a question of acting or being required to act judicially, but of being required to act fairly.'

Those words seem to me to apply to the Gaming Board. The statute says in terms that in determining whether to grant a certificate, the board ' shall have regard only ' to the matters specified. It follows, I think, that the board have a duty to act fairly. They must give the applicant an opportunity of satisfying them of the matters specified in the subsection. They must let him know what their impressions are so that he can disabuse them. But I do not think that they need quote chapter and verse against him as if they were dismissing him from an office, as in *Ridge* v. *Baldwin* [1964] A.C. 40; or depriving him of his property, as in *Cooper* v. *Wandsworth Board of Works* (1863) 14

C.B.N.S. 180. After all, they are not charging him with doing anything wrong. They are simply inquiring as to his capability and diligence and are having regard to his character, reputation and financial standing. They are there to protect the public interest, to see that persons running the gaming clubs are fit to be trusted.

Seeing the evils that have led to this legislation, the board can and should investigate the credentials of those who make application to them. They can and should receive information from the police in this country or abroad who know something of them. They can, and should, receive information from any other reliable source. Much of it will be confidential. But that does not mean that the applicants are not to be given a chance of answering it. They must be given the chance, subject to this qualification: I do not think they need tell the applicant the source of their information, if that would put their informant in peril or otherwise be contrary to the public interest. Even in a criminal trial, a witness cannot be asked who is his informer. The reason was well given by Lord Eyre C.J. in *Hardy's* case [*Rex* v. *Hardy*] 24 State Trials 199, 808:

> '... there is a rule which has universally obtained on account of its importance to the public for the detection of crimes, that those persons who are the channel by means of which that detection is made, should not be unnecessarily disclosed.'

And Buller J. added, at p. 818: '... if you call for the name of the informer in such cases, no man will make a discovery, and public justice will be defeated.' That rule was emphatically reaffirmed in *Attorney-General* v. *Briant* (1846) 15 M. & W. 169 and *Marks* v. *Beyfus* (1890) 25 Q.B.D. 494. That reasoning applies with equal force to the inquiries made by the Gaming Board. That board was set up by Parliament to cope with disreputable gaming clubs and to bring them under control. By bitter experience it was learned that these clubs had a close connection with organised crime, often violent crime, with protection rackets and with strong-arm methods. If the Gaming Board were bound to disclose their sources of information, no one would ' tell ' on those clubs, for fear of reprisals. Likewise with the details of the information. If the board were bound to disclose every detail, that might itself give the informer away and put him in peril. But, without disclosing every detail, I should have thought that the board ought in every case to be able to give to the applicant sufficient indication of the objections raised against him such as to enable him to answer them. That is only fair. And the board must at all costs be fair. If they are not, these courts will not hesitate to interfere.

Accepting that the board ought to do all this when they come to give their decision, the question arises, are they bound to give their reasons?

I think not. Magistrates are not bound to give reasons for their decisions: see *Rex* v. *Northumberland Compensation Appeal Tribunal, Ex parte Shaw* [1952] 1 K.B. 338, at p. 352. Nor should the Gaming Board be bound. After all, the only thing that they have to give is their *opinion* as to the capability and diligence of the applicant. If they were asked by the applicant to give their reasons, they could answer quite sufficiently: ' In our opinion, you are not likely to be capable of or diligent in the respects required of you.' Their opinion would be an end of the matter.

Tested by those rules, applying them to this case, I think that the Gaming Board acted with complete fairness. They put before the applicants all the information which led them to doubt their suitability. They kept the sources secret, but disclosed all the information. Sir Stanley Raymond said so in his affidavit: and it was not challenged to any effect. The board gave the applicants full opportunity to deal with the information. And they came to their decision. There was nothing whatever at fault with their decision of January 9, 1970. They did not give their reasons. But they were not bound to do so.

But then complaint is made as to what happened afterwards. It was said that the board did not pin-point the matters on which they thought the explanations were not satisfactory... But I do not see anything unfair in that respect. It is not as if they were making any charges against the applicants. They were only saying they were not satisfied. They were not bound to give any reasons for their misgivings. And when they did give some reasons, they were not bound to submit to cross-examination on them...

Lord Wilberforce and Phillimore L.J. agreed.

Cp. In *Re Pergamon Press* [1971] 1 Ch. 388.

REGINA v. *LIVERPOOL CORPORATION, Ex parte LIVERPOOL TAXI FLEET OPERATORS' ASSOCIATION* [1972] 2 Q.B. 299

Court of Appeal

Liverpool Corporation were the licensing authority for taxi cabs in Liverpool under the Town Police Clauses Act, 1847, which provided in s. 37: ' The commissioners may from time to time license to ply for hire ... such number of hackney coaches or carriages ... as they think fit.' From 1948 the number of licences issued had remained at 300. When, in 1970, the Association heard that the number might be increased they consulted the town clerk who replied that ' no decision had been taken on the number of hackney carriage plates and, before any decision was taken, you have my assurance that interested parties would be fully consulted.' This was in July. In October he again wrote saying, ' I have no doubt that your client will be given an opportunity to make representations, at the appropriate time, should they wish to do so.' The Association was in fact represented at a meeting in July 1971 at which the relevant sub-committee proposed an increase in the number of licences to be granted. The proposal was approved by the Council but the chairman of the committee gave the Association an assurance that no increase would be made until legislation had been passed regulating private-hire vehicles in the city. This assurance was put in writing by the town clerk in August in a letter in which he said that 'no plates in addition to the existing 300 would be issued until proposed legislation had been enacted and come into force'. In spite of these assurances the sub-committee recommended in November 1971 that there should be an increase from January 1972. When they heard of this the Association asked if they could be heard again but were not given an opportunity. The recommendation of the sub-committee was subsequently confirmed by the committee and the council. The Association applied to the court for an order of prohibition to prevent the issue of further licences, an order of mandamus directing the council to hear the Association before deciding whether more licences should be issued and an order of certiorari to quash the resolution of the council sanctioning the increase. They argued that the corporation had failed to exercise their discretion properly.

LORD DENNING M.R. ... [W]hen the corporation consider applications for licences under the Town Police Clauses Act, 1847, they are under a duty to act fairly. This means that they should be ready to hear not only the particular applicant but also any other person or bodies whose interests are affected. In *Rex* v. *Brighton Corporation, ex parte Thomas Tilling Ltd.* (1910) 85 L.J.K.B. 1552, 1555 Sankey J. said: 'Persons who are called upon to exercise the functions of granting licences for carriages and omnibuses are, to a great extent, exercising judicial functions; and although they are not bound by the strict rules of evidence and procedure observed in a court of law, they are bound to act judicially. It is their duty to hear and determine according to law, and they must bring to that task a fair and unbiased mind.'

It is perhaps putting it a little high to say they are exercising judicial functions. They may be said to be exercising an administrative function. But even so, in our modern approach, they must act fairly: and the court will see that they do so.

To apply that principle here; suppose the corporation proposed to reduce the number of taxicabs from 300 to 200; it would be their duty to hear the taxicab owners' association because their members would be greatly affected. They would certainly be persons aggrieved. Likewise suppose the corporation propose to increase the number ... [I]t is the duty of the corporation to hear those affected before coming to a decision adverse to their interests ...

The other thing I would say is that the corporation were not at liberty to disregard their undertaking. They were bound by it so long as it was not in conflict with their statutory duty.

It is said that a corporation cannot contract itself out of its statutory duties. In *Birkdale District Electric Supply Co. Ltd.* v. *Southport Corporation* [1926] A.C. 355 Lord Birkenhead said, at p. 364, that it was

> ' a well established principle of law, that if a person or public body is entrusted by the legislature with certain powers and duties expressly or impliedly for public purposes, those persons or bodies cannot divest themselves of these powers and duties. They cannot enter into any contract or take any action incompatible with the due exercise of their powers or the discharge of their duties.'

But that principle does not mean that a corporation can give an undertaking and break it as they please. So long as the performance of the undertaking is compatible with their public duty, they must honour it. And I should have thought that this undertaking was so compatible. At any rate they ought not to depart from it except after the most serious consideration and hearing what the other party has to say: and then only if they are satisfied that the overriding public interest requires it. The public interest may be better served by honouring their undertaking than by breaking it. This is just such a case. It is better to hold the corporation to their undertaking than to allow them to break it. Just as it was in *Robertson* v. *Minister of Pensions* [1949] 1 K.B. 227 and *Lever Finance Ltd.* v. *Westminster (City) London Borough Council* [1971] 1 Q.B. 222.

Applying these principles, it seems to me that the corporation acted wrongly at their meetings in November and December 1971. In the first place, they took decisions without giving the owners' association an opportunity of being heard. In the second place, they broke their undertaking without any sufficient cause or excuse.

The taxicab owners' association come to this court for relief and I think we should give it to them. The writs of prohibition and certiorari lie on behalf of any person who is a ' person aggrieved,' and that includes any person whose interests may be prejudicially affected by what is taking place. It does not include a mere busybody who is interfering in things which do not concern him; but it includes any person who has a genuine grievance because something has been done or may be done which affects him: see *Attorney-General of the Gambia* v. *N'Jie* [1961] A.C. 617 and *Maurice* v. *London County Council* [1964] 2 Q.B. 362, 378. The taxicab owners' association here have certainly a locus standi to apply for relief.

We have considered what the actual relief should be. On the whole we think it is sufficient in this case to let prohibition issue. The order should prohibit the corporation or their committee or sub-committee from acting on the resolutions of November 16, 1971, December 8, 1971, and December 22, 1971; in particular, from granting any further number of licences pursuant to section 37 of the Town Police Clauses Act 1847 over and above the 300 currently existing, without first hearing any representations which may be made by or on behalf of any persons interested therein, including the applicants in this case and any other matters relevant thereto, including the undertaking recorded in the town clerk's letter of August 11. If prohibition goes in those terms, it means that the relevant committee, sub-committee and the corporation themselves can look at the matter afresh. They will hear all those interested and come to a right conclusion as to what is to be done about the number of taxicabs on the streets of Liverpool.

I would say that the trouble has arisen because the corporation was advised that this undertaking was not binding on them, whereas it certainly was binding unless overridden by some imperative public interest. I am sure that all concerned have been acting as best they can; but nevertheless prohibition in my view should issue so as to prevent the corporation committee acting on those resolutions ...

ROSKILL L.J. ... It has been said by Mr Morland on behalf of the council that the undertaking given by Alderman Craine does not bind the council. He has sought to persuade this court that that is so because to oblige the council now to honour that undertaking would be to fetter the corporation's freedom of action in the performance of its statutory duty to consider other applications for licences after the respective dates mentioned in the resolution of December 22, 1971. It is said that the corporation having lawfully passed that resolution, no prior undertaking, however clearly given, however much in conflict with the resolution, can be allowed to stand in the way of implementing that resolution. It is said that this court should refuse to grant the relief claimed because the court is under as great a duty to protect the interests of possible future licensees as to protect the interests of those who at present hold a monopoly of the existing licences. For my part, I do not think this court is under any duty to protect the interests of either rival group of licensees or would-be licensees. Its duty is to see that in dealing with the conflicting interests the council acts fairly between them. It is for the council and not for this court to determine what the future policy should be in relation to the number of taxi licences which are to be issued in the City of Liverpool ... The power of the court to intervene is not limited, as once was thought, to those cases where the function in question is judicial or quasi-judicial. The modern cases show that this court will intervene more widely than in the past. Even where the function is said to be administrative, the court will not hesitate to intervene in a suitable case if it is necessary in order to secure fairness. It has been said by Mr Morland that there is no precedent for this court to intervene and enforce an undertaking which he claims to be of no legal effect and thus prevent the council giving effect to delegated legislation of the validity of which there is not doubt. For my part, I am not prepared to be deterred by the absence of precedent if in principle the case is one in which the court should interfere. The long legal history of the former prerogative writs and of their modern counterparts, the orders of prohibition, mandamus and certiorari, shows that their application has always been flexible as the need for their use in differing social conditions down the centuries has changed. If I thought that the effect of granting to the applicants the relief sought was to prevent the council validly using those powers which Parliament has conferred upon it, I would refuse relief. But that is not the present case. It seems to me that the relief claimed will in the end, as Mr Morland in effect ultimately conceded, assist the council to perform rather than inhibit the performance of its statutory duties. Lord Denning M.R. has referred to *Birkdale District Electric Supply Co. Ltd.* v. *Southport Corporation* [1926] A.C. 355. The decision of this court in *William Cory & Son Ltd.* v. *London Corporation* [1951] 2 K.B. 476, shows that a local authority such as the council cannot contractually fetter the performance of its statutory duties. But the present case is not such a case... To stop temporarily action on the resolution of December 22, 1971, is not in any way to perpetuate that undertaking; nor should it embarrass the council in carrying out its statutory duties. The council must make up its own mind what policy it wishes to follow; but before doing so it must act fairly to all concerned, to present licensees and to would-be licensees and to others also who may be interested. In the end it may adhere to its present policy or it may not; but in my view this court should not allow the undertaking given by Alderman Craine on August 4 and repeated by the town clerk with the council's authority in the letter of August 11 to be set at naught. The council can at some future date, if it wishes, depart from that undertaking; but if it does so, it must do so after due and proper consideration of the representations of all those interested.

SIR GORDON WILLMER delivered a concurring judgment.

II. PUBLIC LOCAL INQUIRIES

ERRINGTON v. *MINISTER OF HEALTH*

[1935] 1 K.B. 249

Court of Appeal

As part of a general policy of slum clearance, the Housing Act, 1930, authorised local authorities to propose clearance orders for areas containing houses unfit for human habitation if they were satisfied that demolition of the houses was the only way of dealing with the areas satisfactorily. S. 2 of the Act required the authority to submit any clearance order which it made to the Minister of Health for confirmation. Before submitting the order the authority was required to give notice of its intentions in newspapers circulating in the district and to serve notices on the owners, lessees and occupiers of the houses affected. If any of the latter objected, para. 4 of the First Schedule of the Act provided that the Minister ' shall, before confirming the order, cause a local inquiry to be held and shall consider any objection not withdrawn and the report of the person who held the inquiry . . .'

In February 1933 Jarrow Corporation made a clearance order to which Errington and others objected on the grounds, *inter alia*, that the houses were not unfit for human habitation; that the expense to the local authority if the order were confirmed would be more than the town could bear; that no adequate provision had been made, as the statute required, for the rehousing of members of the working class at present living in the houses; and that demolition was not the most satisfactory way of dealing with the area.

The Minister caused a local inquiry to be held. Having considered the report of the inspector who had conducted the inquiry, Ministry officials were inclined to agree with the objectors that it would be more sensible and more in keeping with the corporation's resources if further consideration were given, in consultation with the owners, to the possibility of rendering the houses fit for habitation. The corporation were, however, unwilling to do this and urged the Ministry to receive a deputation to consider the matter. This proposal was rejected by the Ministry on the ground that ' in view of the quasi-judicial function which the Minister has to exercise there would be considerable difficulty in the way of receiving a formal deputation representing one side only '. Eventually, however, officials from the Ministry, together with the inspector who had conducted the inquiry, did visit Jarrow, and inspected the site with the officials of the Corporation, but without meeting the owners. In addition they received written evidence from officials of the corporation who had not been called as witnesses at the inquiry. The Minister subsequently confirmed the clearance order.

The owners applied to the court to have the order quashed under s. 11 (3) of the Act, on the ground that the requirements of the Act had not been complied with. Swift J. held that the Minister was not acting as a judge deciding an issue between the parties but as an administrative officer performing a statutory duty, and that, provided he followed the statutory procedure, he could inform his mind in whatever way he liked. He therefore dismissed the application. The owners appealed.

GREER L.J. . . . The powers of the Minister are contained in the Act and the First Schedule to the Act and under those powers he could, if no objection be taken on behalf of the persons interested in the property, make an Order confirming the order made by the local authority; and in so far as the Minister deals with the matter of the confirmation of a closing order in the absence of objection by the owners it is clear to me, and I think to my brethren, that he would be acting in a ministerial or administrative capacity, and would be entitled to make such inquiries as he thought necessary to enable him to make up his mind whether it was in the public interest that the Order should be made. But the position, in my judgment, is different where objections are taken by those interested in the properties which will be affected by the order if confirmed and carried out. It seems to me that in deciding whether a closing order should be made in spite of the objections which have been raised by the owners the Minister should be regarded as exercising quasi-judicial functions. The effect of the closing order if confirmed would be to diminish greatly the value of the property owned by the objecting parties, and the decision of the Minister is a decision relating to the rights of the objecting parties and, in my view, it is a decision in respect of which he is exercising quasi-judicial functions.

Now it seems to me that if, as I think, the Ministry were acting in a quasi-judicial capacity they were doing what a semi-judicial body cannot do, namely, hearing evidence from one side in the absence of the other side, and viewing the property and forming their own views about the property without giving the owners of the property the opportunity of arguing that the views which the Ministry were inclined to take were such as could be readily dealt with by means of repairs and alterations to the buildings. Whether the surveyor was one of the officials, or whether the borough engineer was one of the officials, we do not know; but we do know this, that by a letter of February 24, 1934, which was sent by the Town Clerk to the Ministry of Health, the views of the borough engineer were put before the Minister before the Minister gave his decision. The borough engineer had not been called at the public inquiry. Those who represented the owners had not had the opportunity of cross-examining him, testing the value of his opinion, and representing to the Minister through the Inspector that no weight should be attached to his view. The view of the borough engineer is expressed in the letter from the Town Clerk to the Ministry on February 24, 1934: ' In any event this does not arise as the Engineer advises that the foundations and structure of the houses, generally speaking, precludes the possibility of their reconstruction into dwelling houses reasonably fit for human habitation.' That is a view which is hardly consistent with the view which had been expressed on behalf of the Borough Council by the barrister who appeared for them at the inquiry. It is an additional reason being urged by the Council on the advice of the borough engineer in order to put pressure upon the Ministry to confirm the order which has been made by them. . .

In order to see what the requirements of the Act are one must look to the First Schedule to the Act. Para. 4 of the Schedule says: ' If no objection is duly made ... the Minister may, if he thinks fit, confirm the order with or without modification.' ... The paragraph goes on: ' but in any other case he shall, before confirming the order, cause a public local inquiry to be held and shall consider any objection not withdrawn and the report of the person who held the inquiry, and may then confirm the order, either with or without modification '. It seems to me that that involves the proposition that the matters there mentioned are the only matters which he is entitled to consider, and that if, instead of directing his mind solely to those matters, he takes into consideration evidence which might have been, but was not, given at the public inquiry, but was given *ex parte* afterwards without the owners having any opportunity whatever to deal with that evidence, then it seems to me that the confirming Order was not within the powers of the Act. . . In my judgment it is true to say that an order made by a quasi-judicial officer based on materials which are not the materials referred to in para. 4 of the First Schedule is an order which is not within the powers of the Act, having regard to the proposition which has been established in common law that a quasi-judicial officer in exercising his powers must do it in accordance with the rules of natural justice, that is to say, he must hear both sides and must not hear one side in the absence of the other.

For these reasons I have come to the conclusion, though the point is not free from difficulty, that we ought to . . . quash the confirming Order made by the Minister of Health.

MAUGHAM and ROCHE L.JJ. delivered concurring judgments.

Appeal allowed. Order of Minister quashed

B. JOHNSON & CO. (BUILDERS) LTD. v. *MINISTER OF HEALTH*　　　　　　　　[1947] 2 All E.R. 395

Court of Appeal

This was another challenge to a compulsory purchase order which had been confirmed by the Minister after a public local inquiry. On this occasion the owners complained that the Minister in reaching his decision had wrongly taken into account correspondence with the local authority before the public inquiry which had not been revealed to the owners. They argued that this was inconsistent with the Minister's quasi-judicial functions under the statute.

LORD GREENE M.R. The duty placed on the Minister with regard to objections is to consider them before confirming the order. He is also to consider the report of the person who held the inquiry. Having done that, his functions are laid down by the last words of the paragraph, *viz.*, ' and may then confirm the order either with or without modification '. Those words are important, because they make it clear that it is to the Minister that Parliament has committed the decision whether he will or will not confirm the order after he has done all that the statute requires him to do. There is nothing in that paragraph, or anywhere else in the Act, which imposes on the Minister any obligation with regard to the objections, save the obligation to consider them. He is not bound to base his decision on any conclusion that he comes to with regard to the objections, and that must be so when one gives a moment's thought to the situation. The decision whether to confirm or not must be made in relation to questions of policy, and the Minister, in deciding whether to confirm or not, will, like every Minister entrusted with administrative duties, weigh up the considerations which are to affect his mind, the preponderating factor in many, if not all, cases being that of public policy, having regard to all the facts of the case . . . [T]he functions of the Minister in carrying these provisions into operation are fundamentally administrative functions. In carrying them out he has the duty which every Minister owes to the Crown, *viz.*, to perform his functions fairly and honestly and to the best of his ability. But his functions are administrative functions, subject only to the qualification that, at a particular stage and for a particular and limited purpose, there is superimposed on his administrative character a character which is loosely described as ' quasi-judicial ' . . . The language which has always been construed as giving rise to the obligations, whatever they may be, implied in the words ' quasi-judicial ' is to be found in the duty to consider the objections, which, as I have said, is superimposed on a process of Ministerial action which is essentially administrative. That process may begin in all sorts of manners – the collection of information, the ascertainment of facts, and the consideration of representations made from all sorts of quarters, and so forth, long before any question of objections can arise under the procedure laid down by the Act. While acting at that stage, to carry the Act into effect or for purposes relevant to it and bearing on it, the Minister is an executive officer of government, and nothing else. The administrative character in which he acts reappears at a later stage because, after considering the objections, which may be regarded as the culminating point of his quasi-judicial functions, there follows something which again, in my view, is purely administrative, *viz.*, the decision whether or not to confirm the order. That decision must be an administrative decision, because it is not to be based purely on the view that he forms of the objections, *vis-à-vis* the desires of the local authority, but is to be guided by his view as to the policy which in the circumstances he ought to pursue. . . [O]n the substantive matter, *viz.*, whether the order should be confirmed or not, there is a third party who is not present, *viz.*, the public, and it is the function of the Minister to consider the rights and the interests of the public...[I]t is completely wrong to treat the controversy between objector and local authority as a controversy which covers the whole of the ground. It is in respect of the public interest that the discretion that Parliament has given to the Minister comes into operation. It may well be that, on considering the objections, the Minister may find that they are reasonable and that the facts alleged in them are true, but, nevertheless, he may decide that he will overrule them. His action in so deciding is a purely administrative action, based on his conceptions as to what public policy demands. His views on that matter he must, if necessary, defend in Parliament, but he cannot be called on to defend them in the courts. The objections, in other words, may fail to produce the result desired by the objector, not because the objector has been defeated by the local authority in a sort of litigation, but because the objections have been overruled by the Minister's decision as to what the public interest demands. . . .

The last phrase about which I might say a word . . . is the phrase ' duty to act fairly.' As I have said, every Minister of the Crown is under a duty, constitutionally, to the King to perform his functions honestly and fairly and to the best of his ability, but his failure to do so, speaking generally, is not a matter with which the courts are concerned. As a Minister, if he acts unfairly, his action may be challenged and criticised in Parliament. It cannot be challenged and criticised in the courts unless he has acted unfairly in another sense, *viz.*, in the sense of having, while performing quasi-judicial functions, acted in a way which no person performing such functions, in the opinion of the court, ought to act . . .

Returning to the present case, certain matters are common ground. It is not disputed by the respondents that the Minister, in coming to his decision whether to confirm or not to confirm a compulsory purchase order, is entitled to have his mind informed in a number of ways. In other words, he is not limited to material contained in the objections – not limited to arguments, evidence, and considerations put forward by the local authority for the purpose of the considerations of the objections, or put forward by the objectors themselves. It is obvious to anyone who has any familiarity with the operations of government departments that matters of high public policy, such as this, are, or may be, under constant consideration and review by the necessary Minister. The problem does not, so to speak, arrive suddenly out of the blue by the putting forward by the local authority of a compulsory purchase order for confirmation. The housing conditions in great cities are the subject of continuous consideration, not merely by one Ministry, but by several. Information may have arrived, reports may have been obtained, representations and arguments may have been put forward by other Ministries, and in a great many cases one would expect to find a fairly bulky file, much of which, if not the whole of it, may bear on some particular application. Obviously, it would be absurd to say that a Minister, in considering whether to confirm the compulsory purchase order, must exclude from his mind information and considerations which have come before him in that sort of way. It is on the obligation alleged, *viz.*, to disclose information of that kind, that the present controversy turns. It is not unfair to say that, generally speaking, the idea that a Minister can be compelled to disclose to anybody information of that kind, which he has obtained as a purely administrative person, is alien to our whole conception of government in this country...

It is further common ground, and indeed, it is clearly established by authority, that statements made by, or obtained from, either of the two quasi-parties to the quasi-*lis* while it is pending, *viz.*, the local authority and the objector, must be disclosed to the other quasi-party. Information so provided and put before the Minister is information given to enable him to do the thing he is doing at that stage, considering the objections, and it has always been naturally said that information of that kind must be disclosed to the other party to give that other party an opportunity of converting it, or making comments upon it. Does that obligation extend to a matter brought to the knowledge of the Minister before he assumes the quasi-judicial role, when his functions are purely administrative and his action in receiving the information and putting it in his file is a purely administrative action? The objectors maintain that, subject to certain qualifications which I will mention, material which is obtained and considered by the Minister and may effect his decision whether or not to give effect to the objections ought to be made available to the objectors, even if it was obtained long before any objections were or could be made. That proposition, if accepted, would involve remarkable results. The Minister may have – if I may describe the thing graphically – in his office a file (it may be a very large file) containing matters bearing on the particular case, or matters bearing generally, for instance, on the state of working class housing in a great city without reference to any particular plot of land. There may be a report which the Minister has obtained as to the state of working class houses in a particular city which makes it perfectly clear that, as a matter of public policy, he ought to do everything he possibly can to make land available for the construction of working class houses. A report of that kind may well induce him to say, when he comes to consider the objections: ' This objector has got, from his point of view, a very strong case. He is going to be dispossessed, and it will mean a great hardship on him,' and matters of that kind, but he may add : ' I have got in my file a report which I obtained a year ago as to housing conditions in this city, and the matter contained in that report makes it imperative, in my view, to confirm this order, so as to carry out what I consider to be the proper public policy.' A report of that kind would, clearly, be relevant to the objections, because, in the case I put, the report is the thing that has induced the Minister to overrule the objections, however sound in the abstract, and taken by themselves, he may consider them to be. The argument, therefore, if carried to that extreme point, would necessarily, as it seems to me, involve the disclosure to the objectors, and to the local authority, of the Minister's file. That is a proposition from which even counsel for the respondents shrank, and he . . . limited the kind of information, the disclosure of which he said was compulsory, to communications received from the other quasi-party to the quasi-*lis*. . . [B]ut that will not do because the principle on which he bases that limited proposition is one which leads inevitably, if it be right, to the acceptance of the larger proposition, and that larger proposition is one which, I venture to think, is quite unacceptable.

. . . I may add one further matter. If material in writing were to be disclosed, why not material which is not in writing? Logically, the proposition would involve that the Minister ought to communicate to the objectors and the local authority, or to the objectors, matters which he had ascertained, perhaps at conferences, long before the compulsory purchase order was ever on the stocks, matter which was locked up in his own recollection. Failure to communicate that to the objector would, on counsel's view, and on the logic of his argument, be just as detrimental as failure to disclose a minute of such an interview, if there happened to be one on the file.

On principle, having regard to the considerations I have endeavoured to express, it appears to me that the obligation implied by the use of the word ' quasi-judicial ' does not extend beyond what HENN COLLINS, J., described in what, if I may say so, appears to me to be an extremely happy phrase in an earlier case. He had formulated it, clearly, with care, and it seems to me to bring out the distinction between the administrative and the executive aspects of the matter. I quote from his decision in *Miller* v. *Minister of Health*, also a case of a compulsory purchase order. There information had been obtained by the Minister in his administrative capacity, including information regarding the views of other government departments as to the suitability of the site in question. HENN COLLINS, J., said in a paragraph which I find very helpful ([1946] 1 K.B. 628):

> ' I think one must remember in approaching these matters that the question what a Minister shall or shall not do when acting administratively is not one that can be determined on any principle of law, nor yet on any principle, as I see it, of natural justice, as between the Minister and any one member of the community. The Minister, acting in his administrative capacity is governed by considerations of ex-

pediency only. He has to decide – ultimately, I suppose, subject to the review and governance of Parliament – what in his view is best for the community. No principle of natural justice as between any individual and the Minister of the Crown has any place in that kind of administration, but when questions as to whether those administrative powers should be exercised have been referred to him by Act of Parliament, in this case the Housing Act, 1936, at that point he has to consider judicially the matter that is so brought before him. That does not mean, as the authorities have shown, that he is not to use any knowledge which has come to him, so to speak, extra-judicially but all the material which has been formulated for his judicial consideration must be [made] available to him on both sides. That is the meaning of his acting with natural justice in a judicial capacity '. . .

COHEN L.J. delivered a concurring judgment. ASQUITH L.J. agreed.

Appeal allowed

FRANKLIN AND OTHERS v. MINISTER OF TOWN AND COUNTRY PLANNING [1948] A.C. 87

House of Lords

The New Towns Act, 1946, provided: ' 1 (1) If the Minister is satisfied, after consultation with any local authorities who appear to him to be concerned that it is expedient in the national interest that any area of land should be developed as a new town . . . he may make an order designating that area as the site of the proposed new town.' The Act further provided, in the First Schedule, that the Minister should in the first instance prepare and publish a draft of the order and para. 3 stated: ' If any objection is duly made . . . the Minister shall, before making the order, cause a public local inquiry to be held with respect thereto, and shall consider the report of the person by whom the inquiry was held.' The Minister published a draft order designating Stevenage as the site of a new town in August 1946. A public local inquiry was held in October. In November the Minister informed the objectors that he intended to make the order. They applied to the court to have the order quashed. They argued *inter alia* that the Minister had made it clear before he considered the objections that he intended Stevenage to be the first new town and that he was biased in his consideration of the objections,[27] and

---

[27] In a speech in Stevenage in May 1946, after recalling the way in which plans for the relief of the density of population in London had developed and setting out the advantages of Stevenage as the site of a new town, the Minister said: ' The New Towns Bill, published twelve days ago, will receive its Second Reading on Wednesday . . . In anticipation of the passage of the Bill – and I have no doubt that it will go through – certain preliminary steps have been taken regarding Stevenage by way of discussion with some of the local authorities concerned . . . I want to carry out a daring exercise in town planning – (Jeers). It is no good your jeering: it is

secondly, that the Act impliedly required the Minister to consider the objections fairly and properly and to give a fair and proper effect to that consideration and this he had failed to do. For his part the Minister swore an affidavit in which he stated that he had ' personally carefully considered all the objections made by the objectors . . . together with the submissions made and evidence given on their behalf.' [28]

LORD THANKERTON. . . . In my opinion, no judicial, or quasi-judicial, duty was imposed on the respondent, and any reference to judicial duty, or bias, is irrelevant in the present case. The respondent's duties under s. 1 of the Act and sch. I thereto are, in my opinion, purely administrative, but the Act prescribes certain methods of or steps in, discharge of that duty. It is obvious that, before making the draft order, which must contain a definite proposal to designate the area concerned as the site of a new town, the respondent must have made elaborate inquiry into the matter and have consulted any local authorities who appear to him to be concerned, and obviously other departments of the Government, such as the Ministry of Health, would naturally require to be consulted. It would seem, accordingly, that the respondent was required to satisfy himself that it was a sound scheme before he took the serious step of issuing a draft order. It seems clear also, that the purpose of

---

going to be done – (*Applause and boos*). (*Cries of* " Dictator ".) . . . The project will go forward. It will do so more smoothly and more successfully with your help and co-operation. Stevenage will in a short time become world famous – (*Laughter*). People from all over the world will come to Stevenage to see how we here in this country are building for the new way of life . . . Local authorities will be consulted all the way through. But we have a duty to perform, and I am not going to be deterred from that duty. While I will consult as far as possible all the local authorities, at the end, if people are fractious and unreasonable, I shall have to carry out my duty – (*Voice*: Gestapo!).'

[28] ' Before causing the said order of 11th November to be made, I personally carefully considered all the objections made by the objectors including the present applicants, together with the submissions made and evidence given on their behalf as appearing in the said transcript. I also carefully considered the report of the said Arnold Morris [the inspector]. Prior to preparing the draft of the said order, I had before me, and had considered, a mass of information collected by my Ministry, including the report of the Royal Commission on the Distribution of Industrial Population, 1940, Sir Patrick Abercrombie's Greater London Plan, 1944, and the reports of the New Towns Committee dated 21st January, 9th April, and 25th July 1946. I had also consulted with all local authorities who appeared to me to be concerned, and also with the Ministry of Agriculture and the Ministry of Health. Subsequent to the preparation of the draft order and up to the time when I caused the said order to be made on 11th November 1946, I obtained no further information, and in deciding to make the said order I had regard to nothing other than the matters set out in par. 8 hereof, and the information above referred to. I came to the conclusion that it was expedient in the national interest that the proposed site should be developed as a new town ' (176 L.T. 314).

inviting objections, and, where they are not withdrawn, of having a public inquiry, to be held by someone other than the respondent, to whom that person reports, was for the further information of the respondent, in order to the final consideration of the soundness of the scheme of the designation; and it is important to note that the development of the site, after the order is made, is primarily the duty of the development corporation established under s. 2 of the Act. I am of opinion that no judicial duty is laid on the respondent in discharge of these statutory duties, and that the only question is whether he has complied with the statutory directions to appoint a person to hold the public inquiry, and to consider that person's report. On this contention of the appellants no suggestion is made that the public inquiry was not properly conducted, nor is there any criticism of the report by Mr Morris. In such a case the only ground of challenge must be either that the respondent did not in fact consider the report and the objections, of which there is here no evidence, or that his mind was so foreclosed that he gave no genuine consideration to them, which is the case made by the appellants. . .

My Lords, I could wish that the use of the word ' bias ' should be confined to its proper sphere. Its proper significance, in my opinion, is to denote a departure from the standard of even-handed justice which the law requires from those who occupy judicial office, or those who are commonly regarded as holding a quasi-judicial office, such as an arbitrator . . . But, in the present case, the respondent having no judicial duty, the only question is what the respondent actually did, that is, whether in fact he did genuinely consider the report and the objections . . .

I am clearly of opinion that nothing said by the respondent was inconsistent with the discharge of his statutory duty, when subsequently objections were lodged, and the local public inquiry took place, followed by the report of that inquiry, genuinely to consider the report and the objections. [His Lordship quoted the passages in the speech relied on by the appellants : and continued :] My Lords, these passages in a speech, which was of a political nature, and of the kind familiar in a speech on Second Reading, demonstrate (1) the speaker's view that the Bill would become law, that Stevenage was a most suitable site and should be that first scheme in the operation, and that the Stevenage project would go forward, and (2) the speaker's reaction to the hostile interruptions of a section of the audience. In my opinion, these passages are not inconsistent with an intention to carry out any statutory duty imposed on him by Parliament, although he intended to press for the enactment of the Bill, and thereafter to carry out the duties thereby involved, including the consideration of objections which were neither fractious nor unreasonable.

I am, therefore, of opinion that the ... contention of the appellants fails, in that they have not established either that in the respondent's speech he had forejudged any genuine consideration of the objections or that he had not genuinely considered the objections at the later stage when they were submitted to him. . .

LORD PORTER, LORD UTHWATT, LORD DU PARCQ and LORD NORMAND concurred.   *Appeal dismissed*

The report of the Franks Committee, 1957
Administrative procedures involving an enquiry or hearing
268. . . . [I]t is relevant to examine what appears to have been the intention of the legislature in enacting that in all these cases there should be a special procedure for the making and hearing of objections. The various planning procedures are of relatively recent origin, but acquisition of land by public authorities has a longer history, and the procedures which now govern it have been developed, by a series of changes, from the procedure on a Private Bill. In the last century a public authority or an undertaking such as a railway company, wishing to acquire land for its purposes, had always to promote a Private Bill, the procedure for which provides for the lodging of objections and for the hearing of the parties by a Parliamentary Committee. The final decision is, of course, that of Parliament, though the Ministers concerned have an opportunity of influencing that decision by submitting a report or evidence to the Committee and by using the Government's majority on the floor of the House. In the course of time it was decided – because of the extension of governmental responsibilities and the resulting increased need to acquire land for public purposes, and also because of the expense of procedure by Private Bill – to take these matters outside the detailed control of Parliament and to entrust the final decision to a Minister.

269. The intention of the legislature in providing for an enquiry or hearing in certain circumstances appears to have been twofold: to ensure that the interests of the citizens closely affected should be protected by the grant to them of a statutory right to be heard in support of their objections, and to ensure that thereby the Minister should be better informed of the facts of the case.

270. In practice third parties are generally permitted to take part in public local enquiries, but in an acquisition case the Minister is only bound to hold a hearing or enquiry when objections are sustained by persons directly interested in the land affected by the proposals. He is not bound to do so if either no objections are raised or the objections raised come from parties without a direct interest in the land or they relate solely to compensation.

271. Although the statutory requirements are merely to hear and consider objections, it must surely be true that an objection cannot reasonably be considered as a thing in itself, in isolation from what is objected to. The consideration of objections thus involves the testing of an issue, though it must be remembered that it may be only a part of the issue which the Minister will ultimately have to determine. If so, then the case against which objections are raised should be presented and developed with sufficient detail and argument to permit the proper weighing of the one against the other. . .

277. It is with these considerations in mind that we shall seek to apply the three principles of openness, fairness and impartiality – to which we have referred in Part I – to the second part of our terms of reference, but we must recall that the third of these three principles, impartiality, cannot be applied here without qualification.

The procedure before the enquiry

281. We consider that the statutory requirements should, where necessary, be amended to compel acquiring and planning authorities to give full particulars of their case in good time before the enquiry . . . in the form of a written statement . . . [A]ny such statement should also summarise the views of any Government Departments or other public authority which the acquiring or planning authority has consulted in the matter. . .

287. We consider that fair play requires that, whenever possible, some statement of the ministerial policy relevant to the particular case should also be made available before the enquiry. We recognise that it will not in all cases be possible for the Minister to make a statement of particular policy, such, for example, as that he is most unlikely to agree to permit development in a ' green belt ' or the building of new offices in London. The statement may often have to consist of an outline of the general approach which the Minister is likely to take in deciding the matter or of the factors which he will take into account. But something should be possible in many cases. If the inspector is asked by the Minister to see that certain points are brought out at the enquiry, this should be disclosed in the statement of policy. When the Minister himself is the acquiring authority the statement of his case as acquiring authority should be sufficiently full to indicate the considerations of policy involved, and no separate statement of policy should then be necessary.

Procedure at the enquiry
The exposition of the case of the public authority

307. . . . [T]he scope of the enquiry should include some examination of the case of the initiating or planning authority. . .

308. ... [W]hether proposals are initiated by a Minister or by a local authority ... the proposals should be fully explained and supported by oral evidence. . .

309. We do not, however, intend by these recommendations that all matters of ministerial policy should be open to discussion at the enquiry. . . [T]he Minister should be free to direct in writing that the whole or any part of his statement of policy should not be open to discussion. . .

Inspectors

292. The question whether inspectors should or should not be independent of the Departments concerned is controversial . . .

293. The main arguments in favour of departmental inspectors are as follows. First, and most important, it is argued that a Minister is responsible for the final decision and that that decision must often be influenced by considerations of Government policy. The ideal would be for the Minister himself to hold the enquiry and thus hear the evidence at first hand. . . [T]he next best course is for one of his own officers, who can be kept in touch with developments in policy, to perform this function. It is further contended that it may be difficult for the Minister to accept full responsibility for a decision taken in his name if the report on the enquiry, which is an important and sometimes vital part of the advice on which the decision is based, is not made by someone within his Department.

294. The second argument is that, particularly in the case of the Ministry of Housing and Local Government, the number of enquiries is sufficient ... to make essential a corps of full-time inspectors, if enquiries are to be arranged and completed with reasonable promptitude.

295. Third, it is argued that highly technical considerations frequently arise, particularly in planning enquiries, which make it advisable for the inspector to be a person constantly engaged in this kind of work and therefore a member of the Department concerned.

296. Lastly, it is argued that the establishment of a corps of independent inspectors, particularly if responsibility for it were given to the Lord Chancellor ... would foster the impression that the process was judicial. It might thus increase rather than decrease public dissatisfaction, the public being the more likely to expect the final decision to be based solely upon the evidence at the enquiry and the report following the enquiry or indeed to expect the inspector to act as a judge and give a decision himself. If, as an alternative ... independent persons were appointed *ad hoc* for each enquiry the whole process might be lengthened because of their unfamiliarity with the conduct of enquiries

and their inability, through lack of knowledge of departmental policy, to give the Minister the kind of advice which he most needs . . .

298. The main arguments advanced in favour of independent inspectors are as follows. First, it is argued that public confidence in the procedure . . . would be increased. . .

299. Second, it is argued that the need for the inspector to be conversant with departmental policy has been exaggerated and that it would be equally satisfactory if the considerations of policy thought to be relevant were placed before the inspector in departmental evidence given at the enquiry. As the Minister would continue to make the final decision, policy would, where necessary, prevail.

300. Third, it is pointed out that several Departments employ independent inspectors and find this arrangement satisfactory.

301. Fourth, it is argued that it would be less embarrassing for Departments to give oral evidence before an independent inspector than before a departmental inspector.

302. Finally, it is said that it would be less difficult to publish the report of an independent inspector than of a departmental inspector, since as an independent person he could more freely comment upon the evidence given, and that it would not be so embarrassing for the Minister to give a decision differing from any published recommendations . . .

303. We recommend that inspectors be placed under the control of a Minister not directly concerned with the subject-matter of their work. This would most appropriately be the Lord Chancellor in England and Wales. Some may say that this would be a change in name only, but . . . we are convinced that here the appearance is what matters. This change, by no longer identifying the inspector in the minds of the objectors with the Department of the deciding Minister, would emphasise impartiality at an important stage of the adjudication and thus do much to allay public misgiving. We see in this no obstacle to the inspectors being kept in close contact with developments of policy in the Departments responsible for the subject-matter of the enquiries.

Inspectors' reports
The case for publication

330. The first argument advanced in favour of publication is that fair play for the citizen requires that he should know how the inspector has reported to the Minister the course of the enquiry and the inspector's assessment of the case in the light of the enquiry . . . [I]t is argued that there is little point in providing for a special procedure in these cases if the process is thereafter secret except for the Minister's final decision.

331. The second argument is that publication would serve to make

these procedures and the ministerial powers which lie behind them better understood and more acceptable to the public generally, since the degree of openness would be increased and the application of national policy to particular local circumstances would be more easily appreciated.

332. The third argument is that the deciding Minister might be expected to seek to reduce as far as possible the chances of having to disagree with the published findings or recommendations of the inspector and would consequently be inclined to present at the enquiry evidence which, it is suggested, is now withheld until the later and secret stage.

333. Fourthly, it is argued that publication, particularly if it took place before the decision and the parties were given an opportunity to seek to correct alleged mistakes of fact in the report, would negative the argument for a formal appeal on fact against the Minister's decision . . .

334. Fifthly, it has been pointed out that . . . the Ministry of Education, whose practice it is to publish inspectors' reports, does not appear to suffer any embarrassment thereby . . .

335. The main arguments against publication are as follows. First, it is argued that the report of the inspector . . . is but one of perhaps many matters which the Minister must take into consideration in arriving at his decision, and that to publish this alone would give a misleading impression and indeed might increase public dissatisfaction in those cases where the Minister found it necessary to differ from the inspector's recommendations.

336. Second, it is argued that publication would tend to transform the inspector's recommendations into a provisional decision, which the public could then set against the final decision of the Minister, and that the Minister ought not to be exposed to the difficulty and embarrassment which would arise from the disclosure of differences between his decision and the recommendations of the inspector. Even if inspectors were placed under the general charge of the Lord Chancellor they would remain civil servants, and emphasis is laid upon the importance of preserving the confidential relationship between Ministers and their official advisers. Any argument based on the practice of the Ministry of Education in publishing reports is, it is said, irrelevant, since its enquiries are carried out by persons from outside the Government service. Moreover, the issue at its enquiries is generally one of site and not of policy, the need for a school having already been separately established.

337. The third argument is that there is in fact no evidence of widespread demand by the public to see inspectors' reports and that the expense of publication in all cases would consequently not be justified . . .

338. Fourth, it is argued that the knowledge that their reports would be published might lead inspectors to be less frank and therefore less helpful to the Minister in their comments and recommendations. Reports might also be completed less promptly because of the greater care needed in drafting.

339. The fifth argument is that since a report must necessarily involve considerable summarisation, its publication would be unlikely to satisfy all parties that they had been adequately reported. . .

343. Our general conclusion is that the right course is to publish the inspector's report. Apart from the arguments in favour of publication to which we have referred we are impressed by the need for some further control beyond that which Parliament, in theory, though not always in practice, can exercise. There is no doubt that publicity is in itself an effective check against arbitrary action. On the assumption that these cases will continue to be decided by Ministers after an enquiry, complete publicity at all stages is impossible, but we think that it should be insisted upon wherever it is possible. Moreover, the publication of the report seems to flow naturally from the fact that the enquiry itself is held in public.

344. Accordingly we recommend that the complete text of the inspector's report should accompany the Minister's letter of decision and should also be available on request centrally and locally.

345. Additionally, we recommend that the parties should have an opportunity, if they so desire, to propose corrections of fact to . . . the inspector's report before the report is tendered to the Minister.

New factual evidence after the enquiry

347. One of the main causes of dissatisfaction at this stage is that after the enquiry, when the parties no longer have any further influence upon the course of events, fresh evidence or new opinions may be sought by or placed before the Department of the deciding Minister, and that this new matter may well determine the final decision . . .

350. We think . . . that it is both desirable and possible to draw a distinction at the post-enquiry stage between new factual evidence on the one hand and advice on policy on the other. We recommend that the Minister should be under a statutory obligation to submit to the parties concerned, for their observations, any factual evidence, whether from his own or another Department or from an outside source, which he obtains after the enquiry. In the definition of factual evidence for the purposes of this recommendation we include expert opinion on matters of fact but not expert assistance in the evaluation of technical evidence given at the enquiry. There may be cases in which it is clearly desirable to give the parties an opportunity to cross-examine on the new evidence.

Reasoned decisions

351. There is a consensus of opinion that the final letter of decision from or on behalf of the Minister should contain full reasons for the decision. . . It is a fundamental requirement of fair play that the parties concerned in one of these procedures should know at the end of the day why the particular decision has been taken. Where no reasons are given the individual may be forgiven for concluding that he has been the victim of arbitrary decision. The giving of full reasons is also important to enable those concerned to satisfy themselves that the prescribed procedure has been followed and to decide whether they wish to challenge the Minister's decision in the courts or elsewhere. Moreover, as we have already said in relation to tribunal decisions, a decision is apt to be better if the reasons for it have to be set out in writing because the reasons are then more likely to have been properly thought out.

352. Accordingly we recommend that the Minister's letter of decision should set out in full his findings and inferences of fact and the reasons for the decision. Since the letter will be accompanied by the full text of the inspector's report it will inevitably reveal where, if at all, the Minister differs from the inspector's findings or inferences of fact or recommendations and also reveal the reasons for those differences. Copies of the letter of decision, together with the full text of the inspector's report, should be made available on request centrally and locally. . .

[Report of the Committee on Tribunals and Inquiries. Cmnd. 218 (1957)]

THE TOWN AND COUNTRY PLANNING (INQUIRIES PROCEDURE) RULES, 1974 [S.I. No. 419]

Statements to be served before inquiry

6. . . . (2) Not later than 28 days before the date of the inquiry . . . the local planning authority shall—

(a) serve on the applicant and on the section 29 parties a written statement of any submission which the local planning authority propose to put forward at the inquiry . . .

(3) Where the Secretary of State or a local authority has given a direction restricting the grant of permission for the development for which application was made or a direction as to how the application was to be determined, the local planning authority shall mention this in their statement and shall include in the statement a copy of the direction and the reasons given for it . . . and where a government department or a local authority has expressed in writing to the local planning authority the view that the application should not be granted either wholly or in

part, or should be granted only subject to conditions . . . and the local planning authority propose to rely on such expression of view in their submissions at the inquiry, they shall include it in their statement. . .

(4) Where the local planning authority intend to refer to, or put in evidence, at the inquiry documents (including maps and plans), the authority's statement shall be accompanied by a list of such documents, together with a notice stating the times and place at which the documents may be inspected by the applicant and the section 29 parties; and the local planning authority shall afford them a reasonable opportunity to inspect and, where practicable, to take copies of the documents.

(5) The local planning authority shall afford any other person interested a reasonable opportunity to inspect and, where practicable, to take copies of any statement served by the Secretary of State under paragraph (1) or by the authority under paragraph (2) and of the other documents referred to in paragraph (4) as well as of any statement served on the authority by the applicant under paragraph (6) of this rule.

(6) The applicant shall, if so required by the Secretary of State, serve on the local planning authority, on the section 29 parties and on the Secretary of State, within such time before the inquiry as the Secretary of State may specify, a written statement of the submissions which he proposes to put forward at the inquiry; and such statement shall be accompanied by a list of any documents (including maps and plans) which the applicant intends to refer to or put in evidence at the inquiry, and he shall, if so required by the Secretary of State, afford the local planning authority and the section 29 parties a reasonable opportunity to inspect and, where practicable, to take copies of such documents.

Appearances at inquiry

7. (1) The persons entitled to appear at the inquiry shall be—
   (a) the applicant;
   (b) the local planning authority;
   (c) where the land is not in Greater London, the council of the administrative county in which the land is situated, if not the local planning authority;
   (d) where the land is not in Greater London, the council of the district in which the land is situated (or the Council of the Isles of Scilly, as the case may be), if not the local planning authority;
   (e) where the land is in a National Park, the National Park Committee (if any), if not the local planning authority;
   (f) any joint planning board constituted under section 1 of the Act (or any joint planning board or special planning board reconstituted under Part I of Schedule 17 to the Act of 1972), where that board is not the local planning authority;

(*g*) where the land is in an area designated as the site of a new town, the development corporation of the new town;

(*h*) section 29 parties;

(*i*) the council of the parish or community in which the land is situated, if that council has made representations to the local planning authority in respect of the application in pursuance of a provision of a development order made under section 24 of the Act;

(*j*) any persons on whom the Secretary of State has required notice to be served under rule 5 (2) (*b*).

(2) Any other person may appear at the inquiry at the discretion of the appointed person.

(3) A local authority may appear by their clerk or by any other officer appointed for the purpose by the local authority, or by counsel or solicitor; and any other person may appear on his own behalf or be represented by counsel, solicitor or any other person. . .

Representatives of government departments at inquiry

8. (1) Where either—

(*a*) the Secretary of State has given a direction restricting the grant of permission for the development for which application has been made, or

(*b*) a government department has expressed in writing the view that the application should not be granted either wholly or in part or should be granted only subject to conditions . . . and the local planning authority have included this view in their statement as required by paragraph (1) or (3) of rule 6,

the applicant may, not later than 14 days before the date of the inquiry apply in writing to the Secretary of State for a representative of his department or of the other government department concerned to be made available at the inquiry.

(2) Where an application is made to the Secretary of State . . . he shall make a representative of his department available to attend the inquiry or, as the case may be, transmit the application to the other department concerned who shall make a representative of that department available to attend the inquiry. . .

(4) A representative of a government department who, in pursuance of this rule, attends an inquiry on an appeal, shall be called as a witness by the local planning authority and shall state the reasons for the Secretary of State's direction or, as the case may be, the reasons for the view expressed by his department . . . and shall give evidence and be subject to cross-examination to the same extent as any other witness.

(5) Nothing in either of the last two foregoing paragraphs shall

require a representative of a government department to answer any question which in the opinion of the appointed person is directed to the merits of government policy and the appointed person shall disallow any such question.

Representatives of local authorities at inquiry

9. (1) Where any local authority has—

   (a) given to the local planning authority a direction restricting the grant of planning permission or a direction as to how an application for planning permission was to be determined; or

   (b) expressed in writing the view that an application for planning permission should not be granted wholly or in part or should be granted only subject to conditions, and the local planning authority have included this view in their statement, as required under rule 6 (3),

the applicant may, not later than 14 days before the date of the inquiry, apply in writing to the Secretary of State for a representative of the authority concerned to be made available to attend the inquiry.

(2) Where an application is made to the Secretary of State under the last foregoing paragraph he shall transmit the application to the authority concerned, who shall make a representative of the authority available to attend the inquiry.

(3) A representative of a local authority who, in pursuance of this rule, attends an inquiry shall be called as a witness by the local planning authority and shall state the reasons for the authority's direction or, as the case may be, the reasons for the view expressed by them and included in the local planning authority's statement under rule 6 (3) and shall give evidence and be subject to cross-examination to the same extent as any other witness.

Procedure at inquiry

10. (1) Except as otherwise provided in these Rules, the procedure at the inquiry shall be such as the appointed person shall in his discretion determine.

(2) Unless in any particular case the appointed person with the consent of the applicant otherwise determines, the applicant shall begin and shall have the right of final reply; and the other persons entitled or permitted to appear shall be heard in such order as the appointed person may determine.

(3) The applicant, the local planning authority and the section 29 parties shall be entitled to call evidence and cross-examine persons giving evidence, but any other person appearing at the inquiry may do so only to the extent permitted by the appointed person.

(4) The appointed person shall not require or permit the giving or production of any evidence, whether written or oral, which would be contrary to the public interest; but save as aforesaid and without prejudice to the provisions of rule 8 (5) any evidence may be admitted at the discretion of the appointed person, who may direct that documents tendered in evidence may be inspected by any person entitled or permitted to appear at the inquiry and that facilities be afforded him to take or obtain copies thereof.

(5) The appointed person may allow the local planning authority or the applicant, or both of them, to alter or add to the submissions contained in any statement served under paragraph (2) or (6) of rule 6, or to any list of documents which accompanied such statement, so far as may be necessary for the purpose of determining the questions in controversy between the parties, but shall (if necessary by adjourning the inquiry) give the applicant or the local planning authority, as the case may be, and the section 29 parties an adequate opportunity of considering any such fresh submission or document; and the appointed person may make in his report a recommendation as to the payment of any additional costs occasioned by any such adjournment. . .

(7) The appointed person shall be entitled (subject to disclosure thereof at the inquiry) to take into account any written representations or statements received by him before the inquiry from any person. . .

Site inspections

11. (1) The appointed person may make an unaccompanied inspection of the land before or during the inquiry without giving notice of his intention to the persons entitled to appear at the inquiry.

(2) The appointed person may, and shall if so requested by the applicant or the local planning authority before or during the inquiry, inspect the land after the close of the inquiry and shall, in all cases where he intends to make such an inspection, announce during the inquiry the date and time at which he proposes to do so.

(3) The applicant, the local planning authority and the section 29 parties shall be entitled to accompany the appointed person on any inspection after the close of the inquiry; but the appointed person shall not be bound to defer his inspection if any person entitled to accompany him is not present at the time appointed.

Procedure after inquiry

12. (1) The appointed person shall after the close of the inquiry make a report in writing to the Secretary of State which shall include the appointed person's findings of fact and his recommendations, if any, or his reason for not making any recommendations.

(2) Where the Secretary of State—
  (*a*) differs from the appointed person on a finding of fact, or
  (*b*) after the close of the inquiry takes into consideration any new evidence (including expert opinion on a matter of fact) or any new issue of fact (not being a matter of government policy) which was not raised at the inquiry,

and by reason thereof is disposed to disagree with a recommendation made by the appointed person, he shall not come to a decision which is at variance with any such recommendation without first notifying the applicant, the local planning authority and any section 29 party who appeared at the inquiry of his disagreement and the reasons for it and affording them an opportunity of making representations in writing within 21 days or (if the Secretary of State has taken into consideration any new evidence or any new issue of fact, not being a matter of government policy) of asking within 21 days for the re-opening of the inquiry.

(3) The Secretary of State may in any case if he thinks fit cause the inquiry to be re-opened, and shall cause it to be re-opened if asked to do so in accordance with the last foregoing paragraph; and, if the inquiry is re-opened, paragraphs (1) and (2) of rule 5 shall apply as they applied to the original inquiry, with the substitution in paragraph (1) of ' 28 ' for ' 42 '.

Notification of decision

13. (1) The Secretary of State shall notify his decision, and his reasons therefor in writing to the applicant, the local planning authority and the section 29 parties and to any person who, having appeared at the inquiry, has asked to be notifed of the decision.

(2) Where a copy of the appointed person's report is not sent with the notification of the decisions, the notification shall be accompanied by a summary of the appointed person's conclusions and recommendations; and if any person entitled to be notified of the Secretary of State's decision . . . has not received a copy of the appointed person's report, he shall be supplied with a copy thereof on written application made to the Secretary of State within one month from the date of the decision. . .

III. REMEDIES

(i) Proceedings against the Crown

In principle public authorities can be sued for their wrongdoings just as a private person can. But there are important differences in practice. Most of the powers of public authorities are derived from statute and statutory powers are frequently given to public authorities to do things which no private person would be empowered to do.

In general actions against the Crown, i.e. the central Government, do not raise particular problems. The Crown Proceedings Act, 1947, authorises actions against the Crown in tort and contract. There are, however, a number of authorities which suggest that Crown contracts may be in a different position from contracts with private individuals in a number of respects; see e.g. *The Amphitrite* [1921] 3 K.B. 500, *Churchward* v. *The Queen* (1865) L.R. 1 Q.B. 173, *New South Wales* v. *Bardolph* (1934) 52 C.L.R. 455 and *Crown Lands Commissioners* v. *Page* (above p. 583).

Other differences are spelt out or referred to in the 1947 Act itself.

THE CROWN PROCEEDINGS ACT, 1947

[10 & 11 Geo. 6. ch. 44]

11. (1) Nothing in Part I of this Act shall extinguish or abridge any powers or authorities which, if this Act had not been passed, would have been exercisable by virtue of the prerogative of the Crown, or any powers or authorities conferred on the Crown by any statute, and, in particular, nothing in the said Part I shall extinguish or abridge any powers or authorities exercisable by the Crown, whether in time of peace or of war, for the purpose of the defence of the realm or of training, or maintaining the efficiency of, any of the armed forces of the Crown.

(2) When in any proceedings under this Act it is material to determine whether anything was properly done or omitted to be done in the exercise of the prerogative of the Crown, the Admiralty or a Secretary of State may, if satisfied that the act or omission was necessary for any such purpose as is mentioned in the last preceding subsection, issue a certificate to the effect that the act or omission was necessary for that purpose; and the certificate shall, in those proceedings, be conclusive as to the matter so certified . . .

21. (1) In any civil proceedings by or against the Crown the court shall, subject to the provisions of this Act, have power to make all such orders as it has power to make in proceedings between subjects, and otherwise to give such appropriate relief as the case may require:
Provided that: —

(a) where in any proceedings against the Crown any such relief is sought as might in proceedings between subjects be granted by way of injunction or specific performance, the court shall not grant an injunction or make an order for specific performance, but in lieu thereof make an order declaratory of the rights of the parties; and

(b) in any proceeding against the Crown for the recovery of land or other property the court shall not make an order for the recovery of the land or the delivery of the property, but may in lieu thereof make an order declaring that the plaintiff is entitled as against the Crown to the land or property or to the possession thereof.

(2) The court shall not in any civil proceedings grant an injunction or make any order against an officer of the Crown if the effect of granting the injunction or making the order would be to give any relief against the Crown which could not have been obtained in proceedings against the Crown . . .

28. (1) Subject to and in accordance with rules of court and county court rules : —

> (a) in any civil proceedings in the High Court or a county court to which the Crown is a party, the Crown may be required by the court to make discovery of documents and produce documents for inspection; and
>
> (b) in any such proceedings as aforesaid, the Crown may be required by the court to answer interrogatories :

Provided that this section shall be without prejudice to any rule of law which authorises or requires the withholding of any document or the refusal to answer any question on the ground that the disclosure of the document or the answering of the question would be injurious to the public interest.

(2) Without prejudice to the proviso to the preceding subsection, any rules made for the purpose of this section shall be such as to secure that the existence of a document will not be disclosed if, in the opinion of a Minister of the Crown, it would be injurious to disclose the existence thereof . . .

40. . . . (2) Except as therein otherwise expressly provided, nothing in this Act shall : —

> (f) affect any rules of evidence or any presumption relating to the extent to which the Crown is bound by any Act of Parliament . . .

(ii) Discretionary remedies

It is not uncommon for statutes which grant powers to public authorities also to prescribe or limit the remedy to which a person aggrieved by their exercise is entitled. This may involve a total exclusion of access to the courts, or may limit the time within which or the ground on which such an application may be made. It is common, for example, for statutes which provide for a Minister to make a decision after holding a public local inquiry in matters relating to town and country planning, housing and the compulsory acquisition of land also to provide that a person aggrieved by the decision may apply to the courts within a limited time on the grounds either that the Minister has exceeded his powers, or has failed to observe the statutory procedure and the aggrieved person has as a result suffered damage. In such cases it is the statute which provides and shapes the remedy. Indeed as with powers so with remedies; the relevant statute must always be a starting point for any consideration of the question whether there is a remedy in a particular case, and its nature and extent, and the extent to which remedies otherwise available have been limited or excluded.

If no remedies are provided by statute or the remedies provided are not to be regarded as exclusive and alternative remedies are themselves not excluded the complainant can fall back on the remedies offered by the courts themselves.

As has been mentioned above these include in principle all the normal remedies available as between subject and subject. In addition, however, the courts have developed and adapted a number of other, discretionary remedies, which may be available in a particular case, to assist someone complaining about the action, inaction or decisions of a public authority. They are the orders of certiorari, prohibition and mandamus, and declaration. The extracts which follow illustrate some of the principles relevant to their use.

PASMORE v. *OSWALDTWISTLE URBAN DISTRICT COUNCIL* [1898] A.C. 387

House of Lords

The Public Health Act, 1875, required local authorities to ' cause to be made such sewers as may be necessary for effectively draining the district for the purposes of the Act '. S. 299 of the Act provided that ' where complaint was made to the Local Government Board that a local authority has made default on providing their district with sufficient sewers ... the Local Government Board, if satisfied after due inquiry, shall make an order limiting a time for the performance of their duty in the matter of such complaint. If such duty is not performed by the time limited in the order, such order may be enforced by writ of mandamus, or the Local Government Board may appoint some person to perform such duty ...' A millowner wanted to empty his factory drains into the local sewers but they were not adequate for the purpose. The local authority refused to make them adequate. Instead of using the statutory procedure he applied to the court himself for a writ of mandamus.

EARL OF HALSBURY L.C. . . . The principle that where a specific remedy is given by a statute, it thereby deprives the person who insists upon a remedy of any other form of remedy ... is one which is very familiar and runs through the law ... I think Lord Tenterden accurately states that principle in the case of *Doe* v. *Bridges* (1831) 1 B. & Ad. 847, 859. He says: ' Where an Act creates an obligation and enforces the performance in a specified manner, we take it to be a general rule that performance cannot be enforced in any other manner ...' The words which the learned judge, Lord Tenterden, uses there appear to be strictly applicable to this case. The obligation which is created by this statute is an obligation which is created by the statute and the statute alone ... There is a specified remedy contained in it, which is an application to the proper Government department. My Lords it seems to me that if ever it were possible to conceive a case in which it would be extremely inconvenient that each suitor in turn should be permitted to apply for a specific remedy against the body charged with the care of the health of the inhabitants of the district in respect of drainage, it is such a case as this... [T]hat shows how important it is that the particular jurisdiction to call upon the whole district to reform their mode of dealing with sewage and drainage should not be in the hands, and should not be open to the litigation, of any particular individual, but should be committed to a Government Department...

LORD MACNAGHTEN. ... The law is stated nowhere more clearly or, I think, more accurately, than by Lord Tenterden... Whether the general rule is to prevail, or an exception to the general rule is to be admitted, must depend on the scope and language of the Act which creates the obligation and on considerations of policy and convenience. It would be difficult to conceive any case in which there could be less reason for departing from the general rule than one like the present.

LORDS MORRIS and JAMES OF HEREFORD concurred.

PYX GRANITE CO. LTD. v. *MINISTRY OF HOUSING AND LOCAL GOVERNMENT* [1960] A.C. 260

House of Lords

The company who wished to quarry on a particular site in the Malvern Hills applied for planning permission which was in part refused and in part granted, but subject to conditions. They subsequently claimed that they did not in any event need permission because the Town and Country Planning (General Development) Order, 1950, provided that 'development authorised by any local or private Act of Parliament' did not need planning permission and that this particular development was authorised by the Malvern Hills Act 1924. They therefore applied to the court for a declaration to this effect. For the Minister it was contended *inter alia* that s. 17 of the Town and Country Planning Act, 1947, provided the only method by which such a question could be determined.

VISCOUNT SIMONDS. ... It was submitted by the respondents that the court has no jurisdiction to entertain the action. It was argued that s. 17 of the Act supplied the only procedure by which the subject could ascertain whether permission is necessary for the development of his land. That section enacts that if any person who proposes to carry out ' any operations on land ... wishes to have it determined ... whether an application for permission in respect thereof is required under this Part of this Act having regard to the provisions of the development order, he may... apply to the local planning authority to determine that question.' This matter is somewhat complicated by the fact that under other sections of the Act the Minister may ' call in ' the application for his own determination. But nothing turns on this, for, whether the application is heard in the first place by the local planning authority and then on appeal by the Minister or is heard in the first place upon a ' call in ' by the Minister, his determination is expressed to be final. The question is whether the statutory remedy is the only remedy and the right of the subject to have recourse to the courts of law is excluded. Obviously it cannot altogether be excluded; for, as Lord Denning has pointed out,[29] if the subject does what he has not permission to do and so-called enforcement proceedings are taken against him, he can apply to the court of summary jurisdiction under section 23 of the Act and ask for the enforcement notice to be quashed, and he can thence go to the High Court upon case stated. But I agree with Lord Denning and Morris L.J. in thinking that this circuity is not necessary. It is a principle not by any means to be whittled down that the subject's recourse to Her Majesty's courts for the determination of his rights is not to be excluded except by clear words. That is, as McNair J. called it in *Francis* v. *Yiewsley and West Drayton Urban District Council*,[30] a ' fundamental rule ' from which I would not for my part sanction any departure. It must be asked, then, what is there in the Act of 1947 which bars such recourse. The answer is that there is nothing except the fact that the Act provides him with another remedy. Is it, then, an alternative or an exclusive remedy? There is nothing in the Act to suggest that, while a new remedy, perhaps cheap and expeditious, is given, the old and, as we like to call it, the inalienable remedy of Her Majesty's subjects to seek redress in her courts is taken away. And it appears to me that the case would be unarguable but for the fact that in *Barraclough* v. *Brown*[31] upon a consideration of the statute there under review it was held that the new statutory remedy was exclusive. But that case differs vitally from the present case. There the statute gave to an aggrieved person the right in certain circumstances to recover certain costs and the expenses from a third party who was not otherwise liable in a court of summary jurisdiction. It was held that that was the only remedy open to the aggrieved person and that he could not recover such costs and expenses in the High Court. ' I do not think ', said Lord Herschell, ' the appellant can claim to recover by virtue of the statute, and at the same time insist upon doing so by means other than those prescribed by the statute which alone confers the right.' Or, as Lord Watson said: ' The right and the remedy are given uno flatu, and the one cannot be dissociated from the other.' The circumstances here are far different. The appellant company are given no new right of quarrying by the Act of 1947. Their right is a common law right and the only question is how far it has been taken away. They do not uno flatu claim under the Act and seek a remedy elsewhere. On the contrary, they deny that they come within its purview and seek a declaration to that effect. There is, in my opinion, nothing in *Barraclough* v. *Brown* which denies them that remedy, if it is otherwise appropriate.

The appropriateness of the remedy was the final point on this part of the case. It was urged that, even if the court had jurisdiction to make the declaration claimed, it was a discretionary jurisdiction which should not be exercised in this case. My Lords, this plea should not, in my opinion, prevail. It is surely proper that in a case like this involving, as many days of argument showed, difficult questions of construction of Acts of Parliament, a court of law should declare what are the rights of the subject who claims to have them determined. I do not dissent from the contention of the respondents that, where the administrative or the quasi-judicial powers of the Minister are concerned, declaratory judgments should not readily be given by the court. But here, if ever, was a case where the jurisdiction could properly be invoked. It might even be thought surprising that the Minister should not be glad to have such questions authoritatively determined. . .

LORDS GODDARD, KEITH OF AVONHOLME, and JENKINS delivered concurring judgments. LORD OAKSEY agreed with the judgment of LORD GODDARD.

PUNTON v. MINISTRY OF PENSIONS AND NATIONAL INSURANCE (No. 2)   [1964] 1 W.L.R. 226

Court of Appeal

The National Insurance Act, 1946, provided in s. 13 that a person who had lost employment by reason of a stoppage of work which was due to a trade dispute at his place of employment was not entitled to unemployment benefit unless he could prove inter alia that he did not belong to a class of workers ' directly interested in the dispute '. There was a stoppage at Punton's place of employment owing to a demarcation dispute between platers and shipwrights. Punton was a plater's helper and not a member of either of the two unions involved. The local insurance officer, the appeal tribunal and the National Insurance Commissioner nevertheless decided that he was directly interested because the amount of work that would be available to him turned on the outcome of the dispute. He applied to the court for a declaration that he was entitled to benefit as the Commissioner had made a decision which was wrong in law.

SELLERS L.J. ... It was submitted that the National Insurance Act, 1946, and the Regulations made thereunder establish a complete code for administering unemployment benefits and for deciding all claims arising under the Act and that the legislature has given exclusive jurisdiction to those bodies set up to determine disputes and has revealed the clear intention of Parliament that the National Insurance Commissioner or the deputy commissioners shall adjudicate finally in all matters which are properly brought before that tribunal.

By section 11 of the Tribunals and Inquiries Act, 1958, a decision of this tribunal can be reviewed by certiorari proceedings. Such proceedings could have given the plaintiffs a decision on the point of law they now seek to have resolved and whatever disadvantages such procedure may have (I can see none in this case where no discovery is required, for instance) it would have expedited the hearing to within six months of the Commissioner's decision on September 20, 1961. Further, although section 9 of that Act provides that any party dissatisfied in point of law with a decision of certain tribunals may appeal to the High Court or require the tribunal to state and sign a case for the opinion of the High Court, the National Insurance Commissioner is not included.

The essence of the National Insurance legislation is that a fund is set up out of which the benefits which are provided by the Act shall be paid. An award in accordance with the procedure of the Act is required as a condition precedent to payment. The award of the National Insurance Commissioner cannot be quashed by the present proceedings for a declaration and there does not appear to be any power to replace it so as to enable the plaintiffs to be paid unemployment benefit if the point of law were to be decided in their favour. The award therefore must stand and it would remain an effective award within the machinery of the National Insurance Act, 1946, whatever view the High Court or any appellate court were to hold of the true construction of the provisions governing unemployment benefit... The fact that... a declaration of this court could not be implemented seems in itself to put the jurisdiction of the court in question...

It is to be observed that under section 43 (3) the right to benefit is not determined by the Minister himself at any stage but by the insurance officer, the local tribunal or the National Insurance Commissioner, and by a proviso to that subsection certain questions, including those concerned with contributions, are excluded from that sequence of determination and appeal, and by subsection (4) provision is made for regulations to provide for a reference to the High Court for decision of any question of law arising in connection with the determination of a question by the Minister and for appeals to the High Court from the decision of the Minister on any such question of law, and the decision in either event is to be final. This express provision for appeal to the High Court, excluding an appeal relating to claims for benefit, supports the submission that the Act provides its own machinery for dealing with benefit resulting in an effective award. . .

It is true that the Court of Queen's Bench has an inherent jurisdiction to control inferior tribunals in a supervisory capacity and to do so by certiorari (which would be the relevant procedure in this case), which enables the court to quash the decision if the inferior court can be shown to have exceeded its jurisdiction or to have erred in law. Neither certiorari nor mandamus usurp the function of a tribunal but require it, having quashed its decision, to hear the case and determine it correctly.

There may be many cases where a summons for a declaration is at least an adequate substitute for certiorari proceedings and where it may have advantages over it with no defects. That would be so where an authoritative statement of the law by the High Court will serve to undermine a decision or order so that it need not be complied with and could not in the light of the pronouncement of the law be successfully enforced. This may arise, for instance, under the Town and Country Planning legislation or the Dock Workers (Regulation of Employment) Order, 1947 but in the present case the plaintiffs claim benefit under the Act in question and the position can be contrasted with that which arose in *Pyx Granite Ltd.* v. *Minister of Housing and Local Government.*[32] Lord Jenkins said ' The company here cannot be said to occupy the position of the undertakers in *Barraclough* v. *Brown.* They are not seeking to enforce statutory rights by methods other than those prescribed by the Act creating them. They are merely seeking to ascertain the extent of their statutory liabilities.' Without employing the methods set out in the Act, that is, without obtaining an award, the plaintiffs cannot enforce the statutory right to unemployment benefit they claim, and the decision in *Barraclough* v. *Brown* is more closely applicable than the many other authorities cited to us. . .

Apart from certiorari there is no machinery for getting rid of the decision of the National Insurance Commissioner and, what is more important, no way of substituting an effective award on which the claims could be paid. It would be out of harmony with all authority to have two contrary decisions between the same parties on the same issues obtained by different procedures, as it were, on parallel courses which never met or could meet and where the effective decision would remain with the inferior tribunal and not that of the High Court. I conceive that to be the case here and it seems to me to lead to a conclusion against the jurisdiction of the High Court in this particular matter. The tribunal is wholly independent and the Commissioner or a deputy commissioner

[32] See above, p. 629.

has to be a barrister or advocate of not less than ten years' standing, and an appeal may be heard if thought desirable by more than one member of the tribunal, and we were told that the tribunal does sometimes sit in banc. It is a statutory judicial tribunal to deal with a special subject-matter where the decisions will frequently be on mixed law and fact and where finality and the minimum of delay are sought to be achieved. There is much to lead to the implication that the jurisdiction of the courts was intended to be excluded and very little to be set against such a conclusion. . .

If I am wrong in holding that the court has no jurisdiction in this matter then I think the matters I have considered, together with the reasons given by Phillimore J., amply support the judge's refusal to make a declaration. Litigants who could have obtained a decision on the point of law within six months should not be encouraged to wait until that time has expired and then come to the courts. . .

DAVIES L.J. . . . Mr Forrest, for the plaintiffs, conceded that, if it is open to them by means of a summons for a declaration to challenge the decision of the commissioner as being wrong in law, it would also be open to an insurance officer so to do in an appropriate case.

To take an imaginary case. The insurance officer disallows a claim for benefit. The matter is taken on appeal to the local tribunal and thence on further appeal to the commissioner. The commissioner decides in favour of the claim and makes an award.

It seems to me that in the light of the provisions of the Acts and of the regulations which have been referred to by my Lord – provisions which emphasise the need for speedy and final decision – it would be quite preposterous to think in those circumstances it would be permissible for the insurance officer to go to the court, perhaps years later, and ask for a declaration that the decision of the commissioner was wrong in law.

DANCKWERTS L.J. agreed.

REGINA v. *PADDINGTON VALUATION OFFICER AND ANOTHER, Ex parte PEACHEY PROPERTY CORPORATION*   [1966] 1 Q.B. 38

Court of Appeal

Peachey Corporation complained that the valuation officer in the Paddington area had prepared the valuation list improperly, and in particular had rated too highly purpose built flats of the kind owned by the Corporation and too low flats in converted houses. They therefore sought an order of certiorari to have the whole list quashed and an order of mandamus directing the valuation officer to make a new list on a proper basis.

LORD DENNING M.R. Before I deal with the facts, I propose to deal with the law: for it helps to see the issues involved.

I. *What is the proper remedy?*

The first question is whether the remedy by certiorari or mandamus is open at all, seeing that there is a remedy given by statute. The statutory remedy is contained in sections 40 to 49 of the Local Government Act, 1948, as amended by sections 1 and 3 of the Lands Tribunal Act, 1949. Summarised, the remedy is this: Peachey Property Corporation, if they are aggrieved, are entitled to make proposals for the alteration of the valuation list. They can propose alterations, either downwards or upwards. On the one hand, they can ask that the values on their Park West flats be reduced. On the other hand, they can ask that the values on other people's flats in converted houses be increased. If the valuation officer does not agree to the proposals, the applicants can appeal to the local valuation court. If that court decides against them, they can appeal to the Lands Tribunal. The decision of the Lands Tribunal is final, save that on a point of law there is an appeal to the Court of Appeal: and thence, in turn, with leave, to the House of Lords.

Mr Eric Blain contended strongly before us that, as Parliament had provided this specific remedy, the applicants ought to go by it. There was a code of procedure, he said, specially designed by Parliament, to deal with grievances such as these. That was their proper course. Indeed, their only course. Such specific remedy being given, they could not resort to the remedy of certiorari or mandamus. He supported this contention by reference to *Pasmore* v. *Oswaldtwistle Urban District Council,*[33] *Rex* v. *City of London Assessment Committee,*[34] and *Stepney Borough Council* v. *John Walker and Sons, Ltd.*[35]

Now these cases certainly warrant the proposition that, if the applicants were attacking the assessment of any one particular hereditament, or any small group of hereditaments, such as all the houses in a particular terrace, their only remedy would be that statutory remedy. By which I mean that, if and in so far as they are attacking particular assessments within a valid valuation list, they must go by the remedy which Parliament has provided, namely, to make proposals to alter those assessments. But if and in so far as they are attacking the valuation list itself and contend that the whole list is invalid (as they do), then I do not think that they are confined to the statutory remedy: for the simple reason that the statutory remedy is in that case nowhere near so convenient, beneficial and effectual as certiorari and mandamus. I suppose that in theory the Peachey Property Corporation might make

[33] [1898] A.C. 387.
[34] [1907] 2 K.B. 764.   [35] [1934] A.C. 365.

proposals for the alteration of every one of the 31,656 hereditaments in the list, but that would in practice be impossible.

Mr Blain conceded this; he suggested, however, that a few test cases might be taken, and proposals could be made for altering those few assessments, and a decision given by the Lands Tribunal. But one side or the other might not agree on what should be taken as test cases. And in any case the procedure would be most deficient because there could be no discovery against the occupiers. I am, therefore, of opinion that the existence of the statutory remedy is no bar to this application. The case falls within the general principle that the jurisdiction of the High Court is not to be certiorari and mandamus (see *Reg.* v. *Medical Appeal Tribunal, ex parte Gilmore*,[36] and also to the remedy by declaration (see *Pyx Granite Company Ltd.* v. *Minister of Housing* [37]).

II. *Is the applicant a ' party aggrieved '?*

The second question is whether Peachey Property Corporation are persons aggrieved so as to be entitled to ask for certiorari or mandamus. Mr Blain contended that they are not persons aggrieved because even if they succeeded in increasing all the gross values of other people in the Paddington area, it would not make a pennyworth of difference to them. Strange as it may seem, owing to the way expenses are borne in the County of London, the rate poundage of Paddington would remain the same even if the assessments of the flats in converted houses were greatly increased. If the assessments were increased by £1,000,000 the rate poundage would be reduced by a penny. I do not think that grievances are to be measured in pounds, shillings and pence. If a rate-payer or other person finds his name included in a valuation list which is invalid, he is entitled to come to the court and apply to have it quashed. He is not to be put off by the plea that he has suffered no damage, any more than the voters were in *Ashby* v. *White*.[38] The court would not listen, of course, to a mere busybody who was interfering in things which did not concern him. It will listen to anyone whose interests are affected by what has been done, just as it did in *Greenbaum's case*,[39] and in *Attorney-General* v. *N. Jie*.[40] So here it will listen to any rate-payer who complains that the list is invalid.

III. *Are certiorari and mandamus available?*

The third question is whether certiorari and mandamus are available in respect of a valuation list. The Divisional Court thought that they were; and Mr Blain did not contend otherwise. The valuation officer is

---

[36] [1957] 1 Q.B. 574.
[37] [1960] A.C. 260, 286, 304.
[38] (1704) 2 Ld.Raymond 938 H.L.
[39] (1957) 55 L.G.R. 129 C.A.   [40] [1961] A.C. 617.

a public officer entrusted with a public duty. He has legal authority or power to determine questions affecting the rights of subjects, namely, to assess the values of hereditaments. This power carries with it the duty to act ' judicially ', which means, I think, fairly and justly in accordance with the statute. If he declines or fails to carry out his duty, he is answerable to mandamus; and the list itself is liable to be quashed on certiorari: see *Rex* v. *Electricity Commission*; [41] *Rex* v. *Manchester Legal Aid Committee, ex parte R. A. Brand & Co. Ltd.*; [42] *Ridge* v. *Baldwin*.[43]

IV. *The resulting chaos*

The fourth question is what is to happen if the valuation list is quashed. It was said that it would be a nullity from the beginning. The rating authority would have to go back to the 1956 list which was based on 1939 values: section 34 (2) of the Local Government Act, 1948. It would be necessary, it was said, to unravel all the assessments and payments since April 1, 1963. The result would be chaos. I do not accept this at all. It is necessary to distinguish between two kinds of invalidity. The one kind is where the invalidity is so grave that the list is a nullity altogether. In which case there is no need for an order to quash it. It is automatically null and void without more ado. The other kind is when the invalidity does not make the list void altogether, but only voidable. In that case it stands unless and until it is set aside. In the present case the valuation list is not, and never has been, a nullity. At most the first respondent – acting within his jurisdiction – exercised that jurisdiction erroneously. That makes the list voidable and not void. It remains good until it is set aside. ' It bears no brand of invalidity on its forehead. Unless the necessary proceedings are taken at law to establish the cause of invalidity and to get it quashed or otherwise upset, it will remain as effective for its ostensible purpose as the most impeccable of orders '. See *Smith* v. *East Elloe R.D.C.* by Lord Radcliffe.[44] No doubt if the list is in due course avoided certiorari must eventually go to quash it [cp. the All E.R. version of this passage which reads ' No doubt if the list is invalid altogether certiorari must in due course go to quash it ']. But I see no reason why a mandamus should not issue in advance of the certiorari; compare *Reg.* v. *Cotham JJ. and Webb, ex parte Williams*.[45] If the existing list has been compiled on the wrong footing the court can order the valuation officer to make a new list on the right footing. . . Once the new list is made and ready to take effect the court can quash the old list. In that case everything done under

[41] [1924] 1 K.B. 171.
[42] [1952] 2 Q.B. 413.
[43] [1964] A.C. 40.
[44] [1956] A.C. 736, 769, 770.   [45] [1898] 1 Q.B. 802.

the old list will remain good. The rates that have been demanded and paid cannot be recovered back. . .

V. *On what grounds will certiorari lie?*

The fifth question is the most important of all. On what grounds will certiorari lie to quash a valuation list? The Divisional Court thought that it would only lie for excess of jurisdiction or error of law on the face of the list. But the word ' jurisdiction ' in this context has innumerable shades of meaning. Some advocates are prone to say that, whenever a tribunal or other body decides wrongly, it exceeds its jurisdiction. It has only jurisdiction, they say, to decide rightly, not to decide wrongly. This is too broad a view altogether. I would say that, if a tribunal or body is guilty of an error which goes to the very root of the determination, in that it has approached the case on an entirely wrong footing, then it does exceed its jurisdiction. Thus where magistrates refused to issue summonses, in spite of the evidence, because they thought that it was undesirable for the prosecution to go on it was held that was tantamount to declining jurisdiction: see *Rex* v. *Adamson*.[46] And when the Board of Education failed to determine the questions asked of them, but answered another not put to them, it was held that they had declined jurisdiction: see *Board of Education* v. *Rice*.[47] Again when licensing justices refused an application on a ground not open to them, it was held that they had exceeded their jurisdiction. See *Rex* v. *Weymouth Licensing Justices, ex parte Sleep*.[48]

These cases confirm me in the view which I expressed in *Baldwin & Francis, Ltd.* v. *Patents Appeal Tribunal* [49] ' . . . if a tribunal bases its decision on extraneous considerations which it ought not to have taken into account, or fails to take into account a vital consideration which it ought to have taken into account, then its decision may be quashed on certiorari and a mandamus issued for it to hear the case afresh.'

But how does this principle apply in regard to the whole of a valuation list (which can be quashed on certiorari) in contrast to particular assessments in the list (in which there is statutory remedy by appeal)? The error must be one which affects the list as a whole, or a large part of it, and not merely particular hereditaments in it. It seems to me that if the valuation officer prepared the list on entirely the wrong basis, contrary to the directions in the statute, it could be quashed. An instance can be found in the books. Suppose in preparing a new list, he simply took the old list and, instead of assessing each hereditament individually, he multiplied the old values three times all the way through. Clearly the list could be quashed: see *Stirk & Sons Ltd.* v. *Halifax*

---

[46] (1875) 1 Q.B.D. 201.   [47] [1911] A.C. 179.
[48] [1942] 1 K.B. 465.   [49] [1959] A.C. 663, 693.

Assessment Committee; [50] *Ladies Hosiery and Underwear Ltd.* v. *West Middlesex Assessment Committee*, by Scrutton L.J.[51]

Again if he took the actual rents paid without making any adjustments (for rates, repairs, services or furniture), clearly the list would be bad. So also if he disregarded the statutory test of ' what a hypothetical tenant might reasonably be expected to pay, and substituted an arbitrary scale of values based on a preconceived formula (such as so many shillings per square foot according to the type of hereditament) then again the list would be quashed. These instances would all be cases where, in the words of the Divisional Court ' . . . the valuation officer has misdirected himself on some fundamental matter or matters which so vitiate the value of his work that it must be regarded as worthless '.

In short, there must be error which goes to the root of the list or a large part of it. . .

SALMON L.J. I entirely agree, subject to one reservation, with Lord Denning M.R.'s exposition of the law relating to certiorari and mandamus. I am not altogether satisfied, that there would be any power to grant mandamus and keep the 1963 valuation list in force by the simple expedient of postponing certiorari until after a new list had been prepared. No doubt it would be convenient, if possible, to follow this course, were the appeal to be allowed; indeed grave inconvenience if not chaos would follow if the 1956 valuation list were to be revived – which both parties at first agreed would be the inevitable result of allowing the appeal. It may be that mandamus can be granted without certiorari, but mandamus cannot be granted if there is a valid valuation list in being. It is not enough that the valuation officer should have prepared the list badly or even very badly. In such a case, he could not be ordered by mandamus to correct his mistakes or make a new list. In order for mandamus to lie, it must be established that he has prepared the list illegally or in bad faith, so that in effect he has not exercised his statutory function at all and that accordingly there is in reality no valid list in existence (*Reg.* v. *Cotham etc. JJ. and Webb, ex parte Williams*).

Accordingly, it seems to me that a finding that the list is null and void is necessarily implicit in an order of mandamus. Having regard to the view however that I take of the facts, the point whether the 1963 list could be temporarily kept alive were mandamus to issue does not arise for decision, and I express no concluded opinion on it. I would add that whatever inconvenience or chaos might be involved in allowing the appeal, the court would not be deterred from doing so if satisfied that the valuation officer had acted illegally. One of the principal functions of our courts is to protect the public from an abuse of power on the part of anyone, such as a valuation officer, entrusted with a public duty

[50] [1922] 1 K.B. 264.   [51] [1932] 2 K.B. 679, 686.

which affects the rights of ordinary citizens. If the valuation officer acted illegally and thereby produced an unjust and invalid list, this would be such an abuse of power and one which the courts would certainly redress. It could be no answer that to do so would produce inconvenience and chaos for the rating authority – otherwise the law could be flouted and injustice perpetrated with impunity.

The real question must be – has the first respondent made an error in law which goes to the root of the whole list and vitiates it? If he has, the list is invalid and the courts must intervene to say so. Otherwise there is no power to issue mandamus or certiorari; *Stirk & Sons, Ltd.* v. *Halifax Assessment Committee*; *Ladies Hosiery and Underwear Ltd.* v. *West Middlesex Assessment Committee*, per Scrutton L.J., *Board of Education* v. *Rice*.

It is not enough for the appellants to show that the list contains many mistakes due to ineptitude, carelessness and stubborn incompetence on the part of the valuation officer and those in authority over him. If it were, the appellants might well succeed. Such mistakes, however, can only be dealt with by the method of proposals and appeals laid down in sections 40 to 44 of the Local Government Act, 1948... Certiorari and mandamus do not lie to correct such errors, but only errors in law going to the root of the valuation list...

DANCKWERTS L.J. .... As I understand the law relating to mandamus and certiorari, the order of mandamus could be issued forthwith so as to secure the making of a proper valuation list: and the making of the order of certiorari could be postponed until the new valuation list has been created. I do not see why this should not be done. It does not seem to me to be right that the appellants should be deprived of the remedies to which I think they are entitled for fear that inconvenience might result...

In the event LORD DENNING and SALMON L.J., DANCKWERTS L.J. dissenting, held that the valuation officer had not made a mistake of law going to the root of the valuation list and therefore refused the orders requested.

CHAPTER XIII

DEPRIVATION OF LIBERTY AND POLICE POWERS OF INVESTIGATION

I. DEPRIVATION OF LIBERTY

The two principal grounds on which someone may be deprived of his physical liberty are by way of arrest, in particular by the police; or by order of the court, which may order detention pending trial, or upon conviction by way of imprisonment, or by way of committal for contempt. Parliament also has the power to commit for contempt but it is never used. A person may also be detained against his will under the Mental Health Act, 1959, and a number of other statutes authorise detention for specific purposes, e.g. the Immigration Act, 1971, in relation to people who are being deported. In times of emergency the powers of arrest and detention are likely to be expanded and detention without trial authorised, e.g. during the 1939–45 war under the Defence Regulations, in particular Regulation 18B, made under the Emergency Powers Act, 1939, and more recently under the Northern Ireland (Emergency Provisions) Act, 1973 and the Prevention of Terrorism (Temporary Provisions) Act, 1976. In a situation where martial law operated arrest and detention without trial might even be justified at common law.

There are a number of different methods of obtaining release. The writ of habeas corpus is available to anyone who can show that his detention is unlawful. In other circumstances an application for bail or a simple appeal may be more appropriate. The Mental Health Act provides for an appeal to a Mental Health Review Tribunal. The Immigration Act, 1971, provides for an appeal to an Immigration Appeal Tribunal. The Northern Ireland (Emergency Powers) Act, 1973, provides for an appeal to a Detention Appeals Tribunal. The action of false imprisonment is available to secure compensation for an unlawful detention.

(i) Arrest

The Magistrates' Courts Act, 1952, s. 1 (1) authorises a magistrate to issue a warrant of arrest, on an information being given to him in writing and substantiated on oath, that any person has, or is suspected of having, committed an offence. There are, however, a large number of cases in which a constable is authorised to arrest without a warrant. At common law a policeman can arrest without a warrant anyone who commits a breach of the peace in his presence and policemen have in addition a general power to take such action as is necessary to prevent a breach of the peace. This may include arrest [see below, pp. 701 ff]. The most general statute authorising arrest without a warrant is the Criminal Law Act, 1967, though many other statutes, both general and local, authorise arrest without a warrant in relation to particular offences, e.g. ss. 1, 4 and 5 of the Public Order Act, 1936.

There is no general power short of arrest to detain a person to search or question him though this power is given in relation to drug offences by the Misuse of Drugs Act, 1971, and by some local statutes, such as the Metropolitan Police Act, 1839, s. 66 in relation to London. This is the kind of power that it is found necessary to give police and troops in times of emergency [see below, p. 762]. This is also true of stopping and searching cars. The Road Traffic Act, 1972, s. 159 [below, p. 665] gives a constable on traffic duty the power to stop a car but not to search it.

CRIMINAL LAW ACT, 1967   [Ch. 58]

2. (1) The powers of summary arrest conferred by the following subsections shall apply to offences for which the sentence is fixed by law or for which a person (not previously convicted) may under or by virtue of any enactment be sentenced to imprisonment for a term of five years, and to attempts to commit any such offence; and in this Act ... ' arrestable offence ' means any such offence or attempt.

(2) Any person may arrest without warrant anyone who is, or whom he, with reasonable cause, suspects to be, in the act of committing an arrestable offence.

(3) Where an arrestable offence has been committed, any person may arrest without warrant anyone who is, or whom he, with reasonable cause, suspects to be, guilty of the offence.

(4) Where a constable, with reasonable cause, suspects that an arrestable offence has been committed, he may arrest without warrant anyone whom he, with reasonable cause, suspects to be guilty of the offence.

(5) A constable may arrest without warrant any person who is, or whom he, with reasonable cause, suspects to be, about to commit an arrestable offence.

(6) For the purpose of arresting a person under any power conferred by this section a constable may enter (if need be, by force) and search any place where that person is or where the constable, with reasonable cause, suspects him to be.

(7) This section shall not affect the operation of any enactment restricting the institution of proceedings for an offence, nor prejudice any power of arrest conferred by law apart from this section.

3. (1) A person may use such force as is reasonable in the circumstances in the prevention of crime, or in effecting or assisting in the lawful arrest of offenders or suspected offenders or of persons unlawfully at large.

(2) Subsection (1) above shall replace the rules of the common law on the question when force used for a purpose mentioned in the subsection is justified by that purpose.

CHRISTIE AND ANOTHER v. LEACHINSKY
[1947] A.C. 573

House of Lords

In the case of an arrest with a warrant the Magistrates' Courts Rules, 1952, para. 73, provides that the warrant should include 'a statement of the offence charged ... or ... the ground on which the warrant is issued', and s. 102 of the Magistrates' Courts Act, 1952, while authorising an arrest by virtue of a warrant even though it is not in the possession of the person arresting requires that it should be shown on demand to the person arrested 'as soon as is practicable'. The present case establishes that on an arrest without a warrant the person arrested must be informed of the true grounds of his arrest.

Leachinsky had been arrested and charged with 'unlawful possession' of cloth, an offence under the Liverpool Corporation Act, 1921. The Act however only authorised arrest for such an offence if the name and address of the person arrested was not known to the police. In this case they were known. Leachinsky subsequently brought an action for false imprisonment against the police. In their defence the police argued that at the time of the arrest they had reasonable grounds for suspecting that Leachinsky had stolen the cloth and an arrest would therefore have been justified without a warrant and apart from the Liverpool Act. The House of Lords held that the police could not rely on this suspicion as they were under an obligation to inform a person arrested of the true grounds of his arrest.

LORD SIMONDS. . . . [T]he law requires that, where arrest proceeds upon a warrant, the warrant should state the charge upon which the arrest is made. I can see no valid reason why this safeguard for the subject should not equally be his when his arrest is made without a warrant. The exigency of the situation, which justifies or demands arrest without a warrant, cannot as it appears to me, justify or demand either the refusal to state the reason of arrest or a mis-statement of the reason. Arrested with or without a warrant the subject is entitled to know why he is deprived of his freedom, if only in order that he may, without a moment's delay, take such steps as will enable him to regain it . . . If, then, this is, as I think it is, the fundamental rule, what qualification if any must be imposed upon it? . . . I think it is clear that there is no need for the constable to explain the reason of arrest, if the arrested man is caught red-handed and the crime is patent to High Heaven. Nor, obviously, is explanation a necessary prelude to arrest where it is important to secure a possibly violent criminal. Nor again, can it be wrongful to arrest and detain a man upon a charge, of which he is reasonably suspected, with a view to further investigation of a second charge upon which information is incomplete. In all such matters a wide measure of discretion must be left to those whose duty it is to preserve the peace and bring criminals to justice. These and similar considerations lead me to the view that it is not an essential condition of lawful arrest that the constable should at the time of arrest formulate any charge at all, much less the charge which may ultimately be found in the indictment. But this, and this only, is the qualification which I would impose upon the general proposition. It leaves untouched the principle, which lies at the heart of the matter, that the arrested man is entitled to be told what is the act for which he is arrested. The ' charge ' ultimately made will depend upon the view taken by the law of his act. In ninety-nine cases out of a hundred the same words may be used to define the charge or describe the act, nor is any technical precision necessary: for instance, if the act constituting the crime is the killing of another man, it will be immaterial that the arrest is for murder and at a later hour the charge of manslaughter is substituted. The arrested man is left in no doubt that the arrest is for that killing. This is I think, the fundamental principle, viz., that a man is entitled to know what, in the apt words of Lawrence L.J., are ' the facts which are said to constitute a crime on his part '.[1] If so, it is manifestly wrong that a constable arresting him for one crime should profess to arrest him for another. Of what avail is the prescribed caution if it is directed to an imaginary crime? And how can the accused take steps to explain away a charge of which he has no inkling?

I turn, then, to the present case which appears to me to present a strange combination of circumstances. For, while I doubt not, that the appellants reasonably suspected the respondent of having committed a felony, yet I must, on the evidence, conclude that they refrained from bringing home to his mind at the time of arrest that that was their suspicion. Their minds, it is clear, were running on the provisions of the Liverpool Act. . .

[I]n the station charge book the charge was entered ' unlawful possession of a quantity of cloth at the warehouse, 196, Beaufort Street on 31.8.42.' And so the matter proceeded. It is clear, then, that whatever may have been the secret thought of the constables at the time of the arrest and detention, they allowed him to think that he was being arrested for being ' in unlawful possession ' of certain goods, an offence, if it be an offence, which was at the most a misdemeanour within the Liverpool Act and could not, except under conditions which did not here obtain, justify an arrest without a warrant, and was described in

[1] [1946] K.B. 124, 147.

terms not calculated to bring home to him that he was suspected of stealing or receiving the goods. In these circumstances the initial arrest and detention were wrongful. He was not aware and was not made aware of the act alleged to constitute his crime but was misled by a statement which was calculated to suggest to his uneasy conscience that he was guilty of a so-called black market offence. It is no answer that the constables had no sinister motive. They had, from the administrative point of view, a perfectly good motive. It will be found in an answer to a question, which, though it related to a later stage of the proceedings, is equally applicable to the earlier, ' Why did you not then charge him with larceny? ' To this the revealing answer was ' Because that larceny was committed at Leicester and it would then be a matter of withdrawing our charge and handing him over to Leicester. Unlawful possession was the most convenient charge at the time until he could be handed over to the Leicester city police.' My Lords, the liberty of the subject and the convenience of the police or any other executive authority are not to be weighed in the scales against each other. This case will have served a useful purpose if it enables your Lordships once more to proclaim that a man is not to be deprived of his liberty except in due course and process of law. . .

Viscount Simon and Lord du Parcq delivered concurring judgments. Lord MacMillan and Lord Thankerton concurred. *Appeal dismissed*

Cp. *Gelberg* v. *Miller* [1961] 1 W.L.R. 153 where the appellant had refused to move his car which was obstructing the highway and the police constable had arrested him ' for obstructing him in the execution of his duty by refusing to move his car and refusing his name and address '. The Attorney-General admitted that in the circumstances there was no power to arrest for obstructing the police but said that there was power to arrest for obstructing the highway under the Metropolitan Police Act, 1839, and that the police could rely on this power, even though the appellant had been charged and convicted only of obstructing the police. Lord Parker C.J. said: ' To my mind it is clear that, by saying that he was arresting him for refusing to move his motor-car, he was informing the appellant of a fact which, in all the circumstances, amounted to a wilful obstruction of the thoroughfare by leaving his car in that position. It seems to me to matter not that the respondent also coupled with that the refusal to give his name and address or the allegation of obstructing him in the execution of his duty. May I test it in this way: supposing the respondent had said nothing but had just arrested him, could it really be said that the appellant did not know all the facts constituting an alleged wilful obstruction of the thoroughfare without having that particular charge made against him at the time? In my judgment, what the appellant knew and what he was told was ample to fulfil the obligation as to what should be done at the time of an arrest without warrant.'

KENLIN v. GARDINER   [1967] 2 Q.B. 510

Divisional Court

When two policemen in plain clothes attempted to question two boys who were going from house to house in what they regarded as suspicious circumstances they attempted to run away. The policemen attempted to detain them saying that they were police officers, and one of them produced his warrant card. The boys were not convinced and resisted. They were subsequently charged with assaulting the police in the execution of their duty contrary to s. 51 (1) of the Police Act, 1964. They appealed against their conviction.

WINN L.J. . . . Of course, in the case of a charge of assault under section 51 (1) of the Police Act, 1964 . . . the defence or justification – I prefer to call it a justification, because it must always be borne in mind that it is for the prosecution to exclude justification and not for the defendant to establish it – the justification of self-defence is available just as it is in the case of any other assault. That is subject to this, that if the self-defence . . . was self-defence against an assault which was justified in law, as, for instance, a lawful arrest, then in law self-defence cannot afford justification . . . So one comes back to the question . . . was this officer entitled in law to take hold of the first boy by the arm – of course the same situation arises with the other officer in regard to the second boy a little later – justified in committing that technical assault by the exercise of any power which he as a police constable in the precise circumstances prevailing at that exact moment possessed?

I regret, really, that I feel myself compelled to say that the answer to that question must be in the negative. This officer might or might not in the particular circumstances have possessed a power to arrest these boys. I leave that question open, saying no more than that I feel some doubt whether he would have had a power of arrest: but on the assumption that he had a power to arrest, it is to my mind perfectly plain that neither of these officers purported to arrest either of these boys. What was done was not done as an integral step in the process of arresting, but was done in order to secure an opportunity, by detaining the boys from escape, to put to them or to either of them the question which was regarded as the test question to satisfy the officers whether or not it would be right in the circumstances, and having regard to the answer obtained from that question, if any, to arrest them.

I regret to say that I think there was a technical assault by the police officer. From which it follows that the justification of self-defence exerted or exercised by these two boys is not negatived by any justifiable character of the initial assault.

WIDGERY J. and LORD PARKER C.J. agreed.

Cp. *Donnelly* v. *Jackman* [1970] 1 W.L.R. 562.

(ii) Detention under the Mental Health Act, 1959

MENTAL HEALTH ACT, 1959 [Ch. 72]

Compulsory admission to hospital...

25. (1) A patient may be admitted to a hospital, and there detained for the period allowed by this section, in pursuance of an application (in this Act referred to as an application for admission for observation) made in accordance with the following provisions of this section.

(2) An application for admission for observation may be made in respect of a patient on the grounds—

(a) that he is suffering from mental disorder of a nature or degree which warrants the detention of the patient in a hospital under observation (with or without other medical treatment) for at least a limited period; and

(b) that he ought to be so detained in the interests of his own health or safety or with a view to the protection of other persons.

(3) An application for admission for observation shall be founded on the written recommendations in the prescribed form of two medical practitioners, including in each case a statement that in the opinion of the practitioner the conditions set out in paragraphs (a) and (b) of subsection (2) of this section are complied with.

(4) ... [A] patient admitted to hospital in pursuance of an application for admission for observation may be detained for a period not exceeding twenty-eight days beginning with the day on which he is admitted, but shall not be detained thereafter unless, before the expiration of that period, he has become liable to be detained by virtue of a subsequent application, order or direction under any of the following provisions of this Act.

26. (1) A patient may be admitted to a hospital, and there detained for the period allowed by the following provisions of this Act, in pursuance of an application (in this Act referred to as an application for admission for treatment) made in accordance with the following provisions of this section.

(2) An application for admission for treatment may be made in respect of a patient on the grounds—

(a) that he is suffering from mental disorder, being—

(i) in the case of a patient of any age, mental illness or severe subnormality;

(ii) in the case of a patient under the age of twenty-one years, psychopathic disorder or subnormality;

and that the said disorder is of a nature or degree which warrants the detention of the patient in a hospital for medical treatment under this section; and

(b) that it is necessary in the interests of the patient's health or safety or for the protection of other persons that the patient should be so detained.

(3) An application for admission for treatment shall be founded on the written recommendations in the prescribed form of two medical practitioners, including in each case a statement that in the opinion of the practitioner the conditions set out in paragraphs (a) and (b) of subsection (2) of this section are complied with; and each such recommendation shall include—

(a) such particulars as may be prescribed of the grounds for that opinion so far as it relates to the conditions set out in the said paragraph (a); and

(b) a statement of the reasons for that opinion so far as it relates to the conditions set out in the said paragraph (b), specifying whether other methods of dealing with the patient are available, and if so why they are not appropriate.

27. (1) Subject to the provisions of this section, an application for the admission of a patient for observation or for treatment may be made either by the nearest relative of the patient or by a mental welfare officer; and every such application shall be addressed to the managers of the hospital to which admission is sought and shall specify the qualification of the applicant to make the application.

(2) An application for admission for treatment shall not be made by a mental welfare officer if the nearest relative of the patient has notified that officer, or the local health authority by whom that officer is appointed, that he objects to the application being made, and, without prejudice to the foregoing provision, shall not be made by such an officer except after consultation with the person (if any) appearing to be the nearest relative of the patient unless it appears to that officer that in the circumstances such consultation is not reasonably practicable or would involve unreasonable delay.

(3) No application for the admission of a patient shall be made by any person unless that person has personally seen the patient within the period of fourteen days ending with the date of the application.

28. (1) The recommendations required for the purposes of an application for the admission of a patient under this Part of this Act (in this Act referred to as ' medical recommendations ') shall be signed on or before the date of the application, and shall be given by practitioners who have personally examined the patient either together or at an interval of not more than seven days.

(2) Of the medical recommendations given for the purposes of any

such application, one shall be given by a practitioner approved for the purposes of this section by a local health authority as having special experience in the diagnosis or treatment of mental disorder; and unless that practitioner has previous acquaintance with the patient, the other such recommendation shall, if practicable, be given by a medical practitioner who has such previous acquaintance.

(4) A medical recommendation for the purposes of an application for the admission of a patient under this Part of this Act shall not be given by any of the following persons, that is to say—

(a) the applicant;

(b) a partner of the applicant or of a practitioner by whom another medical recommendation is given for the purposes of the same application;

(c) a person employed as an assistant by the applicant or by any such practitioner as aforesaid;

(d) a person who receives or has an interest in the receipt of any payments made on account of the maintenance of the patient; or

(e) except as provided by subsection (3) of this section, a practitioner on the staff of the hospital to which the patient is to be admitted, or by the husband, wife, father, father-in-law, mother, mother-in-law, son, son-in-law, daughter, daughter-in-law, brother, brother-in-law, sister or sister-in-law of the patient, or of any such person as aforesaid, or of a practitioner by whom another medical recommendation is given for the purposes of the same application.

29. (1) In any case of urgent necessity, an application for admission for observation may be made in respect of a patient in accordance with the following provisions of this section, and any application so made is in this Act referred to as an emergency application.

(2) An emergency application may be made either by a mental welfare officer or by any relative of the patient; and every such application shall include a statement (to be verified by the medical recommendation first referred to in subsection (3) of this section) that it is of urgent necessity for the patient to be admitted and detained under section twenty-five of this Act, and that compliance with the foregoing provisions of this Part of this Act relating to applications for admission for observation would involve undesirable delay.

(3) An emergency application shall be sufficient in the first instance if founded on one of the medical recommendations required by section twenty-five of this Act, given, if practicable, by a practitioner who has previous acquaintance with the patient and otherwise complying with the requirements of section twenty-eight of this Act so far as applicable to a single recommendation, but shall cease to have effect on the expiration of a period of seventy-two hours from the time when the patient is admitted to the hospital unless—

(*a*) the second medical recommendation required as aforesaid is given and received by the managers within that period; and

(*b*) that recommendation and the recommendation first referred to in this subsection together comply with all the requirements of the said section twenty-eight (other than the requirement as to the time of signature of the second recommendation).

(4) In relation to an emergency application, section twenty-seven of this Act shall have effect as if in subsection (3) of that section for the words ' fourteen days ' there were substituted the words ' three days '. . .

31. (1) An application for the admission of a patient to a hospital under this Part of this Act, duly completed in accordance with the foregoing provisions of this Part of this Act, shall be sufficient authority for the applicant, or any person authorised by the applicant, to take the patient and convey him to the hospital at any time within the following period, that is to say—

(*a*) in the case of an application other than an emergency application, the period of fourteen days beginning with the date on which the patient was last examined by a medical practitioner before giving a medical recommendation for the purposes of the application;

(*b*) in the case of an emergency application, the period of three days beginning with the date on which the patient was examined by the practitioner giving the medical recommendation first referred to in subsection (3) of section twenty-nine of this Act, or with the date of the application, whichever is the earlier. . .

(4) A patient who is admitted to a hospital in pursuance of an application for admission for treatment may apply to a Mental Health Review Tribunal [2] within the period of six months beginning with the day on which he is so admitted, or with the day on which he attains the age of sixteen years, whichever is the later. . .

43. (1) Subject to the following provisions of this Part of this Act, a patient admitted to hospital in pursuance of an application for admission for treatment. . . may be detained in a hospital . . . for a period not exceeding one year beginning with the day on which he was so admitted . . . but shall not be so detained or kept for any longer period

---

[2] S. 3 of the Act provides for the establishment of Mental Health Review Tribunals. The First Schedule of the Act provides that they are to include ' (*a*) a number of persons . . . appointed by the Lord Chancellor and having such legal experience as the Lord Chancellor considers suitable; (*b*) a number of persons . . . being medical practitioners appointed by the Lord Chancellor after consultation with the Minister; and (*c*) a number of persons appointed by the Lord Chancellor after consultation with the Minister and having such experience in administration, such knowledge of social services or such other qualifications or experience as the Lord Chancellor considers suitable '.

unless the authority for his detention . . . is renewed under the following provisions of this section.

(2) Authority for the detention . . . of a patient may, unless the patient has previously been discharged, be renewed under this section—

    (a) from the expiration of the period referred to in subsection (1) of this section, for a further period of one year;

    (b) from the expiration of any period of renewal under paragraph (a) of this subsection, for a further period of two years,

and so on for periods of two years at a time.

(3) Within the period of two months ending on the day on which a patient who is liable to be detained in pursuance of an application for admission for treatment would cease under this section to be so liable in default of the renewal of the authority for his detention, it shall be the duty of the responsible medical officer to examine the patient; and if it appears to him that it is necessary in the interests of the patient's health or safety or for the protection of other persons that the patient should continue to be liable to be detained, he shall furnish to the managers of the hospital where the patient is liable to be detained a report to that effect in the prescribed form . . .

(5) Where a report is duly furnished under subsection (3) or subsection (4) of this section, the authority for the detention . . . of the patient shall be thereby renewed for the period prescribed in that case by subsection (2) of this section.

(6) Where a report under this section is furnished in respect of a patient who has attained the age of sixteen years, the managers or the local health authority, as the case may be, shall, unless they discharge the patient, cause him to be informed, and the patient may, within the period for which the authority for his detention or guardianship is renewed by virtue of the report, apply to a Mental Health Review Tribunal.

Powers and proceedings of Mental Health Review Tribunals

123. (1) Where application is made to a Mental Health Review Tribunal by or in respect of a patient who is liable to be detained under this Act, the tribunal may in any case direct that the patient be discharged, and shall so direct if they are satisfied—

    (a) that he is not then suffering from mental illness, psychopathic disorder, subnormality or severe subnormality; or

    (b) that it is not necessary in the interests of the patient's health or safety or for the protection of other persons that the patient should continue to be liable to be detained; or

    (c) in the case of an application under subsection (3) of section forty-four or subsection (3) of section forty-eight of this Act, that the patient, if released, would not be likely to act in a manner dangerous to other persons or to himself. . .

II. THE INVESTIGATION OF OFFENCES

(i) Police powers of entry, search and seizure

(a) *Entry*

DAVIS v. *LISLE*   [1936] 2 K.B. 434

Divisional Court

Two police constables, one in plain clothes, saw a lorry being repaired on the highway outside a garage. In their view it was causing an obstruction. When they returned five minutes later it had been moved into the garage. The police officers entered the garage to make inquiries. The appellant who was a member of the firm which occupied the garage told them to leave. The constable in plain clothes was in the act of producing his warrant card when the appellant rushed at him and struck him in the chest and stomach with his fist. He was convicted at Old Street Police Court of assaulting a police constable while in the execution of his duty, of obstructing a police constable while in the execution of his duty and of damaging a serge tunic to the amount of 7s. 6d. His appeals to London Quarter Sessions were dismissed. He now appealed to the Divisional Court.

LORD HEWART C.J. ... The point which is raised here with regard to the appellant's first two convictions is whether the officers were at the material time acting in the execution of their duty. In my opinion, they were not, and there are no grounds on which they can be held to have been so acting. The only ground which is put forward in support of the contention that they were so acting seems to me to be quite beside the point. I feel a difficulty in envisaging the legal proposition that because the police officers had witnessed an offence being committed on the highway they were acting in the execution of their duty in entering and remaining on private premises because the offenders then were on those premises. Admittedly, the officers had no warrant entitling them to search the premises. It is one thing to say that the officers were at liberty to enter this garage to make an inquiry, but quite a different thing to say that they were entitled to remain when, not without emphasis, the appellant had said: ' Get outside. You cannot come here without a search warrant.' From that moment on, while the officers remained where they were, it seems to me that they were trespassers and it is quite clear that the act which the respondent was doing immediately before the assault complained of was tantamount to putting forward a claim as of right to remain where he was. The respondent was in the act of producing his warrant card. That was after the emphatic order to ' get out ' had been made. Mr Raphael, with his usual candour, has admitted that, if the finding in the case that the respondent was in the act of producing his warrant card is fairly to be construed as meaning that he was asserting his right to remain on the premises, it is not possible to contend that at that moment the respondent was acting in the execution of his duty. I think it is quite clear that the act of producing his warrant card constituted the making of such a claim. I cannot think that there is any ambiguity about it. The law on the matter seems to me to be reasonably plain. *Great Central Ry. Co.* v. *Bates* [3] seems to me to be in point...

In my opinion it is not possible to maintain the conclusion that at the material time the respondent was acting in the execution of his duty as a constable. But that conclusion by no means disposes of everything contained in this case. It does not dispose of the question whether the assault which was in fact committed was justified. We have not the materials before us which would enable us to determine that question. Nor was appellant prosecuted for assault. He was prosecuted for assaulting and obstructing a police officer in the execution of his duty. Furthermore, the conclusion to which I have come does not affect the third conviction – that of damaging a tunic by ' wilfully and maliciously tearing ' it. On that part of the case no question arises whether at that moment the officer was acting in the execution of his duty and I see no reason why we should interfere with that conviction...

DU PARCQ and GODDARD JJ. delivered concurring judgments.

Appeal allowed as to first two convictions

Cp. *Robson* v. *Hallett* [1967] 2 Q.B. 393.

THOMAS v. SAWKINS [1935] 2 K.B. 249

Divisional Court

On 7 June 1934 the British Union of Fascists held a meeting at Olympia. As a result of the disturbances that occurred inside and outside the meeting, the Home Secretary, Sir J. Gilmour, was asked questions in Parliament on 11 June as to the role of the police on these occasions.

' SIR J. GILMOUR : ...

The question of the extent of the responsibility of the police for preserving order at public meetings was fully considered by a Depart-

---

[3] [1921] 3 K.B. 578. There a railway policeman had entered a warehouse because he had found a door open. He fell into an unfenced pit. His employers claimed that the warehouse owner was liable to reimburse them for the compensation it had paid him for his injury. The court held that the warehouse owner was not liable to pay as the policeman was not on the premises lawfully. Atkin L.J. said: ' [I]t appears to me quite impossible to suggest, merely because a constable may suspect there is something wrong, that he has a right to enter a dwelling house ... It is true that a reasonable householder would not as a rule object ... if the matter was done *bona fide* and no nuisance was caused. But the question is whether the constable has the right to enter.'

mental Committee appointed by one of my predecessors, the right hon. Herbert Gladstone, in 1909, and the present policy is based on the recommendations of that Committee. In accordance with that policy, it is no part of the ordinary duty of the police to deal with interrupters at public meetings held on private premises, and they have no legal authority to enter the premises except by leave of the occupier or the promoters of the meeting or when they have good reason to believe that a breach of the peace is being committed. Nor again is it any part of the duty of the police to act as stewards at a meeting, but the police have been advised by the Home Office that, on extraordinary occasions when there is a definite reason to apprehend disturbance of a serious character, they should make arrangements for policing the meeting inside as well as outside if they are asked to do so by the persons responsible for convening the meeting.

On the present occasion the British Fascists informed the Commissioner that the Fascists did not require the assistance of the police inside the building and at no stage was any request made for police to enter the meeting... I think, however, I ought to point out that, hitherto, the advice as regards police action has been based on the assumption that the stewards of a meeting in dealing with interrupters will act without undue violence and will themselves avoid illegal acts. If this assumption should be found to be unwarranted as regards meetings promoted by any particular organisation, the whole policy of police action inside such public meetings will have to be reviewed...

SIR AUSTEN CHAMBERLAIN: Having regard to the information which they received, did the police take any steps to have a police observer within the meeting?

SIR J. GILMOUR: There is a distinct difference between uniformed police going to a meeting, which is not proper unless they are asked to go, and the police taking such steps as they think are desirable to have the fullest information of these meetings.' [290 H.C.Deb. 5s. c. 1343]

Two months later the Communist party organised a series of meetings in Glamorganshire which were addressed by Alun Thomas. In spite of his objections, the police insisted upon attending them. After they had refused to leave a meeting on 9 August, he lodged a written complaint at the police station. At a meeting on 14 August, he threatened to eject them if they attended his meeting on 17 August. On 15 August he told an audience that 'if it were not for the presence of these people', pointing at the police, 'I could tell you a hell of a lot more'.

The meeting on 17 August was being held in the Caerau Library Hall, which had been hired by Fred Thomas for the purpose, to protest against the Incitement to Disaffection Bill then before Parliament, and to demand the dismissal of the Chief Constable of Glamorgan. It was extensively advertised by posters and notices chalked on the pavements inviting the public to come 'in crowds'. An inspector and two sergeants of the Glamorgan County Police were told by Fred Thomas at the entrance that he had been instructed not to admit the police. They nevertheless entered and sat down in the front row. Alun Thomas asked them to leave but they refused. He therefore went to the police station to lodge a complaint and to undertake that there would be no breaches of the peace if they were immediately withdrawn. On his return to the Hall he again requested the police to leave, but they still refused. He then told them they would be ejected and laid his hand upon the inspector's arm to eject him. Police Sergeant Sawkins pushed Thomas's hand away, saying ' I won't allow you to interfere with my superior officer.' Other police officers entered and no further attempt was made to eject them. Alun Thomas later preferred an information against Sawkins under s. 42 of the Offences against the Person Act, 1861, charging him with assault and battery. The question whether or not an assault had been committed depended on whether Sawkins was entitled to resist being ejected, i.e. whether the police were entitled to enter and remain at the meeting, even though they had been told by the convenors to leave.

The justices were of the opinion that the police officers had reasonable grounds for believing that, if they were not present, there would be seditious speeches and other incitements to violence, and that breaches of the peace would occur, and that they were therefore entitled to enter and remain at the meeting. They therefore dismissed the application. Thomas appealed to the Divisional Court.

LORD HEWART C.J. It is apparent that the conclusion of the justices in this case consisted of two parts. One part was a conclusion of fact that the respondent and the police officers who accompanied him believed that certain things might happen at the meeting which was then about to be held. There were ample materials on which the justices could come to that conclusion. The second part of the justices' finding is no less manifestly an expression of opinion. Finding the facts as they do, and drawing from those facts the inference which they draw, they go on to say that the officers were entitled to enter and to remain on the premises on which the meeting was being held.

Against that determination, it is said that it is an unheard-of proposition of law, and that in the books no case is to be found which goes the length of deciding, that, where an offence is expected to be committed, as distinct from the case of an offence being or having been committed, there is any right in the police to enter on private premises and to remain there against the will of those who, as hirers or otherwise, are for the time being in possession of the premises. When, however, I look at the passages which have been cited from Blackstone's Commentaries, vol. i., p. 356, and from the judgments in *Humphries* v. *Connor* [4] and *O'Kelly* v. *Harvey* [5] and certain observations of Avory J. in *Lansbury* v. *Riley,* [6] I think that there is quite sufficient ground for the proposition that it is part of the preventive power, and, therefore, part of the preventive duty, of the police, in cases where there are such reasonable grounds of apprehension as the

[4] [Below, p. 693.]
[5] [Below, p. 695.]   [6] [1914] 3 K.B. 229.

justices have found here, to enter and remain on private premises. It goes without saying that the powers and duties of the police are directed, not to the interests of the police, but to the protection and welfare of the public.

It was urged in one part of the argument of Sir Stafford Cripps that what the police did here amounted to a trespass. It seems somewhat remarkable to speak of trespass when members of the public who happen to be police officers attend, after a public invitation, a public meeting which is to discuss as one part of its business the dismissal of the chief constable of the county. It is elementary that a good defence to an action for trespass is to show that the act complained of was done by authority of law, or by leave and licence.

I am not at all prepared to accept the doctrine that it is only where an offence has been, or is being, committed, that the police are entitled to enter and remain on private premises. On the contrary, it seems to me that a police officer has ex virtute officii full right so to act when he has reasonable ground for believing that an offence is imminent or is likely to be committed.

I think, therefore, that the justices were right and that this appeal should be dismissed.

AVORY J. I am of the same opinion. I think that it is very material in this particular case to observe that the meeting was described as a public meeting, that it was extensively advertised, and that the public were invited to attend. There can be no doubt that the police officers who attended the meeting were members of the public and were included in that sense in the invitation to attend. It is true that those who had hired the hall for the meeting might withdraw their invitation from any particular individual who was likely to commit a breach of the peace or some other offence, but it is quite a different proposition to say that they might withdraw the invitation from police officers who might be there for the express purpose of preventing a breach of the peace or the commission of an offence.

With regard to the general question regarding the right of the police to attend the meeting notwithstanding the opposition of the promoters, I cannot help thinking that that right follows from the description of the powers of a constable which Sir Stafford Cripps relies on in Stone's Justices' Manual, 1935, p. 208, where it is said that when a constable hears an affray in a house he may break in to suppress it and may, in pursuit of an affrayer, break in to arrest him. If he can do that, I cannot doubt that he has a right to break in to prevent an affray which he has reasonable cause to suspect may take place on private premises. In other words, it comes within his duty, as laid down by Blackstone (Commentaries, vol. i., p. 356), to keep the King's peace and to keep watch and ward. In my view, the right was correctly expressed in *Reg.* v. *Queen's County Justices,*[7] where Fitzgerald J. said: ' The foundation of the jurisdiction [to bind persons to be of good behaviour] is very remote, and probably existed prior to the statute of 1360–1; but whatever its foundation may be, or by whatever language conveyed, we are bound to regard and expound it by the light of immemorial practice and of decision, and especially of modern decisions. It may be described as a branch of preventive justice, in the exercise of which magistrates are invested with large judicial discretionary powers, for the maintenance of order and the preservation of the public peace.' That passage was expressly approved in *Lansbury* v. *Riley*, and the statement of the law which it contains was adopted by Lord Alverstone C.J. in *Wise* v. *Dunning.*[9] In principle I think that there is no distinction between the duty of a police constable to prevent a breach of the peace and the power of a magistrate to bind persons over to be of good behaviour to prevent a breach of the peace.

I am not impressed by the fact that many statutes have expressly given to police constables in certain circumstances the right to break open or to force an entrance upon private premises. Those have all been cases in which a breach of the peace was not necessarily involved and it, therefore, required express statutory authority to empower the police to enter. In my opinion, no express statutory authority is necessary where the police have reasonable grounds to apprehend a breach of the peace, and in the present case I am satisfied that the justices had before them material on which they could properly hold that the police officers in question had reasonable grounds for believing that, if they were not present, seditious speeches would be made and/or that a breach of the peace would take place. To prevent any such offence or a breach of the peace the police were entitled to enter and to remain on the premises, and I agree that this appeal should be dismissed.

LAWRENCE J. delivered a concurring judgment.

Appeal dismissed

5. It is not the function of the police to become involved in civil disputes of any description which do not involve a breach of the peace however much it may be considered that the rights are on one side rather than the other. This applies to a wide variety of public and private activities, and includes disputes at all types of meetings. It is in particular no part of the duty of the police to attend any meeting for the purpose of maintaining general order. The organisers

---

[7] (1882) 10 L.R.Ir. 294, 301.   [8] [1914] 3 K.B. 229, 236.   [9] [Below, p. 697.]

of all meetings are responsible that the business for which the meeting has been called is transacted; it is also for them to provide stewards or like persons for the general control, if necessary, of those present at the meeting . . .

6. The only basis on which the assistance of the police may lawfully be invoked to eject from meetings persons who are not committing, or about to commit, offences is if they are trespassers. If persons have been requested to leave private premises and afforded reasonable time to depart, the owners of or tenants of the premises are lawfully entitled to eject them provided no more force than is reasonably necessary is used. For this purpose they may lawfully authorise other persons including the police to assist them. Although a police officer, however, may be lawfully authorised to assist in the ejection of a trespasser by an occupier, it has been held that he is not under a duty to assist.

7. Since the only basis upon which a police officer can lawfully be authorised to eject persons in cases of this type is that those persons are trespassers, the essential requirement for the police is to establish whether the persons in question are in fact trespassers. With this in mind chief officers of police are likely to approach with great caution any request to intervene with regard to the removal of alleged trespassers.

[Memorandum from the Home Office to the Select Committee of Privileges, Second Report, 1968–9. H.C. 308]

The anxiety of the police to avoid what might be interpreted as provocative actions also underlies their cautious approach to demonstrations and protests on private property. There is a measure of uncertainty even in their power to enter property when a breach of the peace has broken out or when a breach of the peace is anticipated,[10] though the courts are inclined to back them up when they have acted reasonably in all the circumstances.[11] The legal position is a good deal clearer when the police enter at the invitation of those who own or control the property, and recent actions by them have included the ejection of Protestants trying to break up a Christian unity service at St. Paul's Cathedral,[12] the removal from the London Pavilion in Piccadilly Circus of some people (allegedly members of the National Front) who were objecting to the film ' How I Won the

[10] See Williams, *Keeping the Peace* (1967) at 142 *et seq.*
[11] See, e.g., *Robson* v. *Hallett* [1967] 2 All E.R. 407 (breach of the peace had occurred); *McGowan* v. *Chief Constable of Kingston-upon-Hull* [1968] Crim.L.R. 34 (anticipation of breach of the peace).
[12] *The Times*, 23 Jan. 1969, p. 1.

War ',[13] the ejection of some protesters at a Labour Party meeting in Wood Green called to discuss local educational policy [14] and later at a meeting of Haringey council concerned with the same issue,[15] and the clearing of the public gallery at a Greater London Council meeting debating plans to increase rents.[16] Police intervention has been relatively rare on university and college premises, though the police were called in to remove students demonstrating against the installation of the Duke of Beaufort as Chancellor of Bristol University in 1966 [17] and, more recently, they clashed with students after the gates at the London School of Economics had been broken down.[18] There is in general no legal duty on the police to assist in the removal of trespassers and, even where a breach of the peace is involved, much depends on whether they feel it is tactically wise to get involved. Universities and colleges have been left in most circumstances to their own devices.[19]

[D. G. T. Williams, ' Protest and Public Order ', *Cambridge Law Journal* 28 April 1970]

(b) *Search and seizure*

THEFT ACT, 1968 [Ch. 60]

26. (1) If it is made to appear by information on oath before a justice of the peace that there is reasonable cause to believe that any person has in his custody or possession or on his premises any stolen goods, the justice may grant a warrant to search for and seize the same; but no warrant to search for stolen goods shall be addressed to a person other than a constable except under the authority of an enactment expressly so providing.

(2) An officer of police not below the rank of superintendent may give a constable written authority to search any premises for stolen goods—

(a) if the person in occupation of the premises has been convicted within the preceding five years of handling stolen goods or of any offence involving dishonesty and punishable with imprisonment; or

(b) if a person who has been convicted within the preceding five years of handling stolen goods has within the preceding twelve months been in occupation of the premises.

13 *The Times*, 24 Oct. 1967, p. 1.   14 *The Times*, 23 April 1969, p. 2.
15 *The Times*, 29 April 1969, p. 1.   16 *The Times*, 8 May 1968, p. 5.
17 *The Times*, 20 May 1966, p. 14.   18 *The Times*, 25 Jan. 1969, p. 1.
19 See generally *The Hornsey Affair*, by students and staff of the Hornsey College of Art (Penguin, 1969); Harry Kidd, *The Trouble at L.S.E. 1966–1967* (Oxford, 1969); Michael Beloff, ' The L.S.E. Story ', *Encounter*, May 1969, pp. 66–7.

(3) Where under this section a person is authorised to search premises for stolen goods, he may enter and search the premises accordingly, and may seize any goods he believes to be stolen goods.

ELIAS AND OTHERS v. *PASMORE AND OTHERS*

[1934] 2 K.B. 164

King's Bench Division

As a result of a speech he had made at Hunger Marchers' meeting in Trafalgar Square on Sunday, 30 October 1932 a warrant was issued for the arrest of William (Wal) Hannington, the national organiser of the National Unemployed Workers' Movement. In executing it on 1 November Pasmore and another police inspector entered the premises of the headquarters of the movement. In addition to arresting Hannington they seized a number of documents and took them to Scotland Yard. Some of these were returned on the same day and others on 8, 10 and 18 November. Some of those retained, consisting of letters written from Moscow in September by Elias, the chairman of the movement, were used in the trial of Elias on charges of inciting Hannington and Llewellyn to commit the crime of sedition by inciting illwill among His Majesty's subjects. The documents retained were however, not returned after the trials of Hannington and Elias.[20]

The plaintiffs claimed damages for trespass to the premises, the return of the documents and damages for their retention.

HORRIDGE J. .... It was not contended before me that there was any general right of search or seizure, but it was submitted that in certain circumstances there was a right to seize and detain documents; but this contention, if correct, did not in any way justify the seizure and removal of the documents and goods which have already been

[20] Elias was tried at the Central Criminal Court in December 1932 and was sentenced to two years' imprisonment. In sentencing him, Charles J. said: ' The jury have properly and, I think, inevitably found you guilty upon this indictment. One knows from the evidence and from one's own knowledge to an extent that the activities of this National Unemployed Workers' Movement are as inimical to the good interests of the working man as anything one can well imagine. It is only because the British working man is one of the most honest and law-abiding of men in this or any country that not one in a thousand or two thousand is seduced and led astray by this course which you endeavoured to make them take at the command or at the behest and direction of your friends in Moscow. The result of your efforts have been disorder, riot, damage, in various parts of this land. This is a misdemeanour, and the maximum sentence I can pass upon you is in my judgment far, far too short. The offence is a serious one. It is an offence which is dangerous to the peace of this country, and you will be kept in prison for two years' (*The Times*, 13 December 1932). Hannington was charged with attempting to cause disaffection among members of the Metropolitan Police Force contrary to the Police Act, 1919, and sentenced to three months' imprisonment (*The Times*, 9 November 1932).

returned, and I will deal later on in my judgment with the remedy which the plaintiffs have in respect of such seizure and removal.

The propositions put forward with regard to the removal of the remaining documents in bundle 2 (A)[21] were: (1) that there was a right to search the person arrested; (2) that the police may take all articles which were in the possession or control of the person arrested and which may be or are material on a charge against him or any other person; (3) that the police, having lawfully entered, are protected if they take documents which subsequently turn out to be relevant on a charge of a criminal nature against any person whatever; (4) that the police are entitled to retain property taken until the conclusion of any charge on which the articles are material.

In dealing with these different propositions, I only propose to deal with the authorities which seem to me to be the most relevant to this enquiry, although others have been cited to me. (1): As to the right to search on arrest. This right seems to be clearly established by the footnote to *Bessell* v. *Wilson*[22] in the report in the *Law Times,* where Lord Campbell clearly lays down that this right exists, but this right does not seem to me to authorize what was done in this case, namely, to seize and take away large quantities of documents and other property found on premises occupied by persons other than the person of whom the arrest was made.

As to the second contention, I think the case of *Dillon* v. *O'Brien*[23] clearly lays down that constables are entitled upon a lawful arrest by them of a person charged to take and detain property found in his possession which will form material evidence on his prosecution for that crime, and I think, for the reasons hereinafter stated with regard to the third contention, that that would include property which would form material evidence on the prosecution of any criminal charge. This, however, would not justify the seizure of the documents in this case with the exception of the letter signed ' P.C.', a copy of which was found on Hannington, and which is in the bundle 2 (A).

In support of the third contention, the Attorney-General relied on the case of *Pringle* v. *Bremner and Stirling*[24]...

That case seems to me to show that in the opinion of the Lord Chancellor and Lord Colonsay, though the seizure of documents was originally wrongful, if it in fact turned out that the documents seized were documents which might be properly used in a prosecution against any one, then the seizure would become excused. This, however, is a Scotch case, and must not be taken to have been decided on the law

---

[21] [This contained the documents used in the trial of Elias, i.e. the documents retained after 18 November.]

[22] 20 L.T.(O.S.) 233; 1 E. & B. 489; 118 E.R. 518.

[23] 20 L.R.Ir. 300, 316.   [24] 5 M.(H.L.) 55.

of England, and it becomes necessary therefore to consider whether in principle the same doctrine can be applied to a seizure of documents in England. There was no direct authority cited to me in support of the proposition in English law.

In examining the case of *Dillon* v. *O'Brien* [25] and the judgment of Palles C.B., it seems to me that the principle on which he held that there was a right to detain property in the possession of the person arrested is that the interest of the State in the person charged being brought to trial in due course necessarily extends as well to the preservation of material evidence of his guilt or innocence as to his custody for the purpose of trial, and in dealing with the case of *Entick* v. *Carrington* [26] he says [27]: ' The question there was as to the legality of a warrant, not only to seize and apprehend the plaintiff and bring him before a Secretary of State, but also to seize his books and papers. In that case there was no allegation of the plaintiff's guilt, nor that there was reasonable and probable cause for believing him to be guilty, nor that a crime had, in fact, been committed by any one, nor that he had in his possession anything that was evidence of (or that there were reasonable grounds for believing might be evidence of) a crime committed by him or any one else.'

In the case of *Crozier* v. *Cundey*,[28] where a constable having a warrant to search for certain specific goods alleged to have been stolen found and took away these goods and certain others also supposed to have been stolen but which were not mentioned in the warrant and which were not likely to be of use in substantiating the charge of stealing the goods mentioned in the warrant, it was held that the constable was liable to an action of trespass. Abbott C.J. says: [29] ' If those others had been likely to furnish evidence of the identity of the articles stolen and mentioned in the warrant, there might have been reasonable ground for seizing them, although not specified in the warrant.' He also said: ' I have expressed myself in this manner in order to prevent the supposition, that a constable seizing articles not mentioned in the warrant under which he acts, is necessarily a trespasser.' It therefore seems to me that the interests of the State must excuse the seizure of documents, which seizure would otherwise be unlawful, if it appears in fact that such documents were evidence of a crime committed by any one, and that so far as the documents in this case fall into this category, the seizure of them is excused.

The documents coming within this description were all the documents contained in bundle 2 (A) which were marked as exhibits and which were used at the trial of Elias ... In my opinion the seizure of these exhibits was justified, because they were capable of being and were used as evidence in this trial. If I am right in the above view, the

---

[25] 20 L.R.Ir. 300.   [26] 19 How.S.T. 1029.   [27] 20 L.R.Ir. 318.
[28] 6 B. & C. 232; 108 E.R. 439.   [29] 6 B. & C. 232.

original seizure of these exhibits, though improper at the time, would therefore be excused.

As to the fourth proposition, that the police are entitled to retain property the taking of which is excused until the conclusion of any charge on which the articles are material, Wright J. says in the case of *Reg.* v. *Lushington, Ex parte Otto*:[30] ' In this country I take it that it is undoubted law that it is within the power of, and is the duty of, constables to retain for use in Court things which may be evidences of crime, and which have come into the possession of the constables without wrong on their part. I think it is also undoubted law that when articles have once been produced in Court by witnesses it is right and necessary for the Court, or the constable in whose charge they are placed (as is generally the case), to preserve and retain them, so that they may be always available for the purposes of justice until the trial is concluded.' In this case, however, both the trials of Hannington and Elias have been concluded and I think there is no answer now to the claim for their detention after demand and for the £10 claimed as damages for their detention.

The Attorney-General stated that for the purposes of this case only he did not intend to contend that the plaintiffs, because these documents were of a seditious character, could have no property in the exhibits which had been used on the charge against Elias...

There will therefore be judgment for the plaintiffs for £20 damages for trespass [i.e. as regards the documents which were taken but not used at either trial], an order for the return of the documents comprised in 2 (A), £10 damages for detention of those documents, and the defendants must pay the costs of the action.

Judgment for the plaintiffs

In *Chic Fashions (West Wales)* v. *Jones* [1968] 2 Q.B. 312 Lord Denning M.R. noted: ' I will be noticed that Horridge J. relied on the fact that the documents *were* used in evidence at the trial. But I cannot think that it is a necessary condition to justify their seizure. It may often happen that, on investigation, the prosecution decide not to go on with the case. The seizure must be justified at the time, irrespective of whether the case goes to trial or not. It cannot be made lawful or unlawful according to what happens afterwards.'

REGINA v. *WATERFIELD AND ANOTHER*
[1964] 1 Q.B. 164

Divisional Court (Lord Parker C.J., Ashworth and Hinchcliffe JJ.)
The appellants had been convicted of assaulting a police constable in the execution of his duty and of inciting and procuring an assault, contrary

[30] [1894] 1 Q.B. 420, 423.

to the Offences against the Person Act, 1861, which was the relevant statute at the time. Two police constables had been told to keep watch on a car which was parked in a public car park and which the police wanted to examine for evidence that it had been involved in a collision. When the owner Waterfield and the other appellant came to take it away they were told that it was not to be removed. Lynn nonetheless attempted to drive it away, while the constables attempted to stop him. During the attempt the car came into contact with one of the constables. This was the assault which was the subject of the charge.

ASHWORTH J. [delivered the judgment of the court] . . . The first issue raised in this appeal is whether, on the facts as summarised above, the police constables, and in particular Willis, were acting in the due execution of their duty within the meaning of section 38 of the Offences against the Person Act, 1861, under which the charge of assault was brought. The two constables had been told by their sergeant that the car had been involved in a serious offence, although neither of them had any personal knowledge of the circumstances, and it is not disputed that at the time when the incidents now under consideration occurred they were engaged in preventing removal of the car; the question is, whether they were entitled to do this, at any rate without making a charge or an arrest.

It is convenient to emphasise at this point that the alleged offences were committed in King's Lynn and that special powers, for example, those conferred upon the Metropolitan Police under section 66 of the Metropolitan Police Act, 1839, or powers conferred under a special local Act, cannot be relied on as authorising the action of the two police constables . . .

In the judgment of this court it would be difficult, and in the present case it is unnecessary, to reduce within specific limits the general terms in which the duties of police constables have been expressed. In most cases it is probably more convenient to consider what the police constable was actually doing and in particular whether such conduct was prima facie an unlawful interference with a person's liberty or property. If so, it is then relevant to consider whether (a) such conduct falls within the general scope of any duty imposed by statute or recognized at common law and (b) whether such conduct, albeit within the general scope of such a duty, involved an unjustifiable use of powers associated with the duty . . .

In the present case it is plain that the police constables Willis and Brown, no doubt acting in obedience to the orders of their superior officer, were preventing Lynn and Waterfield taking the car away and were thereby interfering with them and with the car. It is to be noted that neither of the appellants had been charged or was under arrest and accordingly the decision in *Dillon* v. *O'Brien and Davis* [31] does not assist the prosecution.

It was contended that the two police constables were acting in the execution of a duty to preserve for use in court evidence of a crime, and in a sense they were, but the execution of that duty did not in the view of the court authorise them to prevent removal of the car in the circumstances. In the course of argument instances were suggested where difficulty might arise if a police officer were not entitled to prevent removal of an article which had been used in the course of a crime, for example, an axe used by a murderer and thrown away by him. Such a case can be decided if and when it arises; for the purposes of the present appeal it is sufficient to say that in the view of this court the two police constables were not acting in the due execution of their duty at common law when they detained the car...

For these reasons appeals against the convictions in respect of the assault on Police Constable Willis must be allowed and the convictions quashed...

Cp. *Ghani* v. *Jones* [1970] 1 Q.B. 693.

HOFFMAN v. *THOMAS*   [1974] 1 W.L.R. 374

Divisional Court

A constable signalled to the defendant to stop while he was driving along the M20 so that he could take part in a census of vehicles. The defendant stopped but refused to be counted and drove on. He was convicted for failing to obey the direction of a constable contrary to s. 22 (1) of the Road Traffic Act, 1972. This provides: ' Where a constable is for the time being engaged in the regulation of traffic in a road ... a person driving ... a vehicle who— (*a*) neglects or refuses to stop the vehicle or to make it proceed in, or keep to, a particular line of traffic when directed so to do by the constable in the execution of his duty, shall be guilty of an offence.'

LORD WIDGERY C.J. .... [I]t is common ground between counsel that there is no statutory power in the highway authority or anybody else to conduct a compulsory census; in other words there is no authority whereby motorists can be compelled to leave the highway and take part in a census exercise ... I turn, therefore, to the section on which this prosecution was based, section 22 (1) of the Road Traffic Act, 1972 ... There some doubt in my mind whether it is proper to describe the constable ... as regulating traffic for present purposes. That a constable has a duty to regulate traffic is unquestioned where the traffic requires regulation, and if this were an instance in which there was a possibility of collision between vehicles, or confusion of

[31] 16 Cox C.C. 245.

vehicles or anything else which required regulation for the conduct
of those vehicles in that sense then I would have had no hesitation in
saying that the first requirement of section 22 had been complied with.
But I have some doubts, although I do not find it necessary to express
a final conclusion on the point, whether it was right to describe the
constable as regulating traffic at all, when all that he was doing was
arbitrarily abstracting or selecting certain vehicles from a stream of
traffic proceeding along its lawful course and causing those vehicles
to enter the census point in order that their drivers may answer questions. I will assume for the moment for the purposes of this judgment
that that was a regulation of traffic but I express some considerable
doubts whether that really is the case.

The real issue here is whether the direction given by the constable
in the circumstances which I have described was a direction given by
him in the execution of his duty. If his duty empowered or authorised
him to order the defendant to go into the census point, so be it; then
I would have no doubt that the constable was acting in the execution
of his duty. But underlying all the argument in this case is the
accepted fact that there was no power to hold a compulsory census,
and no power existed to order the defendant to subject himself to
that census.

In deciding whether that circumstance prevents the direction from
being a direction given in the execution of the constable's duty, I
obtain the greatest assistance from the decision of this court in *Reg.* v.
Waterfield [1964] 1 Q.B. 164 . . .

The approach to the present problem is, if I may say so with respect,
well exemplified in the judgment of Ashworth J. He said, at p. 170:

' In most cases it is probably more convenient to consider what the
police constable was actually doing and in particular whether such
conduct was prima facie an unlawful interference with a person's
liberty or property. If so, it is then relevant to consider whether
(a) such conduct falls within the general scope of any duty imposed
by statute or recognised at common law and (b) whether such conduct, albeit within the general scope of such a duty, involved an
unjustifiable use of powers associated with the duty.'

Looking at that approach, it is perfectly clear that the constable's
action in the instant case did amount to an interference with the
defendant's personal liberty or property. Therefore one has to go on
and consider its justification under the heads to which Ashworth J.
refers. . .

What then is the general duty of a constable in these matters? In
Halsbury's Laws of England, 3rd ed., vol. 30 (1959), p. 129, there is
this statement:

' The first duty of a constable is always to prevent the commission of a crime. If a constable reasonably apprehends that the action of any person may result in a breach of the peace it is his duty to prevent that action. It is his general duty to protect life and property, and the general function of controlling traffic on the roads is derived from this duty.'

In the present instance there is nothing in the case which I can find to suggest that any life or property was endangered at all. There is no reason why the proceedings which were being conducted should give rise to such a danger, and nothing in the facts found to indicate that there was in this case any such danger. So the conception that the constable was acting in the protection of life and property seems to me not to be supported on the facts of the case, and although the right to regulate traffic must necessarily be a very wide one, as I have already indicated, that right does stem from the general duty to protect life and property. It is not a right to regulate traffic for the constable's own personal motives or entertainment; it is fundamentally a right to regulate traffic because of the dangers to life and limb which unregulated traffic can present. Accordingly it seems to me that neither at common law nor by any statutory provision to which we have been referred, had this constable any right to direct the defendant to leave the motorway and go into the census area.

This judgment has been much shortened, as has the argument, by the consensus of agreement that no such statutory right exists. I have come to the conclusion that when the constable made the signal directing the defendant to leave the motorway and go into the census area, he made a signal which he had no power to make either at common law or by virtue of statute, and consequently it seems to me in my judgment that the giving of that signal cannot have been an act in the execution of his duty, and on that ground alone it seems to me that the defendant's argument is successful and should be sustained...

ASHWORTH and MELFORD STEVENSON JJ. agreed.

KURUMA, SON OF KANUI v. THE QUEEN
[1955] A.C. 197.

Privy Council (Lord Goddard C.J., Lord Oaksey and Mr L. M. D. De Silva)

The appellant had been convicted by an Emergency Court in Kenya of being in unlawful possession of two rounds of ammunition contrary to the Kenya Emergency Regulations, 1952, and had been sentenced to death. He had been stopped at a road block. A police constable had run his hands over the outside of his clothing and had felt what he thought was a knife and some ammunition in his shorts. He called his superior who made the appellant take off his shorts. When they were shaken, two rounds of ammunition and a knife fell out. Under the regulations only a police officer of or above the rank of inspector was authorised to search anyone on whom he suspected evidence of the commission of an offence against the Regulations was likely to be found. Neither of the policemen concerned was of or above the rank of inspector. The appellant argued that the evidence which had been illegally obtained ought not to have been admitted at his trial.

LORD GODDARD [delivered the judgment of the court:] ... In their Lordships' opinion the test to be applied in considering whether evidence is admissible is whether it is relevant to the matters in issue. If it is, it is admissible and the court is not concerned with how the evidence was obtained. While this proposition may not have been stated in so many words in any English case there are decisions which support it, and in their Lordships' opinion it is plainly right in principle... There can be no difference in principle for this purpose between a civil and a criminal case. No doubt in a criminal case the judge always has a discretion to disallow evidence if the strict rules of admissibility would operate unfairly against an accused. This was emphasized in the case before this Board of *Noor Mohamed* v. *The King*,[32] and in the recent case in the House of Lords, *Harris* v. *Director of Public Prosecutions*.[33] If, for instance, some admission of some piece of evidence, e.g., a document, had been obtained from a defendant by a trick, no doubt the judge might properly rule it out. It was this discretion that lay at the root of the ruling of Lord Guthrie in *H.M. Advocate* v. *Turnbull*.[34] The other cases from Scotland to which their Lordships' attention was drawn, *Rattray* v. *Rattray*,[35] *Lawrie* v. *Muir*[36] and *Fairley* v. *Fishmongers of London*,[37] all support the view that if the evidence is relevant it is admissible and the court is not concerned with how it is obtained. No doubt their Lordships in the Court of Justiciary appear at least to some extent to consider the question from the point of view whether the alleged illegality in the obtaining of the evidence could properly be excused, and it is true that Horridge J. in *Elias* v. *Pasmore*[38] used that expression. It is to be observed, however, that what the judge was there concerned with was an action of trespass, and he held that the trespass was excused. In their Lordships' opinion, when it is a question of the admission of evidence strictly it is not whether the method by which it was obtained is tortious but excusable but whether what has

---

[32] [1949] A.C. 182, 191–2.
[33] [1952] A.C. 694, 707.
[34] 1951 S.C.(J.) 96.
[35] (1897) 25 Rettie 315.
[36] 1950 S.C.(J.) 19.
[37] 1951 S.C.(J.) 14.
[38] [Above, p. 660.]

been obtained is relevant to the issue being tried. Their Lordships are not now concerned with whether an action for assault would lie against the police officers and express no opinion on that point . . . It is right, however, that it should be stated that the rule with regard to the admission of confessions, whether it be regarded as an exception to the general rule or not, is a rule of law which their Lordships are not qualifying in any degree whatsoever. The rule is that a confession can only be admitted if it is voluntary, and therefore one obtained by threats or promises held out by a person in authority is not to be admitted. It is only necessary to refer to *Reg.* v. *Thompson,*[39] where the law was fully reviewed by the Court for Crown Cases Reserved.

As they announced at the conclusion of the arguments, their Lordships have no doubt that the evidence to which objection has been taken was properly admitted. The ground upon which leave to appeal was given therefore fails and they have humbly advised Her Majesty to dismiss the appeal . . .

KING v. *THE QUEEN* [1969] 1 A.C. 304

Privy Council

The Jamaican police obtained a warrant from a magistrate under the local Dangerous Drugs Act to enter and search premises on which they suspected drugs might be found. It did not, however, as the statute required, name the constable to whom it was addressed, and, although the statute authorised the issue of warrants to cover both search of premises and persons on them, it authorised only search of the premises. There was power under the Constabulary Force Law to arrest a person suspected of being in unlawful possession of ganja but that Act required the suspect to be taken forthwith before a magistrate to be searched. The police nevertheless entered the premises and searched King and found ganja on him. He was subsequently convicted of being in unlawful possession of ganja. He appealed to the Privy Council, arguing that the evidence obtained as the result of illegal search should not have been admitted.

LORD HODSON [delivered the judgment of the court:] . . . The evidence adduced by the prosecution, if accepted as credible as it was, was relevant and amply sufficient to prove the charge. . . [T]he appellant and another man, who was also searched, were told that the police were there to carry out a search for ganja. . . Although the search was not authorised by the Dangerous Drugs Law or the Constabulary Force Law, there was no evidence that the appellant was wilfully misled by the police officers or any of them into thinking that there

[39] [1893] 2 Q.B. 12; 9 T.L.R. 435.

was such authorisation. Corporal Gayle admitted at the trial that he knew that the warrant was to search the premises of Joyce Cohen and that it referred to the search of no-one else. He suspected that the appellant might have had ganja on him and did not offer him the opportunity of being searched in front of a justice of the peace although he knew of that right of a citizen. It can, therefore, be said that he should have had the advantage of a search before a magistrate and the choice of this was never offered to him.

The substantial argument on behalf of the appellant was that, in the discretion of the court, the evidence produced as a result of the search, which was the whole of the evidence against him, ought, though admissible, to have been excluded as unfair to him...

The matter has been discussed in a number of Scottish cases which were reviewed in the Kuruma case [40]. ... There is a passage in the opinion of the Lord Justice General (Lord Cooper) in *Laurie* v. *Muir* [41] which points to some of the difficulties of the question which is involved. He said:

'From the standpoint of principle it seems to me that the law must strive to reconcile two highly important interests which are liable to come into conflict – (a) the interest of the citizen to be protected from illegal or irregular invasions of his liberties by the authorities, and (b) the interest of the State to secure that evidence bearing upon the commission of crime and necessary to enable justice to be done shall not be withheld from courts of law on any merely formal or technical ground. Neither of these objects can be insisted upon to the uttermost. The protection of the citizen is primarily protection for the innocent citizen against unwarranted, wrongful and perhaps high handed interference, and the common sanction is an action of damages. The protection is not intended as a protection for the guilty citizen against the efforts of the public prosecutor to vindicate the law. On the other hand, the interest of the State cannot be magnified to the point of causing all the safeguards for the protection of the citizen to vanish, and of offering a positive inducement to the authorities to proceed by irregular methods.'

The discretion in criminal cases to disallow evidence if the strict rules of admissibility would operate unfairly against an accused has been emphasised before this Board in *Noor Mohamed* v. *The King*,[42] and in the House of Lords in *Harris* v. *Director of Public Prosecutions* [43] it was pointed out by Lord Goddard C.J., in *Kuruma's* case. In that case, he said:

[40] [Above, p. 667.]   [41] 1950 S.C.(J.) 19.
[42] [1949] A.C. 182; [1949] 1 All E.R. 365, P.C.
[43] [1952] A.C. 694; [1952] 1 All E.R. 1044, H.L.

' In their lordships' opinion, the test to be applied in considering whether evidence is admissible is whether it is relevant to the matters in issue. If it is, it is admissible and the court is not concerned with how the evidence was obtained.'

He said later in commenting on the Scottish cases to some of which reference has been made:

' If, for instance, some admission of some piece of evidence, e.g., a document, had been obtained from a defendant by a trick, no doubt the judge might properly rule it out.'

An instance of the exclusion of evidence on appeal on the ground that it has been obtained unfairly, although clearly admissible, is to be found in *Reg.* v. *Payne.*[44] The defendant was taken to a police station following a car collision. He was there asked if he was willing to be examined by a doctor, and it was made clear to him that the purpose of the examination was to see if he was suffering from any illness or disability and that it was no part of the doctor's duty to examine him in order to give an opinion as to his fitness to drive. The defendant then agreed to the doctor's examination. At his trial on charges of driving while unfit through drink and being in charge of a car while likewise unfit, the doctor gave evidence for the prosecution to the effect that the defendant was under the influence of drink to such an extent as to be unfit to drive. On appeal against conviction, although the doctor's evidence was clearly admissible it was held that, in the exercise of his discretion, the chairman of London Sessions should have refused to allow it to be given since, had the defendant realised the doctor would give evidence as to his fitness or unfitness to drive, he might have refused to allow himself to be examined. The appeal was allowed and the conviction quashed. *Callis* v. *Gunn*[45] is another case where the *Kuruma* case was considered. It was held that evidence of finger prints was relevant and admissible. It had been excluded by magistrates and on appeal by the prosecutor, which was allowed, it was held by the Divisional Court that, while the court had an overriding discretion to disallow evidence if its admission would operate unfairly against a defendant, there were no representations by the police officer who took the finger prints and nothing to justify the justices in excluding the evidence. Lord Parker C.J., in referring to the discretion, said that, as he understood it,

'... it would certainly be exercised in excluding the evidence if there was any suggestion of it having been obtained oppressively, by false representations, by a trick, by threats, by bribes, anything of that sort.'

[44] [1963] 1 W.L.R. 637; [1963] 1 All E.R. 848, C.C.A.
[45] [1964] 1 Q.B. 495; [1963] 3 All E.R. 677, D.C.

In *Reg.* v. *Murphy*,[46] Lord MacDermott C.J., giving the judgment of the Courts-Martial Appeal Court, made valuable observations on circumstances which will or will not render it unfair to allow admissible evidence to be given against an accused person. There the appellant, a soldier serving in the army, was charged before a district court-martial with the offence of disclosing information useful to an enemy, contrary to s. 60 (1) of the Army Act, 1955. The substance of that case against him was contained in the evidence of police officers who had posed as members of a subversive organisation with which the authorities suspected the appellant to have sympathies, and had elicited the information the subject of the charge, by asking the appellant questions about the security of his barracks. The appellant was convicted and appealed on the ground that the court-martial ought, in its discretion, to have rejected the evidence. The appellant relied in his argument on the use of the word ' trick ', which appears in *Kuruma's* case and *Callis* v. *Gunn* and in other cases as well. The court reviewed these and other authorities and, commenting on the passage in Lord Parker C.J.'s judgment, to which their lordships have already referred, used this language :

' We do not read this passage as doing more than listing a variety of classes of *oppressive* conduct which would justify exclusion. It certainly gives no ground for saying that any evidence obtained by any false representation or trick is to be regarded as oppressive and left out of consideration. Detection by deception is a form of police procedure to be directed and used sparingly and with circumspection; but as a method it is as old as the constable in plain clothes and, regrettable though the fact may be, the day has not yet come when it would be safe to say that law and order could always be enforced and the public safety protected without occasional resort to it. We find that conclusion hard to avoid on any survey of the preventive and enforcement functions of the police, but it is enough to point to the salient facts of the present appeal. The appellant was beyond any doubt a serious security risk; this was revealed by the trick of misrepresentation practised by the police as already described; and no other way of obtaining this revelation has been demonstrated or suggested. We cannot hold that this was necessarily oppressive or that Lord Parker of Waddington intended to lay down any rule of law which meant that it was the duty of the court-martial, once the trick used by the police had been established, to reject the evidence that followed from it.'

Their lordships agree with the judgment of the Courts-Martial Appeal Court in holding that unfairness to the accused is not susceptible of close definition. It was said :

[46] [1965] N.I.L.R. 138.

'. . . it must be judged of in the light of all the material facts and findings and all the surrounding circumstances. The position of the accused, the nature of the investigation, and the gravity or otherwise of the suspected offence may all be relevant. That is not to say that the standard of fairness must bear some sort of inverse proportion to the extent to which the public interest may be involved, but different offences may pose different problems for the police and justify different methods.'

Having considered the evidence and the submissions advanced, their lordships hold that there is no ground for interfering with the way in which the discretion has been exercised in this case. This is not, in their opinion, a case in which evidence has been obtained by conduct of which the Crown ought not to take advantage. If they had thought otherwise, they would have excluded the evidence even though tendered for the suppression of crime.

Their lordships will humbly advise Her Majesty that the appeal be dismissed.

Appeal dismissed

(c) *The interception of communications*

In October 1956 allegations were made that a barrister had been guilty of unprofessional conduct in obstructing the course of justice and his name was brought to the attention of the Bar Council by the Attorney-General, Sir Reginald Manningham-Buller. After the secretary of the Bar Council had asked the Assistant Commissioner of Police in charge of the Criminal Investigation Department whether he had any information on the matter, the Home Secretary, Major Lloyd George, authorized the disclosure to Sir Hartley Shawcross, the Chairman of the Bar Council, of material obtained as a result of the interception of the telephone communications of a suspected criminal, Billy Hill. He later authorized the disclosure of the same information to the Bar Council. After criticism of his action it was decided to refer the whole question of the interception of communications to a committee of Privy Councillors.

The authority of the Secretary of State to intercept communications

9. The origin of the authority of the Executive to intercept communications is obscure, and it is not surprising that conflicting views about the source of the power have been placed before us. The first public reference to the warrant of the Secretary of State authorising the opening of letters is in the Proclamation of May 25th, 1663, which forbade the opening of any letters or packets by anybody, except by the immediate warrant of the Principal Secretary of State. But long before this date the practice of opening letters had been followed.

10. It is a singular circumstance that the source of the power has never been the subject of judicial pronouncement, and the text-book writers have not discussed it in any fullness . . .

11. The existence of the power from early times has frequently been acknowledged; its exercise has been publicly known; and the manner of its exercise has been the subject of public agitation from time to time, and has been made the subject of debate in the House of Commons and the House of Lords. In the year 1844, a great agitation arose in the country, because the Secretary of State, Sir James Graham, had issued a warrant to open the letters of Joseph Mazzini; and after debates in both Houses of Parliament, two Secret Committees were set up, one of the House of Commons and one of the House of Lords. . . It is significant that both Committees avoided any discussion of the source of the authority upon which the Secretary of State exercised his power, and were content to recognise the existence of the power to intercept communications, and to rely upon the various statutes which refer to the existence of the power.

15. The Committee of the House of Lords had two former Lord Chancellors as members, Lord Brougham and Lord Cottenham, and in their Report the Committee said:

' The Committee have not thought it necessary to attempt to define the Grounds upon which the Government has exercised the Power afforded by public Conveyance of Letters of obtaining such Information, as might be thought beneficial for the public Service; it seems sufficient for the present Purpose to state, that the Exercise of this Power can be traced from the earliest Institutions in this Country for the Conveyance of Letters, from Orders in Council on the 22nd of November, 1626, and 24th of February, 1627 . . . In 1657, upon the first Establishment of a regular Post Office, it was stated in the Ordinance to be the best Means to discover and prevent any dangerous and wicked Designs against the Commonwealth . . . The Power, therefore, appears to have been exercised from the earliest Period, and to have been recognised by several Acts of Parliament . . . The Committee do not find any other Authority for such detaining or opening.'

16. The situation with regard to the opening and detaining of letters and postal packets is substantially the same in 1957 as it was in 1844, for section 58 (1) of the Post Office Act of 1953, which is the Act now governing the opening and detaining of letters, is substantially in the same terms as the earlier statutes of 1908, 1837 and 1710.

33. Section 58 (1) of the Post Office Act, 1953 provides—

' If any officer of the Post Office, contrary to his duty, opens . . . any postal packet in course of transmission by post, or wilfully detains or delays . . . any such postal packet, he shall be guilty of a misdemeanour . . .
Provided that nothing in this section shall extend . . . to the opening,

detaining or delaying of a postal packet . . . in obedience to an express warrant in writing under the hand of a Secretary of State.'

34. Postal packet is defined in section 87 (1) as meaning—

' A letter, postcard, reply postcard, newspaper, printed packet, sample packet, or parcel, and every packet or article transmissible by post, and includes a telegram.'

35. Section 58 of the Act of 1953 reproduces section 56 of the Post Office Act, 1908 which reproduces section 25 of the Post Office (Offences) Act, 1837 which in turn re-enacted without material amendment section 40 of the Post Office (Revenue) Act of 1710.

37. As telegrams are postal packets for the purposes of the Post Office Act of 1953, and are telegraphic messages for the purposes of the Telegraph Act of 1869 by virtue of section 3, it is an offence for an officer of the Post Office to ' open, delay or detain ' a telegram in course of transmission by post unless it is his duty so to do, or the opening, &c., is authorised by the warrant of the Secretary of State, or it is justified on one or other of the grounds mentioned in section 58 (1) of the Post Office Act, 1953.

40. The power to intercept telephone messages has been exercised in this country from time to time since the introduction of the telephone; and until the year 1937, the Post Office acted upon the view that the power, which the Crown exercised in intercepting telephone messages, was a power possessed by any other operator of telephones and was not contrary to law. No warrants by the Secretary of State were therefore issued, and any arrangements for the interception of telephone conversations were made directly between the Security Service or the Police Authorities and the Director-General of the Post Office.

41. In 1937 the position was reviewed by the Home Secretary and the Postmaster-General and it was then decided, as a matter of policy, that it was undesirable that records of telephone conversations should be made by Post Office servants and disclosed to the Police or to the Security Service without the authority of the Secretary of State. Apart from thinking that the former practice was undesirable, the Home Office was of opinion that the power on which they had acted to intercept letters and telegrams on the authority of a warrant issued by the Secretary of State, was wide enough in its nature to include the interception of telephone messages also. It was accordingly decided to act on this view of the law, and it has since been the practice of the Post Office to intercept telephone conversations only on the express warrant of the Secretary of State, that is, upon the authority which had already been recognised in the statutes to which we have referred dealing with letters and telegrams.

51. We are therefore of the opinion that the state of the law might fairly be expressed in this way.

(*a*) The power to intercept letters has been exercised from the earliest times, and has been recognised in successive Acts of Parliament.

(*b*) This power extends to telegrams.

(*c*) It is difficult to resist the view that if there is a lawful power to intercept communications in the form of letters and telegrams, then it is wide enough to cover telephone communications as well.

Purpose, use and extent of the power of interception

63. The great majority of warrants for interception for the purpose of the detection of crime have been, and are now, granted to the Metropolitan Police and Board of Customs and Excise. In what we say below about the interception of communications for the detection of crime, we confine our observations to these two authorities. For the sake of brevity we sometimes refer to them as the ' Police ' and the ' Customs '.

64. The principles on which the Home Office acts in deciding whether to grant an application for a warrant to intercept communications for the detection of crime were first reduced to writing in letters in similar terms sent to the Metropolitan Police and Customs in September 1951. These letters were occasioned by a recent increase in the number of applications and an increase in the number rejected by the Home Office. It was stated in these letters that the procedure of interception was ' an inherently objectionable one ', that ' the power to stop letters and intercept telephone calls must be used with great caution ', and that it must be regarded as ' an exceptional method '. In particular, three conditions were laid down both for the Police and for the Customs that must be satisfied before a warrant could be issued. These were: —

(*a*) The offence must be really serious.

(*b*) Normal methods of investigation must have been tried and failed, or must, from the nature of things, be unlikely to succeed if tried.

(*c*) There must be good reason to think that an interception would result in a conviction.

65. It was indicated in the letter to the Police that what the Home Office regarded as ' serious crime ' were offences for which a man with no previous record could reasonably be expected to be sentenced to three years' imprisonment, or offences of lesser gravity in which a large number of people were involved.

66. The type of crime that the Customs seek to detect is necessarily somewhat different from the violent crime with which the Metro-

politan Police is mainly concerned. The definition of ' serious crime '
upon which the Home Office acts when considering the issue of
warrants to the Customs is that ' the case involves a substantial and
continuing fraud which would seriously damage the revenue or the
economy of the country if it went unchecked '.

67. The arrangements concerning the issue of warrants to the
Security Service are similar, but the objectives of the Security Service
are different from those of the Police or Customs. The Home Office
considers each case. The principles governing the issue of warrants to
the Security Service can be stated in these terms : —

(*a*) There must be a major subversive or espionage activity that is
likely to injure the national interest.

(*b*) The material likely to be obtained by interception must be of
direct use in compiling the information that is necessary to the
Security Service in carrying out the tasks laid upon it by the State.

68. The same provision applies to the Security Service as to the
Customs and Police about the failure of normal means of detection.
But less stress is laid on the need to secure convictions, since the
Security Service is primarily concerned with safeguarding the State
and keeping itself informed about dangers to its security. Besides
securing convictions, the Security Service has the duty to keep up to
date its information covering espionage and subversion and to inform
Ministers and Departments of State about security matters that concern them.

154. We *recommend* that in no circumstances should material
obtained by interception be made available to any body or person
whatever outside the public service.

[Report of the Committee of Privy Councillors on the Interception of
Communications. Cmnd. 283 (1956–7) [47]]

On 17 November 1966 the Prime Minister (Mr Harold Wilson) stated:
' The House will know that, since the publication of the Report of the
" Committee of Privy Councillors appointed to Inquire into the Interception of Communications " in October, 1957, it has been the established
practice not to give information on this subject.

Nevertheless . . . I feel it right to inform the House that there is no
tapping of the telephones of hon. Members, nor has there been since this
Government came into office.

. . . But if there was any development of a kind which required a
change in the general policy, I would, at such moment as seemed compatible with the security of the country, on my own initiative make a
statement in the House about it ' [736 H.C.Deb. 5s. c. 635].

On 3 December 1959, in a case involving the Reading Police, Home
Secretary Butler said that although in his view it should not become a

---

[47] For footnote please see p. 678.

general practice the authority of the Home Secretary was not needed to listen in on an extension with the permission of the subscriber [614 H.C.Deb. 5s. c. 1381]. On 16 December he added: '[A]s the law now stands – it has hitherto been regarded as a fundamental principle of our Constitution that a Minister of the Crown has no power to intervene in the day-to-day operations of the police and in particular in their methods of detecting criminals, bringing blackmailers to justice, and otherwise conducting criminal investigations. Under the constitution, the police possess a measure of independence and autonomy...

Having made the constitutional position clear, I can tell the House that I have no reason to think that there is widespread listening-in by the police... There are many methods of inquiry such as overhearing conversations, reading a letter at the invitation of the recipient, or in a Shakespearian context, standing behind the arras – which may be distasteful but which on occasions it might be necessary for the police to use – [I]t would not be right for me to single out this particular method of investigation from others involving a disclosure by one party without the knowledge and consent of the other... I cannot see that it would be practicable to prohibit the police by legislation from using this means of inquiry' [615 H.C.Deb. 5s. c. 1535].

[47] In para. 119 the Committee noted: ' In our view public concern may be in some degree allayed by knowledge of the actual extent of the interception of letters and telephone messages which has been exercised on a much smaller scale than many people seem to have thought.' It published the figures in the following table.

Number of Interceptions Authorised by the Secretary of State

Year	Police, Customs, Post Office and Security		Drugs, Lotteries and Obscene Publications		Totals	
	Telephones	Letters	Telephones	Letters	Telephones	Letters
1937	17	335	—	221	17	556
1938	20	422	—	288	20	710
1939	29	643	—	330	29	973
1940	125	1,192	—	365	125	1,557
1941	180	833	—	29	180	862
1942	164	512	—	2	164	514
1943	126	327	—	2	126	329
1944	102	213	—	—	102	213
1945	56	90	—	—	56	90
1946	73	139	—	—	73	139
1947	110	162	—	28	110	190
1948	103	156	—	714	103	870
1949	133	183	—	458	133	641
1950	179	232	—	124	179	356
1951	177	261	—	225	177	486
1952	173	237	—	225	173	462
1953	202	240	—	219	202	459
1954	222	223	—	4	222	227
1955	231	205	10	—	241	205
1956	159	183	—	—	159	183

OFFICIAL SECRETS ACT, 1920   [10 & 11 Geo. 5. ch. 75]

4. (1) Where it appears to a Secretary of State that such a course is expedient in the public interest, he may, by warrant under his hand, require any person who owns or controls any telegraphic cable or wire, or any apparatus for wireless telegraphy, used for the sending or receipt of telegrams to or from any place out of the United Kingdom, to produce to him, or to any person named in the warrant, the originals and transcripts, either of all telegrams, or of telegrams of any specified class or description, or of telegrams sent from or addressed to any specified person or place, sent or received to or from any place out of the United Kingdom by means of any such cable, wire, or apparatus, and all other papers relating to any such telegram as aforesaid . . .

(d) *The use of informers*

REGINA v. MEALEY. REGINA v. SHERIDAN
[*The Times*, 30 July 1974]

Court of Appeal

The appellants were applying for leave to appeal against their convictions for conspiracy to rob and other offences, including the possession of a sawn-off shotgun. They argued that their convictions should not stand as they had been the victims of the acts of an agent provocateur, Kenneth Lennon, who had subsequently been found dead. It was suspected that he had been shot by representatives of the I.R.A.

THE LORD CHIEF JUSTICE (LORD WIDGERY). Shortly before his somewhat dramatic death Mr Lennon had made a statement to an officer of the National Council for Civil Liberties, the gist being that he had been associating with Mr Mealey, Mr Campbell and Mr Sheridan in Luton when they had discussed the possibility of robbery and other offences being committed, but had nevertheless been a police informer, and he had criticized the police for having put pressure on him to act as an informer . . .

Their Lordships had looked at statements made by Mr Mealey and Mr Sheridan. The first question was whether the evidence, if admitted, could have affected the verdicts . . .

The first thing that had to be made clear was that there was no evidence, apart from fragmentary evidence, that Mr Lennon was a agent provocateur in the true sense as defined in the Royal Commission on Police Powers (Cmd 3297) in 1928, when an agent provocateur was taken to mean ' a person who entices another to commit an express breach of the law which he would not otherwise have committed and then proceeds or informs against him in respect of such offence '.

His Lordship said, in fairness to Mr Lennon and the police, that it was not established to their Lordships' satisfaction that Mr Lennon came into that category. But that he was a police informer passing information to the police and operating with them was beyond doubt.

So far as the propriety of using such methods was concerned it was right to say that, in these days of terrorism, the police had to be entitled to use the effective weapon of infiltration. In other words it had to be accepted today, if indeed the contrary was ever considered, that it was a perfectly lawful police weapon in appropriate cases. Common sense indicated that, if a police officer or anybody else infiltrated a suspect society, he had to show a certain amount of enthusiasm for what the society was doing if he was to maintain his cover for more than five minutes.

Accordingly one had to expect that the emissary who penetrated the suspect organization did show a certain amount of interest and enthusiasm for the proposals of the organization, even though they were unlawful. Of course, the intruder, the person who found himself placed in the organization, had to endeavour to tread the somewhat difficult line between showing the necessary enthusiasm to keep his cover and actually becoming an agent provocateur, meaning thereby someone who actually caused offences to be committed which otherwise would not be committed at all.

It was impossible to decide positively whether or not Mr Lennon had overstepped the mark. Their Lordships had no reason to suppose that he had done so, but were prepared, for the purposes of the case, to accept that he had without its being established.

Mr O'Connor's submission was: ' If the defendant would not have committed a criminal offence but for the activities of a police officer or an agent provocateur and where those activities are found to be objectively unacceptable to the court, this constitutes a defence.' His Lordship would find it quite impossible to accept as a principle for the practice of the criminal law in this country any test so difficult of construction and so vague in its scope. He did not know what was meant by ' objectively unacceptable ' or who was to decide the question.

It was well-established that the so-called defence of ' entrapment ', which found some place in the law of the United States, found no place in our law. If a crime was brought about by the activities of someone who could be described as an agent provocateur, although that might be important as regards sentence, it did not affect the question of guilty or not guilty.

In *Browning* v. *J. W. H. Watson* (*Rochester*) *Ltd.* ([1953] 1 WLR 1172) Lord Goddard clearly said that, although people were in the category of agents provocateurs and although nobody liked people like that, yet it could not be said that there was a defence to a charge because of their presence, but a modest penalty could be imposed.

The same point was to be found in *R*. v. *McEvilly* ([1974] Crim LR 239) . . .

However, Mr Solley had insisted that it really was a question of evidence which was unfairly obtained. He cited authorities which established the general proposition that a judge in an English criminal trial had a wide discretion to exclude evidence unlawfully obtained. But the point of the present case had nothing to do with evidence unlawfully obtained . . . Finally, reference had been made to *R*. v. *Murphy* ([1965] NI 138).

Nothing which the court had said in the present case was to be taken as approving the action of an agent provocateur when his conduct crossed the line . . . No one who had read Lord Goddard's words about the dislike of such agents in this country should think that the attitude of the court was different in principle from what it was.

Attention had been drawn to the Home Office's guidance to police officers to assist them in drawing the line between acceptable co-operation with suspects and unacceptable provocation of offences. The extracts, so far as they had been made public, were published: ((1969) 119 *New Law Journal* 513). Their Lordships approved them so far as they went.

Cp. *R*. v. *Birtles* [1969] 2 All E.R. 1131.

(e) *The Security Service*

238. On 24th September, 1952, Sir David Maxwell Fyfe, then Home Secretary, issued this Directive to the Director-General of the Security Service, which is the governing instrument today:

' 1. In your appointment as Director-General of the Security Service you will be responsible to the Home Secretary personally. The Security Service is not, however, a part of the Home Office. On appropriate occasion you will have right of direct access to the Prime Minister.

2. The Security Service is part of the Defence Forces of the country. Its task is the Defence of the Realm as a whole, from external and internal dangers arising from attempts at espionage and sabotage, or from actions of persons and organisations whether directed from within or without the country, which may be judged to be subversive of the State.

3. You will take special care to see that the work of the Security Service is strictly limited to what is necessary for the purposes of this task.

4. It is essential that the Security Service should be kept abso-

lutely free from any political bias or influence and nothing should be done that might lend colour to any suggestion that it is concerned with the interests of any particular section of the community, or with any other matter than the Defence of the Realm as a whole.

5. No enquiry is to be carried out on behalf of any Government Department unless you are satisfied that an important public interest bearing on the Defence of the Realm, as defined in paragraph 2, is at stake.

6. You and your staff will maintain the well-established convention whereby Ministers do not concern themselves with the detailed information which may be obtained by the Security Service in particular cases, but are furnished with such information only as may be necessary for the determination of any issue on which guidance is sought.'

273. No one can understand the nature of the co-operation between the Security Service and the police forces unless he realises:

(1) The Security Service in this country is not established by Statute nor is it recognised by Common Law. Even the Official Secrets Acts do not acknowledge its existence. The members of the Service are, in the eye of the law, ordinary citizens with no powers greater than anyone else. They have no special powers of arrest such as the police have. No special powers of search are given to them. They cannot enter premises without the consent of the householder, even though they may suspect a spy is there. If a spy is fleeing the country, they cannot tap him on the shoulder and say he is not to go. They have, in short, no executive powers. They have managed very well without them. We would rather have it so, than have anything in the nature of a ' secret police '.

(2) The Security Service in this country is comparatively small in numbers. In some other countries there is to be found a massive organisation with representatives dispersed throughout the land. Whereas in this country it is and remains a relatively small professional organisation charged with the task of countering espionage, subversion and sabotage.

(3) Those absences (they are not deficiencies) – the absence of powers and the absence of numbers – are made up for by the close co-operation of the Security Service and the police forces. In particular, in London, with the ' Special Branch ' of the Metropolitan Police and in the country with the Chief Constables. If an arrest is to be made, it is done by the police. If a search warrant is sought, it is granted to a constable. The police alone are entrusted with executive power.

[Report of Lord Denning's Inquiry. Cmnd. 2152. 1963]

(f) *The examination of suspects*

THE JUDGES' RULES   [1964] 1 W.L.R. 152

In introducing the revised edition of the Rules which came into effect on 27 January 1964 Lord Parker C.J. said:

' The origin of the Judges' Rules is probably to be found in a letter dated October 26, 1906, which the then Lord Chief Justice, Lord Alverstone, wrote to the Chief Constable of Birmingham in answer to a request for advice in consequences of the fact that on the same circuit one judge had censured a member of his force for having cautioned a prisoner, whilst another judge had censured a constable for having omitted to do so. The first four of the present rules were formulated and approved by the judges of the King's Bench Division in 1912; the remaining five in 1918. They have been much criticised, inter alia, for alleged lack of clarity and of efficacy for the protection of persons who are questioned by police officers; on the other hand it has been maintained that their application unduly hampers the detection and punishment of crime. A committee of judges has devoted considerable time and attention to producing, after consideration of representative views, a new set of rules which has been approved by a meeting of all the Queen's Bench Judges.

The judges control the conduct of trials and the admission of evidence against persons on trial before them: they do not control or in any way initiate or supervise police activities or conduct. As stated in paragraph (e) of the introduction to the new rules, it is the law that answers and statements made are only admissible in evidence if they have been voluntary in the sense that they have not been obtained by fear of prejudice or hope of advantage, exercised or held out by a person in authority, or by oppression. The new rules do not purport, any more than the old rules, to envisage or deal with the many varieties of conduct which might render answers and statements involuntary and therefore inadmissible. The rules merely deal with particular aspects of the matter. Other matters such as affording reasonably comfortable conditions, adequate breaks for rest and refreshment, special procedures in the case of persons unfamiliar with the English language or of immature age or feeble understanding, are proper subjects for administrative directions to the police.'

These rules do not affect the principles

(*a*) That citizens have a duty to help a police officer to discover and apprehend offenders;

(*b*) That police officers, otherwise than by arrest, cannot compel any person against his will to come to or remain in any police station;

(*c*) That every person at any stage of an investigation should be able to communicate and to consult privately with a solicitor. This is so even if he is in custody provided that in such a case no unreasonable delay or hindrance is caused to the processes of investigation or the administration of justice by his doing so;

(*d*) That when a police officer who is making inquiries of any person about an offence has enough evidence to prefer a charge against that person for the offence, he should without delay cause that person to be charged or informed that he may be prosecuted for the offence;

(*e*) That it is a fundamental condition of the admissibility in evidence against any person, equally of any oral answer given by that person to a question put by a police officer and of any statement made by that person, that it shall have been voluntary, in the sense that it has not been obtained from him by fear of prejudice or hope of advantage, exercised or held out by a person in authority, or by oppression.

The principle set out in paragraph (*e*) above is overriding and applicable in all cases. Within that principle the following rules are put forward as a guide to police officers conducting investigations. Non-conformity with these rules may render answers and statements liable to be excluded from evidence in subsequent criminal proceedings.

RULES

I. When a police officer is trying to discover whether, or by whom an offence has been committed he is entitled to question any person, whether suspected or not, from whom he thinks that useful information may be obtained. This is so whether or not the person in question has been taken into custody so long as he has not been charged with the offence or informed that he may be prosecuted for it.

II. As soon as a police officer has evidence which would afford reasonable grounds for suspecting that a person has committed an offence, he shall caution that person or cause him to be cautioned before putting to him any questions, or further questions, relating to that offence.

The caution shall be in the following terms :

' You are not obliged to say anything unless you wish to do so but what you say may be put into writing and given in evidence.'

When after being cautioned a person is being questioned, or elects to make a statement, a record shall be kept of the time and place at which any such questioning or statement began and ended and of the persons present.

III. (*a*) Where a person is charged with or informed that he may be prosecuted for an offence he shall be cautioned in the following terms :

' Do you wish to say anything? You are not obliged to say anything unless you wish to do so but whatever you say will be taken down in writing and may be given in evidence.'

(*b*) It is only in exceptional cases that questions relating to the offence should be put to the accused person after he has been charged or informed that he may be prosecuted. Such questions may be put where they are necessary for the purpose of preventing or minimising harm or loss to some other person or to the public or for clearing up an ambiguity in a previous answer or statement.

Before any such questions are put the accused should be cautioned in these terms:

' I wish to put some questions to you about the offence with which you have been charged (*or* about the offence for which you may be prosecuted). You are not obliged to answer any of these questions, but if you do the questions and answers will be taken down in writing and may be given in evidence.'

Any questions put and answers given relating to the offence must be contemporaneously recorded in full and the record signed by that person or if he refuses by the interrogating officer.

(*c*) When such a person is being questioned, or elects to make a statement, a record shall be kept of the time and place at which any questioning or statement began and ended and of the person present.

IV. All written statements made after caution shall be taken in the following manner:

(*a*) If a person says that he wants to make a statement he shall be told that it is intended to make a written record of what he says. He shall always be asked whether he wishes to write down himself what he wants to say; if he says that he cannot write or that he would like someone to write it for him, a police officer may offer to write the statement for him. If he accepts the offer the police officer shall, before starting, ask the person making the statement to sign, or make his mark to, the following:

' I . . . wish to make a statement. I want someone to write down what I say. I have been told that I need not say anything unless I wish to do so and that whatever I say may be given in evidence.'

(*b*) Any person writing his own statement shall be allowed to do so without any prompting as distinct from indicating to him what matters are material.

(*c*) The person making the statement, if he is going to write it himself, shall be asked to write out and sign before writing what he wants to say, the following:

' I make this statement of my own free will. I have been told that I need not say anything unless I wish to do so and that whatever I say may be given in evidence.'

(*d*) Whenever a police officer writes the statement, he shall take down the exact words spoken by the person making the statement, without putting any questions other than such as may be needed to make the statement coherent, intelligible and relevant to the material matters: he shall not prompt him.

(e) When the writing of a statement by a police officer is finished the person making it shall be asked to read it and to make any corrections, alterations or additions he wishes. When he has finished reading it he shall be asked to write and sign or make his mark on the following certificate at the end of the statement:

' I have read the above statement and I have been told that I can correct, alter or add anything I wish. This statement is true. I have made it of my own free will.'

(f) If the person who has made a statement refuses to read it or to write the above mentioned certificate at the end of it or to sign it, the senior police officer present shall record on the statement itself and in the presence of the person making it, what has happened. If the person making the statement cannot read, or refuses to read it, the officer who has taken it down shall read it over to him and ask him whether he would like to correct, alter or add anything and put his signature or make his mark at the end. The police officer shall then certify on the statement itself what he has done.

V. If at any time after a person has been charged with, or has been informed that he may be prosecuted for an offence a police officer wishes to bring to the notice of that person any written statement made by another person who in respect of the same offence has also been charged or informed that he may be prosecuted, he shall hand to that person a true copy of such written statement, but nothing shall be said or done to invite any reply or comment. If that person says that he would like to make a statement in reply, or starts to say something, he shall at once be cautioned or further cautioned as prescribed by rule III (a).

VI. Persons other than police officers charged with the duty of investigating offences or charging offenders shall, so far as may be practicable, comply with these rules.

APPENDIX B

Administrative directions on interrogation and the taking of statements

7. Facilities for defence

(a) A person in custody should be allowed to speak on the telephone to his solicitor or to his friends provided that no hindrance is reasonably likely to be caused to the processes of investigation, or the administration of justice by his doing so...

(b) Persons in custody should not only be informed orally of the rights and facilities available to them, but in addition notices describing them should be displayed at convenient and conspicuous places at police stations and the attention of persons in custody should be drawn to these notices.

Cp. the following letter from the former Deputy Commissioner of the Metropolitan Police Force to the Community Relations Officer of Wandsworth in response to a complaint that the police were unreasonably preventing persons detained from contacting help outside. [*Race Today*, February 1972, p. 59.]

' Dear Mr Boxer,

... I fully understand that it must be difficult for persons outside the Police Service to understand why we decline to discuss the reasons which motivate a Station Officer to refuse a person in custody the facility of communicating with his solicitor, friends or other body. I would stress at once that the respectability or otherwise of the proposed recipient of the communication or, indeed, of the person in custody is irrelevant. Rather, the decision hinges on whether it is in the public interest that a request should be refused. Once anyone is told that a person is in custody there can be no control over that information. The person to whom the information is imparted may in all good faith inform other friends, who may use the information to prevent the investigation. Refusal to permit communication may, for example, in some cases frustrate the fabrication of an alibi, the escape of an accomplice, the disposal of evidence, and many other similar possibilities. The only sure way to ensure that investigations are not hampered is to proscribe any communication until the necessary enquiries have been made ... Having said all this, however, I think, with the benefit of hindsight, that the Station Officer might well have made use of the " Help on Arrest " scheme in this case without any interference with police enquiries. The decision, however, had to be made at the time. It was made in good faith, was not unreasonable and certainly, in my view, affords no basis for precipitate or extreme action on the part of anyone ...

> ROBERT MARK
> *Deputy Commissioner,*
> New Scotland Yard,
> Broadway, London SW1H 0BG '

REGINA v. *MILLS. REGINA* v. *ROSE*
[1962] 3 All E.R. 298

Court of Criminal Appeal (Winn, Lawton and Widgery JJ.)

The appellants were charged with burglary and larceny, cautioned, and then confined in separate cells in a local police station pending trial. The cells were separated by a corridor. The men shouted incriminating remarks to one another across this corridor in which they discussed, *inter alia*, whether the police had ' found all the gear ', how much money was involved, and where it was hidden, and also possible alibis. These remarks were recorded on a tape-recorder placed in an empty cell but at the trial a policeman also said he remembered hearing them. Much of the discussion on the appeal was about the admissibility of the tape-recording, but counsel also argued that the statements themselves ought not to be admitted.

WINN J. [delivered the judgment of the Court:] ... I turn now to the separate submission of counsel for the appellant Rose. This is that the conversations were put in evidence in breach of one or more of the Judges' Rules, albeit counsel was not minded to contend that the use of the tape recorder in the manner which I have endeavoured to indicate was itself objectionable. Counsel referred to ... the Judges' Rules. As the court understood his submission, it was that a man who has been cautioned, as both these appellants were cautioned, and, a fortiori, a man who on being cautioned replied, as the appellant Rose did reply: 'I will keep what I have to say till I get to court' is thereafter in a state of asylum, and the cell into which he is put is his own 'castle' and he should be entitled to feel himself free from any eavesdropping or potential use against him of anything that may have come from his lips during his incarceration in the cell. The court cannot accept that exposition of the effect of the Judges' Rules, nor does it feel that there is any substance at all in the complaint made by counsel for the appellant Rose that this was sharp practice on the part of the police. By saying that the court does not implicitly, let alone expressly, give any approval to a police practice, if anywhere it were to be found to exist – that is not this case – of setting up microphones in cells for the purpose of tape recording what may be said in the cells. These appellants brought on themselves what they suffered by being so fatuous as to shout incriminating observations across a corridor to one another. In so far as reference needs to be made to the rules, it is to be observed that the caution itself says: '... whatever you say will be taken down in writing and may be given in evidence', which, in a sense, is a warning against this type of folly. ..

CHAPTER XIV

PUBLIC PROTEST AND THE
MAINTENANCE OF PUBLIC ORDER

I. PUBLIC MEETINGS AND PUBLIC PROCESSIONS

(i) Riot and unlawful assembly

REGINA v. CUNNINGHAME, GRAHAM AND BURNS
(1888) 16 Cox 420

CHARLES J. [to the jury]...Gentlemen, a riot is a disturbance of the peace by three persons at the least who, with an intent to help one another against any person who opposes them in the execution of some enterprise or other, actually execute that enterprise in a violent and turbulent manner to the alarm of the people. Whether such enterprise be a lawful or an unlawful one does not matter [1]... Now, with regard to an unlawful assembly, what is an unlawful assembly? That has been laid down by the very highest authority in these terms: ' An unlawful assembly is an assembly of persons with the intention of carrying out any common purpose,' and mark, ' lawful or unlawful, in such a manner as to give firm and courageous persons in the neighbourhood of such assembly ground to apprehend a breach of the peace in consequence of it.' Those are the definitions of riot and unlawful assembly, and there can be no doubt that either of those offences is committed, whatever be the end which the persons who commit them have in view...

BEATTY AND OTHERS v. GILLBANKS
(1882) 15 Cox 138

Divisional Court

It was the practice of members of the Salvation Army to march through Weston-super-Mare headed by a band to collect a crowd together and take them to the Salvation Army Hall for a meeting. It was also the

---

[1] [Cp. Phillimore J. in *Field and Others* v. *Receiver of Metropolitan Police* [1907] 2 K.B. at 860, ' [T]here are five necessary elements of a riot – (1) number of persons, three at least; (2) common purpose; (3) execution of inception of the common purpose; (4) an intent to help one another by force if necessary against any person who may oppose them in the execution of their common purpose; (5) force or violence... displayed in such a manner as to alarm at least one person of reasonable firmness and courage.']

689

practice here, as in a number of other places, for the Salvation Army to be attacked in the course of their parades, in this case by the so-called Skeleton Army. After a particularly bad incident on 23 March 1882 the local magistrates purported to ban further parades and when the Salvation Army assembled on 26 March their procession was stopped by the police and Beatty was told that he would be arrested if he refused to disperse. Beatty refused and was arrested but told the others to carry on. They too were arrested. All submitted quietly to their arrest. None of them committed any violent act. The case has therefore become one of the classic statements of the extent to which participants in a peaceful procession can be charged with a criminal offence for refusing to disperse when the police have reasonable grounds for apprehending a breach of the peace by other people who do not want the procession to take place. But though it is a classic it is also limited in its scope and application. The Salvationists were charged with and convicted of unlawful assembly and required to find sureties to keep the peace. Their appeal against that conviction was upheld. It is clear, however, from subsequent cases, that the police can achieve the same result in such circumstances by charging those who are in the position of the appellants in this case with obstructing them in the execution of their duty (see the cases below on action to prevent a breach of the peace).

FIELD J. . . . The appellants . . . belong to a body of persons called the Salvation Army, who are associated together for a purpose which cannot be said to be otherwise than lawful and laudable, or at all events cannot be called unlawful, their object and intention being to induce a class of persons who have little or no knowledge of religion and no taste or disposition for religious exercises or for going to places of worship, to join them in their processions, and so to get them together to attend and take part in their religious exercises, in the hope that they may be reclaimed and drawn away from vicious and irreligious habits and courses of life, and that a kind of revival in the matter of religion may be brought about amongst those who were previously dead to any such influences . . . [A]nd, as has been said by their learned counsel, and doubtless with perfect truth, so far are they from desiring to carry out that object by means of any force or violence, their principles are directly and entirely opposed to any conduct of that kind, or to the exercise or employment of anything like physical force; and, indeed, it appears that on the occasion in question they used no personal force or violence, but, on the contrary, when arrested by the police, they submitted quietly without the exhibition of any resistance either on their own parts or on that of any other member of their body. . . [O]n this 26th day of March they assembled, as they had previously done on other occasions, in considerable numbers at their hall, and proceeded to march thence in procession through the streets of the town of Weston-super-Mare.

Now that, in itself, was certainly not an unlawful thing to do, nor can such an assembly be said to be an unlawful one. Numerous instances might be mentioned of large bodies of persons assembling in much larger numbers, and marching, accompanied by banners and bands of music, through the public streets, and no one has ever doubted that such processions were perfectly lawful. Now the appellants complain that, for having so assembled... they have been adjudged guilty of the offence of holding an unlawful assembly, and have in consequence been ordered to find sureties to keep the peace, in the absence of any evidence of their having broken it... The offence charged against them is ' unlawfully and tumultuously assembling with others to the disturbance of the public peace, and against the peace of the Queen ' ... There is no doubt that the appellants did assemble together with other persons in great numbers... But there was nothing so far as the appellants were concerned to show that their conduct was in the least degree ' tumultuous ' or ' against the peace '... [A]nd it is admitted by the learned counsel for the respondent, that as regards the appellants themselves, there was no disturbance of the peace, and that their conduct was quiet and peaceable. But then it is argued that, as in fact their line of conduct was the same as had on previous similar occasions led to tumultuous and riotous proceedings with stone-throwing and fighting, causing a disturbance of the public peace and terror to the inhabitants of the town, and as on the present occasion like results would in all probability be produced, therefore the appellants, being well aware of the likelihood of such results again occurring, were guilty of the offence charged against them. Now, without doubt, as a general rule it must be taken that every person intends what are the natural and necessary consequences of his own acts, and if in the present case it had been their intention, or if it had been the natural and necessary consequence of their acts, to produce the disturbance of the peace which occurred, then the appellants would have been responsible for it, and the magistrates would have been right in binding them over to keep the peace. But the evidence as set forth in the case shows that, so far from that being the case, the acts and conduct of the appellants caused nothing of the kind, but, on the contrary, that the disturbance that did take place was caused entirely by the unlawful and unjustifiable interference of the Skeleton Army... and that but for the opposition and molestation offered to the Salvationists by these other persons, no disturbance of any kind would have taken place. The appellants were guilty of no offence in their passing through the streets, and why should other persons interfere with or molest them? What right had they to do so? If they were doing anything unlawful it was for the magistrates and police, the appointed guardians of law and order, to interpose. The law relating to unlawful assemblies, as laid down in the books and the cases, affords no support to the view... that persons acting lawfully are to be held responsible and punished merely because other persons are thereby induced to act unlawfully and create a disturbance... Many examples of what are unlawful assemblies are given in Hawkins' Pleas of the Crown, book I, cap. 28, sects. 9 and 10, in all of which the necessary circumstances of terror are present in the assembly itself, either as regards the object for which it is gathered together, or in the manner of its assembling and proceeding to carry out that object. The present case, however, differs from the cases there stated; for here the only terror that existed was caused by the unlawful resistance wilfully and designedly offered to the proceedings of the Salvation Army by an unlawful organisation outside and distinct from them, called the Skeleton Army. It was suggested by the respondent's counsel that, if these Salvation processions were allowed, similar opposition would be offered to them in future, and that similar disturbances would ensue. But I cannot believe that that will be so. I hope, and I cannot but think, that when the Skeleton Army, and all other persons who are opposed to the proceedings of the Salvation Army, come to learn, as they surely will learn, that they have no possible right to interfere with or in any way to obstruct the Salvation Army in their lawful and peaceable processions, they will abstain from opposing or disturbing them. It is usual happily in this country for people to respect and obey the law when once declared and understood, and I hope and have no doubt that it will be so in the present case. But, if it should not be so, there is no doubt that the magistrates and police, both at Weston-super-Mare and everywhere else, will understand their duty and not fail to do it efficiently, or hesitate, should the necessity arise, to deal with the Skeleton Army and other disturbers of the public peace as they did in the present instance with the appellants, for no one can doubt that the authorities are only anxious to do their duty and to prevent a disturbance of the public peace. The present decision of the justices, however, amounts to this, that a man may be punished for acting lawfully if he knows that his so doing may induce another man to act unlawfully – a proposition without any authority whatever to support it. Under these circumstances, the questions put to us by the justices must be negatively answered, and the order appealed against be discharged.

CAVE J. delivered a concurring judgment.

Judgment for the appellants with costs

(ii) Action to prevent a breach of the peace

HUMPHRIES v. *CONNOR*   (1864) 17 Ir.C.L.R. 1

Court of Queen's Bench in Ireland

This was an action for assault in which the plaintiff complained that the defendant, a Constabulary Inspector in Swanlinbar, had assaulted and beaten her and torn and spoiled her clothes. The defence was that the assault, which consisted in the removal of a party emblem, an orange lily which she was wearing, was necessary to prevent a breach of the peace.

O'BRIEN J. . . . The defence states, that the defendant was Constabulary Inspector in the district in which the transaction occurred; and I need not say that it was his duty, as such, to preserve the public peace and prevent a breach of it. The defence also states in substance, that the plaintiff's wearing the orange lily at that time was calculated and tended to provoke animosity among different classes of her Majesty's subjects; that several persons, who were provoked by it, followed the plaintiff, made a great disturbance, and threatened plaintiff with personal violence; that the defendant, in order to preserve the public peace and prevent a breach of it, and in order to prevent plaintiff from such threatened violence, and to restore order, &c., requested plaintiff to remove the lily; that plaintiff refused to do so, and on the contrary continued to wear it, and thereby to excite and provoke those persons to inflict personal violence on her, and to cause such disturbance and threats. It further states, that it was likely the public peace would be broken, and violence inflicted on the plaintiff, in consequence of her continuing to wear the lily; and that in order to preserve the public peace, and protect plaintiff from such threatened violence, the defendant *gently and quietly,* and *necessarily and unavoidably,* removed the lily from plaintiff, doing her no injury whatever, and thereby protected plaintiff from such threatened violence, which would otherwise have been inflicted upon her, and preserved the public peace, which would otherwise have been broken. Such is the substance of the defence... The observations of Baron Alderson in *Cooke* v. *Nethercote,*[2] and in *Regina* v. *Browne,*[3] and those of Baron Parke, in *Kyle* v. *Bell,*[4] show the power which policemen have, even to arrest a party, in order to prevent a breach of the peace being committed or renewed. In another case – *Regina* v. *Hogan*[5] – where it appeared that a man playing the bagpipes at night had attracted a crowd of dissolute persons about him, Coltman J. held that a con-

[2] (1835) 6 C. & P. 744; 172 E.R. 1445.
[3] (1841) C. & M. 314; 174 E.R. 522.
[4] (1836) 1 M. & W. 519; 150 E.R. 540.
[5] (1837) 8 C. & P. 171; 173 E.R. 447.

stable who had directed the man to move on did not exceed his duty by merely laying his hand on the man's shoulder, with that view only.

... It has, however, been urged by plaintiff's Counsel that injurious consequences would result from our decision in defendant's favour – giving to constables a power so capable of being abused. I think it sufficient, in answer to this argument, to say that our decision would not be applicable to a state of facts where the power was abused; and that it would not protect a constable from any unnecessary, excessive, or improper exercise of such power in other cases...

HAYES J.... A constable, by his very appointment, is by law charged with the solemn duty of seeing that the peace is preserved. The law has not ventured to lay down what precise measures shall be adopted by him in every state of facts which calls for his interference. But it has done far better; it has announced to him, and to the public over whom he is placed, that he is not only at liberty, but is bound, to see that the peace be preserved, and that he is to do everything that is necessary for that purpose, neither more nor less. What he does, he does upon the peril of answering to a jury of his country, when his conduct shall be brought into question, and he shall be charged either with exceeding or falling short of his duty. In the present case it is said that it would be a lamentable thing if an individual were to be obstructed and assaulted when doing a perfectly legal act; and that there is no law against wearing an emblem or decoration of one kind or another. I agree with that in the abstract; but I think it is not straining much the legal maxim, *sic utere tuo ut alienum non lædas* – to hold that people shall not be permitted to use even legal rights for illegal purposes. When a constable is called upon to preserve the peace, I know no better mode of doing so than that of removing what he sees to be the provocation to the breach of the peace; and, when a person deliberately refuses to acquiesce in such removal, after warning so to do, I think the constable is authorised to do everything necessary and proper to enforce it. It would seem absurd to hold that a constable may arrest a person whom he finds committing a breach of the peace, but that he must not interfere with the individual who has wantonly provoked him to do so. But whether the act which he did was or was not, under all the circumstances, *necessary* to preserve the peace, is for the jury to decide. The defendant in his defence asserts that it was; and, for the purposes of this demurrer, we must take that assertion to be true. In my opinion the plea is good.

FITZGERALD J. My Brother O'Brien has already intimated that I entertain a doubt – and I may add a very serious doubt – as to the correctness of the judgment of the Court, though I defer to the greater experience and sounder opinions of my Brothers... [T]he doubt which I have is, whether a constable is entitled to interfere with one who is not about to commit a breach of the peace, or to do, or join in any illegal act, but who is likely to be made an object of insult or injury by other persons who are about to break the Queen's peace...

I do not see where we are to draw the line. If a constable is at liberty to take a lily from one person, because the wearing of it is displeasing to others, who may make it an excuse for a breach of the peace, where are we to stop? It seems to me that we are making, not the law of the land, but the law of the mob supreme, and recognising in constables a power of interference with the rights of the Queen's subjects, which, if carried into effect to the full extent of the principle, might be accompanied by constitutional danger. If it had been alleged that the lady wore the emblem with an intent to provoke a breach of the peace, it would render her a wrongdoer; and she might be chargeable as a person creating a breach of the peace.

O'KELLY v. *HARVEY*   (1883) 15 Cox 435

Court of Appeal in Ireland

Shortly after placards announcing a meeting of the Land League in Ireland with Parnell as a speaker had been put up, others appeared calling upon Orangemen to gather together and give him a warm reception.[6] When the Land League met, a local justice of the peace called upon them to disperse and when they refused put his hand on the plaintiff in an attempt to disperse the meeting. The plaintiff brought an action against him for assault.

LAW L.C. [delivered the judgment of the Court:]... The defence... states that the defendant, being a justice of the peace and present, believed and had reasonable grounds for believing that the peace could not otherwise be preserved than by separating and dispersing the plaintiff's Land meeting, and justifies his action on that ground.

---

[6] Orangemen of Fermanagh, will you allow your country to be disgraced by letting a Land League meeting be held (as advertised) at Brookeborough, on 17th Dec. inst., where addresses are to be delivered not only dishonest but treasonable, and opposed to your principles?

When the Government won't protect Protestant life and property, it is time we should do so ourselves, and put a stop to all treasonable proceedings in our loyal county Fermanagh.

Remember the treatment of your brethren at Lough Mask!.! ! Assemble in your thousands at Brookeborough on Tuesday, and give Parnell and his associates a warm reception.

God save the Queen.

Brookeborough, Dec. 4th, 1880   (W. & J. Gibson, Printers, Enniskillen.)

The question then seems to be reduced to this: assuming the plaintiff and others assembled with him to be doing nothing unlawful, but yet that there were reasonable grounds for the defendant believing as he did that there would be a breach of the peace if they continued so assembled, and that there was no other way in which the breach of the peace could be avoided but by stopping and dispersing the plaintiff's meeting – was the defendant justified in taking the necessary steps to stop and disperse it? In my opinion he was so justified ... [T]he duty of a justice of the peace being to preserve the peace unbroken, he is, of course, entitled, and in fact bound to intervene the moment he has reasonable apprehensions of a breach of the peace being imminent ... Accordingly, in the present case, even assuming that the danger to the public peace arose altogether from the threatened attack of another body on the plaintiff and his friends, still, if the defendant believed and had just grounds for believing that the peace could only be preserved by withdrawing the plaintiff and his friends from the attack with which they were threatened, it was I think the duty of the defendant to take that course. This indeed was, as it appears to me, substantially decided here some years ago by the Court of Queen's Bench in the case of *Humphries* v. *Connor* [7] ... During the argument the recent case of *Beatty* v. *Gillbanks* [8] was much relied on by the plaintiff's counsel. I frankly own that I cannot understand that decision, having regard to the facts stated in the special case there submitted to the court, and which appear to me to have presented all the elements necessary to constitute the offence known as 'unlawful assembly'. Field J. quotes a passage from Serjeant Hawkins to the effect that any meeting of great numbers of people, with such circumstances of terror as cannot but endanger the public peace and raise fears and jealousies among the King's subjects, is an unlawful assembly, and suggests that, for this purpose, the 'circumstances of terror' must exist in the assembly itself. Well, even supposing this to be so, what is to be said as to the paragraph of the case which stated that the particular assemblage in question was a terror to the peaceable inhabitants of the town, and especially to those then going to their respective places of worship, and was calculated to endanger, and did endanger, the public peace. I should have thought that an assemblage of that character had in itself sufficient 'circumstances of terror' to make it unlawful. But, again, we find it stated that Beatty and his friends constituting this Salvation Army procession knew they were likely to be attacked on this occasion, as before, by the body which had been organised in antagonism to them, and that there would be fighting, stone-throwing, and disturbance as

[7] [Above, p. 693.]   [8] [Above, p. 689.]

there had been on previous occasions; and further, that they intended, on meeting such opposition, to fight and force their way through the streets and public places as they had done before. I confess I should have thought that this, too, was no bad description of an unlawful assembly. Indeed, I have always understood the law to be that any needless assemblage of persons in such numbers and manner and under such circumstances as are likely to provoke a breach of the peace, was itself unlawful; and this, I may add, appears to be the view taken by the very learned persons who revised the Criminal Code Bill in 1878. But, after all, that decision of Field and Cave JJ. is no authority against the view I take of the case now before us. I assume here that the plaintiff's meeting was not unlawful. But the question still remains, Was not the defendant justified in separating and dispersing it if he had reasonable ground for his belief that by no other possible means could he perform his duty of preserving the peace? For the reasons already given I think he was so justified, and therefore that the defence in question is good; that the order of the Exchequer Division overruling the plaintiff's demurrer thereto should be affirmed; and the plaintiff's appeal to this court be dismissed accordingly.

WISE v. *DUNNING*   [1902] 1 K.B. 167

Divisional Court

This was an appeal from an order of a Liverpool magistrate requiring the appellant to enter into a recognisance in the sum of £100 with two sureties of £50 each to keep the peace and be of good behaviour for the next twelve months, and in default to be imprisoned for three months. The main facts as taken from the judgment of Darling J. were as follows: ' To begin with, we have the appellant's own description of himself. He calls himself a " crusader ", who is going to preach a Protestant crusade. In order to do this he supplied himself with a crucifix, which he waved about, and round his neck were hung beads – obviously designed to represent the rosaries used by Roman Catholics. Got up in this way, he admittedly made use of expressions most insulting to the faith of the Roman Catholic population amongst whom he went. There had been disturbances and riots caused by this conduct of his before, and the magistrate has found that the language of the appellant was provocative, and that it was likely to occur again. Large crowds had assembled in the streets, and a serious riot was only prevented by the interference of the police.'

Other relevant facts are to be found in Lord Alverstone's judgment.

LORD ALVERSTONE C.J. . . . It is not necessary to go at great length into the various authorities which were cited to us; I am not able to find in those authorities any statement of a rule of law which is to be applied in all such cases as this. . . For instance, our attention was called to the opinion of a very learned lawyer and writer, Mr Dicey, with respect to *Beatty* v. *Gillbanks*,[9] and his opinion, as I understood the passage when read, was that the view taken by the Irish Courts is in conflict with that taken by Field J. and Cave J. in that case. But I think that, when *Beatty* v. *Gillbanks* is closely examined, it lays down no law inconsistent with anything stated by the judges in the Irish cases. For this purpose it is sufficient to cite the following passages. In *Beatty* v. *Gillbanks* Field J. said, stating, I think, the law with absolute accuracy: ' Now I entirely concede that every one must be taken to intend the natural consequences of his own acts, and it is clear to me that if this disturbance of the peace was the natural consequence of acts of the appellants they would be liable, and the justices would have been right in binding them over. But the evidence set forth in the case does not support this contention.' O'Brien C.J. in *Reg.* v. *Justices of Londonderry*[10] said: ' No act on the part of any person was proved to shew that it was reasonably probable that the conduct of the defendants would, on the day in question, have provoked a breach of the peace.' It is, in my opinion, important to emphasize that enunciation of the necessary test, because it has been pressed upon us by the appellant's counsel that if the appellant did not intend to act unlawfully himself, or to induce other persons to act unlawfully, the fact that his words might have led other people so to act would not be sufficient.

In *Reg.* v. *Justices of Cork*[11] May C.J. . . . [said]: ' This requisition of sureties must be understood rather as a caution against the repetition of the offence than any immediate pain or punishment. This caution is such as is intended merely for prevention without any crime actually committed by the party, but arising only from a probable suspicion that some crime is intended or like to happen...' Again, in the second case of *Reg.* v. *Justices of Cork*,[12] reported in the same volume, Fitzgerald J., after referring to the authorities, said:[13] ' Without citing further authority we may assume that where it shall be made reasonably to appear to a justice of the peace that a person has incited others by acts or language to a violation of law

[9] [Above, p. 689.]
[10] 28 L.R.Ir. 440, at p. 447. [Like *Beatty* v. *Gillbanks*, this was another Salvation Army case. The Divisional Court quashed orders by the magistrates ordering the appellants to find sureties to keep the peace.]
[11] 15 Cox C.C. 78, at p. 84. [In this case a woman who had, as part of a general campaign, encouraged a tenant to refuse to pay rent to his landlord, was ordered to be bound to her good behaviour for six months, herself in £50 and two sureties in £25 each. She refused and was committed to prison for one month.]
[12] Cox C.C. 149.
[13] Ibid. at p. 155.

and of right, and that there is reasonable ground to believe that the delinquent is likely to persevere in that course, such justice has authority by law, in the execution of preventive justice, to provide for the public security by requiring the individual to give securities for good behaviour, and in default commit him to prison.' I have referred to those cases ... for the purpose of pointing out that, in a number of cases and before different judges, what I may call the essential condition has been stated, substantially in the same way though in different language, that there must be an act of the defendant, the natural consequence of which, if his act be not unlawful in itself, would be to produce an unlawful act by other persons. This case might really be put higher, but I have so far dealt with the matter assuming the facts in favour of the argument of the counsel for the appellant. I think that the local Act,[14] to which we were referred, has a very important bearing on this case. It provides that any person who uses any threatening, or abusive, or insulting words or behaviour with intent to provoke a breach of the peace (which is not this case), or whereby a breach of the peace may be occasioned, may be summoned before the local magistrates and fined... Here we have distinct findings of facts that the appellant held a number of meetings in the public streets; that the highways were blocked by crowds numbering thousands of persons; that very serious contests and breaches of the peace had arisen, and that the appellant himself used, with respect to a large body of persons of a different religion, language which the magistrate has found to be of a most insulting character, and that the appellant challenged any one of them to get up and deny his statements... [I]n considering the natural consequence of a man's acts who has used insulting language in the public streets towards persons of a particular religion, the magistrates are bound to take into consideration the fact that there is a large body of those persons in the town. The appellant also was proved to have stated, with respect to a meeting he intended to hold, that he had received a letter informing him that the Catholics were going to bring sticks, and he told his supporters that the police had refused to give him protection, and he said that he looked to them for protection. On these facts I think no one could reasonably doubt that the police and the magistrates were right in thinking that his language and conduct went very far indeed towards inciting people to commit, or was, at any rate, language and behaviour likely to occasion a breach of the peace. It may be true that, if this case were to be considered with reference only to any particular one of the threats or illegalities which it is suggested the appellant has committed, further evidence would have been necessary;

---

[14] [The Liverpool Improvement Act, 1842.]

but, in my opinion, there was abundant evidence to shew that in the public streets he had used language which had caused an obstruction, which was abusive, which did tend to bring about a breach of the peace, and that he threatened and intended to do similar acts in another place. The fact that he had promised not to hold a meeting at one place, but had held it within a quarter of a mile of that place on the same day, shews, at any rate, that the magistrate was justified in taking precautions to prevent a repetition of his previous conduct...

DARLING J. [having set out the facts:] Now, what was the natural consequence of the appellant's acts? It was what has happened over and over again, what has given rise to all the cases which were cited to us, and what must be the inevitable consequence if persons, whether Protestants or Catholics, are to be allowed to outrage one another's religion as the appellant outraged the religion of the Roman Catholics of Liverpool... In my view, the natural consequence of those people's conduct has been to create the disturbances and riots which have so often given rise to this sort of case. Counsel for the appellant contended that the natural consequence must be taken to be the legal acts which are a consequence. I do not think so. The natural consequence of this ' crusader's ' eloquence has been to produce illegal acts, and that from his acts and conduct circumstances have arisen which justified the magistrate in binding him over to keep the peace and be of good behaviour. In the judgment of O'Brien C.J. in *Reg.* v. *Justices of Londonderry* [15] there is this passage: ' Now I wish to make the ground of my judgment clear, and carefully to guard against being misunderstood... [T]he defendants were bound over in respect of an apprehended breach of the peace; and, in my opinion, there was no evidence to warrant that apprehension.' It is clear that, if there had been evidence to warrant that apprehension, the Chief Justice would have held the magistrates' decision in that case to be right. It is said that *Beatty* v. *Gillbanks* is in conflict with that decision. I am not sure that it is. I am inclined to think that the whole question is one of fact and evidence. But I do not hesitate to say that, if there be a conflict between these two cases, I prefer the law as it is laid down in *Reg.* v. *Justices of Londonderry.* If that be a right statement of the law, as I think it is, the magistrate was perfectly justified in coming to the conclusion he did come to in this case, even without taking into consideration the question of the local Act of Parliament to which we were referred...

CHANNELL J.... I agree... that the law does not as a rule regard an illegal act as being the natural consequence of a temptation which

[15] 28 L.R.Ir. 440, at p. 447.

may be held out to commit it. For instance, a person who exposes his goods outside his shop is often said to tempt people to steal them, but it cannot be said that this is the natural consequence of what he does... [B]ut I think the cases with respect to apprehended breaches of the peace shew that the law does regard the infirmity of human temper to the extent of considering that a breach of the peace, although an illegal act, may be the natural consequence of insulting or abusive language or conduct.

Judgment for the respondent

Cp. *Lansbury* v. *Riley* [1914] 3 K.B. 229.

DUNCAN v. *JONES* [1936] 1 K.B. 218

Divisional Court

At about 1 p.m. on 30 July 1934 about thirty people, including the appellant, collected in the road near the entrance to a training centre for the unemployed. A notice written across the entrance to the street itself read:

SEDITION

Meeting at the Test Centre to-day (now) 1 p.m.

Speakers: R. Kidd (Council for Civil Liberties),

          A. Bing (Barrister-at-Law),

          E. Hanley (Amalgamated Engineers' Union),

          K. Duncan (National Unemployed Workers' Movement),

Defend the right of free speech and public meeting.

A box was placed in the road by the entrance to the training centre. Mrs Duncan, who had been an unsuccessful Communist candidate at the General Election, was about to get up on it when the local chief constable told her that the meeting could not be held there. Mrs Duncan said: 'I'm going to hold it', and stepped on to the box and started to speak. Inspector Jones took her into custody, without any resistance on her part. She was later charged with wilfully obstructing the inspector when in the execution of his duty. The question for decision was whether the respondent was acting in the execution of his duty at the time. It was proved or admitted that on 25 May 1933 after Mrs Duncan had addressed a meeting in the same place, there had been a disturbance in the training centre and the superintendent of the centre had sent for the police to prevent a breach of the peace. He had attributed the disturbance to the meeting. Mrs Duncan had attempted on several previous occasions to hold a meeting there, but had been prevented by the police. It was argued for the respondent that as a result of these events, of further communications from the superintendent of the centre and of reports made by the police in the course of their duty, he had reasonable grounds for apprehending a breach of the peace if the meeting were held and it therefore became his duty to take whatever steps were necessary to prevent it.

The magistrate found Mrs Duncan guilty and fined her 40s. London Quarter Sessions dismissed her appeal. The deputy-chairman stated (i) that in fact (if it be material) the appellant must have known of the probable consequence of her holding a meeting – namely, a disturbance and possibly a breach of the peace – and was not unwilling that such consequences should ensue; (ii) that in fact the respondent reasonably apprehended a breach of the peace; (iii) that in law it thereupon became his duty to prevent the holding of the meeting; (iv) that in fact, by attempting to hold the meeting, the appellant obstructed the respondent when in the execution of his duty.

Mrs Duncan appealed to the Divisional Court on the ground that there was no evidence on which her conviction could be upheld.

LORD HEWART C.J. There have been moments during the argument in this case when it appeared to be suggested that the Court had to do with a grave case involving what is called the right of public meeting. I say ' called ', because English law does not recognize any special right of public meeting for political or other purposes. The right of assembly, as Professor Dicey put it,[16] is nothing more than a view taken by the Court of the individual liberty of the subject. If I thought that the present case raised a question which has been held in suspense by more than one writer on constitutional law – namely, whether an assembly can properly be held to be unlawful merely because the holding of it is expected to give rise to a breach of the peace on the part of persons opposed to those who are holding the meeting – I should wish to hear much more argument before I expressed an opinion. This case, however, does not even touch that important question.

Our attention has been directed to the somewhat unsatisfactory case of *Beatty* v. *Gillbanks*.[17] The circumstances of that case and the charge must be remembered, as also must the important passage in the judgment of Field J., in which Cave J. concurred. Field J. said: ' I entirely concede that every one must be taken to intend the natural consequences of his own acts, and it is clear to me that if this disturbance of the peace was the natural consequence of acts of the appellants they would be liable, and the justices would have been right in binding them over. But the evidence set forth in the case does not support this contention...' Our attention has also been directed to other authorities where the judgments in *Beatty* v. *Gillbanks* have been referred to, but they do not carry the matter any further, although they more than once express a doubt about the exact meaning of the decision. In my view, *Beatty* v. *Gillbanks* is apart from the present case. No such question as that which arose there is even mooted here.

The present case reminds one rather of the observations of Bram-

---

[16] Dicey, *Law of the Constitution* [10th ed., p. 271].
[17] [Above, p. 689.]

well B. in *Reg.* v. *Prebble*,[18] where, in holding that a constable, in clearing certain licensed premises of the persons thereon, was not acting in the execution of his duty, he said: ' It would have been otherwise had there been a nuisance or disturbance of the public peace, or any danger of a breach of the peace.'

The case stated which we have before us indicates clearly a causal connection between the meeting of May, 1933, and the disturbance which occurred after it—that the disturbance was not only post the meeting but was also propter the meeting. In my view, the deputy-chairman was entitled to come to the conclusion to which he came on the facts which he found and to hold that the conviction of the appellant for wilfully obstructing the respondent when in the execution of his duty was right. This appeal should, therefore, be dismissed.

HUMPHREYS J. I agree. I regard this as a plain case. It has nothing to do with the law of unlawful assembly. No charge of that sort was even suggested against the appellant. The sole question raised by the case is whether the respondent, who was admittedly obstructed, was so obstructed when in the execution of his duty.

It does not require authority to emphasize the statement that it is the duty of a police officer to prevent apprehended breaches of the peace. Here it is found as a fact that the respondent reasonably apprehended a breach of the peace. It then, ... became his duty to prevent anything which in his view would cause that breach of the peace. While he was taking steps so to do he was wilfully obstructed by the appellant. I can conceive no clearer case. . .

SINGLETON J. delivered a concurring judgment.   *Appeal dismissed*

PIDDINGTON v. *BATES*   [1960] All E.R. 660

Divisional Court

Piddington had been convicted of obstructing the police in the execution of their duty. He had gone to premises which were being picketed. When told by a police constable that in his view there were enough pickets there already he said: ' I'm going there and you can't stop me. I know my rights. . . If you don't want me to, you'd better arrest me.' He pushed past the policeman and was arrested. At the time he was arrested there were eight employees at work on the premises out of a total work force of twenty-four, though there was no evidence to show that Piddington knew this. There were already two pickets on the front and back entrances and a number of other persons in the road, most of whom were wearing picket badges. The magistrate found that there was no obstruction to the highway, and no disorder, and that no violence was threatened or offered. The police defended their action on the grounds that they had reasonable

18 (1858) 1 F. & F. 325, 326; 175 E.R. 748.

grounds for apprehending a breach of the peace if there were more than two pickets at each entrance.

LORD PARKER C.J. . . . The question here is whether the constables were acting in the course of the execution of their duty when, so it is said, they were obstructed. The court has been referred to a great number of cases, both Irish and English, dealing with the position when a police constable can be said to contemplate a breach of the peace and to take action to preserve it, but I find it unnecessary to refer to those cases. It seems to me that the law is reasonably plain. First, the mere statement by a constable that he did anticipate that there might be a breach of the peace is clearly not enough. There must exist proved facts from which a constable could reasonably have anticipated such a breach. Secondly, it is not enough that his contemplation is that there is a remote possibility but there must be a real possibility of a breach of the peace. Accordingly, in every case it becomes a question whether, on the particular facts, there were reasonable grounds on which a constable charged with this duty reasonably anticipated that a breach of the peace might occur. . .

The learned magistrate found, so far as it is material:

' Having regard to the whole of the evidence the respondent was in my opinion justified in anticipating the possibility of a breach of the peace unless steps were taken to prevent it, and in my opinion it was his duty to decide what those steps should be.'

That is challenged by the appellant, as I understand it, on two grounds. The first . . . is a criticism of the word ' possibility ' of a breach of the peace. It is said that there must be something more than a mere possibility. For my part, I agree with that, but I do not read the finding of the magistrate in the Case as saying that here it was just a mere remote possibility. I think that he was referring to it as what I may call a real possibility. The other point goes to an analysis of the evidence, from which it is said that no reasonable man could possibly anticipate a breach of the peace. It is pointed out there was no obstruction in the street; there was no actual intimidation; and that there were no threats or intimations of violence. It is said that there was really nothing save the fact that picketing was going on to suggest that a breach of the peace was a real possibility.

Every case must depend on its exact facts, and the matter which influences me in this case is the matter of numbers. It is, I think, perfectly clear from the wording of the Case, although it is not expressly so found, that the police knew that in these small works there were only eight people working at the time. They found two vehicles arriving with eighteen people, milling about the street, and trying to form pickets at the doors and, for my part, on that ground alone,

coupled with the telephone call which I should have thought intimated some sense of urgency and apprehension, the police were fully
entitled to think as reasonable men that there was a real danger of
something more than mere picketing to obtain or communicate information or to peaceably persuade. I think that, in those circumstances,
the respondent had reasonable grounds for anticipating that a breach
of the peace was a real possibility. The real criticism, I think, is this:
' Well, to say that only two pickets should be allowed is purely arbitrary. Why two? Why not three? Where do you draw the line? ' For
my part, I think that a police officer charged with the duty of preserving the Queen's peace must be left to take such steps as, on the evidence before him, he thinks are proper. I am far from saying that
there should be any rule that only two pickets should be allowed at
any particular door. There, one gets into an arbitrary area, but, so far
as this case is concerned, I cannot see that there was anything wrong
in the action of this respondent.

Finally, I would like to say that all these matters are so much
matters of degree that I, for my part, would hesitate, except on the
clearest evidence, to interfere with the findings of the magistrates, who
have had the advantage of hearing the whole case and observing the
witnesses. In those circumstances, I am of the opinion that the appeal
of Piddington should be dismissed.

ASHWORTH and ELWES JJ. agreed.

(iii) Obstruction of the highway

ARROWSMITH v. *JENKINS*   [1963] 2 Q.B. 561

Divisional Court

The appellant, Pat Arrowsmith, was prosecuted under s. 121 (1) of the
Highways Act, 1959. This provides: ' If a person, without lawful authority
or excuse, in any way wilfully obstructs the free passage along a highway
he shall be guilty of an offence and shall be liable in respect thereof to a
fine not exceeding forty shillings.'

The obstruction was caused by people attending a meeting addressed
by her in Nelson Street, Bootle. The meeting itself had lasted from 12.35
p.m. to 1 p.m. and it was proved that the road was completely blocked
for five minutes until a way was cleared, through which the police
guided a fire engine and other vehicles. At the request of the police, the
appellant had asked the crowd to draw closer to her, but the street
remained obstructed. She complained that meetings had been held there
before and that the police had on occasions attended to keep a free
passage but that no one had been prosecuted before. She also argued that
before she could be found guilty of the offence it ought to be shown that
she either intended to cause an obstruction or had acted with a wilful
disregard of the consequences.

LORD PARKER C.J. stated the facts and continued: I think that the defendant feels that she is under a grievance because – and one may put it this way – she says: ' Why pick on me? There have been many meetings held in this street from time to time. The police, as on this occasion, have attended those meetings and assisted to make a free passage, and there is no evidence that anybody else has ever been prosecuted. Why pick on me? ' That, of course, has nothing to do with this court. The sole question here is whether the defendant has contravened section 121 (1) of the Highways Act, 1959 . . .

I am quite satisfied that section 121 (1) of the Act of 1959, on its true construction, is providing that if a person, without lawful authority or excuse, intentionally as opposed to accidentally, that is by an exercise of his or her free will, does something or omits to do something which will cause an obstruction or the continuance of an obstruction, he or she is guilty of an offence. Mr Wigoder, for the defendant, has sought to argue that if a person . . . acts in the genuine belief that he or she has lawful authority to do what he or she is doing then, if an obstruction results, he or she cannot be said to have wilfully obstructed the free passage along a highway.

Quite frankly, I do not fully understand that submission. It is difficult, certainly, to apply in the present case. I imagine that it can be put in this way: that there must be some mens rea in the sense that a person will only be guilty if he knowingly does a wrongful act. I am quite satisfied that that consideration cannot possibly be imported in the words ' wilfully obstructs ' in section 121 (1) of the Act of 1959. If anybody, by an exercise of free will, does something which causes an obstruction, then an offence is committed. There is no doubt that the defendant did that in the present case.

I am quite satisfied that quarter sessions were right, and I would dismiss this appeal.

ASHWORTH and WINN JJ. concurred. *Appeal dismissed*

REGINA v. *CLARKE (No. 2)* [1964] 2 Q.B. 315

Court of Criminal Appeal (Lord Parker C.J., Winn and Fenton Atkinson JJ.)

Clarke was charged with incitement to commit a public nuisance by unlawfully obstructing the highway during a demonstration organised by the Committee of 100 during the visit of the King and Queen of Greece in 1963. The evidence of the police was that he had directed the movement of a crowd of about 2,000 in an effort to avoid police cordons and the result had been that the highway had been obstructed. He appealed against his conviction on the grounds that the deputy-chairman of quarter sessions had failed to ask the jury whether there had in the circumstances been a reasonable use of the highway, and had simply asked them whether there had been an obstruction.

LORD PARKER C.J. . . . Mr Elwyn Jones for the defendant . . . refers to the Irish case of *Lowdens* v. *Keaveney*.[19] It is convenient to refer to that case because all the relevant earlier decisions are there mentioned. and in some cases summarised. In that case the defendant was a member of a band playing tunes in the streets of Belfast who went down a street followed by a large crowd. A constable cautioned the band but they went on, persisted in playing and the crowd followed, with the result that the free passage of foot passengers and vehicles was temporarily interrupted. It was held that the conviction must be quashed, the justices having overlooked or omitted to decide the real question which was whether the user of the street was, under the circumstances, unreasonable. . .

Lord O'Brien C.J. . . . pointed out that many processions are perfectly lawful, and that no public nuisance is created by obstruction thereby unless the user of the highway in all the circumstances is unreasonable. He pointed out that there may be considerable, even complete obstruction and yet the use of the street may be quite reasonable. . .

Lowdens v. *Keaveney* is valuable as setting out the true position, as this court understands it, after reviewing the previous cases. Unfortunately in the present case, as I have already said, there was no direction to the jury as to the question of reasonableness or unreasonableness. It may well be that on a proper direction this defendant would, all the same, have been convicted, but the question was really withdrawn from the jury since, they were told that, if in fact there was a physical obstruction that constituted nuisance, and that the defendant, if he incited it, was guilty.

The court feels that this is a case in which they are unable to apply the proviso to section 4 (1) of the Criminal Appeal Act, 1907. It follows that, since there was a material misdirection as to the law, this appeal must be allowed and the conviction quashed.

TYNAN v. *BALMER* [1967] 1 Q.B. 91

Divisional Court

The defendant was the leader of draughtsmen who were on strike at the English Electric factory at Liverpool. He was organising and leading forty pickets moving in a circle on the highway outside the main gate of the factory when he was told by a police constable that what he was doing was an intimidation and an obstruction. He refused however to tell

[19] [1903] 2 I.R. 82.

the men to stop and was arrested and charged with obstructing the constable in the execution of his duty, contrary to s. 51 (3) of the Police Act, 1964. He was convicted and his conviction was upheld by the recorder of Liverpool. He now appealed to the Divisional Court. He argued that his conduct was authorised by s. 2 of the Trade Disputes Act, 1906, which provided: ' It shall be lawful for one or more persons, acting on their own behalf or on behalf of a trade union or of an individual employer or firm in contemplation or furtherance of a trade dispute, to attend at or near a house or place where a person resides or works or carries on business or happens to be, if they so attend merely for the purpose of peacefully obtaining or communicating information, or of peacefully persuading any person to work or abstain from working.'

WIDGERY J.... The recorder deals with the crucial issue in this case, which is whether the action of the pickets was authorised by section 2 of the Trade Disputes Act, in this way. He says:

'... It is, I think, clear that the main purpose of section 2 (1) of the Act of 1906 was to make lawful what was otherwise expressly forbidden by various anti-trade union Acts such as the Conspiracy and Protection of Property Act, 1875. Incidentally, it may well have rendered lawful what would otherwise have been unlawful at common law. If, for example, a person is found standing in a public highway and is instructed by a constable: "Move along there, please", it may well be a valid answer to say: " I am attending at a person's place of work as a peaceful picket in pursuance to the Trade Disputes Act, 1906." But that would not mean that if there was a strike at the Ritz Hotel, all the strikers, numbering perhaps several hundred, could gather in a block in Piccadilly and bring the whole of the traffic to a standstill, and it would make no difference to my mind if, instead of being stationary, they produced the same result by walking round and round in an unbroken circle. If the Trade Disputes Act, 1906, confers any rights to produce what would otherwise be an obstruction in a public highway (and it may be that it does) it only does so to the extent that attendance at a place for the purpose of peacefully obtaining or communicating information or of peacefully persuading people to abstain from working cannot reasonably take place at all without producing that result.'

He then goes on to deal with the question of whether it was reasonably necessary for the purpose of obtaining or communicating information or of peacefully persuading people not to work to have 40 men at the entrance in question, and whether it was necessary that they should be kept circling. In regard to the first of those points he says:

' I can quite see the value, from the point of view of advertising the strike and underlining the number of people involved and demonstrating their solidarity, of having a substantial number of people near the prestige entrance, but, from the point of view of the purposes set out in the Trade Disputes Act, 40 seems to me to be a number far in excess of what was reasonably required. Two or three men would have been sufficient to cope with the cars likely to be passing to and fro – the regular attenders in cars would, after a week, know all about the strike anyhow – and for foot passengers – most of whom would be workers in the factory – quite a few would similarly suffice.'

Then he says in regard to the circling manoeuvre:

' 1 entirely fail to see how the circling manoeuvre would have any bearing on the purposes set out in the Trade Disputes Act; it would hinder rather than facilitate the obtaining or communicating of information (except in so far as it would ensure that vehicles were brought temporarily to a standstill) and its power of persuasion would be nil (except in so far as it would have a deterrent effect). The purposes of the Act could have been achieved just as effectively, indeed more effectively, by a few men lined up as a guard of honour on each side of the way in or out, without blocking it at all. I feel forced to the conclusion that at any rate one of the objects designed to be achieved by having the men circling was the effective sealing off of the area occupied by the circle so as to secure that traffic, particularly vehicular, was brought to a standstill. One of course appreciates what was in the mind of the author (who was not disclosed to me) of the book of instructions which the appellant possessed in recommending that pickets should be kept moving; if they were on a public highway, it made it possible at any rate to argue that they were exercising their ordinary common law right of passing and repassing if they were going to and fro. But I should myself regard that argument as a thin one: if in fact the men created a complete blockage of the highway, they could not be said to be exercising their common law rights merely because the blockage took the form of a revolving circle.'

Accordingly, the recorder held that this action was not justified by section 2 of the Trade Disputes Act, 1906, and dismissed the appeal.

In my judgment, the proper way to approach this question . . . is to ask whether the conduct of the pickets would have been a nuisance at common law as an unreasonable user of the highway. It seems, in my judgment, that it clearly would have been so regarded. One leaves aside for the moment any facilities enjoyed by those acting in furtherance of a trade dispute, and if one imagines these pickets as carrying banners advertising some patent medicine or advocating some political reform, it seems to me that their conduct in sealing off a part of the highway by this moving circle would have been an unreasonable user of the highway.

In so far as it is a question of fact, the recorder takes the same view, and has, as I read his judgment, found that it was an unreasonable user of the highway. Indeed, Mr Pain, appearing for the appellant today, does not seek to argue the contrary.

In my judgment, therefore, if one ignores section 2 of the Trade Disputes Act, 1906, for the moment and considers the position at common law, this action would have been an unreasonable use of the highway, admittedly a nuisance, and a police officer would be fully entitled to take action to move the pickets on.

If one can start from that foundation, it seems to me that the sole question in this case is whether the activity was authorised and made legal by section 2 of the Act of 1906.

As Mr Pain has suggested, it would seem that the genesis of that section is the decision of the Court of Appeal in *J. Lyons & Sons* v. *Wilkins*.[20] ... [I]n that case it was accepted as possible at common law that watching and besetting a man's house would be a nuisance and a wrongful act, quite apart from any obstruction of the highway thereby caused. One should not, in my judgment, therefore regard section 2 as being primarily a highway section, because there may be many other wrongs which could be committed by citizens which are now authorised by that section... [S]ection 2 ... authorises in its simplest terms a person to attend at or near one of the places described if he does so merely for the purpose of peacefully obtaining or communicating information or of peacefully persuading any person to work or abstain from working.

The recorder has found as a fact that the pickets in this case were not attending merely for the purposes described in this section. He has found as a fact that their object at any rate in part was to seal off the highway and to cause vehicles approaching the premises to stop. In my judgment that finding of fact is quite enough to require this court to say that as a matter of law the recorder's judgment in this case should be upheld.

Mr Pain, however, submits that a somewhat different test must be applied. He says that section 2 has put beyond doubt that picketing is a lawful user of the highway, and that as a lawful user of the highway it is not the subject of interference by a constable, provided the picket has reasonable regard for the rights of others. In this case, as I understand him, he says that as the pickets did not in fact cause any actual obstruction to any person, the fact that they were circling in the road had not brought them to the point at which it was proper for

[20] [1899] 1 Ch. 255; 15 T.L.R. 128, C.A.

the police to interfere. In particular, he says that the police might have properly interfered half an hour later when work people were coming out for their lunch and might be obstructed, but had no right to interfere at the time when police constable O'Hare took action in this case.

I cannot accept that this is a proper approach to the problem. Once one accepts that independently of section 2 this action was unlawful and a nuisance, the only question left is whether section 2 by its terms authorises it or not. On the recorder's finding section 2 clearly did not authorise this conduct and it therefore seems to me that this appeal should be dismissed...

LORD PARKER C.J.... Mr Pain conceded that no right was conferred of stopping a pedestrian, apparently on the basis that you could communicate your information by walking alongside him, but he suggested that when you get to a vehicle the section authorised and permitted the stopping of vehicles. I am quite unable to accept that argument, and on the findings of the recorder in this case I am quite clear that an offence was committed.

SACHS J. agreed.   *Appeal dismissed with costs*

HUNT v. *BROOME*   [1974] 2 W.L.R. 58

House of Lords

S. 134 of the Industrial Relations Act, 1974, which replaced s. 2 of the Trades Disputes Act, 1906, provides:

' (1) The provisions of this section shall have effect where one or more persons (in this section referred to as " pickets "), in contemplation or furtherance of an industrial dispute, attend at or near—(*a*) a place where a person works or carries on business, or (*b*) any other place where a person happens to be, not being a place where he resides, and do so only for the purpose of peacefully, obtaining information from him or peacefully communicating information to him or peacefully persuading him to work or not to work. (2) In the circumstances specified in the preceding subsection, the attendance of the pickets at that place for that purpose— (*a*) shall not of itself constitute an offence under section 7 of the Conspiracy and Protection of Property Act, 1875 (penalty for intimidation or annoyance by violence or otherwise) or under any other enactment or rule of law, and (*b*) shall not of itself constitute a tort.'

In the present case a trade union official, having made several unsuccessful attempts to dissuade a lorry driver from wanting to enter the factory which he was picketing finally stood in front of the lorry and refused to move when requested by a police inspector to do so. He was arrested and charged with obstructing the highway contrary to s. 121 of the Highways Act, 1959. The magistrates dismissed the charge on the grounds that the whole incident had only lasted about nine minutes and that this was not an unreasonable amount of time to spend in exercising the defendant's statutory right of peaceful persuasion.

LORD REID: ... [Section 134 (2)] enacts that conduct described in subsection (1) shall not of itself constitute an offence under any enactment. So if the appellant is to be convicted it must be shown that this conduct at the place where the alleged offence was committed exceeded any conduct to which the terms of subsection (1) can apply.

His attendance there is only made lawful by subsection (2) if he attended only for the purpose of obtaining or communicating information or ' peacefully persuading' the lorry driver. Attendance for that purpose must I think include the right to try to persuade anyone who chooses to stop and listen, at least in so far as this is done in a reasonable way with due consideration for the rights of others. A right to attend for the purpose of peaceful persuasion would be meaningless unless this were implied.

But I see no ground for implying any right to require the person whom it is sought to persuade to submit to any kind of constraint or restriction of his personal freedom. One is familiar with persons at the side of a road signalling to a driver requesting him to stop. It is then for the driver to decide whether he will stop or not. That, in my view, a picket is entitled to do. If the driver stops, the picket can talk to him but only for so long as the driver is willing to listen.

That must be so because if the picket had a statutory right to stop or to detain the driver that must necessarily imply that the Act has imposed on those passing along the road a statutory duty to stop or to remain for longer than they chose to stay. So far as my recollection goes it would be unique for Parliament to impose such a duty otherwise than by express words, and even if one envisages the possibility of such a duty being imposed by implication the need for it would have to be crystal clear. Here I can see no need at all for any such implication.

Without the protection of the section merely inviting a driver to stop and then, if he were willing to stop and listen, proceeding to try to persuade him not to go on, would in many cases be either an offence or a tort or both, particularly if more than a very few pickets were acting together. I see no reason to hold that the section confers any other right.

The justices speak of the appellant's ' statutory right peacefully to seek to persuade '. That is not an accurate or adequate statement of the provisions of the section. And their further statement that, ' his statutory right is meaningless unless the picket places himself in such a position that the person to be persuaded is obliged to stop and listen for a reasonable length of time ' is for the reasons I have given wholly erroneous.

There was a suggestion that if a picket does not have a right to stop a driver or pedestrian the same result could be obtained lawfully by a large number of pickets gathering at the same place and doing nothing. The section does not limit the number of pickets and no limitation of numbers can be implied. So if a large number assemble it will not be physically possible in many cases for a driver or pedestrian to proceed.

But if a picket has a purpose beyond those set out in the section, then his presence becomes unlawful and in many cases such as I have supposed it would not be difficult to infer as a matter of fact that pickets who assemble in unreasonably large numbers do have the purpose of preventing free passage. If that were the proper inference then their presence on the highway would become unlawful. *Tynan's* case [1967] 1 Q.B. 91 is a good example of this.

In this case it was not and could not reasonably be maintained that, if the law is as I have stated it, any other conclusion is possible than that the appellant committed the offence with which he has been charged.

I would therefore dismiss this appeal.

Lords Morris of Borth-y-Gest, and Salmon and Viscount Dilhorne delivered concurring judgments. Lord Hodson agreed with Viscount Dilhorne.

(iv) Prohibited places

CHANDLER AND OTHERS v. *DIRECTOR OF PUBLIC PROSECUTIONS* [1964] A.C. 763

House of Lords

The appellants were members or supporters of the Committee of 100. Earl Russell, the founder of the Committee, explained in evidence that their ultimate purpose was to prevent a nuclear war and that their more immediate purpose was to get the facts about nuclear warfare known to the public by any means they could and in particular by pursuing a campaign of non-violent civil disobedience. The appellants decided, as part of the campaign, to have a demonstration at Wethersfield air base on 9 December 1961. It was planned that the bulk of the demonstrators would squat in the roadway by the entrances while the others would try to get into the base and immobilise it by sitting in front of the aircraft for some six hours.

The attempt to get into the base was unsuccessful. The appellants were, however, charged with conspiring to commit and to incite others to commit a breach of s. 1 (1) of the Official Secrets Act, 1911. This provides: ' If any person for any purpose prejudicial to the safety of the state—(a) approaches or is in the neighbourhood of, or enters any prohibited place within the meaning of this Act ... he shall be guilty of felony ...'

They were convicted and sentenced to terms of imprisonment. They appealed on several grounds but in particular on the ground that their purpose was not one prejudicial to the safety of the state. They argued that the trial judge had wrongly excluded evidence and cross-examination designed to show that this was so.

LORD REID.... Counsel for the accused said that they sought to adduce evidence that their purpose was not prejudicial to the interests of the State, and that the basis of the defence was that these aircraft used nuclear bombs and that it was not in fact in the interests of the State to have aircraft so armed at that time there. So, he said, it would be beneficial to the State to immobilise these aircraft. Then counsel further submitted that he was entitled to adduce evidence to show that the accused believed, and reasonably believed, that it was not prejudicial but beneficial to the interests of the State to immobilise these aircraft... [C]ounsel said that his evidence would deal with the effect of exploding a nuclear bomb and at other times reference was made to the possibility of accident or mistake, and other reasons against having nuclear bombs. He said that he wished to cross-examine as to the basic wrongness of the conception of a deterrent force and the likelihood of its attracting hostile attack. In reply the Attorney-General submitted that an objective test must determine whether the purpose of grounding aircraft was a prejudicial purpose, that the accused's beliefs were irrelevant and so was the reasonableness of their beliefs. Havers J.... ruled that the defence were not entitled to call evidence to establish that it would be beneficial for this country to give up nuclear armament or that the accused honestly believed that it would be.

The trial proceeded in accordance with this ruling of the learned judge...

The first word [in section 1 of the Official Secrets Act] that requires consideration is ' purpose '... The accused both intended and desired that the base should be immobilised for a time... [E]ven if their reason or motive for doing what they did is called the purpose of influencing public opinion that cannot alter the fact that they had a purpose to immobilise the base...

Next comes the question of what is meant by the safety or interests of the State. ' State ' is not an easy word. It does not mean the Government or the Executive... And I do not think that it means, as counsel argued, the individuals who inhabit these islands. The statute cannot be referring to the interests of all those individuals because they may differ and the interests of the majority are not necessarily the same as the interests of the State... Perhaps the country or the realm are as good synonyms as one can find and I would be prepared to accept the organised community as coming as near to a definition as one can get.

Who then is to determine what is and what is not prejudicial to the safety and interests of the State? The question more frequently arises as to what or is not in the public interest. I do not subscribe to the view that the Government or a Minister must always or even as a general rule have the last word about that. But here we are dealing with a very special matter – interfering with a prohibited place which Wethersfield was. The definition in section 3 shows that it must either be closely connected with the armed forces or be a place such that information regarding it or damage to it or interference with it would be useful to an enemy. It is in my opinion clear that the disposition and armament of the armed forces are, and for centuries have been, within the exclusive discretion of the Crown and that no one can seek a legal remedy on the ground that such discretion has been wrongly exercised. I need only refer to the numerous authorities gathered together in *China Navigation Co. Ltd.* v. *Attorney-General.*[21] Anyone is entitled, in or out of Parliament, to urge that policy regarding the armed forces should be changed; but until it is changed, on a change of government or otherwise, no one is entitled to challenge it in court. Even in recent times there have been occasions when quite large numbers of people have been bitterly opposed to the use made of the armed forces in peace or in war. The 1911 Act was passed at a time of grave misgiving about the German menace, and it would be surprising and hardly credible that the Parliament of that date intended that a person who deliberately interfered with vital dispositions of the armed forces should be entitled to submit to a jury that government policy was wrong and that what he did was really in the best interests of the country, and then perhaps to escape conviction because a unanimous verdict on that question could not be obtained. Of course we are bound by the words which Parliament has used in the Act. If those words necessarily lead to that conclusion then it is no answer that it is inconceivable that Parliament can have so intended. The remedy is to amend the Act. But we must be clear that the words of the Act are not reasonably capable of any other interpretation.

I am prepared to start from the position that, when an Act requires certain things to be established against an accused person to constitute an offence, all of those things must be proved by evidence which the jury accepts, unless Parliament has otherwise provided. But normally such things are facts and where questions of opinion arise they are on limited technical matters on which expert evidence can be called. Here the question whether it is beneficial to use the armed forces in a particular way or prejudicial to interfere with that use would be a political question – a question of opinion on which

21 [1932] 2 K.B. 197.

anyone actively interested in politics, including jurymen, might consider his own opinion as good as that of anyone else. Our criminal
system is not devised to deal with issues of that kind. The question
therefore is whether this Act can reasonably be read in such a way
as to avoid the raising of such issues.

The Act must be read as a whole and paragraphs (c) and (d) of
section 3 appear to me to require such a construction. Places to
which they refer become prohibited places if a Secretary of State
declares that damage, obstruction or interference there ' would be
useful to an enemy'. Plainly it is not open to an accused who has
interfered with or damaged such a place to a material extent to
dispute the declaration of the Secretary of State and it would be
absurd if he were entitled to say or lead evidence to show that,
although he had deliberately done something which would be useful
to an enemy, yet his purpose was not prejudicial to the safety or
interests of the State. So here at least the trial judge must be entitled
to prevent the leading of evidence and to direct the jury that if they
find that his purpose was to interfere to a material extent they must
hold that his purpose was prejudicial. If that be so, then, in view
of the matters which I have already dealt with, it appears to me that
the same must necessarily apply to the present case.

I am therefore of opinion that the ruling of Havers J. excluding
evidence was right and that his direction to the jury was substantially correct... I think that it was proper to give to the jury a
direction to the effect that if they were satisfied that the intention
and desire of the accused was to procure the immobilisation of these
aircraft in a way which they knew would or might substantially
impair their operational effectiveness then the offence was proved
and they should convict...

LORD DEVLIN. . . . This statute is concerned with the safety and
interests of the State and therefore with the objects of State policy,
even though judged sub specie aetern[it]atis, that policy may be
wrong. If in this statute these words ['safety and interests of the
State '] were given a wider meaning, absurd results would follow.
Rebels and high-minded spies could be heard to argue that defeat
in battle would serve the best interests of the nation because it
would be better off under a different régime. The licence allowed
to them would also have to be allowed to traitors. This point was
dismissed by Mr Foster [counsel for the appellants] as theoretical.
It was said that no jury would, in such circumstances, acquit. But
even if it be looked at purely on the practical plane, the judge has
to decide whether he will allow hours or days to be spent at the
trial in giving an accused the opportunity of expounding his political

views. The court is not the forum for such a debate and the jury is not the body to determine what the interests of the State should be.

... What then in the present case, is the question which the jury had to decide? They were inquiring whether a fact, constituted by statute as an ingredient of a criminal offence, had been proved. The fact to be proved is the existence of a purpose prejudicial to the State – not a purpose which ' appears to the Crown ' to be prejudicial to the State... There is no rule of common law that whenever questions of national security are being considered by any court for any purpose, it is what the Crown thinks to be necessary or expedient that counts, and not what is necessary or expedient in fact... In a case like the present, it may be presumed that it is contrary to the interests of the Crown to have one of its airfields immobilised... But the presumption is not irrebuttable... Men can exaggerate the extent of their interests and so can the Crown. The servants of the Crown, like other men animated by the highest motives, are capable of formulating a policy ad hoc so as to prevent the citizen from doing something that the Crown does not want him to do. It is the duty of the courts to be as alert now as they have always been to prevent abuse of the prerogative. But in the present case there is nothing at all to suggest that the Crown's interest in the proper operation of its airfields is not what it may naturally be presumed to be or that it was exaggerating the perils of interference with their effectiveness...

VISCOUNT RADCLIFFE.... When a man has avowed that his purpose in approaching an airfield forming part of the country's defence system was to obstruct its operational activity, what, if any, evidence is admissible on the issue as to the prejudicial nature of his purpose? In my opinion the correct answer is, virtually none. This answer is not surprising if certain considerations that lie behind the protection of official secrets are borne in mind. The defence of the State from external enemies is a matter of real concern, in time of peace as in days of war. The disposition, armament and direction of the defence forces of the State are matters decided upon by the Crown and are within its jurisdiction as the executive power of the State. So are treaties and alliances with other States for mutual defence... If the methods of arming the defence forces and the disposition of those forces are at the decision of her Majesty's Ministers for the time being, it is not within the competence of a court of law to try the issue whether it would be better for the country that that armament or those dispositions should be different...

LORDS HODSON and PEARCE delivered concurring judgments.

(v) The Public Order Act, 1936

PUBLIC ORDER ACT, 1936   [1 Edw. 8 & 1 Geo. 6. ch. 6]

1. (1) Subject as hereinafter provided, any person who in any public place or at any public meeting wears uniform signifying his association with any political organisation or with the promotion of any political object shall be guilty of an offence:

Provided that, if the chief officer of police is satisfied that the wearing of any such uniform as aforesaid on any ceremonial, anniversary, or other special occasion will not be likely to involve risk of public disorder, he may, with the consent of a Secretary of State, by order permit the wearing of such uniform on that occasion either absolutely or subject to such conditions as may be specified in the order.

(2) Where any person is charged before any court with an offence under this section, no further proceedings in respect thereof shall be taken against him without the consent of the Attorney-General . . .

3. (1) If the chief officer of police, having regard to the time or place at which and the circumstances in which any public procession is taking place or is intended to take place and to the route proposed to be taken by the procession, has reasonable ground for apprehending that the procession may occasion serious public disorder, he may give directions imposing upon the persons organising or taking part in the procession such conditions as appear to him necessary for the preservation of public order, including conditions prescribing the route to be taken by the procession and conditions prohibiting the procession from entering any public place specified in the directions:

Provided that no conditions restricting the display of flags, banners, or emblems shall be imposed under this subsection except such as are reasonably necessary to prevent risk of a breach of the peace.

(2) If at any time the chief officer of police is of opinion that by reason of particular circumstances existing in any borough or urban district or in any part thereof the powers conferred on him by the last foregoing subsection will not be sufficient to enable him to prevent serious public disorder being occasioned by the holding of public processions in that borough, district or part, he shall apply to the council of the borough or district for an order prohibiting for such period not exceeding three months as may be specified in the application the holding of all public processions or of any class of public procession so specified either in the borough or urban district or in that part thereof, as the case may be, and upon receipt of the application the council may, with the consent of a Secretary of

State, make an order either in terms of the application or with such modifications as may be approved by the Secretary of State.

This subsection shall not apply within the City of London as defined for the purposes of the Acts relating to the City police or within the Metropolitan police district.

(3) If at any time the Commissioner of the City of London police or the Commissioner of police of the Metropolis is of opinion that, by reason of particular circumstances existing in his police area or in any part thereof, the powers conferred on him by subsection (1) of this section will not be sufficient to enable him to prevent serious public disorder being occasioned by the holding of public processions in that area or part, he may, with the consent of the Secretary of State, make an order prohibiting for such period not exceeding three months as may be specified in the order the holding of all public processions or of any class of public procession so specified either in the police area or in that part thereof, as the case may be.[22]

(4) Any person who knowingly fails to comply with any directions given or conditions imposed under this section, or organises or assists in organising any public procession held or intended to be held in contravention of an order made under this section or incites any person to take part in such a procession, shall be guilty of an offence.

4. (1) Any person who, while present at any public meeting or on the occasion of any public procession, has with him any offensive weapon, otherwise than in pursuance of lawful authority, shall be guilty of an offence.

(2) For the purpose of this section, a person shall not be deemed to be acting in pursuance of lawful authority unless he is acting in his capacity as a servant of the Crown or of either House of Parliament or of any local authority or as a constable or as a member of a recognised corps or as a member of a fire brigade.

5. Any person who in any public place or at any public meeting—

(a) uses threatening, abusive or insulting words or behaviour, or

(b) distributes or displays any writing, sign or visible representation which is threatening, abusive or insulting,

with intent to provoke a breach of the peace or whereby a breach of the peace is likely to be occasioned, shall be guilty of an offence. . .

7. . . . (2) Any person guilty of . . . [an] offence under this Act shall be liable on summary conviction to imprisonment for a term not exceeding three months or to a fine not exceeding fifty pounds, or to both such imprisonment and fine.[23]

---

[22] Cp. s. 52 of the Metropolitan Police Act, 1839.

[23] [The Public Order Act, 1963, provides in s. 1 (1) that a person guilty of an offence under s. 5 or under the Public Meetings Act, 1908, shall be liable

(3) A constable may without warrant arrest any person reasonably suspected by him to be committing an offence under section one, four or five of this Act.

9. (1) In this Act the following expressions have the meanings hereby respectively assigned to them, that is to say: —

'Chief officer of police' has the same meaning as in the Police Pensions Act, 1921;

'Meeting' means a meeting held for the purpose of the discussion of matters of public interest or for the purpose of the expression of views on such matters;

'Private premises' means premises to which the public have access (whether on payment or otherwise) only by permission of the owner, occupier, or lessee of the premises;

'Public meeting' includes any meeting in a public place and any meeting which the public or any section thereof are permitted to attend, whether on payment or otherwise;

'Public place' means any highway, public park or garden, any sea beach, and any public bridge, road, lane, footway, square, court, alley or passage, whether a thoroughfare or not; and includes any open space to which, for the time being, the public have or are permitted to have access, whether on payment or otherwise;

'Public procession' means a procession in a public place;

'Recognised corps' means a rifle club, miniature rifle club or cadet corps approved by a Secretary of State under the Firearms Acts, 1920 to 1936, for the purpose of those Acts...

BRUTUS v. *COZENS*   [1973] A.C. 854

House of Lords

As part of a demonstration against the apartheid policy of the Government of South Africa the appellant had interrupted a tennis match at Wimbledon by going on to the court, blowing a whistle, scattering leaflets, and trying to give one to a player. He then sat down and had to be removed by the police. He was charged with insulting behaviour whereby a breach of the peace was likely to be occasioned, contrary to s. 5 of the Public Order Act, 1936. The magistrates dismissed the case on the ground that his behaviour was not insulting. On appeal the Divisional Court held that it was, but certified that there was a point of law of general public importance for the House of Lords to consider, namely, 'whether conduct which evidences a disrespect for the rights of others so that it is likely to cause their resentment or give rise to protests from

---

on summary conviction to imprisonment for a term not exceeding three months and/or a fine not exceeding £100, and on conviction on indictment to imprisonment not exceeding twelve months and/or a fine not exceeding £500.]

them is insulting behaviour within the meaning of s. 5 of the Public Order Act, 1936 '.

LORD REID. . . . It is not clear to me what precisely is the point of law which we have to decide. The question in the case stated for the opinion of the court is ' Whether, on the above statement of facts, we came to a correct determination and decision in point of law.' This seems to assume that the meaning of the word ' insulting ' in section 5 is a matter of law. And the Divisional Court appear to have proceeded on that footing.

In my judgment that is not right. The meaning of an ordinary word of the English language is not a question of law. The proper construction of a statute is a question of law. If the context shows that a word is used in an unusual sense the court will determine in other words what that unusual sense is. But here there is in my opinion no question of the word ' insulting ' being used in any unusual sense. It appears to me, for reasons which I shall give later, to be intended to have its ordinary meaning. It is for the tribunal which decides the case to consider, not as law but as fact, whether in the whole circumstances the words of the statute do or do not as a matter of ordinary usage of the English language cover or apply to the facts which have been proved. If it is alleged that the tribunal has reached a wrong decision then there can be a question of law but only of limited character. The question would normally be whether their decision was unreasonable in the sense that no tribunal acquainted with the ordinary use of language could reasonably reach that decision. . . So the question of law in this case must be whether it was unreasonable to hold that the appellant's behaviour was not insulting. To that question there could in my view be only one answer – No.

But as the Divisional Court [1972] 1 W.L.R. 484, have expressed their view as to the meaning of ' insulting ' I must, I think, consider it. It was said, at p. 487 :

' The language of section 5, as amended, of the Public Order Act 1936 . . . is: " Any person who in any public place . . . uses . . . insulting . . . behaviour . . . with intent to provoke a breach of the peace or whereby a breach of the peace is likely to be occasioned, shall be guilty of an offence." It therefore becomes necessary to consider the meaning of the word " insulting " in its context in that section. In my view it is not necessary, and is probably undesirable, to try to frame an exhaustive definition which will cover every possible set of facts that may arise for consideration under this section. It is, as I think, quite sufficient for the purpose of this case to say that behaviour which affronts other people, and evidences a disrespect or contempt for their rights, behaviour which reasonable persons would foresee is likely to cause resentment or protest such as was aroused in this case, and I rely particularly on the reaction of the crowd as set out in the case stated, is insulting for the purpose of this section.'

I cannot agree with that. Parliament had to solve the difficult question of how far freedom of speech or behaviour must be limited in the general public interest. It would have been going much too far to prohibit all speech or conduct likely to occasion a breach of the peace because determined opponents may not shrink from organising or at least threatening a breach of the peace in order to silence a speaker whose views they detest. Therefore vigorous and it may be distasteful or unmannerly speech or behaviour is permitted so long as it does not go beyond any one of three limits. It must not be threatening. It must not be abusive. It must not be insulting. I see no reason why any of these should be construed as having a specially wide or a specially narrow meaning. They are all limits easily recognisable by the ordinary man. Free speech is not impaired by ruling them out. But before a man can be convicted it must be clearly shown that one or more of them has been disregarded.

We were referred to a number of dictionary meanings of ' insult ' such as treating with insolence or contempt or indignity or derision or dishonour or offensive disrespect. Many things otherwise unobjectionable may be said or done in an insulting way. There can be no definition. But an ordinary sensible man knows an insult when he sees or hears it.

Taking the passage which I have quoted, ' affront ' is much too vague a word to be helpful; there can often be disrespect without insult, and I do not think that contempt for a person's rights as distinct from contempt of the person himself would generally be held to be insulting. Moreover, there are many grounds other than insult for feeling resentment or protesting. I do not agree that there can be conduct which is not insulting in the ordinary sense of the word but which is ' insulting for the purpose of this section.' If the view of the Divisional Court was that in this section the word ' insulting ' has some special or unusually wide meaning, then I do not agree. Parliament has given no indication that the word is to be given any unusual meaning. Insulting means insulting and nothing else.

If I had to decide, which I do not, whether the appellant's conduct insulted the spectators in this case, I would agree with the magistrates. The spectators may have been very angry and justly so. The appellant's conduct was deplorable. Probably it ought to be punishable. But I cannot see how it insulted the spectators.

I would allow the appeal with costs.

VISCOUNT DILHORNE. . . . The Public Order Act 1936, by section 5, made it an offence for a person to use threatening, abusive or insulting behaviour whereby a breach of the peace is likely to be occasioned. It does not make any kind of behaviour which is likely to lead to a breach of the peace an offence. Behaviour which evidences a disrespect or contempt for the rights of others does not of itself establish that that behaviour was threatening, abusive or insulting. Such behaviour may be very annoying to those who see it and cause resentment and protests but it does not suffice to show that the behaviour was annoying and did annoy, for a person can be guilty of annoying behaviour without that behaviour being insulting. And what must be established to justify conviction of the offence is not that the behaviour was annoying but that it was threatening, abusive or insulting.

The reaction of those who saw the behaviour may be relevant to the question whether a breach of the peace was likely to be occasioned but it is not, in my opinion, relevant to the question, was the behaviour threatening, abusive or insulting. . .

LORDS MORRIS OF BORTH-Y-GEST, and KILBRANDON delivered concurring judgments. LORD DIPLOCK agreed.

II. OFFENCES AGAINST THE STATE AND EMERGENCY POWERS

(i) Offences against the State

(a) *Treason-felony*

TREASON FELONY ACT, 1848   [11 & 12 Vict. ch. 12]

3. If any person whatsoever shall, within the United Kingdom or without, compass, imagine, invent, devise, or intend to deprive or depose our Most Gracious Lady the Queen, from the style, honour, or royal name of the imperial crown of the United Kingdom, or of any other of her Majesty's dominions and countries, or to levy war against her Majesty, within any part of the United Kingdom, in order by force or constraint to compel her to change her measures or counsels, or in order to put any force or constraint upon or in order to intimidate or overawe both Houses or either House of Parliament, or to move or stir any foreigner or stranger with force to invade the United Kingdom or any other of her Majesty's dominions or countries under the obeisance of her Majesty, and such compassings, imaginations, inventions, devices, or intentions, or any of them, shall express, utter, or declare, by publishing any

printing or writing ... or by any overt act or deed, every person so offending shall be guilty of felony ...

6. Provided always, that nothing herein contained shall lessen the force of or in any manner affect any thing enacted by the Treason Act, 1351 ...

8. In the case of every felony punishable under this Act, every principal in the second degree and every accessory before the fact shall be punishable in the same manner as the principal in the first degree is by this Act punishable; and every accessory after the fact to any such felony shall on conviction be liable to be imprisoned, with or without hard labour, for any term not exceeding two years.

(b) *Sedition*

R. v. *ALDRED*

(1909) 22 Cox 1

Central Criminal Court

The defendant was charged with printing and publishing a seditious libel in the August part of the *Indian Sociologist* which was an organ for advocating the independence of India. In previous parts of the periodical, political assassination had been advocated and Indians who had been convicted and executed for murder had been praised. Immediately following the publication of the July part, an Indian, Madan Lal Dhingra, had murdered Sir William Hutt Curzon Wylie in London, and the printer had been convicted of seditious libel. The defendant had then written to Krishnavarma, the editor and proprietor of the paper, who lived in Paris, and offered to carry on the printing. The August part, printed by him, contained articles by Krishnavarma advocating the principle that ' political assassination is no murder ' and proclaiming Dhingra ' a martyr in the cause of Indian independence '. It also contained an intemperate article by the defendant in which he attempted to justify the methods of Indian ' Nationalists '.

COLERIDGE J., in the course of his summing-up to the jury, said: It is not necessary for me in this case to give you a full, accurate, and comprehensive definition of all that could come under the head of seditious libel, because the prosecution have practically limited their case to one form of seditious libel, and that is, that by a publication for which the defendant was responsible he used language implying that it was lawful and commendable to employ physical force in any manner or form whatsoever against the government of our Lord the King, or towards and against the British liege subjects of our Lord the King; and the case has all turned upon that form or species of seditious libel. Nothing is clearer than the law on this head – namely, that whoever by language, either written or spoken, incites or encourages others to use physical force or violence in some public matter connected with the State, is guilty of publishing a seditious libel. The word 'sedition' in its ordinary natural signification denotes a tumult, an insurrection, a popular commotion, or an uproar; it implies violence or lawlessness in some form; but the man who is accused may not plead the truth of the statements that he makes as a defence to the charge, nor may he plead the innocence of his motive; that is not a defence to the charge... [T]he test is this: was the language used calculated, or was it not, to promote public disorder or physical force or violence in a matter of State? – and I need hardly say that anything in the way of assassination would be comprehended in the definition. That is the test; and that test is not for me or for the prosecution; it is for you, the jury, to decide, having heard all the circumstances connected with the case. In arriving at a decision of this test you are entitled to look at all the circumstances surrounding the publication with the view of seeing whether the language used is calculated to produce the results imputed; that is to say, you are entitled to look at the audience addressed, because language which would be innocuous, practically speaking, if used to an assembly of professors or divines, might produce a different result if used before an excited audience of young and uneducated men. You are entitled also to take into account the state of public feeling. Of course there are times when a spark will explode a powder magazine; the effect of language may be very different at one time from what it would be at another. You are entitled also to take into account the place and the mode of publication. All these matters are surrounding circumstances which a jury may take into account in solving the test which is for them, whether the language used is calculated to produce the disorders or crimes or violence imputed. It is quite true, as the defendant has put before you, that a prosecution for seditious libel is somewhat of a rarity. It is a weapon that is not often taken down from the armoury in which it hangs, but it is a necessary accompaniment to every civilised government; it is liable to be abused, and if it is abused there is one wholesome corrective, and that is a jury of Englishmen such as you. Having said this much, I should like to say by way of comment upon a good deal that has fallen from the defendant in the speech that he has addressed to you – that the expression of abstract academic opinion in this country is free. A man may lawfully express his opinion on any public matter, however distasteful, however repugnant to others, if, of course, he avoids defamatory matter, or if he avoids anything than can be characterised either as a blasphemous or as an obscene libel. Matters of State, matters of policy, matters even of morals – all these are open to him. He may state his opinion freely, he may buttress it by argument, he may try to persuade others to share his views. Courts and juries are not the judges in such matters. For instance, if he thinks that either a despotism, or an oligarchy, or a republic, or even no government at all, is the best way of conducting human affairs, he is at perfect liberty to say so. He may assail politicians, he may attack governments, he may warn the executive of the day against taking a particular course, or he may remonstrate with the executive of the day for not taking a particular course; he may seek to show that rebellions, insurrections, outrages, assassinations, and such-like, are the natural, the deplorable, the inevitable outcome of the policy which he is combating. All that is allowed, because all that is innocuous; but, on the other hand, if he makes use of language calculated to advocate or to incite others to public disorders, to wit, rebellions, insurrections, assassinations, outrages, or any physical force or violence of any kind, then, whatever his motives, whatever his intentions, there would be evidence on which a jury might, on which I should think a jury ought, and on which a jury would decide that he was guilty of a seditious publication... The defendant seems to be under some misapprehension in regard to the distinction which he seems to draw between the language written primarily by this man Krishnavarma and the writing put in by himself as the author. In law there is no such distinction. If he publishes – whoever wrote it – if he publishes he is responsible for what he publishes; and there is no distinction in law to be drawn at all between what he wrote in it and what Krishnavarma or any other person wrote in it. In law he is responsible for everything that appears, and for the effect of the language which is there published... To whom was it addressed? I understood the defendant to lay some claim to sympathy or to praise from the fact that the circulation was not *urbi et orbi*, not to all the world; if it was innocent, why should it not be to all the world? This argument that was used by him by way of exculpation – that it was not published to all the world, that it was only published to persons to whom he thought it was safe to publish it – what does it mean? Does it mean that he was conscious of the effect of the law upon his action? Did he take care to ensure that the numbers should not fall into the hands of these Indian ' Nationalists ', who are, according to the expression in the paper which I have read to you, *primâ facie* the readers of this paper... You have to take into consideration all these facts in arriving at your decision. You are the interpreters to-day of the language used in these articles, and you will say what in your judgment is the effect it was calculated to produce.

Verdict : Guilty

Sentence : Twelve months' imprisonment as a first-class misdemeanant [24]

[24] Cp. *R.* v. *Gaunt* (1947) where the Editor of the *Morcambe and Heysham Visitor* was charged with publishing a seditious libel after he had written an anti-Semitic article which concluded ' If British Jewry is suffering today from the righteous wrath of British citizens, then they have only themselves

(c) *Inciting disaffection*

INCITEMENT TO DISAFFECTION ACT, 1934
[24 & 25 Geo. 5. ch. 56]

1. If any person maliciously and advisedly endeavours to seduce any member of His Majesty's forces from his duty or allegiance to His Majesty he shall be guilty of an offence under this Act.

2. (1) If any person with intent to commit or to aid and abet, counsel or procure the commission of an offence under section 1 . . . has in his possession or under his control any document of such a nature that the dissemination of copies thereof among members of His Majesty's forces would constitute such an offence, he shall be guilty of an offence under this Act. . .

3. . . . (2) No prosecution in England under this Act shall take place without the consent of the Director of Public Prosecutions. . .

4. . . . (3) It is hereby declared that this Act extends to Northern Ireland. . .

POLICE ACT, 1964 [Ch. 48]

53. (1) Any person who causes, or attempts to cause, or does any act calculated to cause disaffection amongst members of any police force, or induces, or attempts to induce, or does any act calculated to induce any member of a police force to withhold his services or to commit breaches of discipline, he shall be guilty of an offence and liable

    (*a*) on summary conviction, to imprisonment for a term not exceed-ing six months or to a fine not exceeding £100, or to both;

    (*b*) on conviction on indictment, to imprisonment for a term not exceeding two years or to a fine, or to both:

(2) This applies to special constables as it applies to members of a police force. . .

(d) *Illegal associations*

PUBLIC ORDER ACT, 1936 [1 Edw. & 1 Geo. 6. ch. 6]

2. (1) If the members or adherents of any association of persons, whether incorporated or not, are—

    (*a*) organised or trained or equipped for the purpose of enabling

---

to blame for their own passive inactivity. Violence may be the only way to bring them to the sense of their responsibility to the country in which they live.' The article appeared shortly after three British servicemen had been murdered by terrorists in Palestine and after there had been some breaking of windows of shops owned by Jews in some northern towns. He was acquitted. See *An Editor on Trial* (1947).

them to be employed in usurping the functions of the police or of the armed forces of the Crown; or

(b) organised and trained or organised and equipped either for the purpose of enabling them to be employed for the use or display of physical force in promoting any political object, or in such manner as to arouse reasonable apprehension that they are organised and either trained or equipped for that purpose;

then any person who takes part in the control or management of the association, or in so organising or training as aforesaid any members or adherents thereof, shall be guilty of an offence under this section;

Provided that in any proceedings against a person charged with the offence of taking part in the control or management of such an association as aforesaid it shall be a defence to that charge to prove that he neither consented to nor connived at the organisation, training, or equipment of members or adherents of the association in contravention of the provisions of this section.

(2) No prosecution shall be instituted under this section without the consent of the Attorney-General. . .

(4) In any criminal or civil proceedings under this section proof of things done or of words written, spoken or published (whether or not in the presence of any party to the proceedings) by any person taking part in the control or management of an association or in organising, training or equipping members or adherents of an association shall be admissible as evidence of the purposes for which, or the manner in which, members or adherents of the association (whether those persons or others) were organised, or trained, or equipped.

(5) If a judge of the High Court is satisfied by information on oath that there is reasonable ground for suspecting that an offence under this section has been committed, and that evidence of the commission thereof is to be found at any premises or place specified in the information, he may, on an application made by an officer of police of a rank not lower than that of inspector, grant a search warrant authorising any such officer as aforesaid named in the warrant together with any other persons named in the warrant and any other officers of police to enter the premises or place at any time within one month from the date of the warrant, if necessary by force, and to search the premises or place and every person found therein, and to seize anything found on the premises or place or on any such person which the officer has reasonable ground for suspecting to be evidence of the commission of such an offence as aforesaid:

Provided that no woman shall, in pursuance of a warrant issued under this subsection, be searched except by a woman.

(6) Nothing in this section shall be construed as prohibiting the employment of a reasonable number of persons as stewards to assist in

the preservation of order at any public meeting held upon private premises, or the making of arrangements for that purpose or the instruction of the persons to be so employed in their lawful duties as such stewards, or their being furnished with badges or other distinguishing signs.

(ii) Emergency powers

(a) *General principles on the use of the armed forces in support of the civil authorities*

Report of the Committee on the Featherstone Riots, 1893

On 7 September 1893 troops opened fire on a rioting crowd at Ackton Hall Colliery at Featherstone, some five miles from Wakefield. There had been disturbances there earlier in the day but the manager had been unable to get police help because of the demands of the Doncaster races. Instead a Captain and 28 infantrymen arrived a little after 4 p.m. When it was discovered that they were at the colliery a crowd gathered and demanded their withdrawal. They withdrew to the station but returned after dark when they saw colliery buildings on fire. At 8.40 p.m. a magistrate read the proclamation from the Riot Act, 1714 (now repealed). At 9.15 p.m. he gave written instructions to Captain Barker to fire. Two people were killed. A Committee consisting of Lord Bowen, Sir Albert Rollitt, M.P., and R. B. Haldane, M.P. (later Lord Haldane) was appointed to investigate.

We pass next to the consideration of the all-important question whether the conduct of the troops in firing on the crowd was justifiable; and it becomes essential, for the sake of clearness, to state succinctly what the law is which bears upon the subject. By the law of this country everyone is bound to aid in the suppression of riotous assemblages. The degree of force, however, which may lawfully be used in their suppression depends on the nature of each riot, for the force used must always be moderated and proportioned to the circumstances of the case and to the end to be attained.

The taking of life can only be justified by the necessity for protecting persons or property against various forms of violent crime, or by the necessity of dispersing a riotous crowd which is dangerous unless dispersed, or in the case of persons whose conduct has become felonious through disobedience to the provisions of the Riot Act, and who resist the attempt to disperse or apprehend them. The riotous crowd at the Ackton Hall Colliery was one whose danger consisted in its manifest design violently to set fire and do serious damage to the colliery property, and in pursuit of that object to assault those upon the colliery premises. It was a crowd accordingly which threatened serious outrage, amounting to felony, to property and persons, and it became the duty of all peaceable subjects to assist in preventing this. The necessary prevention of such outrage on person and property justifies the guardians of the peace in the employment against a riotous crowd of even deadly weapons.

Officers and soldiers are under no special privileges and subject to no special responsibilities as regards this principle of the law. A soldier for the purpose of establishing civil order is only a citizen armed in a particular manner. He cannot because he is a soldier excuse himself if without necessity he takes human life... A soldier can only act by using his arms. The weapons he carries are deadly. They cannot be employed at all without danger to life and limb, and in these days of improved rifles and perfected ammunition, without some risk of injuring distant and possibly innocent bystanders. To call for assistance against rioters from those who can only interpose under such grave conditions ought, of course, to be the last expedient of the civil authorities. But when the call for help is made, and a necessity for assistance from the military has arisen, to refuse such assistance is in law a misdemeanor.[25]

The whole action of the military when once called in ought, from first to last, to be based on the principle of doing, and doing without fear, that which is absolutely necessary to prevent serious crime, and of exercising all care and skill with regard to what is done. No set of rules exists which governs every instance or defines beforehand every contingency that may arise. One salutary practice is that a magistrate should accompany the troops... The military come, it may be, from a distance. They know nothing, probably, of the locality, or of the special circumstances. They... need the counsel of the local justice, who is presumably familiar with the details of the case. But... his absence does not alter the duty of the soldier, nor ought it to paralyse his conduct, but only to render him doubly careful as to the proper steps to be taken. No officer is justified by English law in standing by and allowing felonious outrage to be committed merely because of a magistrate's absence.

The question whether, on any occasion, the moment has come for firing upon a mob or rioters, depends, as we have said, on the necessities of the case. Such firing, to be lawful, must, in the case of a riot like the present, be necessary to stop or prevent such serious and violent crime as we have alluded to; and it must be conducted without recklessness or negligence. When the need is clear, the soldier's duty is to fire with all reasonable caution, so as to produce no further injury than what is absolutely wanted for the purpose of protecting person and property... The justification of Captain Barker and his men must stand or fall entirely by the common law. Was what they did necessary, and no more than was necessary, to put a stop to or prevent felonious crime?

[25] [See *Reg.* v. *Brown* (1841) C. & N. 314; 174 E.R. 522.]

In doing it did they exercise all ordinary skill and caution, so as to do no more harm than could be reasonably avoided?

If these two conditions are made out, the fact that innocent people have suffered does not involve the troops in legal responsibility. A guilty ringleader who under such conditions is shot dead, dies by justifiable homicide. An innocent person killed under such conditions, where no negligence has occurred, dies by an accidental death. The legal reason is not that the innocent person has to thank himself for what has happened, for it is conceivable (though not often likely) that he may have been unconscious of any danger and innocent of all imprudence. The reason is that the soldier who fired has done nothing except what was his strict legal duty.

In measuring with the aid of subsequent evidence the exact necessities of the case as they existed at the time at Ackton Hall Colliery, we have formed a clear view that the troops were in a position of great embarrassment. The withdrawal of half their original force to Nostell Colliery had reduced them to so small a number as to render it difficult for them to defend the colliery premises effectively at night time. The crowd for some hours had been familiarised with their presence, and had grown defiant. All efforts at conciliation had failed. Darkness had meanwhile supervened, and it was difficult for Captain Barker to estimate the exact number of his assailants, or to what extent he was being surrounded and outflanked. Six or seven appeals had been made by the magistrates to the crowd. The Riot Act had been read without result. A charge had been made without avail. Much valuable colliery property was already blazing, and the troops were with difficulty keeping at bay a mob armed with sticks and bludgeons, which was refusing to disperse, pressing where it could into the colliery premises, stoning the fire engine on its arrival, and keeping up volleys of missiles. To prevent the colliery from being overrun and themselves surrounded, it was essential for them to remain as close as possible to the Green Lane entrance. Otherwise, the rioters would, under cover of darkness, have been able to enter in force. To withdraw from their position was, as we have already intimated, to abandon the colliery offices in the rear to arson and violence. To hold the position was not possible, except at the risk of the men being seriously hurt and their force crippled. Assaulted by missiles on all sides, we think that, in the events which had happened, Captain Barker and his troops had no alternative left but to fire, and it seems to us that Mr Hartley was bound to require them to do so.

... [N]o sympathy felt by us for the injured bystanders, no sense which we entertain of regret that, owing to the smallness of the military force at Featherstone and the prolonged absence of a magistrate, matters had drifted to such a pass, can blind us to the fact that, as things stood at the supreme moment when the soldiers fired, their action was necessary. We feel it right to express our sense of the steadiness and discipline of the soldiers in the circumstances. We can find no ground for any suggestion that the firing, if it was in fact necessary, was conducted with other than reasonable skill and care. The darkness rendered it impossible to take more precaution than had been already employed to discriminate between the lawless and the peaceable, and it is to be observed that even the first shots fired produced little or no effect upon the crowd in inducing them to withdraw. If our conclusions on these points be, as we believe them to be, correct, it follows that the action of the troops was justified in law.

[Report of the Committee on the Disturbances at Featherstone. C. 7234 (1893–4)]

The Commission on the Landing of Arms at Howth, 1914

35. In our opinion the military should only, and legally can only, be convened to interfere with, quell, or disperse an unlawful assembly, if that assembly is unlawful in the sense that it has committed or threatens to commit serious and violent crime, as for instance the setting fire to or destruction of buildings or property, the killing, or maiming, or seriously injuring of persons, or if it is resisting or overpowering the King's officers engaged in the execution of the law . . .

38. . . . . [E]ven when the limited and extreme class of cases has been reached, there still remains great room for the exercise of a wise, a scrupulously careful, and a forbearing exercise of discretion. . . The appearance of military – men armed with the apparatus for mortal combat – may instead of composing, do much to inflame the passions of a crowd, and instead of quelling riot may do much to disturb the King's peace. But a second consequence, not noted by the authorities, yet unhappily and emphatically illustrated by the incidents under examination may be this, that the passions are not confined to one side, but that the forces brought on the scene and thus engaged in an unpopular and risky task may in the heat of the moment yield to impulses and commit indiscretions which lead to lamentable, and it may be, to fatal results, even involving persons who are entirely innocent either of disturbance or of crime.

39. What has just been said gives point to our next general observations on the law and practice with regard to the invocation of military aid to assist the civil power. It is to the effect that such invocation should be a last resort, that is a resort when all ordinary, peaceful, and less provocative means have failed. . .

[Report of the Royal Commission Appointed to Inquire into the Events Connected with the Landing of Arms at Howth. Cd. 7631 [26]]

[26] The Commissioners were Lord Shaw of Dunfermline, T. F. Molony and W. D. Andrews.

The Widgery Report, 1972

89. Troops on duty in Northern Ireland have standing instructions for opening fire. These instructions are set out upon the Yellow Card which every soldier is required to carry. Soldiers operating collectively – a term which is not itself defined – are not to open fire without an order from the Commander on the spot. Soldiers acting individually are generally required to give warning before opening fire and are subject to other general rules which provide *inter alia:*

' 2. Never use more force than the *minimum* necessary to enable you to carry out your duties.

3. Always first try to handle the situation by other means than opening fire. If you have to fire:

(*a*) Fire only aimed shots.

(*b*) Do not fire more rounds than are absolutely necessary to achieve your aim '.

The injunction to fire only aimed shots is understood by the soldiers as ruling out shooting from the hip – which they in any case regard as inefficient, indeed pointless – except that in a very sudden emergency, requiring split second action, a shot from the hip is regarded as permissible if it is as well aimed a shot as the circumstances allow.

90. Other stringent restrictions apply to soldiers who have given warning of intention to fire. But the rule of principal significance to the events of 30 January is that which contemplates a situation in which it is not practicable to give a warning. It provides:

' You may fire without warning

13. Either when hostile firing is taking place in your area, and a warning is impracticable, or when any delay could lead to death or serious injury to people whom it is your duty to protect or to yourself; *and then only*:

(*a*) against a person using a firearm against members of the security forces or people whom it is your duty to protect; or

(*b*) against a person carrying a firearm if you have reason to think he is about to use it for offensive purposes.'

The term ' firearm ' is defined as including a grenade, nail bomb or gelignite-type bomb.

91. Though no one has sought to criticise the spirit and intention of these orders, it would be optimistic to suppose that every soldier could be trained to understand them in detail and apply them rigidly. Even if he could, the terms of Rule 13 leave certain questions unanswered and, perhaps, unanswerable:

(i) In the conditions contemplated by Rule 13, is fire to be opened defensively and restricted to that which is necessary to cause the attacker to desist and withdraw, or is he to be treated as an enemy in battle and engaged until he surrenders or is killed?

(ii) In the like conditions, is fire to be withheld on account of risk to others in the vicinity who are not themselves carrying or using firearms? Suppose that in a crowd of youths throwing stones one is identified as holding a nail bomb. Is the soldier then to hold his fire because of risk to those who are only throwing stones?

(iii) When hostile fire is taking place how certain must the soldier be in identifying an object as a firearm? From the front a camera with a telescopic lens may look very much like certain types of sub-machine gun. A television sound recordist holding his microphone aloft could well be taken for someone about to throw a nail bomb. Faced with such a situation does the soldier wait or does he give himself the benefit of the doubt and fire?

92. Furthermore, anomalous situations could arise from the Yellow Card's definition of a firearm. Although the definition does not embrace the petrol bomb, the soldier is authorised to fire against a person throwing a petrol bomb, but only after due warning and if petrol bomb attacks continue and if the thrower's action is likely to endanger life. There is no specific mention of other types of missile, including acid bombs. However, the soldier is authorised to fire, after due warning, ' *against a person attacking* . . . if his action is *likely to endanger life* ', or ' if there is no other way ' for the soldier to protect himself or others ' from the danger of being killed or seriously injured '. So it would presumably be in order under the Yellow Card rules for a soldier to fire on a person hurling bricks or acid bombs or pieces of angle iron from high up on a tall building, but only after giving due warning, which it might not be easy to give.

93. Many people will be surprised to learn that it is not open to the soldier to give warning by firing warning shots. As has already been seen, the soldier is required to ' fire only aimed shots '. Whilst the Yellow Card does not in terms forbid a soldier hard pressed by an advancing mob to fire over their heads, to do so is certainly a breach of the orders. The justification put forward for this somewhat surprising provision is that hooligans would rapidly note and take advantage of the regular firing of shots meant to pass harmlessly by; the carrying of firearms would cease to deter.

94. Soldiers will react to the situations in which they find themselves in different ways according to their temperament and to the prevailing circumstances. The more intensive the shooting or stone-throwing which is going on the more ready will they be to interpret the Yellow Card as permitting them to open fire. The individual soldier's reaction may also be affected by the general understanding of these problems which prevails in his unit. In the Parachute Regiment, at any rate in the 1st Battalion the soldiers are trained to take what may be described as a hard line upon these questions. The events of 30 January and the

attitude of individual soldiers whilst giving evidence suggest that when engaging an identified gunman or bomb-thrower, they shoot to kill or continue to fire until the target disappears or falls. When under attack and returning fire they show no particular concern for the safety of others in the vicinity of the target. They are aware that civilians who do not wish to be associated with violence tend to make themselves scarce at the first alarm and they know that it is the deliberate policy of gunmen to use civilians as covers. Further; when hostile firing is taking place the soldiers of 1 Para will fire on a person who appears to be using a firearm against them without always waiting until they can positively identify the weapon. A more restrictive interpretation of the terms of the Yellow Card by 1 Para might have saved some of the casualties on 30 January, but with correspondingly increased risk to the soldiers themselves.

[Report of the Tribunal Appointed to Inquire into the Events on Sunday 30 January 1972 in Londonderry. H.L. 101, H.C. 220, 18 April 1972]

(b) *Martial law*

EX PARTE MARAIS [1902] A.C. 109

Privy Council [27]

THE LORD CHANCELLOR ... The only ground susceptible of argument urged by the learned counsel was that whereas some of the courts were open it was impossible to apply the ordinary rule that where actual war is raging the civil courts have no jurisdiction to deal with military action, but where acts of war are in question the military tribunals alone are competent to deal with such questions... [T]heir Lordships ... are of opinion that where actual war is raging acts done by the military authorities are not justiciable by the ordinary tribunals, and that war in this case was actually raging, even if their Lordships did not take judicial notice of it, is sufficiently evidenced by the petitioner's own petition and affidavit. Martial law had been proclaimed over the district in which the petitioner was arrested and the district to which he was removed.[28] The fact that for some purposes some tribunals had been permitted to pursue their ordinary course is not conclusive that war

---

[27] The Lord Chancellor, Lords Macnaghten, Shand, Davey, Robertson and Lindley and Sir Henry de Villiers.

[28] Note however the statement of the Privy Council in *Tilonko* v. *Attorney-General of Natal* [1907] A.C. 93: 'The notion that "martial law" exists by reason of the proclamation... is an entire delusion. The right to administer force against force in actual war does not depend upon the proclamation of martial law at all. It depends upon the question whether there is war or not. If there is war, there is the right to repel force by force.'

was not raging. That question came before the Privy Council as long ago as the year 1830 [in *Elphinstone* v. *Bedreechund* 1 Knapp P.C. 316]... Doubtless cases of difficulty arise where the fact of a state of rebellion or insurrection is not clearly established. It may often be a question whether a mere riot, or disturbance neither so serious nor so extensive as really to amount to a war at all, has not been treated with an excessive severity, and whether the intervention of the military force was necessary, but once let the fact of actual war be established, and there is a universal consensus of opinion that the civil courts have no jurisdiction to call in question the propriety of the action of military authorities. The framers of the Petition of Right knew well what they meant when they made a condition of peace the ground of the illegality of unconstitutional procedure.

Report on the death of Mr Sheehy Skeffington, 1916

The effect, so far as the powers of the military authorities are concerned, of a proclamation of martial law within the United Kingdom has often been expounded, but nevertheless, in the crisis which evokes such a proclamation, is not always remembered. Such a proclamation does not, in itself, confer upon officers or soldiers any new powers. It operates solely as a warning that the Government, acting through the military, is about to take such forcible and exceptional measures as may be necessary for the purpose of putting down insurrection and restoring order. As long as the measures are necessary, they might equally be taken without any proclamation at all. The measures that are taken can only be justified by the circumstances then existing and the practical necessities of the case...

The shooting of unarmed and unresisting civilians without trial constitutes the offence of murder, whether martial law has been proclaimed or not. We should have deemed it superfluous to point this out were it not that the failure to realise and apply this elementary principle seems to explain the free hand which Capt. Bower-Colthurst was not restrained from exercising throughout the period of crisis...

[Report of the Royal Commission to Inquire into the Facts Connected with the Treatment of Mr Francis Sheehy Skeffington and Others on 25 April 1916. Cd. 8376]

REX v. *ALLEN*   [1921] 2 Ir.R. 241

MOLONY C.J. It is the sacred duty of this Court to protect the lives and liberties of all His Majesty's subjects, and to see that no one suffers loss of life or liberty save under the laws of the country; but when subjects of the King rise in armed insurrection and the conflict is still raging, it is no less our duty not to interfere with the officers of the

Crown in taking such steps as they deem necessary to quell the insurrection, and to restore peace and order and the authority of the law. . .

[T]he affidavit of Sir Nevil Macready . . . described in some detail the nature of the present rebellion. After stating that on and prior to the 1st July, 1920, and since said date to the present time, a state of open rebellion has been and is in existence in, amongst other places, the County of Tipperary, North Riding, and the County of Tipperary, South Riding, the City and County of Cork and adjoining districts, such state of rebellion amounting to actual war of a guerilla character, he proceeds to give instances of the nature of the operations of the force known as the Irish Republican Army or Irish Volunteers. He says: ' Most of the police barracks in the districts referred to have been destroyed or attacked, and in some cases attacked and injured more than once; many of the police have been killed or wounded in these attacks; ambushes have been prepared by day and night against His Majesty's soldiers and police, and in carrying out these attacks and ambushes members of the rebel organizations have used bombs, rifles, shot guns, revolvers, and large supplies of petrol for the purposes of arson. Numbers of His Majesty's soldiers and police have been attacked and have sustained many casualties, entailing loss of lives and serious injuries. His Majesty's mails have been continually raided, trains have been repeatedly held up, and Government offices have been attacked throughout the country.' In proof of his statement that a state of war exists, he refers to copies of a publication called ' An T'Oglac ', which had from time to time been found in the possession or under the control of members of the rebel army, in which it is stated that war exists between England and Ireland, and he gives figures showing the losses that the Crown forces have sustained in the martial law area since the 1st July, 1920. In view of the facts stated and relied on by Sir Nevil Macready, and which have not been contradicted by any affidavit on behalf of the prisoner, it is impossible not to come to the conclusion that at the time of the Lord Lieutenant's proclamation a state of war actually existed and continued to exist at the time of the arrest of John Allen, and since then down to the present time. . .

Unlike the armed insurrections of the past, where the insurgents met the Crown forces in actual battle, the present insurrection consists exclusively of warfare of a guerilla character, the nature of which is explained by Sir Nevil Macready in the following words: ' The scheme of the said warfare does not entail fighting in distinctive uniforms, or in accordance with the laws of war, but under a system of guerilla attacks, in which inhabitants, apparently pursuing peaceful avocations, constantly come together and carry out guerilla operations, which often result in the death of or serious injuries to members of His Majesty's forces and police at the hands of the people who are posing as peaceful citizens.' During the continuance of such a state of affairs as is described in Sir Nevil Macready's affidavit the Government is entitled and, indeed, bound to repel force by force, and thereby to put down the insurrection and restore public order. As was stated by Lord Halsbury in *Tilonko* v. *Attorney-General of Natal*,[29] ' such acts of justice are justified by necessity by the fact of actual war, and that they are so justified under the circumstances is a fact that is no longer necessary to insist upon, because it has been over and over again so decided by Courts as to whose authority there can be no doubt.' It is unnecessary for us to discuss the cases to which Lord Halsbury refers, such as the *Case of Ship Money*;[30] *R.* v. *Pinney*;[31] *R.* v. *Stratton and others*;[32] *R.* v. *Eyre*;[33] *R.* v. *Nelson and Brand*,[34] to which may be usefully added the reports of three Royal Commissions – ' Featherstone Riots ' (Parliamentary Papers, 1893, 1894, c. 7234); ' Landing of Arms at Howth ' (Parliamentary Papers, 1914, cd. 7631); and ' Re Sheehy Skeffington ' (Parliamentary Papers, 1916, cd. 8376).

It is also clear on the authorities that when martial law is imposed, and the necessity for it exists, or, in other words, while war is still raging, this Court has no jurisdiction to question any acts done by the military authorities (*Ex parte Marais*),[35] although after the war is over persons may be made liable, civilly and criminally, for any acts which they are proved to have done in excess of what was reasonably required by the necessities of the case: *Governor Wall's Case*;[36] *Wright* v. *Fitzgerald*;[37] *Rainsford* v. *Browne*;[38] *Ex parte Milligan*[39] – unless these acts have in the meantime been covered by an Act of Indemnity...

(c) *Powers of investigation in times of emergency*

The Report of the Compton Committee, 1971

On 9 August 1971 342 men were arrested by the security forces in Northern Ireland under the Civil Authorities (Special Powers) Act (Northern Ireland), 1922, as part of a policy of internment announced by the Northern Ireland Prime Minister, Mr Faulkner, on the same day. On 31 August a committee was appointed under Sir Edmund Compton ' to investigate allegations by those arrested ... of physical brutality while in the custody of the security forces...' Their findings in relation to the actual allegations were hampered by the refusal of the complainants to participate. From a constitutional point of view, however, it is the procedures and their use in this particular case, which are important.

[29] [1907] A.C. 93, 95.
[30] 3 State Trials, 825. Holborne's Argument, at p. 976, and per Croke J., at p. 1162.
[31] 3 State Trials, N.S., at p. 2; 3 B. & Ad. 947.
[32] 21 State Trials, at p. 1230.
[33] (1868) Finlason's Report.
[34] Frederick Cockburn's Report.
[35] [1902] A.C. 109.
[36] 28 State Trials, 51.
[37] 27 State Trials, 759.
[38] 2 N.Ir.Jur.Repts. 179.
[39] 4 Wall, U.S. 2.

Government Policy in Relation to Interrogation

46. In the course of our investigation we were requested by Her Majesty's Government to receive a note on the subject of Government policy in relation to interrogation methods. We were asked also to include this note in our report for publication. It runs as follows: —

' NOTE ON INTERROGATION

(1) The general rules governing the custody of detainees and the processes of interrogation have been reviewed from time to time by the Government Departments and agencies concerned in the light of experience gained in the various internal security operations in which H.M.G. have been involved since the last war. The techniques of interrogation currently in use have also been employed in many previous internal security situations. The latest instructions on the rules to be followed were issued in 1965, and were revised in 1967 to provide for the daily inspection by a medical officer in the light of the recommendations in the Report on the Aden situation by Mr Roderic Bowen, Q.C., issued in November, 1966 (Cmnd. 3165).

(2) These general rules include the following safeguards: —
  (a) Medical examination and record of weight of subject on admission and discharge.
  (b) Subjects to be seen daily by a Medical Officer.
  (c) The following are prohibited: —
      (i) Violence to life and person, in particular, mutilation, cruel treatment and torture.
      (ii) Outrages upon personal dignity, in particular humiliating and degrading treatment.
  (d) Subjects are to be treated humanely but with strict discipline.
      (These rules follow the broad principles for the treatment of persons under arrest or detention during civil disturbances as laid down in Article 3 of the Geneva Convention relative to the Treatment of Prisoners of War (1949).)

(3) The precise application of these general rules in particular circumstances is inevitably to some extent a matter of judgment on the part of those immediately responsible for the operations in question. Intelligence is the key to successful operations against terrorists; and the key to intelligence is information regarding their operations, their dispositions, and their plans. When combating a terrorist campaign time is of the essence; information must be sought while it is still fresh so that it may be used as quickly as possible to effect the capture of persons, arms and explosives and thereby save the lives of members of the security forces and of the civil population.

(4) Information can be obtained more rapidly if the person being interrogated is subjected to strict discipline and isolation, with a restricted diet; but violence or humiliating treatment, as explained above, are forbidden. Equally any person undergoing interrogation must be assured of security against either violent treatment by his fellow detainees or recognition by them; the evidence of I.R.A. vengeance against informers underlines the importance of this safeguard.'

47. The evidence we received from the officials we interviewed about the application of the general rules set out in the Government memorandum we reproduce above can be summarised as follows:—

The objectives mentioned in the memorandum may involve the use of the following methods, the circumstances and duration of whose application may vary according to the staff and accommodation available at the interrogation centre and the length of time for which detainees may be left alone or must be kept together:—

(a) Wall Standing

48. Requiring detainees to stand with their arms against a wall but not in a position of stress provides security for detainees and guards against physical violence during the reception and search period and whenever detainees are together outside their own rooms in a holding room awaiting interrogation. It also assists the interrogation process by imposing discipline. Although the security need for this technique could be reduced by an increase of staff sufficient to provide for the separate custody of each individual while in transit between his own room and the interrogation room, there would be increased risks of physical contact between detainees and guards.

(b) Hooding

49. The hood (a black pillow-slip which the detainee is not required to wear while he is being interrogated or while he is alone in his room) reduces to the minimum the possibility that while he is in transit or with other detainees he will be identified or will be able to identify other persons or the locations to which he is moved. It thus provides security both for the detainee and for his guards. It can also, in the case of some detainees, increase their sense of isolation and so be helpful to the interrogator thereafter.

(c) Noise

50. The continuous noise to which detainees may be subjected prevents their overhearing or being overheard by each other and is thus a further security measure. By masking extraneous sound and making communication more difficult it may enhance the detainee's sense of isolation.

(d) *Bread and Water Diet*

51. A diet of bread and water at six-hourly intervals may form part of the atmosphere of discipline imposed upon detainees while under control for the purpose of interrogation. The rules about medical inspection are referred to in paragraph 2 of the Note above.

52. These methods have been used in support of the interrogation of a small number of persons arrested in Northern Ireland who were believed to possess information of a kind which it was operationally necessary to obtain as rapidly as possible in the interest of saving lives, while at the same time providing the detainees with the necessary security for their own persons and identities ...

Common Allegations – Evidence of Supervising Staff

58. The persons supervising the operation commented as follows : —

Hooding

59. It was confirmed that the detainees were required to be kept fully hooded except when interrogated or in rooms by themselves. This meant, therefore, that hooding was confined to journeys outside the centre or movement within it and to the periods when complainants were held jointly or at the wall (see below). We were told that in fact some complainants kept their hoods on when they could have removed them if they wished.

Noise

60. It was confirmed that while the detainees were held together pending interrogation or between interrogations, they were subjected to a continuous hissing noise, or electronic ' mush ', loud enough to mask extraneous sounds and prevent effective oral communication between detainees. The noise was neutral, i.e. no music or speech sounds were intruded.

Posture on the Wall

61. It was confirmed that from time to time pending and between interrogations, the detainees were made to stand against a wall in a required position (facing wall, legs apart, leaning with hands raised up against wall) for anything between 4 and 6 hours, except for periodical lowering of the arms to restore circulation. It was pointed out that the posture was not the same as the search position. This was not a stress posture: that is, the legs were not so wide apart, the arms so stretched up, or the weight of the body put forward to the same extent as in the search position.

62. It was confirmed that detainees attempting to rest or sleep by propping their heads against the wall were prevented from doing so.

If a detainee collapsed on the floor, he was picked up by the armpits and placed against the wall to resume the approved posture . . .

64. We find from our inspection of the records kept at the time of this operation that the men were at the wall for periods totalling as follows: —

Mr. Auld	43½	hours
Mr. Clarke	40	hours
Mr. Donnelly	9	hours
Mr. Hannaway	20	hours
Mr. McClean	29	hours
Mr. McGuigan	14	hours
Mr. McKenna	30	hours
Mr. McKerr	15	hours
Mr. McNally	13	hours
Mr. Shivers	23	hours
Mr. Turley	9	hours

65. We were told that the interrogatees were not made to stand at the wall in the required posture throughout. As stated above, the period of standing was 4–6 hours at a time. At other times they would have been sitting against the wall . . .

Sleep

66. It was confirmed that it was the general policy to deprive the men of opportunity to sleep during the early days of the operation.

Food and Drink

67. The records we examined showed that bread and water was offered at 6-hourly intervals from 1230 on the 11th August until the morning of the 15th August, when the diet began to be increased to normal rations. Hot soup was taken at 2230 on the 13th August by all interrogatees except Mr. McClean who refused it, and we were told that a cereal had been offered earlier that evening.

Weight

68. The records kept by the doctor for each detainee on entering and leaving the centre all show loss of weight during the time spent there . . .

[Report of the Inquiry into the Allegations of Physical Brutality in Northern Ireland. Cmnd. 4823 (November 1971)]

The Parker Report, 1972

The rules in force at the time of the Compton Report had been formulated in 1965 by an inter-departmental committee. Following the publication of the Compton Report the Government appointed a Committee of Privy

Councillors consisting of Lord Parker C.J., Mr Boyd-Carpenter and Lord Gardiner to consider the procedures authorised by them for the interrogation of persons suspected of terrorism.

1. 'Terrorism' no doubt connotes violence, and violence for political ends. This could arise under normal conditions, in which case those suspected of such conduct would be dealt with in the same way as any other persons suspected of crime. We do not, however, construe our terms of reference as including in our inquiry ordinary police interrogation. We have accordingly confined our inquiry to interrogation in circumstances where some public emergency has arisen as a result of which suspects can legally be detained without trial . . .

2. We also read our terms of reference as calling upon us to inquire quite generally into the interrogation and custody of persons suspected of terrorism in such circumstances in the future, and not specifically in connection with Northern Ireland . . .

The techniques and their history

10. Essentially interrogation in depth consists in the main of questions and answers across a table. The techniques which have been criticised are in a sense ancillary activities. While other techniques may be devised in the future, the only techniques in current use are those referred to in the Compton Report, that is, wall-standing, hooding, noise, bread and water diet and deprivation of sleep. . . They have been developed since the War to deal with a number of situations involving internal security. Some or all have played an important part in counter insurgency operations in Palestine, Malaya, Kenya and Cyprus and more recently in the British Cameroons (1960–61), Brunei (1963), British Guiana (1964), Aden (1964–67), Borneo/Malaysia (1965–66), the Persian Gulf (1970–71) and in Northern Ireland (1971).

11. The object of all the techniques undoubtedly is to make the detainee . . . feel that he is in a hostile atmosphere, subject to strict discipline, and that he is completely isolated so that he fears what may happen next. A further object of some of the techniques . . . is one of security and safety. Thus it may be vital in the detainee's own interest that he is not recognised by his fellow detainees. It is also necessary that the detainees should not communicate with each other, or with the outside world, or get to know where they are being held or the identity of their guards. Finally, it is necessary to ensure the safety of the guards and prevent the escape of the detainees . . .

12. One of the unsatisfactory features of the past has been the fact that no rules or guidelines have been laid down to restrict the

degree to which these techniques can properly be applied. Indeed, it cannot be assumed that any U.K. Minister has ever had the full nature of these particular techniques brought to his attention, and, consequently, that he has ever specifically authorised their use . . .

Medical aspects and dangers

14. Provided the techniques are applied as envisaged by those responsible for Service training, the risk of physical injury is negligible. That was the evidence of all the medical witnesses, save that in the case of a detainee suffering from ear damage the condition might be aggravated by the noise.

15. We received a good deal of evidence on the effect of these techniques on mental health. One of the difficulties is that there is no reliable information in regard to mental effects, particularly long-term mental effects, and, as one would expect, the medical evidence varied somewhat in emphasis. Evidence we have received is to the effect that, while the techniques may produce some mental disorientation, this is expected to disappear within a matter of hours at the end of the interrogation. It is true that in a small minority of cases some mental effects may persist for up to two months. There is no evidence of a mental effect lasting longer, though very fairly all the medical witnesses were unable to rule out that possibility, certainly in the case of a constitutionally vulnerable detainee. Moreover, even if the mental effect did not disappear at once, it was impossible to say how far that was due to the techniques employed as opposed to the anxiety state which would be induced by reason of the detainee's continued detention, and, if he gave information, the guilty knowledge which he had of letting down his fellows coupled with the fear of reprisals . . .

17. In the result, we have come to the conclusion that, while long-term mental injury cannot scientifically be ruled out, particularly in the case of a constitutionally vulnerable individual, there is no real risk of such injury if proper safeguards are applied in the operation of these techniques. We deal with suggested safeguards in paragraphs 35 to 42 below.

The value of the techniques and the alternatives

18. There is no doubt that when used in the past these techniques have produced very valuable results in revealing rebel organisation, training and 'Battle Orders'. Interrogation also sometimes had the effect of establishing the innocence both of other wanted people and of the detainee himself.

19. Coming to recent times, the position in Northern Ireland prior to August 1971 was that the Security Forces were in need of hard

intelligence. Information obtained by the R.U.C. by ordinary police interrogation had failed to provide anything but a general picture of the I.R.A. organisation. As a result the Security Forces were hampered in their search for arms and explosives and in addition were liable to harass and antagonise innocent citizens. On the introduction of internment two operations of interrogation in depth took place involving the use of these techniques. In August 1971 12 detainees and in October 1971 two detainees were interrogated in depth.

20. As a direct result of these two operations the following new information was obtained:

(1) Identification of a further 700 members of both I.R.A. factions, and their positions in the organisations.

(2) Over 40 sheets giving details of the organisation and structure of I.R.A. units and sub-units.

(3) Details of possible I.R.A. operations; arms caches; safe houses; communications and supply routes, including those across the border; and locations of wanted persons.

(4) Details of morale, operational directives, propaganda techniques, relations with other organisations and future plans.

(5) The discovery of individual responsibility for about 85 incidents recorded on police files which had previously remained unexplained.

21. It is also not without significance that the rate at which arms, ammunition and explosives discovered in Northern Ireland by the Security Forces increased markedly after 9th August, and much the greater part of the haul has resulted either directly or indirectly from information obtained by interrogation in depth . . .

22. There is of course a danger that, if the techniques are applied to an undue degree, the detainee will, either consciously or unconsciously, give false information. So far as the operations in Northern Ireland are concerned, however, the information given was quickly proved to be correct except in a few cases in which incorrect descriptions were given of persons who could not be identified by name.

23. A further advantage was the ' snowball ' effect generated by following up the information thus obtained. Moreover, the indirect effect of these two operations of interrogation was that further information could be, and was, more readily obtained by ordinary police interrogation.

24. There is no doubt that the information obtained by these two operations directly and indirectly was responsible for the saving of lives of innocent citizens.

25. . . . There is no doubt that in time of war skilled interrogators

can obtain and have obtained valuable information by other means – by guile, by careful grouping of prisoners and monitoring of conversations with the aid of microphones, and by the introduction of ' stool pigeons '. Circumstances in time of war are, however, very different. Large resources are generally available in the form both of skilled interrogators and guards and ample accommodation; certainly as time goes on, if not at the beginning, ample information is available to assist interrogators; there is no need or wish to keep the prisoner's identity secret; and there are often, as in the last War, a number of prisoners who dislike the current enemy regime and are only too willing to talk. Moreover, it is doubtful whether today, when ' bugging ' is a well-known and unfortunately often used technique, its use would produce any information.

26. Considerable and persuasive evidence has been put before us that in counter-revolutionary operations, and in particular in urban guerilla warfare, interrogation as conducted in conditions of war is not very effective. While highly skilled interrogators might succeed in getting valuable information over a substantial period of time, they would be unlikely to obtain it as quickly. This evidence we accept.

Should these techniques be employed?

27. We do not subscribe to the principle that the end justifies the means. The means, in our view, must be such as not only comply with the Directive, but are morally acceptable taking account of the conditions prevailing.

28. ... Some take the view that any attempt to disorientate the mind, to lessen the will so as to make a man more susceptible to oral interrogation is, if not mental torture, at any rate not humane, and that the techniques in any form are humiliating or degrading. Others claim that the techniques produce no more than hardship and discomfort for a short period.

29. The true view, it seems to us, must depend upon the degree to which the techniques are applied [and] ... upon the medical condition of the detainee. What would be intolerable for a man in poor health might amount to no more than inconvenience for a fit man.

30. ... Further, we think that such expressions as ' humane ', ' inhuman ', ' humiliating ' and ' degrading ' fall to be judged ... in the light of the circumstances in which the techniques are applied, for example, that the operation is taking place in the course of urban guerilla warfare in which completely innocent lives are at risk; that there is a degree of urgency; and that the security and safety of the interrogation centre, of its staff and of the detainees are important considerations.

31. Viewed in this way we think that the application of these

techniques, subject to proper safeguards, limiting the occasion on which and the degree to which they can be applied, would be in conformity with the Directive.

32. So far as the moral issue is concerned, we feel that in a limited number of situations, in particular those in which urban guerillas are concerned, the attitude taken up by the witnesses as set out in paragraph 8 [i.e. that the techniques should never be used] is unrealistic and one which is unfair both to the State and to law abiding citizens...

33. We have ... considered the argument that, however careful the selection of detainees for interrogation in depth, it may on occasion involve the interrogation of a man wrongly suspected ... [B]ut it must be remembered that even under normal conditions it is accepted that a person suspected of ordinary crime, who may thereafter be found not guilty, can be subjected to some measure of discomfort, hardship and mental anxiety. Moreover, interrogation in depth may itself reveal the innocence of the detainee and allow of his release from detention.

34. We have come to the conclusion that the answers to the moral question is dependent on the intensity with which these techniques are applied and on the provision of effective safeguards against excessive use... Subject to these safeguards we have come to the conclusion that there is no reason to rule out these techniques on moral grounds and that it is possible to operate them in a manner consistent with the highest standards of our society.

Recommended safeguards

35. It is, however, we think of importance that, except in so far as their use is required for purposes of security and safety, these techniques should only be used in cases where it is considered vitally necessary to obtain information.

36. Whether the techniques are used only for the purposes of security and safety or also for the purpose of obtaining information, care should be taken that they are only applied in conformity with the Directive. Accordingly, we think that there should be guidelines to assist Service personnel as to the degree to which in any particular circumstances the techniques can be applied. We suggest guidelines as opposed to rules because we recognise that it may sometimes be impracticable to comply fully with them. Some discretion must be left to the man in charge of the operation, but any departure from them should be the subject of a special report to his superior officer.

37. We are satisfied that Her Majesty's Forces should neither apply nor be party to the application of these techniques except under the express authority of a U.K. Minister. It follows that if he is to authorise their application he must have full knowledge of what they involve and of the persons to whom they are to be applied. He must, in the

light of the conditions prevailing, decide whether and to what extent their application is necessary. He should also lay down guidelines as to their use for the assistance of Service personnel. These will for obvious reasons have to remain secret and we suggest that the Minister might be advised by a small and experienced Committee whose members are appointed by the Prime Minister after consultation with the Leader of the Opposition. Such a Committee should also be informed of, and keep under review, any new techniques which may in the future be developed...

39. It is, we think, important that there should always be a senior officer present at the interrogation centre who is recognised as being in overall control and who will carry personal responsibility for the operation. The chain of command and responsibility above him and to the Minister should be clear.

40. We think that a panel of highly skilled interrogators should be kept in being. This would, among other things, tend to reduce the number of occasions on which there would be a real necessity to use these techniques. Where it is necessary to use them, it is highly desirable that they should be in the hands of skilled and experienced interrogators, assisted by guards and staff who are under strict discipline. Mr Roderic Bowen, Q.C., recommended that the interrogators employed should be civilians. While not disagreeing with that recommendation in relation to Aden, we do not think that it should be adopted generally. Unless therefore there are other and overriding considerations, for example, difficulties of language, the operation should, in our view, be conducted by Service personnel.

41. We think that a doctor with some psychiatric training should be present at all times at the interrogation centre, and should be in a position to observe the course of oral interrogation. It is not suggested that he should be himself responsible for stopping the interrogation – rather that he should warn the controller if he felt that the interrogation was being pressed too far having regard to the demeanour of the detainee, leaving the decision to the controller. This should be some safeguard both for the constitutionally vulnerable detainee and at the same time for the interrogator.

42. We think that, when these techniques are employed, machinery should be set up to ensure that complaints are passed on to the Ministry concerned and that a person or body should be appointed to investigate any such complaints. In this connection it might be advisable to have a representative of the civil authority present at the interrogation centre. The existence of such machinery for the receipt and investigation of complaints would go a long way to ensure that the operation was conducted within the limits authorised.

In this connection we think it is important that careful records be kept of the movement and treatment of those being interrogated . . .

Lord Gardiner dissented from these conclusions in a minority report.

[Report of a Committee of Privy Councillors Appointed to Consider Authorised Procedures for the Interrogation of Persons Suspected of Terrorism. Cmnd. 4901]

(d) *The Northern Ireland (Emergency Provisions) Act, 1973 ch. 53*

The Report of the Diplock Committee, 1972

The committee was appointed 'to consider what arrangements for the administration of justice in Northern Ireland could be made in order to deal more effectively with terrorist organisations by bringing to book, otherwise than by internment by the Executive, individuals involved in terrorist activities, particularly those who plan and direct, but do not necessarily take part in terrorist acts; and to make recommendations'. The committee made a number of recommendations to facilitate the arrest and trial of those charged with 'terrorist' offences, which were subsequently embodied in the Northern Ireland (Emergency Provisions) Act, 1973. At the same time, however, the committee argued that it would still be necessary to maintain detention without trial, if arrest and trial subject even to these modifications were to be effective in securing the conviction of the guilty. The following passage puts forward the justification for the continuance of detention without trial. This justification and the justification of the modifications of the ordinary criminal processes which the committee proposed, together with the provisions of the Act itself, provide an important measure of the extent to which in a situation of continuing emergency it is felt necessary and justifiable to go in making exceptions to the normal constitutional procedures for dealing with offenders and maintaining order, short of martial law.

(i) *Detention without trial*

12. Article 6 of the European Convention for the Protection of Human Rights and Fundamental Freedoms (the ' European Convention') to which the United Kingdom is a party, lays down certain minimum requirements for a criminal trial in normal times. . .

15. The minimum requirements are based upon the assumption that witnesses to a crime will be able to give evidence in a court of law without risk to their lives, their families or their property. . .

16. This assumption, basic to the very functioning of courts of law, cannot be made today in Northern Ireland as respects most of those who would be able, if they dared, to give evidence in court on the trial of offences committed by members of terrorist organisations. . . In the result with increasingly rare exceptions, the only kind of case in which a conviction of a terrorist can be obtained by the ordinary processes of criminal law is one in which there is sufficient evidence against the accused from one or more of three sources: (1) oral

evidence by soldiers or policemen, whose protection can be more readily ensured; (2) physical evidence, such as finger-prints, and (3) an admissible confession by the accused...

18. Inability to prosecute in other cases does not mean that there is not a continuing flow of information to the security authorities about terrorist organisations and terrorist crimes... But this information is given only upon the understanding that the source will never be disclosed in any circumstances in which it could come to the ear of any member of the IRA...

19. ... *Mutatis mutandis* what we have said is likely to be equally true of terrorism by extremist groups operating from areas which are comparable strongholds of Loyalist opinion.

20. The minimum requirements that we have adopted as the criterion for criminal trial by a court of law, permit of hearings *in camera* where, *inter alia*, the interests of public order or national security so require. But even where the hearing takes place *in camera* they call for the accused to be informed *in detail* of the nature of the accusation against him and to examine or to have examined witnesses against him. We have naturally considered whether any methods could be devised whereby the identity of informants could be kept secret, while still enabling their evidence to be adduced in a court of law. The human difficulty is that nothing would convince them that there was no risk of their anonymity being betrayed. But we ourselves can find no practical way of keeping their identity secret if they gave evidence under any procedure which would fulfil the minimum requirements of trial to which we have referred. One could contemplate the hearing of certain evidence *in camera* with the witness screened from sight, his name and address withheld, the exclusion of the Press and public, and even without the physical presence of the accused himself. But at the absolute minimum the lawyer of the accused would have to be present to hear the witness's evidence in chief and to cross-examine him and for that purpose to take instructions from the accused. Even if the witness's identity were not disclosed to the accused's counsel the details, elicited in cross-examination, of how the witness came to see and hear that to which he testified might often suffice to identify him to the accused. Apart from this, the accused's counsel would be gravely handicapped in testing the witness's credibility unless he were informed who the witness was. To disclose this to counsel but prohibit him from communicating it to the accused would expose him to conflict between his duty to his client and his duty to the State inconsistent with the role of the defendant's lawyer in a judicial process. In any event, in the current polarisation of political views in Northern Ireland, no witness would believe that the lawyers defending a terrorist of either

faction would not disclose to their client all they had learnt about the identity of those who gave evidence against him. . .

27. We are thus driven inescapably to the conclusion that until the current terrorism by the extremist organisations of both factions in Northern Ireland can be eradicated, there will continue to be some dangerous terrorists against whom it will not be possible to obtain convictions by any form of criminal trial which we regard as appropriate to a court of law; and these will include many of those who plan and organise terrorist acts by other members of the organisation in which they take no first-hand part themselves. We are also driven inescapably to the conclusion that so long as these remain at liberty to operate in Northern Ireland, it will not be possible to find witnesses prepared to testify against them in the criminal courts, except those serving in the army or the police, for whom effective protection can be provided. The dilemma is complete. The only hope of restoring the efficiency of criminal courts of law in Northern Ireland to deal with terrorist crimes is by using an extra-judicial process to deprive of their ability to operate in Northern Ireland, those terrorists whose activities result in the intimidation of witnesses. With an easily penetrable border to the south and west the only way of doing this is to put them in detention by an executive act and to keep them confined, until they can be released without danger to the public safety and to the administration of justice. . .

31. The identity and functions of the responsible officers of many of the operational ' battalions ' and ' companies ' in which the Provisional I.R.A., at any rate, is organised are widely known. They can often be verified by the security forces from a plurality of reports obtained from separate sources independent of one another and by statements elicited from self-confessed members of the I.R.A. It is possible that some of the information obtained is wrong. Its probative value is cumulative and derives from such opportunity there may be to check and cross-check information from one source by similar information from other sources, to eliminate the possibility of collusion between different informants or the possibility that information coming from a plurality or informants personally unknown to one another can yet be traced back to a single common source.

32. It is now recognised by those responsible for collecting and collating this kind of information that when internment was re-introduced in August, 1971, the scale of the operation led to the arrest and detention of a number of persons against whom suspicion was founded on inadequate and inaccurate information. Such evidence as we have heard leads us to believe that the security authorities have learnt the lessons of this experience and that the danger of their recommending detention on inadequate evidence is now greatly

reduced. We think, however, that it is a valuable safeguard against abuse of the power of detention that under the new Order [40] the security authorities' case against a suspected terrorist has to be submitted to the consideration of some independent and impartial person or tribunal before any final decision to keep him in detention is reached.

The remaining extracts from the report deal with the modifications the committee proposed to the normal criminal processes, which were embodied in the Northern Ireland (Emergency Provisions) Act, 1973.

The first passage deals with the problems of arrest. The following passages deal with the trial of 'terrorist' offences.

(ii) *Arrest*

43. The requirement that a person arrested should be informed of the reason for his arrest is an appropriate safeguard of the liberty of the subject in normal times when arrests can be made by trained police officers, without hindrance by bystanders, of persons found at the scene of the crime or whose identity is known to them. But this is very different from the only way in which the arrest of most terrorists can be effected in extremist strongholds in Northern Ireland.

44. Here it is not practicable in present conditions for the initial arrest of a suspected terrorist to be made by a police officer. It can only be made by soldiers either when in the course of an armed patrol they believe they recognise a wanted man in the streets or in a passing vehicle or when, as a result of information received, they conduct a surprise search of premises on which terrorists are thought to be present. In the latter case there are often a number of people on the premises whose identities are not known to the members of the search party. In either case the arrest is liable to be hindered by crowds of sympathisers, including women and children, hurling stones and other missiles and possibly carried out under fire from snipers.

45. It is, we think, preposterous to expect a young soldier making an arrest under these conditions to be able to identify a person whom he has arrested as being a man whom he knows to be wanted for a particular offence so as to be able to inform him accurately of the grounds on which he is arresting him. It is impossible to question arrested persons on the spot to establish their identity. In practice this cannot usually be ascertained until they have been taken to the safety of battalion headquarters. Even here it may be a lengthy process, as suspects often give false names or addresses or, giving their true names, which are often very common ones, assert that some

[40] The Detention of Terrorists (Northern Ireland) Order, 1972, made under the Special Powers (Northern Ireland) Act, 1922.

relation or other person of the same name is the real person who is ' wanted ' for a particular offence. It is only when his identity has been satisfactorily established that it is possible to be reasonably certain of the particular ground on which he was liable to arrest and to inform him of it.

48. ... [W]e think that it is justifiable to take the risk that occasionally a person who takes no part in terrorist activity and has no special knowledge about terrorist organisations should be detained for such short time as is needed to establish his identity, rather than that dangerous and guilty men should escape justice because of technical rules about arrest to which it is impracticable to conform in existing circumstances.

49. We accordingly recommend that steps should be taken by legislation

   (1) to confer upon members of the armed services:
      (*a*) Power to arrest without warrant and to remove to any police station or to any premises occupied by the armed forces any person suspected of having committed or being about to commit any offence, or having information about any offence committed or about to be committed by any other person; and
      (*b*) Power to detain any such person in custody for a period of not more than four hours for the purpose of establishing his identity.
   (2) It should be an offence to refuse to answer or to give a false or misleading answer to any question reasonably put for that purpose by a member of the armed forces or a police officer.
   (3) Arrest and detention for up to four hours under the above powers should not be unlawful by reason of the fact that no reason was given or a wrong reason given for the arrest.
   (4) A person arrested or detained under the above powers should be deemed to be in lawful custody, so as to make it an offence to resist arrest or to escape from custody or to aid or abet any person attempting to resist or to escape.

50. ... We contemplate that when the arrested person's identity has been established satisfactorily, he should be released unless wanted by the police either on suspicion of having himself committed an offence or for interrogation as a person suspected of having knowledge of any terrorist organisation or activities. If it is intended to keep him in custody on either grounds he should be re-arrested either by the military police or by a police officer and informed of the ground for his further detention in custody. Our proposal does not involve that questioning prior to re-arrest should be directed to any other purpose than establishing the identity of the person arrested.

(iii) *The trial of 'terrorist' offences*

3. 'Terrorist acts' mentioned in our terms of reference we take to be the use or threat of violence to achieve political ends; and 'terrorist activities' as embracing the actual use or threat of violence, planning or directing or agreeing to its use, and taking active steps to promote its use or to hinder the discovery or apprehension of those who have used or threatened it. All these have long been criminal offences under the ordinary law of the land. They are not new offences created specifically to deal with an emergency...

5. ...The object of the terrorist organisations which concern us is to bring about political change in Northern Ireland by violent means; but terrorist organisations inevitably attract into their ranks ordinary criminals whose motivation for particular acts may be private gain or personal revenge. If those who commit such acts for non-political motives are associated with a known terrorist organisation, the effect on public safety and on public fear is no different because the motive with which they are committed is more base. We do not exclude these from the category of terrorist acts with which we are bound to deal.

6. We are driven therefore to classify the crimes to which our recommendations apply by reference to the legal definition of what constitutes the crime and not by reference to the motives (which may be mixed) which led the offender to commit it. For this purpose we have taken those crimes which are commonly committed at the present time by members of terrorist organisations. Except where otherwise stated in later sections of this Report our recommendations apply to those crimes even though they may have been committed by criminals who are not connected with any terrorist organisation. They fall into seven broad categories:—

(1) All offences under statutes relating to firearms or explosives or other devices used for destructive purposes.

(2) All robberies or assaults involving use of or threats to use firearms or other offensive weapons.

(3) Malicious damage to property by fire.

(4) Intimidation with intent to interfere in the course of justice.

(5) Riot and similar offences under statute.

(6) Other serious offences against person or property.

(7) Membership of an association which is unlawful under Special Powers Regulation 24*a*, and other serious offences under those Regulations. Intended to be also included are conspiracies to commit offences in any of the first five categories, and the cognate crimes of attempting, procuring or being accessory to the commission of any of these offences.

7. ... [I]n certain cases ... legislation would be needed to create a new subdivision of a wider general offence to enable the particular offence to be identified as falling within the categories ... [A]ny list of offences ... should be subject to amendment by statutory instrument as terrorist tactics change or experience shows the need for omissions or additions. We shall hereafter refer to offences ... in the list as ' Scheduled Offences '.

Mode of trial

37. ... We think that matters have now reached a stage in Northern Ireland at which it would not be safe to continue to rely upon methods hitherto used for securing the impartial trial by jury of terrorist crimes, particularly if the trend towards increasing use of violence by Loyalist extremists were to continue. The jury system as a means for trying terrorist crime is under strain. It may not yet have broken down, but we think that the time is already ripe to forestall its doing so.

38. We recommend that for the Scheduled Offences trial by judge alone should take the place of trial by jury for the duration of the emergency.

39. We have considered carefully whether trial without a jury of cases on indictment ought to be undertaken by a single judge or by two or more sitting together... The total strength of the Appeal and High Courts is seven. There are the same number of County Court Judges. This, in itself, would render impracticable trial by a plurality of judges in any significant number of cases and terrorist crime at present constitutes the bulk of the calendar of indictable crime. But we should in any event recommend trial by a single judge. ... Our oral adversarial system of procedure is ill-adapted to the collegiate conduct of a trial of fact. In criminal proceedings, in particular, immediate rulings on admissibility of evidence and other matters of procedure have constantly to be made by the single judge when sitting with a jury. It would gravely inconvenience the progress of the trial and diminish the value of oral examination and cross-examination as a means of eliciting the truth if a plurality of judges had to consult together, albeit briefly, before each ruling was made.

The conduct of the trial
The onus of proof

62. The principal weapons of terrorism in Northern Ireland are firearms, explosives and incendiary devices. Sometimes it is possible for the security forces to catch red-handed a terrorist when he is using them. But many terrorist activities take place at night, immediate capture of the terrorist is hindered by rioting crowds, by sympathisers, and reliable identification by army witnesses is extremely difficult.

Because of this the commonest charges which can be brought against terrorists and proved by army or police witnesses are of being in possession of firearms, ammunition or explosives, etc. These charges arise out of the discovery of these lethal objects by the army or the police in the course of searches of premises or vehicles or as a result of stopping people in the streets for questioning.

63. Legislation in the United Kingdom as well as in Northern Ireland has long provided that if the accused is found to be in possession of firearms or explosives the onus of proving that he had them for a lawful purpose shall lie on him . . .

65. But this still leaves the whole onus of proof of ' possession ' upon the prosecution. Possession of an object in criminal law involves two elements (1) the physical presence of the object in a place where the person accused of being in possession of it is able to exercise control over it; and (2) knowledge on the part of the accused of its actual presence, or knowledge of the likelihood of its being present coupled with a deliberate refraining from finding out for certain whether or not it is.

66. No difficulty arises in proving the first element by the evidence of army or police witnesses who conducted the successful search. But in the circumstances in which firearms and explosives are found in the current emergency in Northern Ireland, proof by the prosecution of the necessary element of knowledge is often impracticable under the existing law.

67. Arms, ammunition and explosives are usually found concealed in vehicles in which several people are travelling, on premises which several people occupy, or dropped or discarded by one of a group of people found in the street at night by an army patrol. The circumstances are such that it is probable that all of them knew of the presence of the lethal object. It is certain that at least one of them did. All that is not certain is which of them knew. . .

70. . . . The remedy which we recommend to deal with the three common types of cases of arms, ammunition or explosives is an amendment of the existing law so as to provide that arms, ammunition or explosives found on any premises shall be deemed to be in the possession of the occupier of those premises and of any person residing at or found on those premises at the time of the discovery unless he proves that he did not know and had no reason to suspect that any arms, ammunition or explosives were there. A similar provision is required in respect of persons present in any vehicle which contains arms, ammunition or explosives. To meet the case of firearms or explosives being discarded by an unidentified member of an identifiable group of persons in the street, a provision is required that any person found in the company of any other person who is carrying

arms, ammunition or explosives shall be deemed to be in possession of them unless he proves that he did not know and had no reason to suspect that such other person was carrying them . . .

The admissibility of confessions

84. If human lives are to be saved and destruction of property prevented in Northern Ireland, it is inescapable that the security authorities must have power to question suspected members of terrorist organisations. . . The whole technique of skilled interrogation is to build up an atmosphere in which the initial desire to remain silent is replaced by an urge to confide in the questioner. This does not involve cruel or degrading treatment. . . But as the rules as to admissibility of confessions have been interpreted in Northern Ireland the mere fact that the technique of questioning is designed to produce a psychological atmosphere favourable to the creation of this rapport is sufficient to rule out as evidence in a court of law anything which the accused has said thereafter. . .

86. We would not condone practices such as those which are described in the Compton Report (Cmnd. 4823) and the Parker Report (Cmnd. 4901) as having been used in the crisis resulting from the simultaneous internment of hundreds of suspects in August 1971. The use of any methods of this kind have been prohibited for many months past. As already mentioned they are, in any event, now regarded as counter-productive. Certainly, the official instructions to the RUC and the army are strict. So are the precautions taken to see that they are strictly observed. There is stationed on permanent call at the centre where suspects are questioned by the police an army medical officer who is not attached to any of the operational units stationed in Northern Ireland, but is sent out on a rota from England for a period of four to six weeks. He conducts a thorough medical examination of each suspect on arrival in the absence of the police and a similar examination at the conclusion of the questioning. He informs the suspect that if he wishes he will be allowed to see the doctor at any time while he is at the centre. The possibility of ill-treatment which injures the suspect physically or mentally going undetected by the doctor is remote. . .

89. . . . We consider therefore that . . . the current technical rules, practice and judicial discretions as to the admissibility of confession[s] ought to be suspended for the duration of the emergency in respect of Scheduled Offences, they should be replaced by a simple legislative provision that:

(1) Any inculpatory admission made by the accused may be given in evidence unless it is proved on a balance of probabilities that it was obtained by subjecting the accused to torture or to inhuman or degrading treatment; and

(2) The accused shall not be liable to be convicted on any inculpatory admission made by him and given in evidence if, after it has been given in evidence, it is similarly proved that it was obtained by subjecting him to torture or to inhuman or degrading treatment.

90. In recommending this exception to the admissibility of confessions we have adopted the wording of Article 3 of the European Convention for the Protection of Human Rights and Fundamental Freedoms...

Admissibility of signed statements

96. ... [W]e think that a minimum but immediate alteration is needed to meet the problem that witnesses to terrorist crimes may be killed or so injured as to be incapable of coming to court, or may flee from Northern Ireland or go into hiding in fear for their own safety, with the result that it is impracticable to produce them to give oral evidence in court.

97. What we recommend is that it should be provided by legislation that:

(1) Any signed written statement, if made by any person to a police officer or members of the armed forces or other person charged with the duty of investigating offences or charging offenders, in the course of investigating any crimes or suspected crime which is a Scheduled Offence, should be admissible as evidence of any fact stated therein of which direct oral evidence by the maker of the statement would be admissible, if it is shown that the maker of the statement:

(a) is dead or is unfit by reason of his bodily or mental condition to attend as a witness; or

(b) is outside the Province and it is not reasonably practicable to secure his attendance, or

(c) all reasonable steps have been taken to find him, but he cannot be found.

(2) The weight to be attached to a statement admitted under (1) should be a matter for the court of trial.

The commission also made recommendations intended to restrict the freedom with which bail was granted and for dealing with young offenders.

[Report of the Commission on Legal Procedures to Deal with Terrorist Activities. Cmnd. 5185 (1973)]

NORTHERN IRELAND (EMERGENCY PROVISIONS) ACT, 1973 [Ch. 53]

Trial and punishment of certain offences

2. (1) A trial on indictment of a scheduled offence [41] shall be conducted by the court without a jury. . .

(4) . . . [W]here the court . . . are not satisfied that the accused is guilty of that offence, but are satisfied that he is guilty of some other offence, which is not a scheduled offence, but of which a jury could have found him guilty on a trial for the scheduled offence, the court may convict him of that other offence.

3. (1) Subject to the provisions of this section, a person to whom this section applies and who is charged with a scheduled offence shall not be admitted to bail except by a judge of the High Court acting in that capacity and, if he is convicted of such an offence, shall not be admitted to bail pending any appeal.

(2) A judge shall not admit any such person to bail unless he is satisfied that the applicant—

(a) will comply with the conditions on which he is admitted to bail; and

(b) will not interfere with any witness; and

(c) will not commit any offence while he is on bail.

(3) Without prejudice to any other power to impose conditions on admission to bail, a judge may impose such conditions on admitting a person to bail under this section as appear to him to be likely to result in that person's appearance at the time and place required or to be necessary in the interests of justice or for the prevention of crime.

(4) Nothing in this section shall prejudice any right of appeal against the refusal of a judge of the High Court to grant bail.

(5) This section applies to persons who have attained the age of 14 and are not serving members of any of Her Majesty's regular naval, military or air forces. . .

5. In any criminal proceedings for a scheduled offence a written statement made and signed by any person in the presence of a constable shall be admissible as evidence of any fact stated therein of which direct oral evidence by him would be admissible, if it is shown that—

(a) the maker of the statement is dead, or is unfit by reason of his bodily condition to attend as a witness or is unfit to attend as a witness, by reason of a mental condition which has arisen since he made the statement; or

[41] See s. 27 below, p. 766.

(*b*) he is outside Northern Ireland and it is not reasonably practicable to secure his attendance; or

(*c*) all reasonable steps have been taken to find him, but he cannot be found.

6. (1) In any criminal proceedings for a scheduled offence a statement made by the accused may be given in evidence by the prosecution in so far as it is relevant to any matter in issue in the proceedings and is not excluded by the court in pursuance of subsection (2) below.

(2) If, in any such proceedings where the prosecution proposes to give in evidence a statement made by the accused, prima facie evidence is adduced that the accused was subjected to torture or to inhuman or degrading treatment in order to induce him to make the statement, the court shall, unless the prosecution satisfies them that the statement was not so obtained, exclude the statement or, if it has been received in evidence, shall either continue the trial disregarding the statement or direct that the trial shall be restarted before a differently constituted court (before whom the statement in question shall be inadmissible).

7. (1) Where a person is charged with possessing a proscribed article in such circumstances as to constitute an offence to which this section applies and it is proved that at the time of the alleged offence—

(*a*) he and that article were both present in any premises; or

(*b*) the article was in premises of which he was the occupier or which he habitually used otherwise than as a member of the public;

the court may accept the fact proved as sufficient evidence of his possessing (and, if relevant, knowingly possessing) that article at that time unless it is further proved that he did not at that time know of its presence in the premises in question, or if he did know, that he had no control over it.

(2) This section applies to vessels, aircraft and vehicles as it applies to premises.

(3) In this section ' proscribed article ' means an explosive firearm, ammunition, substance or other thing (being a thing possession of which is an offence under one of the enactments mentioned in subsection (4) below).[42]

Powers of arrest, detention, search and seizure, etc.

10. (1) Any constable may arrest without warrant any person whom he suspects of being a terrorist.

[42] Subsection (4) lists the Explosive Substances Act, 1883, the Firearms Act (Northern Ireland), 1969, the Protection of the Person and Property Act (Northern Ireland) 1969.

(2) For the purpose of arresting a person under this section a constable may enter and search any premises or other place where that person is or where the constable suspects him of being.

(3) A person arrested under this section shall not be detained in right of the arrest for more than seventy-two hours after his arrest ...

(4) Where a person is arrested under this section, an officer of the Royal Ulster Constabulary not below the rank of chief inspector may order him to be photographed and to have his fingerprints and palm prints taken by a constable, and a constable may use such force as may be necessary for the purpose.

(5) The provisions of Schedule 1 to this Act shall have effect with respect to the detention of terrorists and persons suspected of being terrorists.

11. (1) Any constable may arrest without warrant any person whom he suspects of committing, having committed or being about to commit a scheduled offence or an offence under this Act which is not a scheduled offence.

(2) For the purposes of arresting a person under this section a constable may enter and search any premises or other place where that person is or where the constable suspects him of being.

(3) A constable may seize anything which he suspects is being, has been or is intended to be used in the commission of a scheduled offence or an offence under this Act which is not a scheduled offence.

12. (1) A member of Her Majesty's forces on duty may arrest without warrant, and detain for not more than four hours, a person whom he suspects of committing, having committed or being about to commit any offence.

(2) A person effecting an arrest under this section complies with any rule of law requiring him to state the ground of arrest if he states that he is effecting the arrest as a member of Her Majesty's forces.

(3) For the purpose of arresting a person under this section a member of Her Majesty's forces may enter and search any premises or other place where that person is or, if that person is suspected of being a terrorist or of having committed an offence involving the use or possession of an explosive, explosive substance or firearm, where that person is suspected of being.

13. (1) Any member of Her Majesty's forces on duty or any constable may enter any premises or other place other than a dwelling-house for the purpose of ascertaining whether there are any munitions unlawfully at that place and may search the place for any munitions with a view to exercising the powers conferred by subsection (4) below.

(2) Any member of Her Majesty's forces on duty authorised by a commissioned officer of those forces or any constable authorised by

an officer of the Royal Ulster Constabulary not below the rank of chief inspector may enter any dwelling-house in which it is suspected that there are unlawfully any munitions and may search it for any munitions with a view to exercising the said powers.

(3) Any member of Her Majesty's forces on duty or any constable may—

(a) stop any person in any public place and ... search him for the purpose of ascertaining whether he has any munitions unlawfully with him; and

(b) ... search any person not in a public place whom he suspects of having any munitions unlawfully with him.

(4) A member of Her Majesty's forces or a constable authorised to search any premises or other place or any person under this Act may seize any munitions found in the course of the search unless it appears to the person so authorised that the munitions are being, have been and will be used only for a lawful purpose and may retain and, if necessary, destroy them.

(5) In this section ' munitions ' means—

(a) explosives, explosive substances, firearms and ammunition; and

(b) anything used or capable of being used in the manufacture of any explosive, explosive substance, firearm or ammunition. . .

15. Where any person is believed to be unlawfully detained in such circumstances that his life is in danger, any member of Her Majesty's forces on duty or any constable may enter any premises or other place for the purpose of ascertaining whether that person is so detained there, but a dwelling-house may be entered in pursuance of this section by a member of Her Majesty's forces only when authorised to do so by a commissioned officer of those forces and may be so entered by a constable only when authorised to do so by an officer of the Royal Ulster Constabulary not below the rank of chief inspector.

16. (1) Any member of Her Majesty's forces on duty or any constable may stop and question any person for the purpose of ascertaining that person's identity and movements and what he knows concerning any recent explosion or any other incident endangering life or concerning any person killed or injured in any such explosion or incident.

(2) Any person who fails to stop when required to do so under this section, or who refuses to answer or fails to answer to the best of his knowledge and ability, any question addressed to him under this section, shall be liable on summary conviction to imprisonment for a term not exceeding six months or to a fine not exceeding £400, or both.

17. (1) Any member of Her Majesty's forces on duty or any constable may enter any premises or other place—

(*a*) if he considers it necessary to do so in the course of operations for the preservation of the peace or the maintenance of order; or

(*b*) if authorised to do so by or on behalf of the Secretary of State.

(2) Any member of Her Majesty's forces on duty, any constable or any person specifically authorised to do so by or on behalf of the Secretary of State may, if authorised to do so by or on behalf of the Secretary of State —

(*a*) take possession of any land or other property;

(*b*) take steps to place buildings or other structures in a state of defence;

(*c*) detain any property or cause it to be destroyed or moved;

(*d*) do any other act interfering with any public right or with any private rights of property, including carrying out any works on any land of which possession has been taken under this sub-section.

(3) Any member of Her Majesty's forces on duty, any constable or any person specifically authorised to do so by or on behalf of the Secretary of State may, so far as he considers it immediately necessary for the preservation of the peace or the maintenance of order, wholly or partly close a highway or divert or otherwise interfere with a highway or the use of a highway, or prohibit or restrict the exercise of any right of way or the use of any waterway.

(4) Any person who, without lawful authority or reasonable excuse (the proof of which lies on him), interferes with works executed, or any apparatus, equipment or any other thing used, in or in connection with the exercise of powers conferred by this section shall be liable on summary conviction to imprisonment for a term not exceeding six months or to a fine not exceeding £400, or both.

(5) Any authorisation to exercise any powers under any provision of this section may authorise the exercise of all those powers, or powers of any class or a particular power so specified, either by all persons by whom they are capable of being exercised or by persons of any class or a particular person so specified.

18. (1) Any power conferred by this Part of this Act—

(*a*) to enter any premises or other place includes power to enter any vessel, aircraft or vehicle;

(*b*) to search any premises or other place includes power to stop and search any vehicle or vessel or any aircraft which is not airborne and search any container;

and in this Part of this Act references to any premises or place shall be construed accordingly and references to a dwelling-house shall include references to a vessel or vehicle which is habitually stationary and used as a dwelling.

(2) Any power so conferred to enter any place, vessel, aircraft or vehicle shall be exercisable, if need be, by force.

(3) Any power conferred by virtue of this section to search a vehicle or vessel shall, in the case of a vehicle or vessel which cannot be conveniently or thoroughly searched at the place where it is, include power to take it or cause it to be taken to any place for the purpose of carrying out the search.

(4) Any power conferred by virtue of this section to search any vessel, aircraft, vehicle or container includes power to examine it.

(5) Any power conferred by this Part of this Act to stop any person includes power to stop a vessel or vehicle or an aircraft which is not airborne.

(6) Any person who, when required by virtue of this section to stop a vessel or vehicle or any aircraft which is not airborne, fails to do so shall be liable on summary conviction to imprisonment to a term not exceeding six months or to a fine not exceeding £400, or both.

(7) A member of Her Majesty's Forces exercising any power conferred by this Part of this Act when he is not in uniform shall, if so requested by any person at or about the time of exercising that power, produce to that person documentary evidence that he is such a member.

Offences against public security and public order

19. (1) Subject to subsection (7) below, any person who—
   (a) belongs or professes to belong to a proscribed organisation; or
   (b) solicits or invites financial or other support for a proscribed organisation, or knowingly makes or receives any contribution in money or otherwise to the resources of a proscribed organisation,

shall be liable on summary conviction to imprisonment for a term not exceeding six months or to a fine not exceeding £400, or both, and on conviction on indictment to imprisonment for a term not exceeding five years or to a fine, or both.

(3) The organisations specified in Schedule 2 to this Act [43] are proscribed organisations for the purposes of this section; and any organisation which passes under a name mentioned in that Schedule

---

[43] The organisations proscribed at the time the Act was passed were The Irish Republican Army, Cumann na m'Ban, Fianna na h'Eireann, Sinn Fein, Saor Eire, and The Ulster Volunteer Force.

shall be treated as proscribed, whatever relationship (if any) it has to
any other organisation of the same name.

(4) The Secretary of State may by order add to Schedule 2 to this
Act any organisation that appears to him to be concerned in terrorism
or in promoting or encouraging it.

(5) The Secretary of State may also by order remove an organisation from Schedule 2 to this Act.

(6) The possession by a person of a document addressed to him as
a member of a proscribed organisation, or relating or purporting to
relate to the affairs of a proscribed organisation, or emanating or
purporting to emanate from a proscribed organisation or officer of a
proscribed organisation, shall be evidence of that person belonging
to the organisation at the time when he had the document in his
possession. . .

20. (1) No person shall, without lawful authority or reasonable
excuse (the proof of which lies on him), collect, record, publish, communicate or attempt to elicit, any information with respect to the
police or Her Majesty's forces which is of such a nature as is likely
to be useful to terrorists, or have in his possession any record of or
document containing any such information; and if any person contra-
venes this section, he shall be liable—

(a) on summary conviction to imprisonment for a term not
exceeding six months or to a fine not exceeding £400, or both;

(b) on conviction on indictment to imprisonment for a term not
exceeding five years or a fine, or both. . .

(3) In subsection (1) above the reference to recording information
includes a reference to recording it by means of photography or by
any other means. . .

21. (1) Where any commissioned officer of Her Majesty's forces
or any officer of the Royal Ulster Constabulary not below the rank
of chief inspector is of opinion that any assembly of three or more
persons may lead to a breach of the peace or public disorder or may
make undue demands on the police or Her Majesty's forces he, or
any member of those forces on duty or any constable may order the
person constituting the assembly to disperse forthwith.

(2) Where an order is given under this section with respect to an
assembly, any person who thereafter joins or remains in the assembly
or otherwise fails to comply with the order shall be liable on summary
conviction to imprisonment for a term not exceeding six months or to
a fine not exceeding £400, or both.

23. Any person who in a public place dresses or behaves in such a
way as to arouse reasonable apprehension that he is a member of a

proscribed organisation shall be liable on summary conviction to imprisonment for a term not exceeding six months or to a fine not exceeding £400, or both.

Miscellaneous and general

24. (1) The Secretary of State may by regulations make provision additional to the foregoing provisions of this Act for promoting the preservation of the peace and the maintenance of order.

(2) Any person contravening or failing to comply with the provisions of any regulations under this section or any instrument or directions under any such regulations shall be liable on summary conviction to imprisonment for a term not exceeding six months or to a fine not exceeding £400, or both.

(3) The regulations contained in Schedule 3 to this Act shall be deemed to have been made under this section and to have been approved in draft by each House of Parliament, and may be varied or revoked accordingly . . .

26. (1) A prosecution shall not be instituted in respect of any offence under this Act except by or with the consent of the Director of Public Prosecutions for Northern Ireland. . .

27. (1) In this Act 'scheduled offence' means an offence specified in Part I of Schedule 4 to this Act, subject, however, to any relevant note contained in that Part.

(2) Part II of that Schedule shall have effect with respect to offences related to those specified in Part I of that Schedule.[44]

(3) The Secretary of State may by order amend that Schedule (whether by adding an offence to, or removing an offence from, either Part of that Schedule, or otherwise).

28. (1) In this Act, except so far as the context otherwise requires—

'public place' means a place to which for the time being members of the public have or are permitted to have access, whether on payment or otherwise . . .

---

[44] Part I of Schedule 4 includes such offences at common law as murder or manslaughter (unless the Attorney-General for Northern Ireland certifies in any particular case that the offence is not to be treated as a scheduled offence) and offences under a number of statutes, e.g. the Malicious Damage Act, 1861, the Offences against the Person Act, 1861, the Explosives Substances Act, 1883, the Firearms Act (Northern Ireland), 1969, and the Theft Act (Northern Ireland), 1969 (robbery and burglary where an explosive, firearm or imitation firearm was used). Part II covers inchoate and related offences such as aiding, abetting, counselling, procuring, attempting and conspiring to commit a scheduled offence, and doing an act with intent to impede the arrest or prosecution of someone who has committed a scheduled offence.

'terrorism' means the use of violence for political ends and includes any use of violence for the purpose of putting the public or any section of the public in fear;

'terrorist' means a person who is or has been concerned in the commission or attempted commission of any act of terrorism or in directing, organising or training persons for the purpose of terrorism . . .

29. (1) Any power to make orders or regulations conferred by this Act (except the powers to make orders conferred by Schedules 1 and 3 to this Act) shall be exercisable by statutory instrument . . .

(3) No order or regulations under this Act (except an order under either of the said Schedules) shall be made unless either a draft of the order or regulations has been approved by resolution of each House of Parliament or it is declared in the order or regulations that it appears to the Secretary of State that by reason of urgency it is necessary to make the order or regulations without a draft having been so approved.

(4) Orders and regulations under this Act (except an order under either of the said Schedules and except an order or regulations of which a draft has been so approved) shall be laid before Parliament after being made and, if at the end of the period of 40 days (computed in accordance with section 7 (1) of the Statutory Instruments Act 1946) after the day on which the Secretary of State made an order or regulations a resolution has not been passed by each House approving the order or regulations in question, the order or regulations shall then cease to have effect (but without prejudice to anything previously done or to the making of a new order or new regulations).

30. . . . (2) The provisions of this Act, except sections 1, 9 and 25 to 31 and Schedule 5 to this Act, shall remain in force until the expiry of the period of one year beginning with its passing and shall then expire unless continued in force by an order under this section.

(3) The Secretary of State may by order provide—

(*a*) that all or any of the said provisions which are for the time being in force (including any in force by virtue of an order under this section) shall continue in force for a period not exceeding one year from the coming into operation of the order;

(*b*) that all or any of the said provisions which are for the time being in force shall cease to be in force; or

(*c*) that all or any of the said provisions which are not for the time being in force shall come into force again and remain in force for a period not exceeding one year from the coming into operation of the order.

31. ... (2) The Civil Authorities (Special Powers) Act (Northern Ireland) 1970 shall cease to have effect...

(5) Any instrument made, any direction or authorisation given or any other thing done under any enactment repealed by this Act or any order or regulation made under any such enactment shall, so far as it could have been made, given or done under any provision of this Act, have effect as if it had been made, given or done under that provision ...

(7) Neither any rule of law nor any enactment other than this Act nor anything contained in a commission issued for the trial of any person shall be construed as limiting or otherwise affecting the operation of any provision of this Act for the time being in force, but—

(a) subject to the foregoing, any power conferred by this Act shall not derogate from Her Majesty's prerogative or any powers exerciseable apart from this Act by virtue of any rule of law or enactment ...

(8) This Act shall extend to Northern Ireland only.

SCHEDULE 1
Detention of Terrorists
Part I
Commissioners and Appeal Tribunal

1. For the purposes of this Act there shall be—
   (a) commissioners appointed by the Secretary of State; and
   (b) a Detention Appeal Tribunal (hereafter in this Schedule referred to as ' the Tribunal ') whose members shall be appointed by the Secretary of State.

The Commissioners

3. A commissioner shall be a person who holds or has held judicial office in any part of the United Kingdom or is a barrister, advocate or solicitor, in each case of not less than ten years' standing in any part of the United Kingdom...

The Detention Appeal Tribunal

6. The Tribunal shall consist of such number of members as the Secretary of State may determine...

7. A member of the Tribunal shall be a person who holds or has held judicial office in any part of the United Kingdom or is a barrister, advocate or solicitor, in each case of not less than ten years' standing in any part of the United Kingdom.

8. A commissioner may be appointed to be a member of the Tribunal but shall not act as such in the case of an appeal against a decision of his...

PART II
INTERIM CUSTODY ORDERS AND DETENTION ORDERS
Interim Custody Orders

11. (1) Where it appears to the Secretary of State that a person is suspected of having been concerned in the commission or attempted commission of any act of terrorism or in the direction, organisation or training of persons for the purpose of terrorism, the Secretary of State may make an interim custody order for the temporary detention of that person.

(2) An interim custody order of the Secretary of State shall be signed by the Secretary of State or a Minister of State or Under-Secretary of State.

(3) A person shall not be detained under an interim custody order for a period of more than twenty-eight days from the date of the order unless his case is referred by the Chief Constable to a commissioner for determination, and where a case is so referred the person concerned may be detained under the order only until his case is so determined . . .

(4) A reference to a commissioner shall be by notice in writing, of which a copy shall be sent to the Secretary of State and to the person to whom it relates.

Adjudication by Commissioner

12. Where the case of a person detained under an interim custody order (in this Part of this Schedule referred to as 'the respondent') is referred to a commissioner, the commissioner shall enquire into that case for the purpose of deciding whether or not he is satisfied that—

(a) the respondent has been concerned in the commission or attempted commission of any act of terrorism or the direction, organisation or training of persons for the purpose of terrorism; and

(b) his detention is necessary for the protection of the public.

13. Not less than seven days before the hearing of a case for determination under paragraph 12 above, the respondent shall be served with a statement in writing as to the nature of the terrorist activities which are to be the subject of the inquiry.

14. (1) Proceedings before a commissioner shall take place in private.

(2) The respondent shall, subject to paragraph 17 below, be present on the hearing of a reference unless the commissioner directs his removal on the grounds of his disorderly conduct.

15. On the hearing of a reference, the respondent shall be entitled to give and adduce evidence and may make representations to the commissioner, whether orally or in writing, and may be represented by counsel or a solicitor.

16. On the hearing of a reference a commissioner may—

(a) receive oral, documentary or other evidence, notwithstanding that the evidence would be inadmissible in a court of law;

(b) question any person, including the respondent;

(c) cause inquiries to be made in relation to any matter.

17. Where, in relation to any part of the proceedings, it appears to

the commissioner that it would be contrary to the interests of public security or might endanger the safety of any person for that part of the proceedings to take place in the presence of the respondent, the respondent and his representatives shall be excluded accordingly.

18. Where any part of the proceedings takes place in the absence of the respondent and his representatives in pursuance of paragraph 17 above, the commissioner shall, in so far as the needs of public security and the safety of persons permit, inform the respondent and his representatives of the substance of the matters dealt with during that part of the proceedings.

19. A commissioner may require any person to give evidence on oath or by affirmation, and for that purpose an oath or affirmation in due form may be administered.

20. (1) A commissioner—

  (*a*) may by summons in writing require any person to attend as a witness at such time and place as may be specified in the summons; and

  (*b*) may require any person to answer any question or produce any documents in his custody or under his control which relate to any matter in question on the reference,

but a person shall not be required by a summons to go more than ten miles from his place of residence unless the necessary expenses of his attendance are paid or tendered to him.

(2) A person who, without reasonable excuse, fails to comply with a summons or requirement under sub-paragraph (1) above shall be liable on summary conviction to a fine not exceeding £200 or to imprisonment for a term not exceeding six months, or both...

Detention Orders

24. Where a commissioner decides that he is satisfied in accordance with the provisions of paragraph 12 above, he shall make a detention order for the detention of the respondent, and otherwise shall direct his release.

25. (1) A detention order shall be signed by the commissioner and shall contain a statement of the grounds on which it is made.

(2) A copy of a detention order shall be sent to the respondent and to the Secretary of State.

Part III

Appeals

Notice of appeal

26. (1) Where a detention order has been made in the case of any person, he may within twenty-one days of the making of the order appeal by notice in writing to the Tribunal.

(2) The Tribunal shall cause a copy of the notice of appeal to be sent to the Chief Constable and to the Secretary of State.

27. (1) A notice of appeal shall indicate the grounds of appeal and,

where appropriate, the nature of any fresh evidence which the appellant wishes to tender on the hearing of the appeal...

28. ... [T]he Tribunal shall be deemed to be duly constituted if it consists of three members (or a greater uneven number of members); and the determination of any question before the Tribunal shall be according to the opinion of the majority of the members hearing the appeal.

29. The hearing of an appeal shall be in private.

30. On the hearing of an appeal—
- (*a*) the Tribunal shall consider the record of the proceedings before the commissioner together with any fresh evidence which may be tendered with the consent of the Tribunal;
- (*b*) the appellant may be represented by counsel or a solicitor; and
- (*c*) the appellant shall, subject to paragraph 17 above (as applied by paragraph 33 below), be entitled to be present unless the Tribunal direct his removal on the grounds of his disorderly conduct.

31. The Tribunal may require the attendance of the appellant if this appears to them necessary.

32. On an appeal, the Tribunal shall, if they are of the opinion that the Commissioner's decision should be set aside, allow the appeal and direct the discharge of the appellant; and otherwise they shall dismiss the appeal...

PART IV

SUPPLEMENTAL

Reference for review

35. (1) The Secretary of State may at any time refer to a commissioner the case of any person who is for the time being detained under a detention order, and shall so refer the case of any person who has been detained for one year since the making of a detention order or for six months from the determination of the most recent review under this paragraph.

(2) On any such reference the commissioner shall review the case and, unless he considers that the person's continued detention is necessary for the protection of the public, shall direct his discharge...

(4) Paragraphs 14 to 23 above shall have effect in relation to the proceedings of a commissioner under this paragraph.

Release of persons detained

36. (1) The Secretary of State may direct the discharge at any time of a person detained under an interim custody order.

(2) The Secretary of State may direct the release, subject to such conditions (if any) as he may specify, of a person detained under a detention order.

(3) The Secretary of State may recall to detention a person released subject to conditions under sub-paragraph (2) above, and a person so recalled may be detained under the original detention order...

Interpretation

39. In this Schedule—

'detention order' means an order made by a commissioner for the detention of a person;

'interim custody order' means an order made by the Secretary of State for the temporary detention of a person.

SCHEDULE 3

THE NORTHERN IRELAND (EMERGENCY PROVISIONS) REGULATIONS 1973

Title

1. These regulations may be cited as the Northern Ireland (Emergency Provisions) Regulations 1973.

Road traffic

2. The Secretary of State may by order prohibit, restrict or regulate in any area the use of vehicles or any class of vehicles on highways or the use by vehicles or any class of vehicles of roads or classes of roads specified in the order, either generally or in such circumstances as may be so specified.

Railways

3. The Secretary of State, or any officer of the Royal Ulster Constabulary not below the rank of assistant chief constable, may direct any person having the management of a railway to secure that any train specified in the direction or trains of any class so specified shall stop, or shall not stop, at a station or other place so specified.

Funerals

4. Where it appears to an officer of the Royal Ulster Constabulary not below the rank of chief inspector that a funeral may occasion a breach of the peace or serious public disorder, or cause undue demands to be made on Her Majesty's forces or the police, he may give directions imposing on the persons organising or taking part in the funeral such conditions as appear to him to be necessary for the preservation of public order including (without prejudice to the generality of the foregoing) conditions—

(a) prescribing the route to be taken by the funeral;

(b) prohibiting the funeral from entering any place specified in the directions;

(c) requiring persons taking part in the funeral to travel in vehicles.

Closing of licensed premises, clubs, etc.

5. The Secretary of State may by order require that premises licensed under the Licensing Act (Northern Ireland) 1971, premises registered under the Registration of Clubs Act (Northern Ireland) 1967 or any place of entertainment or public resort shall be closed and remain closed, either for an indefinite period or for a period, or until an event, specified in the order or shall be closed at a particular time either on all days or on any day so specified.

The Gardiner Committee, 1975

After the Northern Ireland (Emergency Provisions) Act, 1973, had been in operation for some time a committee under the chairmanship of Lord Gardiner was appointed 'to consider what provisions and powers, consistent to the maximum extent practicable in the circumstances with the preservation of civil liberties and human rights, are required to deal with terrorism and subversion in Northern Ireland, including provisions for the administration of justice, and to examine the working of the Northern Ireland (Emergency Provisions) Act, 1973; and to make recommendations'. In the course of its report it made a number of recommendations for changes in the Act, in particular in relation to procedures connected with detention.

General considerations

17. The suspension of normal legal safeguards for the liberty of the subject may sometimes be essential, in a society faced by terrorism, to counter greater evils. But if continued for any period of time it exacts a social cost from the community; and the price may have to be paid over several generations. It is one of the aims of terrorists to evoke from the authorities an over-reaction to the violence, for which the terrorists are responsible, with the consequence that the authorities lose the support of those who would otherwise be on the side of government.

18. In the present situation there are neighbourhoods in Northern Ireland where natural social motivation is being deployed against lawful authority rather than in support of it. Any good society is compounded of a network of natural affection and loyalties; yet we have seen and heard of situations in which normal human responses such as family affection, love of home, neighbourliness, loyalty to friends and patriotism are daily invoked to strengthen terrorist activity.

19. The imposition of order may be successful in the short term; but in the long term, peace and stability can only come from that consensus which is the basis of law . . .

20. We acknowledge the need for firm and decisive action on the part of the security forces; but violence has in the past provoked a violent response. The adoption of methods of interrogation 'in depth', which involved forms of ill-treatment that are described in the Compton Report [above, p. 738], did not last for long. Following the report of the Parker Committee [above, p. 743] in 1972, these methods were declared unlawful and were stopped by the British Government; but the resentment caused was intense, widespread and persistent. . .

Trial procedures
Section 5

41. Section 5 of the 1973 Act relates only to criminal proceedings for scheduled offences. It provides that a written statement, made and signed by a person in the presence of a constable, shall be admissible as evidence of any fact stated therein of which the person's direct oral evidence would be admissible if it is shown that the person who made the statement:

(a) is dead or bodily or mentally unfit to attend as a witness; or

(b) is outside Northern Ireland and it is not reasonably practicable to secure his attendance; or

(c) cannot be found after all reasonable steps have been taken to find him.

42. The unsworn statements to which section 5 relates would otherwise be inadmissible as hearsay. The main object of the section was to meet the problem that witnesses to terrorist crimes might be killed or so injured as to be incapable of coming to court, or might flee from Northern Ireland or go into hiding in fear of their own safety, thus making it impracticable to produce them to give oral evidence in court. It was also suggested that the section might lessen the hazards for those who had made statements, as their being killed, injured or intimidated thereafter would not prevent the use of their evidence as recorded in their statements.

43. But the objections to section 5 are twofold. First, the accused has no opportunity to test the statement by cross-examination. Second, the accuracy and quality of the statement might, depending on the circumstances in which it was taken and the character and intelligence of those concerned in making it, be open to grave doubt. It is obvious that these drawbacks were regarded by the Director of Public Prosecutions as making this type of evidence generally unsatisfactory; he issued a direction on 7th August 1973, to the Chief Constable that statements under section 5 were not to be tendered to any court without his authority, and this practice also applies to his staff and those acting on his behalf. In fact, evidence tendered under section 5 has never been used in a trial.

44. Section 5 does not refer specifically to intimidation and it is doubtful how far it can be used to make the statement of an intimidated person admissible or how much protection, if any, it is likely to give such a person. It contributes nothing sufficient to override the objections to its use, which we have already noted. We think evidence admitted under section 5 is so likely to lack evidential value that we recommend that it should be repealed or allowed to lapse.

Section 6

46. Section 6 of the 1973 Act relates to the admission of statements made by the accused and is of special importance because it may be assumed that most of such statements are likely to be in the form of confessions. On reading the section, the question at once arises as to how far it impinges on the position at common law. The words of section 6 (2) which refer to an accused person having been ' . . . subjected to torture or to inhuman or degrading treatment. . .' are taken from Article 3 of the European Convention for the Protection of Human Rights and Fundamental Freedoms. Where the accused has *prima facie* been subjected to ill-treatment of this kind in order to induce him to make the statement, it will be excluded unless the court is satisfied that the statement has not been so obtained. That degree of protection the section undoubtedly gives.

47. But the protection of the common law goes further by excluding statements induced by threats, promises or some form of oppressive conduct. This last element, ' oppressive conduct ', is necessarily difficult to define in this context, but we think it safe to say that a finding upon it calls for a review of all the relevant circumstances, including the nature of the investigation, the public interest and the position of the accused. Moreover, the common law goes an important step beyond this. Perhaps in recognition of the infinite variety of the circumstances in criminal cases, it has conferred on judges a judicial discretion to exclude certain forms of evidence even when legally admissible. This has been proclaimed on various occasions and was described by Lord Parker of Waddington thus in *Callis* v. *Gunn* [1964] 1 Q.B. 495 at 501:

' . . .as is well known, in every criminal case a judge has a discretion to disallow evidence, even if in law relevant and therefore admissible, if admissibility would operate unfairly against a defendant. I would add that in considering whether admissibility would operate unfairly against a defendant one would certainly consider whether it had been obtained in an oppressive manner by force or against the wishes of an accused person. That is the general principle. . .[45]

48. . . . It is difficult to conclude that Parliament intended to withdraw from the judiciary a well-established discretion of the important nature indicated without saying so in clear terms. Judges presiding over the trials of scheduled offences in Northern Ireland during the last year have held that this discretion remains vested in them and have exercised it when the interests of justice so required.

[45] See also *Noor Mohamed* v. *R.* [1949] A.C. 182 at 192; *Harris* v. *D.P.P.* [1952] A.C. 694 at 707; *Kuruma* v. *R.* [1955] A.C. 197 at 204; and *R.* v. *Murphy* [1965] N.I. 138 at 142–3.

49. In the belief that this is the correct view, we do not suggest that section 6 should be repealed. . .

50. . . . But the construction we favour, which leaves the judicial discretion unimpaired, should be stated expressly and no longer left to be inferred.

The Committee rejected proposals for further changes aimed at withholding the identity of witnesses by means of such methods as the use of screens and voice scramblers and, if necessary, the exclusion of the defendant and his counsel during part of the hearing; and the admission of hearsay evidence when it would be too dangerous for a witness to appear in person. The grounds for rejecting them can be found in its discussion of the existing detention procedures below. It also rejected a proposal that once a *prima facie* case had been established a defendant should be obliged to testify.

Existing and proposed offences
Offence of terrorism

70. We considered the creation of a new offence of being concerned in terrorism in the following terms:

> ' Any person who is concerned in the commission or attempted commission of any act of terrorism or in directing, organising, training or recruiting persons for the purpose of terrorism shall be liable on conviction on indictment to imprisonment for a term not exceeding 15 years.'

Many of the most dangerous terrorists do not themselves commit specific offences, but they are responsible for directing, organising, training or recruiting others to commit acts of terrorism. Such persons could be indicted, if the evidence were available, for conspiracy at common law; this crime is difficult to prove and often involves intricate questions of law. We therefore recommend the creation of this simpler statutory offence, which should be included in schedule 4 to the 1973 Act. We hope that its introduction would result in prosecutions for this offence of some people who now can only be dealt with by the detention procedure. Many young people, including children, have been recruited to commit acts of terrorism by various terrorist groups. . . The proposed crime of terrorism is extended to include recruitment. The definition of terrorist under section 28 (1) of the 1973 Act does not include recruitment and we recommended that it should be amended to do so.

71. We also considered the amendment of the definition of terrorism in section 28 (1) of the 1973 Act in the following terms:

> ' Terrorism means the use of violence for political or sectarian ends and includes any use of violence for the purpose of putting the public or any section of the public in fear.'

This extension of the definition of terrorism is necessary because, although most acts of terrorism are politically motivated, many are not; and, of the latter, the majority are undoubtedly acts of terrorism with apparent sectarian motivation. Therefore, to eliminate the possibility of a successful but unmeritorious, technical defence that the alleged act of terrorism had a sectarian but not a political motivation, we recommend this extension to the definition in section 28 (1) of the 1973 Act. . .[46]

The News Media

73. The view has been expressed to us that the news media must bear a degree of responsibility for the encouragement of terrorist activity in Northern Ireland. Interviews with terrorist leaders on television and radio and the practice of some newspapers in accepting advertisements from paramilitary groups may provide propaganda platforms for those whose aim is the violent overthrow of lawful government. There is a tendency, which exists elsewhere, towards sensational reporting of shootings and bombing incidents which lends a spurious glamour both to the activities themselves and to the perpetrators. In addition there are ill-founded and false allegations against the security forces.

74. There can be no question of introducing censorship in a free society in time of peace. But this does not mean that nothing can be done. We recommend that it be made a summary offence for editors, printers and publishers of newspapers to publish anything which purports to be an advertisement for or on behalf of an illegal organisation or part of it.

75. The authority of the Press Council extends to all newspapers and magazines within the United Kingdom, including Northern Ireland . . . In the present situation, we suggest that the Press Council should closely examine the reconciliation of the reporting of terrorist activities with the public interest.

76. Finally, the Governors of the British Broadcasting Corporation and the Independent Broadcasting Authority should re-examine the guidance they give to programme controllers or companies about contact with terrorist organisations and the reporting of their views and activities.

Detention
Present procedures

121. The detention of an alleged terrorist follows an arrest under section 10 of the 1973 Act and the procedures for his detention and

---

[46] The Committee also recommended the creation of an offence of wearing any form of disguise in a public or open place or in the vicinity of a dwelling house without just cause or reasonable excuse.

eventual release are set out in Schedule 1 to the Act. The procedure begins with the making by the Secretary of State of an interim custody order for the temporary detention of the suspected terrorist. The order is usually made after his arrest, although it can be made before arrest. It can only be made on the authority of the Secretary of State and is usually signed by him, although it can be signed by a Minister of State or Under-Secretary of State.

122. Before an order can be made, it must appear to the Secretary of State that the person is suspected of having been concerned in the commission or attempted commission of an act of terrorism or in the direction, organisation or training of persons for the purpose of terrorism. Before the Secretary of State can reach a conclusion as to whether or not any of these criteria is *prima facie* satisfied, police and army intelligence reports and other information are evaluated, graded and summarised by the security agencies and officials in the Northern Ireland Office. The information about and allegations against the suspected terrorist are then presented in summary form, with recommendations, to the Secretary of State. The decision whether or not to make an interim custody order will be based upon this evidence, but will be related to current security and political situations at local and general level in Northern Ireland. Thus far the procedure has been executive in character; at this stage it becomes quasi-judicial.

123. A suspected terrorist cannot be detained under an interim custody order for more than 28 days unless his case is referred by the Chief Constable of the Royal Ulster Constabulary to a Commissioner for determination. Once the referral has taken place the suspected terrorist can be detained until his case is determined. At present many months may elapse between the referral and determination of the case. Not less than seven days before the hearing of his case the suspected terrorist must be served with a notice in writing specifying the nature of the terrorist activities alleged against him. Because there is frequently a long time between the referral and the date of the hearing of a case, he may not receive this notice for many months.

124. The hearing of the case is before one of about 20 Commissioners, most of whom are Scottish sheriffs, English circuit judges or part-time recorders. . .

126. At the hearing, the Commissioner's task is to enquire into the case for the purpose of deciding whether or not he is satisfied that:

(*a*) the suspected terrorist has been concerned in the commission or attempted commission of any act of terrorism, or the direction, organisation or training of persons for the purpose of terrorism; and

(*b*) his detention is necessary for the protection of the public.
Most Commissioners apply a standard of proof to be equated with the phrase ' a very high degree of probability '. If such a standard is reached, they are ' satisfied '.

127. If the Commissioner is satisfied that (*a*) and (*b*) above are established, he must make an order detaining the suspect. Otherwise, he must direct his release. Therefore at this stage the decision to detain or release is made quasi-judicially and independently of the executive branch of government.

128. The hearing before the Commissioner, which can last between one and four days, is held in private and has become adversarial in form. Leading counsel are often engaged by both the Crown and the ' respondents ' as the suspected terrorists are called; the Crown pays the legal costs of both sides. Counsel for the Crown have always been members of the English Bar, and counsel for the respondents have been members of the Northern Ireland Bar. This decision was made to reduce the risks to the Northern Ireland Bar and the pressure which would be brought upon their limited numbers if they were instructed to appear for the Crown in detention proceedings.

129. A hearing cannot be held in the absence of the respondent. Individual respondents or groups of respondents have often refused to attend hearings. This has resulted in the time of witnesses and Commissioners being wasted and in an overall delay in the disposal of cases. At present there is a complete refusal by all Republican respondents to attend hearings, with the result that no Republican cases are being disposed of.

130. The evidence for the Crown is given almost exclusively by Army officers and police officers, who are usually members of Special Branch. Normally they gave their evidence behind screens, so that they cannot be identified by the respondent or his legal advisers. Sometimes voice scramblers are used as a further precaution. Occasionally, despite these precautions, respondents do identify witnesses. It is necessary that the identity of many witnesses should not be revealed, for their own safety and also in the general interests of public security. A serious consequence of the concealment of identity of witnesses is that the respondent's lawyer is handicapped in the cross-examination which is essential for an effective adversarial procedure.

131. The evidence given by these witnesses is, in the main, hearsay – first-hand, second-hand or even of remoter degree. It is derived from various sources, such as eye-witnesses of terrorist activities or from relations and neighbours of respondents and accomplices of respondents. Much of it is derived from information from paid informers, who receive payment varying from beer money to weekly wages and

even substantial lump sums; some of them have criminal records. They do not attend the hearings, either because it would be too dangerous for them to do so, or because they are afraid. Evidence from such sources, requires penetrating examination. The provenance or pedigree of the hearsay has to be probed in order that the credit-worthiness of the informants and the accuracy of their information or the weight of the evidence can be evaluated.

132. Such probing cannot be done in the hearing of the respondent or his lawyers, because the lives of the sources or informants would be at risk, and in consequence necessary counter-terrorist intelligence would cease to come to the security forces. For this reason Crown witnesses frequently have to refuse to answer questions or have to give evasive answers in open session. The procedure allows for such evidence to be given in camera; with the respondent and his lawyers temporarily excluded from the hearing. The result is that, although the respondent can be cross-examined as to his credit, his accuser cannot be. In most cases the important evidence is given during sessions held in camera and the respondent and his lawyers are necessarily unaware of it. During these sessions the Crown lawyers and the Commissioners have regard for the interests of the respondent and do their best to probe and evaluate the hearsay evidence.

133. At the conclusion of the restricted session, the Commissioner informs the respondent and his lawyers of the nature of the evidence given in camera, and his reasons for hearing it in this manner. The information given by the Commissioner is in precis form. The content of it is dependent upon security considerations and may be of minimal or no assistance to the respondent or his lawyers in the cross-examination of Crown witnesses and the meeting of allegations.

134. Usually respondents give evidence on their own behalf, although some Republicans, as a matter of principle, have taken no active part in the hearings and do not give evidence. If respondents give evidence, they are liable to cross-examination by the Crown. However, such cross-examination is necessarily limited in scope and value because the cross-examiner is inhibited from asking any questions which might indicate the nature of the evidence given in camera or the identity of an informant.

135. If the Commissioner signs a Detention Order, the respondent may appeal to the Appeals Tribunal consisting of three members. Until recently Commissioners did not sit as members of the Tribunal, with the consequence that no members of the Tribunal had direct experience of the atmosphere and difficulties of Commissioners' hearings. The decisions of the Appeals Tribunal seem in many cases to have been reached upon evaluation of the written notes made by the Commis-

sioners at the hearing, and of documentary evidence, some of which was not produced or explained in oral evidence at the hearing before the Commissioner.

136. When a person has been made subject to a detention order and any subsequent appeal has been unsuccessful, he may be released from custody either by decision of a Commissioner when the case is referred to him for review by the Secretary of State, or by direction of the Secretary of State. Both methods of release have been extensively used in the past 12 months. The first is quasi-judicial in form and the second is an executive action.

137. The Secretary of State is obliged to refer to a Commissioner for review, the case of any person who has been detained for more than one year since the making of a detention order or for six months from the determination of the last review. The procedure at a review is similar to that at the original hearing before the Commissioner, but the hearings are much shorter. Four or more reviews can be completed in a day.

138. On a review, the Commissioner must direct the discharge of the detainee, unless he considers that his continued detention is necessary for the protection of the public. Unfortunately, only scanty information is available for the Commissioner's consideration. Some information will be available about the nature and general level of terrorist activity in the detainee's home community. However, little or no information will be available upon which the Commissioner can decide the important question of the detainee's attitude. As the male detainee will have been incarcerated in the Maze in a large compound for many months, there will be little guidance as to whether or not he has had a change of heart.

Criticism of present detention procedures

150. We have received evidence and heard witnesses about the detention of terrorists procedures now in operation... Much of the evidence has been critical... and we consider that this criticism is well-informed, based upon experience and justified...

152. The most cogent criticism was that the procedures are unsatisfactory, or even farcical, if considered as judicial. The adversarial method of trial is reduced to impotence by the needs of security. The use of screens and voice scramblers, the overwhelming amount of hearsay evidence and the in camera sessions are totally alien to ordinary trial procedures. The quasi-judicial procedures are a veneer to an enquiry which, to be effective, inevitably has no relationship to common law procedures.

153. The introduction of the quasi-judicial procedures was well intentioned. Its object was to give the person suspected of terrorism

every opportunity consistent with security to challenge and test the allegations made against him. Its apparent similarity to the ordinary judicial process has had the side effect of tending to bring the ordinary processes of law in Northern Ireland into disrepute.

154. Strong criticism was made of the nature of the evidence tendered before the Commissioners. This criticism is valid to the extent that the adversarial quasi-judicial procedures are unsatisfactory for testing the reliability of evidence from paid informers and accomplices of terrorists. The most effective testing of such evidence can only with safety be conducted in a situation of the utmost confidentiality.

155. The delays, now about six months, which occur before the persons suspected of terrorism have an adjudication by a Commissioner are serious, especially as a substantial proportion of detainees are at present being released on first hearing because both the criteria laid down in paragraph 12 of schedule 1 of the 1973 Act have not been satisfied. We consider that the blame for these delays can be attributed to the basic unsuitability of the system and procedures for the numbers of people passing through them.

156. It was said that the Commissioners varied in quality and consistency of approach. We think that this contention has some validity. Commissioners sit alone exercising an alien jurisdiction. When they first sit they are totally unfamiliar with Northern Ireland with all its regional and cultural nuances. They have to take a note of the evidence, assess the evidence and be on their guard for a breach of security in an atmosphere of screens, voice scramblers and pseudo-adversarial contest. These factors indicate the desirability of a tribunal sitting in plurality. Nevertheless we are satisfied that the Commissioners have acted with fairness and conscientiousness.

157. The review procedure by the Commissioners was almost universally condemned. This in our view was no fault of the Commissioners but resulted from the almost complete lack of worthwhile material available to the Commissioners in the conduct of a review.

158. In the light of these criticisms we recommend that the existing arrangements provided in schedule 1 to the 1973 Act be repealed and replaced by the provisions below.

Proposed Detention Procedures

159. The deprivation of the liberty of an individual by extra-judicial process is a very serious decision for the government of a civilised democratic country to take and can be justified only if that individual's continued presence in the community would seriously endanger the general security of the public. We therefore recommend that the sole and ultimate responsibility for the detention of individuals should be that of the Secretary of State, onerous as that may be. His responsibility

for detention should not be capable of delegation to any Minister of State or Under-Secretary of State; in the absence or unavailability of the Secretary of State for Northern Ireland, this responsibility can be discharged by another Secretary of State. . .

160. Nevertheless the public interest and the interests of individuals suspected of terrorism require the existence of a body, independent of the executive, to carry out an effective investigation of individual cases. We therefore recommend the creation of a Detention Advisory Board to carry out the investigation of the cases of individuals proposed for detention. The Board should have advisory duties but no executive power to detain.

Detention Advisory Board

161. We recommend that the enquiry should take place in private and that witnesses should be questioned individually and alone, without legal representation. The Board should have full powers to question any person and to obtain documents relevant to the enquiry. An accurate assessment of the information requires uninhibited investigation. We appreciate that this method of enquiry would deprive the person suspected of terrorism of the basic rights of legal representation and cross-examination. Yet we are convinced it would have a greater opportunity of reaching the truth than the adversarial quasi-judicial method, to the real benefit of any person wrongly suspected of terrorism and of any person whose release would not seriously endanger the general security of the public. We recommend that the detainee should have the right to make written representations to the Secretary of State who should refer them to the Board and should consider them himself. The detainee should also have the right to appear before the Board, but not to be legally represented or present when other witnesses are being questioned.

162. We recommend that members of the Board be whole time holders of judicial office in England and Wales or Scotland. . .

163. We recommend that membership of the Board be limited to seven to ensure continuity, three of whom should constitute a division for investigating cases. The deprivation of a citizen's liberty by executive action and extra-judicial process is such a grave step that the responsibility for investigating a case, and making recommendations which may lead to a detention order, merits consideration by more than one person, however carefully selected. It would be impossible for an individual at the same time to probe in depth by questioning a witness, to take a note of the questions and answers, and to evaluate the evidence in the context of other information and documents . . .

165. Delay has been a serious defect in the present procedures and

our proposals are designed to prevent delays ... We recommend that from the date of the making of the provisional custody order:

(a) 7 days be allowed for service of a written notice upon the detainee setting out the nature of the terrorist activities alleged against him;

(b) a further 21 days be allowed for the Board to submit their written report to the Secretary of State;

(c) a further 7 days be allowed for the Secretary of State's decision as to whether to make a confirmed custody order or to direct the detainee's release.

Any non-compliance with these time limits should entitle the detainee to automatic release.

Criteria for Detention

166. ... At present, one of the criteria for the making of a Detention Order is that the detention of an individual is necessary for the protection of the public. We recommend the raising of this criterion so that a person should be detained only if his freedom would seriously endanger the general security of the public. This higher criterion reflects our concern that detention, while it remains, should be used sparingly. The other existing criterion, in our view, is still appropriate, but we recommend that it should be amended to include the recruitment of persons for the purpose of terrorism and the definition of terrorism recommended in paragraph 71 should apply. ...

[Report of a Committee to Consider Measures to Deal with Terrorism in Northern Ireland (January 1975) Cmnd. 5847]

(e) *The Prevention of Terrorism (Temporary Provisions) Act, 1976*

Until 1974 the Northern Ireland (Emergency Provisions) Act, 1973, was the most extensive Act on the statute book dealing with the problems of disorder on the scale that has been experienced in Northern Ireland and its application was confined to Northern Ireland. The Public Order Act, 1936, remained the principal United Kingdom Act dealing with political disorder and its provisions reflected the disorder with which it was endeavouring to cope in the 1930s. Although some of its provisions are still relevant they have proved inadequate to deal with the new problems of the 'urban guerrilla'. Following a number of bomb attacks in England the Government introduced the Prevention of Terrorism (Temporary Provisions) Act, 1974 (replaced in 1976 by the Prevention of Terrorism (Temporary Provisions) Act, 1976), to meet the demand for wider powers to deal with these newer problems. Although intended to be temporary it provides an important ingredient in the discussion of the question as to the measures a democratic state can and should take in its own self-defence, similar to those raised in relation to espionage, and the freedom to form associations and groups who have as their object a departure from the existing constitutional system and its methods of securing political, social and economic changes.

PREVENTION OF TERRORISM (TEMPORARY PROVISIONS) ACT, 1976   [Ch. 8]

Part I

Proscribed Organisations

1. (1) Subject to subsection (6) below, if any person—

(a) belongs or professes to belong to a proscribed organisation;

(b) solicits or invites financial or other support for a proscribed organisation, or knowingly makes or receives any contribution in money or otherwise to the resources of a proscribed organisation; or

(c) arranges or assists in the arrangement or management of, or addresses, any meeting of three or more persons (whether or not it is a meeting to which the public are admitted) knowing that the meeting is to support, or to further the activities of, a proscribed organisation, or is to be addressed by a person belonging or professing to belong to a proscribed organisation,

he shall be liable—

(i) on summary conviction to imprisonment for a term not exceeding six months or to a fine not exceeding £400, or both, and

(ii) on conviction on indictment to imprisonment for a term not exceeding five years or to a fine, or both.

(2) Any organisation for the time being specified in Schedule 1 to this Act is a proscribed organisation for the purposes of this Act; and any organisation which passes under a name mentioned in that Schedule shall be treated as proscribed, whatever relationship (if any) it has to any other organisation of the same name.

(3) The Secretary of State may by order add to Schedule 1 to this Act any organisation that appears to him to be concerned in terrorism occurring in the United Kingdom and connected with Northern Irish affairs, or in promoting or encouraging it.

(4) The Secretary of State may also by order remove an organisation from Schedule 1 to this Act.

(5) In this section ' organisation ' includes an association or combination of persons.

(6) A person belonging to a proscribed organisation shall not be guilty of an offence under this section by reason of belonging to the organisation if he shows that he became a member when it was not a proscribed organisation and that he has not since then taken part in any of its activities at any time while it was a proscribed organisation.

In this subsection the reference to a person becoming a member of an organisation shall be taken to be a reference to the only or last occasion on which he became a member.

(7) The court by or before which a person is convicted of an offence under this section may order the forfeiture of any money or other property which, at the time of the offence, he had in his possession or under his control for the use or benefit of the proscribed organisation.

2. (1) Any person who in a public place—
   (a) wears any item of dress, or
   (b) wears, carries or displays any article,

in such a way or in such circumstances as to arouse reasonable apprehension that he is a member or supporter of a proscribed organisation, shall be liable on summary conviction to imprisonment for a term not exceeding six months or to a fine not exceeding £400, or both.

(2) A constable may arrest without warrant a person whom he reasonably suspects to be a person guilty of an offence under this section.

(3) In this section ' public place ' includes any highway and any other premises or place to which at the material time the public have, or are permitted to have, access whether on payment or otherwise.

PART II

EXCLUSION ORDERS

3. (1) The Secretary of State may exercise the powers conferred on him by this Part of this Act in such way as appears to him expedient to prevent acts of terrorism (whether in the United Kingdom or elsewhere) designed to influence public opinion or Government policy with respect to affairs in Northern Ireland.

(2) An order under section 4, 5 or 6 of this Act is referred to in this Act as an ' exclusion order '.

(3) An exclusion order may be revoked at any time by a further order made by the Secretary of State.

4. (1) If the Secretary of State is satisfied that any person—
   (a) is or has been concerned (whether in Great Britain or elsewhere) in the commission, preparation or instigation of acts of terrorism, or
   (b) is attempting or may attempt to enter Great Britain with a view to being concerned in the commission, preparation or instigation of acts of terrorism,

the Secretary of State may make an order against that person prohibiting him from being in, or entering, Great Britain.

(2) In deciding whether to make an order under this section against a person who is ordinarily resident in Great Britain, the Secretary of State shall have regard to the question whether that person's con-

nection with any territory outside Great Britain is such as to make it appropriate that such an order should be made.

(3) An order shall not be made under this section against a person who is a citizen of the United Kingdom and Colonies and who—

(*a*) is at the time ordinarily resident in Great Britain, and has then been ordinarily resident in Great Britain throughout the last 20 years, or

(*b*) was born in Great Britain and has, throughout his life, been ordinarily resident in Great Britain, or

(*c*) is at the time subject to an order under section 5 of this Act. . . .

[5.] (2) In deciding whether to make an order under this section against a person who is ordinarily resident in Northern Ireland, the Secretary of State shall have regard to the question whether that person's connection with any territory outside Northern Ireland is such as to make it appropriate that such an order should be made.

(3) An order shall not be made under this section against a person who is a citizen of the United Kingdom and Colonies and who—

(*a*) is at the time ordinarily resident in Northern Ireland, and has then been ordinarily resident in Northern Ireland throughout the last 20 years, or

(*b*) was born in Northern Ireland and has, throughout his life, been ordinarily resident in Northern Ireland, or

(*c*) is at the time subject to an order under section 4 of this Act. . . .

6. (1) If the Secretary of State is satisfied that any person—

(*a*) is or has been concerned (whether in the United Kingdom or elsewhere) in the commission, preparation or instigation of acts of terrorism, or

(*b*) is attempting or may attempt to enter Great Britain or Northern Ireland with a view to being concerned in the commission, preparation or instigation of acts of terrorism,

the Secretary of State may make an order against that person prohibiting him from being in, or entering, the United Kingdom.

(2) In deciding whether to make an order under this section against a person who is ordinarily resident in the United Kingdom, the Secretary of State shall have regard to the question whether that person's connection with any territory outside the United Kingdom is such as to make it appropriate that such an order should be made.

(3) An order shall not be made under this section against a person who is a citizen of the United Kingdom and Colonies.

7. (1) As soon as may be after the making of an exclusion order, notice of the making of the order shall be served on the person against whom it is made, and the notice shall—

(*a*) set out the rights afforded to him by this section, and

(*b*) specify the manner in which those rights are to be exercised.

(2) Subsection (1) above shall not impose an obligation to take any steps to serve a notice on a person at a time when he is outside the United Kingdom.

(3) If a person served with notice of the making of an exclusion order objects to the order, he may within 96 hours of service of the notice—

(a) make representations in writing to the Secretary of State setting out the grounds of his objection, and

(b) include in those representations a request for a personal interview with the person or persons nominated by the Secretary of State under subsection (4) below.

(4) Where representations are duly made under this section, the Secretary of State shall, unless he considers the grounds to be frivolous, refer the matter for the advice of one or more persons nominated by him.

(5) Where a matter is referred for the advice of one or more persons nominated by the Secretary of State and the person against whom the order was made—

(a) included in his representations a request under subsection (3) (b) above, and

(b) has not been removed, with his consent, from Great Britain, Northern Ireland or the United Kingdom, as the case may be, under section 8 of this Act,

that person shall be granted a personal interview with the person or persons so nominated.

(6) After receiving the representations and the report of the person or persons nominated by him under subsection (4) above, the Secretary of State shall, as soon as may be, reconsider the case.

(7) Where representations are duly made under this section the Secretary of State shall, if it is reasonably practicable, notify the person against whom the order was made of any decision he takes as to whether or not to revoke the order.

8. Where a person is subject to an exclusion order and notice of the order has been served on him, the Secretary of State may have him removed from Great Britain, Northern Ireland or the United Kingdom, as the case may be, if—

(a) he consents, or

(b) no representations have been duly made by him under section 7 of this Act, or

(c) where such representations have been duly made by him, he has been notified of the Secretary of State's decision not to revoke the order.

9. (1) If any person who is subject to an exclusion order fails to comply with the order at a time after he has been, or has become

liable to be, removed under section 8 of this Act from Great Britain, Northern Ireland or the United Kingdom, as the case may be, he shall be guilty of an offence.

(2) If any person—

  (a) is knowingly concerned in arrangements for securing or facilitating the entry into Great Britain, Northern Ireland or the United Kingdom of, or

  (b) in Great Britain, Northern Ireland or the United Kingdom knowingly harbours,

a person whom he knows, or has reasonable cause to believe, to be a person who is subject to an exclusion order and who has been, or has become liable to be, removed from there under section 8 of this Act, he shall be guilty of an offence.

(3) A person guilty of an offence under subsection (1) or subsection (2) above shall be liable—

  (a) on summary conviction to imprisonment for a term not exceeding six months, or to a fine not exceeding £400, or both, or

  (b) on conviction on indictment to imprisonment for a term not exceeding five years, or to a fine, or both.

Part III

General and Miscellaneous

10. (1) If any person—

  (a) solicits or invites any other person to give or lend, whether for consideration or not, any money or other property, or

  (b) receives or accepts from any other person, whether for consideration or not, any money or other property,

intending that the money or other property shall be applied or used for or in connection with the commission, preparation or instigation of acts of terrorism to which this section applies, he shall be guilty of an offence.

(2) If any person gives, lends or otherwise makes available to any other person, whether for consideration or not, any money or other property, knowing or suspecting that the money or other property will or may be applied or used for or in connection with the commission, preparation or instigation of acts of terrorism to which this section applies, he shall be guilty of an offence.

(3) A person guilty of an offence under subsection (1) or subsection (2) above shall be liable—

  (a) on summary conviction to imprisonment for a term not exceeding six months, or to a fine not exceeding £400, or both, or

  (b) on conviction on indictment to imprisonment for a term not exceeding five years or to a fine, or both.

(4) A court by or before which a person is convicted of an offence under subsection (1) above may order the forfeiture of any money or other property—

(*a*) which, at the time of the offence, he had in his possession or under his control, and

(*b*) which, at that time, he intended should be applied or used for or in connection with the commission, preparation or instigation of acts of terrorism to which this section applies.

(5) This section and section 11 of this Act apply to acts of terrorism occurring in the United Kingdom and connected with Northern Irish affairs.

11. (1) If a person who has information which he knows or believes might be of material assistance—

(*a*) in preventing an act of terrorism to which this section applies, or

(*b*) in securing the apprehension, prosecution or conviction of any person for an offence involving the commission, preparation or instigation of an act of terrorism to which this section applies,

fails without reasonable excuse to disclose that information as soon as reasonably practicable—

(i) in England and Wales, to a constable, or

(ii) in Scotland, to a constable or the procurator fiscal, or

(iii) in Northern Ireland, to a constable or a member of Her Majesty's forces,

he shall be guilty of an offence.

(2) A person guilty of an offence under subsection (1) above shall be liable—

(*a*) on summary conviction to imprisonment for a term not exceeding six months, or to a fine not exceeding £400, or both, or

(*b*) on conviction on indictment to imprisonment for a term not exceeding five years, or to a fine, or both. . . .

12. (1) A constable may arrest without warrant a person whom he reasonably suspects to be—

(*a*) a person guilty of an offence under section 1, 9, 10 or 11 of this Act;

(*b*) a person who is or has been concerned in the commission, preparation or instigation of acts of terrorism;

(*c*) a person subject to an exclusion order.

(2) A person arrested under this section shall not be detained in right of the arrest for more than 48 hours after his arrest; but the Secretary of State may, in any particular case, extend the period of 48 hours by a further period not exceeding 5 days.

(3) The following provisions (requirement to bring arrested person before a court after his arrest) shall not apply to a person detained in right of the arrest.

The said provisions are—

Section 38 of the Magistrates' Courts Act 1952,

Section 29 of the Children and Young Persons Act 1969,

Section 321 (3) of the Criminal Procedure (Scotland) Act 1975,

Section 132 of the Magistrates' Courts Act (Northern Ireland) 1964, and

Section 50 (3) of the Children and Young Persons Act (Northern Ireland) 1968.

(4) In Scotland section 295 (1) of the Criminal Procedure (Scotland) Act 1975 (chief constable may in certain cases accept bail) shall not apply to a person detained in right of an arrest under this section.

(5) The provisions of this section are without prejudice to any power of arrest conferred by law apart from this section.

13. (1) The Secretary of State may by order provide for—

(a) the examination of persons arriving in, or leaving, Great Britain or Northern Ireland, with a view to determining—

(i) whether any such person appears to be a person who is or has been concerned in the commission, preparation or instigation of acts of terrorism, or

(ii) whether any such person is subject to an exclusion order, or

(iii) whether there are grounds for suspecting that any such person has committed an offence under section 9 or 11 of this Act,

(b) the arrest and detention of persons subject to exclusion orders, pending their removal pursuant to section 8 of this Act, and

(c) arrangements for the removal of persons pursuant to section 8 of this Act.

(2) An order under this section may confer powers on examining officers . . . including—

(a) the power of arresting and detaining any person pending—

(i) his examination,

(ii) the taking of a decision by the Secretary of State as to whether or not to make an exclusion order against him, or

(iii) his removal pursuant to section 8 of this Act,

(b) the power of searching persons, of boarding ships or aircraft, of searching in ships or aircraft, or elsewhere and of detaining articles—

(i) for use in connection with the taking of a decision by the Secretary of State as to whether or not to make an exclusion order, or

(ii) for use as evidence in criminal proceedings.

14. (1) In this Act, unless the context otherwise requires— . . .

' terrorism ' means the use of violence for political ends, and includes any use of violence for the purpose of putting the public or any section of the public in fear....

(3) Any reference in a provision of this Act to a person's having been concerned in the commission, preparation or instigation of acts of terrorism shall be taken to be a reference to his having been so concerned at any time, whether before or after the coming into force of that provision.

(4) When any question arises under this Act whether or not a person is exempted from the provisions of section 4, 5 or 6 of this Act, it shall lie on the person asserting it to prove that he is.

(5) The provisions of Schedule 3 to this Act shall have effect for supplementing sections 1 to 13 of this Act.

(6) Any power to make an order conferred by section 1, 13 or 17 of this Act shall be exercisable by statutory instrument and shall include power to vary or revoke any order so made....

(8) An order made under section 13 of this Act shall be subject to annulment in pursuance of a resolution of either House of Parliament.

(9) No order under section 1 or 17 of this Act shall be made unless—

(a) a draft of the order has been approved by resolution of each House of Parliament, or

(b) it is declared in the order that it appears to the Secretary of State that by reason of urgency it is necessary to make the order without a draft having been so approved.

(10) Every order under section 1 or 17 of this Act (except such an order of which a draft has been so approved)—

(a) shall be laid before Parliament, and

(b) shall cease to have effect at the expiration of a period of 40 days beginning with the date on which it was made unless, before the expiration of that period, the order has been approved by resolution of each House of Parliament, but without prejudice to anything previously done or to the making of a new order....

17. (1) The provisions of—

sections 1 to 13 of this Act,

section 14 of this Act except in so far as it relates to order under subsection (2) (a) or (b) below,

subsection (2) (c) below, and

Schedules 1 to 3 to this Act

shall remain in force until the expiry of the period of twelve months beginning with the passing of this Act and shall then expire unless continued in force by an order under subsection (2) (a) below.

(2) The Secretary of State may by order provide—

(a) that all or any of the said provisions which are for the time being in force (including any in force by virtue of an order under this paragraph or paragraph (c) below) shall continue in force for a period not exceeding twelve months from the coming into operation of the order;

(b) that all or any of the said provisions which are for the time being in force shall cease to be in force; or

(c) that all or any of the said provisions which are not for the time being in force shall come into force again and remain in force for a period not exceeding twelve months from the coming into operation of the order.

(3) On the expiration of any provision of this Act, section 38 (2) of the Interpretation Act 1889 (effect of repeals) shall apply as if that provision of this Act was then repealed by another Act. . . .

SCHEDULE 1

PROSCRIBED ORGANISATIONS

Irish Republican Army

SCHEDULE 3

SUPPLEMENTAL PROVISIONS FOR SECTIONS 1 TO 13

PART II

OFFENCES, DETENTION, ETC.

Prosecution of offences

3. Proceedings shall not be instituted—

(a) in England and Wales for an offence under section 1, 2, 9, 10 or 11 of this Act, except by or with the consent of the Attorney General, or

(b) in Northern Ireland for an offence under section 9, 10 or 11 of this Act, except by or with the consent of the Attorney General for Northern Ireland.

Search warrants

4. (1) If a justice of the peace is satisfied that there is reasonable ground for suspecting that—

(a) evidence of the commission of an offence under section 1, 9, 10 or 11 of this Act, or

(b) evidence sufficient to justify the making of an order under section 1 of this Act or an exclusion order,

is to be found at any premises or place, he may grant a search warrant authorising entry to the premises or place.

(2) An application for a warrant under sub-paragraph (1) above shall be made by a member of a police force of a rank not lower than the rank of an inspector, and he shall give his information to the justice on oath.

(3) The warrant shall authorise the applicant, and any other member of any police force, to enter the premises or place, if necessary by force, and to search the premises or place and every person found therein and to seize anything found on the premises or place, or on any such person, which any member of a police force acting under the warrant has reasonable grounds for suspecting to be evidence falling within sub-paragraph (1) above.

(4) If a member of a police force of a rank not lower than the rank of superintendent has reasonable grounds for believing that the case is one of great emergency and that in the interests of the State immediate action is necessary, he may by a written order signed by him give to any member of a police force the authority which may be given by a search warrant under this paragraph.

(5) Where any authority is so given, particulars of the case shall be notified as soon as may be to the Secretary of State. . . .

Powers of search without warrant

6. (1) In any circumstances in which a constable has power under section 12 of this Act to arrest a person, he may also, for the purpose of ascertaining whether he has in his possession any document or other article which may constitute evidence that he is a person liable to arrest, stop that person, and search him.

(2) Where a constable has arrested a person under the said section, for any reason other than for the commission of a criminal offence, he, or any other constable, may search him for the purpose of ascertaining whether he has in his possession any document or other article which may constitute evidence that he is a person liable to arrest. . . .

Scheduled offences

8. Offences under sections 9, 10 and 11 of this Act shall be scheduled offences for the purposes of the Northern Ireland (Emergency Provisions) Act 1973; and accordingly in Part I of Schedule 4 to that Act there shall be inserted after the paragraph 13 inserted

there by paragraph 7 of Schedule 2 to the Northern Ireland (Emergency Provisions) (Amendment) Act 1975 the following paragraph: —

   ' *Prevention of Terrorism (Temporary Provisions) Act* 1976
   13A. Offences under the following provisions of the Prevention of Terrorism (Temporary Provisions) Act 1976—

     (*a*) section 9 (breach of exclusion orders);
     (*b*) section 10 (contributions towards acts of terrorism);
     (*c*) section 11 (information about acts of terrorism).'

POSTSCRIPT

The manuscript of this book was completed in August 1974, though some additions and changes have been made since then. It is impossible, however, to keep pace with all the changes that are taking place. And this is particularly the case at a time like the present when many of the most fundamental aspects of the existing Constitution are under scrutiny and being adapted and modified to meet new challenges. Listed below are some of the additions and modifications that should be taken into account when reading the materials set out in the preceding pages.

Chapter I. The difficulties facing a head of state who attempts to exercise the power of dismissal vested in him have been highlighted by the dismissal by the Governor-General of Australia of Prime Minister Whitlam on 11 November 1975. A statement of the grounds of his action can be found in *The Times*, 12 November 1975.

Chapter II. To the 1931 example of a temporary agreement to depart from the principle of collective responsibility with regard to a particular issue must now be added the freedom granted by the Labour Government in 1975 to Ministers opposed to Britain remaining in the European Economic Community to campaign in favour of her leaving [see 884 H.C. Deb. 5s. c. 1746, 23 January 1975 and 889 H.C. Deb. 5s. c. 351 (Written answers), 7 April 1975].

Chapter III. It is becoming an accepted practice for Ministers to appoint special advisers to assist them in their work in their Departments. The Labour Government, for example, stated on 21 November 1974 that it proposed to appoint 15 full-time and 11 part-time special advisers [881 H.C. Deb. 5s. c. 502 (Written answers)].

On 3 July 1975 Prime Minister Wilson announced that he had appointed a standing committee to advise him on applications from senior civil servants who wanted to take up commercial appointments within two years of their leaving the service [894 H.C. Deb. 5s. c. 495 (Written answers)].

Chapter IV. The House of Commons (Disqualification) Act, 1957 has been replaced by the House of Commons (Disqualification) Act, 1975 (Ch. 24). The new Act brings up to date the list of disqualifying offices and makes minor changes in the wording and arrangements of the sections. The principles remain the same.

On 12 June 1975 the House of Commons agreed to publish a

register of Members' interests [893 H.C. Deb. 5s. c. 735]. The first register was published on 27 November 1975.

The experience of the past two years has brought to the fore again the whole question of alternative systems of voting, including proposals for the introduction of the alternative vote in single-member constituencies and some form of proportional representation in three- or four-member constituencies. It is worth recalling that this is a question considered by the Royal Commission on Electoral Systems of 1910 (Cd. 5352) as well as by the Speakers' Conferences of 1917 (Cd. 8463), 1930 (Cmd. 3636), 1944 (Cmd. 6543) and 1969 (Cmnd. 3550). In 1918 the Boundary Commissioners were actually instructed to prepare a scheme involving proportional representation for 100 borough constituencies, but the proposals were subsequently rejected by the House of Commons. A Bill to introduce the alternative vote (which received its second reading in the House of Commons on 2 February 1931 [247 H.C. Deb. 5s. c. 1467]) lapsed on the collapse of the Labour Government in 1931. Reference should also be made to the practice and experience of other countries, e.g. Germany, and, of course, Northern Ireland.

Chapter V. The proposals of the Labour Government set out on p. 214 have been embodied in the Industry Act, 1975 (Ch. 68).

The reference to the positive aspects of Ministerial responsibility should be supplemented by a reference to the articles by G. Ganz, ' Allocation of Decision-Making Functions ', in *Public Law* (1972), pp. 215 and 299.

In dealing with the Parliamentary Commissioner in the context of the responsibility of Ministers of the Central Government one should not forget the appointment of National Health Service Commissioners under the National Health Reorganisation Act, 1973 (Ch. 32) or the Commissions for Local Administration under the Local Government Act, 1974 (Ch. 7).

Chapter VI is already beginning to have an old-fashioned look about it, even though it still accurately states the present position. The publication of Sir Leslie Scarman's Hamlyn Lectures on ' The New Dimensions of English Law ' has been the occasion for renewed discussions of the question whether the United Kingdom should have a Bill of Rights and, if so, the form it should take. As the United Kingdom is already a signatory of the European Convention of Human Rights, one proposal is that that Convention, or a modified version of it, should be incorporated directly into English law by statute. The Court of Appeal in *R.* v. *Secretary of State for Home Affairs, ex parte Bhajan Singh* [1973] 2 All E.R. 1081, has already, on its own initiative, referred to the Convention to resolve a problem of interpretation of the Immigration Act, 1971. This still leaves open the questions whether any future Bill of Rights should be entrenched in some way, whether it should place a constitutional limit on the legislative powers of Parliament, enforceable by a court, and if so whether this should be an existing court or one especially established for the purpose. Equally problematic is, how, if this was desired, one would actually go about the process of incorporating such a fundamental change in the Constitution. Some of the difficulties of the more radical approach have led to a more moderate proposal which leaves the final say with Parliament, allowing it to reverse any decision by a court that a statute infringed the Bill of Rights. The court's role would then be similar in effect to the delaying power of the House of Lords. Indeed, the uncertainties surrounding the role of the House of Lords as a check on the activities of the elected House is one of the grounds for suggesting a Bill of Rights and the courts as an extra or alternative check.

The second challenge to the existing position is the publication by the Government of its White Paper, ' Our Changing Democracy: Devolution to Scotland and Wales ' on 27 November 1975, and in particular its proposals for a Scottish Assembly. This long-awaited event now makes it possible to make an overall assessment of the probable impact of devolution on the existing Constitution in a way that was premature while only the report of the Royal Commission on the Constitution (Cmnd. 5460) was available.

The third challenge, already touched on in this and later chapters is Britain's membership of the European Economic Community.

Chapters V, VI and VII should all be read in the light of (i) Britain's membership of the EEC, whose principal institutions have powers of initiative and implementation which put them, within the area of their jurisdiction, on a par with the Government and Parliament of the United Kingdom, as regards matters affecting the internal affairs of the United Kingdom; (ii) the proposals for devolution, fragmenting the constitutional arrangements of the United Kingdom in a way which was previously confined to Northern Ireland, which go well beyond the traditional limits of delegated local authority as exemplified in the existing forms of Local Government touched on in chapter IX; and finally (iii) the fundamental question of the continued adherence to the political principle to which the existing constitutional arrangements give effect, namely that of unlimited legislative power of the Government for the time being, subject only to the short delaying power of the House of Lords. The function and power of a Second Chamber in the existing or any future Constitution is in fact as important an aspect of this issue as the more recently discussed question of a possible Bill of Rights.

Chapter VII should also now contain a reference to the Referendum Act, 1975 (Ch. 33) and its implications.

Chapter VII. The report of the Renton Committee on ' The Preparation of Legislation ' [Cmnd. 6053] contains a brief description of the present legislative process and the factors affecting the present style of legislation (cp. Lord Denning's remarks at p. 284, above). The Committee commended the increasing readiness of Governments to produce Green and White Papers (above p. 481) and recommended that the explanatory memoranda accompanying Bills should be more informative. Where a Bill was long and complicated the explanation should, in its view, be set out in a White Paper.

On 3 November 1975 the Labour Government accepted the proposal made in the First Report of the Select Committee on Procedure on European Secondary Legislation [H.C. 294 of 1974–5] that a Standing Committee should be established, on the lines of the Standing Committee on Statutory Instruments (above p. 383) to consider some of the documents and proposals referred to the House by the sifting Committee (above p. 312). [See 890 H.C. Deb. 5s. c. 28.] The government also agreed that as far as possible time should be found not only for a discussion of original proposals but also of any substantial amendments. It repeated, however, the difficulties expressed by its predecessors in making available to Parliament information in the course of negotiations in the Council of Ministers.

So far as the provision of economic information is concerned (above p. 325ff.) the Industry Act, 1975 provides in s. 271 and the Fifth Schedule that the Treasury is to keep available for public use a macro-economic model suitable for demonstrating the likely effect on economic events in the United Kingdom of a number of different assumptions about, e.g. government economic policies, which would enable forecasts to be made about, e.g. the level of the gross domestic product, unemployment and the balance of payments, etc.

Chapter X. Following the publication of extracts from the diaries of Richard Crossman an attempt was made to restrain further publication on the grounds, *inter alia*, that the extracts contained accounts of Cabinet discussions, including expressions of opinion by individual Ministers, and of advice given to Ministers by civil servants [*A.-G.* v. *Jonathan Cape Ltd.* [1975] 3 W.L.R. 606]. The Lord Chief Justice accepted the argument that an injunction could be granted to restrain the publication of an account of Cabinet discussions if it could be shown that the public interest in free and frank discussion in the Cabinet would otherwise be damaged. He rejected the argument that an injunction could be granted to restrain the publication of advice given to Ministers by civil servants. In the particular case he refused to grant an injunction on the ground that, having regard to the fact that the events described had occurred 10 years previously, publication would not inhibit free discussion in the present Cabinet.

Prime Minister Wilson had already announced on 11 April 1975 the appointment of a Committee of Privy Councillors to reconsider the principles which should govern publication by former Ministers of their memoirs [889 H.C. Deb. 5s. c. 483 (Written answers)] (cf. above p. 436). Its report was published in January 1976 [Cmnd. 6386]. It sets out the current principles and makes recommendations. It suggests that Ministers should not reveal matters which would contravene the requirements of national security or be injurious to Britain's relations with other countries or information ' the publication of which would be destructive of the confidential relationships . . . which may subsist between Minister and Minister, Ministers and their advisers, and between either and outside bodies and private persons '. This meant *inter alia* that they should not reveal or discuss the opinions of other Ministers expressed in Cabinet or the advice given to them by individual civil servants. Nor should they make public assessments or criticism of individual civil servants who had served them. In general they thought that the embargo so far as the views of their colleagues were concerned should continue for 15 years, and for the life of the civil servant, so far as civil servants were concerned.

The Labour Government announced in the Queen's Speech on 19 November 1975 its intention to bring in legislation to amend the Official Secrets Acts.

Chapter XI. The Government published in November 1975 a ' Review of the Findings of Research Study on Supplementary Benefits Appeal Tribunals ' by Professor Kathleen Bell. The passages on tribunals should be supplemented by a reference to M. Herman, ' Administrative Justice and Supplementary Benefits ' (1972) and the article by Professor Bell, ' Administrative Tribunals since Franks ', in *Social and Economic Administration*, 4 (1970), p. 279.

Chapter XII. The case of *Punton* v. *Ministry of Pensions* (above p. 631) should be read together with *R.* v. *Preston Tribunal, ex parte Moore* [1975] 1 W.L.R. 624, in which the Court of Appeal expressed reluctance to interfere by way of certiorari with decisions of Supplementary Benefit Appeal Tribunals.

Chapter XIV. The Northern Ireland (Emergency Provisions) Act, 1973 has been amended by the Northern Ireland (Emergency Provisions) Act, 1975 (Ch. 62) in the light of the report of the Gardiner Committee. S. 9 of the new Act replaces the detention procedures set out in Schedule 1 to the 1973 Act. Under the new provisions, set out in Schedule 1 to the 1975 Act, it is the Secretary of State who makes the final decision whether or not a person held under an

Interim Custody Order is to be made subject to a Detention Order. In reaching his decision he is advised by an Adviser to whom he must refer the case within 14 days of the Interim Order being made. The Adviser conducts his inquiry informally, without the modified adversarial procedure used by the Commissioners under the 1973 Act. Although the detainee may make representations, may have legal advice and assistance in preparing these, and may request to be heard in person, no provision is made for legal representation or for examination or cross-examination of witnesses on his behalf. The Secretary of State makes his decision in the light of the Adviser's Report. If a detention order is not made within seven weeks the detainee must be released, though provision is made for extensions of up to three weeks to enable the Adviser to complete his Report.

S. 4 of the new Act amends s. 3 (1) of the 1973 Act and provides that bail may be granted ' (a) by a judge of the Supreme Court; or (b) by a judge of the Court of trial, on adjourning the trial . . .'. It also provides that the section is not to apply to scheduled offences tried summarily or which the Director of Public Prosecutions for Northern Ireland has certified as suitable for summary trial.

S. 7 repeals s. 5 of the 1973 Act. S. 8 provides that ss. 6 and 7 of the 1973 Act shall not apply to summary trials.

S. 11 authorises search for and seizure of radio transmitters. A member of the armed forces on duty or a constable may enter any premises or place other than a dwelling-house to conduct a search for that purpose. In the case of a dwelling-house the authority of a commissioned officer or an officer of the Royal Ulster Constabulary not below the rank of chief inspector is needed. They may also stop any person in a public place for the purpose of searching him, and search anyone anywhere if they suspect he has a transmitter with him. Any transmitter found can be seized.

S. 12 adds to the offences set out in s. 19 (1) of the 1973 Act the offence of soliciting or inviting a person to become a member of a proscribed organisation or to carry out on its behalf orders, directions given or requests made by a member.

S. 13 replaces s. 20 (1). It extends the offence set out there to the collection of information about persons holding judicial office, officers of any court and prison officers. It also creates a new offence of collecting or recording information likely to be useful to terrorists in planning or carrying out any act of violence.

INDEX OF SUBJECT MATTER